The Social Psychology of Aggression

The second edition of this textbook provides a thoroughly revised, updated and expanded overview of social psychological research on aggression.

The first part of the book covers the definition and measurement of aggression, presents major theories and examines the development of aggression. It also discusses the role of situational factors in eliciting aggression, and the impact of using violent media.

The second part of the book focuses on specific forms and manifestations of aggression. It includes chapters on aggression in everyday life, sexual aggression and domestic violence against children, intimate partners and elders. There are two new chapters in this part addressing intergroup aggression and terrorism. The concluding chapter explores strategies for reducing and preventing aggression.

The book will be essential reading for students and researchers in psychology and related disciplines. It will also be of interest to practitioners working with aggressive individuals and groups, and to policy makers dealing with aggression as a social problem.

Barbara Krahé is Professor of Social Psychology at the University of Potsdam, Germany. Her main research interests are in the area of applied social psychology, focusing on sexual aggression, decision making about sexual assault, and the impact of media violence on aggression. She is an active member of the International Society for Research on Aggression (ISRA).

The Social Psychology of Aggression

Second edition

Barbara Krahé

Psychology Press
Taylor & Francis Group

LONDON AND NEW YORK

Second edition published 2013
by Psychology Press
27 Church Road, Hove, East Sussex BN3 2FA

Simultaneously published in the USA and Canada
by Psychology Press
711 Third Avenue, New York NY 10017

Psychology Press is an imprint of the Taylor & Francis Group, an informa business

1 0 0 7 2 9 6 5 2 1

First edition published 2001 by Psychology Press

British Library Cataloguing in Publication Data
A catalogue record for this book is available from the British Library

Library of Congress Cataloging-in-Publication Data
Krahé, Barbara.
    The social psychology of aggression / Barbara Krahe.—2nd ed.
        p. cm.
    Includes bibliographical references and index.
    1. Aggressiveness.   2. Social psychology.   I. Title.
    BF575.A3.K73 2013
    302.54—dc23   2012018578

ISBN: 978-1-84169-874-8 (hbk)
ISBN: 978-1-84169-875-5 (pbk)
ISBN: 978-0-203-08217-1 (ebk)

Typeset in Times New Roman
by Swales & Willis Ltd, Exeter, Devon

MIX
Paper from
responsible sources
FSC
www.fsc.org   FSC® C004839

Printed and bound in Great Britain by
TJ International Ltd, Padstow, Cornwall

For Charlotte and Justin

Contents

Series preface

Social Psychology: A Modular Course, edited by Miles Hewstone, aims to provide under-graduates with stimulating, readable, affordable, and brief texts by leading experts committed to presenting a fair and accurate view of the work in each field, sharing their enthusiasm with students, and presenting their work in an approachable way.

The series will appeal to those who want to go deeper into the subject than the traditional textbook will allow, and base their examination answers, research projects, assignments, or practical decisions on a clearer and more rounded appreciation of the research evidence.

Also available in this series:

Attribution
by Friedrich Försterling

Attitudes and Attitude Change
by Gerd Bohner and Michaela Wänke

Group performance
by Bernard A. Nijstad

Prosocial Behaviour
by Hans-Werner Bierhoff

Social Cognition
by Herbert Bless, Klaus Fiedler, and Fritz Strack

For more information about this series please visit the *Social Psychology: A Modular Course* website at www.psypress.com/socialmodular

Preface

In the decade since the first edition of this book was published, social psychological research on aggression has gone through a period of fast and steady growth. New evidence has emerged on the problems that have challenged aggression researchers for a long time, and completely new aspects have appeared on the agenda, raising new questions and offering new answers about aggressive behaviour. A case in point is the introduction of the construct of relational aggression, which broadened the scope of behaviours studied under the label of aggression, required new measurement tools, and stimulated a new look at gender differences in aggressive behaviour.

For the second edition, all of the chapters were thoroughly revised and updated, and readers will note that the reference list consists predominantly of sources that were published in the last ten years. Two new chapters have been added, addressing the problem of aggression between social groups (Chapter 9) and presenting the findings of research on international terrorism as a worldwide problem (Chapter 10). In addition, several new sections have been added to the chapters of the first edition.

- Chapter 1 has been extended to include a discussion of *proactive*/*reactive* as well as *direct*/*indirect* aggression, and presents original items from key instruments that measure aggressive behaviour.
- Chapter 2 now includes a more extensive section on the role of *hormones* in aggression.
- In Chapter 3, a new section on *narcissism* and aggression has been added, and the section on the role of *self-control* in regulating aggression has been expanded.
- Chapter 4 contains a new section on *social exclusion* as a trigger of aggressive behaviour.
- Chapter 5 has a new section that presents *content analyses* of violent media and a summary of meta-analytic findings on the link between media violence and aggression.
- Chapter 6 contains a new section on *aggressive driving*, and the sections on school and workplace aggression and aggression in the sports world have been expanded.
- Chapter 7 includes a new section on *witnessing family violence* as a form of domestic violence against children.

- Chapter 8 has been revised in order to integrate the section on definitions of sexual aggression with prevalence studies based on legal or research definitions, contrasting both with rape definitions in everyday discourse.
- Chapter 11 offers a more extensive discussion of *learning processes* in the context of prevention.

As a new feature, each chapter concludes by suggesting a number of "tasks to do" to prompt the readers to go beyond the contents presented in the text and embark on their own investigation of key aspects of aggression related to the part of the world in which they live.

Acknowledgements

I would very much like to thank Craig Anderson and Jeff Bryson for their valuable and constructive comments on the manuscript, which have greatly helped to improve its final shape. I am also grateful to the members of my team at Potsdam, Marianne Hannuschke, Claudia Ahlert, Fabian Kirsch, Johanna Reiche, and Isabell Schuster, for their reliable help. Deep thanks go to my family, Peter, Charlotte, and Justin, for their unfailing encouragement and support during the ups and downs of working on this second edition.

Introduction

The report on the "Global Burden of Armed Violence 2011" issued by the Geneva Declaration on Armed Violence and Development estimated that, between 2004 and 2009, 396 000 people died each year around the world in intentional killings as a result of interpersonal violence, gang violence, or economically motivated crime. A further 55 000 people worldwide died each year as a result of armed conflicts, political violence, or terrorism (Geneva Declaration on Armed Violence and Development, 2011, p. 43). These figures are assumed to be conservative estimates, as many countries do not have reliable incidence reporting systems and are likely to under-report violent deaths. The number of fatalities, shocking as it is, represents only the tip of the iceberg as far as the scale of aggression worldwide is concerned. Another global report, the "World Report on Violence and Health" published by the World Health Organization in 2002, presented data on the prevalence of various forms of interpersonal violence, including sexual violence, and violence against children, intimate partners, and elders. It also addressed collective violence between social, ethnic, and national groups (Krug, Dahlberg, Mercy, Zwi, & Lozano, 2002). In his foreword to the report, Nelson Mandela stated:

> The twentieth century will be remembered as a century marked by violence. It burdens us with its legacy of mass destruction, of violence inflicted on a scale never seen and never possible before in human history . . . a legacy that reproduces itself, as new generations learn from the violence of generations past, as victims learn from victimizers, and as the social conditions that nurture violence are allowed to continue.

In the same year, and in stark contrast to Mandela's view, Pinker (2011, p. xxi) claimed that "violence has declined over long stretches of time, and today we may be living in the most peaceable era of our species' existence." He argued that although rates of violence have decreased over the course of the centuries, people find it hard to appreciate this decline because societies have become less tolerant of violence, and the scope of what is condemned as violent action has broadened as a result. In a historical analysis of violence that started with a prehistoric case more than 5000 years ago, Pinker presented extensive data to demonstrate that rates of violent death in its various shapes and forms have declined over the centuries. With regard to the extreme levels of violence seen in two world wars in the first half of the twentieth century, he concluded: "Together with whatever ideological, political, and social currents put the world at risk in the first half of the twentieth century, those decades were also hit by a run of extremely bad luck" (Pinker, 2011, p. 209).

The squarely opposite appraisals by Mandela and Pinker mark the extreme poles of thinking about the scale of violence in modern-day societies. On close reading, both analyses reveal many difficulties involved in comparing data on violence across historical periods, countries, and – not least – methodologies that allow such divergent conclusions to be drawn. These problems will also become apparent throughout this volume.

The analysis in this book takes a broad perspective on aggression that extends beyond severe forms of physical violence (see Chapter 1 for conceptual distinctions), based on the definition of aggression as any behaviour carried out with the intention of harming another person. This definition places a wide range of behaviours beyond the infliction of severe physical harm on the agenda of aggression research. Given the complexity of human aggression, it is obvious that no single discipline can offer a comprehensive understanding of its manifestations, causes, and consequences. Therefore it should be stated at the outset what issues are at the focus of the *social psychological* perspective on aggression adopted in this volume, and what aspects fall within the realm of other fields.

From a social psychological point of view, aggression is conceptualised as a social problem in interactions between individuals and between groups, resulting from the joint influence of the personal characteristics of the actors and the situational and societal conditions in which their behaviour takes place. Accordingly, when considering *manifestations* of aggression, the focus will be on aggressive behaviour that occurs in social relationships between individuals and/or groups and that is prompted by certain features of social situations. This means that other forms of aggression, such as self-destructive behaviour, psychopathological or criminal forms of aggression, or the destruction of material objects, will not be included in the discussion. Similarly, in terms of *explaining* the occurrence of aggressive behaviour, the focus will be on individual differences that emerge in the course of development and interact with situational states as well as factors in the social environment. Other causal influences, such as hormonal processes, are considered only insofar as they influence a person's readiness to engage in aggressive interactions. Finally, our examination of the *consequences* of aggression will focus on the social functioning of both victims and perpetrators in the context of their interpersonal relationships, excluding such issues as the forensic or psychiatric treatment of aggressive offenders and clinical help for targets of aggressive behaviour in coping with their victimisation.

In addition to stating what will, and will not, be covered in the chapters to follow, the present volume should be positioned in the existing social psychological literature on aggression. Readers looking for a concise summary of the main issues and findings of aggression research will find a chapter on aggression in every textbook of social psychology. Those seeking in-depth analyses of particular topics will find excellent collections of specialised papers in recent handbooks and edited volumes, such as those by Flannery, Vazsonyi, and Waldman (2007), Forgas, Kruglanski, and Williams (2011), and Shaver and Mikulincer

(2011). The present volume takes an intermediate position between these two levels of specificity. It aims to provide an up-to-date and critical overview of aggression research from a social psychological perspective, so as to inform readers about the central concepts, issues, and findings in the study of aggression. Furthermore, it is intended to create a knowledge base from which the more specialised literature can be approached.

Aggression research has made enormous progress in the last decade. The majority of studies included in this new edition have been published since the first edition came out in 2001, resulting in an almost complete renewal of the original reference list. This is not to say that the older sources have become obsolete. Instead, it is a reflection of the fact that the older studies have informed new research that built on their findings and developed them further. For example, interventions to reduce gang violence or sexual aggression were made more effective based on systematic evaluations that revealed the limited success of earlier programmes.

The last ten years have seen new constructs, such as relational aggression, social exclusion, and the study of self-control, become firmly established on the agenda of aggression research. They have also seen a growing interest in understanding new forms of aggression, such as cyberbullying, as well as forms that pose an ever increasing threat to people's well-being, such as terrorist violence. And they have seen impressive methodological progress, reflected, for example, in a rapid growth in the number of meta-analytic reviews, integrating the findings from individual studies, and in an increasing number of longitudinal studies covering extensive periods of time. These developments have made a huge contribution towards improving our knowledge about aggression and violence.

A preview of the chapters

The dual role of social psychological aggression research as a basic and an applied field of study is reflected in the chapters of the present volume. In the first part, basic issues of definition, measurement, and explanation will be discussed which are of general significance to the understanding of aggressive behaviour irrespective of its specific manifestations. In the second part of the book, this body of knowledge will be applied to the analysis of specific forms of aggressive behaviour.

Chapter 1 sets the stage by presenting definitions and characteristic features of aggressive behaviour and introducing the main methodologies for measuring aggression. The advantages and limitations of studying aggression in the artificially created settings of the psychological laboratory or in the realistic contexts of naturally occurring situations play an important part in this discussion.

Chapter 2 presents an overview of theories explaining aggressive behaviour, dividing them into approaches that stress the biological foundations of aggressive behaviour and those that explain aggression as the result of psychological processes. It will become clear that there is a considerable diversity of views on the causes of individuals' aggressive behaviour and the processes that lead to aggression. The General Aggression Model (DeWall & Anderson, 2011) will be presented as a framework that integrates personal and situational input variables, internal psychological processes, and social consequences of aggression into a comprehensive theoretical model.

Chapter 3 is concerned with the development of individual differences in aggressive behaviour and with the stability of such differences over the lifespan. In addition to examining patterns of stability and change in aggression during childhood and adolescence, we shall discuss personality dispositions that can account for individual differences in aggression in adulthood, such as trait anger, narcissism, and lack of self-control. Furthermore, gender differences in aggression will be discussed. Traditionally it has been assumed that men are more aggressive than women, and this assumption is well supported, at least for physical aggression. The focus on male aggression has meant that women's aggressive behaviour has been largely neglected by researchers in the past. However, there are now signs of an increasing interest in female aggression, stimulated in part by the introduction of the concept of relational aggression and by the perceived increase in female participation in domestic violence.

In Chapter 4, situational factors will be examined which are assumed to facilitate aggressive behaviour and can explain why individuals are more likely to act aggressively in some situations than in others. The discussion includes the role of aggressive cues that enhance the salience of aggression as a potential response, the experience of social exclusion as a precipitator of aggression, the disinhibiting effects of alcohol, and the role of environmental stressors, such as heat and crowding. Throughout this chapter it will be shown that no matter how powerful situational factors are as determinants of behaviour, they do not affect individuals in a uniform way. Therefore, for a proper assessment of the determinants of aggression, the impact of situational factors needs to be considered in interaction with individual difference variables.

Chapter 5 focuses on the effects of violent media contents on aggressive behaviour in viewers. This chapter addresses an issue that has attracted intense controversy, particularly in public debate and in confrontation between social scientists and the media industry. Three aspects will be at the focus of the analysis: (a) the strength of the evidence addressing the general question of whether exposure to violent media contents leads to increased aggression in viewers, in particular children and adolescents, both in the short term and over time; (b) the psychological processes by which violent media stimuli may increase users' aggression; and (c) the role of pornography in promoting aggression generally, and sexual aggression in particular.

The first five chapters present basic concepts and psychological processes that play a role in explaining who is likely to show aggressive behaviour under what circumstances. The research covered in these chapters highlights the interaction between individual dispositions and situational influences, both in the development of aggressive behaviour over time and in the emergence of aggression in a particular context. In combination, this research lays the foundations for a more detailed examination of specific forms of aggression in different domains of life, which is offered in the second part of the book.

Chapter 6 examines different forms of aggression that are common in everyday life in the public sphere. Bullying at school and in the workplace are forms of aggression that are characterised by an imbalance of power between perpetrators and victims and typically take place over extended periods of time. Both forms of aggression can have severe negative consequences for the victims, and there is evidence to suggest that the victims of bullying at school are at higher risk of being victimised again in the workplace. Aggressive driving is another form of aggression that is common in everyday life, not least because road traffic presents many frustrations. Finally, this chapter reviews research on aggression and violence in the context of the sports world, as shown by competitors as well as spectators.

Chapter 7 deals with aggression in a domestic context and covers issues such as the physical, sexual, and psychological abuse of children, violence against intimate partners, and abuse of elders in the family. Unlike aggressive behaviour in the public domain, these forms of aggression occur in the confined sphere of the home, making it easier for perpetrators to conceal their aggression and more difficult for their victims to attract attention to their plight. At the same time, they are particularly traumatising because the victims are harmed by the very people whom they love and trust.

The same holds true for sexual aggression, which is the topic of Chapter 8. The majority of sexual assaults involve individuals who know each other, often in the context of intimate relationships. We shall review a large body of evidence on the widespread prevalence of sexual aggression in heterosexual and same-sex relationships. Explanations for sexual aggression at the societal and the individual level will be discussed, as well as factors associated with increased vulnerability to sexual victimisation. Following a review of research on the consequences of sexual assault for the victims, the final section explores a new and controversial issue on the agenda of sexual aggression research, namely women's sexual aggression against men.

In addition to a thorough update and extension of the chapters from the previous edition, this new edition contains two new chapters. The first of these, Chapter 9, examines the problem of aggression and violence between social groups. Following a discussion of two influential social psychological explanations of intergroup conflict, the *theory of realistic group conflict* and *social identity theory,* it presents research on gang violence and on hate crimes involving aggression towards targets selected on the basis of their ethnic group membership, religious affiliation, or sexual orientation. It also reviews evidence on the conditions under which people behave aggressively when in the midst of a crowd.

The second new chapter, Chapter 10, addresses the issue of terrorism as a worldwide problem. Research is presented that seeks to explain why people are attracted to terrorism to the point of sacrificing their own life and why, of a large number of disenchanted individuals, few end up committing terrorist acts of violence. It will also be asked why terrorists find support for their violent actions in their communities, and how the experience or fear of terrorist violence affects people's attitudes, behaviours, and psychological well-being.

Finally, Chapter 11 discusses strategies aimed at controlling and preventing aggressive behaviour. Given the scope of aggression and violence, stopping individuals and groups from acting aggressively towards others is a daunting task and, as annual crime statistics reveal, so far success has been limited. First, proposals for controlling aggression will be reviewed that are potentially applicable to many forms of aggressive behaviour. This review includes measures targeting the individual aggressors in an attempt to change their emotions, cognitions, and behaviour. We shall also look at societal-level interventions, in particular with regard to the deterrent function of capital punishment and the potential effectiveness of tighter gun-control legislation. This will lead on to measures custom-tailored to deal with specific forms of aggression, such as gang violence, domestic violence, and sexual aggression. It is evident that this chapter in particular will have to look beyond the boundaries of social psychological research to include relevant contributions from sociology, criminology, and other neighbouring fields.

In conclusion, this book aims to offer up-to-date and critical coverage of the current state of social psychological knowledge on aggression and violence. It presents research on the prevalence, causes, and consequences of aggressive behaviour in its numerous manifestations, and it illustrates strategies for prevention and intervention. Although we are still a long way from providing a conclusive answer to the question of why aggression and violence occur and what can be done to make the world a more peaceful place for the interactions of individuals, social groups, and political and cultural units, the evidence covered in these chapters will show that we are making progress.

1   Defining and measuring aggression

Everybody knows and uses the word "aggression." Entering it as a search term into Google returns about 50 million entries. It derives from the Latin verb "aggredi", which means "to approach" or "to go to," and has found its way from Latin into a wide range of different languages. But what exactly do we mean when we talk about aggression? Is aggression always a bad thing or can it also be good? Should people refrain from it altogether or is there something like a "healthy" level of aggression that enables people to stand up for themselves in different domains of life? How can we explain why people engage in aggressive behaviour and why some individuals seem to be more aggressive than others? Why is it that a person may be calm and composed in one situation but fly off the handle in another?

Just try and raise these questions with your friends, and you are bound to discover that there is considerable diversity in how people think and feel about aggression, including the question of whether a specific behaviour is an act of aggression or not. Is it aggression to spread rumours about an unfriendly colleague or is this just common workplace behaviour? Is it aggression to smack a child on its bottom or is this just part of normal child-rearing? Is it a form of sexual abuse for a father to take a bath with his 6-year-old daughter, and what if the daughter is not 6, but 13 years old? And is there such a thing as "positive aggression" in the sense of being assertive and forceful?

These questions show that when we talk about aggression, we are talking about a social construction. What is – or is not – considered aggression is determined on the basis of shared values and normative beliefs that vary not only between societies but also over time. As we shall see, corporal punishment was considered a legitimate way of disciplining children until fairly recently, and is still seen and practiced as such by many parents across the world. Similarly, questioning a husband's right to force his wife to have sex with him at his convenience, and calling it sexual aggression instead, is a relatively recent development in the western world, and is a view that is by no means universally shared around the globe.

Given the variety of views about aggression as they are voiced in everyday discourse, it is necessary to begin by taking a close look at the meaning of our key concept as it is commonly used and understood in social psychological research on aggression. To evaluate the research presented in this volume, it is important to be aware of the understanding of aggression on which this work is based. We need to establish a consensus about the basic criteria for deciding whether or not a given behaviour should be classified as aggressive, and to think about ways of categorising different forms of aggression so as to gain an understanding of the multiplicity of forms in which aggressive behaviour presents itself.

In addition to dealing with the definition of aggression, a closer look at the available methods and data sources for measuring it is required to facilitate a critical appraisal of the current body of knowledge. Among psychologists, it is commonplace to state that research findings cannot be properly understood without considering the methods by which they were obtained. However, in the public debate about aggression, conclusions about causes and consequences of aggression are typically traded without much concern for their methodological foundations. A case in point is the controversy about the detrimental effects of exposure to media violence, in which each side refers to research results selected to corroborate their views without acknowledging that differences in conclusion often result from differences in methodology. Therefore it seems appropriate that a review of the scholarly literature on aggression should start by looking at the definitions and methodological strategies adopted in this body of research.

What is aggression?

The term "aggression" is as firmly established in ordinary language as it is in the vocabulary of social psychologists. Unfortunately, using the same term does not necessarily imply agreement about what exactly it is supposed to mean, and this is clearly the case with aggression. For example, when prompted for their understanding of aggression, laypersons often talk about "good" or "healthy" aggression as opposed to "bad" aggression. However, most social psychologists have focused on aggression as a negative form of social behaviour that causes problems between individuals, groups, and societies.

Beyond the basic consensus about conceptualising aggression as a form of negative or antisocial behaviour, more precise definitions are needed to lay down the criteria for a specific behaviour to be categorised as "aggressive." A classic definition was proposed by Buss (1961, p. 1), who characterised aggression as "a response that delivers noxious stimuli to another organism." However, this purely behaviourist definition is too broad in some ways and too narrow in others. It is too broad because it includes many forms of behaviour that should not be categorised as aggression, such as accidental infliction of harm. At the same time, it is too narrow because it excludes all non-behavioural processes, such as thoughts and feelings, and behaviours that are intended to cause harm but which, for whatever reason, fail to achieve their objective.

Additional aspects were subsequently included to address the limitations of a purely behaviourist definition (for a comprehensive discussion, see also Tedeschi & Felson, 1994, Chapter 6). For a person's behaviour to qualify as aggression, the behaviour must be carried out with the *intention* of inflicting harm on the target, which in turn presupposes the *anticipation* that the action will produce a particular outcome. Introducing these additional criteria means that *excluded* from the definition are behaviours that result in unintended harm or injury (e.g., by accident or through lack of foresight). At the same time, the definition *includes* behaviours that are aimed at harming another person but which, for whatever reason, do not have the intended consequences. According to this criterion, a gunshot that misses its target represents an aggressive act even though not a hair on the target's head may have been harmed. Focusing on the person's intention to harm also allows non-action, such as the deliberate withholding of care or failure to help a person in need, to be classified as aggressive. A further specification refers to the desire of the target person to *avoid* the harmful treatment. This is to exclude cases of harm inflicted with the target person's consent, such as painful medical procedures or injury inflicted in the context of sadomasochistic sexual practices.

A concise definition that takes these considerations into account was offered by Baron and Richardson (1994, p. 7). They suggested that the term "aggression" should be used to describe "*any form of behavior directed toward the goal of harming or injuring another living being who is motivated to avoid such treatment.*" Their definition is widely accepted (Parrott & Giancola, 2007), and it has also been adopted in the present volume. Broadly speaking, "harm" denotes any form of treatment that is not wanted by the target persons, such as causing them physical injury, hurting their feelings, damaging their social relationships by spreading rumours about them, or taking away or destroying their cherished possessions. It is important to add that, of course, individuals may act aggressively against themselves up to the point of taking their own life. However, this form of self-inflicted harm does not fall within the above definition, as it does not involve harming "another person who is motivated to avoid such treatment." Therefore self-harm is outside the focus of the social psychological perspective on aggression adopted in this volume.

In terms of distinguishing aggression from other forms of social behaviour, the definition offered by Baron and Richardson (1994) has three important implications:

(1) Aggressive behaviour is characterised by its underlying motivation (to harm or injure another living being), *not* by its consequences (whether or not harm or injury actually occurs). This means that a behaviour is regarded as aggressive if it was guided by the intention to harm, even if no damage was done to the target. As noted above, a shot fired from a gun may miss its target, but if it was intended to hit the target, pulling the trigger is nonetheless an aggressive act.

(2) A necessary feature of the intention to harm is the actor's understanding that the behaviour in question has the potential to cause harm or injury to the target. If one person's actions lead to harm or injury of another, but the actor could not have anticipated that the behaviour could lead to those adverse effects, they do not represent instances of aggression. They could be due to carelessness or incompetence, but they do not reflect an intention to harm.

(3) Defining aggression as behaviour that the target would want to avoid means that actions that may cause harm but which are performed with the target's consent, such as painful medical treatment, do not represent instances of aggression.

Aggression can take a great variety of specific forms. Rather than presenting a long and necessarily incomplete list of behaviours that are categorised as aggressive, it is useful to try to identify aspects by which different manifestations of aggression may be distinguished. There are different taxonomies proposed in the literature (e.g., Parrott & Giancola, 2007), each highlighting different aspects. A list of the many faces of aggressive behaviour that is considered useful for capturing the research presented in this volume is presented in Table 1.1.

As with any typology, some forms of aggression may fit into more than one category. This is true, for example, for relational aggression, which is often treated as a response modality that is distinguished from physical aggression, but it is also seen as a form of indirect aggression because it involves acting against other people behind their back (Archer & Coyne, 2005). Furthermore, the different aspects are not mutually exclusive, and indeed they need to be considered in conjunction to properly understand specific forms of aggression.

Table 1.1 The many faces of aggressive behaviour

Aspect	Examples
Response modality	
Verbal	• Shouting or swearing at someone
Physical	• Hitting or shooting someone
Postural	• Making threatening gestures
Relational	• Giving someone *"the silent treatment"*
Immediacy	
Direct	• Punching someone in the face
Indirect	• Spreading rumours about someone behind their back
Response quality	
Action	• Making another person engage in unwanted sexual acts
Failure to act	• Withholding important information from a colleague at work
Visibility	
Overt	• Humiliating someone in front of others
Covert	• Sending threatening text messages to a classmate
Instigation	
Proactive/unprovoked	• Grabbing a toy from another child
Reactive/retaliative	• Yelling at someone after having been physically attacked
Goal direction	
Hostile	• Hitting someone out of anger or frustration
Instrumental	• Taking a hostage to secure a ransom
Type of harm	
Physical	• Broken bones
Psychological	• Fears and nightmares
Duration of effects	
Transient	• Minor bruises
Lasting	• Long-term inability to form relationships
Social units involved	
Individuals	• Intimate partner violence
Groups	• Riots and wars

For example, aggression can be driven by primarily hostile rather than instrumental motives, expressed overtly, in physical terms, and reactively as a response to a preceding provocation.

Although most of the distinctions in Table 1.1 are self-explanatory, some of them require further comment. In the last ten years or so, much emphasis has been placed on the distinction between *direct* and *indirect* aggression. Direct aggression involves a face-to-face confrontation between the aggressor and the target, whereas indirect aggression is aimed at harming other people behind their back by spreading rumours about them or otherwise damaging their peer relationships (Björkqvist, Lagerspetz, & Österman, 1992). As noted above, the term *relational aggression* is also used by some authors instead of indirect aggression to denote aggression aimed at damaging the target person's social relationships (Crick & Grotpeter, 1995). Because indirect/relational aggression can be inflicted covertly, without the target being aware of the aggressor's identity, it represents an alternative strategy for harming another person when the costs of engaging in direct forms of aggression would be high (see also Chapter 3 for a detailed discussion of direct and indirect aggression in the context of gender differences).

The distinction between hostile and instrumental aggression refers to the psychological *function* of the aggressive behaviour for the actor. The primary motive for aggressive behaviour may be either the desire to harm another person as an expression of negative feelings, as in *hostile* aggression, or the aim of achieving an intended goal by means of the aggressive act, as in *instrumental* aggression. The two types of motivation for aggressive behaviour frequently coexist. Nevertheless, we shall see when discussing theories of aggressive behaviour that it makes sense to look at them separately, because different psychological processes may be involved (however, for a critical analysis of the instrumental/hostile distinction, see Bushman & Anderson, 2001).

An additional feature to be considered when defining aggression refers to the normative appraisal of the behaviour in question. There has been some controversy as to whether or not the aspect of *norm violation* should be included among the defining features of aggression, which is why it was not listed in Table 1.1. Disciplinary measures used by teachers and acts of physical self-defence are examples of behaviours that satisfy the criteria of intention, expectancy, and the target's desire to avoid them, and should accordingly be classified as aggressive. Yet they are covered by social norms that turn them into accepted forms of social behaviour. Therefore it has been argued that behaviour should only be considered aggressive if it involves the violation of a social norm. However, as Berkowitz (1993) has pointed out, defining aggression in terms of norm-violating or socially unacceptable behaviour has the problem that the normative evaluation of a behaviour frequently differs depending on the perspectives of the parties involved. For example, some people regard corporal punishment as an acceptable and effective child-rearing practice, while others consider it to be an unacceptable form of aggression.

A similar point can be made with regard to the distinction between *legitimate* and *illegitimate* aggression. Capital punishment, for example, satisfies all elements in the definition by Baron and Richardson (1994). Actions are carried out with the intention and expectancy of inflicting harm on the convicted person, who is motivated to avoid such treatment. However, these actions are legitimised in the laws of many countries. Is it therefore appropriate to regard them as aggression, provided that the legal procedures are properly conducted? Although many people will reject this idea, others may have a different view. In the absence of explicit legal regulations, the question of legitimacy becomes even more difficult. Are violent acts committed by separatist movements or marginalised minorities legitimate or illegitimate forms of aggression? It is obvious that the answer to this question will depend to a large extent on the position a person takes in the underlying controversy. Therefore, although issues of norm violation and legitimacy are highly relevant, for example, when analysing dynamics of intergroup encounters or justifications for aggressive behaviour, they are problematic to accommodate as critical features in a basic definition of aggression.

Before turning from the definition to the measurement of aggressive behaviour, we should briefly look at the meanings of three related terms, namely antisocial behaviour, coercion, and violence. *Antisocial behaviour* denotes behaviour that violates social norms of appropriate conduct (DeWall & Anderson, 2011). It is a broader construct than aggression in that it includes behaviours that are not intended to harm other people, such as vandalism or lying. *Coercion* is defined by Tedeschi and Felson (1994, p. 168) as "an action taken with the intention of imposing harm on another person or forcing compliance." Defined in this way, coercion can be seen as a form of instrumental aggression. Coercive action can take the form of threats, punishments, or bodily force, and it is directed as much at gaining compliance as at causing harm. Coercion is seen as a form of social influence, which highlights the social nature of this type of behaviour and brings it conceptually closer to processes of communication and interaction not previously examined in the context of aggression.

In contrast to antisocial behaviour and coercion, which are broader constructs than aggression, the term *violence* is more narrow in meaning and is restricted to behaviours carried out with the intention of causing serious harm that involve the use or threat of *physical force*, such as hitting someone over the head, or – in the ultimate form – taking another person's life. Thus not all instances of aggression involve violence (e.g., shouting at someone would be described as aggressive, but not violent), but all acts of violence qualify as aggression. Violence is defined by social psychologists as "the infliction of intense force upon persons or property for the purposes of destruction, punishment, or control" (Geen, 1995, p. 669), or as "physically damaging assaults which are not socially legitimised in any way" (Archer & Browne, 1989, p. 11). These definitions by psychologists are in line with the definition proposed by the World Health Organization, which describes violence as "the intentional use of physical force or power, threatened or actual, against oneself, another person, or against a group or community, that either results in or has a high likelihood of resulting in injury, death, psychological harm, maldevelopment or deprivation" (Krug et al., 2002, p. 4). A functional typology of violence has been presented by Mattaini, Twyman, Chin, and Lee (1996), who identified six potential functions of violent behaviour: (1) change of, or escape from, aversive situations; (2) positive reinforcement (i.e., attainment of a particular goal); (3) release of negative affective arousal; (4) resolution of conflict; (5) gaining of respect; and (6) attack on a culturally defined "enemy," (i.e., a member of a devalued out-group).

A special form of violence has been termed structural violence and denotes societal conditions that entail harmful consequences for certain social groups. Structural violence is seen as a latent feature of social systems that leads to social inequality and injustice – for example, by institutionalising a power hierarchy between men and women which leaves women largely unprotected against male sexual coercion (Lubek, 1995). In the present analysis, the focus will be on violence between individuals and social groups, but issues of structural violence will also be touched upon in several places in the course of this volume.

How to measure aggression

Obtaining measures of aggressive behaviour poses particular challenges for researchers due to its potentially harmful nature. When studying prosocial behaviour, creating situations in which research participants may give help to others is not problematic from an ethical point of view. By contrast, it would be highly unethical to set up experimental situations in which research participants are given the opportunity to inflict genuine harm on another person, to make them targets of other participants' aggressive behaviour, or to expose them to treatments that are expected to increase the likelihood of subsequent aggression. With regard to studying aggression in real life outside the laboratory, other problems arise. With the exception of unusual circumstances, such as war or civil unrest, acts of severe aggression are relatively rare in everyday life, and are therefore hard to measure in natural contexts. Therefore the methodological toolbox available to aggression researchers is quite limited. Table 1.2 presents an overview of the different methods used by social psychologists to study aggressive behaviour as well as aggressive thoughts and feelings.

Broadly, measures of aggression rely either on observation or on reporting. Observational methods enable researchers to gain first-hand evidence of aggressive behaviour in a given situation, either in the laboratory or in the field. Measures based on reporting provide them

Table 1.2 Summary of methods for studying aggression

Observing behaviour in natural contexts	• Naturalistic observation
	• Field experiments
Observing behaviour in the laboratory	• Essay evaluation paradigm
	• Teacher–learner paradigm
	• Competitive reaction time paradigm
	• Hot sauce paradigm
	• Cold water paradigm
Collecting reports of aggressive behaviour, thoughts, and feelings	• Self-reports of aggressive behaviour
	• Parent or teacher reports
	• Peer nominations
	• Measures of anger and hostility
	• Implicit Association Text
	• Projective techniques
Using official records	• Crime statistics
	• Archival data

with second-hand accounts of aggressive behaviour that can cover longer periods of time and a wider spectrum of situations. The approaches in each group have both strengths and limitations, as will become evident in the following discussion.

Observing aggressive behaviour in natural contexts

Observing aggression "in the field" (i.e., under natural conditions) is a good strategy because information can be collected in an unobtrusive way without people realising that their behaviour is being observed and recorded. With a behaviour such as aggression that everybody knows to be socially undesirable, this is a particular asset because it avoids the problem of measurement *reactivity* (i.e., people's tendency to change their usual patterns of behaviour because they are aware that they are under observation). At the same, the fact that people are not made aware that they are being observed – and therefore have no chance to opt out – poses particularly strict ethical constraints on this type of method. Observational measures in natural contexts mainly come in two forms: *naturalistic observation* in which the researcher records behaviour as it unfolds naturally without manipulating the situation in any way, and *field experiments* that involve a systematic yet unobtrusive manipulation of certain variables to observe the effects of that manipulation on the likelihood of aggressive behaviour.

Naturalistic observation

One aim of observation in natural contexts is to obtain a picture of the various forms of aggression in a particular setting, and the frequency with which they occur. For example, Graham and Wells (2001) conducted an observational study in 12 bars in Ontario, Canada, to record the frequency of aggressive incidents among young adults. Aggressive incidents were defined as involving "personal violation (verbal insults, unwanted physical contact), behavior that was offensive according to the norms of the place, or a dispute in which the participants had personal investment" (p. 197). Trained observers were positioned in different parts of the bar and recorded each aggressive incident. They observed, for example, that 77.8% of the incidents involved men only, 3.4% of them involved women only, and the remaining incidents involved both men and women. In a third of all incidents, severe physical aggression (e.g., kicking, punching, brawling) took place.

The use of naturalistic observation with children is illustrated by a study by Ostrov and Keating (2004). Trained observers watched preschool children during a free play situation and recorded their behaviour as physical aggression (e.g., hitting, pushing, punching), verbal aggression (e.g., antagonistic teasing, calling mean names), or relational aggression (e.g., excluding from playgroup, ignoring a peer). Frequency counts of behaviours in each category were summed up to yield physical, verbal, and relational aggressiveness scores for each child.

In this type of research, the natural flow of behaviour is first recorded, then broken down into more fine-grained units of analysis, and finally assigned to the pre-defined categories.

Questions of when and where to sample behaviour and how to define the basic units of analysis are central to this methodological approach (e.g., Wehby & Symons, 1996). Moreover, it is important to check how reliably the units can be assigned to the different categories by examining the correspondence achieved by independent coders.

Field experiments

Another line of research using observation in natural contexts is directed at exploiting inconspicuous everyday situations to examine the link between certain antecedent conditions and subsequent aggressive responses. Unlike naturalistic observation, where there is no interference with the situation itself, field experiments involve the unobtrusive variation of one or more variables in order to assess their impact on aggressive behaviour as the dependent variable. For example, to test the prediction that de-individuation (not being personally identifiable; see Chapter 9) would lower the threshold for aggression, Rehm, Steinleitner, and Lilli (1987) asked a group of fifth-grade students to dress in identical T-shirts for their sports lessons, ostensibly so that a new teacher would find it easier to tell them apart from members of the opposing team who wore their own clothes. The number of aggressive acts during the ensuing handball game was recorded by two independent observers who were unaware of the experimental hypotheses. Students who were wearing the uniform T-shirts committed more aggressive acts than students who were wearing their own clothes, supporting the prediction that anonymity increases the likelihood of aggressive behaviour.

As another example of a field experiment, Baron (1976) studied behaviour in a common traffic situation to test the hypothesis that drivers would show more aggressive behaviour when they were frustrated. Frustration was manipulated by the time that a confederate took to move his car when the traffic lights turned green (Baron, 1976). The dependent variable was drivers' aggressive behaviour, defined in terms of latency and duration of horn honking. In support of his prediction, Baron showed that the drivers, who were unaware that they were taking part in an experimental study, honked faster and longer when the confederate took longer to move his car. Similarly, a field experiment by Harris (1974) showed that people waiting in a queue responded more aggressively if a confederate jumped in close to the head of the queue (high frustration) than when he jumped in closer to the end of the queue (low frustration).

Despite their advantages in terms of allowing the analysis of naturally occurring behaviour uncontaminated by social desirability concerns, many additional variables may operate in field situations which are not under the experimenter's control. Suppose, for example, that the queue-jumping approach was to be used to study the aggressive responses of people waiting for a bus. There would be a problem if, in some of the trials, the bus for which people were waiting was 15 minutes late at the time of the experimental intervention, creating an additional and powerful source of frustration that might contaminate the effects of the queue-jumping manipulation. In addition, a key feature of experimental research, namely the random allocation of participants to experimental conditions, is often not possible in natural contexts without making people aware that they are part of an experiment.

Observing aggressive behaviour in the laboratory

The lack of control over so-called "third variables" that might interfere with the experimental variations and problems with the assignment of respondents to experimental treatments are the main reasons why the vast majority of observational studies on aggressive behaviour have been conducted as *laboratory experiments*. In this setting, situations can be created by the investigator to meet three essential criteria:

(1) that respondents are exposed to an experimental manipulation aimed at influencing their aggressive response tendencies
(2) that they can be randomly assigned to the experimental and control conditions
(3) that many factors which might influence participants' behaviour over and above the experimental treatment can be controlled.

Experimental studies of aggression need to resort to paradigms in which participants can show behaviour *intended* to harm another person without actually allowing real harm to be inflicted on anyone. Several experimental paradigms have been developed to address this challenge by creating situations in which participants are given the opportunity to deliver a range of different aversive stimuli to another person without actually causing them any harm (Ritter & Eslea, 2005). Each paradigm uses a somewhat different cover story to disguise the true purpose of the measure.

(1) The *teacher–learner* paradigm. This paradigm uses the set-up of an alleged learning experiment in which one person adopts the role of a teacher and presents a word association learning task to another person, the learner. In the first round, pairs of words are presented to the learner. In the second round, only the first word of each pair is presented, and the learner has to correctly remember the second word of the pair. Errors made by the learner are punished by the teacher through administering aversive stimuli. Unbeknownst to the participants, assignment to the two roles is rigged so that the participant always ends up as the teacher, and the learner is a confederate of the experimenter. The participant's choice of punishment intensity represents the measure of aggressive behaviour. In the original version of this paradigm, punishments are delivered in the form of electric shocks, the strength of which is determined by the teacher. This procedure, which is probably better known from the famous study of obedience by Milgram (1974) than from the context of aggression research, was pioneered by Buss (1961). He developed an "aggression machine" that enabled respondents to choose the *intensity* and the *duration* of electric shocks which they thought would be delivered to the learner whenever he made a mistake (no shocks were actually delivered, but respondents received mild shocks in a trial run to convince them that the device was genuine). In later studies, electric shocks were replaced by other aversive stimuli, such as loud noise (e.g., Edguer & Janisse, 1994) or air blasts to the throat (Verona & Sullivan, 2008), and the intensity and duration chosen by the participant

were used as measures of aggressive behaviour. The teacher–learner paradigm provides an experimental framework in which the effects of a variety of independent variables on aggression may be studied (Baron & Richardson, 1994). Differences in aggressive responding may be examined, for example, as a function of respondents' group membership (male vs. female; prisoners vs. students) or situational manipulations (different degrees of frustration or physiological arousal). However, a criticism of the teacher–learner paradigm has been that if they accept the cover story, participants may be motivated by prosocial concerns in that they want to help the alleged learner to improve his task performance, rather than show aggressive behaviour. In addition, it can only measure proactive/unprovoked aggression, as the learner has no opportunity to retaliate. These problems were addressed, at least to some extent, in other paradigms.

(2) The *essay evaluation* paradigm. In this paradigm, the aggressive behaviour consists of delivering negative evaluations of an essay purportedly written by the target person. This paradigm has been used to investigate aggressive behaviour in response to preceding frustration or provocation, and was first introduced by Berkowitz (1962). Participants are told that they are to provide a written solution to a problem-solving task which will then be evaluated by a fellow participant, who is in fact a confederate of the experimenter. They are also informed that the evaluation will be expressed in terms of the number of electric shocks delivered by the evaluator, with one shock indicating the best possible and ten shocks indicating the worst possible evaluation. Irrespective of the quality of their solution, participants then receive either few or many shocks, depending on whether they are in the provocation or control condition. In the second and main phase of the experiment, the roles are reversed and the participant gets the chance to evaluate the solution provided by the other person. The number of shocks administered indicates the strength of the aggressive response. Typically, more shocks are administered to a target person who is seen as responsible for a negative evaluation of the actor in the first round of the experiment, supporting the hypothesis that provocation leads to aggression. The essay evaluation paradigm has been modified by later studies that replaced electric shocks with other aversive stimuli, such as the level of negative verbal feedback in the essay evaluation (e.g., Krahé & Bieneck, 2012). Vasquez, Denson, Pedersen, Stenstrom, and Miller (2005) adapted the paradigm to use feedback about participants' performance on an anagram task rather than an essay, and used the length of time for which participants made the target persons submerge their hands in unpleasantly cold water as a measure of aggression. Beyond addressing the role of anger or provocation, this experimental set-up allows researchers to examine additional variables moderating the effects on aggression. A case in point is Berkowitz and LePage's (1967) well-known study on the so-called "weapons effect", which will be examined in more detail in Chapter 2. They showed that when participants were angered they showed more aggression towards the person who was the source of the anger in the presence of an aggression-related cue (such as a revolver) than in the presence of a neutral object (such as a badminton racket).

(3) The *competitive reaction time (CRT)* paradigm. Using a different cover story, this widely used paradigm leads participants to believe that they are engaging in a competitive reaction time task against another participant. It is also referred to as the Taylor Aggression Paradigm (TAP), as it was first introduced by Taylor (1967). When a visual cue appears on a screen, the participants have to press a button, and the person who presses the button first is the winner of that trial. Before each trial, the participants have to set the intensity of the aversive stimulus delivered to their opponent in case they win, which represents the measure of aggressive behaviour. In the original version developed by Taylor (1967), electric shocks were used as aversive stimuli. Because success and failure of the naive participants are in fact predetermined by the experimenter, each genuine participant receives, as well as delivers, a set number of shocks in the course of the task. In order to make sure that participants perceive the shocks to be aversive but not painful, each participant's threshold of unpleasantness is established in a pilot phase. As the naive participants are always programmed to win the first trial, the intensity they set for the first trial yields a measure of proactive or unprovoked aggression. After the first trial that they lost and in which they received a shock from their alleged opponent, participants' subsequent intensity levels reflect the strength of their reactive or retaliative aggression. Rather than delivering electric shocks, recent studies have used other aversive stimuli, such as unpleasantly loud noise (Bartholow & Anderson, 2002), and measured the intensity and duration chosen by the participant as a measure of aggressive behaviour. Yet other studies have replaced the electric shocks with points deducted from an opponent so as to reduce the other person's reward (e.g., Stadler, Rohrmann, Steuber, & Poustka, 2006).

As noted by Giancola and Parrott (2008), there is ample evidence for the validity of the CRT as a measure of aggressive behaviour. Several studies have shown that the extent to which participants deliver aversive stimuli was significantly correlated with trait measures of aggression (see, however, Ferguson & Ruda, 2009, for disconfirming evidence) and also differentiated between individuals with and without a history of violence. In their own study, Giancola and Parrott (2008) showed that the intensity of electric shocks was more closely related to trait measures of physical aggression than to trait measures of verbal aggression, anger, or hostility, as one would expect from a measure intended to inflict physical harm. A criticism raised about the standard format of the CRT concerns the absence of a non-aggressive response option. Participants can only choose to deliver more or less aversive shocks or noise blasts, the procedure does not allow them to refrain from delivering aversive stimuli altogether. To address this criticism, modifications have been proposed to include non-aggressive response options (Bushman, 2002; Reidy, Shirk, Sloan, & Zeichner, 2009).

(4) The *hot sauce* paradigm. This strategy for measuring aggression also consists of delivering unpleasant stimuli to a target person, this time in the form of setting the amount of hot spicy sauce to be consumed by a target person who allegedly dislikes this kind of food (Lieberman, Solomon, Greenberg, & McGregor, 1999; McGregor et al., 1998). Participants are first made to taste the sauce themselves before being given the

chance to allocate a portion to a person whom they believe strongly dislikes spicy food. The selected quantity of sauce is weighed and constitutes the measure of aggressive behaviour. Using this method, Ayduk, Gyurak, and Luerssen (2008), found that participants allocated more hot sauce to a target person who rejected them as a potential partner in the experiment than to a target person who chosen them as a partner. Meier and Hinsz (2004) showed that participants allocated more hot sauce to a target person when they were in a group than when they acted individually and gave more hot sauce to each target when targets were in a group rather than encountered as individuals. Barlett, Branch, Rodeheffer, and Harris (2009) extended the method by giving their participants a choice of sauces that differed in their degree of hotness. Using a combined index of the hotness of the sauce selected and the quantity assigned to the target person, they were able to show that participants who had played a violent video game subsequently showed more aggressive behaviour than those who had played a non-violent video game. The hot sauce measure yields an easily quantifiable index of aggressive behaviour. Moreover, it is ethically feasible because it does not lead to any harmful effects other than, perhaps, temporary discomfort in the participants as a result of having to test a small quantity of the sauce themselves.

Each of the paradigms discussed so far uses deception (concealing the true purpose of the experiment) to make participants believe that they are harming another person. In addition to obtaining ethical approval for the chosen procedures beforehand, it is important to stress that participants in these experiments have to be carefully debriefed to explain the true purpose of the experiment, and to reassure them that they did not inflict any real harm on another person.

Critique of laboratory measures of aggressive behaviour

Although the experimental procedures discussed in this section have generated a strong body of knowledge on aggressive behaviour, their prominence has not been uncontroversial. The main challenge refers to their validity – that is, the extent to which they (a) represent the underlying theoretical construct of aggression (construct validity), and (b) can explain aggressive behaviour occurring outside the laboratory in the "real world" (external validity). In terms of construct validity, the criticism has been raised that the different approaches are potentially susceptible to alternative interpretations of what is taken to be aggressive behaviour. In the teacher–learner paradigm, participants may choose high levels of shock because they want to help the learner to accomplish his learning task more effectively. In the essay evaluation paradigm, high shock intensities may similarly reflect compliance with the cover story, namely to provide critical feedback on a person's problem-solving success. In the competitive reaction time paradigm, participants' responses may be motivated by competitiveness rather than by aggression. As far as external validity is concerned, critics have pointed out that the artificial and impoverished nature of many laboratory settings is a far cry from those contexts in which aggression occurs as a social problem in the real world.

Thus it has been questioned whether evidence gained from laboratory studies can contribute to a better understanding of aggression as it occurs in natural contexts. Without being able to review the controversy in detail (see Anderson & Bushman, 1997; Berkowitz, 1993; Ritter & Eslea, 2005 for comprehensive discussions), two main lines of reasoning have been advanced in defence of the use of laboratory experiments in the study of aggression:

(1) Experimental procedures for measuring aggressive behaviour can be said to have high construct validity (i.e., to measure the same underlying construct) if they meet the following requirements. First, a person's responses should be correlated across different indicators of aggression, such as duration and intensity of shocks versus negative verbal feedback or amount of hot sauce. This means that if Person A delivers more intensive electric shocks than Person B, then Person A should also give more negative feedback or allocate more hot sauce compared with Person B. Secondly, the different measures of aggression should be triggered by the same antecedent conditions. This means that if the induction of negative affect is found to elicit higher shock intensities compared with a control condition, it should equally result in higher amounts of hot sauce or more intense noise blasts being administered to a target person. Integrating results from over 100 published studies, Carlson, Marcus-Newhall and Miller (1989) examined these aspects of construct validity, and concluded that "critics have gone too far in rejecting outright the thesis that specific aggression measures typically index a common behavioral disposition" (p. 386).

(2) The second criticism refers to a lack of external validity (i.e., the failure to generalise to aggressive behaviour in the real world). This criticism was tackled by Anderson and Bushman (1997; Bushman & Anderson, 1998). They conducted a meta-analysis including 53 studies of laboratory and real-world aggression to explore the correspondence between the two sources of data across a range of independent variables. Meta-analysis is a statistical procedure in which the results from a number of individual studies are converted to a common metric and then integrated into a quantitative index of effect size, indicating the magnitude of the difference between two variables, such as location of a study in the laboratory versus the real world, across the entire range of studies (Glass, McGaw & Smith, 1981). More specifically, Anderson and Bushman (1997) looked for converging evidence concerning the role of individual difference variables (sex, trait aggressiveness, and type A personality; see Chapter 3) and situational variables (provocation, alcohol, media violence, anonymity, and temperature; see Chapters 4 and 5) as determinants of aggressive behaviour. With the exception of temperature, for which the laboratory evidence was inconsistent both in itself and with field research, they found substantial convergence across the two data sources. In both laboratory and field research, aggression was found to increase as a function of provocation, alcohol consumption, anonymity, and exposure to violent media content. Aggression was also found to be higher in both settings for men (physical aggression only) and for individuals with high trait aggressiveness and type A behaviour patterns. It is worth noting, however, that the magnitude of the effects varied across the two approaches. For example, the effect of violent media content was found to be higher in laboratory

experiments than in field studies, whereas the link between trait aggressiveness and behavioural aggression was stronger in field studies than in the laboratory. As Bushman and Anderson (1998) have pointed out, these differences are conceptually plausible. They argue that the stronger effect size for the impact of trait aggressiveness on aggressive behaviour found in field studies was to be expected, because laboratory studies mostly involve relatively homogeneous samples of college students, whereas variability in trait aggressiveness is greater among the largely unselected samples observed in many field studies. In contrast, the effect of media violence on aggressive behaviour was expected to be stronger in the laboratory, because the time interval between exposure to media violence and measurement of subsequent aggression is typically shorter in laboratory experiments, and extraneous influences that might undermine the impact of the media stimuli can be controlled more effectively in the laboratory.

In conclusion, the analysis by Anderson and Bushman (1997) shows that the unquestionable advantage of laboratory experiments (i.e., their ability to test causal hypotheses in a controlled context) is not necessarily undermined by a lack of external validity (for a similar appraisal, see Berkowitz, 1993). Therefore laboratory studies are of prime importance for testing cause–effect hypotheses and illuminating conceptual links between instigating variables, aggressive behaviour, and its consequences. On the other hand, they do not allow researchers to study severe manifestations of aggressive behaviour which would be unethical to elicit deliberately. Therefore, there is clearly a need for additional methodological tools for studying aggressive behaviour.

Collecting reports of aggressive behaviour

Obtaining behavioural records through direct observation is not always feasible. As noted above, the dangerous and potentially damaging nature of aggressive acts prevents researchers from creating conditions in their laboratories under which such behaviours might be observed. Moreover, many aggressive acts occur without prior warning, or only come to light after they have been performed. This is typically the case for acts of violence, such as physical assault, rape, or homicide. In these cases, researchers have to rely on reports of aggressive behaviours rather than gaining first-hand evidence of their occurrence. In other contexts, research questions may be focused not on behaviours, but on internal variables, such as aggressive thoughts and fantasies, that are not open to observation. An overview of different strategies for collecting reports about aggression is presented in the third part of Table 1.2. Most of these methods are commonly used techniques of data collection that can be applied to the measurement of aggression.

Self-reports of aggressive behaviour

In this approach, participants are asked to provide reports of their own aggressive behaviour. The reports can either refer to general patterns of behaviour that reflect trait aggression, such as how characteristic particular aggressive behaviours are for the person, or they can refer to the frequency of specific behaviours shown in the past, such as how many times in the last year the person has spread rumours about a colleague at work.

Probably the best-known general measure of dispositional or trait aggression relying on self-reports is the Aggression Questionnaire (AQ) developed by Buss and Perry (1992). Based on the earlier Buss-Durkee Hostility Inventory (Buss & Durkee, 1957), the AQ measures the habitual tendency to engage in physical aggression and verbal aggression. In addition, it contains two scales measuring individual differences in anger and hostility, seen as important affective correlates of aggressive behaviour. Box 1.1 shows the full set of all 29 items of the AQ together with mean scores for men and women in the original study by Buss and Perry (1992). You can assess your trait aggression by completing the items in Box 1.1 and comparing your mean score on each scale with the original sample.

The AQ has been translated into several other languages (e.g., Herzberg, 2003, for a German version; Santisteban, Alvarado, & Recio, 2007, for a Spanish version), and has undergone some extensions (Buss & Warren, 2000) and modifications (Bryant & Smith, 2001). It remains one of the most widely used instruments for measuring trait aggression.

As can be seen from the items in Box 1.1, the behavioural scales of the AQ are limited to the measurement of direct physical and verbal aggression. Other self-report measures have recently been developed to measure individual differences in indirect and relational aggression. The Richardson Conflict Response Questionnaire (RCRQ; Richardson & Green, 2003) contains 10 items that measure direct verbal and physical aggression (e.g., "threw something at them," "yelled or screamed at them") and 10 items that measure indirect, relational aggression (e.g., "gossiped about the person behind their back") as behaviours shown when angry.

Recording self-reports of aggression is not limited to the perpetrator perspective. It is also a viable strategy for collecting evidence on victimisation by aggressive others. For example, Forrest, Eatough, and Shevlin (2005) developed the Indirect Aggression Scales (IAS) that contained the same set of items from the aggressor perspective (e.g., "criticised another person in public") and from the target perspective ("someone criticised me in public").

Another aspect of indirect aggression is captured in the Displaced Aggression Questionnaire (DAQ) by Denson, Pedersen, and Miller (2006). The DAQ was designed to measure individual differences in the tendency to engage in displaced aggression. Displaced aggression is said to occur when people shift their aggressive response to a provocation or frustration away from the original source onto an innocent target (see Chapter 2 for a more detailed discussion). The DAQ was developed to capture stable individual differences in the tendency to displace aggression, and consists of three subscales, addressing Angry Rumination (e.g., "I often find myself thinking over and over about things that have made me angry"), Revenge Planning ("I have long living fantasies of revenge after the conflict is over"), and Displaced Aggression at the behavioural level ("I take my anger out on innocent others").

Each of the measures discussed so far was designed to assess aggressive behaviour in a wide range of contexts. In addition, self-report measures are available that are custom-tailored to specific manifestations of aggressive behaviour in different domains, such as sexual aggression, aggressive driving, or school bullying. In the area of sexual aggression,

BOX 1.1   Items from the Aggression Questionnaire (AQ) by Buss and Perry (1992).
(Copyright American Psychological Association. Reprinted with permission)

Where do you stand on trait aggression?
Response scale:

1	2	3	4	5
Extremely				*Extremely*
uncharacteristic				*characteristic*
of me				*of me*

Physical Aggression
- Once in a while I can't control the urge to strike another person.
- Given enough provocation, I may hit another person.
- If somebody hits me, I hit back.
- I get into fights a little more than the average person.
- If I have to resort to violence to protect my rights, I will.
- There are people who pushed me so far we came to blows.
- I can think of no good reason for ever hitting a person.*
- I have threatened people I know.
- I have become so mad that I have broken things.

Verbal Aggression
- I tell my friends openly when I disagree with them.
- I often find myself disagreeing with people.
- When people annoy me, I may tell them what I think of them.
- I can't help getting into arguments when people disagree with me.
- My friends say that I'm somewhat argumentative.

Anger
- I flare up quickly but get over it quickly.
- When frustrated, I let my irritation show.
- I sometimes feel like a powder keg ready to explode.
- I am an even-tempered person.*
- Some of my friends think I'm a hothead.
- Sometimes I fly off the handle for no good reason.
- I have trouble controlling my temper.

Hostility
- I am sometimes eaten up with jealousy.
- At times I feel I have gotten a raw deal out of life.
- Other people always seem to get the breaks.
- I wonder why sometimes I feel so bitter about things.
- I know that "friends" talk about me behind my back.
- I am suspicious of overly friendly strangers.
- I sometimes feel that people are laughing at me behind my back.
- When people are especially nice, I wonder what they want.

Please give each item a number from 1 to 5 depending on how characteristic it is of you.

Reverse the coding on the items marked with * so that high scores always mean high aggressiveness. Then compute the mean of the items for each scale.

In the Buss and Perry (1992) study, men had significantly higher scores on Physical Aggression, Verbal Aggression, and Hostility, but not on Anger. The sex difference was largest on the Physical Aggression scale.

You can compare your mean score on each scale with the following mean scores derived from Buss and Perry (1992, Table 3), based on U.S. college students:

Scale	Men (n = 612)	Women (n = 641)
Physical aggression	2.70	1.98
Verbal aggression	3.04	2.70
Anger	2.42	2.38
Hostility	2.66	2.52

one of the most widely used instruments is the Sexual Experiences Survey (SES) developed by Koss et al. (2007). The SES can be used to obtain both self-reports of sexual aggression and, in a parallel format, self-reports of sexual victimisation. In the original version, which was developed in the 1980s (Koss & Oros, 1982; Koss, Gidycz, & Wisniewski, 1987), the scales were phrased to assess men's sexual aggression and women's sexual victimisation. In the revised version by Koss et al. (2007), the items are worded in a gender-neutral manner, so that both men and women can be asked about their experiences as perpetrators as well as victims of sexual aggression. It presents a list of different sexual acts, combined with a list of different coercive strategies, and respondents are asked to indicate how many times since the age of 14 or in the last year they engaged in or experienced each specific combination. An example of the format of the SES is presented in Box 1.2.

The SES is widely used to examine the scale of sexual aggression and to explore risk factors as well as consequences of sexual aggression and victimisation. A discussion of research based on the SES will be presented in Chapter 8.

Self-reports of aggressive behaviour can be combined with other-reports (i.e., reports of another person's behaviour) to examine the dynamics of aggressive interactions and to assess the correspondence between self- and other-reports. This type of approach is prominently represented by the "Conflict Tactics Scales" developed by Straus (1979) to measure intimate partner violence. In the latest version, the Conflict Tactics Scales 2 (CTS2), respondents are asked to indicate which of a list of behaviours representing psychological aggression, physical assault, and sexual coercion they have shown against their partner in the past year (Straus, Hamby, Boney-McCoy, & Sugarman, 1996). In addition, they are asked to indicate, for the same set of behaviours, how many times their partner showed the respective behaviour towards them. This enables researchers to examine the agreement between couples about the behaviour shown by each of the partners and to see whether intimate partner aggression is mutual or just shown by one partner in a relationship. Research based on the CTS will be reviewed in Chapter 7. A similar set of scales addressing aggression in parent–child interactions was developed by Straus, Hamby, Finkelhor, Moore, and Runyan (1998).

One problem with the use of self-reports is that aggression is a socially undesirable behaviour, and respondents are aware that they are being asked to report behaviour that makes them appear in a negative light. This renders self-report measures susceptible to response distortions in the direction of social desirability, resulting in an under-reporting of aggressive behaviour (for a discussion of this point regarding the AQ, see Becker, 2007). In many cases there is no alternative to asking people to report on their aggressive behaviour, as there are no other reliable sources one could consult instead. However, in some contexts it is feasible to rely on information from third parties who can provide information about the aggressive behaviour of research participants.

Parent or teacher reports of aggressive behaviour

In studies measuring aggression in childhood and adolescence, parents and teachers may be recruited as informants. They have first-hand knowledge of a target person's aggressive

BOX 1.2 **Example items from the Short Form of the Sexual Experiences Survey**
(see Koss et al., 2007, for the full item list)

Item 2 of the Short Form Perpetration (SES-SFP)

Perpetration Item	How many times in the past 12 months?				How many times since age 14?			
I had oral sex with someone or had someone perform oral sex on me without their consent by:	0	1	2	3+	0	1	2	3+
a. Telling lies, threatening to end the relationship, threatening to spread rumors about them, making promises about the future I knew were untrue, or continually verbally pressuring them after they said they didn't want to.	☐	☐	☐	☐	☐	☐	☐	☐
b. Showing displeasure, criticizing their sexuality or attractiveness, getting angry but not using physical force after they said they didn't want to.	☐	☐	☐	☐	☐	☐	☐	☐
c. Taking advantage when they were too drunk or out of it to stop what was happening.	☐	☐	☐	☐	☐	☐	☐	☐
d. Threatening to physically harm them or someone close to them.	☐	☐	☐	☐	☐	☐	☐	☐
e. Using force, for example holding them down with my body weight, pinning their arms, or having a weapon.	☐	☐	☐	☐	☐	☐	☐	☐

Item 2 of the Short Form Victimization (SES-SFV)

Victimisation Item	How many times in the past 12 months?				How many times since age 14?			
Someone had oral sex with me or made me have oral sex with them without my consent by:	0	1	2	3+	0	1	2	3+
a. Telling lies, threatening to end the relationship, threatening to spread rumors about me, making promises I knew were untrue, or continually verbally pressuring me after I said I didn't want to.	☐	☐	☐	☐	☐	☐	☐	☐
b. Showing displeasure, criticizing my sexuality or attractiveness, getting angry but not using physical force, after I said I didn't want to.	☐	☐	☐	☐	☐	☐	☐	☐
c. Taking advantage of me when I was too drunk or out of it to stop what was happening.	☐	☐	☐	☐	☐	☐	☐	☐
d. Threatening to physically harm me or someone close to me.	☐	☐	☐	☐	☐	☐	☐	☐
e. Using force, for example holding me down with their body weight, pinning my arms, or having a weapon.	☐	☐	☐	☐	☐	☐	☐	☐

behaviour, and can provide behavioural ratings that can then be examined for their convergence with each other and with the person's self-reports. Parent ratings of aggression are particularly useful for studying aggression in young children. An example is provided by Tremblay et al. (1999), who asked parents to rate their children on a list of 11 items addressing physical aggression, such as" bites," "kicks," and "takes away things from others." Similarly, teachers can provide ratings of a child's aggressive behaviour. For example, the teacher form of the Preschool Social Behavior Scale (PSBS-T) developed by Crick, Casas, and Mosher (1997) consists of 16 items on which preschool teachers are asked to rate the children in their class in terms of relational aggression (e.g., "Tells others not to play with or be a peer's friend") and overt aggression (e.g., "Hurts other children by pinching them"). In a recent study of adolescents, self-reported use of violent media was related to teacher reports of the participant's aggressive behaviour in school to examine the link between media violence use and aggression (Krahé & Möller, 2011).

Peer nominations

Whereas parents and teachers are typically asked to rate research participants on a number of items describing aggressive behaviour, peers are asked to nominate (i.e., select from their group) individual children who fit certain behavioural descriptors. Students in a class might be asked to nominate classmates who, for instance, "attack others without reason," "say nasty things to other children even if they had done nothing wrong" or "take other children's possessions" (Kokko, Pulkkinen, Huesmann, Dubow, & Boxer, 2009). The more nominations participants receive, the higher their aggression score. Peer nominations have also been used to measure indirect forms of aggression, as in the Direct–Indirect–Aggression Scale (DIAS) by Björkqvist et al. (1992), for example to nominate a peer who says unpleasant things behind the person's back. Using this approach, Kokko et al. (2009) demonstrated significant correlations of $r = 0.43$ between peer-nominated aggression at age 8 years and peer-nominated aggression at age 19 years for both boys and girls in an American sample, and a correlation between peer-nominated aggression at age 8 years and peer-nominated aggression at age 14 years of $r = 0.38$ for girls and $r = 0.35$ for boys in a Finnish sample. These correlations are impressive, given that different peers provided the ratings at the two measurements.

Measures of aggressive affect: anger and hostility

In addition to eliciting reports of aggression at the behavioural level, researchers are often interested in studying the affective concomitants of aggressive behaviour, most notably *anger* and *hostility*. Standardised scales have been developed to capture individual differences in the disposition to experience affective states that are relevant to aggressive behaviour. As shown in Box 1.1, Buss and Perry's (1992) "Aggression Questionnaire" contains two such scales, measuring dispositional anger and hostility. Another pertinent measure of anger is the State–Trait Anger Expression Inventory (STAXI) developed by Spielberger (1996). The

STAXI addresses five facets of anger and the way it is characteristically expressed. The State–Anger scale asks participants to describe how they feel at a particular moment in time (e.g., "I feel angry," "I feel irritated"), the Trait–Anger scale addresses the habitual tendency to experience these affective states, the Anger/In and Anger/Out scales refer to individual differences in the tendency to direct anger towards others in the social environment as opposed to directing it towards the self, and the Anger/Control scale measures the extent to which people try to keep their anger under control (Forgyas, Forgyas, & Spielberger, 1997). The STAXI is available in many languages, and has been established as a reliable and valid measure of anger in a variety of domains (for a review, see Eckhardt, Norlander, & Deffenbacher, 2002).

Measure of aggressive cognitions: the Implicit Association Test (IAT)

Given the undesirable nature of aggression, self-reports of aggressive thoughts, feelings, and behaviours are susceptible to the problem of systematic under-reporting. Therefore measures of aggressive cognitions have been developed that cannot be easily distorted in the direction of social desirability. Several studies have adapted the Implicit Association Test (IAT), first developed as a measure of attitudes (Greenwald, McGhee, & Schwartz, 1998), for the measurement of aggressive cognitions and aggression-related self-construals (for a review, see Richetin & Richardson, 2008). The IAT is designed to tap into aggressive cognitions in an unobtrusive way by examining the speed with which aggression-related stimuli are recognised. It is based on the assumption that the strength of the association between a target category (e.g., self vs. other) and an attribute category (e.g., aggressive vs. non-aggressive) can be inferred from the speed with which participants can recognise particular combinations of the target and the attribute category. Participants are presented with a list of words that refer to either the target category (e.g., I, ME vs. THEM, YOU) or the attribute category (e.g., AMBUSH, CHOKE vs. HELP, COMFORT; see Richetin, Richardson, & Mason, 2010). For each word, they are asked to indicate as fast as they can whether it refers to the category in question (e.g., press the left key if it is a word related to "me" and press the right key if it is a word related to "other") or whether it refers to the attribute category in question (e.g., press the right key if it is an aggressive word, press the left key if it is a nonaggressive word). If participants respond faster to aggression-related words when they share the same key as the "me" words than when they share the same key as the "other" words, this is regarded as an indication that "me" and "aggression" are closely related in the person's self-concept.

Scores on the Aggression IAT are interpreted as a measure of stable dispositions towards aggression, and they have been used to predict aggressive behaviour in specific situations. So far, there is some evidence that individual differences in aggressiveness may be used to predict aggressive behaviour in laboratory contexts. For example, Richetin et al. (2010) found that participants' implicit aggression scores on the IAT predicted their negative behaviour towards a target person, but only after a preceding provocation by the same person. A study by Gollwitzer, Banse, Eisenbach, and Naumann (2007) showed that IAT scores may be useful as unobtrusive outcome measures in the evaluation of interventions designed to reduce aggression. Other studies have shown that the IAT can also detect changes in aggression-related self-concept as a result of situational influences. In research on exposure to media violence, it has been found that playing a violent video game for brief periods of time leads to shorter reaction times for aggressive words associated with the self than playing a non-violent game (Bluemke, Friedrich, & Zumbach, 2010; Uhlmann & Swanson, 2004).

Projective techniques

Another approach for exploring the affective and cognitive correlates of aggressive behaviour involves the use of projective techniques in which participants are presented with ambiguous stimulus material and asked to generate a response. Their responses are then scored for aggressive content by trained raters. The most well-known projective technique for the measurement of aggression is the Picture Frustration Test (PFT) by Rosenzweig (1945). It consists of a set of cartoon drawings, each depicting a situation that involves some mild to moderate form of everyday frustration. An example is shown in Figure 1.1.

The person who caused the frustration (e.g., the driver responsible for splattering the pedestrian) makes a comment that is designed to attenuate or add to the initial frustration. The participant suggests a verbal response from the perspective of the frustrated person in the cartoon, and responses across all cartoons are coded for aggressive content (Rosenzweig, 1976). For example, responses are categorised as "extraggression" if they are directed at the social environment, or as "intraggression" if they are directed towards the self, a distinction similar to the STAXI scales of Anger/in and Anger/out. A children's version of the PFT is also available, and an example situation is "A girl on a swing is telling another girl that she is planning to keep the swing all afternoon" (Rosenzweig, Fleming, & Rosenzweig, 1948).

Apart from the time-consuming task of coding free-response statements into a manageable set of categories, the reliability of such codings (i.e., their consistency across independent raters and across repeated codings by the same rater) has been difficult to achieve (Rosenzweig, Ludwig, & Adelman, 1975). Moreover, responses to the PFT have been found to be affected by social desirability concerns. Taken together, these problems explain why the use of projective techniques is no longer widespread in the social psychological analysis of aggression.

The methods for obtaining records of aggressive behaviour can be used to study aggressive behaviour over time. In addition, self-reports of aggressive thoughts and feelings, such as anger, and measures that assess the accessibility of aggressive thoughts in a person's self-concept can be used to predict aggressive behaviour in the course of an individual's development. *Longitudinal studies* provide an important methodological tool for testing hypotheses about the emergence and change of aggressive behaviour that cannot be addressed in short-term experimental studies. They follow the same group of participants over two or more points in time to examine patterns of change at the intra-individual level and to test

Figure 1.1 Example from the Rosenzweig Picture Frustration Test (PFT). (From Rosenzweig, 1945, p. 4. Copyright John Wiley & Sons, Inc. Reprinted with permission).

hypotheses about the prospective links between certain risk factors and aggression. For example, Ostrov and Godleski (2009) combined teacher ratings and observational data to demonstrate that impulsivity and hyperactivity predicted aggressive behaviour in preschool children over a 4-month period. A Spanish study by Carrasco, Holgado, Rodriguez, and del Barrio (2009) showed that higher levels of parents' hostility predicted more aggressive behaviour in their children over a period of 2 years. In a unique study covering a period of 40 years and including three generations, Huesmann, Dubow, and Boxer (2011) explored the links between parents' and children's aggression at different points in their lives. They found, for example, that parents' aggression measured when they were 8 years of age correlated at $r = 0.24$ with their children's aggressive personality assessed 40 years later, when the parents were 48 years old.

Using official records

Rather than asking individuals about their own behaviour or that of others, researchers can derive information about aggressive behaviour from publicly available databases. These data sources are not compiled for research purposes, and therefore researchers are limited to whatever information has been recorded.

Crime statistics

Official records of reported crime are compiled by most countries, and these figures can be used by aggression researchers who want to study criminal forms of aggression. For example, the Uniform Crime Reporting (UCR) Program in the USA, which was started in 1929, presents detailed information about the rates of different forms of criminal violence, broken down by a range of demographic characteristics, such as perpetrator and victim sex or, age, and also by geographic location (see www.fbi.gov/about-us/cjis/ucr/ucr). For instance, it tells us that 15 241 cases of murder and non-negligent manslaughter were reported in 2009, corresponding to a rate of 5 cases per 100 000 inhabitants. This figure compares with 23 438 cases or a rate of 9.4 per 100 000 inhabitants for the year 1990. Crime statistics can be used to examine changes in crime rate in covariation with legal measures to address research questions about aggression. For example, they can help to answer the question of whether murder rates go up when the death penalty is abolished, or whether the tightening of gun control legislation is followed by a decrease in the number of gun-related homicides. We shall come back to crime statistics when we discuss these questions in later chapters.

A possibly less obvious candidate for the study of aggression is the analysis of meteorological records that provide data on average annual temperatures and comparisons between geographic regions. Meteorological data have been used as an important source for studying the link between temperature and aggression. Historical analyses revealed that riots were more frequent in hotter regions and during hotter periods of the year, and this observation was followed by systematic analyses relating temperature scores and violent crime rates within and across different regions to further explore the link. By relating crime statistics to weather records, Anderson and his colleagues found, for example, that the incidence rates of serious and deadly assault were higher in years with a higher average temperature, whereas robbery figures remained unaffected by temperature (Anderson, Bushman & Groom, 1997, Study 1; for a more detailed discussion of this research, see Chapter 4).

Another example of the use of archival data in the study of aggression comes from the domain of sexual violence. In the USA, such data have been used to demonstrate a link, within different states, between the circulation rate of pornographic magazines and the number of rapes documented in annual crime statistics (e.g., Jaffee & Straus, 1987; Scott & Schwalm, 1988). However, these studies nicely illustrate the problem of inferring causal pathways from associations between frequency data of this kind. It may not be unreasonable to suspect that both the popularity of pornographic magazines and the incidence of rape could be expressions of a third variable, such as the prevalence of a macho gender stereotype among the male population, which was not captured by the design of the study.

Finally, newspaper reports have been used as another form of archival records by aggression researchers. For example, Mullen (1986) referred to this data source in his analysis of violent behaviour by lynch mobs. Based on newspaper reports of 60 lynchings in the USA between 1899 and 1946, Mullen demonstrated that the larger the mob relative to the number of victims, the more savage the lynch mobs were in their atrocities. Mullen used these data to argue that the larger the mob, the more difficult it is for members to retain self-focused attention that is important for inhibiting violent behaviour. We shall return to this issue in our discussion of intergroup aggression in Chapter 9.

Summary

- This chapter was designed to create a basis for the understanding and critical appraisal of empirical research to be discussed in the course of this volume. A definition of aggression was presented that focuses on three aspects, namely *harmful consequences*, *intention and expectancy of inflicting harm*, and *desire by the target person to avoid the harmful treatment*. Dimensions for classifying aggressive acts were discussed to provide a framework for the systematic description of different forms of aggressive behaviour.
- The research strategies reviewed in this chapter clearly show that a variety of methods are available for the social psychological analysis of aggression. Ethical constraints prevent researchers from setting up situations in which participants are given the opportunity to harm another person. Therefore experimental analogues have been developed that facilitate the study of behaviours intended to harm another person without causing any actual harm. Evidence was presented which shows that findings obtained in contrived laboratory settings correspond in many areas to findings obtained from studies conducted in the real world.
- When first-hand observation is not feasible, a range of methods are available for collecting reports of aggressive behaviour. Self-reports, parent or teacher reports, peer nominations, and projective techniques have a firm place in social psychological aggression research. Archival records such as crime statistics and even weather data provide an additional data source that can be used to establish the rates of different violent offences and to examine covariations of crime rates and a range of other variables.

Tasks to do

(1) Plan the design of an experiment using the *competitive reaction time* paradigm to study the effect of frustration on aggression.
(2) Find out how you score on the Aggression Questionnaire presented in Box 1.1, and compare your score with the Buss and Perry sample at the bottom of the box.

(3) Visit the official crime statistics database in your country, find out the most recent figure available for annual homicide rates, and compare this rate with the figures recorded 10 and 20 years earlier.

Suggested reading

Anderson, C. A., & Bushman, B. J. (1997). External validity of "trivial" experiments: The case of laboratory aggression. *Review of General Psychology, 1*, 19–41.

Carlson, M., Marcus-Newhall, A., & Miller, N. (1989). Evidence for a general construct of aggression. *Personality and Social Psychology Bulletin, 15*, 377–389.

2 Theories of aggression

Aggressive behaviour causes harm and suffering to individuals and groups on a large scale, and incurs enormous social and material costs for societies. Therefore the search for theories that may explain *why* people engage in aggressive behaviour has been a prime task for researchers for a long time, not least because understanding the factors that instigate aggressive behaviour is a first step towards prevention. In this chapter, the most important lines of theorising will be presented and discussed in terms of their contribution to understanding the origins and causes of aggressive behaviour. The purpose of this discussion is twofold – first, to highlight the diversity of approaches from different disciplines that have been offered to explain aggressive behaviour, and secondly, to build up a stock of theoretical constructs pertaining to different aspects of aggressive behaviour that can be applied later to the understanding of specific forms of aggression in different areas of life.

As a starting point, Table 2.1 presents an overview of the major theoretical explanations of aggression as a form of social behaviour. Their core assumptions about what causes aggression are presented along with a summary statement about their empirical support that is, of course, to be substantiated by a more detailed discussion in the course of this chapter.

The approaches in the top half of Table 2.1 are based on biological concepts and principles, whereas the approaches in the bottom half of the table address psychological processes. Rather than seeing them as competing or even mutually exclusive, biological and psychological explanations are best regarded as complementary, stressing different aspects of aggression as a complex form of social behaviour. The next sections will introduce each of the approaches in turn, paying special attention to the answers they provide to two closely related questions:

(1) Is aggression an innate quality of human nature?
(2) Is it possible for aggressive behaviour to be changed, pre-empted, or controlled?

Biological explanations

In this section, we shall look at four lines of research that refer to biological principles in explaining aggression, namely the ethological approach, the sociobiological approach, the

Table 2.1 Major theories of aggression: An overview

	Aggression conceptualised as . . .	Main database	Empirical evidence
Biological approaches			
Ethology	. . . internal energy released by external cues; steam-boiler model	Animal studies	No support as a model for human aggression, but still popular in lay discourse
Sociobiology	. . . product of evolution through natural selection	Animal studies and correlational studies in humans	Support for correlational but not causal links
Behaviour genetics	. . . transmitted as part of genetic make-up	Twin and adoption studies	Support for the predictive value of genetic similarity
Hormonal explanations	. . . influenced by male sex hormones and cortisol	Comparisons of violent and non-violent individuals	Some empirical support
Psychological approaches			
Freudian psychoanalysis	. . . a destructive instinct	Case studies	No quantitative empirical evaluation, but important source for the F-A hypothesis
Frustration–aggression (F–A) hypothesis	. . . a likely response to frustration, likelihood enhanced by aggressive cues	Experimental studies	Supported by empirical evidence
Cognitive neo-associationist model and excitation transfer theory	. . . a result of affect elicited by aversive stimulation that is interpreted as anger	Experimental studies	Supported by empirical evidence
Learning theory	. . . a result of reinforcement, either direct or indirect (observed)	Experimental and observational studies	Supported by empirical evidence
Social information processing models	. . . a result of social information processing, enactment of learned scripts	Experimental and longitudinal studies	Supported by empirical evidence
The General Aggression Model (GAM)	. . . a result of personal and situational input variables eliciting affective, cognitive, and physiological responses	Correlational experimental, and longitudinal studies	Integrating findings from the psychological approaches

behaviour genetic approach, and the study of hormonal influences on aggression. Biological approaches to aggression focus on the roots of aggressive behaviour in the biological nature of humans, rather than their psychological functioning.

The ethological view: aggression as an internal energy

Among the biological approaches to aggression, one of the earliest contributions came from the field of ethology, which is concerned with the comparative study of animal and human behaviour. As one of the field's pioneers, Konrad Lorenz (1966) offered a model of aggression that dealt specifically with the issue of how aggressive energy is developed and released in both animals and humans. His core assumption was that the organism continuously builds up aggressive energy. Whether and when this energy will be released and lead to an aggressive response depends on two factors: (a) the level of aggressive energy inside the organism at any one time, and (b) the strength of external stimuli capable of triggering an aggressive response. In his *hydraulic model*, also known as the *steam-boiler model*, Lorenz assumed that aggressive energy is produced continuously inside the organism until it is released by an external cue, such as the appearance of a rival in competition for a mating partner. If the amount of energy rises above a certain level without being released by an external stimulus, it will overflow, leading to spontaneous aggression. According to this model, aggressive behaviour is the inevitable consequence of the continuous production of aggressive energy. Even if it were possible to remove all instigating stimuli, this would not abolish aggressive behaviour. As Lorenz (1966, p. 269) put it, such an attempt would be "as judicious as trying to counteract the increasing pressure in a continuously heated boiler by screwing down the safety valve more tightly."

Although Lorenz regarded aggression as a pervasive and inevitable feature of human nature, he saw the possibility of releasing aggressive energy in a controlled and socially acceptable way, e.g., through sports activities. In this way, levels of aggressive energy would be kept below the critical threshold above which violent outbursts and other highly destructive forms of aggression would be likely to occur. According to Lorenz, "the main function of sports today lies in the cathartic discharge of aggressive urge" (1966, pp. 271–272).

When transferring this model from animal to human aggression, it has to be explained why the inhibition against killing members of their own species, widely observed among animals, clearly does not generalise to humans. Here Lorenz (1966) argued that strong inhibitions against intra-species killing were superfluous in the early history of mankind, when fists and teeth were the only (relatively innocuous) weapons with which to attack one another. With the development of ever more sophisticated and lethal weapons, the fact that there is no innate inhibition to counterbalance the potential for destroying one's own species has given rise to basically uncontrolled levels of aggression and violence.

Psychologists have challenged Lorenz's application of his findings from animal studies to human aggression (e.g., Lore & Schultz, 1993). An important criticism is directed at the implication that once the internal reservoir of aggressive energy has been used up by an aggressive act, it is impossible to trigger another aggressive response for as long as it takes for the organism to rebuild a sufficient energy level. Sadly, there is ample evidence from school shootings and other instances of multiple killings that humans can perform several aggressive behaviours in quick succession, and that one aggressive act often serves to precipitate, rather than suppress, further aggressive acts. Neither of these observations is compatible with the depletion effect assumed by the steam-boiler model. Furthermore, Lorenz's belief in the cathartic release of aggressive energy through sports activities is contradicted both by a large literature on sports aggression (see Russell, 2008, and Chapter 6 of this volume) and by research debunking the catharsis hypothesis (see Bushman, 2002, and Chapter 11 of this volume). Given that there is little support for Lorenz's ethological model as an explanation of human aggression, you may wonder why it has been presented here at all. The reason is that it still remains widely popular in everyday discourse when people are suggesting explanations, and indeed cures, for aggression. Enabling readers to participate in this discourse well-equipped with critical arguments to challenge popular myths about aggression is one of the goals of the present volume.

The sociobiological view: aggression as a product of natural selection

Sociobiology is concerned with analysing the biological foundation of social behaviour on the basis of the evolutionary principle of natural selection. It also offers an explanation of aggression which includes both human and animal behaviour, focusing on the long-term, "ultimate" mechanisms that shape and promote aggression through the generations. Rooted in Darwin's (1859) theory on "the origin of species", evolutionary theory is based on the idea that in order for a behaviour to be genetically transmitted within a species, it has to be *adaptive*. Behaviours are adaptive to the extent that they enhance the chances of survival of the species as a whole in the environment in which it lives.

Concise presentations of the general tenets of evolutionary thinking about social behaviour have been provided by Daly and Wilson (1994) and Buss and Shakelford (1997). Applying the principle of evolution through natural selection to the study of aggression, aggressive behaviour directed at fighting off attackers as well as rivals in mate selection is seen as adaptive in the sense of enhancing the reproductive success of the aggressor (Archer, 1995). By virtue of their ability to control access to female mating partners, the more aggressive members of a species are likely to be more successful in passing their genes on to the next generation, thus favouring the natural selection of aggressive behaviour. Their genetic make-up will slowly spread at the expense of less aggressive, and therefore less reproductively successful, members. However, aggression may be a potentially costly and maladaptive behaviour in certain cases. For example, when faced with an opponent of superior fighting power, it incurs the risk of being killed. Therefore the functional mechanism seen as driving the evolution of aggressive behaviour is a cost-benefit calculus (Archer, 2009). As it would be maladaptive to engage in aggressive behaviour when the risk of being overpowered by the opponent is high, it would be functional from the point of view of reproductive success to withdraw from confrontations that involve an opponent of superior strength and fighting power.

Evidence cited to support the sociobiological account of aggression mainly comes from studies of animals, which have been used to generate and test hypotheses about aggressive behaviour in humans. For example, the observation that members of some species respond to cues indicating fighting power, such as opponent size, and refrain from attacking a stronger opponent, has led to the hypothesis that size and physical strength might be correlated with aggression in humans. Studies showing a positive correlation between height and physical aggression in boys and men support this line of reasoning. For example, Archer and Thanzami (2007) found significant correlations between physical aggression scores on the Aggression Questionnaire (see Chapter 1) and body weight ($r = 0.25$) as well as height ($r = 0.34$) in a sample of young men.

Arguably the most controversial contribution of the sociobiological approach in the aggression domain refers to its explanation of sexual aggression (Malamuth & Heilmann, 1998). From an evolutionary point of view, sexual aggression is an optional, if high-risk mating strategy for those men who have limited opportunities for reproduction through consensual sexual relationships (Thornhill & Thornhill, 1991). This view implies that the potential for rape is part of the evolutionary inheritance of all males. It also implies that reproduction is the main functional basis for rape, not necessarily in the rapist's conscious awareness, but in terms of the evolutionary significance of his behaviour. To substantiate their arguments, proponents of the sociobiological explanation of rape refer to two main sources of data: (a) evidence from animal studies of forcible mating behaviours in different species (e.g., Brown, 2000); and (b) crime statistics, showing that the vast majority of rape victims are young women at the peak of their reproductive capacity and that men of low socio-economic status (indicating reduced reproductive opportunities by non-aggressive means) account for a disproportionate percentage of convicted rapists. Both data sources have been fundamentally challenged by critics of the sociobiological approach (Travis, 2003a), and the controversy is far from being settled. We shall return to the arguments of both sides of this debate in more detail in Chapter 8.

In summary, sociobiologists view aggression as a form of behaviour that has evolved in animals as well as humans because of its potential to enhance an individual's reproductive success, thereby facilitating the selective transmission of aggressive genes to future genera-tions. The fact that aggression is universally observed in human societies is seen as corrobo-rating the evolutionary account, although differences between cultures in the level of aggression have been acknowledged (Ferguson & Beaver, 2009). The evidence presented in support of the evolutionary account is largely correlational – for example, the covariation of physical strength and physical aggression – precluding statements about cause-effect rela-tionships. Furthermore, alternative hypotheses may be advanced for many of the findings. For instance, the greater tendency of taller and stronger men to engage in physical aggres-sion may be the result of learning through reinforcement in the individual's socialisation history. Although evolutionary and socialisation hypotheses are often discussed as incom-patible, integrations between the two approaches have been suggested, such as in Malamuth's (1998) "confluence model" of rape discussed in Chapter 8. By drawing attention to the roots of aggressive behaviour in the ancient genetic heritage of the human species and explaining how it may be passed on through the generations, the evolutionary approach has made an important contribution to the theoretical debate about the causes of aggression.

Behaviour genetics: is aggression hereditary?

As noted above, the sociobiological argument holds that aggression has evolved because it is instrumental in enhancing the reproductive success of individuals and species. Central to this line of reasoning is the assumption that the propensity for aggressive behaviour is part of an individual's genetic make-up. This assumption has been addressed in the field of behaviour genetics, which is directed at exploring the role of genetic similarity in explaining personal characteristics and behaviour. Specifically, behaviour geneticists have sought to demonstrate that genetically related individuals are more similar in terms of their aggressive tendencies than individuals who are not genetically related.

Because most children are raised by their biological parents, to whom they are also genetically related, the effects of "nature" and "nurture" normally coincide in individual development. Therefore, to separate the influences of family environment and heritability, special methods are needed. *Adoption studies* are capable of separating the influence of genetic and environmental factors by comparing individuals with their biological parents (shared genes) and with their adoptive parents (shared environment). If children are more similar in their aggressive behaviour to their biological parents than to their adoptive parents, this is an indication that shared genes are more influential than shared environment. Conversely, if adopted children are more similar in aggression to their adopted parents than to their biological parents, this suggests a stronger role of environmental compared with genetic factors. A second methodological approach is provided by *twin studies* that compare identical and fraternal twins in terms of how similar they are in their aggressive tendencies. Identical twins share 100% of their genetic make-up, whereas fraternal twins have only 50% of their genes in common. Therefore evidence that identical twins are more similar than fraternal twins in their aggressive behaviour would indicate that aggression is to some extent genetically transmitted.

Evidence from both twin and adoption studies was reviewed by Miles and Carey (1997). They conducted a meta-analysis of 22 studies in which ratings of aggressive or antisocial behaviour had been obtained either from the respondents themselves or, in the case of young children, from their parents. Two further studies were included in which actual aggressive behaviour had been observed. The authors concluded from their findings that shared genetic make-up plays a large role in similarities in self-ratings as well as parent ratings of aggressiveness, explaining up to 50% of the variance. Taking into account the different age groups included in the meta-analysis, they suggest furthermore that the relative importance of genetic and environmental influences in shaping aggression may change in the course of development. Shared genes were found to be more powerful than shared environmental influences in explaining similarities in aggression in adulthood, whereas the reverse pattern was found for children and adolescents. However, an important qualification of these conclusions comes from the two studies that used behavioural observation as measures of aggression. In these studies, the impact of shared environment was substantially greater than that of genetic similarity. A later meta-analysis by Rhee and Waldman (2002) including 51 twin and adoption studies also found substantial effects of genetic similarity, explaining 41% of the variance, but environmental influences were even stronger, accounting for 59%.

DiLalla and Gottesman (1991) also found in their study of antisocial behaviour that genetic similarity was more influential on questionnaire measures than on behavioural indicators, such as criminal convictions. At the same time, they concluded from their review of adoption studies that genetic factors and environmental factors may have an additive effect. Individuals whose biological as well as adoptive parents were criminal had the highest likelihood of becoming criminal themselves, followed by individuals whose biological parents, but not adoptive parents, had criminal records. The risk of the latter group becoming criminal was found by several studies to be substantially higher than that of the group whose adoptive parents were criminal but whose biological parents were not, suggesting that genes are relatively more influential than shared environment. A recent meta-analysis by Burt (2009) comparing physical aggression and rule breaking as distinct aspects of antisocial behaviour concluded that genetic similarity played a greater role, and environmental factors played a lesser role, in aggressive as compared with rule-breaking behaviour.

On balance, the available evidence suggests that genetic make-up must be regarded as a potentially important source of individual variation in aggression. A precise assessment of the magnitude of its impact relative to environmental influences is difficult, hampered by various methodological problems that have been noted throughout the literature (Tedeschi & Felson, 1994, Chapter 1). For example, studies analysing genetic vs. environmental influences on criminality often failed to distinguish between violent and non-violent crimes. This distinction is crucial if the aim is to determine the heritability of aggressive behaviour in particular, rather than antisocial or deviant behaviour in general (see also Burt, 2009). Furthermore, studies combining both self-report and observation are needed to resolve the issue of why the two types of measures produce diverging evidence on the strength of genetic influences.

With regard to the question of whether or not aggression is an inevitable part of human nature and individual character, research showing the impact of genetic factors has sometimes been construed as suggesting a deterministic, and thus pessimistic, view – if an individual carries the aggressive genes, then he or she will grow up to be aggressive and violent. However, such a view is rejected by behaviour geneticists. They stress that an individual's genetic make-up may predispose him or her towards becoming an aggressive person, but environmental factors play a crucial role in determining whether or not that predisposition will actually be expressed in aggressive behaviour. As noted by van Goozen, Fairchild, Snoek, and Harold (2007), a genetic disposition towards aggressive behaviour may become manifested in behaviour in a negative family environment, or it may be suppressed in a positive environment. As children inherit the genetic disposition towards aggression from their parents, they are likely to grow up in a more aggression-prone family environment (Moffitt, 1993). To complicate matters further, children with a genetic disposition towards aggression may elicit negative responses from their social environment through their aggressive behaviour, also pointing to the interactive influences of nature and nurture.

Hormones and aggression

Another line of biological research on aggression is concerned with the role of hormones in explaining variations in aggressive behaviour (for a review, see van Goozen, 2005). An obvious candidate for examination is the male sex hormone testosterone, both to account for individual differences among men in their aggressive tendencies, and to explain the widely demonstrated gender differences in physical aggression. Testosterone is related to the activation of fight impulses and the inhibition of flight or avoidance behaviour, thereby increasing the likelihood of an aggressive response. A meta-analysis of 18 studies conducted by Archer, Birring, and Wu (1998) found that highly aggressive men had higher levels of testosterone than non-aggressive men. However, van Goozen (2005, p. 287) concluded that the link between male sex hormones and aggression appears to be much weaker in humans than in animals, which may be explained by the fact that human aggression is more socially regulated.

With regard to situational variations in testosterone levels, Klinesmith, Kasser, and McAndrew (2006) conducted an interesting experimental study. They asked male participants to handle a gun or a children's toy for 15 minutes and measured testosterone levels before and after. Men who had handled the gun showed a significant increase in testosterone levels, whereas those who had handled the toy did not. Those who had handled the gun also showed more aggressive behaviour in a subsequent phase, as measured by the hot sauce paradigm (see Chapter 1), and this effect could be at least partly explained by the increase in testosterone levels.

Cortisol has been examined as another hormonal correlate of aggression, as it is related to the experience and management of stress. Low cortisol levels have been linked to fearlessness, risk taking, and insensitivity to punishment. Longitudinal studies have shown that low levels of resting cortisol in boys predict aggressive behaviour over time (e.g., Shoal, Giancola, & Kirillova, 2005; see also McBurnett, Lahey, Rathouz, & Loeber, 2000). Psychological under-reactivity, as indicated by low cortisol levels, seems to be a characteristic feature of aggressive and antisocial behaviour, due to its disinhibiting function (for a review, see van Goozen et al., 2007). By way of explanation, it has been argued that individuals with low levels of cortisol are less susceptible to the fear of punishment that would prevent them from engaging in aggressive behaviour (Raine, 1996). Terburg, Morgan, and van Honk (2009) recently proposed that it is the combination of high testosterone and low cortisol levels (i.e., a high testosterone-cortisol ratio) that predicts high levels of aggression. The aggression-stimulating effect of high testosterone levels is not counterbalanced by the inhibitory effect of cortisol, resulting in unmitigated aggressive behaviour.

Although the research discussed in this section shows that dispositional and situational differences in testosterone and cortisol may be related to aggressive behaviour, it is clear that hormones do not shape aggressive behaviour in a deterministic fashion. They work together with a wide range of factors in the social environment that may reinforce or attenuate the impact of biological influences on aggression.

Psychological explanations

The theoretical approaches considered so far have referred to biological processes in explaining aggression. We shall now turn to contributions that focus on the psychological mechanisms involved in aggressive behaviour. It is worth noting, though, that the earliest line of theoretical development in this tradition, namely Freud's psychoanalytic account of aggression, also started off from a biological construct by conceptualising aggressive behaviour as the expression of a genetically rooted *instinct*.

Freudian psychoanalysis: aggression as a destructive instinct

In his *dual instinct theory*, Freud (1920) proposed that individual behaviour is driven by two basic forces which are part and parcel of human nature: the life instinct (*Eros*) and the death instinct (*Thanatos*). Whereas Eros drives the person towards pleasure seeking and wish fulfilment, Thanatos is directed at self-destruction. Due to their antagonistic nature, the two instincts are a source of sustained intrapsychic conflict that can be resolved by diverting the destructive force away from the individual on to others. Thus acting aggressively towards another person is seen as a mechanism for releasing destructive energy in a way that protects the intrapsychic stability of the actor. In his notion of *catharsis*, Freud acknowledged the possibility of releasing destructive energy through non-aggressive expressive behaviour (e.g., jokes), but with only temporary effects. According to this view, aggression is an inevitable feature of human behaviour beyond the control of the individual. It is interesting to note that Freud revised his earlier model, focusing on Eros only, and added a destructive force after witnessing the violence of World War I (Ekstein, 1949; for a review of psychoanalytic thinking on aggression following Freud, see also Jaffe, 1982).

Empirical evidence in support of Freud's theorising is scarce and largely based on case studies without the stringent operationalisations required in modern-day quantitative studies. Nonetheless, his ideas have played a significant role in promoting the understanding of aggression insofar as they inspired the influential frustration-aggression hypothesis, which will be considered next.

The frustration-aggression hypothesis and the role of aggressive cues

Instinct-related explanations of aggression have met with a critical reception, not least because of a shortage of empirical evidence to support them (see Baron & Richardson, 1994). However, the idea that there is a force within the organism which, in conjunction with external events, leads to aggressive behaviour has been central to an influential line of research that postulated an aggressive *drive* as motivating aggressive behaviour. Unlike an instinct, a drive is not an ever present, continuously increasing source of energy, but is activated only if the organism finds itself deprived of the means of satisfying a vital need. A drive, then, serves as a goal-directed, energising force directed at terminating a state of deprivation.

In the *frustration-aggression hypothesis* (Dollard, Doob, Miller, Mowrer, & Sears 1939), aggression is seen as triggered by frustration. Frustration is defined as an external interference with the goal-directed behaviour of the person. The experience of frustration activates the desire to restore the path to goal attainment, and aggressive behaviour results from the drive to remove the source of the interference. For example, in the field experiment by Harris (1974) discussed in Chapter 1, a person waiting in a queue is pursuing a goal-directed activity, such as buying a train ticket at a busy ticket office. If someone else jumps the cue and cuts in just in front, the person's goal-directed activity is blocked (i.e., frustrated). This releases aggressive energy to restore the goal-directed activity (e.g., by pushing the person aside).

In the first version of the frustration-aggression hypothesis, Dollard et al. (1939) assumed that frustration would always trigger aggression, and that aggression would always be attributable to a preceding frustration. However, it quickly became clear that not every frustration leads to an aggressive response. Alternatively, frustrated individuals may withdraw from the situation or become upset. Moreover, not every aggressive act is the result of a preceding frustration. Acts of instrumental aggression carried out to achieve a particular goal, such as robbing a bank to resolve a desperate financial situation, do not necessarily entail a previous frustration. Therefore the earlier assumption of a deterministic relationship between frustration and aggression was changed into a probabilistic version by Miller (1941), one of the authors of the original theory. He stated that "frustration produces instigations to a number of different types of response, one of which is an instigation of some form of aggression" (p. 338). In this revised view, aggression is not the only but merely a possible response to frustration. To the extent that the aggressive act reduces the strength of the underlying drive, it becomes self-reinforcing – there is an increasing likelihood that an aggressive response will be shown following subsequent frustrations.

Displaced aggression

Whether or not frustration will result in an aggressive response depends on the influence of moderating variables. Fear of punishment for overt aggression or unavailability of the frustrator are factors that may inhibit aggression following a frustration. These moderators may also explain why aggression is frequently "displaced" away from the frustrator on to a more easily accessible or less intimidating target. The concept of *displaced aggression* plays a role in understanding aggression not only in response to frustration, but particularly in response to provocation. Frustration and provocation are related, yet distinguishable constructs. Whereas frustration focuses on goal blockage, provocation refers to an interpersonal encounter. However, the two concepts converge, for example, when the provocation takes the form of exposing another person to frustrating events, such as insoluble tasks or failure in a competition. Therefore research on displaced aggression after a provocation is also relevant to understanding the frustration-aggression link. A meta-analysis of 40 studies by Marcus-Newhall, Pedersen, Carlson, and Miller (2000) found consistent evidence for the displacement of aggression from the source of the frustration or provocation on to a less powerful or more accessible target.

Subsequent research into "triggered displaced aggression" has provided further insights into the psychological processes involved in the path from frustration or provocation to aggression (Miller, Pedersen, Earleywine, & Pollock, 2003). Triggered displaced aggression describes the outcome of a sequence of events which starts with the experience of a frustration or provocation that activates the desire to retaliate. If this desire cannot be acted out, a relatively mild subsequent provocation, the "trigger," may elicit a disproportionately strong aggressive response (Pedersen, Gonzales, & Miller, 2000). For example, a man who is told off at work by his boss, against whom he cannot retaliate because the boss is too powerful, may react with an outburst of verbal abuse in response to a mildly teasing comment from his wife when he gets home. The same comment might have been dismissed as a joke in the absence of the prior provocation. Experimental research has shown that participants who were first exposed to a provocation without being able to retaliate and then encountered a mildly provoking trigger showed much stronger aggressive responses than participants who were exposed to the same trigger without being previously provoked (Vasquez et al., 2005).

To explain displaced triggered aggression, two processes have been proposed (Miller et al., 2003). The first is the elicitation of negative arousal by the initial provocation that is still present when the trigger is encountered, and is intensified by the trigger. The second process refers to rumination about the initial provocation that is maintained because the person is unable to deliver an aggressive response to the source of the frustration. The anger elicited by the original provocation is kept on the back burner and is caused to flare up again by the trigger. As both arousal and rumination subside over time, triggered displaced aggression is likely to occur primarily when the trigger is encountered shortly after the initial provocation. However, Miller et al. (2003) have discussed a number of situational and personal variables that may lead to displaced triggered aggression even over extended periods of time, such as the importance of the goal that is being impeded, or the dispositional tendency to engage in ruminative thinking (for a discussion of research on rumination and aggression, see Chapter 3).

Aggressive cues

If aggression is seen as just one of various different possible responses to frustration, the question arises as to when people are likely to choose aggressive behaviour over alternative responses when they are experiencing a frustration. One answer to this question comes from research into the role of aggressive cues that are present in the situation. Aggressive cues can be any stimuli with an aggressive meaning that increase the salience of aggressive thoughts, such as the presence of weapons, or being reminded of the names of famous boxing champions. It is assumed that if aggression-related cues are present, individuals are more likely to select an aggressive response when angered or provoked.

In a much cited study, Berkowitz and LePage (1967) demonstrated that angered participants subsequently showed more aggressive behaviour in the presence of aggressive cues than in the presence of neutral cues. Half of their participants were angered by receiving negative feedback for a problem-solving task from an alleged co-participant (who was in fact a confederate of the experimenter), while the other half received positive feedback. Both groups were then given the opportunity to evaluate the other person's performance on the task by administering electric shocks (ranging from one shock, indicating a very positive evaluation, to a maximum of 10 shocks, indicating a very negative evaluation). The number of electric shocks delivered represented the measure of aggressive behaviour. To manipulate the role of aggressive cues, the setting was created such that participants saw:

(1)   a 38 mm calibre revolver and a 12 gauge shotgun allegedly left behind by the other student in the experiment (associated weapons condition)
(2)   the same weapons allegedly left behind by a third student in an earlier experiment (unassociated weapon condition)
(3)   two badminton rackets and shuttlecocks (neutral objects condition), *or*
(4)   no objects at all (control condition).

Figure 2.1 presents the number of shocks administered in the different conditions. After receiving negative feedback, participants delivered significantly more shocks in the presence of a weapon than in the presence of a neutral object or in the no object control condition. Whether the weapon was associated or unassociated with the person who was the source of the negative evaluation made no difference. Significantly fewer shocks were delivered by the non-angered participants, and the availability of aggressive cues had no effect on the aggressive behaviour in this group.

Although subsequent studies did not always replicate the effect, with some failing to find a weapons effect and others finding an effect in the non-angered participants as well, overall support for the role of aggression-related cues in facilitating aggressive behaviour is impressive. From their meta-analysis of 57 studies, Carlson, Marcus-Newhall, and Miller (1990, p. 632) concluded that "aggression-related cues present in experimental settings act to increase aggressive responding." In an experimental study of aggressive driving behaviour, Ellison-Potter, Bell, and Deffenbacher (2001) showed that participants who drove past billboards bearing aggressive messages while steering through a course in a driving simulator committed more acts of aggressive driving (speeding, driving through red lights, and killing pedestrians) than participants exposed to non-aggressive billboard messages (for more research on aggressive driving, see Chapter 6). By way of explaining the underlying processes, cognitive priming has been offered as the key mechanism. Being exposed to aggressive cues enhances the accessibility of aggressive cognitions that in turn facilitate aggressive behaviour. We shall come back to the role of aggressive cues as situational primes in Chapter 4.

Thus, starting off as a drive model, the frustration-aggression hypothesis has been developed into a more complex approach, stressing the cognitive appraisal of situational

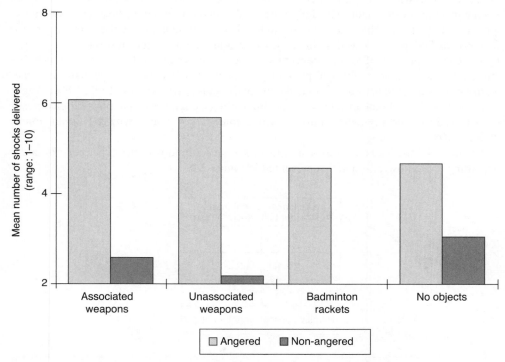

Figure 2.1 Angered participants delivered more electric shocks in the presence of a weapon. No participants were run in the badminton racket/non-angered condition. The means for angered participants between the associated and unassociated weapons conditions and between the badminton rackets and the no objects conditions were not significantly different. (Adapted from Berkowitz & LePage, 1967, Table 2. Copyright American Psychological Association).

cues as a crucial mediator between an anger-eliciting event and an aggressive response. This line of thinking was developed further by Berkowitz (1989) in his cognitive neo-associationist model to be discussed next.

Cognitive neo-associationism: the role of anger

In trying to explain why frustration leads to aggression in some circumstances but not in others, Berkowitz (1989, 1993, 2008) proposed that negative affect in the form of *anger* and its cognitive appraisal are important mediators between frustration and aggression. Frustration leads to aggression only when it arouses negative affective states. Some frustrations may be perceived as challenges, such as struggling to play the piano well, and remain unrelated to aggression, whereas other frustrations may be perceived as accidental, such as being slowed down by an elderly pedestrian when rushing to catch a bus. Although they may elicit anger, the anger response is likely to be weaker in these situations than if the frustration was considered to be deliberate, such as another driver cutting in to take the last empty space in a crowded car park. Viewed in this way, frustrations can be seen as just one example of a more general category of aversive events that elicit negative affect. Other types of aversive stimulation, such as fear, physical pain, or psychological discomfort, can equally instigate aggression through their capacity to make the person angry (Berkowitz, 1997, 1998). Anger is defined as "a syndrome of relatively specific feelings, cognitions, and physiological reactions linked associatively with an urge to injure some target" (Berkowitz & Harmon-Jones, 2004, p. 108).

The process that leads from exposure to an aversive stimulus to the experience of anger according to Berkowitz's model is presented in Figure 2.2.

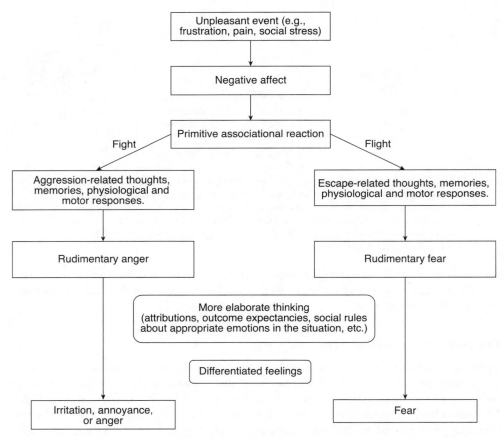

Figure 2.2 The cognitive neo-associationist model of aggression. (Adapted from Berkowitz, 1993, p. 57. Copyright McGraw-Hill Companies. Reprinted with permission).

Berkowitz proposed that unpleasant stimuli give rise to unspecific negative feelings that evoke two immediate reactions – *fight* and *flight*. In a swift and automatic appraisal process that occurs with little or no conscious awareness, the fight impulse is associated with aggression-related thoughts, memories, and behavioural responses, whereas the flight impulse is associated with escape-related responses. These responses serve to quickly channel the initially undifferentiated negative affect into the more specific emotional states of (rudimentary) anger or (rudimentary) fear. In a subsequent more elaborate and controlled appraisal process, the person *interprets* these basic or rudimentary feelings. They are considered in relation to the situational input, and the person enters into a more specific and consolidated emotional state of anger *or* fear. The final emotional state is "a collection of particular feelings, expressive motor-reactions, thoughts and memories that are associated with each other" (Berkowitz, 1993, p. 59). It should be noted that pitting "fight" against "flight" shows parallels with research reviewed earlier into the antagonistic role of testosterone and cortisol as instigators and inhibitors of aggression, respectively, but in the present context the focus is on cognitive rather than physiological processes.

Although the model stops at the level of emotional responses, it is assumed that when the evaluation gives rise to feelings of anger, irritation, or annoyance, an aggressive response becomes likely. For example, when a child is hit by a stone thrown by a classmate, he will immediately experience pain associated with negative affect, probably a combination of anger, inducing the urge to fight, and fear, inducing the urge to run away. Depending on the context and the child's past experience, either the anger or the fear response is likely to dominate and guide his further analysis of the situation. Before deciding how to respond, the child will engage in a more careful appraisal process, including an assessment of his classmate's motives. If he concludes that his classmate threw the stone on purpose, the immediate feeling of anger will be consolidated, and retaliation (i.e., aggression) will be contemplated as an appropriate response.

Because all the components of the emotional experience are associated with each other, the activation of one component is assumed to trigger other components relative to the strength of their association, hence the term "associationism." For example, activating memories of past aversive events can give rise to aggressive thoughts and feelings, which may then increase the likelihood of aggressive behaviour in a new situation or towards a target that is completely unrelated to the initial aversive event.

From the above discussion it is clear that, according to Berkowitz, aggression is only one of several possible responses to aversive stimulation, depending on a chain of processes involving feelings and cognitive appraisals. This implies that aggression is not an inevitable feature of human behaviour, but rather a potential one, which is facilitated or suppressed by the emotional experience elicited by the aversive event and its subsequent cognitive processing.

Excitation transfer theory: anger and the attribution of arousal

The cognitive appraisal of physiological arousal is also at the core of another influential theory of aggression, the excitation transfer model proposed by Zillmann (1979). Like the cognitive neo-associationist model, excitation transfer theory highlights the role of negative arousal as a powerful stimulant of aggression. Building on Schachter's (1964) two-factor theory of emotion, Zillmann (1979) proposed that the intensity of an anger experience is a function of two components: (a) the strength of the physiological arousal generated by an aversive event, and (b) the way in which the arousal is explained and labelled. For example, every motorist is familiar with the sudden increase in physiological arousal that occurs after a narrow escape from a dangerous traffic situation, such as stopping one's car inches away from a pedestrian who stepped out into the road from behind a parked car. Whether or not this arousal will be interpreted as anger depends largely on the appraisal of the situation. If the pedestrian is an adult, then the driver's arousal is likely to be experienced as anger about the other person's carelessness. However, if that person is a young child, feelings of relief are likely to prevail over feelings of anger. Thus the interpretation of physiological arousal elicited by an aversive event is crucial for the link between the aversive event and a potential aggressive response. The associations proposed by the excitation transfer model are shown in Figure 2.3.

Zillmann argued that the effects of frustration as a trigger for aggressive behaviour can be augmented by physiological arousal from a neutral source, unrelated to anger, through a process of misattribution. If physiological arousal from a neutral activity, such as climbing up a flight of stairs or riding a bike, is still present when the person encounters an anger-eliciting situation, such as being verbally attacked, the earlier neutral arousal (excitation) is

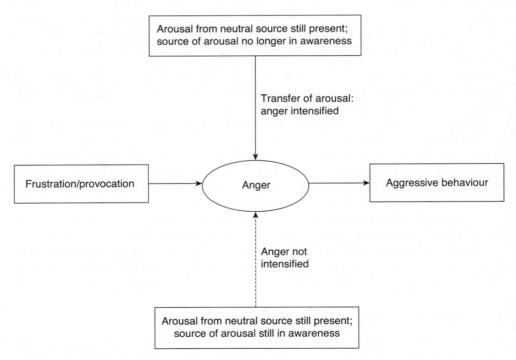

Figure 2.3 Zillmann's (1979) excitation transfer theory.

transferred on to the anger-related arousal and falsely attributed as anger. As a result, the strength of the subsequent aggressive response is increased. However, this misattribution will only occur if the person is no longer aware of the source of the neutral arousal. This in turn means that excitation transfer can only take place within a relatively narrow time window in which arousal from the neutral source is still sufficiently high, yet the actor is no longer aware of its origin.

To support the excitation transfer model, Zillmann and Bryant (1974) conducted an experiment in which the participants had to perform either a physically non-arousing task (threading discs on a wire) or an arousing task (pedalling a bike ergometer for 1 minute). Two minutes later they received a provocation from another person in the form of an aversive noise, another 6 minutes later, they were given the opportunity to administer aversive noise blasts to the person who had provoked them with the noise, using an intensity scale from 1 to 10. The findings are shown in Figure 2.4.

As predicted by the model, participants in the bike condition, who were still aroused from the physical exercise at the time of the provocation, administered louder noise blasts than did

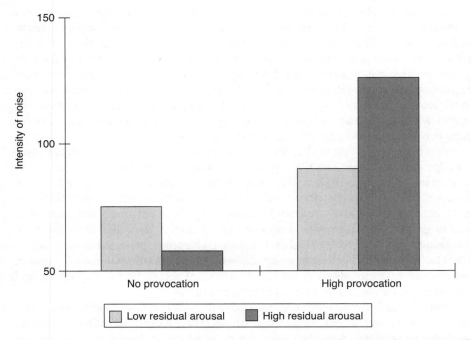

Figure 2.4 High residual arousal at the time of provocation intensifies aggressive responses. The sum of intensity scores (accumulated over all trials) in the no provocation conditions is significantly different from the high provocation/high residual arousal condition. In the high provocation condition, intensity scores of low and high residual arousal are also significantly different. (Adapted from Zillmann & Bryant, 1974, Table 2. Copyright American Psychological Association).

participants in the disc-threading condition, who did not feel any neutral arousal that might have augmented the anger elicited by the provocation.

The excitation transfer model deals with the combined effects of physiological arousal and its cognitive appraisal on the emotional experience of anger. By influencing attributions of physiological arousal, aggressive response tendencies can be strengthened, as shown by Zillmann and Bryant (1974). By the same token, misattributions of arousal may be used to weaken aggressive response tendencies. If people are led to believe that their arousal was caused by a pill rather than by the provocation they experienced from another person, they perceive themselves as less angry and react less aggressively than those who are not offered a neutral explanation for their arousal (Younger & Doob, 1978). Therefore this approach also supports the view of aggression as a potential but by no means inevitable form of human behaviour.

The social cognitive approach: aggressive scripts and social information processing

The importance of cognitive processes in the formation of an aggressive response has been stressed throughout the preceding sections. The way in which people think about an aversive event and about the emotional reaction they experience as a consequence is critical in determining the level of anger as well as the likelihood and strength of an aggressive response. The social cognitive approach further extends this perspective by studying individual differences in aggression as a function of differences in social information processing. In particular, two issues have been explored by this research: (a) the development of cognitive schemata that guide aggressive behaviour; and (b) characteristic ways of processing social information that distinguish between aggressive and non-aggressive individuals.

Cognitive schemata referring to situations and events are called "scripts." Scripts consist of knowledge structures that describe "appropriate sequences of events in a particular context" (Schank & Abelson, 1977, p. 41). These knowledge structures are acquired through experience with the respective situations, either at first hand or vicariously (e.g., through the media). In his social cognitive approach, Huesmann (1988, 1998) proposed that social behaviour in general, and aggressive behaviour in particular, is controlled by behavioural repertoires acquired in the process of early socialisation. From these behavioural experiences, scripts develop as abstract cognitive representations containing the characteristic features of the critical situation, expectations about the behaviour of the participants involved, and beliefs about the consequences of different behavioural options.

For example, if children have repeatedly responded (or seen others responding) to conflict situations by showing aggressive behaviour and thereby settled the conflict to their advantage, they develop a generalised cognitive representation in which aggression and success are closely linked. In subsequent conflict situations, this representation is likely to be activated, leading to further aggressive behaviour. Inherent in aggressive scripts are normative beliefs that guide the individual's decision as to whether or not a specific response is appropriate under the given circumstances. Thus children may develop the normative belief that one can hit back if attacked by a peer in a fight, but not if one is hit by an adult as a disciplinary measure. In a study by Huesmann and Guerra (1997), a significant correlation was found between the endorsement of normative beliefs approving aggressive behaviour and actual aggressive behaviour. Failure to learn the normative restrictions imposed on the manifestation of overt aggression will lead to the repeated display of inappropriate aggression that may form the basis for long-term adjustment problems (Eron, 1987).

Whether or not an aggressive script is activated and guides the person towards responding in an aggressive fashion depends to a significant extent on the initial cognitive processing of the information that precedes the behavioural act. Following the perception of another person's behaviour, the individual looks for an interpretation of that behaviour. Several studies show that individuals with a history of aggressive behaviour selectively prefer interpretations that attribute the other's behaviour to hostile intentions, especially when the actor's behaviour is ambiguous (Geen, 1998). This "hostile attribution bias" may then activate an aggressive script and increase the probability that an aggressive reaction will be selected from the individual's response repertoire (for a more detailed discussion of the hostile attribution bias, see Chapter 3).

The role of scripts as cognitive blueprints that shape aggressive behaviour has been demonstrated in different domains. For example, Vandello and Cohen (2003) showed that cultural scripts about male honour predicted the acceptance of physical violence by a man betrayed by his female partner, and also predicted a more positive view of victimised women remaining with their abusive partners rather than leaving the relationship. Similarly, the more strongly certain known risk factors for sexual aggression, such as drinking alcohol in a sexual encounter, were rooted in adolescents' sexual scripts, the more they were inclined to accept sexual aggression as normative and to engage in sexually aggressive behaviour (Krahé, Bieneck, & Scheinberger-Olwig, 2007).

Another influential model of the role of social information processing in aggression has been proposed by Dodge (2006; Fontaine & Dodge, 2009). His *social information processing (SIP)* model sees the development of social behaviour as a transactional process in which individuals are both influenced by their social environment and are themselves actively involved in shaping that environment. With regard to aggression, or more broadly antisocial behaviour, the SIP model specifies a sequence of social-cognitive processes that pave the way to aggressive behaviour. The first step, *encoding of cues*, involves the perception and encoding of the social stimulus, such as receiving a derogatory comment from a peer. In the second step, *interpretation of cues*, attributions are made about intent and causality (e.g., Did this person mean to be nasty to me or was he just generally in a bad mood?). In the third step, *clarification of goals*, individuals engage in a process of identifying and prioritising their interests in the situation (e.g., to remain friends with the other person or to save face by retaliating). Depending on the goals that are identified, possible responses are generated in the fourth step (*response access or construction*), such as dismissing the remark as funny or responding with an angry comment. In the fifth and final step, the sequence ends with the selection of a response that is then enacted in the situation (*response selection*). It is clear from this five-step model that the individual may leave the pathway to aggression at any of the stages, depending on the appraisal processes and their outcomes. In support of the SIP model, Fontaine and Dodge (2009) presented evidence to show that antisocial youths (a) encode fewer social cues, (b) are more likely to attribute another person's ambiguous behaviour to hostile intentions, (c) are more likely to activate goals that are harmful to social relationships, (d) generate more aggressive and fewer nonaggressive behavioural options, and (e) evaluate aggressive responses more favourably.

The script model and the SIP model both stress the role of the cognitive appraisal of aggressive cues and of potential responses, based on past behaviour and generalised knowledge structures. The development of aggressive scripts as well as the emergence of patterns of information processing conducive to aggressive responding are shaped by an individual's experiences in the course of socialisation (i.e., through the process of learning). Therefore it is time now to turn to the role of learning in the acquisition and performance of aggressive behaviour.

Learning to be aggressive: the role of reinforcement and imitation

There is no doubt that aggression is, to a significant degree, the product of learning processes (Bandura, 1983). The potential importance of genetic dispositions notwithstanding, it is clear that social experiences in the process of development shape an individual's propensity to engage in aggressive behaviour. Learning is defined as behaviour change through experience, and two mechanisms in particular can explain the acquisition of aggressive behaviour: (a) *instrumental learning*, which is behaviour change through direct reinforcement, and (b) *modelling*, which is behaviour change through vicarious reinforcement.

Instrumental learning involves the experience of being rewarded for aggressive behaviour, either by achieving a desired goal through the aggressive act or by winning social approval for showing aggressive behaviour. Children who are praised by their parents for "standing up for themselves" after being provoked, or who succeed in getting hold of a desired toy by grabbing it from another child, learn that aggressive behaviour pays off, and they are encouraged by the positive effects of their behaviour to perform similar aggressive acts in the future. Modelling refers to learning by imitation. Watching others engage in aggressive behaviour also increases the likelihood of aggressive behaviour in the observer, particularly if the models are attractive and/or similar to the observer, and if they are seen being rewarded for their aggression.

In a classic study, Bandura, Ross, and Ross (1961) pioneered the *Bobo doll paradigm*, in which children were shown adult models behaving in either an aggressive or a non-aggressive way towards a large inflatable clown figure called Bobo. When the children were subsequently given the opportunity to play with the doll, those who had watched the aggressive model showed more aggressive behaviour towards Bobo than those who had watched the non-aggressive model. These findings suggest that observing an aggressive model may lead to the *acquisition* of the observed behaviour even if the model is not seen to be reinforced for his or her behaviour. In predicting whether or not the learned behaviour will actually be *performed*, the perceived consequences of the model's as well as the observer's behaviour do play an important role. Bandura, Ross, and Ross (1963) showed in a later study that an aggressive model elicited more imitative aggression when he was praised for his aggressive behaviour than when he was punished (i.e., beaten up by the target of the aggression). Thus the more positive the consequences of the aggressive behaviour for the model, the greater is the likelihood of imitation by the observer. The model's behaviour as well as its consequences serve as external stimuli that elicit aggressive response tendencies in the observer. The observers' normative standards with regard to the adequacy of the model's behaviour and their self-efficacy beliefs (i.e., the conviction that they are capable of performing the behaviour with the intended effects) serve as internal mechanisms that regulate aggressive behaviour. Repeated experiences of direct reinforcement of aggressive behaviour or repeated exposure to models who successfully engage in aggression accumulate over time to give rise to dispositional tendencies of aggression and to the development of cognitive scripts that promote aggressive behaviour.

Both direct reinforcement and imitation play a role in explaining aggression in a variety of domains, as will be seen in the next chapters. The social learning perspective has been a particularly prominent theoretical approach for conceptualising the effects of media violence on aggressive behaviour. Exposure to violent media models can be regarded as a paradigmatic case of observational learning and vicarious reinforcement, as will be discussed in Chapter 5.

The social interactionist model: aggression as coercive social influence

The final theoretical contribution to be reviewed in this chapter was proposed by Tedeschi and Felson (1994) to extend the analysis of aggressive behaviour into a broader "social interactionist theory of coercive actions." They used the concept of coercive action rather than aggression for two reasons: (a) because they saw it as less value-laden, avoiding the qualification of harm-doing as legitimate or illegitimate, and (b) because it includes threats and punishments as well as bodily force as important strategies for inflicting harm on, or obtaining compliance from, an unwilling target.

Whereas most of the approaches reviewed in the previous sections focused on hostile or impulsive aggression, the social interactionist model is concerned with the instrumental function of coercive actions. It postulates that coercive strategies are used to inflict harm on the target or to make the target comply with the actor's demands in the service of three major goals: (a) to control the behaviour of others, (b) to restore justice, and (c) to assert and protect positive identities (Tedeschi & Felson, 1994, p. 348). Coercive actions are conceptualised as outcomes of a decision-making process in which the actor first makes a general decision to use coercive rather than non-coercive means, and then chooses a particular form of coercion from the range of available options. For example, a person whose goal it is to make a wealthy relative change his will in her favour has to decide first whether to use non-coercive social influence, such as ingratiation or gentle persuasion, or coercive strategies, such as threats or physical harm. If a decision is made in favour of coercive influence, then the next step is to decide what particular form of coercion will be most successful in achieving the intended goal.

Three forms of coercive actions are at the core of the theory. The first is *threat* (i.e., the communication of an intention to harm the target person), with special emphasis on contingent threat that makes the infliction of harm contingent upon the target's refusal to comply with the aggressor's demands. The second form of coercive action is *punishment*, that is, an act performed with the intention of inflicting harm on the target person, and the third form is *bodily force* (i.e., the use of physical contact to compel or constrain the behaviour of another person). The choice of a coercive strategy is determined by the intention of achieving a particular immediate or "proximate" outcome, which in turn is motivated by the aim of reaching a valued terminal goal. These motivational underpinnings of coercive actions are illustrated in Figure 2.5.

The actor's decision to use threats or bodily force is seen as prompted by the intention of obtaining *compliance* from the target person with his or her demands. However, compliance is not a goal in itself, but is motivated by the desire to reach a terminal outcome, such as getting the target to hand over resources or provide services to the aggressor. In contrast, punishment is carried out as a coercive action with the intention of *harming* the target person, with the ultimate goal of restoring justice, defending one's superior status, or deterring the person from carrying out particular unwanted actions.

To explain the decision-making process that leads to the performance of coercive actions, Tedeschi and Felson draw on several lines of theorising, some of which have been discussed earlier in this chapter. Weighing the costs and benefits attached to each option plays an important role. The actor considers the subjective value of the intended goal, the probability that it will be reached successfully by the contemplated action, and the magnitude and probability of potential negative effects. Past learning experiences in similar situations hold

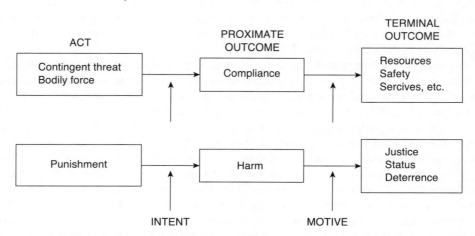

Figure 2.5 The motivational foundations of coercive actions. (Adapted from Tedeschi & Felson, 1994, p. 164. Copyright American Psychological Association).

vital cues for assessing the probability of different outcomes as well as their costs and benefits. Moreover, the actor's attitudes and values determine whether a particular behaviour, such as corporal punishment of children, is seen as an acceptable coercive strategy. Referring to socio-cognitive processes, the ease with which scripts for different types of coercive vs. non-coercive courses of action are cognitively accessible to the actor is seen as another critical factor. For example, if an individual habitually uses coercive strategies, coercive scripts will be activated more readily in a new situation because they have been rehearsed more frequently in the past.

The contribution of the social interactionist approach is to place aggression in the context of other forms of social behaviour designed to exert influence over others. It is stressed that aggression, as a particular form of coercive action, is just one potential influence strategy, and that the individual decides in a rational choice process whether or not to resort to that strategy in a given situation. Therefore, rather than being driven to aggressive behaviour by innate instincts or intense negative affect, individuals are seen here as having control over their aggressive response repertoire and using it strategically in social interactions.

Putting it all together: the General Aggression Model (GAM)

The different approaches reviewed in this chapter reflect the multiplicity of theories designed to understand aggressive behaviour. The biological approaches concentrated on the role of individual differences based on genetic and hormonal influences, whereas the psychological approaches highlighted the interplay of affective states, cognitive processes, and learning experiences in the course of socialisation for the implementation of aggressive responses.

A comprehensive model that integrates aspects of many of the theories discussed so far is the "General Aggression Model (GAM)" developed by Anderson and his co-workers (DeWall & Anderson, 2011). The GAM aims to explain how aggressive behaviour emerges both in specific situations and over time. At the single episode level, the GAM presents an account of how certain input variables in the person and the situation come together to elicit affective, cognitive, and arousal processes that may pave the way for aggressive behaviour via automatic and controlled appraisals. In addition, the GAM seeks to explain how aggression develops over time as part of an individual's personality. The part of the GAM that conceptualises the processes operating in a single episode is presented in Figure 2.6.

The GAM assumes that the starting point of an aggressive interaction lies in individual dispositions, such as trait anger, and external stimuli, such as aggressive cues, that meet in a particular situation and evoke an interrelated set of internal processes in the actor. They elicit an internal state that is characterised by specific cognitions, feelings, and arousal symptoms. For example, someone who is easy to anger may only need a small provocation from a stranger to enter into a state of fury, characterised by aggressive thoughts ("This person is an idiot"), negative feelings ("This person makes me mad"), and bodily symptoms ("I can feel my blood pressure rising"). This internal state in turn gives rise to

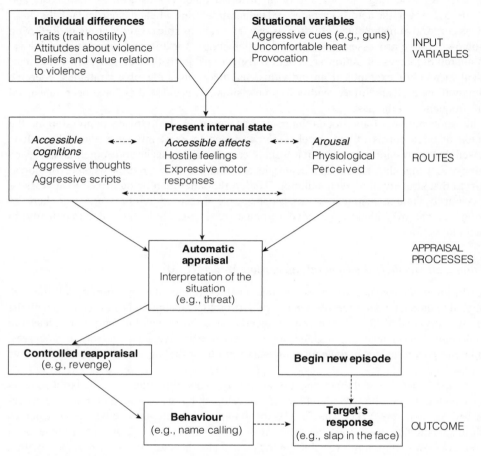

Figure 2.6 The General Aggression Model (GAM). (Based on Anderson & Dill, 2000, and Lindsay & Anderson, 2000).

a fast automatic appraisal of the situation (e.g., "This person's behaviour is outrageous"). In the subsequent reappraisal stage, the initial evaluation of the situation is considered in a more controlled and elaborate way, leading to the selection and enactment of a behavioural response. Depending on the reappraisal, this response will either be aggressive ("This person annoyed me on purpose and therefore I will retaliate in kind") or non-aggressive ("Let's try to calm down"). The behavioural decision may trigger a response from the target that marks the beginning of a new episode and may further escalate or de-escalate the conflict.

Beyond the single episode, the GAM also offers a perspective on the development of aggression over time. Each aggressive episode is seen as a social learning trial in which aggression-related knowledge structures are rehearsed and reinforced. The more often a person engages in aggressive behaviour without negative consequences, the lower the threshold becomes for choosing to act aggressively in the future, the more readily aggressive scripts are accessed, and the more rapidly aggressive cognitions are activated. In combination, these processes work to more firmly establish aggression in individuals' behavioural repertoires, eventually making it part of their personality (Anderson & Carnagey, 2004).

The GAM incorporates ideas and findings from several of the theoretical approaches discussed in the course of this chapter, such as the neo-associationist model of anger in response to aversive stimuli or the role of aggressive scripts. It provides a structure that helps us to understand the complex processes through which particular input variables, such as violent media stimuli or biographical experiences of abuse, can lead to aggressive behaviour as the critical outcome variable. DeWall, Anderson, and Bushman (2011) recently elaborated the usefulness of the GAM as a model for understanding different forms of violent behaviour and for designing violence prevention progammes.

To conclude this review of theoretical approaches for understanding aggression, one important point of comparison relates to their implications for the controllability and prevention of aggressive behaviour. The early instinct-related view entails a basically pessimistic view, but it has not played a major role in modern aggression research due to the lack of empirical support. As Berkowitz (1993, p. 387) pointed out, "people have a *capacity* for aggression and violence, but not a biological urge to attack and destroy others that is continually building up inside them." This view is supported by theories that emphasise the mediating role of cognitions and learning as well as decision-making processes. These theories imply the possibility of strengthening the inhibitory forces against aggression, and they acknowledge the individual's freedom to decide against acting aggressively in favour of alternative courses of action.

Summary

- Theoretical explanations of aggressive behaviour include both biological and psycho-logical lines of thinking and research.
- Biological models refer to evolutionary and genetic principles and the role of hormones in explaining aggression. The ethological perspective regards the manifestation of overt aggression as a function of an internal aggressive energy that is released by aggression-related external cues. The sociobiological approach postulates that aggression has developed as an adaptive form of social behaviour in the process of evolution. Evidence from the field of behaviour genetics suggests that the propensity to act aggressively is at least partly influenced by genetic dispositions. Finally, there is some evidence that hormones, such as testosterone and cortisol, are involved in regulating aggressive behaviour and explaining individual differences in the propensity to engage in aggression.

- Early psychological models also assumed aggression to be an innate response tendency. Freud's view of aggression as an expression of the antagonism of Eros and Thanatos inspired the frustration-aggression hypothesis, which sees aggression as driven by the desire to overcome frustration.
- Subsequent psychological approaches widened the frustration-aggression hypothesis into a more general model of negative affect, and highlighted the role of cognitive factors, learning experiences, and decision-making processes in eliciting aggressive responses. According to cognitive neo-associationism and excitation transfer theory, negative affect (caused by a range of adverse stimuli, such as frustration, pain, or noise) is a powerful trigger of selective information processing that enhances the probability of aggressive behaviour.
- Social-cognitive approaches refer to the role of aggressive scripts (i.e., generalised knowledge structures of how and when aggressive behaviour may be enacted) and sequential appraisal processes that lead to the choice of an aggressive response. From the perspective of learning theory, aggression becomes part of an individual's repertoire through direct reinforcement as well as observational learning and imitation of aggressive models. The social interactionist model examines aggression as an instrumental strategy of social influence.
- The General Aggression Model integrates assumptions on the affective, cognitive and arousal-based antecedents of aggressive behaviour from different models into a comprehensive framework.
- The psychological explanations of aggression share the assumption that aggressive behaviour is not inevitable but depends on the operation of a variety of promoting and inhibiting factors located both within the person and in the environment.

Tasks to do

(1) Watch the original video of Bandura's Bobo doll experiment on YouTube (www.youtube.com/watch?v=jWsxfoJEwQQ&feature=related).
(2) Sit down for ten minutes and think back to situations that made you angry in the course of the last week. Write down how you responded in these situations, and then analyse your responses with reference to the theories discussed in this chapter.
(3) Ask five people you know, who are not psychologists, how they would explain aggression. Compare their answers with the theories discussed in this chapter. How much difference or overlap do you see?

Suggested reading

Archer, J. (2009). The nature of human aggression. *International Journal of Law and Psychiatry, 32*, 202–208.

Berkowitz, L., & LePage, A. (1967). Weapons as aggression-eliciting stimuli. *Journal of Personality and Social Psychology, 7*, 202–207.

DeWall, C. N., & Anderson, C. A. (2011). The General Aggression Model. In P. Shaver & M. Mikulincer (Eds), *Human aggression and violence: Causes, manifestations, and consequences* (pp. 15–33). Washington, DC: American Psychological Association.

Huesmann, L. R. (1998). The role of information processing and cognitive schema in the acquisition and maintenance of habitual aggressive behavior. In R. G. Geen & E. Donnerstein (Eds), *Human aggression: Theories, research and implications for social policy* (pp. 73–109). San Diego, CA: Academic Press.

3 Development of aggression and individual differences

It is clear from everyday observation that people differ in predictable ways in their tendency to show aggressive behaviour. Some go ballistic at the slightest provocation, others are almost impossible to fall out with, and there is a broad spectrum in between. In this chapter we shall take a closer look at the development of individual differences in aggression and relate them to other psychological characteristics. The first section takes a necessarily selective look at the wide developmental literature on aggression, focusing on the role of social experience in shaping an aggressive personality from early childhood onwards. This will be followed by a review of the evidence on personality variables associated with aggressive behaviour that can help to clarify some of the processes underlying differences in dispositional aggression. Finally, gender will be examined as an individual difference variable to put the common-sense notion that men are more aggressive than women to the test of systematic empirical investigation.

The discussion in this chapter will be limited to research with a primary focus on individual differences in aggression. Studies considering individual differences as moderators of particular forms of aggression, such as intimate partner violence or aggressive driving, will be reviewed in their respective contexts.

Development of aggressive behaviour in childhood and adolescence

Aggression is to a certain extent an age-normative behaviour in childhood and adolescence (Loeber & Hay, 1997). Aggressive behaviour is common in these periods, and then becomes less prevalent in the course of further development. From this point of view, aggression is a transient phenomenon in the life course. However, there are children and adolescents who deviate from this normal course of development by showing high and persistent levels of aggressive behaviour that are not considered age-normative. The developmental psychology of aggression is concerned both with demonstrating patterns of change in aggressive behaviour in the course of childhood and adolescence, and with identifying the causes of stable, high levels of aggression in a small group of individuals.

When trying to understand the developmental dynamics of aggression, the following questions are of key importance and will guide our discussion (Loeber & Hay, 1997):

(1) When does aggressive behaviour first appear and what forms does it take in childhood, adolescence, and early adulthood?
(2) How stable are early manifestations of aggressive behaviour as children get older?
(3) Does the development of aggressive behaviour follow a pattern of escalation whereby milder forms of aggression are followed by more severe aggressive behaviours?
(4) What are the emotional and cognitive antecedents of aggressive behaviour?
(5) What is the role of the social environment (parents, peers, and neighbourhoods) in the formation and persistence of aggressive behaviour patterns?

Emergence and manifestations of aggression in childhood and adolescence

The first precursors of individual differences in aggression emerge very early in life. At about 3 months of age, a child is able to recognise anger in adults' facial expressions. This is followed by the expression of anger by the child in response to frustration in the second half of the first year. Although young children still lack the ability to foresee the consequences of their actions, and are therefore unable to intentionally inflict harm on others, as required by our definition of aggressive behaviour (see Chapter 1), it is nonetheless possible to identify certain early affective and behavioural indicators that are predictive of individual differences in aggression later on. For example, the Cardiff Infant Contentiousness Scale (CICS; Hay et al., 2010) was developed to address six aspects of the use of physical force in social interactions and the expression of anger in babies: *doesn't want to let go of toys, pulls hair, hits out at other people, bites, has angry moods,* and *has temper tantrums.* Reports elicited from parents and other informants when the children were between 5 and 8 months of age predicted the use of physical force against peers observed in a free play situation in the laboratory when the children were between 11 and 15 months old (Hay et al., 2010).

Aggression in conflicts with peers and adults becomes more frequent during the second and third years of life in the form of temper tantrums and the intentional use of physical force (Tremblay et al., 1999), although overt physical aggression tends to decline after about 30 months of age (Alink et al., 2006). At the same time, indirect and relational forms of aggression begin to emerge as children's verbal skills and understanding of social relationships develop (Vaillancourt, 2005). In the early school years, gender differences in aggression become apparent. Boys show higher levels of physical aggression than do girls, who are more likely to engage in indirect and relational forms of aggression (see the final section of this chapter). Although the two forms of aggression were substantially correlated, a meta-analysis by Card, Stucky, Sawalani, and Little (2008) found that only direct aggression was uniquely related to externalising problems, such as attentional deficits and delinquency, whereas indirect aggression was uniquely associated with internalising problems, such as depression and anxiety. These differential associations were confirmed in a 10-year longitudinal study of an all-male sample from adolescence to adulthood (Fite, Raine, Stouthamer-Loeber, Loeber, & Pardini, 2010).

An important change in the pattern of aggressive behaviour from childhood to adolescence is that aggression and violence tend to become more socially organised. Juvenile gangs assemble adolescents who share aggressive norms and mutually reinforce their aggressive behaviour patterns. Gangs are attractive to highly aggressive individuals and account for a high proportion of juvenile aggression, including fighting between rival gangs. Although gang violence is still largely seen as a male phenomenon, reports of girl gangs engaging in serious aggression are becoming increasingly frequent (see also Chapter 9). However, there does seem to be a gender difference in that girls' aggressive behaviours are replaced by non-aggressive strategies of conflict resolution to a greater extent, whereas boys' tendencies to use aggression to resolve social conflicts more frequently persist into adolescence and early adulthood.

Stability of aggressive behaviour and patterns of change

An important question is whether children with aggression levels that are higher than normative for their age group remain highly aggressive in subsequent periods of development. Longitudinal studies have produced evidence that aggressive behaviour is indeed relatively stable over time (for a review, see Farrington, 2007). Based on data from 16 studies exploring the stability of male aggressiveness, Olweus (1979) estimated stability coefficients of $r = 0.76$ over a 1-year period, $r = 0.69$ over a period of 5 years, and $r = 0.60$ over a 10-year period. These figures suggest that aggression is almost as stable as intelligence, even over extended periods of time.

In a large-scale longitudinal study involving six sites in three countries (Canada, New Zealand, and the USA) and covering an age range from 6 to 15 years, childhood physical aggression predicted violent delinquency in adolescent boys, but the link was inconsistent for girls (Broidy et al., 2003). Several long-term studies have shown that aggression in childhood is linked to aggressive behaviour in later life. Following a sample of boys over five measurements from age 12 to age 24, Barker et al. (2007) found two stable developmental trajectories. For the majority of their sample (87%), low levels of aggression were found at each point over the 12-year period. At the same time, a highly aggressive subgroup at age 12 (13%) showed continuously high levels of aggression over time, with a peak at age 18. Boys in the high aggression trajectory performed significantly worse than the non-aggressive group on a series of cognitive tests, indicating a link between cognitive deficits and aggression. In a Finnish study, the stability of peer nominations of aggression obtained at the ages of 8 and 14 years was $r = 0.35$ for boys and $r = 0.38$ for girls, and the link between peer-nominated aggression at age 14 and aggression in adulthood (a composite measure of self-reports obtained at ages 36 and 42) in the same participants was $r = 0.33$ for men and $r = 0.29$ for women (Kokko et al., 2009, Figure 1).

In a study that covered a period of 30 years, Temcheff et al. (2008) found significant links between peer-nominated aggression in childhood and self-reports of aggression towards children and spouses in adulthood. The link was mediated by low educational attainment in adolescence, and the authors discuss the possibility that educational achievement may act as a protective factor to buffer the risk of aggressive children carrying their dispositions into adulthood.

Table 3.1 Pairwise correlations of aggression over time in the Columbia County Longitudinal Study. (Adapted from Huesmann et al., 2009, Table I, p. 143. Copyright Wiley Publications)

Aggression at	Age 8	Age 19	Age 30	Age 48
Age 8	–	.23***	.15*	.13*
Age 19	.37***	–	.44***	.45***
Age 30	.35***	.61***	–	.56***
Age 48	.29***	.41***	.56***	–

Correlations for n = 420 females above the diagonal, correlations for n = 436 males below the diagonal.

Finally, a 40-year longitudinal study by Huesmann, Dubow, and Boxer (2009) also demonstrated significant links between physical aggression in childhood, adolescence, and adulthood. In their Columbia County Longitudinal Study, the authors obtained peer nominations of aggression at age 8 and used a combined index of self-reported severe physical aggression and aggressive personality as a measure of aggression at the ages of 19, 30, and 48. The correlations between the aggression measures over time for male and female participants are presented in Table 3.1.

Table 3.1 not only reveals a very consistent pattern of significant correlations for both genders, but it also shows that the stability is higher in adulthood than in the transition from childhood to age 19. For example, the correlation between aggression at age 30 and aggression at age 48 was $r = 0.56$ for both men and women. Another way of looking at the issue of stability used by Huesmann et al. (2009) was to identify the proportion of participants who remained consistently high (above the median) or low (below the median) in aggression over the 40 years of the study. This analysis showed that 37% of participants who were low in aggression at age 8 remained low in the three subsequent waves, and 35% of participants who scored above the median at age 8 remained in the high aggression group throughout the study.

An important message that emerges from these findings is that aggression at a young age is not a problem that children can be expected to outgrow as they get older. To explain the stability of aggression in the course of development, two interlocking processes have been proposed (Caspi, Elder, & Bem, 1987). Through the first process, *cumulative continuity*, aggression is maintained because of its own consequences that accumulate over time. For example, highly aggressive children often experience academic failure (e.g., Patterson, DeBaryshe, & Ramsey, 1989), which may increase anger and hostility and thereby consolidate aggressive behaviour. According to the second process, *interactional continuity*, aggression is maintained through the responses it elicits in others. For example, highly aggressive children are socially rejected by non-aggressive peers, which may lead them to selectively associate with other aggressive peers, creating an environment in which aggression is socially accepted (Martino, Ellickson, Klein, McCaffrey, & Edelen, 2008).

However, even though high stability coefficients were found for aggressive behaviour from childhood into adolescence and early adulthood, it is important to recognise that there is also the possibility of changes in aggression over time. For example, an individual who was non-aggressive as a child may become an aggressive adolescent (i.e., show late onset of aggression). Alternatively, an aggressive child may become less aggressive over time (i.e., show a decline in aggressive behaviour). There is evidence to support both patterns of change. For example, Kingston and Prior (1995) measured aggression in a group of Australian children on three occasions between the ages of 2–3 and 7–8 years, and identified three distinct groups. The first and largest group, comprising 55% of the boys and 41% of the girls, was the stable group that showed similar levels of aggression at the age of 2 and at the age of 8. The second group, consisting of 31% of the boys and 24% of the girls, showed a decrease in aggression from age 2 to age 8. The final group consisted of children with low levels of aggression at age 2 whose level of aggressive behaviour went up from the age of 5. These children showed an increase in aggression. Each of the latter two groups displayed variability in their aggressive behaviour over time, albeit in different directions. In a study following adolescents from Grades 7 to 11, Martino et al. (2008) found that almost half of their sample showed an increase (23%) or a decrease (22%) in aggression over the 4-year period, compared with 37% whose level of aggression remained consistently low and 17% who remained consistently high.

Overall, there is evidence of a continuous decline in aggression as a function of age (Broidy et al., 2003; Loeber & Stouthamer-Loeber, 1998), so desistance may reflect the age-normative pattern of development with regard to aggressive behaviour. However, it is equally clear that there is a substantial proportion of aggressive children who do not show a decline but exhibit an increase or escalation of aggressive behaviour in adolescence and adulthood. *Short-term escalation* denotes a rapid increase in violence among individuals who only start to become aggressive relatively late. *Long-term escalation* refers to a gradual increase in the severity of aggressive actions from childhood to adolescence. At a group level, evidence of long-term escalation comes from studies that have explored the cumulative onset curves for different forms of aggression varying in severity. An example of this approach is provided in Figure 3.1. It presents Loeber and Hay's (1997) analysis of the age at which minor aggression, physical fighting, and severe violence became apparent in boys' behaviour.

Figure 3.1 indicates that comparatively minor forms of aggression (annoying others, bullying) showed the earliest onset, followed by physical fighting. Despite its later onset, physical fighting showed a steeper increase than minor aggression, and by the age of 15 years, the two curves reached similar prevalence levels. The latest and slowest-rising onset was observed for violence (strongarming, assault, and forced sex). As would be expected, its prevalence at age 16 years, although standing at almost 20%, was substantially lower than the prevalence rates for the two less serious forms of aggression.

In addition to describing different patterns of development, it is crucial to identify their correlates at the level of the person and the social environment. Moffitt's work on the distinction between *adolescence-limited* and *life-course persistent* aggressive and antisocial behaviour exemplifies this approach (Moffitt, 1993, 2007). She argues that life-course

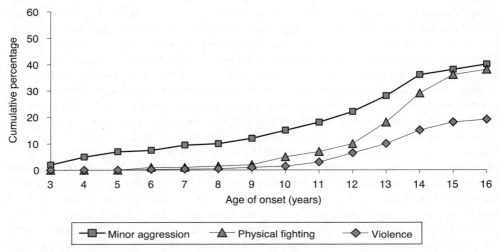

Figure 3.1 Cumulative onset of minor aggression, physical fighting, and violence in boys. (Adapted from Loeber & Hay, 1997, p. 379. Copyright Annual Reviews).

persistent antisocial behaviour is associated with specific risk factors and manifestations that distinguish this developmental pattern from adolescent-limited antisocial behaviour. Table 3.2 summarises some of the differences between the two developmental trajectories.

The life-course persistent antisocial behaviour pattern is assumed to start in early child-hood, originating from a combination of neuropsychological deficits and adverse social conditions. Individuals with a life-course persistent pattern of antisocial behaviour typically show early cognitive and affective deficits and are often born into a high-risk family

Table 3.2 Two prototypes of antisocial behaviour over the life course (Based on Moffitt, 2007)

Life-course persistent antisocial behaviour	Adolescence-limited antisocial behaviour

• Originates in early childhood
• Early neurodevelopmental risk factors
  − Cognitive deficits
  − Difficult temperament
  − Hyperactivity
• Exacerbated by high-risk social environment
  − Inadequate parenting
  − Family conflict
  − Rejection by peers
• Associated with violent crime in adulthood
	• Emerges in puberty as a virtually normative pattern of behaviour
	• Psychological discomfort during the "maturity gap"
	• Desire for autonomy
	• Desistance from antisocial behaviour when adopting adult roles
	• Social mimicry of antisocial models
	• Associated with non-violent delinquent offences in adulthood

environment. As noted by Moffitt (2007, p. 50), "Over the first two decades of development, transactions between the individual and the environment gradually construct a disordered personality with hallmark features of physical aggression and antisocial behavior persisting to midlife."

By contrast, individuals with an adolescence-limited pattern typically do not show developmental abnormalities in early childhood, and come from normal family backgrounds. They are described as "otherwise ordinary healthy youngsters" who take up aggressive and antisocial behaviour in adolescence out of discomfort about experiencing a "maturity gap" (i.e., the feeling that their biological maturation is not matched by social maturation because they are denied access to adult role behaviour and entitlement) (Moffitt, 2007, p. 50). Engaging in aggressive and antisocial behaviour to demonstrate autonomy in relation to parents and to hasten social maturation is seen by these adolescents as a normative pattern of behaviour, which is given up once they grow into adult social roles. Rather than being driven by neuropsychological deficits and adverse family conditions, adolescence-limited aggression results from social mimicry (i.e., the imitation of and attraction to antisocial peers).

Support for the distinction between the two developmental prototypes comes from several large-scale longitudinal studies reviewed by Moffitt (2007), including the famous "Dunedin Study", of which she is a co-author. In this ongoing study, which started in Dunedin, New Zealand in 1972, more than 1000 children were first studied at age 3 and were then followed every 2–3 years up to the age of 38 as per the latest wave. The study has accumulated an extremely rich set of data from the different developmental stages, including adult mental health and personality measures, criminal offending, and work-related and economic measures (e.g., Moffitt, Caspi, Harrington, & Milne, 2002).

However, other authors have cautioned against regarding adolescent-limited antisocial behaviour as a kind of "benign" form of aggression. When they compared adolescent-limited aggressive individuals with continuously non-aggressive individuals, Roisman et al. (2010) found that adolescent-limited individuals differed significantly from continuously non-aggressive individuals on a number of childhood risk factors, such as showing a more difficult temperament in early childhood and experiencing less maternal sensitivity in infancy and childhood. The authors concluded that although the individual and environmental risk factors of adolescent-limited aggressive youths may be less extreme than those of the early-onset, life-course persistent individuals, they "clearly experience risks during their preadolescent years that have been reliably linked with later antisocial behavior" (Roisman et al., 2010, p. 309).

In conclusion, the longitudinal studies reviewed in this section showed that there is evidence for both stability and change in aggressive behaviour in the course of childhood and adolescent development. With regard to stability, Moffitt (1993) argued that only a small group of highly aggressive children fall into the life-course persistent group and account for the observed stability of aggressive behaviour. However, as shown by other studies (e.g., Barker et al. 2007; Huesmann et al., 2009, Roisman et al., 2010), such stability is also due to a comparatively large group of individuals who show little aggression throughout the different developmental stages. At the same time, there is evidence for both escalation and decline of aggression in individual biographies. To understand these different trajectories, it is necessary to take a closer look at the emotional and cognitive processes involved in the instigation and regulation of aggressive behaviour.

Emotional and cognitive processes associated with individual differences in aggression

To understand why some children are more aggressive than others and continue to be so in the course of development, both affective and cognitive processes have been examined. The psychological theories of aggression reviewed in Chapter 2 explained how hostile affect (i.e., anger) and hostile information processing pave the way to aggressive behaviour, not only in a given situation but also over time. It was shown that children with deficits in affective regulation and impulse control are more likely to develop and sustain aggressive behaviour patterns. These children are often perceived as having a difficult temperament, and find it hard to constrain their aggressive impulses in an age-appropriate way (Kingston & Prior, 1995). Looking specifically at girls, a longitudinal study by Fontaine et al. (2008) found that girls on a trajectory of high hyperactivity and high physical aggression between the ages of 6 and 12 were significantly more likely to report physical aggression in intimate relationships at the age of 21.

Individual differences in anger are thought to be more closely related to reactive aggression (i.e., aggression shown in response to a provocation) than to proactive or unprovoked aggression (Hubbard, McAuliffe, Morrow, & Romano, 2010). For example, children who showed more anger when losing in a game, as established through physiological data and observations of anger expression, were also rated by their teachers as more reactively aggressive, but not as more proactively aggressive (Hubbard et al., 2002). With regard to empathy, a review by Lovett and Sheffield (2007) found that, across a range of studies, aggressive adolescents showed lower levels of empathy than their non-aggressive peers. However, the evidence from childhood studies was less clear, with some studies finding no relationship or even a positive association between aggression and empathy.

At the level of general cognitive functioning, the possible impact of low intelligence and attention deficit disorders has been addressed by a small number of studies. The available evidence suggests that both variables may be linked to aggression, but the exact nature of the link and interactions with other variables has yet to be clarified. Among more specific cognitive precursors to aggression, aggression-related attitudes were found to play an important role. For example, Erdley and Asher (1998) found that children who saw aggression as a legitimate form of social behaviour showed higher levels of actual aggressive behaviour (as evidenced by peer ratings and the children's own responses to ambiguous interactions described in hypothetical scenarios). The difference in aggressive behaviour as a function of legitimacy beliefs was found for both boys and girls, but levels of aggression were generally lower for girls than for boys.

Beliefs about the legitimacy of aggression can be seen as part of individuals' aggressive scripts, developed on the basis of direct and vicarious learning experiences (Huesmann,

1998; see also Chapter 2). Another feature of the scripts of children who show high levels of aggression is the perception of hostile intent in others. Children with a *hostile attributional style* interpret their peers' behaviour in the light of a pre-existing knowledge structure that sees potentially harmful behaviour by others as the expression of their hostile intentions. Dodge (2006) argued that, in young children, equating (hostile) intent with (negative) outcome is a common reaction when they experience harm from others. In the course of socialisation, children learn to acquire a benign attributional style – that is, they learn to consider the possibility that the other person's actions were not intended to be harmful.

According to this view, a learning process is required to make benign attributions, and children who maintain a hostile attributional style beyond early childhood show deficits in this learning process. Every time they attribute behaviours of others to hostile intentions and react with an aggressive response, the link between the perception of hostile intent and aggression is reinforced, a cycle which may account for the long-term stability of aggressive behaviour. A meta-analysis including 41 studies with over 6000 participants confirmed the link between hostile attributional style and aggression in children (Orobio de Castro, Veerman, Koops, Bosch, & Monshouwer, 2002). However, very few of the located studies included girls, and therefore gender differences could not be examined.

The connection between hostile knowledge structures and aggression over time was demonstrated in a longitudinal study by Burks, Laird, Dodge, Pettit, and Bates (1999). They obtained mother and teacher ratings of aggressive behaviour in kindergarten and Grade 8. In Grade 8 they also assessed children's attributions of hostile intent in response to hypothetical conflict scenarios and their hostile knowledge structures (i.e., the salience of hostility-related thoughts). In support of their hypotheses, Burks et al. (1999) found that children who had hostile knowledge structures were more likely to attribute hostility in a specific social encounter, and were also rated as more aggressive by their mother and teacher. In addition, they found that the link between early aggression and aggressive behaviour in Grade 8 was mediated by hostile knowledge structures. Thus individual differences in aggression may be the result of schematic, habitual ways of information processing that suggest aggression as an adequate response in social interactions. The propensity towards hostile attributions may be socially shared, and thus reinforced, among peers. A study of adolescents by Halligan and Philips (2010) found significant correlations within peer groups in their tendency to attribute hostile intent, and the link was particularly close in reciprocal friendships. Thus it appears that the stability of hostile attributional styles is also promoted through associations with like-minded peers.

The hostile attribution bias is particularly relevant to the understanding of *reactive aggression* – that is, aggression shown in response to a provocation (Hubbard et al., 2010). Children who tend to see their peers' behaviour as driven by hostile intent feel provoked more easily and have a lower threshold for aggressive retaliation. A meta-analysis by Card and Little (2006) found that reactive aggression was more strongly related to adjustment problems than proactive aggression in children and adolescents.

Further cognitive deficits have been shown to be characteristic of highly aggressive individuals, such as difficulties in remembering the details of conflict scenarios as well as in generating non-confrontational and compromise-oriented solutions to those conflicts (Lochman & Dodge, 1994). Even though these socio-cognitive deficiencies may, in principle, be targeted by specific interventions, Eron (1994) noted that such interventions have been largely unsuccessful. In his view, the main reason why maladaptive forms of information processing are so resistant to change lies in the fact that aggressive scripts are learned very early on and applied successfully in the course of development: "The payoff is very good, so that despite occasional or even frequent punishment it is difficult to unlearn, and thus the behaviour persists under the regulation of well-established cognitions" (Eron, 1994, p. 8). To reduce this positive payoff, the normative beliefs that support the script and the positive feelings associated with script enactment need to be challenged.

Social influences on the development of aggression

A variety of adverse social conditions have been examined as potentially responsible for individual differences in aggression. Harsh parental discipline was found to be linked to higher levels of subsequent aggressiveness (Farrington, Ttofi, & Coid, 2009), which makes sense not least because physical punishment is viewed by the child as an acceptable form of conflict resolution. In the same way, children exposed to abuse and parental rejection were shown to display higher levels of aggression later in life (Huesmann et al., 2009; see also Chapter 7). Economic pressure may trigger and exacerbate negative parental behaviour by increasing hostility in parents that is directed against the children, as shown in a 3-year longitudinal study by Williams, Conger, and Blozis (2007). Furthermore, the role of learning by observation is highlighted by findings that witnessing violence, both directly in the family and indirectly in media portrayals, increases the likelihood of aggressive behaviour (Widom, 1989; see also Chapters 5 and 7).

Peer relationships constitute another powerful source of social influence that is relevant to aggression. Aggressive children are rejected by their peers from as early as the age of 6, and rejection is associated with subsequent increases in aggression. The more a child's behaviour is dominated by aggression (i.e., the less he or she displays non-aggressive forms of behaviour), the more unanimous is the rejection and the more extreme is the resulting social isolation. As a result of being marginalised by their non-aggressive peers, aggressive children tend to associate with other aggressive peers, entering social systems, such as violent gangs, that further promote aggressive norms (Halligan & Philips, 2010) and aggressive behaviour (Patterson et al., 1989). Thus they become trapped in a situation where social acceptance depends on the committal of further acts of aggression. Moreover, the experience of peer rejection may reinforce existing tendencies to engage in reactive aggression, precipitating further social rejection (Hubbard et al., 2010).

Loeber and Hay (1997) noted that in adolescence and young adulthood aggressive behaviour tends to become more harmful, not least because so many male adolescents have access to firearms, knives, and other weapons (Verlinden, Hersen, & Thomas, 2000). Although rates of youth homicide have declined in recent years, homicide remains the second leading cause of death among 10- to 24-year olds in the USA, according to the Centers for Disease Control and Prevention (CDC, 2010). The figures for 2007 show that 86% of all juvenile homicide victims were male, and 84% were killed with a firearm.

This section has traced the emergence of individual differences in aggression from early childhood to adolescence, but development does not stop there. Adults differ as much as children and adolescents in their aggressive response tendencies. The next section will therefore examine the relationship between personality and aggression in adulthood.

Personality and aggression in adulthood

According to the General Aggression Model (GAM) presented in Chapter 2, aggressive behaviour varies as a function of individual difference variables. Such variables denote personality characteristics or "traits" that remain relatively stable over time, and can help to explain why not all people behave equally aggressively in a given situation. In this section, personality traits will be discussed that have been linked to individual differences in aggressive behaviour through shaping both affective and cognitive processes. In addition, the role of stable differences in self-esteem and self-regulation will be examined in relation to their effects on aggressive behaviour. Consistent with our focus on the social psychology of aggression, the discussion will be limited to constructs that play a role in explaining stable differences in aggression in normal individuals, excluding constructs that are primarily relevant in explaining severe forms of aggression and violence in the context of psychopathology and criminal offending. A summary of the personality constructs and their relationship with aggression is presented in Table 3.3.

Trait anger and trait hostility

As was shown in Chapter 2, anger and hostility feature in several theoretical accounts of aggression as key components of trait aggressiveness. Anger involves physiological arousal and preparation for aggression, and represents the emotional or affective component of trait aggression. Hostility consists of feelings of ill will and injustice, and represents the cognitive component. Both constructs are measured by separate subscales in the Aggression Questionnaire (AQ; Buss and Perry, 1992) (see Chapter 1). There is ample evidence that

Table 3.3 Personality variables associated with individual differences in aggression

Associated with higher aggression	*Associated with lower aggression*
<ul><li>Trait anger and hostility</li><li>Irritability</li><li>Emotional susceptibility</li><li>Rumination</li><li>Hostile attributional style</li><li>Narcissism</li></ul>	<ul><li>Dissipation</li><li>Perspective taking</li><li>Self-control</li></ul>

individuals who are habitually prone to anger and hostility show more aggressive behaviour in situations that elicit these affective and cognitive responses. In a meta-analysis by Bettencourt, Talley, and Valentine (2006), trait anger was established as a significant predictor of aggressive behaviour following a provocation. A study by Tafrate, Kassinove, and Dundin (2002) found that individuals who scored high on trait anger experienced more anger episodes that lasted for longer periods of time and were more likely to engage in verbal aggression on their part than those who scored low on trait anger.

Irritability

Irritability refers to the habitual "tendency to react impulsively, controversially, or rudely at the slightest provocation or disagreement" (Caprara, Perugini, & Barbaranelli, 1994, p. 125). Habitually irritable people, as identified by the Caprara Irritability Scale (Caprara et al., 1985), which consists of items such as "I think I am rather touchy," were found to show increased levels of aggression compared with non-irritable individuals. The difference was particularly pronounced if the respondents had previously been frustrated. Similarly, irritability augmented the differences in aggressive behaviour observed in response to exposure to aggressive cues (for a summary, see Caprara et al., 1994). In a study by Giancola (2002a), highly irritable participants administered more painful electric shocks as a measure of aggressive behaviour (see Chapter 1). Drinking alcohol increased aggressive behaviour in highly irritable but not in less irritable participants, although this pattern was only found for the male subgroup. The meta-analysis by Bettencourt et al. (2006) confirmed the link between trait irritability and situational aggression across a broader range of studies.

Emotional susceptibility

Emotional susceptibility is defined as an individual's tendency "to experience feelings of discomfort, helplessness, inadequacy, and vulnerability" (Caprara et al., 1994, p. 125). Like irritability, it is presumed to indicate a generally higher readiness (or lower response threshold) for aggressive behaviour. The findings reported by Caprara and his colleagues for emotional susceptibility largely parallel the effects they found for irritability. Emotionally susceptible participants showed more aggressive behaviour, particularly following prior frustration. They also showed a larger increase in aggression following physical exercise, lending support to Zillmann's excitation transfer model (see Chapter 2). The meta-analysis by Bettencourt et al. (2006) also found that individual differences in emotional susceptibility predicted aggressive behaviour, particularly following provocation. The two constructs of irritability and emotional susceptibility thus seem to be associated with individual differences in affective or hostile aggression.

Rumination

Rumination and dissipation represent the opposite poles of a continuum that describes the extent to which people are preoccupied with aggressive cognitions following an aggression-eliciting stimulus. Low ruminators/high dissipators quickly get over a provocative or hostile encounter without investing much time and effort in thinking about the experience. Ruminators, on the other hand, remain cognitively preoccupied with the hostile experience and are more likely to plan and elaborate retaliative responses. In order for ruminative vs. dissipative tendencies to show an effect, sufficient time must be allowed between the hostile or provoking stimulus event and the aggressive response. The more time elapses, the less likely it should be that dissipators will show an aggressive response, whereas in ruminators such a response should become more likely. Although some people may be generally more prone to rumination than others in all areas of life, the contents of the ruminative thoughts are important for the link with aggression. Peled and Moretti (2010) showed that only the tendency to ruminate about anger was linked to aggression, whereas the tendency to ruminate about feelings of sadness was associated with depression. Similarly, Bettencourt et al. (2006) found in their meta-analysis that trait rumination was associated with observed aggressive behaviour only in the context of provocation. These findings highlight once more the interaction between the person (here the tendency to ruminate) and the situation (here the elicitation of anger) in explaining aggressive behaviour.

Although dissipation/rumination is conceptualised as a stable individual difference variable, it is possible to demonstrate the role of rumination or dissipation by inducing the two modes in experimental studies. In a study in which participants were either instructed to ruminate about a provocation or distracted from thinking about it, those in the rumination condition reported significantly higher levels of anger after a 25-minute interval, and also showed more aggressive behaviour after a minor triggering event (Bushman, Bonacci, Pedersen, Vasquez, & Miller, 2005). Further clarifying the path from rumination to aggression, a series of studies by Denson, Pedersen, Friese, Hahm, and Roberts (2011) showed that rumination leads to a reduction in self-control, which in turn lowers the threshold for aggressive behaviour. We shall return to the link between low self-control and aggression later in this chapter.

Hostile attributional style and perspective taking

Hostile attributional style, defined as a person's habitual tendency to interpret the ambiguous behaviour of others as an expression of their hostile intent, has already been discussed earlier in this chapter in relation to the development of aggressive behaviour patterns in childhood and adolescence. It also features as a personality correlate of aggression in adults. Attributional style not only affects the way in which people interpret actions directed at them individually, but also shapes their social perceptions in general. As Dill, Anderson, Anderson, and Deuser (1997, p. 275) graphically described it, these people "tend to view the world through blood-red tinted glasses." Attributional style is a cognitive disposition, and does not depend on the experience of affective arousal (i.e., anger) as a result of being personally affected by others' apparently hostile actions. However, this cognitive disposition may go hand in hand with affect-based dispositions towards aggression. Dill et al. (1997) showed that irritability and trait aggressiveness predicted the extent to which participants attributed aggressive thoughts to the actor in a scenario describing an ambiguous social interaction.

The hostile attributional style can be seen as part of a person's aggressive script that is shaped through social experience, as described above (see also Chapter 2). The more often an aggressive script is rehearsed, the more easily hostile schemata can be accessed, making it more likely that behaviour shown by others is interpreted as an expression of hostile intent (Huesmann, 1998). Thus aggressive behaviour and hostile attributions are mutually reinforcing. Takarangi, Polaschek, Hignett, and Garry (2008) demonstrated that distorted memory plays an important part in this process. They gave participants word lists containing neutral and violence-related terms and asked them to recall which of the words had been presented in an earlier phase of the experiment. Highly aggressive participants were significantly more likely to falsely remember violent words as having been included in the earlier list. A parallel but weaker effect was found for a situational manipulation in which participants were primed by reading a word list referring to insults (e.g., "idiot," "loser," "incompetent"), or were given a list of neutral words. Those who had seen the insult words were more likely to falsely remember having seen violent words than those who had received the neutral words. Hostile attributional style is seen as an important variable contributing to individual differences in trait anger, as noted by Wilkowski and Robinson (2008). However, these authors argue that angry individuals are not only prone to fast and automatic hostile interpretations of situational cues, they are also less likely to engage in more effortful cognitive processes that might correct the initial hostile attributions. The failure to revise spontaneous hostile attributions through more elaborate information processing was also stressed by Dodge (2006) in his developmental account of the hostile attribution bias discussed earlier in this chapter.

Whereas the hostile attribution bias enhances aggressive behaviour, *perspective taking* is a cognitive variable associated with the inhibition of aggressive responses. Perspective taking refers to a person's ability to orient him- or herself non-egocentrically to the perspective of another person (Richardson, Green & Lago, 1998). The role of perspective taking in inhibiting aggressive behaviour has been established by a variety of studies (Miller & Eisenberg, 1988). For example, Richardson, Hammock, Smith, Gardner, and Signo (1994) showed that individuals who scored high on dispositional perspective taking were less likely to report aggressive behaviour and also less likely to respond in an aggressive way to a provocation. In a subsequent study, Richardson et al. (1998) found that individuals who scored high on dispositional perspective taking were more likely to choose a non-aggressive response to a verbal attack (as opposed to an aggressive response) than low perspective-takers. This was only true, however, if the attacker's verbal insults increased in aggressiveness from the beginning to the end of the interaction. If the verbal insults decreased from high to low levels during the interaction, no effect of perspective taking emerged. The need to understand an aggressive opponent's behaviour is probably greater if the opponent's aggression becomes more extreme in the course of the interaction than if an initially aggressive opponent becomes less aggressive over time. Therefore high perspective takers may have chosen non-aggressive (i.e., de-escalating) responses to a greater extent when the opponent showed increasing levels of aggression.

Self-esteem and narcissism

In everyday discourse, it is commonly believed that aggressive individuals have low self-esteem and engage in aggressive behaviour to increase their feelings of self-worth. However, systematic research shows the link between self-esteem and aggression to be more complicated. Reviews of the literature have found several studies demonstrating a link between low self-esteem and aggression, but also identified studies that showed the reverse relationship, a curvilinear relationship or no link at all (Ostrowsky, 2010; Walker & Bright, 2009). To make sense of this conflicting evidence, a theoretical analysis is needed as to why and how low or high self-esteem should be linked to aggression. To begin with, there is agreement among researchers that having genuinely high self-esteem, reflected in objective achievements and mirrored in a positive evaluation by others, works as a protective factor against aggression. Low self-esteem has been linked to aggression via the experience of shame and humiliation that elicits anger and thereby promotes aggressive behaviour (Walker & Bright, 2009). However, other authors have argued that aggression requires risk taking and confidence of success, which are typically absent in people with low self-esteem (Baumeister, Bushman, & Campbell, 2000). They suggest that it is unrealistically high ("inflated") but fragile self-esteem that leads to aggressive behaviour and introduced the concept of "narcissism" to denote this problematic type of self-esteem. Narcissism is characterised by a grandiose view of superiority and a sense of entitlement that leads to aggression when one is challenged by others (Baumeister et al., 2000). Several measures have been developed to measure individual differences in narcissism, such as the Narcissistic Personality Inventory (NPI; Raskin & Terry, 1988), which contains items such as "If I ruled the world it would be a much better place" (for a review, see Soyer, Rovenpor, Kopelman, Mullins, & Watson, 2001).

From the perspective of narcissism, aggression is seen as serving an ego-protective function, and it is activated to restore a threatened sense of personal superiority. Therefore narcissists are particularly prone to aggressive behaviour in response to stimuli perceived as a threat to a positive sense of self-worth, such as negative feedback or provocation. To differentiate narcissism from high self-esteem, it can be said that "an individual with high self-esteem thinks he or she is good; a narcissistic individual thinks he or she is better" (Taylor, Davis-Kean, & Malanchuk, 2007, p. 131). In line with Berkowitz's cognitive neo-associationist model of aggression (see Chapter 2), Baumeister and Boden (1998) stipulated that a threat to self-esteem precipitates aggression by eliciting anger. To the extent that negative appraisal is perceived as unjustified, it evokes anger which in turn increases the probability of an aggressive response.

There is evidence from correlational and experimental studies that narcissism is related to aggression in a wide range of areas, including laboratory aggression, domestic violence, aggressive driving, and even murder and assault (Baumeister & Boden, 1998; Lustman, Wiesenthal & Flett, 2010; Walker & Bright, 2009). Consistent with the proposition that narcissists engage in aggression to cope with threats to their fragile self-esteem, the meta-analysis by Bettencourt et al. (2006) found a significant link between narcissism and aggression in situations involving a provocation, but not in neutral situations. Narcissists have also been found to show more aggression in response to negative feedback that was delivered in public than to negative feedback delivered in private (Ferriday, Vartanian, & Mandel, 2011). Bushman, Baumeister, Thomaes, Ryu, Begeer, & West (2009, Study 1) obtained separate measures of self-esteem and narcissism and found that the combination of high self-esteem and high narcissism produced the highest levels of direct aggression in a competitive reaction time measure of aggression (see Chapter 1). In a further study, Bushman et al. (2009, Study 3) replicated the findings in a realistic context using the essay evaluation paradigm (see Chapter 1). Students first received either positive or negative feedback about an essay from a fellow student, and were then asked to assign a grade to the feedback that would count towards the other student's course mark. The lowest grades (indicating the highest level of aggression) were assigned by students who scored high on both self-esteem and narcissism. The self-esteem measure on its own was unrelated to aggressive behaviour in both studies, supporting the importance of ego threat as incorporated in narcissism in prompting aggressive behaviour.

Although the theoretical concept of narcissism links it primarily to provoked and direct aggression against the source of the provocation, recent studies have also demonstrated a link with unprovoked aggression and aggression displaced on to a third party. Reidy, Foster, and Zeichner (2010) used a competitive reaction time task to classify their participants as *unprovoked aggressors* (those who chose to deliver an aversive shock to an alleged opponent even before they received the first shock), *retaliative aggressors* (those who only delivered aversive shocks after receiving a shock from their opponent), and *non-aggressors* (those who refrained from delivering shocks altogether). They found that unprovoked aggressors scored significantly higher on a trait measure of narcissism than both the provoked aggressor and the nonaggressor groups. With regard to displaced aggression, Twenge and Campbell (2003) studied narcissists' aggressive responses after a social rejection, which should be a powerful form of ego threat. In a series of experiments, they found that narcissists not only reacted more angrily to social rejection and showed more direct aggression against the person rejecting them, but also behaved more aggressively towards a third party. Corroborating the idea that narcissists' higher aggression is contingent upon the experience of ego threat, no difference between high and low narcissists' aggressive behaviour was found following social acceptance. We shall examine social rejection as a situational trigger of aggression in more detail in Chapter 4.

In summary, a substantial body of evidence has demonstrated that narcissism, defined as an inflated but vulnerable feeling of self-worth, predisposes individuals to engage in aggressive behaviour, particularly in situations that involve a threat to their self-esteem.

Recent research has identified components of narcissism that may be particularly maladaptive as far as aggression is concerned. For example, Reidy, Zeichner, Foster, and Martinez (2008) found that entitlement (e.g., "I will never be satisfied until I get all that I deserve") and exploitation (e.g., "I find it easy to manipulate people") were the two sub-dimensions of narcissism as measured by the NPI most closely related to aggressive behaviour in a competitive reaction time task, whereas other dimensions, such as vanity and self-sufficiency, were unrelated to aggression. These findings suggest that narcissism represents a construct with multiple aspects referring to an exaggerated sense of self-worth, not all of which may be related to aggression. A second line of research has been directed at breaking down narcissism into different domains of self-esteem. For example, Widman and McNulty (2010) found that a specific measure of sexual narcissism, with components such as sexual entitlement and a grandiose sense of sexual skills, predicted men's engagement in sexual aggression better than a global measure of narcissism. In a meta-analysis that looked at differences in narcissism scores over time, Twenge, Konrath, Foster, Campbell, and Bushman (2008) found a significant generational shift over a period of 25 years, with greater endorsement of the narcissism items on the NPI in more recent studies. Given the strong evidence that links narcissism to aggression, this does look like a worrying trend. On a more positive note, Thomaes, Bushman, Orobio de Castro, Cohen, and Denissen (2009) conducted a school-based field experiment with adolescents and were able to show that a brief self-affirmation intervention in which participants were asked to write a paragraph on their most important personal values reduced aggressive behaviour in high narcissists over a 1-week period.

Lack of self-control

A further aspect of the self that is relevant to the understanding of individual differences in aggression is *self-control*. This construct refers to internal restraints that should inhibit the release of aggressive response tendencies. Several authors have suggested that some individuals' chronic deficits in self-control are responsible for their criminal behaviour (for a review, see Gottfredson, 2007). The fact that many criminals commit a variety of different offences, together with the observation that criminal behaviour is often accompanied by a lack of self-control in other areas (e.g., heavy smoking, excessive alcohol consumption), supports the idea of a general self-control problem underlying aggressive behaviour (Baumeister & Boden, 1998). Lower self-control was also related to physical violence against a dating partner in a study by Archer, Fernández-Fuertes, and Thanzami (2010, Study 2). Research on *impulsivity*, which is the opposite of self-control, demonstrated that it was linked to aggression, although, according to Bettencourt et al.'s (2006) meta-analysis, only in situations that involved provocation. This finding suggests that individual differences in self-control may be particularly influential in the regulation of reactive aggression. A meta-analysis that examined gender differences in impulsivity found no differences between men and women on measures of general impulsivity or in measures of effortful control (Cross, Copping, & Campbell, 2011).

The role of self-control in the regulation of aggressive behaviour has also been confirmed in experimental studies using *ego-depletion* manipulations – that is, preventing participants from engaging in self-control by forcing them to allocate mental resources to another task. Stucke and Baumeister (2006) depleted their (hungry) participants' self-regulation resources by asking them to refrain from eating tempting sweets placed in front of them, before exposing them to a provocation from the experimenter in the form of negative feedback. As a measure of aggression, participants were asked to provide feedback on the experimenter that would affect the extension of his job. Stucke and Baumeister hypothesised that participants who had been asked not to eat from the sweets in front of them would have to use their self-control resources to refrain from taking a sweet. They would therefore be less able to suppress the urge to aggress against the experimenter who provoked them than participants in a control condition who were told they could eat as many sweets as they liked. This was exactly that they found. Participants who were made to concentrate on stopping themselves from eating the sweets gave significantly more negative evaluations of the experimenter than those in the control condition. In two further studies, Stucke and Baumeister (2006) replicated the findings using another method of ego-depletion. Participants were made to watch an extremely boring film and those in the experimental condition were asked to carefully monitor their facial expression so as not to give away how bored they were. These participants evaluated the experimenter more negatively after he provoked them than participants who were just told to relax while watching the film.

Using the hot sauce paradigm as a measure of aggression (see Chapter 1), DeWall, Baumeister, Stillman, and Gailliot (2007) replicated this finding by asking participants to refrain from eating either a doughnut, requiring a high level of self-control, or a radish, requiring low self-control. They found that those in the doughnut condition administered more hot sauce after a provocation than those in the radish condition. This study also suggests that self-control primarily involves cognitive activity, as there was no difference in anger between depleted and non-depleted participants. Furthermore, depleting self-control had no effect on aggression in the absence of provocation, indicating that self-control depletion disinhibits rather than instigates aggression (DeWall et al., 2007, Study 2). Although the experimental findings demonstrate situational variations in self-control, they can also contribute to the understanding of individual differences in aggression by showing that self-control, enabling people to suppress their aggressive impulses, is a limited cognitive resource.

The evidence reviewed in this section points to a number of personal characteristics that can help to explain why individuals differ in their readiness to act aggressively even when exposed to the same situational conditions. However, as shown by the comprehensive meta-analysis conducted by Bettencourt et al. (2006), the majority of the personality variables considered in this section only predict aggression in situations that activate the respective affective or cognitive processes – for example, by presenting a provocation. This finding supports the General Aggression Model (see Chapter 2) by showing that it is the interaction of individual differences and features of the situation that shapes the aggressive response.

Gender differences in aggressive behaviour

Gender is another stable characteristic of the person that is relevant to aggression. In this section we shall first discuss evidence on the emergence and development of gender differences in aggression through childhood and adolescence, followed by a review of the evidence on gender differences in adulthood. In both cases it will be important to distinguish between direct (physical and verbal) aggression and indirect (relational) aggression.

Gender differences in aggression during childhood and adolescence

Developmental research has revealed that gender differences in aggressive behaviour emerge early in life, and that the gap between boys and girls widens as they get older, at least as far as physical aggression is concerned (for reviews, see Archer & Coté, 2005; Hay, 2007). Loeber and Stouthamer-Loeber (1998) have summarised the evidence on gender differences in aggressive behaviour in different developmental periods, as shown in Table 3.4.

Table 3.4 indicates that gender differences in aggression are established from preschool age onwards, and there is evidence that they may start to emerge as early as in toddlerhood (Alink et al., 2006). The overall direction of these differences is towards higher levels of aggression in boys, with the exception of indirect aggression, which is found to be more common in girls. With regard to gender constellations of aggressors and targets, Archer and Coté (2005) summarised evidence showing that boys tend to be more physically aggressive than girls in same-sex encounters, whereas girls tend to be more physically aggressive than boys in opposite-sex encounters. With regard to self-reported verbal aggression, meta-analytic evidence provided by Archer (2004) revealed a significant gender difference. He used the difference (d) between mean aggression scores for males and females as a measure of effect size that indicates the magnitude of the difference between the two gender groups. Boys were found to be more verbally aggressive than girls, and the difference increased from childhood (6–11 years of age, effect size in the male direction of $d = 0.19$) to adolescence (11–17 years of age, effect size of $d = 0.36$). In the younger age group, the gender difference was smaller for verbal aggression ($d = 0.19$) than for physical aggression ($d = 0.26$), but in the adolescent group the effect sizes for verbal and physical aggression were almost identical.

Some recent research using observational methods and teacher reports has found that girls are more relationally aggressive than boys from as early as preschool age onwards. By contrast, several studies using peer reports have failed to support the gender difference (for a summary, see Crick, Ostrov, & Kawabata, 2007). In a meta-analysis including 148 studies and a total of over 70 000 children, Card et al. (2008) found that boys scored higher than girls

Table 3.4 Evidence for gender differences in aggression in childhood and adolescence (Reprinted from Loeber & Stouthamer-Loeber, 1998, p. 253. Copyright American Psychological Association)

Developmental period	Manifestation	Gender differences
Infancy	• Frustration and rage	No
Toddlerhood	• Instrumental aggression	Few
Preschool	• Personal aggression	Yes
	• Physical fighting	
Elementary school	• Indirect aggression	Yes
Middle and high school	• Group and gang fighting	Yes
	• Aggravated assault	
	• Sexual violence	
	• Homicide	

on direct (i.e., verbal and physical) aggression. The gender difference was negligible for relational aggression, such as harming others' social relationships behind their back (for similar meta-analytic findings, see also Scheithauer, Haag, Mahlke, & Ittel, 2008). Therefore it appears that the gender gap for physical aggression is not matched by a gap in relational aggression, either in the same or the opposite direction.

Moreover, Loeber and Stouthamer-Loeber (1998) noted that not only the level of aggression but also its developmental course appears to be different for boys and girls. A greater proportion of girls start to become aggressive in adolescence without a previous history of aggression, and girls' involvement in serious violence peaks earlier than that of boys. However, more recent longitudinal findings showed that a high proportion of girls diagnosed with conduct disorder in adolescence also had elevated levels of aggression in childhood, and that childhood-onset aggression may be more common in girls than was previously assumed (Keenan, Wroblewski, Hipwell, Loeber, & Stouthamer-Loeber, 2010).

To explain gender differences in physical aggression and why they seem to widen between early childhood and adolescence, several possible mechanisms have been proposed (Hay, 2007). One is that the more rapid maturation by girls in infancy promotes greater self-regulation skills, which enable girls to better control their anger. Another proposed explanation is that higher rates of rough-and-tumble play among boys spill over into aggression and bring about the development of norms condoning aggression. Indeed, boys and girls were found to differ in their normative approval of aggression (Huesmann & Guerra, 1997). Importantly, there are pressures created by gender role expectations that affect aggressive behaviour in boys as well as girls. For example, the norm that boys should not hit girls may explain why girls were found to be more aggressive than boys in opposite-sex encounters. Gender-role norms prohibiting overt aggression in girls may serve to curb aggression in girls, or may lead them to restrict their aggressive behaviour to the private sphere. The latter possibility will be examined more closely in the context of intimate partner violence (see Chapter 7), where the role of women as perpetrators has been intensely debated.

How pronounced are gender differences in aggression in adulthood?

The view that men are generally more aggressive than women is well supported by everyday observation, crime records, and lay beliefs about gender differences. Men consistently outnumber women by a wide margin as perpetrators of violent crime. Table 3.5 illustrates this claim with statistical data taken from the Uniform Crime Reports in the USA (U.S. Department of Justice, 2010) and from the Police Crime Statistics for the Federal Republic of Germany (Bundeskriminalamt, 2010).

The data in Table 3.5 are not strictly comparable across the two countries because the underlying legal definitions are somewhat different, and the US figures refer to the number of arrests whereas the German data refer to the number of suspects identified. Nevertheless, they serve to illustrate that men are similarly over-represented in statistics for violent crime in both countries. In addition to official crime statistics, many studies have confirmed that

Table 3.5 Overrepresentation of men in violent crime: data from the USA and Germany

	USA, 2009	*Germany, 2009*
Murder and non-negligent manslaughter	89.6	87.2
Rape	98.7	99.0
Robbery	88.2	91.0
Aggravated assault	78.0	85.2

Sources: US data: US Department of Justice, 2010, Table 42, data refer to persons arrested; German data: Bundeskriminalamt, 2010, p. 85, data refer to persons identified as suspects. The figures indicate the percentage of arrestees/suspects who were male.

physical aggression is predominantly shown by men. For example, Archer, Holloway, and McLoughlin (1995) found that 61% of a sample of male students had been involved in a fight during the 3 years prior to the study. A substantial number of respondents reported that either they (11%) or their opponent (18%) had drawn blood. In 15% of all fights, the police had been involved, and in 8% arrests had been made. Unfortunately, no comparable data on women's involvement in fights were reported. Men are also far more likely to own a gun than are women. In a study by Cairns and Cairns (1994), 51% of the boys under the age of 16 reported owning a gun, whereas the corresponding figure for girls was only 5%.

With regard to the overall differences between men and women in aggressive behaviour, several meta-analytical reviews have found that men show higher levels of physical aggression compared with women in early adulthood (e.g., Archer, 2004; Eagly & Steffen, 1986; Hyde, 1984). Findings from cross-cultural studies also support this conclusion (e.g., Archer & McDaniel, 1995). In the most recent meta-analysis by Archer (2004), the largest difference in physical aggression was found for young adults (aged 18–30 years), but the difference remained significant beyond that age. The findings from Archer's analysis referring to self-reports of aggressive behaviour are presented in Table 3.6. The measure of effect size reported in Table 3.6 is *d*, a difference score, with higher values denoting a larger gender difference. Positive *d* scores indicate that males score higher than females, whereas negative *d* scores denote higher scores in females than in males.

In each age group, positive *d* scores were found for physical aggression, indicating that men scored higher on measures of physical aggression than did women. Men were also found to be significantly more verbally aggressive in each of the three age groups, but the difference was less pronounced than for physical aggression in the two younger age groups. A small gender difference in indirect, relational aggression in the female direction was found for the group of 18- to 21-year-olds. Above the age of 21, this difference was no longer apparent, indicating that in adulthood men and women become more similar in their use of relational aggression.

Whether or not gender differences in aggression have become smaller over time has been a contentious issue. Crime statistics can be used to examine the possibility that the gender gap in physical aggression is narrowing, but they do not present a conclusive picture. For example, the Uniform Crime Report (U.S. Department of Justice, 2010, Table 35) has

Table 3.6 Meta-analytic evidence on gender differences in adult aggression (Adapted from Archer, 2004, Table 5. Copyright American Psychological Association).

Age group (years)	Overall	Physical	Verbal	Indirect/ relational
18–21	0.46	0.66	0.35	–0.11
	(33)	(44)	(35)	(19)
22–30	0.29	0.60	0.22	
	(7)	(8)	(9)	–0.01
> 30	–0.01	0.25	0.26	(7)
	(4)	(8)	(7)	

Positive *d* scores indicate higher scores for males, negative *d* scores indicate higher scores for females. The number of studies for each effect size is given in parentheses.

revealed that although arrests for aggravated assault declined overall from 2005 to 2009, the decline was less pronounced for females (–2.8%) than for males (–8.1%). However, the reverse pattern was found for homicide and non-negligent manslaughter, which declined by 13.5% for females and by only 8.7% for males. Some meta-analyses of research studies comparing men's and women's levels of aggression found that earlier studies tended to show larger gender differences than more recent publications (e.g., Hyde, 1984), and this finding has been interpreted as suggesting that socialisation is more important in eliciting gender differences than biological processes. However, Knight, Fabes, and Higgins (1996) demonstrated that the earlier and later studies differed not only with regard to their publication date, but also in their use of different methodologies. Different methodologies in turn are systematically related to different magnitudes of gender differences. When these methodological differences were taken into account in Knight et al.'s re-examination of studies included in Hyde's (1984) meta-analysis, the "year of publication effect" disappeared.

Explaining gender differences in aggression

Three main lines of theorising have been proposed to account for the observed gender differences in aggression: the hormonal explanation, the sociobiological model, and the social role model.

(1) The *hormonal* explanation attributes men's higher aggressive tendencies to the male sex hormone testosterone. Studies involving subhuman species provide some support for the role of testosterone in aggression shown by male animals (Archer, 1988). However, as discussed in Chapter 2, there is less support for the role of testosterone in explaining differences in human aggression. Cross-sectional studies comparing testosterone levels in men who differed in aggressive behaviour found some evidence of a covariation of testosterone and aggression (see reviews by Archer, 1991; Archer, Birring, & Wu, 1998;

Benton, 1992). The claim that testosterone plays a crucial role in aggression would require evidence that intra-individual variations in testosterone levels are accompanied by corresponding fluctuations in physical aggression. In particular, the dramatic increases in testosterone levels during puberty should lead to parallel increases in aggressive behaviour. In a longitudinal study that followed boys from the beginning to the end of puberty, Halpern, Udry, Campbell, and Suchindran (1993) failed to demonstrate a covariation of testosterone levels and aggression. Archer's (2004) meta-analysis also found no evidence of a substantial increase in the gender gap in physical aggression that would parallel the increase in testosterone levels in boys at puberty.

(2) The *evolutionary* or sociobiological account stresses the adaptive value of male aggression in securing access to female mating partners (e.g., Archer & Coté, 2005; see also Chapter 2). This claim is supported by the finding that it is primarily *young* men who are responsible for the higher rates of male physical aggression, as reflected in crime statistics as well as controlled studies. According to the evolutionary perspective, men's display of aggression is designed to demonstrate their status and power and thereby to enhance their success in the reproductive competition with other men. Therefore situations that involve a threat to a man's status should be particularly likely to elicit aggression as a means of restoring power and status. Similarly, men whose status is continuously low or under threat should be more violent than high-status men. Support for this proposition has been offered by Archer et al. (1995), who found that compared with students (a relatively high-status group), unemployed men were significantly more likely to have been involved in a fight following public humiliation or a dispute over money or property. However, it should be emphasised that the observed link is only correlational, and does not identify low status as a *cause* of proneness to fight.

To explain men's greater involvement in intergroup conflicts, such as wars, Van Vugt (2011) proposed the "male warrior hypothesis." This hypothesis argues that forming coalitions with other men to procure and protect resources has favoured the evolution of a "tribal brain" that increases men's propensity to engage in intergroup conflict. In support of this view, Van Vugt cited evidence that men are more competitive than women in intergroup situations, more likely to discriminate against out-groups, and more eager to defend their group against external threat.

Women's tendency to prefer indirect to direct forms of aggression can also be explained from an evolutionary perspective (Archer & Coté, 2005). From a cost-benefit point of view, indirect aggression carries a lower risk of physical injury in competitions with other women for access to attractive mating partners. Protecting themselves from risk of injury is seen as more important for women than for men because their offspring are more dependent on their continuous care and nurturance than on their fathers (Cross & Campbell, 2011). Consistent with this reasoning, several studies have reported positive correlations between the use of indirect aggression and dating popularity and/ or number of dating partners among girls (Pellegrini & Long, 2003). In conclusion, indirect aggression by women may be seen as a less risky form of intimidating potential rivals in the competition for attractive male partners, thereby increasing their reproductive fitness (Vaillancourt, 2005).

(3) The *social role* model proposes that aggressive behaviour is regulated by male and female gender roles adopted in the process of socialisation (Eagly, 1987; Eagly & Wood, 1999). According to this approach, biological sex has little explanatory power in itself, but is linked to differences in aggressive behaviour via differential social roles associated with masculinity and femininity (Richardson & Hammock, 2007). This model argues that the male gender role is associated with assertiveness and dominance, which facilitate aggression, whereas the female gender role is associated with characteristics such as nurturance and empathy, which prohibit the display of aggressive behaviour. The finding that women are more likely to experience feelings of guilt and anxiety when engaging in aggressive behaviour supports the idea that aggression is incompatible with female role prescriptions (Campbell, 2006). It follows from this line of reasoning that gender differences in aggression should disappear if role demands are removed, and several studies have found this to be the case. For example, in a study by Lightdale and Prentice (1994), gender differences disappeared when participants were de-individuated (i.e., tested under conditions of anonymity). Participants had to play a video game in which they could attack their opponents by dropping bombs. Figure 3.2 displays the

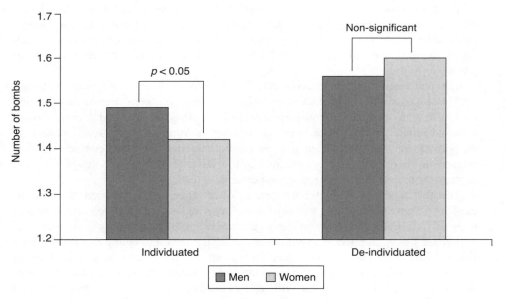

Figure 3.2 Gender differences in aggression as a function of individuation vs. de-individuation. (Adapted from Lightdale & Prentice, 1994, p. 41. Copyright Sage Publications).

findings for men and women under de-individuated vs. individuated conditions, using the log-transformed data reported by Lightdale and Prentice (1994, Table 3).

When participants were "individuated" (i.e., when they were personally identified by large name badges), men dropped significantly more bombs on their virtual opponents than did women. However, in the de-individuated condition, where they could drop the bombs under the cloak of anonymity, women were no less aggressive than men. The meta-analysis of 64 studies by Bettencourt and Miller (1996) further showed that gender differences in aggression are reduced when provocation is involved. Arguably, aggression in response to provocation or under conditions of anonymity is less at odds with female role prescriptions, and the decrease in gender differences under these circumstances attests to women's sensitivity to gender role norms. In the same vein, a meta-analysis by Bettencourt and Kernahan (1997) of the impact of aggressive cues on aggressive behaviour found that, in the absence of provocation, women were significantly less responsive to aggressive cues than were men. However, under conditions of provocation, men and women both showed increased levels of aggression when presented with aggressive cues.

The impact of masculine gender-role socialisation on men's aggressive behaviour has been highlighted by research on hypermasculinity, also referred to as the "macho personality pattern" (Mosher & Sirkin, 1984). This construct seeks to explain individual differences in aggression between men. The macho personality pattern consists of three related components: (a) calloused sexual attitudes towards women, (b) the perception of violence as manly, and (c) the view of danger as exciting. Since aggression is deeply ingrained in the male gender stereotype, macho men are expected to show aggressive behaviour to a greater extent than men who do not endorse this hypermasculine role. In support of this reasoning, positive correlations were found between the endorsement of the macho personality pattern and aggression (Mosher & Sirkin, 1984). In an experimental study by Reidy, Shirk, Sloan, and Zeichner (2009), hypermasculine men were more aggressive towards a female confederate in terms of delivering electric shocks in a competitive reaction time paradigm (see Chapter 1) than men who scored lower on hypermasculinity, particularly when they were led to believe that the woman had rejected the traditional female gender role.

The social role approach explains gender differences in social behaviour as the result of the individual's adaptation to particular social structural conditions and role requirements, varying over time and across societies (see Figure 3.3). The evolutionary approach sees the roots of this adaptive process in the early history of the human species, focusing on differences in reproductive strategies between men and women. This view leaves little room for variations in aggression across cultures and historical periods, and indeed views evidence of cross-cultural similarity in aggression as supportive of its claims. Although evolutionary and social role explanations stress different processes underlying gender differences in aggression, they are not necessarily incompatible. As has been noted by Eagly and Wood (1999), the two approaches can be fruitfully combined if they are placed along a continuum from distal to proximal influences. The evolutionary account is concerned with so-called

Figure 3.3 Iranian women practising their shooting skills (1986).
Source: Jean Gaumy/Magnum Photos/Agentur Focus. Reprinted with permission.

distal factors that explain the long-term emergence of gender differences in the human species, whereas the socialisation approach emphasises the *proximal* influences that impinge on individuals in the course of their development.

Summary

*   Aggressive behaviour emerges in early childhood, with boys generally displaying higher levels of aggression than girls from preschool age onwards. In age-normative patterns of development, aggression declines as children get older, giving way to non-aggressive strategies of conflict resolution. However, if aggressive behaviour persists into adolescence, it becomes more harmful in its consequences and is more often socially organised in the form of gangs and group violence.
*   Individual differences in aggression show considerable stability from childhood to early adulthood. Nonetheless, there are some children who start off with a high level of aggression that declines as they grow older, while others show a late onset of aggression in adolescence without a previous history of aggressive behaviour. The acceptance of

aggression as legitimate and the habitual perception of hostile intent in others were found to be important cognitive antecedents of aggression in childhood and adolescence. Exposure to violence in the family, including harsh parental punishment, and peer rejection are environmental factors linked to individual differences in aggression.

- In adults, individual differences in trait anger and hostility, irritability, emotional susceptibility, and dissipation vs. rumination following an aggression-eliciting stimulus have been linked to differences in aggression. Moreover, hostile attributional bias (i.e., the tendency to interpret others' behaviour as hostile) was found to predict adults' aggressive behaviour. Research on narcissism has shown that it is not low self-esteem but unrealistically high and fragile self-esteem that makes individuals susceptible to aggressive behaviour. Individuals holding inflated and/or unstable views of themselves are more easily threatened in their self-esteem and are more likely to show aggression to restore a positive self-appraisal. Finally, research on self-control and aggression has demonstrated that the failure to control aggressive impulses may explain individual differences in aggression, and that depleting resources for self-control facilitates aggressive behaviour.

- Research on gender differences in aggression has established that men are more physically aggressive than women. Men also score higher than women on measures of verbal aggression, although the difference is smaller than for physical aggression. However, recent research on aggressive women suggests that women may choose indirect, relational forms of aggression to a greater extent than do men. There is no conclusive evidence so far on the role of the male sex hormone testosterone in explaining higher levels of male aggression over time. The debate on how to explain gender differences in aggression has focused on the evolutionary vs. the social role approach. The evolutionary approach attributes gender differences in aggression to differential reproductive strategies in men and women, whereas the social role approach emphasises the significance of gender-specific roles and norms to which men and women have to adapt in their social behaviour. Recent theorising has offered an integrative perspective in which evolutionary hypotheses refer to the distal roots of gender differences in the development of the human species, and socio-cultural explanations refer to the proximal influence of socialisation processes in individual development.

Tasks to do

(1) Visit the website of the Dunedin Longitudinal Study (http://dunedinstudy.otago.ac.nz) to find out more about the findings of this exciting study that has been following the same group of people for almost 40 years.

(2) Develop your own small-scale measure of the hostile attribution bias. Write down two scenarios in which one person causes harm to another but there is ambiguity as to whether the actor did this on purpose. Then write down three items referring to the scenarios that can capture a person's hostile attributional style.

(3) Design an experimental study to test the hypothesis that gender differences in aggression are due to the salience of masculine and feminine gender roles.

Suggested reading

Archer, J. (2004). Sex differences in aggression in real-world settings: A meta-analytic review. *Review of General Psychology, 8*, 291–322.

Bettencourt, B. A., Talley, B. A. J., & Valentine, J. (2006). Personality and aggressive behavior under provoking and neutral conditions: A meta-analytic review. *Psychological Bulletin, 132*, 751–777.

Tremblay, R. E., Hartup, W. W., & Archer, J. (Eds) (2005). *Developmental origins of aggression*. New York: The Guilford Press.

4 Situational elicitation of aggressive behaviour

In the previous chapter, we looked at the development of aggressive behaviour and at individual characteristics to address the question of why some people are more aggressive than others in precisely the same situation. In this chapter, the reverse question will be asked, namely why people are more likely to act aggressively in some situations and not in others. The importance of frustration and provocation in eliciting aggressive behaviour has already been discussed in Chapter 2. In the present chapter we shall consider further variables explaining situational variations in aggressive behaviour. First, research on aggressive cues that trigger aggressive behaviour will be examined, stressing the role of automatic information processing in the instigation of aggression. The second section will examine the experience of social exclusion as a trigger for aggressive behaviour. The third section is devoted to the role of alcohol as a powerful situational influence on aggression and to the processes by which it lowers the threshold for engaging in aggressive behaviour. Finally, evidence will be reviewed on the impact of temperature and other stressors in the physical environment on aggressive behaviour.

In each of these areas it will become clear that situational characteristics, even if influential in themselves, interact with personal characteristics that actors bring to the situation, and it is the interaction between the situation and the person that holds the clue to understanding aggressive behaviour. A complementary perspective on the link between situational characteristics and aggression is to ask what features of a situation are likely to *reduce* or *inhibit* aggression. This question refers to the prevention and control of aggression, and will be discussed in that context in Chapter 11.

Examining the situational dynamics of aggression and violence is an area where social psychology meets sociology, in particular micro-sociology. This sociological perspective is concerned with the analysis of interactions between individuals and within small groups. It differs from the social psychological approach primarily in the focus on qualitative, interpretative methods, including direct observation of aggressive confrontations and the analysis of case studies, rather than the quantitative methods that predominate in social psychology. A comprehensive micro-sociological analysis of violence that discusses the situational unfolding of aggression and complements the evidence presented in this chapter has been provided by Collins (2008).

Aggressive cues

The frustration-aggression hypothesis, discussed in Chapter 2, states that frustration increases the likelihood of an aggressive response, while acknowledging that other, non-aggressive responses may also be shown in response to frustration. The question arises, therefore, what the circumstances are that facilitate aggression as a consequence of frustration or, more generally, negative arousal. One answer has been that the presence of aggression-related cues in the immediate environment promotes aggression by increasing the accessibility of aggressive thoughts, which in turn enhance the likelihood of choosing an aggressive response (see Figure 4.1). In their famous "weapons experiment which was discussed in Chapter 2, Berkowitz and LePage (1967) demonstrated that angered participants acted more aggressively towards the source of the provocation when a firearm was present in the lab room than in the presence of a badminton racket (a neutral object) or in a no-object control condition in which no objects were present. This experiment highlighted the importance of *aggressive cues in the environment* in triggering aggressive responses. As shown in the meta-analysis by Carlson et al. (1990), Berkowitz and LePage's findings were corroborated by many subsequent studies. In addition, Carlson et al. identified an effect, albeit weaker, of aggressive cues on participants in a neutral mood state. This finding suggests that negative arousal may not be a necessary condition for situational cues to affect aggressive behaviour.

Figure 4.1 Aggressive cues can be found everywhere, even in the kitchen. (Egg moulder. Copyright INVOTIS B. V. Reprinted with permission).

The psychological mechanism underlying the impact of aggressive cues on aggressive cognitions and behaviour is referred to as "priming" (Todorov & Bargh, 2002). *Primes* are stimuli that activate specific mental concepts which in turn feed into subsequent judgements and behaviours. For example, media depictions of violence, words with an aggressive meaning, or names of people associated with violent crime are clearly associated with aggressive connotations. Being exposed to these stimuli facilitates the ease with which aggressive cognitions come to mind and the likelihood that aggressive behaviour will be shown.

Using a standard reaction time paradigm, Anderson, Benjamin, and Bartholow (1998) showed that exposure to weapon primes does indeed enhance the accessibility of aggression-related cognitions, even in individuals who were not previously angered or frustrated. They presented their participants with series of word pairs, with the first word of each pair acting as a prime. Primes were either aggression-related (weapon words) or neutral (animal words). Following the silent reading of the prime word, participants were instructed to read the second (target) word of the pair out loud as fast as they could. Reaction times for reading the target word were used as the dependent variable. The target word was either aggression-related or neutral. As aggressive primes were assumed to activate aggressive thoughts, it was predicted that weapon primes would lead to shorter reaction times when reading aggressive target words compared with either neutral target words or animal primes. The findings from the study are presented in Figure 4.2.

As Figure 4.2 shows, participants were significantly faster in reading out aggressive target words when they had been primed by a weapon word than when the prime had been an animal word. Moreover, reaction times within the aggressive prime group were shorter for

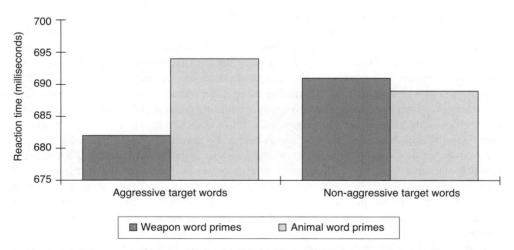

Figure 4.2 Effects of aggressive vs. non-aggressive primes on reaction times for aggressive and neutral target words. (Adapted from Anderson, Benjamin, & Bartholow, 1998, Table 2. Copyright Sage Publications).

the aggressive than for the non-aggressive target words. A second study conducted by Anderson et al. (1998) using visual stimuli as primes (pictures of weapons vs. pictures of plants) confirmed this result.

The literature on the weapons effect suggests that the very fact that a weapon is visually present in the situation increases the likelihood of aggressive responses. Further research has demonstrated that the effect is not limited to weapons, but extends to other aggression-related stimuli as well. People associated with aggressive events (e.g., because they happened to be present in a particular situation or featured in a particular aggressive film) can acquire aggressive cue value and increase the salience of aggressive thoughts through their mere presence (Carlson et al., 1990).

Aggressive cues work automatically – that is, without conscious monitoring or awareness – as shown by the finding that even primes presented subliminally (i.e., below the threshold of conscious perception) were found to influence subsequent cognitions. Bargh and Pietromonaco (1982) exposed their participants to subliminally presented word lists in which 0%, 20%, or 80% of the words were related to hostility (e.g., "hostile," "insult," "inconsiderate"). The words were briefly flashed up on a computer screen while the participants were working on a vigilance task. In a second, seemingly unrelated part of the experiment, they received a scenario describing a person showing mildly hostile behaviour (e.g., not opening the door to a salesman) and were asked to rate the person on a number of traits related to hostility. As expected, the participants who had been presented with the word list in which 80% of the words were related to hostility rated the stimulus person as significantly more hostile than the participants in the 0% or 20% conditions. No difference between the priming conditions was found for traits unrelated to hostility. These findings suggest that even subliminally presented cues related to hostility activate corresponding mental concepts related to hostility that impinge on subsequent judgements.

However, for cues such as weapons to serve as primes of aggressive cognitions, it is crucial that they are associated with aggression rather than with other cognitive constructs. This was demonstrated in a set of studies comparing the susceptibility of hunters and non-hunters to weapons as aggressive cues (Bartholow, Anderson, Carnagey, & Benjamin, 2005). The argument was that hunters would have more differentiated knowledge structures than non-hunters, which would lead them to associate hunting weapons (e.g., shotguns and long-range rifles) with pleasurable sports activities, but to associate assault guns (e.g., handguns and assault rifles) with harming other human beings. By contrast, non-hunters should associate both types of weapons primarily with aggression. Drawing on Berkowitz's cognitive neo-associationist model (see Chapter 2), Bartholow et al. predicted that in the group of hunters the accessibility of aggressive cognitions and likelihood of aggressive behaviour would be higher in the presence of pictures of assault weapons than in the presence of hunting guns, whereas non-hunters would associate both types of weapons equally with aggression.

In the first study, hunters and non-hunters were exposed to a set of six pictures each of hunting weapons and assault weapons. Nature scenes were included as non-aggressive control stimuli. The participants were shown colour pictures of these stimuli randomly paired with target words that had either an aggressive meaning (e.g., "attack") or an anti-aggressive meaning (e.g., "comfort"). They were asked to read each word out loud as quickly as they could. The difference between the reaction times when reading out aggressive and anti-aggressive target words was the critical dependent variable. Higher difference scores indicated shorter response times (and thus better cognitive accessibility) of aggressive compared with anti-aggressive words. In the second study, the participants were randomly presented with either a hunting gun picture or an assault gun picture and then engaged in a competitive reaction time task where they could deliver an aversive noise blast to an alleged opponent (see Chapter 1). The intensity of the noise blasts set by the participants constituted the measure of aggressive behaviour. The findings are presented in Figure 4.3.

As predicted, hunters displayed a more pronounced "weapons effect," in terms of faster reaction times when reading out aggression-related words relative to anti-aggressive words, following the presentation of the assault weapons as opposed to the hunting weapons. For non-hunters, no differentiation between the two weapons primes was expected. Unexpectedly, however, non-hunters showed a stronger weapons effect following the presentation of the hunting guns. A parallel pattern was found for aggressive behaviour, shown in the bottom diagram. Hunters assigned louder noise blasts to an alleged opponent following the presentation of the assault guns than following the presentation of the hunting guns. Non-hunters assigned louder noise blasts after viewing the hunting weapons than after viewing the assault weapons, although this difference was not significant.

These findings lead to two main conclusions. First, they suggest that the aggressive meaning of a situational cue is not an inherent property of the stimulus itself, but is assigned on the basis of the perceiver's pre-existing knowledge structures and past behavioural experience. Hunters and non-hunters clearly had different knowledge structures with regard to hunting weapons. Secondly, the findings support the General Aggression Model (GAM) (see Chapter 2) by showing that differences in the accessibility of aggressive cognitions are linked to differences in aggressive behaviour.

Although the research reviewed in this section was conducted in artificial laboratory settings, it has important implications for the understanding of aggression in natural, everyday contexts. Weapons and other objects or images associated with aggression are widely available in a variety of social settings. They are an integral part of children's toy boxes and video game libraries, and omnipresent in the world of film and television (for a discussion of violent media contents as aggressive cues, see Chapter 5). The present discussion has shown short-term effects of aggressive cues confined to a single experimental session, but social cognitive priming research also has a message to convey regarding the repeated exposure to aggressive cues: the more frequently the primes are encountered, the more easily aggressive cognitions and behavioural response options are activated, making them chronically accessible over time. As noted by Todorov and Bargh (2002, p. 58), "people who are repeatedly exposed to stimuli related to aggression can develop chronically accessible knowledge structures, which would automatically affect the interpretation of new aggression-related events." In this way, repeated exposure to aggressive cues is one

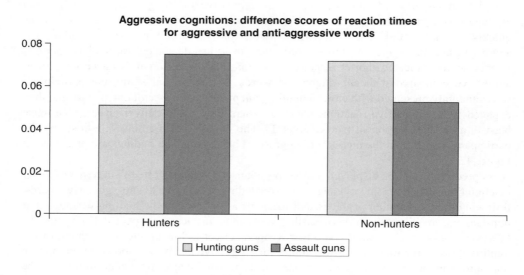

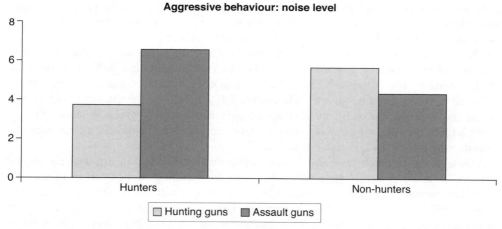

Figure 4.3 The meaning of aggressive cues for hunters and non-hunters. (Adapted from Figure 2 (Aggressive cognitions) and Figure 3 (Aggressive behaviour) of Bartholow et al., 2005. Copyright Elsevier Science).

pathway that contributes to the emergence of individual differences in the proneness to aggression.

Social exclusion

Being accepted and liked by others serves several vital needs fur humans. It gives individuals the experience of belonging and connectedness, helps them to maintain feelings of self-worth, and provides them with a sense of control over their social relationships. The experience of being rejected by another person or being excluded from a social group threatens these vital needs and is a powerful source of negative affect. Several overlapping terms are used in research that addresses the impact of the experience of not belonging on aggressive behaviour (Williams, 2007a, p. 427). *Ostracism* refers to ignoring and excluding individuals or groups by other individuals or groups, *rejection* involves an explicit declaration that an individual or group is not wanted, and finally *social exclusion* describes the experience of being kept apart from others. Although each of these constructs emphasises somewhat different aspects, they share the common core of describing experiences that undermine a person's need for social approval and social connectedness. Therefore they will be treated as synonyms for the purposes of the present discussion. A large body of research has shown that social exclusion results in feelings of sadness and anger, even when it comes from complete strangers or an apparently randomised computer programme (for reviews, see Leary, Twenge, & Quinlivan, 2006; Williams & Wesselmann, 2011; Zadro, 2011). In fact, Williams and Warburton (2003) described ostracism as a form of indirect aggression that often elicits aggressive responses, directed either against the excluding agents or against third parties.

A widely used paradigm for studying social exclusion in the laboratory is the "Cyberball" game, a ball-tossing game in which a person is excluded from the tossing exchanges of two or more other players (Williams, 1997). In addition to making participants engage in real-life ball-tossing rounds, the Cyberball game was developed by Williams, Cheung, and Choi (2000) as a computer-based version (see "Tasks to do" at the end of this chapter). Using this paradigm, a large number of studies have shown that participants who are excluded by other players experience strong feelings of anger, even when the exclusion lasts for only a few minutes, comes from members of a disliked out-group, or is thought to have been randomly generated by a computer programme (Williams, 2007b).

Another experimental strategy for studying the effects of social exclusion is the "Life Alone" paradigm developed by Twenge, Baumeister, Tice, and Stucke (2001). Participants are provided with false feedback about the projected development of their social relationships in the future. In the social exclusion condition, they are informed that based on alleged personality test scores they will most probably end up being alone for the greater part of their future life. For example, the text of the feedback provided by Twenge et al. (2001, p. 1060) reads as follows:

> You're the type who will end up alone later in life. You may have friends and relationships now, but by your mid-20s most of these will have drifted away. You may even marry or

have several marriages, but these are likely to be short-lived and not continue into your 30s. Relationships don't last, and when you're past the age where people are constantly forming new relationships, the odds are you'll end up being alone more and more.

The paradigm also includes a social *inclusion* condition, which provides feedback about successful relationships in the future, and a negative comparison condition unrelated to social relationships in which participants are told that they are particularly likely to be accident-prone in the future. Of course, participants are carefully debriefed at the end of the experimental session to make sure that they realise the feedback was bogus. Twenge et al. (2001) showed that participants in the social exclusion group behaved significantly more aggressively towards an experimenter (in the form of giving negative feedback relevant to his job promotion prospects) who had insulted them previously than did participants in the social inclusion or the accident-proneness conditions.

Finally, Leary, Tambor, Terdal, and Downs (1995) designed a "Get Acquainted" paradigm to manipulate social rejection. After a brief group discussion to enable them to get acquainted, participants are asked to name two group members with whom they would like to work on the experimental task. Bogus feedback is then provided to participants about the choices of the other group members. In the social rejection condition, they are told that no one has chosen them to work with, in the social inclusion condition they learn that everyone wants to work with them. When the participants thought that they had been rejected by the other group members, their self-esteem was significantly reduced (Leary et al., 1995).

Each of these three paradigms has generated conclusive evidence about the negative effects of social exclusion on self-esteem and feelings of control (Williams, 2007a). The experience of social exclusion has been described as a feeling of "social pain" that is no less intense than the feeling of physical pain, and brain imaging studies have revealed that being rejected in a Cyberball game activated the same areas of the brain as the infliction of physical pain (Eisenberger, Lieberman, & Williams, 2003). There are at least two common ways of reacting to this aversive experience. One is to try to restore social inclusion through ingratiation and behaving in a socially desirable way. Another is to engage in aggressive behaviour, fuelled by the experience of anger about the rejection. Williams (2007a,b) has reviewed a large body of evidence demonstrating that socially excluded participants were more likely to engage in aggressive behaviour across a range of measures of aggression discussed in Chapter 1, such as the noise blast paradigm (Twenge et al., 2001, Experiment 4) or the hot sauce paradigm (Warburton, Williams, & Cairns, 2006).

In explaining the effects of social exclusion, Williams (2007a) proposed a two-stage process. The first, immediate response is seen as a *reflexive*, automatic experience of social pain experienced as a result of the exclusion. This response is largely unaffected by individual differences or contextual variables in the situation, and is followed by feelings of anger, sadness, and helplessness. A meta-analysis of 192 studies by Blackhart, Nelson, Knowles, and Baumeister (2009) found significantly less positive affect in rejected participants than in accepted or control participants, although the effect was relatively small. The reflexive and automatic effects on self-esteem are illustrated by the fact that information which should have lessened the impact of perceived exclusion is not taken into consideration at this stage. In a study by Zadro, Williams, and Richardson (2004) using the Cyberball paradigm, participants were either included (i.e., received about a third of all tosses in a three-player situation) or excluded (i.e., received no further tosses after the first two rounds). Half of the participants in the inclusion and exclusion conditions were told that they played the game with other human players, and the other half were told that they played against a computer. The impact of these manipulations on participants' self-esteem immediately after 6 minutes of playing the game is presented in Figure 4.4. As expected, when they thought they played with other human participants, the excluded participants reported significantly lower self-esteem than the included participants. More importantly, the effect was equally strong among participants who thought that the tossing sequence had been determined by a computer.

With time to reflect on the exclusion episode, a second process sets in that involves a more *controlled* cognitive appraisal. As shown in a series of experiments by DeWall, Twenge, Gitter, and Baumeister (2009), rejected individuals generated more hostile thoughts, which in turn predicted more aggressive behavioural responses. This second phase of responding to social exclusion is influenced by stable dispositions and the features of the situation. For example, Twenge and Campbell (2003) showed that narcissists, whose self-esteem is inflated

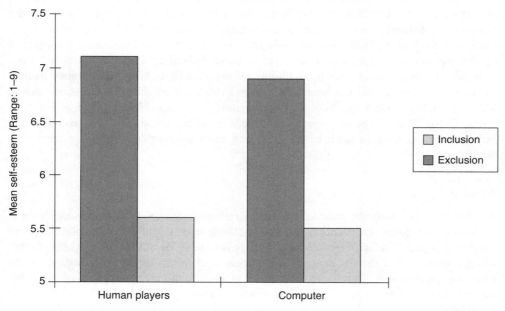

Figure 4.4 Effects of social exclusion in a Cyberball game on self-esteem, depending on whether tosses were thought to be determined by human players or a computer programme. (Adapted from Zadro, Williams, & Richardson, 2004, Table 1. Copyright Elsevier Science).

and particularly vulnerable to threat, were more aggressive after rejection than non-narcissists (for a discussion of narcissism and aggression, see Chapter 3). Similarly, a study by Ayduk et al. (2008) found that individuals high in rejection sensitivity, who anxiously expect and readily perceive social rejection, showed more aggressive behaviour following social rejection in a laboratory situation than those low in rejection sensitivity.

Situational variables have also been identified as moderators of the rejection-aggression link. Arguing that social rejection undermines an individual's sense of control and that aggression is a means of regaining control, Warburton et al. (2006) conducted an experiment in which participants were either excluded or included. Subsequently, they were exposed to an aversive noise blast that they could either terminate or could not control. Their findings showed that excluded participants who were given situational control over the aversive noise were not more aggressive in the hot sauce paradigm than participants in the inclusion condition. By contrast, excluded participants who were denied situational control over the aversive noise assigned four times more hot sauce to the target person than any of the other groups. The critical role of control has also been demonstrated in a study by Wesselmann, Butler, Williams, and Pickett (2010). They showed that participants responded more aggressively to the experience of rejection when it occurred unexpectedly than when they had seen it coming on the basis of the experimenter's previous behaviour.

Although the present discussion has focused on single episodes of social exclusion as a situational trigger of aggressive behaviour, it is of course important to consider the effects of continuous and cumulative experiences of social exclusion over time. Many recent school shootings and also workplace killings were committed by individuals enraged by the experience of rejection in the form of being bullied at school or dismissed from their jobs (Leary, Kowalski, Smith, & Philipps, 2003). Similarly, social rejection by parents and/or peers in childhood has been linked to individual differences in aggression later in life (e.g., Hale, VanderValk, Akse, & Meeus, 2008; Lansford, Malone, Dodge, Pettit, & Bates, 2010). Taken together, the evidence discussed in this section suggests that the experience of social exclusion is both a short-term and a long-term risk factor for aggressive behaviour.

Alcohol

Alcohol induces a situation-specific, transient state that may explain why individuals show aggression in a particular situation and not in others. It is part of everyday psychological wisdom that people tend to become more aggressive under the influence of alcohol. In this section we will ask if there is conclusive empirical evidence to support this proposition. In addition, research will be presented that seeks to identify the mechanisms involved in the alcohol-aggression link and to clarify the pathways through which alcohol affects aggressive behaviour.

From the evidence available to date, it seems safe to conclude that alcohol is a key factor when it comes to explaining aggressive behaviour. Alcohol plays an important role in the perpetration of violent crime, such as homicide (Parker & Auerhahn, 1999) and domestic violence, including the physical and sexual abuse of children, sexual aggression, and wife battering (Barnett, Miller-Perrin, & Perrin, 2011). It features prominently in many forms of group violence, such as sports violence, rioting, and vandalism (Russell, 2004). In 50% of all violent incidents reported in the British Crime Survey 2009–2010, victims indicated that the offender(s) had been under the influence of alcohol (Flatley, Kershaw, Smith, Chaplin, & Moon, 2010, p. 77). Alcohol is also implicated in a range of aggressive behaviour on college campuses (Wells, Mihic, Tremblay, Graham, & Demers, 2008).

However, the finding that alcohol is often involved in the performance of aggressive behaviour does not necessarily suggest that alcohol is the *cause* of an individual's aggressive actions. It may be the case that both the tendency to get drunk and the performance of aggressive behaviour are caused by a third variable, such as lack of impulse control, or that alcohol affects the likelihood of aggressive behaviour in an indirect way (e.g., by lowering a person's frustration level). In addition, it is possible that the aggression-promoting effects of alcohol consumption occur only in the presence of particular features of the situation, such as provocation or prior frustration.

To make things even more complicated, there are at least two ways in which alcohol can affect aggressive behaviour. The first is through its *pharmacological effects*, which alter the physiological functioning of the body. The second is through its *psychological effects*, through the knowledge of having drunk alcohol. People hold intuitive theories about the link between alcohol and aggression (e.g., that alcohol may serve as an excuse for antisocial behaviour, commonly known as "blaming the bottle"), and they have expectations about the changes induced by alcohol (Phil & Sutton, 2009). Knowing that one has drunk alcohol activates beliefs about the effect of alcohol over and above the changes that occur at the physiological level.

Meta-analyses and qualitative reviews point towards a causal influence of alcohol on aggression. For example, Ito, Miller, and Pollock (1996) found an average effect size of $d = 0.54$ across 49 studies that compared intoxicated and sober participants' aggressive behaviour. Across 60 studies, Bushman (1997) found an effect size of $d = 0.50$ for male participants, but only $d = 0.13$ for women. To separate the pharmacological and psychological effects of alcohol on aggression, the "balanced placebo design" has been developed as the method of choice (Bushman & Cooper, 1990). This experimental design includes a total of four groups, as shown in Figure 4.5.

(1) Participants in the *alcohol group* are correctly informed that they are going to receive an alcoholic drink. They will experience both physiological changes and psychological effects as a result of the alcohol.
(2) Participants in the *control group* are correctly informed that they will receive a non-alcoholic drink, and therefore experience neither pharmacological nor psychological effects.
(3) Participants in the *placebo group* are told they will receive an alcoholic drink, but in fact they are given a non-alcoholic drink. Therefore they may experience alcohol-related expectations, but no pharmacological changes.

		Alcohol expected	
		Yes	No
Alcohol received	Yes	Alcohol	Anti-placebo
	No	Placebo	Control

Figure 4.5 The balanced placebo design for studying the alcohol–aggression link (based on Bushman & Cooper, 1990).

(4) In the final group, called the *anti-placebo group*, participants are led to believe that they consumed a non-alcoholic drink when in fact they received an alcoholic drink. They experience pharmacological changes but no psychological effects because they are unaware of having drunk alcohol.

The pharmacological effect of alcohol is most clearly discernible by comparing the control group with the anti-placebo group. Neither group thinks they have received alcohol, thereby eliminating alcohol-related expectancies, but the anti-placebo group does in fact receive an alcoholic drink. If the participants in the anti-placebo group behave more aggressively than those in the control group, the difference can be explained as a result of the physiological changes caused by the alcohol.

The psychological effects of alcohol can be assessed most conclusively by comparing the placebo group with the control group. Neither group receives alcohol, so there are no pharmacological effects, and any differences between them can be attributed to the operation of alcohol-related expectancies. By comparing the alcohol group and the placebo group, the combined impact of the pharmacological and psychological effects of alcohol on aggression can be established.

Bushman and Cooper (1990) conducted a meta-analysis that included 30 studies addressing the impact of alcohol on aggression in men. They found that neither the pharmacological effect on its own (the difference in aggressive behaviour between the anti-placebo group and the control group, $d = 0.06$) nor the psychological effect alone (the difference between the placebo group and the control group, $d = 0.10$) were significant. However, a significant difference of $d = 0.61$ was found between the alcohol group and the placebo group, which both thought they had consumed alcohol although only the alcohol group had actually done so. This finding suggests that the pharmacological changes induced by alcohol promote aggressive behaviour only in combination with the psychological effect (i.e., the belief that alcohol had been consumed). A second but smaller significant difference was found between the alcohol group and the control group which differed in terms of both pharmacological and psychological effects. In this comparison, the pharmacological and expectancy effects of alcohol cannot be separated, because the alcohol group both expects and receives alcohol, whereas the control group both expects and receives a non-alcoholic drink. However, this comparison may still be the most relevant one in terms of real-life significance. As Bushman and Cooper (1990) pointed out, people usually know whether or not they have consumed alcohol, which activates beliefs about how they are likely to be affected by its pharmacological effects. Unfortunately, the authors did not compare the placebo group (expectancy, but no alcohol) against the anti-placebo group (alcohol, but no expectancy) to answer the question which of the two processes is more influential.

The role of alcohol-related expectancies as triggers of aggression was highlighted by Subra, Muller, Bègue, Bushman, and Delmas (2010). Using a priming paradigm, they demonstrated that participants showed shorter reaction times in recognising aggression-related words after they were subliminally presented with images of alcoholic beverage bottles than following a priming with non-alcoholic beverage bottles. The priming effect of alcoholic beverage bottles was as strong as the effect elicited by images of weapons as aggression-related primes. In a second study, Subra et al. showed that participants who had seen bottles of alcohol acted more aggressively in terms of negative evaluations of a confederate who had previously angered them than those presented with non-alcoholic beverage bottles. Again, the effect of alcohol-related primes on aggression was as strong as the effect of aggression-related primes. These findings are important because they suggest that the mere presence of alcohol-related cues may trigger cognitive associations with aggression and elicit aggressive behaviour, even when there is no anticipated or even actual consumption of alcohol.

In a naturalistic laboratory experiment, Leonard and Roberts (1998) also showed that actually consuming alcohol is not a necessary condition for eliciting aggression. They addressed the pharmacological and expectancy effects of alcohol in married couples with or without a history of husband physical aggression towards the wife. Husbands in one group received an alcoholic drink and were correctly informed about it (the alcohol group), while husbands in a second group were led to believe they would receive an alcoholic drink, but in fact received a non-alcoholic drink (the placebo group), and husbands in a third group both expected and received a non-alcoholic drink (the control group). All couples then engaged in a discussion about the most controversial issue in their relationship which they had previously identified. Observations of the couples' verbal exchanges during the discussion yielded three scores for each partner: a *negativity score* composed of negative reactions towards the partner, a *problem-solving score* consisting of attempted solutions to the conflict, and a *positivity score*, including behaviours such as smiles and laughter. In the present context, the negativity scores are of greatest interest. To establish common levels of negativity unaffected by alcohol, couples discussed the second most controversial issue in their relationship prior to the introduction of the alcohol manipulation, so that alcohol-related effects could be established relative to this baseline. Figure 4.6 shows how the negativity scores for husbands and wives changed from baseline following the alcohol manipulation.

For the husbands in the alcohol group, a significant increase in negativity towards their partner was observed after the administration of alcohol. By contrast, the placebo group did not show an increase in their negativity scores from baseline level. As expected, no differences were observed in the control group between baseline and drinks administration,

The wives in the alcohol condition, who had been exposed to an intoxicated husband but had not received any drinks themselves, showed parallel changes in negativity scores to their intoxicated partners. This finding is interpreted by Leonard and Roberts (1998) as an indication of the negative reciprocity in dyadic conflict. It demonstrates that alcohol intoxication by one partner in a conflict situation is sufficient to initiate an aggressive interaction and to trigger aggressive behaviour in the other partner, who did not consume any alcohol at all. The negativity scores of the wives in the placebo condition who merely believed that their husband had received alcohol were not affected. As expected, no changes were observed in the wives' negativity scores in the control condition. Finally, it should be noted that couples both with and without a history of previous aggression were affected by the alcohol manipulation in the same way, disconfirming the authors' initial hypothesis that alcohol would have a stronger effect on couples with an already established pattern of dyadic aggression.

One methodological issue in the experimental literature on the alcohol-aggression link refers to the observation that the most clear-cut effects of alcohol in increasing aggression were found in studies that did not provide participants with a non-aggressive response alternative. In these studies, the respondents could only be relatively less aggressive (i.e., by administering fewer or shorter electric shocks or blasts of noise), but they could not avoid giving an aggressive response altogether (see Bushman & Cooper, 1990, Table 2). In their meta-analysis, Ito et al. (1996) found that the effect of alcohol on aggression was indeed stronger in studies that did not include a non-aggressive response alternative. However, intoxicated persons were still more aggressive than sober persons in studies that did provide participants with an option for responding in a non-aggressive fashion.

With regard to alcohol dose, the results are not entirely clear. Bushman and Cooper (1990) found no effect of alcohol dose across four studies that used different dosage levels. However, in their meta-analysis of a larger sample of 49 studies, Ito et al. (1996) did find that the differences in aggression between sober and intoxicated individuals increased as a function of alcohol dose.

Far fewer studies are available that have examined the effects of drugs other than alcohol on aggressive behaviour (Bushman, 1993; Kretschmar & Flannery, 2007), and they mostly focus on particular domains or forms of aggression. In a longitudinal study on men's sexual aggression, Swartout and White (2010) found a significant relationship between the use of marijuana and other illicit drugs and the perpetration of sexual aggression, which remained

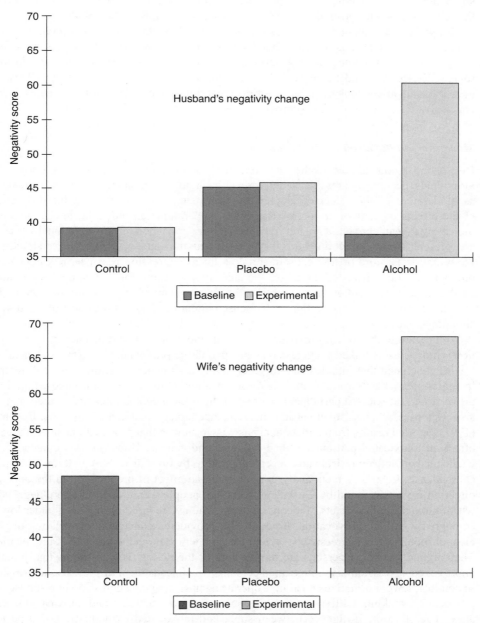

Figure 4.6 Increase in negativity scores from baseline in married couples as a function of the husband's intoxication. (Adapted from Leonard & Roberts, 1998, Table 5. Copyright American Psychological Association).

significant after controlling for concurrent alcohol use. In a meta-analysis of 96 studies on the role of drugs other than alcohol, Moore, Stuart, Meehan, Rhatigan, Hellmuth, and Keen (2008) presented a fine-grained analysis of a range of drugs in relation to different forms of intimate partner aggression. They found that cocaine use in particular was significantly associated with psychological, physical, and sexual aggression against a partner. In their review, Kretschmar and Flannery (2007) concluded that the strength of the link between drug use and violent behaviour varies for different drugs, and that so far the evidence is less conclusive than for the alcohol-aggression link.

Moderators of the alcohol-aggression link

Despite the strong support for the alcohol-aggression link, it is clear that not all intoxicated individuals become aggressive. Therefore it is important to identify variables that act as moderators of the effect of alcohol on aggression and can account for differences in the effects of alcohol on aggression. Such moderators can either lie in the situation, indicating that alcohol has a greater impact on aggression when certain situational variables are present at the same time, or they can lie in the person, suggesting that alcohol consumption is more or less consequential as far as aggression is concerned, depending on stable characteristics of the actor. We shall first examine four situational moderators of the impact of alcohol on aggression that have received particular attention in the literature: provocation, frustration, self-focused attention, and the presence of aggressive situational cues.

With regard to the role of *provocation*, several studies have found that alcohol consumption is more closely linked to aggression when people are provoked. In his review, Gustafson (1994) concluded that intoxicated and sober participants generally showed little difference in aggressive behaviour in the absence of provocation. However, if confronted with a mild provocation, intoxicated participants increased the frequency and intensity of their aggressive responses, whereas sober participants remained largely unaffected. Similarly, Bushman (1997) reported results from a meta-analysis which showed that provocations have a greater effect on intoxicated participants than on sober individuals. However, this evidence was challenged on both empirical and conceptual grounds by Ito et al. (1996). In terms of empirical evidence, Ito et al.'s meta-analysis established an effect of provocation in the opposite direction from that found by Gustafson. Although people were generally more aggressive when intoxicated, the effects of alcohol on aggression were *more* pronounced under low as compared with high provocation. Ito et al. also provided a conceptual explanation of why alcohol should affect aggressive behaviour to a greater extent in the absence of provocation. They argued that sober persons are more aware of the normative constraints that prohibit unprovoked aggression than intoxicated persons, which leads them to show less aggression. In contrast, fewer normative constraints operate against showing aggression in response to a provocation, making it a less undesirable course of action for sober and intoxicated people alike. Therefore the difference between sober and intoxicated individuals should be less pronounced under provocation.

A similar pattern was predicted by Ito et al. (1996) for the effects of *frustration* on the aggressive tendencies of sober and intoxicated individuals. Unlike provocation, which is caused by the actions of another person, frustration arises from any obstacle blocking the individual's attainment of a particular goal. Ito et al. predicted that there would be small differences between sober and intoxicated participants after experiencing a frustration – that is, in a situation where aggression may be seen as a justified response. By contrast, larger differences were expected in the absence of frustration, when intoxicated participants were thought to be less aware than sober participants of the inappropriateness of aggressive responses. However, the findings from their meta-analysis point in the opposite direction to those found for provocation – intoxicated participants were even more aggressive than sober participants following high as compared with low levels of frustration. To explain this somewhat puzzling result, Ito et al. (1996) provided several methodological explanations for the divergent findings concerning provocation and frustration, and they also suggested an interesting conceptual distinction: Provocation may be more likely to give rise to anger arousal, leading to affective aggression, whereas frustration may be more likely to elicit instrumental aggression directed at removing the perceived obstacle. This difference in the motives for aggression triggered by provocation as opposed to frustration may form the basis for explaining the differential effects of the two moderators on the alcohol-aggression link, but further research is needed to support this line of reasoning (Pedersen, Aviles, Ito, Miller, & Pollock, 2002).

Self-focused attention, the third moderator variable considered by Ito et al. (1996), is generally thought to be impaired under the influence of alcohol (e.g., Hull, Levenson, Young, & Sher, 1983). When intoxicated, individuals are less able to concentrate on the self and to monitor their behaviour than they would be in a sober state. However, inducing self-focus in intoxicated participants who are aware of their alcohol consumption (i.e., who are in the alcohol condition of the balanced placebo design) might lead these participants to try extra hard to compensate for alcohol-related cognitive impairment. Therefore differences between sober and intoxicated participants in aggressive behaviour should be less pronounced under high as compared with low self-awareness. This prediction was confirmed in Ito's et al. (1996) meta-analysis when all 49 studies were considered simultaneously: sober and intoxicated participants behaved more similarly the higher their self-focused attention. However, when only studies that used high doses of alcohol were examined, the difference was reversed. Highly intoxicated participants and sober participants behaved more similarly when their self-focused attention was low. This finding suggests that attempts to counteract the deleterious effects of alcohol through increased self-focused attention are successful only at relatively low levels of intoxication.

The presence of *aggressive cues* has been examined as a further moderator of the effects of alcohol on aggression. We saw earlier in this chapter that aggression-related cues may serve to highlight aggression as a behavioural option, but does this effect apply in the same way to sober and intoxicated individuals? Research that has examined the impact of threats present in a situation, such as an opponent's indication that he or she will set high shock levels in the competitive reaction time paradigm (see Chapter 1), shows that threat increases aggression in both sober and intoxicated individuals, but that the effect is far stronger in those under the influence of alcohol (e.g., Taylor, Gammon, & Capasso, 1976). Other evidence suggests that intoxicated persons only respond to explicit, salient external cues (Leonard, 1989). If these cues highlight aggression, such as aggressive behaviour from a fellow participant, then an aggressive response is likely to be shown. However, if salient cues are non-aggressive, such as social pressure to set low levels of shock, then behaviour becomes less aggressive. Because sober individuals can attend to a greater variety of situational stimuli as well as to their personal norms, their behaviour is less affected by the salience of cues. Consistent with this reasoning, Giancola and Corman (2007) showed that when intoxicated participants working on a competitive reaction time task were distracted, they showed less aggression compared with a non-distracted control group. The distraction task prevented them from paying full attention to the aggressive cues, the shock levels set by their opponent, thereby reducing their aggressive responses.

Among the person characteristics that affect the link between alcohol and aggression, many of the individual difference variables examined in Chapter 3 have been shown to play a role, such as trait anger, hostile rumination, and irritability. With regard to trait anger, alcohol seems to have a greater effect as a trigger of aggressive behaviour in individuals who are dispositionally anger-prone (Giancola, 2002b), and those characterised by low levels of anger control (Parrott & Giancola, 2004). Similarly, individuals with high levels of dispositional aggression scored higher on alcohol-related aggression and hostility, and the more participants reported they drank, the stronger was the link between dispositional rumination and aggression (Borders, Barnwell, & Earleywine, 2007). Giancola (2002a) found a greater effect of alcohol on aggression in individuals who scored high on irritability, but this effect was limited to the men in his sample.

Another candidate for explaining individual differences in the alcohol-aggression link is weight, particularly in men. There is a stereotype of the "big, drunk, aggressive guy" that may be incorporated by heavier men as part of their identity, magnifying the effect of alcohol on aggression. Comparing an alcohol group and a placebo group, DeWall, Bushman, Giancola, and Webster (2010) found that alcohol was linked to higher levels of aggression in heavier men, but not in lighter men or in women. They concluded that "alcohol reduced the inhibition for heavy men to 'throw their weight around' and intimidate others by behaving aggressively" (De Wall et al., 2010, p. 622). However, it should be noted that they did not control for height in their studies, so not everyone who was heavy might have been "big."

Finally, one potential moderator that has yielded mixed findings with regard to the alcohol-aggression link is gender. Earlier reviews converged on the conclusion that the aggression-enhancing effect of alcohol is similar in men and women (Bushman & Cooper, 1990; Gustafson, 1994). However, subsequent studies did find gender differences, if not always in the same direction. As noted above, Giancola (2002a) found that higher irritability magnified differences in aggressive behaviour between sober and intoxicated men, but no parallel effects were found for women. Borders et al. (2007) found that rumination interacted with alcohol consumption in women, but not in men. In an experimental study, Giancola et al. (2009) found that both men and women delivered more electric shocks to an opponent when under the influence of alcohol, but that the effect was stronger for men than for women. Giancola and Zeichner (1995) suggested that men and women may express their aggressive tendencies differently when under the influence of alcohol. In their study, men showed increased levels of shock intensity *and* shock duration as a function of alcohol consumption, whereas women only chose longer shock durations when intoxicated, which is regarded as a more subtle indicator of aggression than shock intensity.

Explanations for the alcohol-aggression link

Several theoretical assumptions have been proposed to explain *how* the tendency to show aggressive behaviour is affected by alcohol consumption. Two main lines of theorising will be briefly described here (for a review, see Bégue & Subra, 2008).

The first approach focuses on the *pharmacological* effects of alcohol. It comprises several hypotheses that address different consequences of alcohol consumption. The "disinhibition hypothesis" claims that alcohol directly affects the centre of the brain which controls aggressive behaviour. According to this view, alcohol sets free aggressive impulses because it demobilises the individual's ability to suppress and avoid aggressive tendencies. However, the finding that participants who received alcohol, but were unaware of it (the anti-placebo condition of the balanced placebo design), were not found to be more aggressive than participants who neither expected nor received alcohol (the control condition) argues against the assumption of such a direct link between alcohol and aggression. The "arousal hypothesis" suggests that the stimulant effects of alcohol are responsible for its aggression-enhancing effect. However, evidence concerning alcohol-induced arousal and aggression is limited, and results obtained for other stimulant drugs have been described by Chermack and Giancola (1997) as inconsistent.

The second approach is concerned with the psychological mechanisms by which alcohol consumption may trigger aggressive behaviour (for a summary, see Quigley & Leonard, 2006). It may be further subdivided into two explanations, referring to expectancy and myopia, respectively. The *expectancy hypothesis* proposes that the effects of alcohol on aggression are due at least in part to people's knowledge that they have consumed alcohol. This knowledge is associated with alcohol-related expectancies, which include cultural norms excusing or condoning aggressive behaviour under the influence of alcohol. Alcohol-related expectancies (i.e., beliefs about the effects of alcohol) were shown to be important for the pharmacological effects to occur. As noted earlier, the meta-analysis by Bushman and Cooper (1990) showed that the pharmacological effects depend on the presence of alcohol-related expectancies. People who believe that alcohol causes people to engage in aggressive behaviour should be more likely to engage in aggression when intoxicated than individuals who do not subscribe to this belief. This was found to be the case in several field studies (e.g., Leonard, Collins, & Quigley, 2003), correlational studies (Barnwell, Borders, & Earleywine, 2006), and laboratory experiments (Davis, 2010).

Another explanation attributes the psychological effects of alcohol on aggression to the disruption of cognitive information processing. The *alcohol myopia model (AMM)* first introduced by Steele and Josephs (1990), suggests that alcohol has an indirect effect on aggression by reducing the attentional capacity of the individual, hampering a comprehensive appraisal of situational cues. Alcohol narrows down attention, making people "short-sighted" (myopic) with regard to the perception and processing of situational information. As a result, only the most salient cues present in a situation are attended to, and if these cues suggest aggressive rather than non-aggressive responses, aggressive behaviour is likely to be shown. Intoxicated people pay insufficient attention to inhibitory cues that might suppress aggressive behaviour. Laplace, Chermack, and Taylor (1994) proposed that attentional impairment should be more pronounced in people who are not used to drinking alcohol, who should therefore be more aggressive following a high dose of alcohol intake than moderate or heavy drinkers. The findings from their study support this proposition. A review of the AMM by Giancola, Josephs, Parrott, and Duke (2010) concluded that there was compelling support for the role of impaired attentional processes in explaining alcohol-related aggression. Evidence discussed earlier in this chapter about attention to aggressive cues as a moderator of the alcohol-aggression link is also consistent with the AMM. This model has important implications for the prevention of alcohol-related aggression, as it involves the prediction that salient anti-violence cues present in a situation should reduce aggressive behaviour. Giancola and Corman (2007) have provided evidence that when distracted so that they were unable to attend to provocation cues, intoxicated participants showed less aggressive behaviour than a sober comparison group.

In summary, several conclusions can be drawn from the literature on alcohol-related aggression.

(1) There is ample evidence that individuals show more aggressive behaviour when intoxicated than when sober. This evidence comes from controlled laboratory studies, including research using the balanced placebo design, as well as from studies in a variety of real-life contexts, using both self-reports and observational methods. It seems that, in general, men are more strongly affected than women, but the evidence on gender differences is not conclusive.

(2) The link between alcohol and aggression is affected by variations in the situation. Provocation, frustration, lack of self-focused attention, and the presence of aggressive cues have been identified as relevant variables accounting for differences in the effect of alcohol on aggressive responses.

(3) It seems clear that the pharmacological changes induced by alcohol are largely responsible for its aggression-enhancing effect, but only when combined with alcohol-related expectancies.

(4) Alcohol affects aggression in an indirect way. Cognitive interpretations are seen as the most promising explanations of the effects of alcohol on aggression. They emphasise that alcohol impairs a person's information-processing capacities, including

attention to the normative constraints that would suppress aggressive responses in a sober state.

Heat and other environmental stressors

Ambient temperature is another situational determinant of aggression that has been widely explored in the literature. Most of the research refers to the so-called "heat hypothesis", which states that uncomfortably high temperatures increase aggressive behaviour (Anderson et al., 1997). Since the late nineteenth century, scientists have observed that aggression levels vary as a function of temperature, being higher at hot than at comfortable temperatures. More recent research in social psychology has developed three methodological approaches for studying the temperature-aggression link (Anderson & DeLisi, 2011).

The first approach is concerned with identifying *geographic region effects* by showing that aggression is more prevalent in geographic regions with hotter, as compared to cooler, climates.

The second approach is designed to identify *time period effects* through examining variations in the level of aggression as a function of temperature changes within a region over time (season, month, or time of day).

Finally, research looking for *concomitant heat effects* manipulates temperature in the laboratory and examines differences in aggressive behaviour in relation to variations in temperature.

Evidence from each of the three approaches has been summarised by Anderson (2001). Before we present a brief review of the main findings, it is important to clarify what exactly has been examined as aggressive behaviour in these studies. Consistent with the proposition that uncomfortably high temperature affects aggression by eliciting negative affect, affective (or hostile) aggression is most pertinent to the heat hypothesis. Aggressive acts that have a strong affective component of anger and hostility, such as homicide, assault, rioting, and rape, are therefore expected to be more strongly affected by temperature than acts of instrumental aggression, such as robbery, theft, or, possibly, international warfare. Both the geographic region approach and the time period approach rely heavily on archival data, in particular meteorological records and crime statistics, to examine the link between high temperatures and aggression (for a discussion of the use of archival data, see Chapter 1).

Evidence for the heat hypothesis

Studies based on the *geographic region approach* mostly compared northern and southern areas of the USA. They showed with high consistency that, as predicted by the heat hypothesis, violent crime is more widespread in the hotter regions of the south than in the cooler regions of the north (Anderson, Anderson, Dorr, DeNeve, & Flanagan, 2000). However, this observation is merely correlational, and tells us little about any causal influence of temperature on aggression. Variations in geographical location are associated with a host of other social structural variables that could be responsible, solely or in part, for observed regional differences in aggression. However, it is possible to control for the potential influence of demographic and socio-economic factors, such as population size, ethnic composition, unemployment rate, educational background, and age composition. When this was done, the link between temperature and violent crime remained across a range of studies, suggesting that temperature may play a causal role in eliciting aggression (Anderson et al., 2000).

However, the heat hypothesis is only one of several explanations for the higher rate of violent crime in the southern regions of the USA. An alternative explanation was proposed by Nisbett (1993). He argued that higher rates of violent crime in the south result from a particular "Southern culture of honour," which can be traced back to the historical roots of settlement and survival in the south. The Southern culture of honour is characterised by a greater acceptance of the use of violence, both for self-protection and in response to an insult or provocation as a way of restoring one's honour. Nisbett (1993) reported that Southerners showed greater anger in response to a provocation and were more likely to produce aggressive solutions to an interpersonal conflict following a provocation. Similarly, Cohen, Nisbett, Bowdle, and Schwarz (1996) showed that, following an insult, Southerners were more upset and more likely to engage in aggressive behaviour than Northerners.

A limitation of the geographic region approach is that it can only provide data about the co-occurrence of high temperature and violent crime. Moreover, it examines the temperature-aggression link at a highly aggregated level (i.e., at the level of entire regions and large populations). Therefore it does not allow immediate inferences about the link between exposure to high temperature and aggression within the individual person, as is stated in the heat hypothesis. On the other hand, geographic region studies have the advantage of providing large and reliable data sets about the criterion variable (i.e., violent crime). Murder and assault rates, for example, are reported and recorded continuously over time. Therefore geographic region studies are able to complement evidence from other sources in evaluating the heat hypothesis (for a more detailed critique of the geographic region approach, see also Anderson, Bushman, & Groom, 1997).

Time period studies avoid some of the methodological problems of the geographic region approach. They examine variations in aggression over different periods of time within a given population, and are therefore less affected by the confounding influence of socio-structural variables. This approach also supports the heat hypothesis by showing that violent crime rates are higher in the summer months than during the winter period, and in hotter than in cooler summers (Anderson, 2001; Anderson & Anderson, 1998). For example, the rates of murder, assault, and rape were found to be highest in the summer months across several studies, and the daily rates of emergency calls to police stations were found to increase as temperatures went up. Figure 4.7 illustrates the distribution of assault cases over the year course based on Anderson's (1989) aggregation of data across seven large data sets accumulated between 1883 and 1977.

As predicted by the heat hypothesis, Figure 4.7 shows a clear peak of assault rates in the summer months. Comparing years with different average temperatures and with hotter vs.

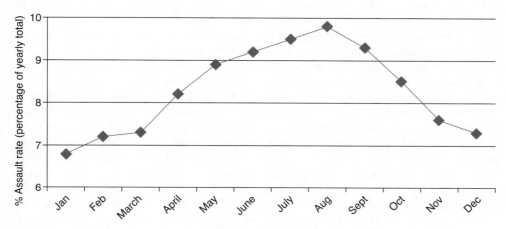

Figure 4.7 Variations in assault rates over the course of the year aggregated across seven data sets. (Reprinted from Anderson, 1989, p.85. Copyright American Psychological Association).

cooler summers, Anderson et al. (1997) found further support for the heat hypothesis and the particular impact of heat on affective aggression: both homicide and serious assault were more prevalent in hotter years and hotter summers, but property-related crime was unaffected by variations in temperature. In addition to these studies from the USA, support for a link between temperature oscillation and the rate of armed political conflict within tropical regions has been provided by Hsiang, Meng, and Cane (2011). They analysed rates of armed conflict in El Niño years (with higher temperatures) and in La Niña years (with lower temperatures) between 1950 and 2004, and found significantly higher rates of armed conflict in the warmer periods of the El Niño years in the regions affected by El Niño-La Niña oscillations.

Critics of the time period approach have argued that rather than reflecting a causal effect of the aversive effects of high temperatures, the increase in violence could be explained by differences in people's routine activities (Cohen & Felson, 1979). People tend to spend more time outdoors in the summer months and in years with hotter as opposed to cooler summers. This may create more opportunities for aggressive encounters with others, leading to higher rates of violent crime. Anderson (1989) argued against this interpretation by pointing out that rates of domestic violence are also higher in the summer months, although families probably spend more time at home together in the winter months. Looking at the covariation of temperature and aggression within the context of baseball matches in which the opportunities for aggression are standardised across matches, higher temperatures interacted with in-game provocation to predict aggressive moves. When provocation was high (as defined by the number of times a team mate had been hit by a member of the opposing team), the rate of aggressive retaliation increased significantly in proportion to the temperature during the match (Larrick, Timmerman, Carton, & Abrevaya, 2011; for a discussion of aggressive behaviour in a sports context, see Chapter 6).

The third approach addressing the heat hypothesis is the *concomitant heat paradigm*. It involves manipulating temperature levels in laboratory settings and observing variations in aggressive behaviour as a function of variations in temperature. Here intra-individual associations are observed between exposure to heat and aggressive behaviour, using very different behavioural criteria of aggression (mostly electric shocks) to the other two paradigms.

The concomitant heat approach is illustrated by a study by Vrij, van der Steen, and Koppelaar (1994), who showed a sample of police officers a virtual-reality display of a burglary that involved a face-to-face confrontation with the suspected burglar. The participants were asked to respond to the incident as they would do in real life in their job, using laser beams as simulated weapons. During the experiment the room temperature was systematically varied. One group was exposed to a comfortable temperature of 21°C (70°F), and the other was tested in an uncomfortably warm room at 27°C (81°F). The main dependent measures were (a) ratings of the negative affect elicited by the confrontation with the burglar, (b) perceptions of the burglar as aggressive, (c) perceived threat from the burglar, and (d) self-rated tendency to shoot. The effects of the temperature manipulation on these judgements are displayed in Figure 4.8.

All four dependent variables showed a significant effect of room temperature, supporting the heat hypothesis. Participants tested at an uncomfortably warm room temperature perceived the suspected burglar as more aggressive, reported more negative affect, and perceived greater

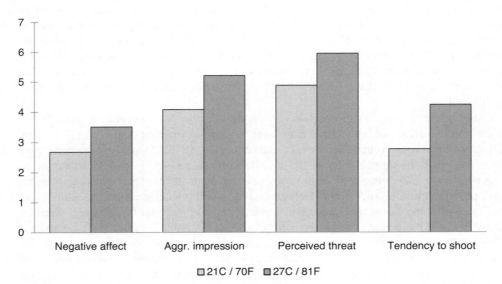

Figure 4.8 Effect of room temperature on police officers' responses to a burglary scenario. (Adapted from Vrij, van der Steen & Koppelaar, 1994, Table 1. Copyright Wiley Publishing).

threat. In support of the heat hypothesis, they also indicated stronger intentions to use their firearms against the suspect than participants who were tested at a comfortable room temperature. However, other laboratory studies found a curvilinear relationship between temperature and aggression, demonstrating a decrease in aggression with very high temperatures. On the basis of a meta-analysis of 11 studies, Anderson et al. (2000) concluded that the results of laboratory studies on the heat hypothesis remained inconsistent.

A methodological limitation of the concomitant heat paradigm is that participants know that their behaviour is being observed by the experimenter, and they may often become aware of the link between artificially created high temperatures and the tasks they are expected to perform. Given that it seems part of intuitive psychological wisdom that aggression will increase with temperature (Anderson & Anderson, 1998, Study 1), the possibility cannot be ruled out that participants' intuitive theories about the heat-aggression relationship affect their behaviour in the experimental settings.

Evidence addressing the temperature-aggression link has, with very few exceptions, been limited to the aggression-enhancing effects of uncomfortably *high* temperatures. No corresponding effect has been found for uncomfortably low temperatures in natural settings. The explanation offered by Anderson et al. (2000) is that people are generally better equipped to protect themselves against the cold than they are to escape from excessive heat, so they are able to reduce cold-related discomfort more easily than heat-related discomfort.

The finding that exposure to high temperatures promotes aggression can be explained with reference to Berkowitz's (1993) cognitive neo-associationist model of affective aggression described in Chapter 2. Uncomfortably high temperatures represent aversive stimuli that activate aggression-related thoughts and feelings, giving rise to aggressive behaviour. Drawing on the General Aggression Model (GAM) (see Chapter 2), Anderson (2001) proposed that heat-induced discomfort may increase hostile affect and prime aggressive cognitions, both of which increase the likelihood of an aggressive response in social interactions that occur under aversively hot conditions.

The implications of studies that support the heat hypothesis are worrying in the face of global warming. If increases in temperature are systematically related to increases in violent crime, then the continuous rise in global temperature will represent a risk factor for the rise in violent crime. Based on archival data on the link between temperature and violent crime in the USA over a 48-year period from 1950 to 2008, Anderson and DeLisi (2011) estimated the scale of this threat, as shown in Figure 4.9. This analysis predicts that an increase in temperature of 8° Fahrenheit (or 4.4° Celsius) would increase the murder and assault rate by 34 cases per 100 000 citizens.

Research on the heat hypothesis should alert both policy makers and the general public to the fact that the adverse effects of global warming are not restricted to our natural environment, but also pose a threat to the social functioning of human communities. At the same time, this line of research has important implication for violence prevention. As noted by Anderson et al. (2000), keeping temperatures at a comfortable level by means of air conditioning may help to bring down violence rates, and may be particularly useful in settings such as prisons, factories, and schools where violence is a problem.

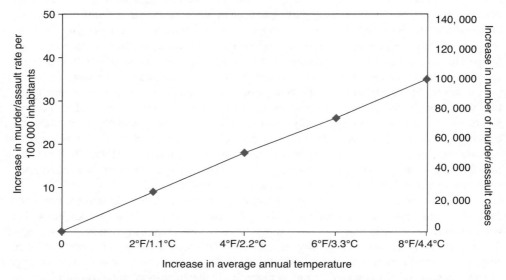

Figure 4.9 Estimates of the effect of global warming on murders and assaults per year based on rates of murder and assault in the USA during the period 1950–2008. (Adapted from Anderson & DeLisi, 2011, p. 256. Copyright Psychology Press).

Other stressors in the physical environment

In this concluding section, we shall briefly examine the role of three further environmental stressors that promote aggressive behaviour: crowding, noise, and air pollution.

Crowding refers to the perception of spatial density as unpleasant and aversive. Note that crowding is a subjective experience, whereas density is a physical concept that is defined in terms of the number of people per space unit. This distinction is important because the same level of spatial density may give rise to feelings of crowding in some people but not in others. Similarly, the same level of spatial density may be perceived as pleasantly busy in some settings (e.g., at an open-air concert) and unpleasantly crowded in others (e.g., in a packed train compartment). Whereas density cannot be linked to aggression in a conclusive fashion, crowding has been found to increase the likelihood of aggression in a variety of settings, such as bars (Green & Plant, 2007), prisons (Lahm, 2008), and overcrowded living conditions for families (Regoeczi, 2008). Experimental evidence suggests that the aggression-enhancing effect of crowding is mediated by negative affective arousal elicited by the subjective perception of spatial constraint (Lawrence & Andrews, 2004). Furthermore, it seems that men are more likely than women to respond to crowding with aggressive behaviour (Regoeczi, 2008). This finding is consistent with the negative affect explanation, in that men have consistently been found to claim more personal space than women, and are therefore more likely to be adversely affected by restrictions of their territorial claims (e.g., Leibman, 1970; Patterson, Mullens, & Romano, 1971).

Noise is another environmental stressor linked to aggression. As an aversive stimulus, noise can trigger or reinforce aggressive behaviour. In a study by Geen and O'Neal (1969), participants were shown either a violent or a non-violent film and subsequently instructed to deliver electric shocks to another person as a punishment for errors on a learning task. While they administered the shocks, half of the participants in each group were exposed to a loud noise. It was found that the noise manipulation led to higher aggression only among those who had previously watched the violent film. Another consequence of noise is that it impairs the person's tolerance of frustration, thereby increasing aggressive behavioural tendencies following a frustration (Donnerstein & Wilson, 1976). Thus noise operates as a reinforcer of aggressive response tendencies in individuals who are already in a state of increased readiness for aggressive behaviour. However, it does not seem to be the noise per se that facilitates aggression, but rather the fact that noise is often an uncontrollable aversive event. If the noise was perceived as controllable by the individual, its impact on aggressive behaviour was substantially reduced (Geen & McCown, 1984).

Finally, *air pollution* has been found to be a reinforcer of aggressive response tendencies in much the same way as crowding and noise. Studies examining the effect of cigarette smoke on aggression found that individuals exposed to cigarette smoke showed more hostility towards others (not only towards the person producing the smoke) as well as aggressive behaviour than a control group not exposed to smoky conditions (Jones, 1978; Zillmann, Baron, & Tamborini, 1981). The role of unpleasant smells in promoting aggression was examined in the context of the negative affect escape model (Baron & Bell, 1976). This model predicts that moderate levels of an unpleasant smell lead to an increase in aggression, while aggression levels drop again as the unpleasant smell becomes more intense. Support for this prediction was found in a study by Rotten, Frey, Barry, Milligan, and Fitzpatrick (1979).

Summary

- Aggression-related cues, social exclusion, alcohol, and temperature have been identified as situational variables that have a significant influence on aggressive behaviour. More limited evidence is available on the impact of other external stressors, such as crowding, noise, and air pollution, but it appears that these features of the physical environment also increase or reinforce aggressive behaviour.
- The "weapons effect," first demonstrated by Berkowitz and LePage (1967), refers to situational cues, such as weapons or other violence-related primes, that enhance the cognitive availability of aggression as a response option. The weapons effect was strongest in individuals who were previously angered, and who were therefore already in a state of heightened angry arousal. However, it has also been demonstrated in people

who were in an affectively neutral state. Therefore the mere presence of an aggression-related cue seems to increase the probability of an aggressive response.

- There is consistent evidence that being rejected or excluded by others precipitates aggressive behaviour. Social exclusion thwarts vital needs for belonging, self-esteem, and control, and aggression is a common response to this experience. Whereas the immediate social pain experienced when a person is excluded by others is a reflexive response that is largely independent of personal or situational influences, individual and contextual factors affect the subsequent more controlled processing of the exclusion experience. Chronic experience of social exclusion has long-term effects on psychological well-being, and may explain individual differences in aggression.
- The claim that people are more likely to act aggressively when under the influence of alcohol is supported by a large body of research. Alcohol affects aggressive behaviour through both pharmacological and psychological effects. The pathway from alcohol consumption to aggressive behaviour seems to be mediated by attentional deficits. Under the influence of alcohol, individuals' attention capacity is impaired, and they only attend to the most salient stimuli. Awareness of the normative constraints that inhibit aggressive behaviour is reduced, undermining an important mechanism in the self-regulation of aggressive behaviour.
- The effect of temperature on aggression has also been widely demonstrated across different methodological paradigms. Comparing hot vs. cold regions or hot vs. cold time periods within a region, it was found that aggression, especially violent crime, is generally higher under conditions of high temperature, supporting the "heat hypothesis." Experimental studies that have explored differences in aggression as a function of variations in temperature also provide some support for the heat hypothesis, but the evidence is less conclusive.
- Finally, the general proposition that stressors in the physical environment cause negative affective arousal which in turn gives rise to aggressive responses is further supported by studies that have looked at crowding, noise, and poor air quality in relation to aggression. These stressors can both elicit and intensify aggressive behaviour.

Tasks to do

(1) When you leave your house tomorrow, look out for aggressive cues in your environment (e.g., billboards, shop window displays, movie advertisements, etc.). At the end of the day, make a list of the cues you have seen.

(2) Find out more about the Cyberball paradigm as a measure of social exclusion (www1. psych.purdue.edu/~willia55/Announce/cyberball.htm).

(3) Check the latest crime statistics in your country for the rates of violent crime (e.g., murder, assault) committed when under the influence of alcohol.

Suggested reading

Anderson, C. A., & DeLisi, M. (2011). Implications of global climate change for violence in developed and developing countries. In J. P. Forgas, A. W. Kruglanski, & Williams, K. D. (Eds), *The psychology of social conflict and aggression* (pp. 249–265). New York: Psychology Press.

Collins, R. (2008). *Violence: A micro-sociological theory.* Princeton, NJ: Princeton University Press.

Giancola, P. R., Josephs, R. A., Parrott, D. J., & Duke, A. A. (2010). Alcohol myopia revisited: Clarifying aggression and other acts of disinhibition through a distorted lens. *Perspectives on Psychological Science, 5,* 265–278.

Todorov, A., & Bargh, J. A. (2002). Automatic sources of aggression. *Aggression and Violent Behavior, 7,* 53–68.

5   Media violence and aggression

In the public debate on aggression and violence, media influences are blamed by many people for the apparently increasing levels of aggression, especially among children and adolescents. A cursory and occasional sampling is sufficient to convince the everyday observer that television programmes are full of aggressive episodes, often of a highly violent nature, that are easily accessible even to young viewers. The same is true for movies, comic books, and, in particular, video games. In addition, surveys regularly present alarming figures of the time that children from preschool age onwards spend using violent media. These observations lead many people to believe that the portrayal of violence in the media affects the level of aggression in society. Some critics even argue that media consumption in general, irrespective of its aggressive content, contributes to aggression and antisocial behaviour. At the same time, the claim that violent media contents cause users to become more aggressive has been vigorously disputed, not only by the media industry but also by some researchers in the field.

The present chapter will review the current state of the debate on the link between media violence and aggression. Even though the discussion will be limited to effects on aggression, it is important to note that eliciting aggressive behaviour is not the only detrimental outcome attributed to violent media. Fear, for example, is another common and adverse result of exposure to media violence (Smith & Donnerstein, 1998). An extensive literature, both in psychology and in media science, is available to address the link between media violence and aggression, focusing on television, movies, and video games as the most widely used media, but also including music (Fischer & Greitemeyer, 2006) and even texts from the Bible (Bushman, Ridge, Das, Key, & Busath, 2007). The chapter will be organised as follows.

To begin with, some data will be presented about the *prevalence and forms of violence* in today's media diet and about the *extent to which violent media are used*, especially by children and adolescents, who are seen as particularly vulnerable to media influences. We shall then address the general question of whether there is a (*causal*) *link* between exposure to media violence and aggression. Recent meta-analyses will be examined that bring together a large number of individual studies and thus provide the most robust estimates of the strength of the association between media violence and aggression. The *short-term effects* of media violence on aggressive thoughts, feelings, and behaviours will be considered, and theoretical explanations of the underlying processes will be reviewed. This will be followed by a discussion of the processes that explain the *long-term effects* of habitual exposure to violent media. A special section will be devoted to research on *pornography* as a specific type of media content, combining aggression and sexuality, on aggression in general, and sexual aggression in particular. Finally, ways of *preventing or mitigating* the aggression-enhancing effects of media violence exposure will be examined.

It is important to note that the scientific debate about media-induced aggression is *not* based on the assumption of a simple mono-causal relationship between media violence and aggression. Such an assumption would hold that exposure to media violence causes aggression regardless of other influences. Instead, it is recognised in the debate that media violence is only one of many factors potentially leading to aggression. As will become clear in the course of our discussion, the effects of heavy use of violent media may be exacerbated by other factors causing of aggression (e.g., exposure to real-life violence within the family), or they may be attenuated (e.g., by teaching critical viewing skills). At the same time, heavy use of violent media may itself exacerbate the influence of other risk factors for aggressive behaviour.

Prevalence and use of violent media contents

There are two premises to the claim that media violence produces harmful effects on viewers. First, evidence is required that violence and aggression are widely present in media programmes. Secondly, it must be shown that exposure to such violent contents is substantial among both children and adults. The first issue has been addressed by a wide range of studies providing content analyses of different media in a variety of countries. For example, the National Television Violence Study (1997) showed that 57% of the programmes sampled across 23 channels in the USA in 1994 and 1995 contained violent episodes. Similarly, in an analysis of 1162 programme hours on 10 German television channels during 2002 and 2003, Grimm, Kirste, and Weiß (2005) found that 58% of all programmes contained at least one violent episode, and 33% of all violent interactions were presented as resulting from socially accepted motives.

Analysing data from the National Television Violence Study, Wilson et al. (2002) found that programmes directed at children aged 12 years or younger contained more violence and showed more positive consequences of violence than programmes produced for older audiences. In a more recent analysis of ten TV programmes screened in the UK, Coyne, Robinson, and Nelson (2010) established that violent acts were committed at a rate of 42.5 acts per hour. Reality TV programmes, such as *Big Brother*, contained substantially more violence (61.5% of all violent acts counted) than non-reality programmes, such as *Eastenders*. The most common form of aggression was verbal aggression, such as yelling/arguing (38.39%), insulting (30.60%), and name calling (9.31%).

Violent content is also rife in movies. Examining a sample of 74 animated films rated "G" (which means suitable for a general audience), Yokota and Thompson (2000) found that each film contained at least one scene of violence. Pointing out that direct physical violence is not the only form of aggression displayed in films, Coyne and Whitehead (2008) looked for instances of indirect aggression in 47 animated Disney films. Indirect aggression was defined as social exclusion (e.g., malicious gossip, excluding others from the group), malicious humour (e.g., making gestures behind a person's back, playing practical jokes), guilt induction (e.g., exerting undue pressure and influencing others by making them feel guilty), and finally, indirect physical aggression (e.g., plotting and kidnapping). A total of 584 acts of indirect aggression were identified in the 47 films. The most indirectly aggressive Disney films were *Aladdin* (20 acts per hour), *Cinderella* (19.2 acts per hour), and *Pinocchio* (18.4 acts per hour; for an analysis of cartoon violence, see also Kirsh, 2012).

Content analyses of video games unanimously suggest that violent scenes are just as or even more frequent in this medium as they are in movies and television shows. More than 20 years ago, Braun and Giroux (1989) found a violence rate of 71% for a sample of 21 arcade games. Since then, the hardware and software of game technology have improved dramatically, graphics and sound effects have become highly realistic, and modern games often show a technical quality similar to that of films. Dietz (1998) analysed 33 best-selling video games and found that about 79% contained some form of violence. A content analysis by Haninger and Thompson (2004) of 396 video games that were rated "T" (for "teens") showed that 94% of them had violent content. An analysis of popular games in Germany also concluded that many games rated by the self-regulating body of the media industry as suitable for children and adolescents contained substantial levels of violence (Höynck, Mößle, Kleimann, Pfeiffer, & Rehbein, 2007). In addition to identifying high levels of violent content in contemporary video games, Smith, Lachlan, and Tamborini (2003) found that games directed at children often involve forms of violence that correspond to everyday forms of aggression, such as slapping, boxing, or kicking.

Finally, analysing the popular medium of music videos, Smith and Boyson (2002) found an average rate of violent content of 15%. However, there was substantial variation by genre, with rap videos having a significantly higher percentage of violent acts (29%) than rock (12%) or rhythm and blues (9%) videos. In addition, there is growing concern about misogynous and men-hating texts in music that are hallmarks of popular artists, such as Eminem and Christina Aguilera (Adams & Fuller, 2006; Fischer & Greitemeyer, 2006).

In addition to counting the number of games that feature violence, a qualitative analysis of the way in which violence is presented is useful for understanding the underlying mechanism of media violence effects on aggression. For example, evidence that violence is frequently rewarded by positive consequences in media depictions would support an explanation based on social learning principles (see Chapter 2). Smith et al. (2004) have provided a contextual analysis of the use of guns in television programmes and video games. They analysed a total of 2586 hours of television programmes screened in 1997 that contained 4284 gun-related violent interactions, and a sample of 10 hours of playing the 60 video games most popular in 1999. A summary of their main findings is presented in Table 5.1.

Table 5.1 Portrayals of gun use in violent interactions on television and in video games (Adapted from Smith et al., 2004, Table 3, p. 593. Copyright Taylor & Francis)

Percentage of acts	Television gun use (n = 4284 acts)	Video game gun use (n = 116 interactions)
Involving lethal violence	92%	99%
Involving repeated violence	69%	89%
Involving blood and gore	30%	79%
Involving protection of life	35%	95%
Involving anger	19%	3%
Involving retaliation	2%	1%
Presented as justified	33%	95%
Involving rewards	30%	27%
Involving punishments	43%	0%
Showing no pain	49%	n.a.
Showing extreme harm	60%	61%
Accompanied by humour	29%	28%

In both types of media, almost all scenes involving the use of a gun by an actor towards a target depicted lethal violence. In video games, virtually all acts of gun-related violence were presented as justified, compared with about a third of the acts on television. Very few of these acts were carried out in retaliation, which suggests that proactive, unprovoked aggression is the predominant form of violence shown in these media.

Surveys show that the use of media is a prominent leisure activity for children and adolescents. In 2009, children and adolescents in the USA between the ages of 8 and 18 were found to spend 4.29 hours watching television, 1.29 hours using a computer, and 1.13 hours playing video games on a typical day (Rideout, Foehr, & Roberts, 2010). A recent representative survey of German adolescents aged 12 to 19 found average daily usage times of 2.03 hours for watching television, 2.18 hours for computer and Internet use, and 1.05 hours during the week and 1.20 hours at weekends for playing video games (Medienpädagogischer Forschungsverbund Südwest, 2010).

With regard to violent movies, Worth, Chambers, Nassau, Rakhra, and Sargent (2008) asked a random sample of over 6000 adolescents in the USA aged 10 to 14 whether they had seen titles on a list of 40 violent movies rated "R" for violence in the USA and "18" ("suitable only for adults") in the UK. Across the 40 movies, the average rate of 10 to 14-year olds who had seen them was 12.5%, but the percentage was substantially higher for a number of specific titles. For example, the horror film *I Know What You Did Last Summer* had been seen by 44% of the sample. Extrapolating from this figure to the population as a whole, the authors concluded that the movie had been seen by more than 9 million viewers under the age of 14 years, a million of whom would have been just 10 years of age.

Arguably, video games are even more popular as entertainment media. Even in the age group of 65 years or over, 23% report playing video games (Lenhart & Macgill, 2008), and among adolescents and young adults user rates are close to 100%. In a survey conducted in the USA in 2008, 97% of teenagers aged 12 to 17 reported playing video games, 31% reported playing every day. In terms of the preferred game content, about a third of gaming teenagers reported that at least one of their three favourite games was rated "Mature," with boys outnumbering girls by three to one in this group (Lenhart, Kahne, Middaugh, Macgill, Evans, & Vitak, 2008).

In the German survey cited above, only 20% of the participants reported not playing games at all, whereas 45% reported playing several times a week (Medienpädagogischer Forschungsverbund Südwest, 2010). Of those participants who were aware of the age ratings for video games, 81% of boys (but only 36% of girls) had played games rated as unsuitable for their age group, and 71% of boys (and 45% of girls) reported that violent games were used by many or most of their peers. Another representative survey of more than 44 000 15-year-olds in Germany found that 55% of boys (compared with 9% of girls) reported playing games rated 16+ several times a month, and 48% of boys (compared with 5.2% of girls) reported regularly playing games rated 18+ (Rehbein, Kleimann, & Mößle, 2009). These figures need to be seen in the context of strict legal regulations in Germany that prohibit the sale of these games to minors.

From the evidence reviewed in this section, two points have become clear: (a) violence is prominently present across a range of different media, and (b) violent content is widely consumed not only by adults, but also by a younger, especially male, audience. Against this background, we can now turn to the question of whether exposure to media violence really leads to increased aggression in viewers.

How strong is the link between media violence and aggression?

Research designs and examples

To explore the association between media violence use and aggression, three main methodologies have been used:

(1) cross-sectional studies relating self-reports of violent media use to aggressive behaviour measured through observation, peer nominations, or self-reports
(2) experimental studies that assign participants randomly to a violent media condition or a non-violent media condition and then observe the short-term differences in aggressive behaviour in the two groups
(3) longitudinal studies that follow the same group of participants over several measurements to relate media violence use at an earlier point in time to aggressive behaviour observed later.

As an example of *cross-sectional studies,* Krahé and Möller (2011) studied a sample of 1688 seventh- and eighth-grade students who reported their use of different genres of TV series, films, and video games. Frequency reports for each genre were weighted by ratings of violent content obtained from media experts to yield a measure of media violence use. Class teachers provided ratings of aggressive and prosocial behaviour for each student. The more media violence participants used, the higher their aggressive behaviour and the lower their prosocial behaviour as rated by their class teacher. When the participants' normative perceptions of aggression were taken into account, the direct links of media violence use with aggressive as well as prosocial behaviour were reduced. This finding indicates that the more the participants used violent media, the more they saw aggression as socially acceptable, and the more they regarded aggression as acceptable, the more aggressive behaviour they reported.

The *experimental approach* is illustrated by research by Carnagey and Anderson (2005), who explored the importance of reward and punishment of violent action in a video game for subsequent aggressive cognitions, affect, and behaviour. All participants played a racing game, *Carmaggedon 2*, but they were randomly assigned to one of three different conditions:

(1)   a condition in which killing competitors and pedestrians was rewarded by giving extra points
(2)   a condition in which killing competitors and pedestrians was punished by deducting points
(3)   a non-violent condition in which killing pedestrians or competitors was not possible.

Blood pressure and pulse were recorded as measures of arousal to make sure that the three versions did not differ in terms of their arousal quality. State hostility after the 20-minute playing period was measured as an index of aggressive affect (Experiment 1). A word completion test presenting words that could be completed to yield either an aggressive or a non-aggressive meaning was used as a measure of aggressive cognition (Experiment 2), and the duration and intensity of noise blasts administered in a competitive reaction time task (see Chapter 1) were used to measure aggressive behaviour (Experiment 3). The results are shown in Figure 5.1.

For aggressive affect, the findings revealed that both groups engaging in violent actions in the video game experienced higher levels of state hostility than the group that could not engage in violent actions. For aggressive cognition and aggressive behaviour, the participants in the reward group scored significantly higher than those in the punishment group and those in the non-violent control group. The latter two groups did not differ significantly in either cognitions or behaviour. The finding that violence which is rewarded by positive consequences promotes aggressive thoughts as well as aggressive behaviour is consistent with social learning and socio-cognitive models of aggression (see Chapter 2).

Finally, a prominent example of *longitudinal studies* that have addressed the link between media violence and aggression is the Columbia Television Violence Study (Huesmann & Miller, 1994). This study started in 1960 with a sample of 875 children that comprised the entire population of third graders in a community in Columbia County, New York. Ten years later, 427 of the original participants, who were then 18 years of age, were re-interviewed. A

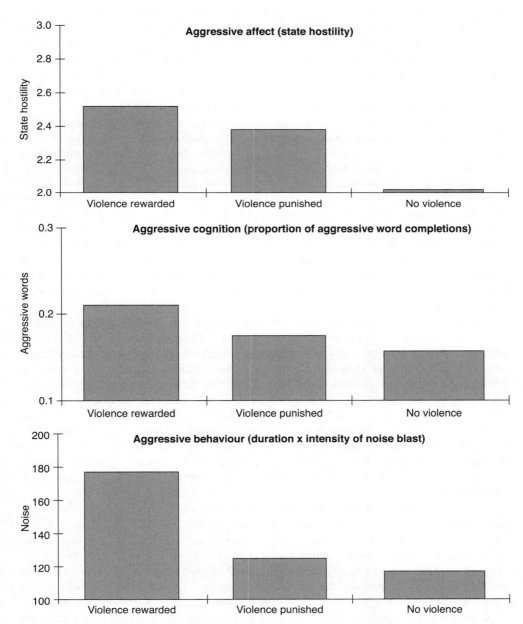

Figure 5.1 Effects of reward and punishment of violence in video games. (Adapted from Carnagey & Anderson, 2005, Table 2. Copyright Sage Publications).

further 12 years later, in 1982, data were collected from 409 of the original participants, who by then had reached the age of 30. At the first assessment, measures of aggressive behaviour were obtained for each child on the basis of peer nominations. Exposure to TV violence was assessed by asking the mothers to name their child's most-watched TV programmes, which were then rated by experts for level of violent content. Aggressive behaviour and exposure to TV violence were measured again at the subsequent two data points, and additional data about criminal offences were collected at the last data point.

Cross-lagged panel analyses were conducted in which the correlation between Time 1 TV violence exposure and Time 2 aggression was compared with the correlation between Time 1 aggression and Time 2 TV violence exposure. No evidence was found for a longitudinal link between exposure to TV violence and aggression in girls. However, in boys, exposure to TV violence at Time 1 was significantly correlated at $r = 0.24$ with aggression at Time 2, whereas aggression at Time 1 was unrelated to TV violence exposure at Time 2. The path model that presents the relationships for the sample of 184 boys for whom complete data were available from both Time 1 and Time 2 is shown in the top half of Figure 5.2. For the 162 male participants who were still in the sample at Time 3, 22 years after the start of the study, a significant path of $r = 0.18$ was found from exposure to TV violence at the age of 8 and conviction for violent crime at the age of 30, as shown in the bottom half of Figure 5.2. The reverse path, from earlier TV violence use to later aggression, was weaker but also significant.

Thus, for boys, there was clear evidence that childhood exposure to TV violence predicted aggressive behaviour over a period as long as 22 years. The magnitude of the link was not dramatic, which is unsurprising given the host of other factors that affected participants in the course of that period. However, the findings show that at least part of the variance in aggressive behaviour in adulthood can be explained by differences in the preference for violent TV programmes 22 years earlier. Other studies, including cross-national comparisons, have provided similar findings (Huesmann & Eron, 1986). For girls, the evidence remains inconclusive. A longitudinal study by Huesmann, Moise-Titus, Podolski, and Eron (2003) found parallel links among men and women between exposure to TV violence in childhood and aggression in adulthood, but studies on the impact of violent computer games also showed stronger effects for male than for female players (e.g., Bartholow & Anderson, 2002).

Longitudinal studies enable researchers to address two alternative explanations of the relationship between TV violence and aggression: (a) that viewing TV violence makes viewers more aggressive (the "socialisation" hypothesis), or (b) that more aggressive individuals are more strongly attracted by violent TV programmes (the "selection" hypothesis). The pattern of results shown in Figure 5.2 supports the socialisation hypothesis but provides little support for the selection hypothesis. The path from exposure to TV violence at the age of 8 to aggression at the age of 18 was significant, whereas the path from aggression at age 8 to exposure to TV violence at age 18 was not. The path from aggression at age 8 to exposure to TV violence at age 30, although significant, was smaller than the path from TV violence at age 8 to aggression at age 30.

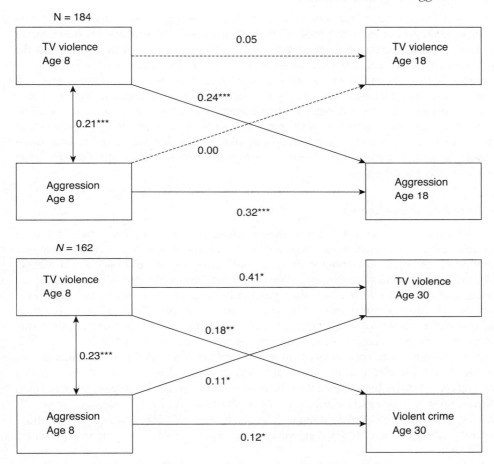

Figure 5.2 Longitudinal link between exposure to media violence and aggression in a sample of boys followed over a period of 22 years. (Adapted from Huesmann & Miller, 1994, pp. 169–170. Copyright Plenum Press).

Note: Dashed lines indicate non-significant links.

   Although there was only limited evidence for a selection effect in these data, other studies did find that highly aggressive individuals selectively prefer violent media (Anderson et al., 2003). There is no inherent contradiction between the two processes, as they can be mutually reinforcing. Indeed the "downward spiral" model of Slater, Henry, Swaim, and Anderson (2003) proposes that although more aggressive individuals may show a preference for violent media in the first place, the more intense use of these media may reinforce their aggressive tendencies over time.

The question of whether exposure to media violence is a *causal* risk factor for aggression cannot be addressed in cross-sectional studies that merely show a correlation between media violence use and aggression. Experimental studies can test causal hypotheses about the short-term effects of media violence exposure by systematically varying the level of violence in media contents. Longitudinal studies enable researchers to test the hypothesis that differences in the habitual use of media violence are linked to differences in aggression over extensive periods of time. Although longitudinal studies cannot demonstrate cause-effect relationships because it is impossible to randomly assign participants to different levels of habitual exposure to media violence, they can demonstrate that the use of violent media remains a significant predictor of aggression over time even when controlling for other known risk factors for aggression.

Evidence from meta-analyses

Over the last 20 years, several extensive meta-analytic reviews of studies on the association between media violence exposure and aggression have been published in the scholarly literature. These reviews combined *different methodologies* (correlational, experimental, and longitudinal studies), *different media* (television, movies, video games, and comic books), and *different outcome variables* (aggressive cognitions, feelings, and behaviour, physiological arousal, and prosocial behaviour) across samples from *different countries*. The standard measures of effect size capturing the strength of the association are r (the correlation between media violence use and outcome variables), and d (the difference between exposure to violent as opposed to non-violent media). In addition to the quantitative reviews based on effect sizes, there are several comprehensive qualitative reviews covering the extensive literature on the effects of violence on television (e.g., Murray, 2008; Gunter, 2008), in video games (e.g., Bensley & Van Eenwyk, 2001; Anderson, Gentile, & Buckley, 2007), or across different media (e.g., Anderson et al., 2003; Browne & Hamilton-Giachritsis, 2005; Savage, 2008). A summary of the major meta-analytic studies is presented in Table 5.2.[1]

The figures presented in Table 5.2 indicate a fairly consistent pattern across the different meta-analyses. The correlations are mostly in the region of 0.15 to 0.25, with stronger effect sizes for experimental studies using laboratory measures of aggressive behaviour. Critics who dispute the claim that using violent media increases aggressive thoughts, feelings, and behaviour have argued that due to methodological problems with some of the available evidence, the strength of the link between media violence exposure and aggression is overestimated (e.g., Ferguson 2007a). To address this criticism, Anderson et al. (2010) identified a list of "best practice" criteria that allowed them to separate good- from

---

1 The meta-analyses of video game violence by Anderson (2004) and Anderson and Bushman (2001) are not presented in the table because the studies in these analyses were also included in the most recent analysis published by Anderson et al. (2010). For the same reason, the meta-analysis by Ferguson (2007b) is excluded because of its overlap with Ferguson (2007a).

Table 5.2 Summary of meta-analytic studies on the link between media violence use and aggression-related outcomes

I. Different media

Year	Author(s)	Number of studies	Age	Type of media	Methodology C = Cross-sectional E = Experimental L = Longitudinal	Effect size(s)/outcomes
2006	Bushman & Huesmann	431	All ages	TV, movies, video games, music, and comic books	C, E, L	Aggressive behaviour: $r = 0.19$ Aggressive cognition: $r = 0.18$ Angry feelings: $r = 0.27$ Physiological arousal: $r = 0.26$ Prosocial behaviour: $r = -0.08$
2008	Savage & Yancey	26	All ages	Television and movies	C, E, L	Criminal aggression E: $r = 0.06$ C: $r = 0.16$ L: $r = 0.12$
2009	Ferguson & Kilburn	25	All ages	Television, video games, and movies	C, E, L	Overall aggression: $r = 0.14$ Proxy (laboratory) measures: $r = 0.25$ Physical aggression: $r = 0.10$ Violence: $r = 0.07$

(Continued)

Table 5.2 Continued

II. Television

Year	Author(s)	Number of studies	Age	Type of media	Methodology C = Cross-sectional E = Experimental L = Longitudinal	Effect size(s)/outcomes
1991	Wong et al.	12	Children and adolescents	Television	E	Overall aggression: $r = 0.20$ ($d = 0.40$) Laboratory experiments: $r = 0.27$ ($d = 0.56$) Field experiments: $r = 0.09$ ($d = 0.19$)
1994	Paik & Comstock	217	All ages	Television	C, E	Overall aggression: $r = 0.31$ Experiments: $r = 0.39$ Cross-sectional surveys: $r = 0.19$ Effect size declined with age
1998	Hogben	30	All ages	Television	C, E, L	Overall aggression: $r = 0.10$ ($d = 0.21$) Presentation of inaccurate ($r = 0.12$; $d = 0.25$) vs. accurate ($r = 0.05$; $d = 0.10$) consequences of violence TV violence presented as justified ($r = 0.15$; $d = 0.30$) vs. unjustified ($r = 0.00$; $d = 0.00$) Higher effect sizes in more recent studies
2002b	Anderson & Bushman	280	All ages	Television	C, E, L	Cross-sectional: $r = 0.18$ Laboratory experiments: $r = 0.23$ Field experiments: $r = 0.19$ Longitudinal: $r = 0.17$
2007	Christensen & Wood	13	Children and adolescents	Television	E	$r = 0.23$ Higher effect size for children aged 6–10 years than for younger and older participants

To facilitate comparisons, d scores reported by Wong et al. (1991) and Hogben (1998) were converted into r values; see www.stat-help. com/. . ./Converting%20effect%20sizes%202009-06-25.xls

(Continued)

Table 5.2 Continued

III. Video games

Year	Author(s)	Number of studies (period)	Age	Type of media	Methodology C = Cross-sectional E = Experimental L = Longitudinal	Effect size(s)/outcomes
2001	Sherry	25 (1975–2000)	Up to 22 years	Video games	C, E	Overall aggression: $r = 0.15$; stronger effects in post-1995 studies $r = 0.11$ (experiments); $r = 0.16$ (surveys) $r = 0.09$ (behavioural measures); $r = 0.19$ (paper-and-pencil measures)
2007a	Ferguson	25 (1995–2005)	All ages	Video games	E, non-experimental	Aggressive behaviour: $r = 0.29$ (experimental); $r = 0.15$ (non-experimental) Aggressive cognition: $r = 0.25$ (experimental); $r = 0.13$ (non-experimental) Physiological arousal: $r = 0.27$ (experimental)
2010	Anderson et al.	136 (until 2008)	All ages	Video games	C, E, L	Aggressive behaviour: $r = 0.19$ overall; $r = 0.24$ best practice studies Aggressive cognition: $r = 0.16$ overall; $r = 0.18$ best practice studies Aggressive affect: $r = 0.14$ overall; $r = 0.12$ best practice studies Prosocial behaviour: $r = -0.10$ overall; $r = -0.11$ best practice studies Empathy/desensitisation: $r = -0.18$ overall; $r = -0.19$ best practice studies Physiological arousal: $r = 0.18$ No difference between Asian and western studies

poor-quality studies. For example, studies were classified as "good practice" if they compared violent games with games that did not contain violence rather than using comparison games that did include some violence, or if they used measures of violent game playing rather than total time spent playing video games regardless of their content. As shown in Table 5.2, studies meeting the "best practice" criteria produced somewhat higher effect sizes compared with the total sample of studies on four of the five outcome variables considered. Thus on the basis of these data there is no support for the claim that the effects of violent media are overestimated because of the poor quality of the available studies.

Following Cohen (1988), r values in the region of ±0.10 are considered small, those in the region of $r = \pm 0.30$ are considered medium, and those in the region of ±0.50 or higher are considered large effects. By this standard, the effect sizes obtained in the media violence meta-analyses fall into the small to medium range. However, this does not mean that they are without practical significance, as has been claimed by some critics (e.g., Ferguson, 2010). Rosenthal (1990) demonstrated that a correlation of $r = 0.20$ between media violence and aggression shifts the odds of someone with high media violence use showing high levels of aggressive behaviour from 50:50% (the odds if aggression was completely unrelated to media violence use) to 60:40%. This means that of 100 high users of media violence, 60% will fall into the high aggression group, compared with 40% of low media violence users, if all other things are equal in the two groups. Considering how widely violent media are available and used around the world, this difference of 20% translates into a large number of individuals who may become more aggressive as a result of using violent media. As Sparks and Sparks (2002) have pointed out, if only one person in several hundred thousand viewers was inspired by a violent movie to commit a violent act, the consequences of several million people watching that movie would be dramatic.

In addition to the information presented in Table 5.2, the meta-analyses revealed a host of specific findings. For example, Bushman and Huesmann (2006) found that age interacted with methodology in that the effects were stronger for adults than for children in laboratory experiments, and stronger for children than for adults in longitudinal studies. The most extensive analysis of violent video game effects by Anderson et al. (2010) revealed substantial differences depending on methodology on some of the outcome variables, such as much stronger effects for aggressive affect and cognitions from experimental studies compared with longitudinal and cross-sectional studies.

Taken together, the meta-analytic evidence indicates that there is a link between the use of media violence and aggression. Experimental as well as longitudinal studies suggest that violent media stimuli may have a causal influence on aggression. However, as noted by Huesmann (2010a), this is not to say that violent media use "determines" aggressive behaviour. Not every heavy user of violent media will be highly aggressive, just as not every drunken driver will cause a fatal accident, but the risk of aggression is increased among the high user group. Media violence may reinforce the effects of other risk factors, particularly exposure to violence in the real world (Browne & Hamilton-Giachritsis, 2005). The role of moderator variables in explaining individual differences in the susceptibility to violent media effects will be discussed later in this chapter. First, however, we will take a closer look at theoretical explanations of the underlying process that lead from media violence as the input variable to aggressive behaviour as the outcome variable. Different explanations address the short-term effects of a single episode of exposure to media violence and the long-term effects of repeated use of violent media over extended periods of time.

Explaining the short-term effects of media violence use

This section will address the question of how exposure to media violence enhances viewers' aggressive response tendencies in the period following the presentation of the aggressive content. The General Aggression Model (GAM) (DeWall & Anderson, 2011) introduced in Chapter 2 provides a conceptual framework which proposes that physiological arousal, aggressive affect, and aggressive cognitions pave the way for media violence as a situational input variable to elicit aggressive behaviour. In addition, media violence may instigate aggressive behaviour through a process of observational learning. The key mechanisms underlying the effects of exposure to violent media stimuli on immediate aggressive responses are presented in the top half of Figure 5.3, and will be discussed in turn.

(1) Exposure to violent media stimuli leads to an *increase in physiological* as well as *affective arousal* in the form of state anger and hostility. As shown in Table 5.2, the meta-analyses by Bushman and Huesmann (2006) and Ferguson (2007a) found evidence that violent media stimuli increase physiological arousal, with effect sizes of $r = 0.26$ and $r = 0.27$, respectively. This increased arousal may facilitate aggression by enhancing the person's activity level and strengthening dominant responses (i.e., behaviours that are most easily activated). For example, individuals confronted with a provocation are more likely to respond aggressively if they are already in a state of increased arousal, as suggested by Zillmann's (1979) excitation transfer model discussed in Chapter 2. This model suggests that arousal caused by a media stimulus may be added to the arousal caused by a provocation or other adverse stimulation and mislabelled as anger if the person is no longer aware of the source of the initial arousal, thus reinforcing an aggressive response (Zillmann & Bryant, 1974).

(2) Whereas physiological measures provide a quantitative index of arousal, affective arousal reflects the subjective perception of the quality of arousal. Several studies have demonstrated that exposure to violent media stimuli may elicit feelings of state anger and hostility that trigger subsequent aggressive behaviour. Bushman and Huesmann (2006) found an effect size of $r = 0.27$ for the link between media violence and angry affect across all types of methods and media genres, Anderson et al. (2010) reported an effect size of $r = 0.29$ from experimental studies of video game violence.

(3) Violent media stimuli may activate *aggressive thoughts, feelings, and self-concepts.* Watching media depictions of aggressive interactions increases the ease with which users can access their own aggressive thoughts and feelings. The underlying mechanism is a priming process whereby a particular external stimulus, such as an aggressive act, guides the individual's attention to the congruent mental constructs, such as aggressive

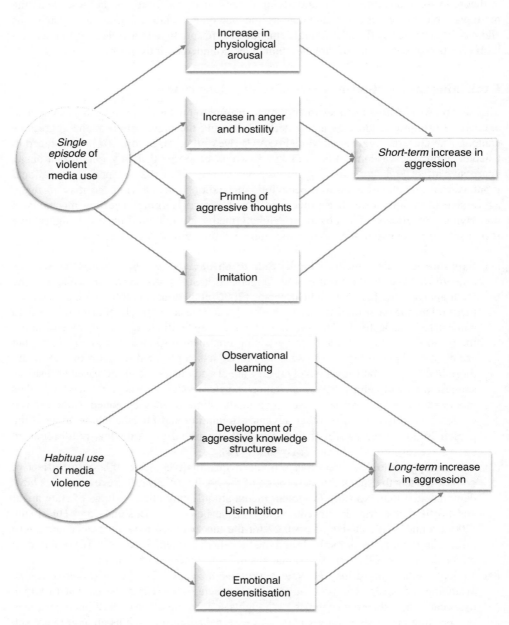

Figure 5.3 Short-term and long-term effects of media violence.

cognitions, thus lowering the threshold for using them to interpret social information (for a general discussion of priming and aggressive cues, see Chapter 4). Asking participants to list their thoughts after watching a violent or non-violent videotape, Bushman (1998) found that respondents who had watched the violent videotape produced more aggressive associations to homonyms with both an aggressive and a non-aggressive meaning (e.g., "box," "punch"). They were also faster in identifying letter strings making up aggressive words than were respondents who had been shown a non-violent videotape (see also Bushman & Anderson, 2002). Bösche (2010) replicated the faster recognition times for aggression-related words after playing a violent compared with a non-violent video game. In addition, he found faster accessibility of positively valenced words in the violent game condition, which indicates that violent entertainment is linked to positive associations.

Beyond violence in films and video games, recent research has examined violent lyrics in music as triggers of aggressive responses. In research by Fischer and Greitemeyer (2006), men who were asked to listen to songs with lyrics that disparage women (e.g., "Superman" by Eminem, and "Self-Esteem" by Offspring) recalled more negative attributes about women and behaved more aggressively towards a female experimenter than did men who listened to neutral lyrics. In a second study, women who had listened to songs with men-hating lyrics (e.g., "You Oughta Know" by Alanis Morrisette, and "Can't Hold Us Down" by Christina Aguilera) displayed more aggression towards a male confederate. In a study of violent music videos, Lennings and Warburton (2011) found that the lyrics alone, even when the visual channel was removed, increased aggression, as measured by the hot sauce paradigm (see Chapter 1), compared with a control group.

Furthermore, there is evidence that even brief periods of media violence use may activate aggression-related aspects of players' self-concept. Playing a violent video game for 10 or 20 minutes increased the speed with which aggression-related words were associated with the self in an Implicit Association Test (IAT) (see Chapter 1), compared with a non-violent control condition, eliciting a process of learning aggressive self-views (Bluemke et al., 2010; Uhlmann & Swanson, 2004). No parallel effects were found on explicit self-report measures of aggression, which suggests that the effects of violent media cues operated at the unconscious or automatic level. The link between violent media use and the self was highlighted further in a study by Fischer, Kastenmüller, and Greitemeyer (2010). Their participants played either a violent (boxing) game or a non-violent (bowling) game. In each condition, half of the participants could personalise their game character by modelling its physical appearance on themselves. The other half played the respective game with a non-personalised character. Participants playing the personalised violent game subsequently administered more hot sauce to another person as a measure of aggressive behaviour than those playing the non-personalised violent game, and both groups acted more aggressively than the players of the non-violent game in either the personalised or non-personalised condition. The effects were mediated by self-activation (feeling strong, active, and motivated) that was higher in the personalised than in the non-personalised violent game conditions.

However, it seems that not only do aggressive media contents prime aggressive cognitions, but also the priming of aggressive thoughts then leads to a preference for violent media contents. Langley, O'Neal, Craig, and Yost (1992) first activated aggressive cognitions by asking participants to compose short stories using words from a list of aggressive (as opposed to non-aggressive) terms. Next, they were given a choice of different film clips described as varying in aggressive content. Participants who had written aggression-related stories during the priming task expressed a greater preference for the violent film clips than those who had written a story based on the neutral words. These findings support the idea of a vicious cycle between media violence and aggression, in that media violence fosters aggressive cognitions just as aggressive cognitions create preferences for violent media.

(4) A further process that explains the short-term effects of exposure to violent media stimuli is *imitation*. Exposure to aggression may instigate social learning processes that result in the acquisition of new behaviours. As we saw above, much of the aggression portrayed in the media is rewarded or at least goes unpunished. Moreover, it is often shown by attractive characters with whom viewers can identify. As social learning theory suggests, learning through imitation is particularly likely under these circumstances (Bandura, 1983; for a more detailed discussion, see Chapter 2). The most obvious way in which aggression portrayed in the media is incorporated in the recipients' behavioural repertoire is reflected in "copycat aggression." Studies conducted as early as the 1960s showed that children imitate the behaviours performed by adult role models (Bandura et al., 1963). Direct imitation, or "copycat violence," also features with some regularity in crime reports. Deliberate as well as accidental killings were shown to have resulted from children's re-enactments of scenes they had observed in the media. Although this evidence is largely anecdotal, finding a close resemblance of a specific method of killing in a real-life murder case to a fictional murder in the media points to a possible translation of virtual reality into real life. In addition, real events that receive widespread media attention, such as hijackings, are also well documented in the literature to trigger copycat violence, including the effect of self-killings by prominent public figures on subsequent suicide rates (the "Werther effect") (Hittner, 2005; Niederkrotenthaler et al., 2009).

Individual differences and features of the violent media input as moderators of short-term effects

Violent media stimuli clearly do not affect all people to the same extent. Several studies have demonstrated that individuals differ in their aggressive responses to media violence depending on trait aggression and trait hostility. Anderson and Carnagey (2009) showed that playing a violent video game increased the accessibility of aggressive cognitions compared with a non-violent control group only among participants who scored high on trait aggression (for similar results, see Giumetti & Markey, 2007). However, in a study by Anderson (1997), playing a violent game increased hostile affect only among participants who scored low on trait hostility. An explanation for the latter finding may be that for individuals high on trait hostility, hostile feelings are chronically accessible, so that the violent game as a short-term aggressive prime has no additional effect on them. By contrast, people who are not habitually hostile are induced by the prime to activate aggression-related affective states.

Bushman (1995, Study 3) explored the impact of media violence on aggressive behaviour shown by participants high vs. low in trait aggressiveness, who were randomly assigned to watch a violent or non-violent film clip. The noise blast paradigm was used to yield a measure of unprovoked aggression (noise selected for the first round) and a measure of provoked aggression (noise selected from the second round onwards; see Chapter 1). On the measure of unprovoked aggression, both aggressive and non-aggressive individuals were equally affected by the violent film in that they set higher noise levels than participants who watched a non-violent film. However, on the measure of provoked aggression the aggression-enhancing effect of the violent film was significantly more pronounced for the aggressive than for the non-aggressive participants.

The impact of short-term exposure to media violence is also affected by users' past experience with violent media contents. For example, Bartholow, Sestir, and Davis (2005) showed that after playing a violent video game for 20 minutes, high habitual users of violent video games were more aggressive on a competitive reaction task than were low habitual users. High users also scored lower on empathy and higher on trait hostility than did low users, and these differences partly explained the differences in aggressive behaviour (see also Anderson & Dill, 2000). There is also evidence that the more regularly violent media stimuli are used, the more positive feelings they elicit. Habitual players enjoyed playing violent games more than non-regular players, (Bösche, 2010), and habitual exposure to violent media stimuli was associated with greater pleasant arousal in response to violent film clips, but not in response to sad or funny clips (Krahé, Möller, Huesmann, Kirwil, Felber, & Berger, 2011).

The different ways in which violence is presented also have an impact on the strength of the link between media violence use and aggression (for a review, see Barlett, Anderson, & Swing, 2009). In the study by Carnagey and Anderson (2005) discussed earlier, aggressive cognitions and behaviour were higher when the game was programmed so that violent actions were rewarded than when they were punished (see Figure 5.1). Barlett, Harris, and Bruey (2008) varied the amount of blood that was visible during the playing of a violent computer game. In the condition where large amounts of blood were displayed, participants showed significantly higher arousal, state hostility, and number of aggressive words in a word completion task. Similarly, Barlett, Harris, and Baldassaro (2007) found that playing a violent video game with a controller in the shape of a realistic gun led to a larger increase in arousal from baseline than playing the same game with a standard controller. A recent study by Williams (2011) examined the effect of physical similarity between players and their game characters on players' physical state anger after playing a violent or a non-violent game. Participants were either instructed to create an avatar that resembled them in various physical features, such as skin colour, height, build, and hairstyle, or they were given an avatar that looked dissimilar to them. As expected, a main effect for violence level was found, with higher state anger after playing the violent game than after playing the non-violent game. However, a significant interaction was found between the violence level of the game and the physical resemblance of the main character. Participants who had played the violent game with an avatar resembling themselves were significantly more angry than those who had played the violent game with a dissimilar avatar or those who had played a non-violent game with either the similar or the dissimilar avatar. These findings are consistent with the effects reported by Fischer et al. (2010) for the comparison of personalised and non-personalised game characters. In combination, these studies suggest that the more realistically violence is presented in video games, the more likely it is to promote aggressive behaviour.

Regarding differences between passive exposure to media violence as opposed to active involvement, Polman, Orobio de Castro, and van Aken (2008) compared children who were actively playing a violent or non-violent video game with a group of children who passively observed the actions of the first group shown on a television screen. This ensured that the participants in both groups received exactly the same input and only differed in terms of active involvement. Aggressive behaviour was measured through peer nominations (see Chapter 1). The results showed that boys in the violent-active condition were more aggressive than boys in the passive-violent condition who had merely observed the play moves of the active group. However, they were no more aggressive than boys in the active-non-violent condition. No effects of involvement or violence level of the game were found for girls.

With regard to the role of gender more generally, evidence was presented at the beginning of this chapter that boys are far more attracted to violent media than are girls. Whether they are differentially affected when exposed to the same level of violent content has not been established conclusively in the literature. The meta-analysis by Anderson et al. (2010) found no significant gender differences in the effect sizes for the link between media violence use and aggression, and findings from studies with all-female samples showed that women are also affected by violent media. Anderson and Murphy (2003) found higher levels of aggression in woman who had played a violent compared with a non-violent game, and Fischer and Greitemeyer (2006) showed that women who had listened to men-hating lyrics acted more aggressively towards a male target person than women who had listened to neutral lyrics. However, other studies found no effect of violent media stimuli on women (e.g., Bartholow & Anderson, 2002; Deselms & Altman, 2003; Polman et al., 2008; see also the Columbia Television Violence Study described earlier in this chapter; Huesmann & Miller, 1994). Given that violent media actors are typically male, women cannot identify with aggressive media models in the same way as men, which may account for their lower preference for this type of media and, possibly, their lower levels of aggression following exposure to violent contents. This line of reasoning is supported by the finding that women playing a violent game with a female avatar showed more aggressive thoughts in a word completion task than women playing the same game with a male avatar (Eastin, 2006).

Explaining the long-term effects of media violence use

To explain the impact of habitual use of media violence on aggressive behaviour, several interlocking processes have been proposed (for a summary, see Huesmann & Kirwil, 2007). The most widely studied mechanisms are presented in the bottom half of Figure 5.3. It should be noted that none of these mechanisms is specific to violent media contents; they pertain to the long-term effects of exposure to violence in real life as well as in the virtual reality of the media. Therefore many of the general theories of aggression discussed in Chapter 2 can also inform the understanding of media violence effects over time.

(1) *Observational learning* plays a key role in the adoption of aggression as part of the individual's behavioural repertoire. Just as real-life models are imitated, particularly if their aggressive behaviour is followed by positive consequences, as shown by Bandura et al. (1961, 1963), media models are a powerful source of learning by imitation. Violent media characters are typically presented as strong, powerful, and acting in pursuit of a good cause, making them appealing models to imitate. Huesmann et al. (2003) found positive correlations between childhood identification with same-sex aggressive media characters and aggression measured 17 years later in both men and women. Moreover, children who perceived television violence as "real" were significantly more aggressive as young adults. A longitudinal study of Japanese children showed that playing video games in which violence was committed by an attractive as opposed to a less attractive actor predicted higher levels of hostility and aggression 12 months later (Shibuya, Sakamoto, Ihori, & Yukawa, 2008).

(2) Observational learning is not limited to the imitation of specific acts of aggression; it also involves the acquisition of more general *aggressive knowledge structures*, or scripts. According to the General Aggression Model, repeated exposure to violent media promotes the learning, rehearsal, and reinforcement of pro-aggression beliefs and attitudes, hostile perceptions, and expectations as well as the acquisition of behavioural scripts (Bushman & Anderson, 2002). The more frequently people encounter violence in media depictions or engage in virtual violence in electronic games, the more likely they are to develop positive attitudes about the use of aggression in interpersonal conflicts, to see others' behaviour as hostile and antagonistic, and to access aggressive scripts when planning behavioural responses. In a study of third to fifth graders, Gentile and Gentile (2008) showed that playing violent video games predicted a higher tendency to attribute hostile intent to others 5 months later, which in turn was linked to higher physical aggression (for a discussion of the hostile attribution bias, see Chapter 3). Habitual violent video game play was also associated with higher trait hostility in an adolescent sample studied by Gentile, Lynch, Linder, and Walsh (2004), and trait hostility in turn was associated with the involvement in physical fights, as well as with arguments with teachers. These links support the role of violent media use in promoting hostile schemata that lower the threshold for aggressive behaviour.

Media violence also affects aggressive behaviour through changing users' world view. The more often individuals encounter violence in the media, the more prevalent they assume it to be in the real world. This is thought to be due to the increased accessibility of aggression-related cognitions in heavy users of violent media, whereby accessibility is seen as a function of the frequency and recency of exposure, and the vividness of memory representations of violence (Shrum, 1996). Demonstrating the role of vividness, it was shown that the more references people made to blood and gore in their recollections of violent scenes they had seen in movies or on TV, the higher they estimated the prevalence of crime and violence to be in the real world (Riddle, Potter, Metzger, Nabi, & Linz, 2011). Because habitual users of media increasingly come to see the world as a hostile and dangerous place, they are more likely to feel threatened and provoked by other people's actions and to respond with aggressive behaviour.

The role of media violence in eliciting aggressive thoughts and feelings is relevant to understanding the activation of aggressive scripts. The more violence individuals see in the media, the more often they encounter stimuli relevant to their aggressive scripts. Over time, the frequent activation of aggressive scripts will make them more easily accessible, thus enhancing the likelihood that they will be used to interpret incoming stimuli. Children are particularly susceptible to this effect, because their aggressive scripts are still more malleable than those of adults (Huesmann, 1998).

(3) A further long-term effect of using violent media that is relevant to the explanation of aggression is *disinhibition*. Exposure to violent media contents may weaken viewers' inhibitions against aggression by making aggression appear to be a common and accepted feature of social interactions. As shown earlier in this chapter, many violent acts are presented as justified without showing the suffering of victims, which undermines the perception of violence as antisocial and harmful. Thus they increase the belief that aggression is a common and acceptable form of behaviour. As noted by Huesmann (1998), such normative beliefs are an integral part of aggressive scripts and are used to decide which behavioural options will be activated in a given situation. Consistent with this proposition, Huesmann and Kirwil (2007) reported longitudinal evidence that normative beliefs about aggression in adulthood were predicted by childhood preferences for violent media contents and that the normative acceptance of aggression partly mediated the link between childhood exposure to violence and adult aggressive behaviour. Presenting aggression as justified was correlated with higher hostility and aggression assessed 1 year later in the Japanese study by Shibuya et al. (2008). Furthermore, in a study of German adolescents, Möller and Krahé (2009) found that the more participants played violent video games, the more accepting they were of physical aggression in interpersonal conflict situations as assessed 30 months later. Acceptance of aggression as normative was significantly associated with both physical aggression and a hostile attributional style.

(4) Finally, habitual exposure to violent media stimuli has a lasting effect on aggression through a process of *desensitisation*. In general terms, desensitisation refers to the gradual reduction in responsiveness to an arousal-eliciting stimulus as a function of repeated exposure. In the context of media violence, desensitisation more specifically describes a process "by which initial arousal responses to violent stimuli are reduced, thereby changing an individual's 'present internal state'" (Carnagey, Anderson, & Bushman, 2007, p. 491). In particular, desensitisation to violent media stimuli is thought to reduce anxious arousal. Fear is a spontaneous and probably innate response of humans to violence. As with other emotional responses, repeated exposure to media violence can *decrease* negative affect because violent stimuli lose their capacity to elicit strong emotions the more often the stimulus is presented (Anderson & Dill, 2000).

Several studies have demonstrated that, in the long term, habitual exposure to media violence may reduce anxious arousal in response to depictions of violence. Research has found that the more time individuals spent watching media depictions of violence, the less emotionally responsive they became to violent stimuli (e. g., Averill, Malstrom, Koriat, & Lazarus, 1972), and the less sympathy they showed for victims of violence in the real world (e.g., Mullin & Linz, 1995). In a series of studies with children aged 5 to 12, Funk and colleagues demonstrated that habitual use of violent video games was associated with reduced empathy with others in need of help (Funk, Baldacci, Pasold, & Baumgardner, 2004; Funk, Buchman, Jenks, & Bechtoldt, 2003).

Bartholow, Bushman, and Sestir (2006) used event-related brain potential (ERP) data to compare responses by users of violent and non-violent video games to violent stimuli, and relate them to subsequent aggressive responses in a laboratory task. They found that the more violent games the participants played habitually, the less ERP activity they showed in response to violent pictures and the more aggressively they behaved in the subsequent task. No effect of habitual media violence use was found on ERP responses to negative stimuli without violence (such as pictures of accident victims or disfigured babies), indicating that desensitisation was specific to the violent content of the media diet. Using skin conductance levels as a measure of arousal during exposure to a violent film clip, Krahé et al. (2011) found that the more participants were used to violent media, the less physiological arousal they showed while watching graphic scenes of violence and the more pleasant arousal they reported to have experienced during the clips. Higher pleasant arousal was associated with faster recognition of aggression-related words, demonstrating the associations between affective and cognitive processes postulated by the General Aggression Model. Participants in this study were also shown sad and funny film clips, for which no association with habitual media violence was found, which again demonstrates that the effects are specific to violent media contents.

Further evidence for the desensitising role of media influences comes from a wide range of studies into the effects of pornography on sexual aggression. Experimental studies have shown that participants exposed to violent pornography rated the impact of a subsequently presented rape scenario on the victim as significantly less severe and expressed more permissive attitudes about sexual violence than those who had not previously been exposed to the pornographic material (e.g., Linz, Donnerstein, & Adams, 1989; Mullin & Linz, 1995). The desensitising effect of violent pornography is not limited to men, but has been found to affect women as well (Krafka, Linz, Donnerstein, & Penrod, 1997). The evidence linking pornographic media contents to aggression will be reviewed in more detail in the next section.

Effects of pornography

Pornography is broadly defined as "media material used or intended to increase sexual arousal" (Allen, D'Alessio, & Brezgel, 1995, p. 259). It includes presentations of nudity, consensual sexual interactions, and the use of coercion and violence in the context of sexual interactions. A review of the different ideological positions concerning the effects of pornography and the appropriate societal responses to deal with them was provided by Linz and Malamuth (1993). In this section, we shall focus on the empirical evidence generated by the debate about the harmfulness of pornography with regard to aggression.

Content analyses show that violence has a firm place in pornography. Analyzing 50 videos at the top of the list of pornography sales and rentals in 2004 and 2005, Bridges, Wosnitzer, Scharrer, Sun, and Liberman (2010) established that aggression is an integral feature of this genre. Of a total of 304 scenes that were analysed, 88% showed acts of physical aggression, such as spanking or gagging, and 48% contained verbal aggression. Only 10% of all scenes contained positive behaviours, such as kissing or verbal compliments. Most of the aggressive behaviours were shown by a male actor towards a female target, and 95% of the targets responded either with expressions of pleasure or in a neutral way to the aggressive treatment. These findings clearly contradict the dismissal of violent pornography as "comparatively rare in the real world" by Ferguson and Hartley (2009, p. 323). Moreover, sexual content has also found its way into the popular medium of video games (Brathwaite, 2007).

There is evidence that exposure to pornographic media contents, at least occasionally, is widespread from early adolescence onwards. In a study by Kraus and Russell (2008), 83% of participants reported that they had watched sexually explicit media contents between the ages of 12 and 17. For online pornography, Sabina, Wolak, and Finkelhor (2008) found an exposure rate of 93% for boys and 62% for girls up to the age of 17. In a representative German study, two-thirds of 14- to 17-year-olds reported having seen pictures or films of sexual acts (BRAVO, 2009).

Two methodological strategies have dominated research on the link between pornography and aggression. The first is correlational and examines the link between consumption of pornography and aggression. Correlations are computed either at a societal level by linking circulation rates of pornographic material to prevalence rates of violent crime and sexual offences (for a review, see Bauserman, 1996), or at an individual level by relating self-reported consumption of pornographic material to some measure of aggressive behaviour (e.g., Bonino, Ciairano, Rabaglietti, & Cattelino, 2006). The second approach is experimental and compares individuals exposed to different media contents (e.g., pornographic vs. neutral material, depictions of consensual vs. coercive sexual interactions, sexually violent vs. non-sexually violent material) in terms of the effect on subsequent aggressive behaviour (e.g., Donnerstein, 1984). The issue of whether or not pornography use is a risk factor for aggressive behaviour needs to be broken down into several more specific questions.

Is there a link between the use of pornography and sexual as well as non-sexual aggression?

Several studies have documented a significant association between pornography use and sexual aggression (Malamuth, Addison, & Koss, 2000). In an experimental study by Yao,

Mahood, and Linz (2010), men were assigned to play either a sexually oriented video game or a comparison game without sexual content. Those who had played the sexually charged game scored significantly higher on a measure of sexual harassment and were faster at responding to words that sexually objectify women (e.g., "slut", "bitch") in a lexical decision task. A longitudinal study by Brown and L'Engle (2009) revealed that boys who used pornographic material at the age of 13 were more accepting of sexual harassment 2 years later, and Ybarra, Mitchell, Hamburger, Diener-West, and Leaf (2011) found that adolescents who used pornography were six times more likely to engage in sexual aggression over a 3-year period. A cross-sectional study by Vega and Malamuth (2009) established a positive correlation between pornography use and sexual aggression in men, after controlling for a range of personality and attitudinal risk factors. However, the link was strongest in men with high scores on other risk factors for sexual aggression. Further studies with sex offenders (Kingston, Fedoroff, Firestone, Curry, & Bradford, 2008) and with adolescents (Alexy, Burgess, & Prentky, 2009) reached a similar conclusion. These results are consistent with more comprehensive reviews of the literature (Kingston, Malamuth, Fedoroff, & Marshall, 2009; Seto, Maric, & Barbaree, 2001). Seto et al. (2001) argued that the effect of pornography was likely to be transient in men not predisposed to sexual aggression, as these men would not normally seek out violent pornography. Experimental evidence included in a meta-analysis by Allen, D'Alessio, and Brezgel (1995) yielded an overall effect size of $r = 0.13$ for exposure to pornography on subsequent (non-sexual) aggression in the laboratory, but the effects varied depending on the level of violence in the pornographic material.

Is violent pornography more closely related to aggression than non-violent pornography?

Pornographic material containing violence has been found to have a greater impact on subsequent aggression than non-violent sexual stimuli. The meta-analysis by Allen, D'Alessio, and Brezgel (1995) examined the pornography-aggression link separately for three types of stimuli: (a) violent sexual behaviour, (b) non-violent sexual behaviour, and (c) presentations of nudity. The findings from their analysis are presented in Figure 5.4.

Figure 5.4 shows that depictions of nudity produced a small decrease in aggression. Both violent and non-violent pornography were found to increase aggressive behaviour. In interpreting these findings, it is important to bear in mind that all studies included in this meta-analysis were experiments involving only brief exposure to violent pornography. The fact that measurable effects of such limited exposure were obtained suggests that even small effect sizes are not to be dismissed. Although the effect size is higher for violent than for non-violent pornography, the difference is not significant. Therefore the authors concluded that "violent content, though possibly magnifying the impact of pornography, is unnecessary to producing aggressive behavior" (Allen, D'Alessio, & Brezgel, 1995, p. 271). Donnerstein (1984) suggested that non-violent pornography may only affect individuals whose readiness for aggressive behaviour is already high (e.g., due to previous frustration, alcohol

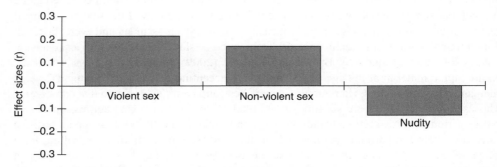

Figure 5.4 Meta-analytic effects of different types of pornography on aggression in experimental
studies. (Based on Allen, D'Alessio, & Brezgel, 1995, p. 271. Copyright Oxford University
Press).

consumption, or arousal from a different source) (see the discussion of excitation transfer
theory in Chapter 2).

Is there a difference between violent pornography and portrayals of non-sexual violence in their effects on aggression?

This question is important because it pits the sexual against the violent aspects of pornography,
and addresses the role of sexual arousal in precipitating aggression. Donnerstein conducted
a series of studies that compared participants' aggressive responses following the presentation
of a non-violent pornographic film, a violent pornographic film, and a non-sexual violent
film (for a summary, see Donnerstein, 1984). In addition, some of the studies explored the
effect of previous provocation – assumed to lower the threshold for aggressive behaviour –
on responses to the different films. In one of the experiments, male participants were
either angered or not angered by a female confederate, were then shown one of three films,
and subsequently had the opportunity to aggress against the female confederate by
means of electric shocks of varying intensity. The main results of this study are presented in
Figure 5.5.

The findings in Figure 5.5 suggest that it is not so much the sexual but the aggressive
contents of the materials which instigate aggression. The non-sexual violent film led to
significantly more aggression than the non-violent sexual film. The highest levels of
aggression were observed for the film that combined both sexual and violent contents. Prior
provocation led to higher levels of aggression as a response to both types of aggressive films,
but the pattern across the films was not affected by provocation.

The primary dependent variable in this study was shock intensity, which is a non-sexual
aggression measure. However, Donnerstein also measured sexually aggressive responses
following exposure to the films. Again, exposure to violence, even without sexual content,
was associated with a greater likelihood of aggression (willingness to use force and

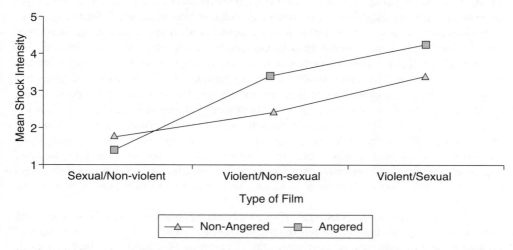

Figure 5.5 Aggression against a female confederate as a function of anger and film type. (Adapted from Donnerstein, 1984, p. 76. Copyright Academic Press).

willingness to rape) than exposure to the non-violent sex film. However, it would be premature to conclude that non-violent pornography is innocuous with regard to aggression. Paik and Comstock's (1994) meta-analysis yielded a substantially higher effect size for violent and non-violent erotica combined than for non-sexual violence. This finding is consistent with Zillmann's (1998) "sexual callousness model". Zillmann suggests that the degrading portrayal of women in pornography may promote sexual callousness towards women that facilitates male aggression directed at female targets. His model points to the role of attitudinal variables as mediators between sexual/violent media contents and subsequent aggression, which will be addressed in the next section.

Does pornography affect attitudes that are relevant to aggression, in particular rape-supportive attitudes?

This question reflects the possibility that pornographic media contents may have an indirect negative effect on aggression by promoting attitudes conducive to aggressive behaviour. As shown by content analyses, many pornographic films contain violence against women which is seemingly enjoyed by the targets or portrays initially reluctant women changing their mind after forceful attempts by the man to engage in sexual contact (Bridges et al., 2010). Such presentations may foster the view that women enjoy aggressive sexual tactics and that they are usually willing to have sex even if they initially reject a man's advances. For example, Peter and Valkenburg (2007, 2008) found significant correlations between pornography use and the sexual objectification of women among Dutch adolescents, and an experimental study of Japanese men showed a significant increase in participants' rape myth acceptance following exposure to a pornographic video (Ohbuchi, Ikeda, & Takeuchi, 1994).

Evidence from both correlational and experimental studies suggests that the distinction between non-violent and violent pornography is again important in clarifying the link between pornography and attitudes that condone sexual aggression. Linz (1989) examined the experimental evidence on the effects of short-term (less than an hour) and long-term (more than an hour) exposure to pornographic materials. Under short-term exposure, little evidence was found for an increase in rape-supportive attitudes and judgements following exposure to sexually explicit material compared with a control group exposed to a neutral film. Studies comparing short-term exposure to non-violent vs. violent pornography yielded more consistent results: violent pornography led to stronger rape-supportive and antisocial attitudes than non-violent sexual material. A parallel picture emerged with regard to the long-term effects. There were more negative effects of violent than of non-violent pornography.

A subsequent meta-analysis by Allen, Emmers, Gebhardt, and Giery (1995) included both experimental and correlational studies to provide quantitative assessments of the strength of pornography effects on rape-supportive attitudes. A total of 24 studies were included in the analysis, eight of which were correlational (i.e., relating self-reports of exposure to pornography to rape-supportive attitudes). The remaining 16 studies were experimental (i.e., exposure to pornography was manipulated and then related to measures of rape-supportive attitudes). The experimental evidence yielded a significant, albeit small effect size of $r = 0.15$. Again, violent pornography was more strongly related to rape-supportive attitudes than were non-violent sexual depictions, but the effect was still present for non-violent pornography. As evidenced by an average effect size of $r = 0.02$, the correlational studies reviewed by Allen, Emmers et al. (1995) failed to support the claim that individuals with more exposure to pornographic material hold more rape-supportive attitudes. However, a more recent meta-analysis by Hald, Malamuth, and Yuen (2010) found a significant effect size of $r = 0.18$ across nine studies of the link between pornography use and attitudes supporting violence against women. Distinguishing between violent and non-violent pornography, they found that attitudes condoning violence against women were related significantly more closely to violent than to non-violent pornography use ($r = 0.24$ vs. $r = 0.13$). A cross-sectional study of German adolescents showed that violent pornography consumption, but not overall pornography use, correlated significantly with the normative acceptance of sexual aggression (Krahé, 2011).

Although the question of whether exposure to pornographic media contents is a risk factor for aggression continues to be the subject of controversy (e.g., Ferguson & Hartley, 2009; Kingston et al., 2009), the evidence reviewed in this section suggests a number of conclusions:

(1) Many pornographic media contain depictions of violence against women that is seemingly enjoyed by the targets, and pornography is widely used from adolescence onwards.

(2) There is evidence of a link between explicit depictions of sexual acts and both sexual and non-sexual aggression, but no evidence of an effect for images of nudity. The effect sizes reported in meta-analyses are similar in magnitude to the effects found for non-sexual depictions of violence in the media, as shown in Table 5.2.

(3) Pornographic material that contains depictions of violence is more likely to elicit aggressive behaviour than non-violent pornography. Violent content and sexual content seem to have an additive effect, as non-sexual violence triggers more aggression than sexual stimuli without violence, but violent pornography that combines sexual and aggressive cues produces a further increase in aggression.

(4) Research with sex offenders has shown a stronger association between pornography use and aggression in individuals who are at higher risk of aggression due to other risk factors.

(5) Finally, many studies have found an effect of pornography on rape-supportive attitudes and the sexual objectification of women, which suggests that pornography affects sexual aggression indirectly via a greater acceptance of violence against women. Given that a substantial body of evidence shows that rape-supportive attitudes predict sexual aggression, the effect of pornography on these attitudes has important implications in terms of understanding the risk factors for sexual aggression (e.g., Lanier, 2001; White & Kowalski, 1998). We shall return to the role of rape-supportive attitudes in explaining sexual aggression in Chapter 8.

Preventing and mitigating the effects of media violence

It has become clear in the course of this chapter that media presentations of violence may affect viewers' aggressive behaviour through a number of different routes. What, then, can be done to prevent or mitigate these adverse effects? Theoretical models that explain the long-term effects of exposure to violent media as a result of observational learning, aggressive scripts, and desensitisation suggest that interventions should start at an early age when aggressive scripts are not yet consolidated and therefore more amenable to change.

Compared with the large number of studies seeking to demonstrate an effect of media violence use on aggression, the current body of knowledge about effective intervention strategies is limited, and the majority of the available studies focused only on short-term changes in experimental settings (for reviews, see Anderson et al., 2003; Cantor & Wilson, 2003). Typically, interventions designed to mitigate the aggression-enhancing effects of media violence exposure focus on either or both of two outcome variables: restricted consuming and critical consuming. Restricted consuming refers to an overall reduction in media exposure and to the substitution of violent with non-violent media content. Critical consuming refers to the promotion of an understanding of how media violence influences users, and of the mechanisms by which violence is presented as acceptable, successful, and detached from negative consequences. Critical consuming is therefore directed at increasing an important aspect of media literacy, namely the ability to analyse and evaluate media (Kirsh, 2010).

Focusing on restricted overall media use, Robinson, Wilde, Navracruz, Haydel, and Varady (2001) demonstrated the efficacy of an intervention with third and fourth graders over a period of 6 months. The intervention included a 10-day complete turn-off of television, videos, and video games, followed by a prescribed budget of no more than 7 hours of screen time per week. Participants in the intervention group showed not only a reduction in media use compared with the control group, but also a significant decrease in peer-rated aggression as well as observed verbal aggression from baseline to post-test. However, no parallel intervention effects were apparent in parent ratings of aggression.

Byrne (2009), on the other hand, focused exclusively on the aspect of critical consuming. She compared two intervention conditions with a control group in a sample of fourth and fifth graders. In the "basic condition," students received a lesson on the negative effects of media violence, how to avoid these effects, and how to critically evaluate the aggressive behaviour of media characters, using violent clips as examples. In the "activity condition," participants were given the same instruction but were additionally required to write a paragraph about what they had learned, and were videotaped reading it aloud. No difference was found between the activity and the control conditions immediately post-intervention and at the 6-month follow-up, whereas the basic condition showed a significant *increase* in the willingness to use aggression, indicating a boomerang effect.

Using a combined approach of reducing media violence use *and* promoting critical consuming, Rosenkoetter, Rosenkoetter, Ozretich, and Acock (2004) conducted an intervention over a 12-month period with children from first to third grade. The intervention was designed to cut down the amount of violent television viewing and to reduce the identification with violent TV characters. It produced different effects for boys and girls. Girls in the intervention group scored higher than girls in the control group on knowledge about the effects of TV violence, and lower on TV violence viewing as well as identification with violent TV characters. The effect of the intervention on reducing peer-nominated aggression was significant only for boys. In a subsequent study with children from first to fourth grade, Rosenkoetter, Rosenkoetter, and Acock (2009) implemented a similar programme over a 7-month period with an immediate post-intervention measurement and an 8-month follow-up. Participants in the intervention group reported watching less violent television and expressed more critical attitudes about media violence than those in the control group, both immediately post-intervention and 8 months later. The short-term effect of reduced identification with violent characters was no longer present at the follow-up. No effect of the intervention on peer-rated aggression was found, either immediately post-intervention or at the 8-month follow-up.

In a German study by Möller, Krahé, Busching, and Krause (2012), a sample of 683 seventh and eighth graders were assigned to two conditions: a 5-week intervention or a no-intervention control group. Measures of exposure to media violence and aggressive behaviour were obtained about 3 months prior to the intervention (Time 1) and about 7 months post-intervention (Time 2). The intervention group showed a significantly larger decrease in the use of violent media from Time 1 to Time 2 than the control group. Participants in the intervention group also scored significantly lower on self-reported aggressive behaviour (physical and relational aggression) at Time 2 than those in the control group, but the effect was limited to those with high levels of initial aggression. Further analyses revealed that the effect of the intervention on aggressive behaviour was mediated by an intervention-induced decrease in the normative acceptance of aggression.

Overall, the limited evidence that evaluates systematic interventions to reduce media violence use and to mitigate its harmful effects presents a mixed picture, ranging from positive effects to no effects, and unintended boomerang effects. Potter and Byrne (2007) stressed the importance of evaluative mediation in comparison to factual mediation (i.e., merely providing facts about the media, or media production). Furthermore, even within the studies on evaluative mediation, it appears that a focus on critical consumption with instructions limited to presenting facts about media violence is ineffective or may even backfire, whereas theory-based formats that involve *active* involvement seem to be more successful.

A second approach to prevention is directed at the limitation of access of children and adolescents to violent media content. Various age classification systems have been developed to identify media with violent content and designate them as unsuitable for certain age groups (for a summary of the most common rating systems in the USA, see Bushman & Cantor, 2003; for information about the British Board of Film Classification (BBFC) film ratings in the UK, see www.bbfc.co.uk; for the Pan European Game Information (PEGI) system, see www.pegi.info/en). Ratings either employ content labels or age labels, and a meta-analysis of parent polls by Bushman and Cantor (2003) showed that parents overwhelmingly preferred content-based ratings. Empirical analyses revealed several problems with rating systems (for a summary, see Gentile & Anderson, 2006). First, parents are either not familiar with the ratings or do not use them to regulate their children's media diet (Gentile, 2010). Secondly, media that are rated as suitable for children and adolescents often contain substantial levels of violence, and there appears to be a trend over time towards greater tolerance of violent content in media that are accessible to a young audience. A historical analysis of movies rated between 1950 and 2006, conducted by Nalkur, Jamieson, and Romer (2010), found a steady increase in violent content in films rated as PG-13 (designated as containing content inappropriate for children under 13 years of age). Thirdly, ratings are often not matched by consumer perceptions of the same titles, especially with regard to cartoons and fantasy games, which undermines their perceived validity (Funk, Flores, Buchman, & Germann, 1999; Walsh & Gentile, 2001). Finally, and probably most difficult to resolve, warning labels have been found to enhance the appeal of violent media to those whom they should protect. Demonstrating a "forbidden fruit" effect, Bijvank, Konijn, Bushman, and Roelofsma (2009) asked children and adolescents to evaluate the attractiveness of video games that came with different age recommendations or with different violent content indicators taken from the PEGI system. Consistent with their predictions, the authors found that adding an age label to a video game made it more attractive to children under the indicated age, and that adding a warning label about violent content similarly increased the attractiveness of the game, particularly to boys. Psychological reactance theory provides a theoretical explanation of the forbidden fruit effect (Brehm, 1966). It stipulates that having the freedom of choice is a basic need in humans, and that reactance arises as an unpleasant emotional state in response to restrictions of that sense of freedom. An increase in the perceived attractiveness of the denied option is seen as a psychological response that serves to restore the freedom of choice and enable individuals to alleviate the feeling of reactance. These findings raise questions about the effectiveness of rating systems and highlight the challenges involved in protecting children and adolescents from exposure to violent media contents.

Summary

- Aggression and violence are widely present in films, television programmes, and computer games, including those aimed at children and adolescents. Individuals of all age groups spend a lot of time using these media. Meta-analytic evidence integrating the findings of experimental, cross-sectional, and longitudinal studies provides support for the proposed link between the use of violent media contents and aggression across a range of different media.
- Violent media contents are particularly likely to affect viewers' aggressive tendencies if the violence is presented as successful or goes unsanctioned, if it is presented as justified and not leading to any pain or harm to the victim. In addition, consistent with social learning theory, aggression shown by powerful or much admired media figures is more likely to elicit aggressive behaviour. Individual differences have been observed in response to aggressive media, suggesting that habitually aggressive and hostile individuals appear to be particularly affected by violence in the media.
- Violent media stimuli may affect aggressive behaviour through different mechanisms. Short-term exposure to media violence leads to an increase in physiological arousal and aggressive affect, increases the accessibility of aggressive thoughts, and instigates the imitation of aggressive acts as observed or performed in the virtual reality.
- Habitual exposure to violence in the media creates the basis for sustained observational learning that promotes the development of aggressive knowledge structures, such as hostile expectations and attributional styles, and the formation of aggressive scripts. Through the portrayal of violence as normal and appropriate, media violence strengthens the normative acceptance of aggression that disinhibits aggressive behaviour. Finally, repeated exposure to violent media cues leads to desensitisation (i.e., reduced physiological and affective responsiveness to violent media stimuli), which is also reflected in a decrease in empathic concern for the plight of others who are in need of help.
- Evidence examining pornography demonstrates a link between sexually explicit media depictions and aggression, particularly for material that combines sex with violence. Pornography showing non-consensual sex increases aggressive behaviour, both in experimental settings and over time. Furthermore, violent pornography has been found to promote rape-supportive attitudes, which in turn are linked to sexually aggressive behaviour.

- To prevent or mitigate the adverse effects of media violence, two broad approaches have been adopted. First, interventions have been designed to reduce consumption and promote critical viewing through educating users about the potential risks of media violence use. Secondly, media rating systems have been designed to protect children and adolescents from the influence of violent media. However, the current rating systems are fraught with a number of problems, not least the creation of a "forbidden fruit effect", by making violent media more attractive to those whom they were designed to protect.

Tasks to do

(1) Look up the media rating systems in your country to find out what categories are used and how violence features in the criteria for assigning age labels.
(2) Go through your library of DVDs and video games and give each title a violence score on a scale ranging from 0 (not violent at all) to 4 (very violent), on the basis of how you remember the film or game. Then compare your score with the age ratings printed on the box.
(3) Pick a random 30-minute slot from your favourite TV channel and count the number of violent acts you observe during this period.

Suggested reading

Anderson, C. A., Berkowitz, L., Donnerstein, E., Huesmann, L. R., Johnson, J. D., Linz, D., Malamuth, N. M., & Wartella, E. (2003). The influence of media violence on youth. *Psychological Science in the Public Interest, 4*, 81–110.

Huesmann, R. L., & Kirwil, L. (2007). Why observing violence increases the risk of violent behavior by the observer. In D. J. Flannery, A. T. Vazsonyi, & I. D. Waldman (Eds), *The Cambridge handbook of violent behavior and aggression* (pp. 545–570). Cambridge: Cambridge University Press.

Kirsh, S. J. (2012). *Children, adolescents, and media violence* (2nd edn). Thousand Oaks, CA: Sage.

Malamuth, N. M., Addison, T., & Koss, M. P. (2000). Pornography and sexual aggression: Are there reliable effects and can we understand them? *Annual Review of Sex Research, 11*, 26–91.

6   Aggression as part of everyday life

Up to now, we have been talking about aggression as a general construct covering a wide range of different manifestations. In the chapters to come, the focus will shift towards a closer analysis of specific forms of aggressive behaviour, each carrying its unique characteristics. We shall begin in the present chapter by examining the prevalence and consequences of aggression in four areas of everyday life where it is commonplace, namely in school, at the workplace, on the roads, and in the sports world. Chapter 7 then moves to the protected realm of the family, where aggression is nonetheless a sad reality in the form of sexual, physical and emotional abuse of children, as well as violence against partners and elders. Chapter 8 focuses on sexual aggression, most notably against women, but it will also consider the problem of male sexual victimisation. Chapter 9 will discuss the different forms of aggression and violence that arise from confrontations between social groups, such as gangs, ethnic groups, and mobs. Finally, Chapter 10 will review the growing literature that seeks to understand terrorism as a particular form of group-based aggression.

Bullying at school

The last 30 years have seen the development of a large research literature dealing with aggressive interactions in school and work settings (Olweus, 1978; Randall, 1997). *Bullying*, "*mobbing*," and workplace aggression are forms of aggressive behaviour in these settings directed at victims who cannot easily defend themselves. Bullying is carried out with the intention of inflicting harm on the target person, thus meeting the core definition of aggressive behaviour (see Chapter 1). In addition, bullying is characterised by two further features: (a) it involves an imbalance of power between the aggressor and the victim, resulting, for example, from differences in physical strength or status in a job hierarchy, and (b) it is carried out repeatedly and over time. Thus single aggressive confrontations and aggressive behaviour towards a target of equal strength or status would fall outside the definitional boundaries of bullying (for a review of bullying definitions, see Smith, Cowie, Olafsson, & Liefooghe, 2002).

Bullying can take both direct forms, such as physical and verbal attacks, and indirect forms, such as relational aggression (i.e., behaviour directed at damaging the victim's peer relationships) (for an explanation of the distinction between direct and indirect aggression, see Chapter 1). With the advent of modern communication technology, *cyberbullying* has appeared on the scene as a new mode of bullying. Cyberbullying is carried out by means of modern technology, such as computers, mobile phones, or other electronic devices, to inflict intentional harm on a peer repeatedly and over time. Like traditional bullying, it involves a power differential between the aggressor and the target (Patchin & Hinduja, 2006). Sending threatening emails, posting derogatory comments about a marginalised classmate on Internet platforms, or circulating photos designed to embarrass or humiliate another person of lesser popularity or status are all examples of cyberbullying. Unlike face-to-face bullying, cyberbullying is not limited to a relatively small audience but can humiliate and intimidate a target on a large scale and under the cloak of anonymity (Dooley, Pyzalski, & Cross, 2009).

Different methods have been employed to study bullying (for a review, see Griffin & Gross, 2004). First, there is a range of *self-report* instruments that ask participants to indicate the frequency with which they engaged in bullying behaviour or experienced bullying (or both) during a certain period of time, such as the last month or the last year. Self-reports can be elicited either through general questions (see, for example, the study by the World Health Organization, 2004, described below) or through multiple items that specify different behavioural forms of bullying. It is important to provide participants with a clear definition of bullying to ensure that they respond on the basis of the same understanding of the term. A second methodological approach involves *peer nominations* in which peers are asked to name those members of their class or work group that engage in, or are made to suffer from, a range of different behaviours representing bullying. Bully or victim scores are assigned to individuals based on the aggregated peer nominations. In a third approach, parents and teachers can be asked to provide assessments of a child's bully and/or victim status, and employees can be asked to nominate colleagues who bully, or are bullied by, others. Finally, direct observation can be used in certain settings, such as school breaks or office meetings, whereby trained observers record the frequency and the social context of bullying.

This section will summarise the extant literature on the prevalence, risk factors, and consequences of bullying during childhood and adolescence, and will discuss the evidence on the effectiveness of anti-bullying programmes. Wherever possible, we shall refer to meta-analytic studies, which have the advantage of integrating results from a number of individual studies, thereby yielding more solid conclusions.

Prevalence of bullying

The most extensive research programme on the causes, manifestations, and consequences of bullying has been conducted in Norway by Olweus and his colleagues (Olweus, 1994). In a sample of 130 000 Norwegian pupils aged between 8 and 16, 9% reported being bullied, and 7% admitted bullying others "frequently" or at least "now and then." A literature review by Schuster (1996) found that victimisation rates varied widely across the 23 studies included, ranging from 3% to almost 90%. This variation is due in large part to methodological differences between studies, such as the time period considered, the source of data (self-reports vs. other-reports of victimisation and perpetration), and the broadness of the operational definition of bullying (e.g., requirement for serious and lasting consequences or for a power imbalance between perpetrator and victim). Although virtually all children will experience some form of upsetting treatment by older or stronger peers in the course of their school career, counts of bullying should be limited to those experiences that are repeated and persistent over time and involve an unequal balance of power. Studies adopting this more restrictive definition suggest a prevalence rate of victimisation of 5–10%, with figures for the perpetration of bullying being slightly lower (Carney & Merrell, 2001).

An international survey conducted in collaboration with the World Health Organization asked 11- to 15-year-olds in 40 countries about their experiences as bullies and as victims (Craig et al., 2009). Two questions were asked: (1) How often have you been bullied at school during the last couple of months?, and (2) How often have you taken part in bullying another student/other students in the last couple of months? The response options ranged from "I have not been bullied/I have not bullied" to "Several times a week." The questions were preceded by the following definition of bullying:

> We say a student is *being bullied* when another student, or a group of students, say or do nasty and unpleasant things to him or her. It is also bullying when a student is teased repeatedly in a way he or she doesn't like, or when he or she is deliberately left out of things. But it is *not bullying* when two students of about the same strength fight and quarrel. It is also *not bullying* when the teasing is done in a friendly and playful way.
>
> (Currie et al., 2008, p. 159)

The main findings based on responses from over 200000 participants are presented in Figure 6.1.

Across all 40 countries, 10.7% of respondents reported bullying others, 12.6% reported having been bullied, and 3.6% reported being both bullies and victims. Bullying rates were consistently higher for boys than for girls, and victimisation rates were higher for girls than for boys in most countries. A striking finding that can be gleaned from Figure 6.1 is the wide variation between the different countries. As the questions and instructions were the same in each country, this variation cannot readily be attributed to methodological differences. Additional analyses would be required linking the different rates to other aspects of variation between countries, such as features of the school system, differences in other forms of aggression, or general tolerance of aggression, to understand the high variability. A further finding from the survey was that a substantial minority of respondents reported both bullying behaviour and victimisation experiences. These so-called "bully-victims" have also been identified in many other studies as a particularly problematic group (Georgiou & Stavrimides, 2008; O'Brennan, Bradshaw, & Sawyer, 2009).

Salmivalli (2010) has pointed out that bullying needs to be examined in a group context, looking not only at the roles of bullies and victims but also at those of peer witnesses who may assist or encourage the bullies, intervene on behalf of the victim, or remain passive bystanders. Bullying frequently happens on a social stage, and the responses of those

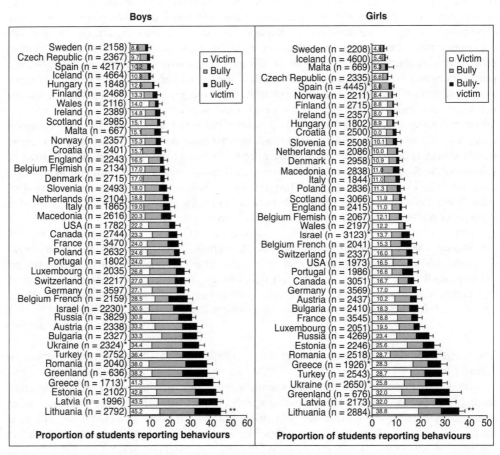

Figure 6.1 Rates of bullying and of being bullied among 11- to 15-year-olds reported in 2006 in 40 countries/regions. (Reprinted with permission from Craig et al., 2009, p. 219. Copyright Elsevier Science.)

witnessing the bullying behaviour of the aggressor may critically affect the course of events. Research based on the "participant role" approach has identified four different roles over and above those of the bully and victim: assistants of bullies, reinforcers of bullies, defenders of the victim, and outsiders (Salmivalli, Lagerspetz, Björkqvist, Österman, & Kaukiainen, 1996). The higher the number of students in a classroom who condone bullying by assisting or reinforcing the bully, the more prevalent bullying behaviour was found to be. Conversely, the more students are willing to defend the victim, the lower the rates of bullying and the less adverse the effects on victims' social adjustment (Salmivalli, 2010). Unfortunately, however, many bystanders are reluctant to intervene on behalf of victims, despite holding negative attitudes about bullying. In an Australian study by Rigby and Johnson (2006), fewer than 10% of secondary school boys and girls said that they would "certainly" intervene if they witnessed verbal or physical bullying. Removing obstacles for defenders coming forward in support of victims is therefore an important objective for intervention efforts (see below).

Comparing traditional face-to-face bullying with cyberbullying, research suggests that rather than representing a distinct form of bullying, cyberbullying simply adds additional channels through which it is possible to bully others, and that those who engage in cyberbullying are also likely to show bullying behaviour of the traditional form (Raskauskas & Stoltz, 2007; Werner, Bumpus, & Rock, 2010). These two studies found no evidence for a greater likelihood of victims of traditional bullying to engage in cyberbullying as a less risky form of retaliation.

Risk factors for bullying and victimisation

Beyond exploring the overall prevalence rates for bullying, it is important to ask what puts children and adolescents at risk of becoming victims or perpetrators of bullying. A recent meta-analysis integrating results from 153 individual studies provides some answers to this question by examining both personal characteristics and contextual variables associated with being a victim, a bully, or acting in both roles as a bully-victim (Cook, Williams, Guerra, Kim, & Sadek, 2010). Some risk factors were present in each of the three groups, whereas others were unique to the different roles. For example, low social problem-solving skills and internalising symptoms, such as anxiety, were individual-level risk factors for membership of each of the three groups, as were negative family environment and low peer status as contextual risk factors (see Cook et al., 2010, Table 9). Among the unique predictors, it was found that poor academic performance predicted bullying, but not victimisation or membership of the bully-victim group. Furthermore, holding negative attitudes about others was a unique risk factor for bullying, and lack of social competence was more characteristic of victims and bully-victims than of bullies. Male gender was found to be a small but significant risk marker for being a bully and a bully-victim, but was unrelated to the risk of being a victim in this analysis. Cook et al. (2010) concluded that the group of bully-victims had the greatest number of risk factors, corroborating earlier research, and they pointed out that this group should be particularly targeted by intervention efforts.

Consequences of bullying

Being the target of bullying often brings long-term misery to the victims. It undermines their mental and physical health and even entails an increased risk of suicide. A meta-analysis of 11 studies addressing the association between bullying and psychosomatic symptoms found that victims of bullying were twice as likely to report psychosomatic symptoms as non-victims, as reflected by an overall odds ratio of 2.00 (Gini & Pozzoli, 2009).[1] However, it should be noted that, with two exceptions, the studies included in this meta-analysis measured bullying victimisation and psychosomatic symptoms concurrently, and therefore cannot provide information about any causal or temporal ordering of the two.

Recent research has shown that victims of traditional bullying as well as cyberbullying are at increased risk of suicidal thoughts and actual suicide. A survey of about 2000 randomly selected middle-school students in the USA revealed that victims of traditional bullying were 1.7 times more likely than non-victims to attempt suicide, and victims of cyberbullying were 1.9 times more likely to do so than non-victims (Hinduja & Patchin, 2010). A Finnish study by Klomek et al. (2009) examined the link between bullying and victimisation at the age of 8 and attempted and completed suicides before the age of 25 in a sample of more than 5300 children. Their study also yielded troubling results, as shown in Table 6.1.

Being a victim was associated with an increased suicidal risk. Among girls, the odds ratio shows that those who were frequently bullied at age 8 were 6.3 times more likely to have attempted or completed suicide before the age of 25 than those not bullied at age 8. This figure is adjusted for conduct disorders and depression assessed at age 8, which would be additional risk factors of suicide. Another longitudinal study found that victimised girls were more susceptible to suicidal thoughts and behaviour than were victimised boys (Heilbron & Prinstein, 2010).

Being a bully may also have long-term negative consequences (Hawker & Boulton, 2000). Table 6.1 shows that suicide rates were elevated not only for victims, but also for bullies.

Table 6.1 Attempted or committed suicide before the age of 25 years in relation to bullying or victimisation at the age of 8 years (Adapted from Klomek et al., 2009, p. 257. Copyright American Academy of Child and Adolescent Psychiatry).

	Victims			*Bullies*		
	Never	*Sometimes*	*Frequently*	*Never*	*Sometimes*	*Frequently*
Boys						
%	0.5	1.2	2.9	0.5	1.0	3.9
OR*		1.9	3.8		1.3	1.8
Girls						
%	0.8	1.0	3.3	1.1	0.7	0.0
OR*		1.5	6.3		0.7	—

* OR (Odds ratios) adjusted for conduct disorders and depression at age 8 years. ORs indicate the increased probability of attempted or completed suicide in the bully and victim groups compared with the non-bully and non-victim groups.

1 The odds ratio indicates the factor by which the likelihood of an outcome variable (in this case attempting suicide) changes if a given risk factor (in this case being bullied) is present. Odds ratios greater than 1 indicate an increase in the likelihood, whereas odds ratios smaller than 1 indicate a decrease in the likelihood.

Similarly, the meta-analysis by Gini and Pozzoli (2009) revealed that the odds of bullies reporting psychosomatic symptoms were 1.65 times higher than for non-bullies. However, the highest risk was found for the bully-victim group (with an odds ratio of 2.22). This finding underlines once more that bully-victims are a particularly problematic group.

Several studies have addressed the question of whether engaging in bullying during childhood and/or adolescence is a risk factor for other forms of aggression in subsequent developmental periods. Basile, Espelage, Rivers, McMahon, and Simon (2009) reviewed a large body of evidence which showed that bullying shares many individual and contextual risk factors with sexual aggression, suggesting that male bullies may be at greater risk of engaging in sexual aggression. Similarly, Corvo and deLara (2010) discussed evidence of an overlap of risk factors for bullying and violence against intimate partners, arguing that both should be seen as expressions of a more general tendency to engage in aggression in social relationships. Adopting such a broader perspective on bullying also has important implications for anti-bullying interventions. For example, interventions that address shared risk factors, such as poor problem-solving skills, may be beneficial not only with regard to bullying but also in reducing the risk of other forms of interpersonal aggression.

Interventions

Responding to the evidence on adverse effects of bullying, many schools introduced anti-bullying policies, aimed at encouraging victims of bullying to come forward and at persuading bystanders to report peers who bully other schoolmates (Samara & Smith, 2008; Sherer & Nicholson, 2010). In the UK, the first privately run school was opened in 1999 to give a small group of severely victimised adolescents the opportunity to learn in a protected school environment without fear of further bullying. In addition, interventions to prevent bullying in schools have mushroomed. However, meta-analytic examinations of the effectiveness of anti-bullying interventions yielded discouraging findings. In a review of 16 studies conducted between 1980 and 2004 in the USA and several European countries, Merrell, Gueldner, Ross, and Isava (2008) found only small intervention effects. There was some indication that students in the intervention groups reported higher self-esteem and social competence, and that teachers' knowledge about bullying was increased, but the key criterion of success, namely a reduction in bullying behaviour, was not achieved across the range of studies, as indicated by an overall effect size of $d = 0.04$. The analysis also yielded evidence of counterproductive effects (again small in magnitude), in that feeling safe at school decreased and feelings of anxiety increased after the intervention.

Including a broader sample of 42 studies, all employing experimental designs with a non-intervention control group and random assignment of participants to the intervention or control conditions, Ferguson, San Miguel, Kilburn, and Sanchez (2007) found an overall effect size of $r = 0.12$ for a reduction in bullying behaviour. In interventions that specifically targeted groups identified as being at high risk for aggression, the effects were somewhat stronger, but still in the small range ($r = 0.19$). These authors also concluded that "school-based anti-bullying programs are not practically effective in reducing bullying or violent behaviours in the schools" (Ferguson et al., 2007, p. 410). However, as noted in our discussion of the meaning of small effect sizes in relation to the media violence-aggression debate in Chapter 5, dismissing effects of this magnitude as trivial may be disputed, given the large number of students who are affected by bullying worldwide and the dramatic impact bullying may have on their well-being. Even if only a small proportion of victims could be spared the experience as a result of school-based interventions, this would amount to a large number of people in absolute terms. However, it is clear that the effectiveness of anti-bullying interventions needs to be weighed against the costs involved in their implementation. On this basis, the meta-analytic evidence shows that the available programmes have not been doing well.

Workplace aggression

Aggression against weaker members of the peer group is not limited to the school setting, but also happens to people at work. Workplace aggression, also called workplace bullying (e.g., Notelaers, De Witte, & Einarsen, 2010), refers to behaviours that are intended to make another person feel miserable at work over longer periods of time. The target persons are unable to defend themselves due to an imbalance of power between perpetrator and victim, because the bully has a higher status (e.g., a boss bullying a subordinate) or a stronger position among peers (e.g., a man bullying a woman of equal status in a male-dominated work group). Schat and Kelloway (2005, p. 191) have defined workplace aggression as "behavior by an individual or individuals within or outside an organisation that is intended to physically or psychologically harm a worker or workers and occurs in a work-related context." This definition covers aggression by colleagues at work as well abusive behaviour by outsiders, such as patients in a hospital or customers in a shop. The term "workplace violence" denotes those acts of workplace aggression that are intended to cause physical harm.

The most common way of measuring workplace bullying is through self-reports of victimisation, as exemplified by the *Revised Negative Acts Questionnaire* (NAQ-R; Einarsen, Hoel, & Notelaers, 2009). This measure contains 22 items addressing three dimensions: (a) work-related bullying (e.g., "being exposed to an unmanageable workload"), (b) person-related bullying (e.g., "being the subject of excessive teasing and sarcasm"), and (c) physically intimidating bullying (e.g., "threats of violence or physical abuse or actual abuse"). Substantial correlations were found between victimisation scores on the NAQ-R and psychosomatic complaints and intentions to leave (Einarsen et al., 2009). A particular form of workplace bullying that has attracted widespread attention is *sexual harassment*. Fitzgerald (1993, p. 1070) has defined sexual harassment as "any deliberate or repeated sexual behavior that is unwelcome to the recipient, as well as other sex-related behaviors that are hostile, offensive, or degrading." Such definitions of sexual harassment based on the subjective perception of the target are the most common approach in psychological studies of workplace sexual harassment (however, for alternative definitions based on objective criteria, see O'Leary-Kelly, Bowes-Sperry, Bates, & Lean, 2009).

Theoretical explanations of workplace bullying focus on the concepts of stressors, stress, and strain (Hershcovis & Barling, 2010). Stressors are measurable properties of the work environment, stress refers to the subjective experience and representation of these stressors by the individual, and strain describes how the individual responds to the stressors. The research reviewed in this section demonstrates how stressors, such as ill-defined roles, interact with stress, such as a person's affective negativity, to increase the risk of workplace bullying and adversely affect individual well-being and organisational functioning. Theoretical accounts of sexual harassment as a special form of workplace bullying claim that gender inequalities in society at large are reflected in gender hierarchies in organisational contexts, making sex-related aggression an easy option for men to assert status and dominance (Berdahl, 2007).

Prevalence of workplace aggression

Compared with the large number of studies that have addressed bullying at school, workplace aggression has been less well researched. The evidence suggests that victimisation rates for workplace aggression are similar to those obtained for school bullying. Incidence rates over 6 to 12 months are in the range of 3–10% (for reviews, see Hoel, Rayner & Cooper, 1999; Randall, 1997; Schuster, 1996). However, as with school bullying, there is wide variation between studies, and victimisation rates are higher if the time period is extended or broader definitions are used (McDonald, 2012). For example, in Rayner's (1997) survey of more than 1100 part-time university students, just over half of the respondents indicated that they had experienced some form of workplace bullying in their jobs. Cyberbullying has been identified as a new form of workplace aggression. A study by Privitera and Campbell (2009) found that 10% of employees across a range of employment sectors reported having been bullied via electronic media over the last 6 months, compared with a rate of 34% for face-to-face bullying.

Studies of sexual harassment at work have mainly focused on women as victims (for a review, see O'Donohue, Downs, & Yeater, 1998). Studies including both men and women show that victimisation rates are indeed substantially higher for women than for men (Fitzgerald & Ormerod, 1993). Confirming the gender imbalance from the perpetrator side, Perry, Schmidtke, and Kulik (1998) found that men had a significantly higher propensity than women to engage in sexually harassing behaviour. With regard to the prevalence of sexual harassment, it was estimated that one in two women will experience sexual harassment at some point in her working life (Fitzgerald, 1993). Other studies have supported this estimate. For example, O'Hare and O'Donohue (1998) found that 69% of the women they surveyed reported at least one incident of gender harassment. Schneider, Swan, and Fitzgerald (1997) collected reports from women in two organisations, a private-sector company and a university. In total, 68% of the respondents in the private company reported at least one incident of sexual harassment in the 2 years preceding the survey. Of these, 66% rated the experience as offensive or extremely offensive. In the university sample, 63% of the respondents reported at least one experience of sexual harassment, and 48% of these rated the experience as offensive or extremely offensive. There is also evidence that sexual harassment commonly occurs in combination with other, non-sexual forms of workplace bullying (Lim & Cortina, 2005).

Risk factors for workplace aggression

To understand who is likely to be affected by workplace bullying, both individual and organisational characteristics have been considered (for a review, see McDonald, 2012). Just as some people may be more likely to engage in, or experience, bullying in the workplace, there may be certain features of the work environment that allow bullying to be more common. A large-scale study by Smith, Singer, Hoel, and Cooper (2003) showed that the experience of bullying at school may predispose victims to later experiences of workplace bullying. Respondents who were victimised at school were more likely to have been bullied at work in the last 5 years than respondents who had not been bullied at school. However, it is important to note that the relationship was inferred on the basis of retrospective reports of school bullying that may have been inaccurately recalled or distorted in the light of subsequent experiences of bullying in the workplace.

A meta-analysis of 90 victimisation studies by Bowling and Beehr (2006) found a small effect size for negative affectivity of the victim as a predictor of experiencing bullying in the workplace. Negative affectivity describes the tendency to experience distress, to be highly sensitive to negative events, and to have a pessimistic view of the self. No effects were found for victim age or gender, but Hoel et al. (1999) noted that men are mostly bullied by other men, whereas women are bullied by men as well as by women. Notelaers et al. (2010) found a small but significant negative association between level of qualification and experience of workplace bullying, which suggests that bullying is somewhat less common at higher levels of qualification. By contrast, some studies suggest that sexual harassment is more commonly directed at higher-status women, who are seen as violating traditional female gender roles and assuming characteristics that are more desirable in men (O'Leary-Kelly et al., 2009).

Higher effect sizes were found by Bowling and Beehr (2006) for risk factors inherent in the work environment, particularly work constraints, role conflict, and role ambiguity. Leymann (1993) suggested that power differentials within organisations play an important role. He found that 37% of all bullying incidents involved a person in a senior position who bullied a subordinate, 44% involved individuals of the same hierarchical position, and only a minority of victims were bullied by someone in a lower hierarchical position. Poor leadership quality, reflected by authoritarian management methods and communication problems, is an important organisational characteristic that allows workplace bullying to develop and persist.

Organisational characteristics also play an important role in understanding and predicting sexual harassment. In their meta-analysis, Willness, Steel, and Lee (2007) found that organisational climate was the strongest predictor of sexual harassment. Aspects of organisational climate conducive to sexual harassment are lack of sanctions for harassers and perceived risks of complaining for victims, both of which are indicators of a tolerance of sexual harassment. A second organisational risk factor for sexual harassment is a masculine work environment that can be defined in terms of the workplace gender ratio or gendered power hierarchy with a predominance of men in more senior positions. A prime example of a masculine work environment is the military, and many studies have identified sexual harassment as a problem in this domain (Fitzgerald, Magley, Drasgow, & Waldo, 1999; see also the list of studies included in the meta-analysis by Chan, Lam, Chow, & Cheung, 2008). Another setting in which male dominance is combined with a strong power hierarchy is academia. Even though women account for a large proportion of students and relatively low-status clerical workers, men hold the majority of senior positions. Evidence of widespread sexual harassment in academic institutions has been provided by several studies (e.g., Hill & Silva, 2005; Paludi, 1990). In addition to aspects of workplace structure, gender stereotypes shared at a more general level contribute to sexual harassment. An important aspect here is the difference between men and women in terms of perceiving sexually charged comments and behaviours as inappropriate and offensive (Hunter & McClelland, 1991; Jones & Remland, 1992).

Consequences of workplace aggression

The meta-analysis by Bowling and Beehr (2006) found that workplace bullying was associated with significant impairment of the victims' well-being and work-related functioning (see also Aquino & Thau, 2009). Bullying was associated with feelings of frustration, experiencing negative emotions at work, and depression, with effect sizes of around 0.30. It showed negative links of similar strength with job satisfaction and organisational commitment. A large-scale French study revealed a significant association between workplace bullying and sleep disturbance (Niedhammer, David, Degioanni, Drummond, & Philipp, 2009). Bowling and Behr also found effects of bullying on turnover intentions and counterproductive work behaviour, indicating that bullying involves costs not only for the individual member of the workforce but also for the organisation as a whole.

Another meta-analysis of 55 studies by Hershcovis and Barling (2010) examined the effects of bullying on a range of negative outcomes, distinguishing between bullying by supervisors, co-workers, and people from outside the organisation (e.g., customers). The results showed that being bullied by a supervisor was significantly more damaging than being bullied by co-workers, as indicated by higher psychological distress and intention to leave, reduced job satisfaction, and lower work performance. Being bullied by a co-worker in the workplace was more damaging than being bullied by someone from outside the workplace.

Just like workplace bullying in general, sexual harassment has serious consequences both for the victims and for the institution or organisation involved. Meta-analyses by Willness et al. (2007) and Chan et al. (2008) have identified significant negative effects of sexual harassment on a range of physical and mental health outcomes, including an increased risk of developing post-traumatic stress disorder (PTSD) (for the definition of PTSD, see Chapter 7). They also found negative effects on global job satisfaction, organisational commitment, and work group productivity. Victims of sexual harassment had higher rates of absenteeism and job turnover than non-victimised members of the workforce, indicating that tolerance of sexual harassment is not only painful for the victims but also costly for the organisation (Sims, Drasgow, & Fitzgerald, 2005). No gender differences in the adverse consequences of sexual harassment were found by Chan et al. (2008), but age played a role as a moderator, with younger employees being more negatively affected.

In trying to respond to sexual harassment, denial (ignoring the offensive behaviour) and avoiding contact with the harasser are common coping strategies. If these strategies fail, victims of harassment often feel that they have no other option but to leave their job. Only a small proportion of harassment incidents are reported and lead to formal complaint procedures (O'Donohue et al., 1998; Welsh, 2000).

Interventions

Overall, the existing evidence suggests that exposure to workplace bullying, which by definition is experienced over a prolonged period of time, has adverse effects on employees' well-being and job functioning. It also incurs costs for the organisation itself, as victims of bullying show poorer work performance and increased turnover rates. Despite growing evidence of these negative effects, there has been little systematic research on interventions and their evaluations. Given the finding that bullying is more widespread in work environments with high levels of stress and problematic handling of occupational roles, an obvious intervention strategy is to reduce the stress levels within the organisation by fostering a positive organisational climate (Duffy, 2009). A critical review of specific intervention approaches has been provided by Saam (2010).

The first sections of this chapter on aggression as part of everyday life have examined two forms of aggression in the public sphere: school bullying and workplace aggression, both of which have been found to have lasting negative effects on their victims. Although the research literature has provided some converging evidence, the majority of the findings are based on cross-sectional surveys that cannot disentangle cause-effect relationships. For example, it could be the case that the negative affectivity identified as higher in victims of bullying is a result of, rather than a risk factor for, workplace bullying. Similarly, role ambiguity could be the result rather than the cause of bullying in the workplace. Research on the outcomes of victimisation is also mostly cross-sectional, thus precluding a causal interpretation of the findings. For example, it may be possible that individuals are targeted as victims because of their emotional vulnerability or lower job performance, rather than developing these problems as a result of being bullied. Research using prospective designs – for example, with children who start at a new school or employees who start at a new organisation without any previous history of contact – would help to illuminate the mechanisms involved in bullying at schools and in the workplace, both at the level of the individuals involved and at the level of the social system in which they interact.

Aggressive driving

Another everyday context in which aggression is frequently observed is driving a car. Most motorists would have to admit that they become angry with other road users at least occasionally, and may have engaged in aggressive behaviour towards them. Moving through traffic potentially involves many frustrations. Drivers may find their progress impeded due to a high volume of traffic or through the behaviour of other motorists, they may have difficulty finding a free space when they are in a hurry to park their car, or they may feel provoked by the assertive or dangerous driving style of others. Thus it is not surprising that frustration-related anger is often experienced in a driving context and that it gives rise to aggressive behaviour. In this section we shall review the extensive research literature that has examined the role of personal and situational variables affecting aggressive driving. Many studies have found associations between aggressive driving and accident involvement, so understanding risk factors for driving aggression and the underlying processes involved has significant practical implications for improving road safety (Galovski, Malta, & Blanchard, 2006; Mann, Zhao, Stoduto, Adlaf, Smart, & Donovan, 2007).

Definition and measurement

Aggressive driving may be defined as "any behavior intended to physically, emotionally, or psychologically harm another within the driving environment" (Hennessy & Wiesenthal, 2001, p. 661). This definition is consistent with the general definition of aggression as a behaviour carried out with the intention of harming another person (see Chapter 1). It consists of a range of specific actions, which vary in terms of the severity of harm inflicted and the potential to create dangerous traffic situations. Hennessy and Wiesenthal (2002) have differentiated between mild driver aggression (e.g., horn honking or hand gestures) and driver violence (e.g., fighting or deliberate contact). Aggressive driving motivated by the intention to harm needs to be distinguished from *reckless* or *assertive driving* (i.e., driving in a risky and selfish manner), which may cause harm to other drivers, but the harm is accidental rather than deliberate (Hennessy & Wiesenthal, 2002). However, other authors have suggested a broader definition of driving aggression that includes aggressive driving and reckless/assertive driving, defining it as "a dysfunctional pattern of social behaviors that constitutes a serious threat to public safety" (Houston, Harris, & Norman, 2003, p. 269). Most scales eliciting reports of aggressive driving are based on this broader definition, including both behaviours motivated by the intent to harm, such as swearing at other drivers, and behaviours motivated by the desire to make progress, such as speeding, that constitute a threat to safety on the roads (for a summary of measures, see Van Rooy, Rotton, & Burns, 2006).

Although some authors have used aggressive driving and road rage as interchangeable and the two constructs clearly overlap, road rage more narrowly denotes extreme acts of aggressive driving, involving assaultive behaviour with the intention of causing bodily harm and possible homicide (Ellison-Potter et al., 2001). Road rage is a criminal offence and is far less common than the more general construct of aggressive driving, which includes behaviours such as honking the horn when annoyed, or swearing at other drivers. Some authors have identified road rage as a psychological disorder (Ayar, 2006).

The most common method of assessing aggressive driving is through drivers' self-reports. Several instruments have been developed that present different forms of aggressive driving behaviour and ask drivers to indicate how frequently they have engaged in each behaviour in the past (Van Rooy et al., 2006). Reports of aggressive driving obtained through self-reports have been linked to personality traits as risk factors (e.g., Lustman et al., 2010), and also to reports of accident involvement as a correlate of aggressive driving (e.g., Mann et al., 2007). Moreover, several studies have used modern communication technology, such as beepers or mobile phones, to elicit state measures of anger and reports of aggressive driving while participants are actually on the road (Hennessy & Wiesenthal, 1999). Box 6.1 presents items from two instruments used to elicit self-reports of aggressive driving.

The *Driving Anger Expression Inventory (DAX)* by Deffenbacher, Lynch, Oetting, and Swaim (2002) measures drivers' general propensity to engage in aggressive behaviour when they are angry while driving. It consists of four subscales, referring to (a) verbal aggression, (b) personal physical aggression, (c) using one's vehicle to express aggression, and (d) displacing aggression onto people other than the annoying motorist. Hennessy and Wiesenthal's (1999) *State Behaviour Checklist* provides a brief assessment tool for use in specific driving situations when drivers are contacted while driving and asked to indicate whether they have engaged in aggressive driving in the previous 5 minutes of their journey.

A second, less frequently used approach is to study aggressive driving in a driving simulator to obtain data analogous to real-life behaviour behind the wheel. Participants are exposed to different traffic situations in the virtual reality of the driving simulator to record their aggressive behaviour (e.g., Deffenbacher, Deffenbacher, Lynch, & Richards, 2003). This approach typically yields lower correlations with risk factors or antecedents, such as state or trait anger (Nesbit, Conger, & Conger, 2007). A good example of the use of driving simulators to observe aggressive driving under controlled conditions is the study by Ellison-Potter et al. (2001). Their simulated driving task was designed as follows:

> The actual simulation task was programmed to include several potentially frustrating events (e.g., jaywalking, slow vehicles ahead, tailgating, general traffic congestion). The simulation included nine incidents of jaywalking involving 52 pedestrians, seven traffic lights, all of which were programmed to turn red when the subject approached them, and 116 other vehicles on the road. Hence, participants had the opportunity to hit pedestrians 9 times, run a red light 7 times, and hit another vehicle 116 times. Opportunities for off-road collisions were unlimited.
>
> (Ellison-Potter et al., 2001, p. 436)

Dependent measures were the average speed, number of red lights run, number of collisions, and number of pedestrians killed. We will turn to the findings from this experiment shortly.

BOX 6.1   Items measuring general and situation-specific aggressive driving behaviour (Adapted from Deffenbacher et al., 2002, Table 1; Hennessy & Wiesenthal, 1999, p. 423)

Example Items from the *Driving Anger Expression Scale* (DAX; Deffenbacher et al., 2002, Table 1)

How *often* do you *generally* react or behave in the manner described *when you are angry or furious while driving*?

Verbal aggressive expression

- I call the other driver names aloud
- I make negative comments about the other driver aloud
- I yell questions like "Where did you get your license?"

Personal physical aggressive expression

- I try to get out of the car and tell the other driver off
- I try to force the other driver to the side of the road
- I stick my tongue out at the other driver

Use of vehicle to express anger

- I drive right up on the other driver's bumper
- I speed up to frustrate the other driver
- I flash my lights at the other driver

Displaced aggression

- I yell at the people who are riding with me
- I take my anger out on other people riding with me
- I take my anger out on other people later on

Items from the *State Behaviour Checklist* (Hennessy & Wiesenthal, 1999, p. 423)

Please indicate whether you have employed the following behaviours during the last five minutes of this particular commute:

- Horn honking at other drivers out of frustration
- Purposely tailgating other drivers
- Flashing your high beams at another driver out of frustration
- Hand gestures at other drivers
- Swearing at other drivers

Finally, there are some field experiments, conducted under naturalistic conditions, which studied the impact of situational variables, such as heat, time pressure, or status of the offending car, and used horn honking as a measure of aggressive driving (for a summary, see Ellison-Potter et al., 2001). However, the validity of observations of horn honking as a measure of aggression is questionable, as drivers may also use it as a way of communicating with other drivers that is not necessarily based on intent to harm.

Anger and aggressive driving

Anger has been identified as a critical antecedent of aggression while driving. As noted above, moving through traffic can involve many frustrations. Therefore the frustration-aggression hypothesis and its extension in the cognitive neo-associationist model of aggression, both discussed in Chapter 2, can offer theoretical explanations of why aggression is frequently shown while driving. Traffic-related frustrations represent aversive stimuli that may trigger aggressive behaviour through the elicitation of anger. A meta-analysis by Nesbit et al. (2007) that included 28 samples found an average correlation of $r = 0.37$ between state anger and drivers' aggressive behaviour.

The state-trait model of driving anger by Deffenbacher and colleagues (e.g., Deffenbacher et al., 2003) proposes that state anger experienced in a specific traffic situation varies as a function of individual differences in trait driving anger, that is the extent to which a person is habitually prone to experience anger while driving. However, the model assumes that trait anger translates into state anger only in situations that involve frustrations, such as traffic congestion or provocative behaviour by other drivers. Correlational evidence supports this differential link between trait and state driving anger under high vs. low frustration conditions (Deffenbacher, Lynch, Oetting, & Yingling, 2001). Experimental studies that measured anger in response to pre-programmed traffic situations have yielded less conclusive results. In support of the state-trait model, a driving simulator study by Deffenbacher et al. (2003) found no difference between drivers who scored high and low in dispositional driving anger in low impedance situations, which involved no frustrations, but individual differences in driving anger did affect driving behaviour in high impedance situations. After they were made to drive under conditions where their progress was impeded, participants who scored high on trait driving anger reported significantly more state anger and a greater urge to be verbally and physically aggressive than did participants who scored low on trait anger.

Personal risk factors for aggressive driving

In addition to trait anger, several other personal characteristics have been linked to aggressive driving behaviour. Harris and Houston (2010) found significant correlations between aggressive driving and boredom susceptibility (i.e., an aversion to repetitive experiences of any kind). Boredom susceptibility is a component of sensation seeking, a personality trait characterised by the need for varied, novel, complex, and intense sensations and experiences to maintain an optimal level of arousal, associated with a high propensity towards risk taking

(Zuckerman, 2007). Lustman et al. (2010) established a link between aggressive driving and high levels of narcissism, defined as a grandiose feeling of superiority and a sense of entitlement that leads to aggression when challenged by others (see Chapter 3). However, the link was influenced by gender and by trait aggression. With regard to gender, it was found that among those who scored low on narcissism, men reported more aggressive driving than did women, whereas among those with high levels of narcissism, women reported more aggressive driving than did men. Regarding the interaction between narcissism and self-reported anger in frustrating driving scenarios, the combination of high narcissism and high anger yielded the highest aggressive driving scores. Another driving simulation study with men found that the more participants reported an obsessive passion for driving (example item: "I have difficulties controlling my urge to drive"), the more aggressively they drove as rated by independent observers (Philippe, Vallerard, Richer, Vallières, & Bergeron, 2009).

Age

Age is another personal characteristic linked to aggressive driving. Several studies suggest that aggressive driving is more common among younger than among older motorists (Vanlaar, Simpson, Mayhew & Robertson, 2008). There is evidence from official statistics on accident involvement and registered violations, as well as from self-reports, that aggressive driving declines with age (e.g., Åberg & Rimmö, 1998; Blockley & Hartley, 1995; Lajunen & Parker, 2001). In addition, there is evidence of an interactive effect of gender and age. Young *male* drivers have a disproportionately high risk of accident involvement and aggressive driving, and the gender gap diminishes with age. Lajunen and Parker (2001) found that age was associated with a decrease in aggressive driving behaviour among their male but not their female respondents.

Gender and gender-related self-concept

With regard to the role of gender, studies using self-reports of driving behaviour overwhelmingly suggest that men are more prone to aggressive driving (Vanlaar et al., 2008). In a study of motorists from the UK, Finland, and the Netherlands, Parker, Lajunen, and Summala (2002) found that male drivers reacted more aggressively than female drivers when other drivers impeded their progress or showed inconsiderate and impatient driving behaviour. Several other studies have confirmed this gender difference with respect to aggressive driving (e.g., Åberg & Rimmö, 1998; Blockley & Hartley, 1995; Ellison-Potter et al., 2001; Lawton, Parker, Manstead, & Stradling, 1997). However, when aggressive driving was subdivided into mild driver aggression (e.g., horn honking out of frustration, hand gestures) and driver violence (e.g., physical confrontations, chasing other vehicles), a more differentiated picture of the role of gender differences emerged. Hennessy and Wiesenthal (2001) found that men scored higher on a measure of driving violence than women, but no gender differences emerged with respect to mild driver aggression. A subsequent study narrowed down the higher prevalence of driving violence in men to a combination of male gender and endorsement of a vengeful attitude to driving (Hennessy & Wiesenthal, 2002). Driving vengeance is conceptualised by these authors as an individual difference variable of the desire to harm others in the driving environment in response to a perceived wrongdoing or injustice on the part of the other driver.

A further body of research has examined gender-related self-concept rather than biological sex as a correlate of aggressive driving. Aggression in general and driving aggression in particular have been highlighted as central elements of the masculine gender role. The social role model (Eagly & Wood, 1999; see Chapter 3) posits that gender differences in aggression are the result of an individual's social learning experiences. They are rooted in differential gender role socialisation that rewards males for being assertive and dominant and females for being caring and submissive. Within each gender group, individuals differ in the extent to which they endorse traditional gender stereotypes of masculinity and femininity as part of their self-schemata (Bem, 1981). A subgroup of men were identified who show an exaggerated endorsement of the masculine gender role in the form of a "macho personality." Macho men were found to report higher levels of aggressive driving in a German study by Krahé and Fenske (2002) compared with men who did not endorse this hypermasculine self-concept. In a study that addressed women's gender-related self-concept, femininity was associated with lower levels of driving aggression, when trait aggression was controlled for, suggesting that femininity buffered aggressive driving (Krahé, 2005). A study by Özkan and Lajunen (2005) that included both men and women obtained similar results. Masculinity was associated with higher levels of aggressive driving, whereas femininity was linked to lower aggressive driving scores in both genders. The highest rate of aggressive driving was found for those who scored high on masculinity and low on femininity, again pointing to the role of a hypermasculine self-concept as a risk factor for aggressive driving.

Contextual risk factors

It has already become clear that aggressive driving is not only a function of drivers' personal characteristics, but is also critically affected by features of the driving context. Two contextual risk factors have received particular attention in research on aggressive driving: traffic congestion and anonymity. In addition, exposure to risk-glorifying media has been examined as an instigator of aggressive driving in the form of intentional violation of traffic rules.

Traffic congestion

Consistent with the proposition that frustration may increase aggression, congested traffic conditions that frustrate drivers' goal of making swift progress have been found to precipitate aggressive driving. Hennessy and Wiesenthal (1999) studied commuters whose route was either low or high in traffic volume, and contacted them via mobile phones during their journey to elicit ratings of driver stress and driving behaviours. Drivers on the high-volume traffic routes reported significantly more acute stress and more aggressive driving behaviours than commuters on the low congestion route. Similarly, Harris and Houston (2010) reported that more tailgating occurred in heavy traffic. Hennessy, Wiesenthal, and Kohn (2000) found significantly higher levels of acute driver stress under high than under low traffic congestion conditions, and in situations of high as opposed to low time urgency, especially for drivers who were dispositionally prone to stress while driving.

Anonymity

Aggressive behaviour is generally more prevalent under conditions of anonymity (see Chapter 9), and driving a car provides such conditions. Although it is possible to identify the car, the aggressive driver's personal identity is typically concealed from others. Supporting the role of anonymity, Harris and Houston (2010) found that drivers reported more aggressive driving when they were alone in the car than when passengers were present, and an observational field study by Wiesenthal and Janovjak (1992) found that drivers in cars with tinted windows committed more deliberate violations of traffic rules. However, these are correlational findings that could be due to differences in the personalities of drivers who chose to drive cars with tinted windows, rather than reflecting the causal role of anonymity. By contrast, Ellison-Potter et al. (2001) used an experimental manipulation of anonymity by telling their participants to imagine that the vehicle assigned to them in the driving simulator was an open-top convertible that would enable others to identify them personally (no anonymity), or that the vehicle was a convertible with the top closed, so that others would be able to identify the car, but not them personally (anonymity). A significant effect of the anonymity manipulation was found on all measures of aggressive driving. Participants drove faster in the anonymous condition (on average 43 miles/hour or 69 km/hour) than in the identifiable condition (on average 40 miles/hour or 64 km/hour). Moreover, they drove through more red lights, were involved in more collisions, and killed more pedestrians, as shown in Figure 6.2.

Risk-glorifying media

A final contextual factor relevant to the understanding of aggressive driving is the use of risk-glorifying media. For example, racing games in which drivers engage in speeding and other high-risk manoeuvres may contribute to more risky driving behaviour in the real world, which includes aggressive behaviour towards other drivers. A series of studies by Fischer and colleagues demonstrated that playing virtual racing games increased players' positive evaluations of risk taking, the accessibility of risk-promoting cognitions, and also risky behaviour in a driving simulator (e.g., Fischer, Greitemeyer, Morton, Kastenmüller, Postmes, Frey et al., 2009; Fischer, Kubitzki, Guter, & Frey, 2007). Fischer et al. (2009) showed that the effects were evident only for racing games in which the violation of traffic rules was rewarded, and were mediated by a change in participants' self-concept in the direction of seeing themselves as reckless drivers. A meta-analysis including 11 studies found an overall effect size of 0.66 between the use of media that glorify risky driving and risk-taking

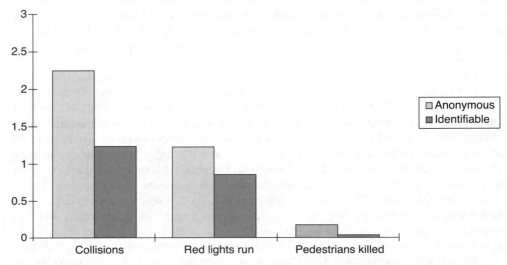

Figure 6.2 Differences in aggressive driving as a function of driver anonymity. (Adapted from Ellison-Potter et al., 2001, Table 1. Copyright Wiley-Blackwell).

behaviour in simulated driving contexts (Fischer, Greitemeyer, Kastenmüller, Vogrincic, & Sauer, 2011). Although these experimental studies only demonstrated short-term effects of playing racing games, it can be assumed on the basis of theorising and research on other media effects that the habitual use of risk-glorifying media will have a more persistent impact on users' driving behaviour (for a discussion of the pathways from media use to behaviour, see Chapter 5).

Interventions

Aggressive driving behaviour is clearly a safety hazard on the roads, which raises the question of how to prevent people from driving in a way that may harm others. The research reviewed in this section suggests two potential avenues: (a) targeting the aggressive driver; and (b) changing the contextual conditions that precipitate aggressive driving. Given the important role of anger in eliciting aggressive driving behaviour, interventions that target aggressive drivers have focused on promoting better control of anger (for a general discussion of the anger management approach, see Chapter 11). Deffenbacher, Filetti, Lynch, Dahlen, and Oetting (2002) assigned participants who scored high on driver anger to an 8- to 9-week intervention that included three groups: one group focused on relaxation techniques, the second group received an intervention that combined relaxation exercises and cognitive techniques designed to promote cognitive appraisals of situations that would reduce anger while driving, and the third group was a non-intervention control condition. Measures of driver anger and aggressive driving behaviour were collected at baseline prior to the intervention, immediately after the intervention, and at a follow-up after 4 weeks. Both intervention conditions led to a significant reduction in driving anger immediately after the intervention, but the difference from the control condition was no longer significant at the 4-week follow-up. The self-reported likelihood of aggressive driving decreased significantly in both intervention groups, and was lower than in the control group immediately post-intervention. At the 4-week follow-up, only the combined cognitive training and relaxation group differed significantly from the control group. Constructive ways of dealing with frustrating traffic situations (e.g., trying to think of positive things to do, paying even closer attention to the other person's driving to avoid an accident) increased in both intervention groups and remained higher than in the control group at the follow-up measurement.

In addition to helping anger-prone drivers to control their anger and develop non-aggressive ways of dealing with driving-related frustrations, changes in the driving context may be an effective way of reducing driver stress (Asbridge, Smart, & Mann, 2006). For example, promoting the use of public transport or introducing electronic traffic control systems may reduce congestion on the roads, thereby decreasing the experience of frustration. A study by Wiesenthal, Hennessy, and Totten (2000) explored the potential of music to buffer driver stress. They studied commuters who were using a route with either a high or a low traffic density, and randomly assigned them to either a music condition in which they were asked to listen to their favourite music during the entire journey, or a control group that was instructed not to listen to music (or any other media) during their journey. Participants were contacted by telephone twice during their journey and responded to a set of items measuring driver stress (e.g., "Trying but failing to overtake is frustrating me"). The findings from the study are presented in Figure 6.3.

A significant interaction was found between traffic congestion levels and the effects of music on driver stress. Under conditions of low congestion, driver stress was generally low, regardless of whether the participants had been listening to music or not. However, when congestion was high, participants listening to their favourite music were significantly less stressed than those in the non-music condition. These findings are consistent with the results of other research showing that pleasant music may buffer the effects of frustration on aggressive affect, cognition, and behaviour (Krahé & Bieneck, 2012; see also Chapter 11).

In summary, many studies have shown that driving through traffic is associated with a high potential for frustration. Consistent with theoretical accounts that have identified frustration as a powerful instigator of anger (see Chapter 2), frustrations encountered while driving give rise to anger, which in turn may trigger aggressive behaviour. For example, being slowed down by heavy traffic or provoked by the behaviour of other drivers instigates state anger that can lead to various forms of aggressive behaviour. Furthermore, being in the anonymity of one's car was found to lower the threshold for aggressive driving. The degree of state anger experienced in a frustrating traffic situation depends on the driver's dispositional proneness to anger. Additional personal characteristics that are related to differences in

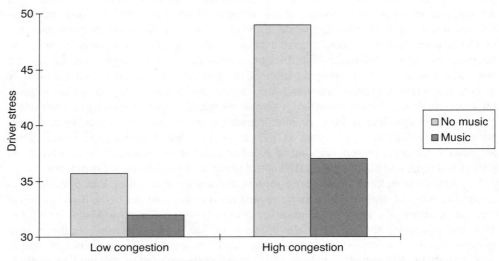

Figure 6.3 Music as a buffer of driver stress under high and low congestion. (Adapted from
Wiesenthal et al., 2000, Figure 1. Copyright Wiley-Blackwell).

aggressive driving include age and gender, with younger motorists and men featuring
more prominently among aggressive drivers. The reliance on self-reports of driving
anger and aggressive drivers is a limitation of many studies in this area, but there are
also experimental studies that have used observations of driving behaviour in simulated
conditions or in natural contexts to test causal hypotheses about risk factors for aggressive
driving.

Aggression in the sports world

Sporting events provide a context for aggressive behaviour by the athletes involved as well
as by spectators. As Russell (1993, p. 181) has noted, "outside of wartime, sport is perhaps
the only setting in which acts of interpersonal aggression are not only tolerated but
enthusiastically applauded by large segments of society." In this section we shall review the
limited body of research on aggressive behaviour among athletes as well as among spectators
who witness aggressive behaviour in the sports arena (for more detailed reviews, see Kimble,
Russo, Bergman, & Galindo, 2010; Russell, 2008; Young, 2012).

   Two forms of aggression can be observed among competitors in sports events: *instrumental
aggression*, which is carried out in order to promote the chances of winning, and *hostile
aggression*, which arises from the desire to harm another person as an expression of negative
feelings (see Figure 6.4; for the distinction between hostile and instrumental aggression,

see Chapter 1). Although it is often difficult to distinguish between these two kinds of motivation, behaviours in football, such as illegal tackling, tripping, or holding an opponent, would be examples of instrumental aggression, whereas behaviours such as shouting at the referee or hitting a teammate are examples of hostile aggression (Coulomb-Cabagno & Rascle, 2006). As with aggressive driving, predictors of aggressive behaviour in sport can be divided into two categories: personal characteristics of the actors involved, and contextual variables, such as aggression levels inherent in different sports or the outcome of contests in terms of defeat or victory.

Aggression by competitors

Among personal risk factors for aggressive behaviour by competitors in sports events, several studies have identified gender as a marker of differences in the perceived legitimacy of aggressive behaviours and in the perpetration of aggressive acts. For example, male basketball players rated rule-violating behaviours as more legitimate than did female players

Figure 6.4 An example of sports aggression. (Copyright dpa. Reprinted with permission).

(Duda, Olson, & Templin, 1991). In an observational study including 90 soccer games and 90 handball games in France, Coulomb-Cabagno and Rascle (2006) found that male players committed more acts of both instrumental and hostile aggression than did women across departmental, regional, and national levels of competition in both types of sport. In a study with male hockey players, Weinstein, Smith and Wiesenthal (1995) showed that endorsement of a masculine gender identity was related to aggressive playing behaviour, and that more aggressive players were rated as more competent by teammates as well as coaches. With regard to personality variables, Bushman and Wells (1998) found that individual differences in high-school ice hockey players' levels of trait aggression were related to the penalties they incurred for aggressive behaviour during the season (e.g., tripping), whereas no correlation was found with penalties for non-aggressive rule breaking (e.g., delaying the game). A significant correlation was found by Maxwell (2004) between athletes' anger rumination and their self-reported aggressive behaviour (for a discussion of the construct of anger rumination, see Chapter 3)

In terms of contextual risk factors, Reifman, Larrick, and Fein (1991) and Larrick et al. (2011) found that the higher the temperature on the day of the match, the more aggressive acts baseball players committed against fellow players. This finding is consistent with other research on the heat hypothesis, discussed in Chapter 4. Frank and Gilovich (1988) reported a series of studies which showed that colour of team uniform is linked to players' aggression, in particular the colour black. They argued that the colour black is associated with connotations of evil and badness, and should therefore serve as a cue affecting both the perceptions of others and the players' self-concept (for a discussion of the role of aggressive cues, see Chapter 4). In the first study, they established that those teams in the national football and hockey leagues who were wearing black were rated as more malevolent by participants who knew little about either sport and simply had to rate the teams based on photographs of their uniforms. The second study used archival records from 15 years of national league matches to demonstrate that teams who wore black received more penalties than their opponents who wore uniforms of other colours. Two teams had switched from non-black to black uniforms during this period, and that change was accompanied by an increase in the number of penalties received.

In a further experimental study, students who were knowledgeable football fans and experienced referees watched identical football scenes that were manipulated such that the players wore either black or white uniforms. Across two different episodes of playing, both students and referees indicated a greater willingness to assign penalties to the teams when they were wearing black than when they were shown in white uniforms, although the actions on the pitch had been exactly the same. The effect was even more pronounced among the referees than among the students. The findings for the referees are shown in Figure 6.5.

In the final experiment, Frank and Gilovich (1988) made participants wear either black or white sports shirts when choosing games in which they wanted to compete against another team. The games on offer were selected so as to differ in terms of aggressiveness (e.g., a dart gun duel or a putting contest). Participants were asked to choose five games, and the aggressiveness level of the five choices was used as a measure of aggression. Before donning

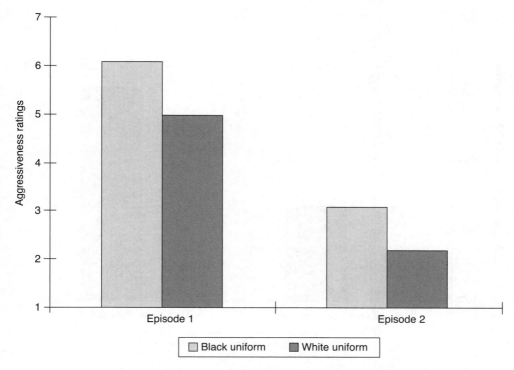

Figure 6.5 Experienced referees' ratings of aggressiveness of football teams wearing black or white uniforms. (Based on Frank & Gilovich, 1988, p. 80. Copyright American Psychological Association).

the black or white shirt, each participant made a choice of games while wearing their normal clothes, and when they put on the black or white shirts they were told that they would from then on be referred to as "the black team" or "the white team." The findings are shown in Figure 6.6.

The participants wearing black shirts and being referred to as "the black team" chose significantly more aggressive games than the participants wearing white shirts and being called "the white team." However, the groups did not differ in the choices made under individualised conditions when they were wearing their normal clothes (for a discussion of the role of uniforms in undermining people's sense of individuality and adherence to personal norms, to create a state of de-individuation, see Chapter 9). The findings by Frank and Gilovich (1988) indicate that the colour black is an aggression-related cue that affects people's self-perceptions and the way in which their behaviour is judged by others.

In addition to studies that have looked at athletes' aggressive behaviour on the field, another body of research has examined their aggressive behaviour outside the sports context. This research, which has been reviewed by Kimble et al. (2010), failed to produce consistent evidence that athletes are generally more aggressive than non-athletes, nor is there evidence

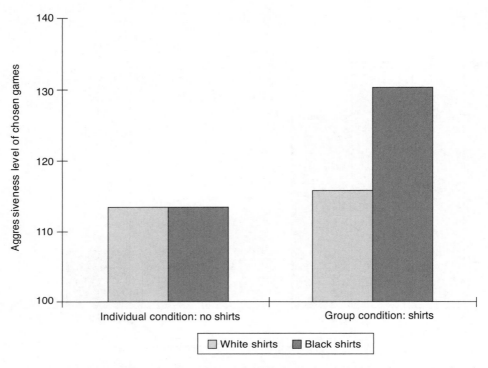

Figure 6.6 Students' choice of competitive games differing in level of aggressiveness as a function of wearing black or white shirts. (Adapted from Frank & Gilovich, 1988, Table 4. Copyright American Psychological Association).

that sports engagement serves as a protective factor against aggression, as would be suggested by the catharsis hypothesis (for a discussion of the notion of catharsis, see Chapters 2 and 11).

Aggression by spectators

A second body of research has assessed the impact of watching sports aggression on spectators' aggressive tendencies. Simons and Taylor (1992) have pointed out that sports which require extensive physical contact are more likely to elicit aggressive tendencies in the spectators. Arms, Russell, and Sandilands (1979) found that respondents exposed to a wrestling competition (stylised aggression) or an ice hockey match (realistic aggression) subsequently showed greater hostility and punitiveness than spectators of a swimming contest (non-aggressive condition). This finding directly contradicts the notion of symbolic catharsis, derived from psychoanalytic theorising, which suggests that aggressive tension may be reduced by observing aggressive sports. Interestingly, Wann, Carlson, Holland,

Jacob, Owens, and Wells (1999) showed that individuals who engaged in, or liked to watch, aggressive sports particularly adhered to the idea that aggressive tensions may be relieved through sporting activity. Several other studies reviewed by Russell (2004) further supported the claim that the more aggression is shown by the players, the more aggression is displayed by those who are watching.

There is evidence that aggression which builds up in the context of watching a sports event may spill over into other domains. Sachs and Chu (2000) analysed police records spanning a 3-year period to examine the association between football events and the number of police calls to a domestic violence incident. They found that the number of police dispatches was higher at weekends than during the rest of the week and, more importantly, that the increase was substantially greater for weekends when there was a football event than for non-football weekends.

Contextual factors, such as the outcome of the game and alcohol use, were found to play a role in a file analysis of discipline cases at a university in the USA over a period of 4 years. Coons (1995) examined differences in the number of discipline cases during football game weekends and non-football game weekends. She discovered that significantly more discipline incidents occurred during football weekends than during non-football weekends, and during home games compared with away games. Perhaps counterintuitively, the number of discipline incidents was significantly higher when the team had won than when it had lost the game. Almost half of the incidents involved the consumption of alcohol, highlighting the link between alcohol and aggressive behaviour discussed in Chapter 4. A similar finding was reported by Moore, Shepherd, Eden, and Sivarajasingam (2007) for rugby fans, who were surveyed after a match that ended in a victory, a defeat, or a draw of their favoured team. Those in the victory and draw groups rated themselves as more aggressive compared with a group of fans who were surveyed before the game, but those in the defeat group did not.

Addressing changes in physiological responses, Bernhardt, Dabbs, Fielden, and Lutter (1998) conducted two studies in which they measured the testosterone levels of spectators at a baseball match (Study 1) or a televised World Cup football match (Study 2) both before and after the match. They found that testosterone levels increased from baseline among those participants who saw their favourite team win, and decreased among those who saw their favourite team lose. Given the link between testosterone levels and aggression discussed in Chapter 2, these findings can help to explain why aggression may be increased more by a victory than by a defeat of the spectator's favourite team. Over the course of two seasons, White, Katz, and Scarborough (1992) found significantly higher rates of women admitted to hospital for domestic violence injuries after victories of the local football team than after lost games. To explain their findings, the authors suggested that "viewing a hypermasculine activity in which force is used to successfully overcome others increases the likelihood that male spectators will become physically aggressive with their partners" (White et al., 1992, p. 158). However, it should be noted that the data are only correlational, showing a co-variation between wins and losses on the one hand and domestic violence incidents on the other, and therefore they do not provide evidence of a causal influence of game outcomes on fans' perpetration of domestic violence.

With regard to personal characteristics, the gender difference found for aggressive behaviour by competitors is mirrored among fans. Male adolescents rated aggressive behaviour in a range of different sport scenarios as significantly more legitimate that did their female age-matched peers (Conroy, Silva, Newcomer, Walker, & Johnson, 2001). Wann, Haynes, McLean, and Pullen (2003) found that men reported a significantly greater likelihood than did women that they would commit anonymous hostile acts of physical aggression (e.g., "trip the star player of the rival team" and even "murder the star player of the rival team"). For both genders, however, positive correlations were found between identification with their own team and willingness to commit acts of hostile aggression towards the rival team.

Fan identification has consistently been identified as a predictor of aggressive behaviour. Van Hiel, Hautman, Cornelis, and De Clercq (2007) showed that the more football fans identified with their favourite team, the more physical and verbal aggression they reported showing in the context of football matches. In a field study, Wann, Carlson, and Schrader (1999) asked spectators at a college basketball match to complete a measure of how much they identified with their team prior to the match. After the match, participants were asked to indicate how many acts of instrumental verbal aggression (e.g., yelling at an official, opposing player, or coach because they thought this would help their team to win) and hostile verbal aggression (e.g., yelling at an official, opposing player, or coach because they were mad at him or her and wanted to show their anger) they had shown in the course of the match. Fans who identified strongly with their team reported significantly higher rates of both instrumental and hostile verbal aggression than did fans who identified less strongly. A subsequent study found that fans who identified strongly with their team were more likely to commit anonymous acts of physical hostile aggression against the rival team when their team had lost than after a victory (Wann, Culver, Akanda, Daglar, De Divitiis, & Smith, 2005).

Fan identification with a team not only predicts the behaviour of individuals, but is also crucially important for understanding the problem of collective spectator aggression or "hooliganism," which is notorious in the context of football matches. Several studies have found a link between trait measures of physical aggression and involvement in sports riots (for a review, see Russell, 2004). In their explanation of football hooliganism, Murphy, Williams, and Dunning (1990) have argued that this phenomenon is a form of aggression typically shown by young working-class males. They identified a subculture of aggressive masculinity, "predominantly, but not solely lower class" (p. 13), which provides the normative framework for the violent behaviour shown by football fans. Alcohol use and the level of violence on the pitch exacerbated the influence of masculinity norms on spectators' aggressive behaviour (Dunning, Murphy, & Williams, 1986). The significance of violence-condoning social norms in explaining football hooliganism was also apparent in an Italian study, in which violent fans cited "solidarity with the fan club" as their primary motive for participating in disturbances around football matches (Zani & Kirchler, 1991). The assertive nature of the game itself as well as the aggression displayed by the players in the course of the match provide additional cues that may reinforce aggressive tendencies in the spectators.

In addition to considering the individual actor, examining hooliganism as an intergroup phenomenon helps us to understand aggressive escalation in the context of football matches. Stott, Hutchison, and Drury (2001) provided a qualitative analysis that compared the behaviour of English and Scottish fans during the 1998 Football World Cup in France. They sought to understand why the English supporters were repeatedly involved in violent clashes with local youths, whereas the Scottish supporters were not. Stott et al. identified situational variables, such as perceived hostility from the out-group and lack of police protection against illegitimate violent out-group activities, that led English fans to close ranks and view their aggressive responses as legitimate. By contrast, Scottish fans perceived their relationship with the local youths as friendly and legitimate, and were disapproving of violent behaviour shown by members of their in-group. The Scottish supporters cited a further reason for abstaining from aggressive behaviour, which is interesting from an intergroup perspective. One of them was quoted by Stott et al. (2001, p. 372) as saying that "No one causes trouble at Scottish games any more 'cause it makes the English look bad." This statement shows that the dynamics involved in the regulation of intergroup conflict need to be examined not just in terms of the immediate relationships between the groups involved, but also taking into consideration the more complex issues of strategic differentiation from third parties. We shall look at other forms of intergroup aggression and discuss theoretical explanations of intergroup behaviour in more detail in Chapter 9.

To address the problem of violence associated with sports events, a variety of strategies and control mechanisms are available (for a summary, see Russell, 2008). These include legal measures, such as banning identified hooligans from attending matches or prohibiting the sale of alcohol before matches, and organisational measures, such as enforcing strategic seating arrangements for opposing fan groups and segregating rival fan clubs on their way to and from the stadium (see, for example, in the UK the Violent Crime Reduction Act, 2006, www.legislation.gov.uk/ukpga/2006/38/contents, and the 1989 Football Spectators Act, www.legislation.gov.uk/ukpga/1989/37/contents). In addition, measures can be directed at athletes as well as at spectators to promote anger management or induce positive affect that is incompatible with anger responses (see also Chapter 11). Finally, the strategic positioning of peaceful role models in aggressive crowds may be an effective approach, which is suggested by social learning theory (see Chapter 2), but systematic evaluations in the context of sporting events have yet to be conducted.

Summary

- Aggression is a widespread feature of many domains of public life. The school, the workplace, the road, and the sports arena are common venues for aggressive encounters. A large body of research has examined the prevalence of and potential risk factors for these forms of aggression.
- School bullying is a form of aggressive behaviour that is characterised by an imbalance of power between aggressor and victim and by taking place over a prolonged period of time. It can take the form of both physical and relational aggression, and is recognised

as a problem across many countries. Cyberbullying is a new form of harassment involving the use of electronic devices that allows perpetrators to remain anonymous and reach a large audience. Some studies suggest that the experience of being bullied in school makes victims vulnerable to long-term psychological problems, including later experience of bullying in the workplace and an increased risk of suicide.

- Workplace aggression refers to behaviours intended to make another person feel miserable at work over a prolonged time period, and it is also defined by a power differential between victim and perpetrator. It is more prevalent in environments characterised by a high level of work stress. Sexual harassment is a specific form of workplace aggression, and consists of sex-related behaviours that are unwanted by the recipient or perceived as hostile, offensive, or degrading. It is directed primarily at women and is more common in male-dominated work environments. Workplace aggression has been linked to significant impairments of victims' job satisfaction and psychological well-being, and is also costly at the organisational level in terms of high rates of absenteeism and turnover.

- Aggressive driving may cause significant safety hazards on the roads. It is more common among male than female drivers, and its prevalence decreases with age. Personality variables, such as trait aggression and trait anger, are associated with aggressive driving behaviour, but situational variables, such as anonymity and frustrating traffic conditions that impede progress, are equally important. These conditions contribute to the experience of driver stress that lowers the threshold for aggressive behaviour. Therefore strategies for reducing driver stress may also be effective in reducing aggressive driving.

- Aggression by competitors in sports events can be based on either instrumental or hostile motives. Male athletes show a greater acceptance of aggression and are also more likely to engage in aggressive behaviour on the field. Aggressive cues, such as black uniforms, have been found to increase aggressive behaviour and to affect the perception of behaviour as aggressive by third parties. The impact on spectators of observing aggression has also been widely demonstrated, and there is some evidence that it may spill over into other forms of aggression, such as domestic violence. The extent to which spectators identify with their team is an important aspect of understanding fan aggression and the dynamics of confrontations between rival groups of fans.

Tasks to do

(1) Reflect on whether you have experienced bullying at school and/or in a work setting, as defined in this chapter. Ask a male friend and a female friend about their experience of bullying.

(2) Find out whether you are prone to aggressive driving. Indicate how often you have shown the behaviours described in the top half of Box 6.1 in the last month, using a scale ranging from 0 (never) to 5 (almost every time I drove my car), and compute your personal score by averaging across the items.

(3) Watch the trailer for the film *Green Street Hooligans* (or *Green Street*, as it is called in the UK), directed by Lexi Alexander in 2005, which features violent confrontations between rival hooligan groups (www.cinemagia.ro/trailer/hooligans-huliganii-de-pe-green-street-1180). The story and screenplay were written by a former hooligan who became an author and adviser to the British Government on how to tackle football disorder.

Suggested reading

Craig, W., Harel-Fisch, Y., Fogel-Grinvald, H., Dostaler, S., Hetland, J., Simons-Morton, B., et al. (2009). A cross-national profile of bullying and victimization among adolescents in 40 countries. *International Journal of Public Health, 54*, 216–224.

Galovski, T. E., Malta, L. S., & Blanchard, E. B. (2006). *Road rage: Assessment and treatment of the angry, aggressive driver.* Washington, DC: American Psychological Association.

Russell, G. H. (2008). *Aggression in the sports world.* New York: Oxford University Press.

Willness, C. R., Steel, P., & Lee, K. (2007). A meta-analysis of the antecedents and consequences of workplace sexual harassment. *Personnel Psychology, 60*, 127–162.

Young, K. (2012). *Sport, violence and society.* London: Routledge.

7   Aggression in the family

The ideal image of family life is one of warmth, affection, and mutual respect. At the same time, it is a sad fact that aggression is widespread in family relationships. Physical, sexual, and emotional abuse of children, intimate partner violence, and elder abuse and neglect are recognised as serious social problems worldwide. In addition, many children are forced to witness aggression and violence in their family. As Gelles (1997, p. 1) stated in the opening sentence of his book, "People are more likely to be killed, physically assaulted, hit, beat up, slapped, or spanked in their own homes by other family members than anywhere else, or by anyone else, in our society." For example, of the 13 636 homicides reported in the USA in 2009, 4385 victims (32.3%) were killed by a member of their own family (Federal Bureau of Investigation, 2009). The rate for Germany, using a broader definition of family that included cohabitating partners, divorced partners, foster parents, and children, was 43.3% in the same year (Bundeskriminalamt, 2010, p. 61).

Drawing on the general definition of aggression as behaviour carried out with the intention to harm (see Chapter 1), violence in the family can be defined as any form of *behaviour that is carried out with the intention to inflict harm on a family member or a close other, for example a stepchild, residing in the same household* (Barnett et al., 2011; Gelles, 2007). Family violence, also referred to as domestic violence, is an umbrella term that covers a range of different aggressive behaviours, such as abusing children, acting violently towards a spouse, or depriving dependent elders of proper care. Despite the diversity of manifestations, the different forms of family violence share a number of characteristics that set them apart from aggression and violence outside the family context. Some of these characteristics are listed in Table 7.1.

Domestic violence typically occurs behind the closed door of the family home and is therefore difficult for outside observers to detect. This enables perpetrators to carry out abusive actions repeatedly and over extended periods of time. If and when third parties suspect or recognise aggression in a family, they are frequently unwilling to take action because they do not want to become involved in what is considered to be other people's private business. The desire to protect the integrity of the family is not limited to external observers, but is often shared by witnesses within the family, as well as by the victims themselves. Children abused by a family member may not disclose their experience to others

Table 7.1 Shared characteristics of different forms of family violence

- Shielded from outside observation
- Taking place over extended periods of time
- Exploiting and betraying a relationship of trust
- Involving a power differential between perpetrators and victims
- Including both acts of commission (active harm infliction) and acts of omission (withholding proper care)
- Reluctance by victims to disclose abuse
- Transgenerational transmission
- Victim–perpetrator cycle

because they do not want to appear as troublemakers or liars, battered women may try to cover up their partner's violent behaviour to salvage the image of an intact family, and abused elders may fear being placed in institutional care if they speak to others about the abuse. All of these concerns act against identifying the victims and reporting the perpetrators of family violence, making it difficult to estimate true prevalence rates and to make help available to those who need it. At the same time, there is growing evidence about the long-term adverse effects of family violence. Both experiencing and watching family violence have been found to increase the risk of violent behaviour in the victims and witnesses themselves, often creating a transgenerational cycle of violence that is difficult to break. In addition, childhood experiences of abuse put victims at risk of further victimisation in the course of adolescence and early adulthood.

This chapter provides an overview of the current state of knowledge on the prevalence, causes, and consequences of family violence. The study of family violence is a truly inter-disciplinary endeavour, and the present chapter cannot do justice to the extensive literature in different fields. Several recent sources provide comprehensive overviews (e.g., Barnett et al., 2011; White, Koss, & Kazdin, 2011). In keeping with the social psychological perspec-tive adopted in this volume, we shall concentrate on the psychological analysis of family violence as a form of interpersonal behaviour to understand perpetrators' actions and analyse the effects on the victims.

First, we shall look at children as targets of family violence and review research on physical and sexual abuse, psychological maltreatment, and the witnessing of intrafamilial aggression. In the second section, physical aggression between partners will be discussed. Reflecting the scope of the available evidence, the focus will be on aggression in heterosexual partnerships, but the problem of violence in gay and lesbian relationships will also be considered. The issue of *sexual violence* between intimate partners will be discussed in Chapter 8, where it will be considered as part of a more general analysis of the causes and consequences of sexual aggression beyond the domestic sphere. Finally, as we move along the chronological life course, we shall examine the increasingly pressing social problems of elder abuse and neglect.

Each of the following sections will present recent research findings on the *scale* (or prevalence) of different forms of family violence, including an examination of variables associated with an increased risk of family violence, and on the *effects* of each form of family violence on the victims, drawing on evidence from longitudinal studies wherever it is available. An important issue refers to the identification of risk factors for family violence at the individual, interpersonal, community, and societal levels. As noted consistently throughout the literature, different forms of family violence are often related and/or can be traced back to a common set of underlying causes and facilitating conditions. Therefore, we will present theoretical explanations pertaining to the different forms of family violence in the final section.

Child maltreatment

Due to their status as relatively powerless members of the family system, children are particularly at risk of becoming targets of aggressive behaviour from parents, older siblings, and other adult family members. As Tedeschi and Felson (1994, p. 287) have noted, "people who rarely if ever use coercion with others make an exception in the case of their children." Child maltreatment occurs in several different forms, as shown in Table 7.2.

In this section, research findings will be presented on three major forms of child maltreatment: physical abuse, sexual abuse, and emotional or psychological abuse. In addition, we

Table 7.2 Forms of child abuse and neglect (Based on World Health Organization, 2006, p. 10)

Physical abuse	Intentional use of physical force against a child that results in, or has a high likelihood of resulting in, harm to the child's health, survival, development, or dignity. This includes hitting, beating, kicking, shaking, biting, strangling, scalding, burning, poisoning, and suffocating
Sexual abuse	Involvement of a child in sexual activity that he or she does not fully comprehend, is unable to give informed consent to, or for which the child is not developmentally prepared, or else that violates the laws or social taboos of society. Children can be sexually abused by both adults and other children who are – by virtue of their age or stage of development – in a position of responsibility, trust, or power over the victim
Emotional/ psychological abuse	Isolated incidents or a pattern of failure over time on the part of a parent or caregiver to provide a developmentally appropriate and supportive environment. Acts in this category may have a high probability of damaging childrens' physical or mental health, or their physical, mental, spiritual, moral, or social development
Neglect	Isolated incidents or a pattern of failure over time on the part of a parent or other family member to provide for the development and well-being of the child – where the parent is in a position to do so – in one or more of the following areas: • health • education • emotional development • nutrition • shelter and safe living conditions.

shall review the growing literature on the effects of witnessing violence in the family on children's development. Child neglect, although it accounts for the majority of cases reported to child protection agencies, will not be considered in detail because it is often hard to establish to what extent it is based on the intent to harm required by our definition of aggressive behaviour.

Physical abuse

As shown in Table 7.2, physical abuse is defined as the use of physical force intended to harm the child's health, survival, development, or dignity. One form of parental behaviour meeting this definition is corporal punishment. Corporal punishment is still practised by many parents, at least occasionally, as an accepted means of disciplining children, despite the introduction of legal bans in many countries (Zolotor & Puzia, 2010). For example, a survey in the UK revealed that only about a third of parents said that they had never smacked their child, with 37% of parents of 2- to 5-year-olds and 32% of parents of 6- to 10-year-olds reporting having smacked their child in the last year. Around half of the parents agreed with the opinion that it is sometimes necessary to smack a naughty child (Department for Children, Schools, and Families, 2007).

Although corporal punishment is carried out with the intention of harming the child, researchers have suggested that the term "physical abuse" should be limited to those acts of corporal punishment that result in serious injury. As suggested by Gershoff (2002, p. 540), "behaviors that do not result in significant physical injury (e.g., spanking, slapping) are considered corporal punishment, whereas behaviors that risk injury (e.g., punching, kicking, burning) are considered physical abuse." Even milder forms of physical punishment, however, have been shown to be related to higher levels of aggressive behaviour in children. A meta-analysis of 88 studies by Gershoff (2002) found significantly higher levels of aggression, both in childhood (weighted effect size of $d = 0.36$) and in adulthood (weighted effect size of $d = 0.57$), in individuals who had been exposed to corporal punishment.[1] This analysis was restricted to studies investigating corporal punishment rather than more serious forms of physical assault. Similar associations were observed in a cross-national study including China, India, Italy, Kenya, the Philippines, and Thailand (Gershoff et al., 2010). Furthermore, a longitudinal study by Straus and Paschall (2009) revealed detrimental effects of corporal punishment on children's cognitive development.

Prevalence of physical abuse

Data on the number of children who suffer physical abuse in their family come from two sources: (a) official records from child protection or law enforcement agencies and (b) parent

---

1 Weighted effect size means that the effect size from each study is weighted by the number of participants in that study, so that studies with larger samples have a greater impact on the overall effect size estimate.

reports in surveys and research studies. The full extent of physical violence against children is hard to establish from either source because many acts of child abuse go unreported or undetected. In addition, sources differ in terms of the definitions they use, and these differences have a bearing on the number of cases that fall within the boundaries of the respective categories of maltreatment. Nevertheless, the available figures are meaningful in that they can be seen as reflecting the lower boundary of the problem. An overview of annual incidence figures for different forms of child victimisation in the USA has been provided by Finkelhor (2011), and a summary of figures from a large range of other countries can be found in the report by Krug et al. (2002) for the World Health Organization.[2]

For the USA, data on child maltreatment reported to child protection agencies are compiled annually in the National Child Abuse and Neglect Data System (NCANDS). The most recent data available for 2008 revealed that 123 599 children were victims of physical abuse and that 602 fatalities occurred as a result of physical abuse (U.S. Department of Health and Human Services, 2009). Another large study, the Fourth National Incidence Study on Child Abuse and Neglect (NIS-4) conducted during 2005 and 2006, identified 323 000 children as victims of physical abuse, corresponding to a rate of 4.4 per 1000 children (Sedlak et al., 2010). In England, recent statistics from the Department for Education (2010) showed that 6300 children had been on the Child Protection Register for physical abuse in the year ending March 2010. When fatal child maltreatment was examined, 276 cases were identified in England for the period 2005–2009, representing a rate of 0.63 cases per 100 000 children under the age of 18. Severe physical assault was the most common cause, accounting for one in four deaths (Sidebotham, Bailey, Belderson, & Brandon, 2011).

In addition to official statistics, self-reports by victims or reports by caregivers are another relevant source of information. Such data were collected by Finkelhor, Turner, Ormrod, and Hamby (2009), who found that 4.4% of their representative sample of children and adolescents under the age of 18 had experienced physical abuse, although this figure also included abuse by someone outside the family. Looking more specifically at violence within the family, a representative survey of 11- to 17-year olds conducted by the National Society for the Prevention of Cruelty to Children (NSPCC, 2011) in England revealed that 3.8% of them had suffered severe physical violence from a parent at least once. A Swedish study including a large community sample revealed that 15% of participants had been hit by a parent, but only 7% of them had disclosed the experience to the authorities (Annerbäck, Wingren, Svedin, & Gustafsson, 2010).

When compared with earlier figures, the more recent data show a decline in physical abuse rates (e.g., Annerbäck et al., 2010; Finkelhor, 2011; Sedlak et al., 2010), and there is some indication that legislation banning parents from using physical force against their children is having an effect (Zolotor & Puzia, 2010). However, the most recent figures clearly demonstrate that a substantial proportion of children remain exposed to physical

---

2 The incidence rate is the number of separate incidents recorded within a specified period of time. It differs from the prevalence rate, which is the number of individuals who have experienced at least one critical incident within a specified time period.

aggression from parents and other trusted individuals, with severe implications for their physical, mental, and emotional well-being.

Risk factors for physical abuse

In the search for variables associated with an increased likelihood of physical abuse of children, researchers have looked at characteristics of the perpetrators (such as gender and personality), social circumstances (such as poverty and poor housing), and vulnerability factors in the victim (such as disability or difficult temperament) (Wolfe, 2011). As far as the sex of the abuser is concerned, some sources suggest that women are more frequently involved in physical child abuse than men. A simple explanation for this difference could be that women are mostly responsible for childcare, especially with young children, and are therefore more likely to encounter problems in interacting with the child that may prompt physical aggression. In studies that controlled for differences due to childcare responsibility (e.g., by comparing women with men who were also the primary caretakers), the difference was reversed, with higher abuse rates being found for men (Featherstone, 1996). More recent incidence studies have found that biological mothers and fathers were represented equally as perpetrators of physical abuse of their children, but where children were abused by a step-parent or a parent's partner, men were over-represented as perpetrators by a wide margin (Sedlak et al., 2010). Single parents living with a new partner were found in some studies to be more likely to physically abuse their children, as were parents who had problems with alcohol and drug abuse (Barnett et al., 2011; Sedlak et al., 2010). With regard to socio-contextual variables, poverty and poor housing, living in a violence-prone neighbourhood, and poor social support were linked to a higher rate of physical abuse of children, creating higher levels of stress for parents (Barnett et al., 2011). Finally, among child-related factors, the risk of physical abuse was found to remain relatively stable from early childhood to adolescence, and boys and girls were equally affected by physical abuse.

However, all of the links established between child abuse and specific predictor variables suffer from the problem that the predictors are often related (e.g., poverty and lack of social support) or influenced by a third variable (e.g., single-parent status). Therefore it is difficult to precisely assess the impact of any single risk factor in the complex, multicausal pathway to abuse. In a rare prospective longitudinal study, Brown, Cohen, Johnson, and Salzinger (1998) measured a variety of demographic, familial, parenting, and child risk factors for childhood abuse in 1975, 1983, and 1986. Between 1991 and 1993 they collected information, through self-reports and official records, on whether or not abuse had occurred in the mean time. The findings reported by Brown et al. for physical child abuse are presented in Table 7.3. The odds ratios indicate the factor by which the likelihood of physical abuse increased when the respective risk factor had been present.

As Table 7.3 reveals, the highest risk of physical abuse was found for maternal sociopathy (i.e., antisocial personality disorder) which was associated with an almost fivefold increase in the probability of abuse. Among the demographic risk factors, dependency on welfare featured most prominently, with the risk of abuse being 3.74 times higher than in families not

Table 7.3 Prospective risk factors for physical child abuse. (Adapted from Brown et al., 1998, p. 1070. Copyright Elsevier Science)

	Odds ratio
Demographic risk factors	
Mother's low education	2.59
Low religious attendance	2.22
Mother's young age	3.52
Single parent	2.26
Welfare	3.74
Familial risk factors	
Early separation from mother	4.08
Mother's dissatisfaction	2.44
Mother's external locus of control	2.16
Mother's sociopathy	4.91
Poor marital quality	1.98
Mother's serious illness	2.06
Parenting risk factors	
Mother's low involvement	2.68
Father's low involvement	3.18
Father's low warmth	3.24
Child risk factors	
Pregnancy or birth complications	2.45

Note: The odds ratio indicates by how much the risk of physical abuse increases if the risk factor is present.

dependent on state welfare. Low paternal warmth was most prominent among the parenting risk factors, while complications during pregnancy and birth were the only significant risk factors associated with the child. Because the risk factors were measured several years *before* establishing the occurrence of abuse, it is possible to examine the effects of the risk factors on the likelihood of physical abuse. A recent meta-analysis by Stith et al. (2009) integrating findings from 155 studies largely confirmed the risk factors identified by Brown et al. (1998). Additional risk factors that emerged from their meta-analysis included parents' experience of childhood abuse, parents' proneness to anger and hyper-reactivity, as well as parents' anxiety and depression.

Consequences of physical abuse

Clearly, suffering bodily harm at the hands of their own parents or other family members is a potentially traumatic experience for children. Therefore it is not surprising that many victims show serious and long-term impairments with regard to their psychological well-being, their social relationships, and their social behaviour generally. Low self-esteem, anxiety, self-destructive as well as suicidal behaviour, and the inability to engage in trusting relationships with others are commonly reported effects of physical abuse in childhood (Gilbert, Widom, Browne, Fergusson, Webb, & Janson, 2009; Salzinger, Rosario, Feldman, & Ng-Mak, 2007). Longitudinal studies have also revealed significant paths from childhood physical abuse to illicit drug use and a number of drug-related problem behaviours, such as dropping out of school, in adolescence and young adulthood (Huang et al., 2011; Lansford, Miller-Johnson, Berlin, Dodge, Bates, & Pettit, 2007).

Of particular relevance in the context of this volume is the question of whether the experience of physical abuse is associated with a greater likelihood of aggressive behaviour as the child grows up. The longitudinal study by Lansford et al. (2007) found that children identified as victims of physical abuse when they were 5 years old were significantly more likely to show aggressive behaviour towards a relationship partner at the age of 21.

There is some evidence that the increased risk of future aggressive behaviour is a specific consequence of experiencing physical abuse, and is not found in victims of other forms of abuse. Prino and Peyrot (1994) analysed the effects of physical abuse in comparison with physical neglect (failure to provide food, clothing, supervision, medical care, etc.), and found that the two types of maltreatment were associated with distinctly different effects on the children's aggressive and prosocial behaviour. Whereas the physically abused children showed high levels of aggression, the neglected children showed high levels of withdrawal. Both abused and neglected children scored significantly lower on prosocial behaviour than the non-abused comparison group. The differential effects of abuse in relation to other adverse childhood experiences were also demonstrated by O'Keefe (1995) in a study of children who had witnessed violence between their parents, some of whom had also experienced physical abuse themselves. She found that physically abused children were more likely to develop aggressive behaviour problems than children who had witnessed intimate partner violence but had not been abused themselves. However, subsequent longitudinal evidence showed that witnessing family violence was related to a range of antisocial behaviours in the absence of physical abuse (Sousa et al., 2011). The meta-analysis by Kitzmann, Gaylord, Holt, and Kenny (2003) did not find significant differences across a range of negative outcomes between children who had witnessed physical abuse and children who had suffered abuse themselves. In addition, a high comorbidity was found for experiencing and witnessing family violence, with heightened effects on the likelihood of later antisocial and aggressive behaviour (Wolfe, Crooks, Lee, McIntyre-Smith, & Jaffe, 2003). Research on the effects of witnessing family violence will be discussed later in this section.

A specific aspect of the link between childhood experience of physical abuse and subsequent aggression refers to the likelihood that abused children will themselves become abusive parents. The notion of an intergenerational transmission of abuse, leading to a "cycle of violence," features prominently in the literature (Maas, Herrenkohl, & Sousa, 2008). Longitudinal studies showed that individuals who were physically abused as children were more likely to become abusive parents (Berlin, Appleyard, & Dodge, 2011; DePaul & Domenech, 2000; Merrill, Thomsen, Crouch, May, Gold, & Milner, 2005). In addition, physical abuse in adolescence was found to predict a higher risk of engaging in intimate partner violence in young adulthood (Fagan, 2005).

However, it is important to realise that the relationship is not a deterministic one in the sense of all abused children growing up to be abusive. Although the risk is higher than among non-abused children, only a minority of abused children later become abusers themselves. Childhood abuse should be seen as a risk factor that acts in combination with other adverse conditions (Milner & Crouch, 1999). Zuravin, McMillen, DePanfilis, and Risley-Curtiss (1996) addressed the question of whether certain characteristics of the abuse experience were differentially related to the likelihood of becoming an abuser. They found that abused women who had succeeded in breaking the cycle of violence had had a better attachment relationship with their primary caretakers at the time of the abuse than those who went on to abuse their own children.

Taken together, there is strong evidence from longitudinal studies that the experience of physical abuse has severe, often prolonged negative consequences for the affected children. However, evidence is only beginning to emerge on factors that account for individual differences in responding to the abuse, including the potential role of protective factors that might mitigate its adverse effects (Chu, Pineda, DePrince, & Freyd, 2011). Whereas the severity of the abuse, the presence of more than one form of abuse, and high levels of parental stress have been named as factors associated with poorer coping, good social relationships and the presence of a supportive adult were found to buffer the adverse effects of physical abuse (Collinshaw, Pickles, Messer, Rutter, Shearer, & Maughan, 2007).

Sexual abuse

Sexual abuse is commonly defined as sexual contact between a child and an adult that is carried out for the sexual stimulation of the perpetrator. Sexual abuse is tied to an unequal power relationship between victims and perpetrators, whereby the perpetrators exploit their age or maturational advantage, their position of authority over the victim, or resort to the use of force or trickery (Kendall-Tackett & Marshall, 1998, p. 48).

Beyond this broad consensus, there are substantial variations in the legal definitions of child sexual abuse across countries, and in the research definitions adopted across studies. These differences relate to the age limit that is used to define childhood, the minimum age difference between the victim and the perpetrator, and the nature of the sexual acts considered abusive. All of these aspects have implications for collecting and comparing data about the rates of victimisation and perpetration. A distinction that seems to be universally accepted in the literature is that between contact abuse, involving physical contact between victim and perpetrator (e.g. touching or penetration of the body), and non-contact abuse (e.g. exhibitionism, voyeurism, use of child pornography).

Rates of and risk factors for sexual abuse

As with physical abuse, several data sources are available for estimating the scale of child sexual abuse, each of which has its own problems. One data source consists of reports from child protection agencies. These figures only include the cases that have come to the attention of the authorities, and therefore underestimate the true rate of sexual abuse. Another source is provided by large-scale victimisation surveys, which typically yield retrospective reports of sexual abuse in childhood.

Official agency data from the National Child Abuse and Neglect Data System (NCANDS) showed 65 964 reports of sexual abuse in 2008, accounting for 9.5% of all cases in the database (U.S. Department of Health and Human Services, 2009). Data from the Fourth National Incidence Study on Child Abuse and Neglect (NIS-4) conducted in 2005 and 2006 identified 135,300 children as victims of sexual abuse, corresponding to a rate of 183 per 100 000 children (Sedlak et al., 2010). In England, 2500 children were on the Child Protection Register for sexual abuse in the year ending March 2010 (Department for Education, 2010). Based on cases reported to the police, the latest German figures for the year 2009 showed a rate of 13.8 cases per 100 000 children (Bundeskriminalamt, 2010). Like the US figures quoted above, this figure includes sexual abuse by family members, acquaintances, and strangers. Nonetheless, the data are relevant with regard to intra-familial sexual abuse, given that a large proportion of sexually abusive acts are committed by members of the child's family. It is estimated that 75–80% of sexual abusers are known to their victim, with male family members accounting for a substantial proportion of perpetrators (Kendall-Tackett & Marshall, 1998).

A second data source is provided by self-report surveys in which respondents are asked to indicate whether or not they experienced sexual abuse when they were children. The problem here is that these reports are collected retrospectively, and memories may have been affected by experiences that occurred after childhood. In addition, studies vary substantially in terms of how the critical abuse questions are phrased (Finkelhor, 1986, Appendix 1). Despite these limitations, self-report surveys are valuable because they can uncover those cases of abuse that were not reported to the authorities. Data from a representative survey of children and adolescents up to the age of 17 that was conducted in the USA by Finkelhor, Turner, Ormrod, Hamby, and Kracke (2009) found that 6.1% of those surveyed had been sexually victimised in the past year. Survey data from the National Society for the Prevention of Cruelty to Children (NSPCC, 2011) for the UK revealed that 11.8% of young adults and 4.8% of adolescents aged 11–17 years had experienced contact sexual abuse. However, these data include extra-familial abuse.

As the international evidence shows, sexual abuse must be seen as a pervasive threat in children's lives. No demographic or family characteristics have as yet been identified to rule out the possibility that a child will be or has been sexually abused (Finkelhor, 1994). A large research literature has investigated factors that increase children's risk of sexual abuse. With respect to the perpetrator, it was shown that the vast majority of sexual abusers are male. According to a variety of sources, 80–95% of child abusers are male (Browne, 1994). For example, in the NIS-4 study, 87% of all identified sexual abusers were male. Among stepparents or a parent's new partner, men accounted for 97% of the perpetrators (Sedlak et al., 2010). On the victim side, the importance of age and gender has been demonstrated consistently in the literature. The rates of sexual abuse increase with age from middle childhood to early adolescence, peaking at around the age of 12 (Barnett et al., 2011). Girls are consistently more at risk of sexual abuse than boys, as shown in recent international analyses of studies based on community and student samples (Pereda, Guilera, Forns, & Gómez-Benito, 2009a,b), particularly in cases of intra-familial abuse. Finkelhor (1986) found that about 50% of the female victims but only 20% of the male victims were abused by a member of their family. However, researchers agree that even though boys may experience sexual abuse at a lower rate than girls, the possibility of systematic under-reporting of victimisation of boys needs to be considered. Traditional gender stereotypes portray girls as more typical victims of sexual abuse, and make it harder for boys and men to identify themselves as victims, due to shame and the fear of being perceived as homosexual (Romano & De Luca, 2001).

The study by Brown et al. (1998) already mentioned in the context of physical abuse also provided data on risk factors for sexual abuse. Risk factors were identified prospectively before children were followed over a 17-year period during which sexual abuse victimisation was assessed. The risk factors that significantly predicted sexual abuse in the course of this period are listed in Table 7.4. The strongest risk factors identified in this analysis were the child being handicapped (i.e., requiring special education), maternal sociopathy, negative life events, and the presence of a stepfather in the family.

Consequences of sexual abuse

Sexual abuse is a traumatising experience that may lead to both immediate and long-term impairment in many, if not most victims. A wide range of problems were found with notable

Table 7.4 Prospective risk factors for child sexual abuse. (Adapted from Brown et al., 1998, p. 1071. Copyright Elsevier Science)

	Odds ratio
Demographic risk factors	
Mother's young age	2.26
Father's death	2.62
Familial risk factors	
Mother's sociopathy	6.27
Negative life events	4.43
Presence of a stepfather	3.32
Harsh punishment	3.22
Parenting risk factors	
Unwanted pregnancy	3.10
Child risk factors	
Child gender (female)	2.44
Handicapped child	11.79

Note: The odds ratio indicates by how much the risk of sexual abuse increases if the risk factor is present.

consistency to be more prevalent among victims of childhood sexual abuse than in non-abused comparison groups (for reviews, see Barnett et al., 2011; Gilbert et al., 2009; Hillberg, Hamilton-Giachritsis, & Dixon, 2011; Senn, Carey, & Vanable, 2008). This section will highlight some domains of psychological functioning that are adversely affected by the experience of sexual abuse. In addition, there is a large body of evidence on potential moderators of the magnitude of negative effects (e.g., nature of the abusive act, duration and frequency of the abuse, age of victim, age of offender, etc.), which is beyond the scope of the present discussion. This evidence has been well covered by Barnett et al. (2011). A conceptual framework for integrating the variety of adverse effects of childhood sexual abuse is the *traumagenic dynamics model* proposed by Finkelhor (1987). A traumagenic dynamic is an experience that distorts the child's self-concept, view of the world, and affective functioning. The four distinct dynamics identified in the model are presented in Table 7.5.

Traumatic sexualisation, betrayal, stigmatisation, and powerlessness denote four broad processes by which childhood sexual abuse undermines children's development. They provide a frame of reference for the diversity of symptoms that occur in the immediate aftermath of the abuse experience as well as over extended periods of time.

Among the initial effects of sexual abuse, which occur within the first 2 years after the abuse, higher rates of depression, loneliness, and suicidal ideation have been identified in

Table 7.5 Consequences of childhood sexual abuse: the traumagenic dynamics model (Based on Finkelhor, 1987)

Dynamic	Explanation

Traumatic sexualisation	• Undermining of the child's healthy sexual development by:
	  – rewarding the child for age-inappropriate sexual behaviour
	  – making the child use sexual behaviour as a strategy for manipulation others
	  – making the child give distorted meaning and importance to certain parts of their anatomy
	  – inducing misconceptions about sexual behaviour and sexual morality
	  – linking sexuality to feelings of anxiety and unpleasant memories

Betrayal	• Discovery that someone on whom they depended and whom they trusted wished to cause them harm • Encompassing both the perpetrator and other family members who fail to come to the child's support
Stigmatisation	• Negative messages about the self communicated to the child around the experience. These messages may come from the abuser and those who become aware of the abuse, but can also occur in the form of self-stigmatisation as victims realise that sexual abuse is regarded as deviant • Stigmatisation varies according to gender, with female victims more likely to be stigmatised as seductive and male victims more likely to be stigmatised as homosexual
Powerlessness	• Experience of the child's wishes repeatedly being ignored and overruled by the abuser • Experience of being unable to escape the unwanted sexual attention and avoid harm and injury

victim samples. Many victims show the symptomatology of post-traumatic stress disorder (PTSD) as an immediate reaction and/or as a long-term consequence of the abuse. Indeed, Kendall-Tackett, Williams, and Finkelhor (1993) concluded that PTSD is one of two core symptoms which seem to be more common in victims of sexual abuse than in other clinical groups and which carry particular diagnostic relevance (the second core symptom being sexualised behaviour; see below). As a category of the *Diagnostic and Statistical Manual of Mental Disorders, Fourth Edition (DSM-IV)* (American Psychiatric Association, 1994), PTSD is characterised by the persistent re-experiencing of the traumatic event in the form of flashbacks and distressing dreams, a persistent state of emotional numbing and avoidance of trauma-related stimuli, and persistent symptoms of physiological arousal, such as inability to sleep and concentration problems.

Behavioural problems, such as sleep disturbances, hyperactivity, and aggression, are also common as initial responses to the trauma of sexual abuse. Victims often attempt to dissociate themselves from the experience of abuse and deny feelings of shame and anger – a coping strategy that makes them more susceptible to the development of dissociative personality disorders. In addition, lowered self-esteem and feelings of worthlessness are common reactions to the experience of sexual abuse.

Evidence from many sources suggests that the adverse effects of childhood sexual abuse frequently extend into adolescence and adulthood (Barnett et al., 2011, p. 226). As noted above, high rates of PTSD have been found in survivors a long time after the abuse itself. The same is true for higher rates of depression, anxiety, and poor self-esteem among adults who were abused as children. In addition, a variety of mental health problems have been linked to the experience of sexual abuse in childhood (e.g., Cutajar, Mullen, Ogloff, Thomas, Wells, & Spataro, 2010). Following a sample of female victims of intrafamilial sexual abuse over a period of 23 years, Trickett, Noll, and Putnam (2011) found a wide range of problems in the areas of mental health, cognitive development, and sexuality compared with a non-victimised comparison group. These authors studied mother-child dyads and established that children born to abused mothers scored twice as high on a cumulative index of developmental risk factors, such as premature birth and involvement of child protection agencies, compared with children born to non-abused mothers.

Childhood sexual abuse and sexuality in adolescence and adulthood

Given that sexual abuse involves an infringement of the victim's sexual integrity and self-determination, sexual development is particularly likely to be negatively affected by the experience of abuse. In Finkelhor's (1987) traumagenic dynamics model of the effect of childhood sexual abuse, "traumatic sexualisation" is identified as a key mechanism leading from sexual abuse to specific sexuality-related symptoms and adjustment problems. Although many of the symptoms found in relation to sexual abuse can also be observed as a result of other forms of childhood traumatisation, sexualised behaviour appears to be a specific consequence of sexual abuse. Its prevalence is significantly higher among survivors of sexual abuse than in other clinical groups (Kendall-Tackett et al., 1993).

Sexuality-related problems manifest themselves in different ways depending on the victim's stage of development. In childhood, evidence of inappropriate sexual behaviour has consistently been found at a higher rate among abuse victims compared with either non-abused children or children affected by other types of clinically relevant experiences. Indeed the majority of the behavioural symptoms listed by Barnett et al. (2011, pp. 222–223) for school-age survivors of sexual abuse are sexuality related. Their list includes sexualised behaviour, sexual preoccupation, precocious sexual knowledge, seductive behaviour, excessive masturbation, sex play with others, sexual language, genital exposure, and the sexual victimisation of others.

In adolescence, preoccupation with sexuality remains characteristic of abuse survivors. Several sources suggest that childhood sexual abuse is associated with early sexualisation, manifested in a lower age at first sexual intercourse and a higher number of sexual partners (e.g., Chandy, Blum, & Resnick, 1996; Miller, Monson, & Norton, 1995). Kendall-Tackett et al. (1993) summarised findings from two studies in which 38% of adolescents who had been abused as children were classified as promiscuous (Cahill, Llewelyn, & Pearson, 1991). A meta-analysis by Noll, Shenk, and Putnam (2009) revealed that victims of sexual assault had a significantly increased rate of adolescent pregnancy.

In late adolescence and adulthood, problems in initiating and maintaining intimate relationships are consistently reported in the literature for victims of child sexual abuse. These problems are also reflected in higher divorce rates among abuse victims compared with non-abused samples. In addition to the difficulty in establishing close emotional bonds, many survivors show problems of sexual adjustment (Feiring, Simon, & Cleland, 2009). Victims of sexual abuse have been found to be more sexually anxious, to experience more sexual guilt, to have lower sexual self-esteem, and to be more likely to seek sexual therapy (Browne & Finkelhor, 1986). Furthermore, there is evidence of a link between sexual abuse in childhood and high-risk sexual behaviour, such as having multiple partners, having unprotected sex, and engaging in prostitution (Arriola, Louden, Doldren, & Fortenberry, 2005).

The majority of studies focused on female victims of childhood sexual abuse. Studies that included male victims suggest that boys and girls are similarly affected by the experience of sexual abuse (Romano & De Luca, 2001). However, two potential effects of the abuse experience specific to male victims have been considered in the literature. The first is the possibility that childhood experience of sexual abuse may be linked to the development of a homosexual orientation, mediated by the victim's uncertainty about his sexual identity. However, evidence to support this link is limited (Browne & Finkelhor, 1986; Beitchman, Zucker, Hood, daCosta, & Akman, 1991). Secondly, a recent meta-analysis found that male abuse victims were at higher risk of becoming perpetrators of sexual aggression, indicating a victim-to-perpetrator cycle (Seto & Lalumière, 2010).

A particularly worrying consequence of childhood sexual abuse is *revictimisation* – that is, an increased risk of sexual victimisation in later developmental stages. Many individual studies and several reviews have shown that both male and female victims of child sexual abuse had an increased risk of sexual victimisation in adolescence and adulthood (Aosved, Long, & Voller, 2011; Krahé, Scheinberger-Olwig, & Schütze, 2001; Messman-Moore,

Walsh, & DiLillo, 2010). To explain the pathway from child sexual abuse to later sexual victimisation, a number of studies have shown that victims of sexual abuse develop sexual behaviour patterns that put them at increased risk of sexual victimisation, such as a having more casual sexual contacts, having more sexual partners, and habitually drinking alcohol in the context of sexual encounters (e.g., Fargo, 2009; Krahé, Scheinberger-Olwig, Waizenhöfer, & Kolpin, 1999; Testa, Hoffman, & Livingston, 2010). In addition, heavy drinking and drug use, which have been identified as common problems in victims of sexual abuse, contribute to the risk of revictimisation, given the strong links between alcohol use and sexual victimisation (Testa & Livingston, 2009; see also Chapter 8). Thus evidence from child sex abuse research and from the literature on sexual victimisation in adolescence and adulthood converges on the conclusion that the experience of childhood sexual abuse puts both male and female victims at greater risk of later sexual victimisation. Furthermore, there is evidence that rape prevention programmes directed at young adults are largely ineffective in women with a history of child sexual abuse (Blackwell, Lynn, Vanderhoff, & Gidycz, 2004).

Psychological maltreatment

In the literature, several terms are used to denote parental behaviours that lead to the impairment of the child's psychological well-being. Mattaini, McGowan, and Williams (1996, p. 225) refer to *emotional maltreatment* as consisting of "acts that result in the impairment of a child's emotional or mental health, such as verbal abuse and belittlement, symbolic acts designed to terrorize a child, and lack of nurturance or emotional availability by caregivers." O'Hagan (1995, p. 456) adopted a more restricted definition of *emotional abuse* as referring to "the sustained, repetitive, inappropriate emotional response to the child's experience of emotion, and its accompanying expressive behaviour." He distinguished emotional abuse from *psychological abuse*, consisting of behaviours that impair the development of mental faculties. For the purposes of the present chapter, we shall use the broad term *psychological maltreatment*, which combines both cognitive and emotional impairments and denotes "the ensemble of abusive psychological acts committed by the parents and also encompasses all acts of omission that result in emotional, cognitive, or educational neglect" (Fortin & Chamberland, 1995, p. 276). According to Barnett et al. (2011, pp. 107–108), psychological maltreatment can take a variety of forms: rejecting, degrading, terrorising, isolating, missocialising (i.e., permitting or encouraging antisocial or delinquent behaviour), exploiting (e.g., using a child for pornography or prostitution), ignoring the child, or restricting the child's physical movements.

Prevalence of and risk factors for psychological maltreatment

In the NCANDS database, psychological maltreatment accounted for 7.6% of all cases of abuse and neglect in 2008, corresponding to a total of 52,532 victimised children (U.S. Department of Health and Human Services, 2009). Data from the Fourth National Incidence Study on Child Abuse and Neglect (NIS-4) conducted in 2005 and 2006 identified 148,500 children as victims of emotional abuse, corresponding to a rate of 2 per 1000 children (Sedlak et al., 2010). In England, 12 300 children were on the Child Protection Register for emotional abuse in the year ending in March 2010 (Department for Education, 2010). However, experts agree that under-reporting to official agencies is a particular problem with regard to psychological maltreatment for two main reasons: (a) it is more difficult for observers to decide what exactly constitutes psychological maltreatment as compared, for instance, with physical abuse, and (b) psychological maltreatment is less likely to produce visible effects. Statistics based on cases reported to official agencies therefore represent the lower boundaries of the problem.

Higher rates of psychological maltreatment were found in surveys that elicited self-reports from parents about different forms of psychological maltreatment of their children (e.g., insulting, swearing, refusing to talk). Vissing, Straus, Gelles, and Harrop (1991) showed that 63% of parents in a representative national sample reported engaging in one of these behaviours when interacting with their child over the previous 12 months. Straus et al. (1998) collected data based on the *Parent-Child Conflict Tactics Scales*, which address five forms of psychological aggression: yelling, threatening to spank the child, cursing, name-calling, and threatening to send the child away. They found that 85% of parents showed one of these forms of psychological aggression towards their child in the 12 months prior to the survey. Christensen (1999) provided data based on health visitors' reports from a Danish sample of 28 000 children, which showed that 6% of children aged between 1 and 2 years, 13% of children aged between 2 and 3 years, and 17% of children aged between 3 and 4 years had been subjected to emotional abuse, defined as constant exposure to verbal insults, confinement, threats, and rejections.

As with physical abuse, the question arises as to whether there are any characteristics of the children that would make them more vulnerable to psychological maltreatment. Due to the relatively low number of cases officially reported and substantiated, evidence on this issue is limited. However, there are indications that the risk of psychological maltreatment increases with the child's age and is slightly higher for girls than for boys (Miller-Perrin & Perrin, 2007).

Consequences of psychological maltreatment

As one might expect, one area in which psychological maltreatment has been shown to have detrimental effects on children is the formation of trusting relationships with others and the development of social skills. In addition, children exposed to psychological maltreatment have been found to show deficits in both their intellectual and affective development. Barnett et al. (2011, pp. 110–111) listed a number of effects of psychological maltreatment on infants and children, as presented in Table 7.6.

In addition to its immediate effects during childhood, psychological maltreatment can lead to lasting psychological problems that extend into adulthood. Victims of childhood psychological abuse have been found to have lower self-esteem and to exhibit higher levels of anxiety and depression as well as higher levels of psychopathology in adulthood (e.g.,

Table 7.6 Effects of psychological maltreatment observed in infants and children. (Reprinted with permission from Barnett et al., 2011, pp. 110–111. Copyright Sage Publications)

Interpersonal maladjustment/social incompetence	• Insecure attachment to caregiver • Antisocial functioning • Aggression • Sexual maladjustment • Dependency • Low empathy • Social phobia	• Difficulties making and retaining friends • Difficulties with peers
Intellectual deficits/ learning problems	• Academic problems • Lower educational achievement • Deficits in cognitive ability • Impaired moral reasoning	• Deficits in problem solving and intelligence • Lack of creativity
Affective–behavioural problems *Interpersonal thought problems*	• Aggression, hostility, anger • Disruptive classroom behaviour • Noncompliant behaviour • Lack of impulse control • Self-abusive behaviour • Anxiety • Low self-esteem	• Shame and guilt • Conduct disorder • Hyperactivity and distractability • Pessimism and negativity • Dependence on adults for help, support, and nurturance
Physical health problems	• Hypertension • Metabolic syndrome	• Inflammatory disease

Finzi-Dottan & Karu, 2006; Spertus, Yehuda, Wong, Halligan, & Seremetis, 2003). A study by Gross and Keller (1992) even found psychological maltreatment to be a stronger predictor of depression and low self-esteem than physical abuse. Additional evidence suggests that childhood psychological maltreatment may be a risk factor for subsequent victimisation, in particular sexual victimisation. In the study by Krahé et al. (1999), women who reported that they had felt worthless in their families as children were significantly more likely to experience sexual victimisation in adolescence and early adulthood. Parallel revictimisation patterns as a function of emotional maltreatment in childhood were found for male victims of same-sex and heterosexual sexual aggression (Krahé et al., 2001). Finally, several studies found that victims of psychological maltreatment in childhood were at higher risk of becoming abusive partners and parents (Taft, Schumm, Marshall, Panuzio, & Holtzworth-Munroe, 2008; Zurbriggen, Gobin, & Freyd, 2010).

Witnessing violence in the family

It has been increasingly recognised that witnessing violence between parents and other family members has adverse effects on children even if they are not directly targeted themselves. For example, 9.8% of children in the representative survey by Finkelhor et al. (2009) reported having witnessed a family assault in the past year. In a study of children identified as at risk for child abuse, 8–25% of mothers from four different sites reported that their child had witnessed physical aggression between them and their partner. When their children were asked, 27–46% stated that they had seen grown-ups hit each other in their home (Litrownik, Newton, Hunter, English, & Everson, 2003). Although experts agree that a large number of children are exposed to violence between their parents, establishing the exact scale of the problem is hampered by differences in the way that exposure to family violence has been defined and measured (for a methodological critique, see Knutson, Lawrence, Taber, Bank, & DeGarmo, 2009).

There is evidence from many studies that witnessing family violence has adverse effects on children's mental health and psychological well-being, and the effects of exposure to interparental violence are similar to those of experiencing abuse directed at the child him- or herself (see the summary of problems by Barnett et al., 2011, p. 115). Adverse effects of being in a violent family environment can occur from birth, and there is evidence of social, emotional, and cognitive deficits, health problems, and post-traumatic stress from infancy and early childhood onwards (Lewis-O'Connor, Sharps, Humphreys, Gary, & Campbell, 2006). Recent meta-analyses have integrated the evidence into overall estimates of negative outcomes (Kitzmann et al., 2003; Wolfe et al., 2003). The meta-analysis by Evans, Davies, and DiLillo (2008) included 60 studies that examined the effects of witnessing violence between intimate partners on their children's internalising (e.g., anxiety, depression) and externalising (e.g., aggression, delinquency) problem behaviour, as well as traumatisation. Significant effect sizes of $d = 0.48$ and $d = 0.47$ were found for the difference between children who witnessed violence and those who did not on the measures of internalising and externalising behaviour problems, respectively. In addition, children exposed to violence were significantly more likely to develop trauma symptoms, with a strong effect size of $d = 1.54$ (although only a small number of studies assessed these negative outcomes). The sex of the child made no difference to the effect of witnessing family violence on internalising problems, but boys were significantly more likely than girls to develop externalising problems. A subsequent meta-analysis by Chan and Yeung (2009) replicated the significant associations of witnessing family violence with internalising and externalising problems as well as PTSD, although with somewhat lower effect sizes. In their sample of studies, they found that boys and girls were equally affected.

Witnessing violence between parents has also been linked to an increased risk of aggressive behaviour towards a partner in adolescence and adulthood. A study by Milletich, Kelley, Doane, and Pearson (2010) found that young adults who had witnessed violence between their parents in childhood were more likely to behave aggressively towards a dating partner. Furthermore, Turcotte-Seabury (2010) showed that the link between exposure to interparental violence in childhood and aggressive behaviour towards a partner was mediated by deficiencies in anger management. In a prospective longitudinal study, Smith, Ireland, Park, Elwyn, and Thornberry (2011) followed participants from adolescence (14–18 years) through young adulthood (21–23 years) into adulthood (29–31 years). Parents were also included in the study, and provided reports of intimate partner violence in their own relationship at Time 1. On the basis of these reports, researchers were able to categorise participants into those with and without a history of exposure to intimate partner violence, before assessing their involvement in intimate partner violence. As predicted, participants who had witnessed violence in their parents' relationship were significantly more likely to engage in aggression towards an intimate partner, both in young adulthood and in adulthood.

The research reviewed in this section demonstrates that children are indeed vulnerable to experiencing violence within the family. Incidence rates for physical and sexual abuse, psychological maltreatment, and exposure to violence between parents show that many children experience violence in their family environment. Moreover, it is clear that these adverse experiences inflicted by people whom they trust and depend on, and which occur in the very sphere that should provide protection and security, can cause lasting harm to victims' physical, intellectual, emotional, and social development. Although the different forms of child maltreatment have been considered individually in this section, they often co-occur, leaving many children poly-victimised (Finkelhor, 2011). As noted earlier, individuals exposed to family violence in childhood have a higher risk of showing aggressive behaviour in their intimate relationships and in interactions with their own children. In addition, they are at higher risk for victimisation in close relationships later in life.

Intimate partner violence

In this section we shall look at the problem of physical aggression between partners in intimate relationships. Sexual aggression between intimate partners will be examined in Chapter 8, which is devoted to a more general discussion of sexual aggression beyond the family setting. For the purposes of the present discussion, *intimate partner violence* is defined as the perpetration or threat of an act of physical violence, by one partner towards the other, in the context of an intimate relationship. This definition is open with regard to the sex of the perpetrator and the victim, and includes both heterosexual and same-sex relationships. Intimate partner violence is recognised as a serious problem worldwide, even though the prevalence rates vary enormously not only between but also within countries (for reviews of the international evidence, see Archer, 2006; Krahé, Bieneck, & Möller, 2005; Krug et al., 2002).

Prevalence of intimate partner violence

Three main data sources provide information on the scale of intimate partner violence: (a) figures from representative crime victimisation surveys, (b) crime statistics showing the proportion of violent crime committed towards an intimate partner, and (c) findings from research studies, mostly using the Conflict Tactics Scales (CTS) to elicit reports of victimisation by, as well as perpetration of, physical aggression towards an intimate partner (Straus, 1979; Straus et al., 1996). These sources portray very different pictures of the involvement of men and women as victims and perpetrators of intimate partner violence, and have fuelled an intense debate about the extent and direction of gender differences with respect to this form of aggressive behaviour (Perilla, Lippy, Rosales, & Serrata, 2011).

Victimisation surveys identify women as more vulnerable to intimate partner violence than men. Figure 7.1 presents data on the incidence of three forms of intimate partner violence, namely simple assault, aggravated assault, and robbery, from the National Crime Victimization

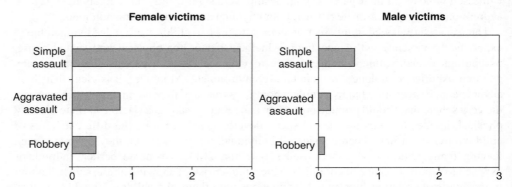

Figure 7.1 Average annual rate of non-fatal intimate partner victimisation in the USA, by type of
crime, for the period 2001–2005. Rate per 1000 individuals aged 12 years or older. (From
the National Crime Victimization Survey, http://bjs.ojp.usdoj.gov/content/pub/pdf/ipvus.
pdf).
Simple assault: an attack without a weapon resulting either in no injury, minor injury (for
example, bruises, black eyes, cuts) or in undetermined injury requiring less than 2 days of
hospitalisation. Also includes attempted assault without weapon.
Aggravated assault: an attack or attempted attack with a weapon, regardless of whether or
not an injury occurred and attack without a weapon when serious injury results.
Robbery: completed or attempted theft, directly from a person, of property or cash by
force or threat of force, with or without a weapon, and with or without injury.

Survey (NCVS) in the USA for the period 2001–2005. The figures show a clear gender
imbalance, with substantially higher victimisation rates for women than for men.

Women are also more likely than men to suffer injuries as a result of the partner's
aggressive actions (e.g., Rennison & Welchans, 2000), to the extent that they are more likely
to be killed by an intimate partner. The crime statistics in the Uniform Crime Reports reveal
that of the 750 homicide victims killed by a spouse in 2009, 609 were female, and of the 601
homicides that involved boyfriends or girlfriends, 472 victims were female (Uniform Crime
Reports, 2009, Expanded Homicide Data, Table 10).

For England and Wales, findings from the British Crime Survey (BCS) 2010/11 revealed
that 16.1% of the women and 6.9% of the men surveyed had experienced physical force by
an intimate partner at least once since the age of 16 (Chaplin, Flatley, & Smith, 2011). For
incidents in the last 12 months, 2.2% of women and 1.3% of men reported the use of physical
force by an intimate partner. A report by the Crown Prosecution Service (2010) quoting the
number of individuals prosecuted for intimate partner violence in England and Wales in
2009–2010 revealed that 93% of the defendants were male and 85% of the victims were
female.

Studies using the Conflict Tactics Scales (CTS) (Straus, 1979) or the revised Conflict
Tactics Scales (CTS2) (Straus et al., 1996) yield a different picture. In this measure,
participants are presented with a list of minor and severe acts of physical aggression and

asked to indicate whether and how many times they have shown the behaviour in question towards an intimate partner. Parallel items are included to measure experiences of victimisation by an intimate partner. In addition, a scale measuring injuries suffered by or inflicted on a partner is included. The items of the *physical assault scale* and the *injury scale* of the CTS2 are shown in Box 7.1.

The physical assault scale is subdivided into five items that measure what is considered to be minor physical assault (Items 1 to 5) and seven items that measure severe physical assault (Items 6 to 12). In addition to the items presented in Box 7.1, the CTS2 contains three further scales, measuring *psychological aggression* (defined as communications intended to cause psychological pain to a partner, such as insults or verbal abuse), *sexual aggression*, and *negotiation* as a non-aggressive form of conflict resolution in relationships.

A large body of evidence has shown that on the CTS women feature as much as or even more than men as perpetrators of physical aggression towards a partner. A review including 62 empirical studies found that up to two-thirds of women had used some form of physical aggression towards a heterosexual partner (Williams, Ghandour, & Kub, 2008). In a German study of young adults, all gender differences that were found on the items of the CTS2 were in the direction of women scoring higher than men on the perpetration of physical aggression by a partner, and men scoring higher than women on victimisation by physical aggression from a partner (Krahé & Berger, 2005). In a meta-analysis including 82 studies using either the original CTS or the revised CTS2 presented in Box 7.1, Archer (2000) found that women were slightly more likely than men to show physical aggression towards a partner ($d = -0.05$). A subsequent meta-analysis by Archer (2002) on the individual items of the CTS also revealed significant gender differences on seven out of nine items, but in different directions. Women were more likely than men to throw something at their partner, to slap, kick, bite, or punch them, or to hit them with an object. On the other hand, men were more likely than women to push, grab or shove, beat up, choke, or strangle a partner. No differences were found for using a knife or gun, and the higher rate of women who had threatened to use a knife or gun disappeared once outliers (studies with extreme values) were removed.

At the same time, there is little doubt that men's aggression towards an intimate partner is more dangerous. The effect sizes obtained by Archer (2000) for the injury subscale revealed that men were significantly more likely to inflict injury on their partner, with an effect size of $d = 0.15$. This finding may explain why men feature more prominently as perpetrators of interpersonal violence in crime statistics. If their actions are more likely to lead to injuries, there is an increased likelihood that they will be reported to the police and find their way into official records.

Unsurprisingly, the claim derived from the CTS studies that women are at least as involved as men in the perpetration of intimate partner violence has proved highly controversial. Not only is it at odds with data from crime statistics and victimisation surveys, it also contradicts notions of femininity and masculinity that are firmly ingrained in gender stereotypes (Rudman & Glick, 2008). Critics have argued that the over-representation of women as perpetrators of intimate partner violence in studies using the CTS is distorted because this instrument records acts of violence without considering their context. In particular, it does

BOX 7.1 Items of the Physical Assault Scale and the Injury Scale of the Revised Conflict Tactics Scales (CTS2). (Adapted from Straus et al., 1996, Appendix Part 3. Copyright Sage Publications)

Instruction: No matter how well a couple gets along, there are times when they disagree, get annoyed with the other person, want different things from each other, or just have spats or fights because they are in a bad mood, are tired, or for some other reason. Couples also have many different ways to settle their differences. This is a list of things that might happen when you have differences. Please indicate how many times you did each of the things in the past year.

How often did this happen:

1	2	3	4	5	6	B	N
Once in the past year	Twice in the past year	3–5 times in the past year	6–10 times in the past year	11–20 times in the past year	More than 20 times in the past year	Not in the past year, but happened before	This has never happened

	1	2	3	4	5	6	B	N
1. I threw something at my partner that could hurt.	☐	☐	☐	☐	☐	☐	☐	☐
2. I twisted my partner's arm or hair.	☐	☐	☐	☐	☐	☐	☐	☐
3. I pushed or shoved my partner.	☐	☐	☐	☐	☐	☐	☐	☐
4. I grabbed my partner.	☐	☐	☐	☐	☐	☐	☐	☐
5. I slapped my partner.	☐	☐	☐	☐	☐	☐	☐	☐
6. I used a knife or gun on my partner.	☐	☐	☐	☐	☐	☐	☐	☐
7. I punched or hit my partner with something that could hurt.	☐	☐	☐	☐	☐	☐	☐	☐
8. I choked my partner.	☐	☐	☐	☐	☐	☐	☐	☐
9. I slammed my partner against a wall.	☐	☐	☐	☐	☐	☐	☐	☐
10. I beat up my partner.	☐	☐	☐	☐	☐	☐	☐	☐
11. I burned or scalded my partner on purpose.	☐	☐	☐	☐	☐	☐	☐	☐
12. I kicked my partner.	☐	☐	☐	☐	☐	☐	☐	☐
13. My partner had a sprain, bruise or small cut because of a fight with me.	☐	☐	☐	☐	☐	☐	☐	☐
14. My partner still felt physical pain the next day because of a fight we had.	☐	☐	☐	☐	☐	☐	☐	☐
15. My partner passed out from being hit on the head in a fight with me.	☐	☐	☐	☐	☐	☐	☐	☐
16. My partner went to a doctor because of a fight with me.	☐	☐	☐	☐	☐	☐	☐	☐
17. My partner needed to see a doctor because of a fight with me, but didn't.	☐	☐	☐	☐	☐	☐	☐	☐
18. My partner had a broken bone from a fight with me.	☐	☐	☐	☐	☐	☐	☐	☐

Note. Items 1–5 describe behaviours classified by Straus et al. as *"minor physical assault,"* Items 6–12 represent *"severe physical assault,"* and Items 13–18 form the *"injury"* scale.

not consider whether the behaviour shown is an act of unprovoked aggression or a response to a previous attack, so that an act of self-defence by a woman would be counted in the same way as the initial assault by her male partner.

It is now widely acknowledged by researchers that intimate partner violence is not a unitary phenomenon, but comprises different forms, contexts, and underlying dynamics. Kelly and Johnson (2008) have distinguished three types of intimate partner violence, which differ in terms of the involvement of men and women as perpetrators and victims. The first type is called *coercive controlling violence*, involving emotionally abusive intimidation and physical violence. It is a stable relationship feature and is more often shown by men than by women. The second type, called *violent resistance*, occurs in response to a coercive controlling partner, and is more often shown by women than by men. The third and most common type is called *situational couple violence*, arising *ad hoc* from everyday conflict situations rather than being a stable pattern in a relationship. This form of intimate violence is shown equally by men and women. If progress is to be made in understanding the role of gender in violence between heterosexual partners, greater attention needs to be paid to the specific forms and contexts in which assaults on intimate partners take place (Frieze, 2000).

The problem of intimate partner violence in same-sex relationships has received far less attention. Some studies have demonstrated substantial levels of intimate partner violence among gay and lesbian couples (e.g., Bartholomew, Regan, White, & Oram, 2008; West, 2002). Comparing physical violence in same-sex relationship with findings from studies of heterosexual couples, the available evidence suggests that the prevalence rates are similar (for a review, see Messinger, 2011). Evidence comparing same-sex and heterosexual couples within the same study has yielded mixed results. Blosnich and Bossarte (2009) analysed data from a representative sample in the USA and found no differences between same-sex and heterosexual partner constellations in the rates of physical violence. By contrast, Rhodes, McCoy, Wilkin, and Wolfson (2009) found that gay men had a higher probability of being victimised by an intimate partner than did heterosexual men. Analysing data from a representative victimisation survey, the National Violence Against Women Survey, Messinger (2011) found that rates of victimisation of women were higher in same-sex relationships (25%) than in heterosexual relationships (21%). Men were substantially more often victimised by another man in a homosexual relationship (33%) than by a woman in a heterosexual relationship (7.5%). This means that victimisation rates in same-sex relationships were higher than those in heterosexual relationships for both men and women, and that lesbian women were somewhat more physically aggressive towards their partners than were heterosexual men.

Overall, it has become clear that physical aggression is a major problem in intimate relationships, although the question of the gender distribution of aggressors and victims has not been resolved conclusively. The controversy surrounding the use of the Conflict Tactics Scales as a measure of intimate partner violence has highlighted the need to consider not only the aggressive acts per se but also the context in which they occur, such as differences in physical strength, related to differences in the potential to cause serious harm, and the proactive or reactive nature of the aggressive behaviour. In terms of the scale of intimate partner violence, a large body of evidence has been accumulated in recent years from a wide range of countries around the world. In fact, one could say that the study of intimate partner violence is the only area of aggression research for which empirical studies are available from countries that are not typically represented in mainstream psychological research (Krahé & Berger, 2005; Krug et al., 2002).

Risk factors for intimate partner violence

In the search for risk factors for violence towards intimate partners, individual, situational, and relationship variables have been examined to find out (a) who is susceptible to behaving violently towards an intimate partner, (b) what situational conditions increase the likelihood of intimate partner violence, and (c) what characterises relationships that are at risk for intimate partner violence (for a review, see Aldarondo & Castro-Fernandez, 2011).

Among individual-level variables, particular attention has been paid to the socio-demographic and personal characteristics of men who abuse their female partners. A meta-analysis of risk factors for physical partner abuse by Stith, Smith, Penn, Ward, and Tritt (2004) showed that younger, less educated, and less affluent men were more likely to abuse their partners. However, personality variables were more closely associated with the risk of partner abuse in men than these socio-demographic characteristics. Endorsement of the traditional male gender role and attitudes condoning violence, dispositional proneness to anger, and attachment difficulties, particularly jealousy, were found to increase the likelihood that men would become abusive towards an intimate partner (Stith et al., 2004, p. 88). The body of evidence looking at risk factors for women's use of physical violence towards an intimate partner is smaller, but has found largely similar associations (Barnett et al., 2011; Hamberger & Holtzworth-Munroe, 2009). In addition, as noted earlier in this chapter, childhood exposure to family violence, whether as a target or as a witness, increases the risk of engaging in violence in later relationships both for men and for women (Edwards, Desai, Gidycz, & VanWynsberghe, 2009; Smith, Ireland et al., 2011).

In addition to considering individual risk factors for intimate partner violence, several authors have proposed distinctions between different types of batterers characterised by different risk factors and patterns of aggressive behaviour. An influential typology was developed by Holtzworth-Munroe and Stuart (1994), who distinguished between three types of male batterers on the basis of three dimensions: severity of violence, generality of violence beyond the intimate relationship, and evidence of psychopathology.

(1) The first group consists of *family-only* batterers, whose violent behaviour is limited to members of their own family, who do not show signs of psychopathological disorders, and whose violence is generally less severe and does not extend to sexual and/or psychological abuse. This group is estimated to account for about 50% of male batterers.
(2) *Dysphoric/borderline* batterers constitute the second group. Their violence is rooted in emotional instability and psychiatric disorders. Their aggression is mainly directed towards their family, but extra-familial violence and criminal behaviour occur occasionally. About 25% of men who abuse their partners are estimated to fall into this group.

(3) *Generally violent/antisocial* batterers, who show violent behaviour both within and outside their family, and who engage in sexual and psychological aggression in addition to physical violence, form the third group. Their general tendency to engage in violent behaviour means that they are likely to have a criminal record. In addition, alcohol and substance abuse are frequently found in this group, which is estimated to account for 25% of male batterers.

A fourth group was later identified and labelled *low-level antisocial* men characterised by moderate levels on the three dimensions of severity, generality, and psychopathology (Holtzworth-Munroe, Meehan, Herron, Rehman, & Stuart, 2000). The differentiation between these types of abusive men has been supported by several studies. A longitudinal study by Holtzworth-Munroe, Meehan, Herron, Rehman, and Stuart (2003) concluded that men who were assigned to one of these types showed behaviour consistent with the typology over a 3-year period. For example, men classified as family-only batterers at the beginning of the study continued to limit any aggressive behaviour they manifested to the family context, and showed less severe aggression than the borderline/dysphoric and generally aggressive types. Typologies such as this show that men who abuse their partners are not a homogeneous group. They come to relationships with different personal characteristics and biographical experiences, and show predictable differences in the severity and generality of their aggressive behaviour.

Among the *situational variables* linked to an increased risk of violence between partners, alcohol consumption plays a major role. As we saw in Chapter 4, there is consistent evidence that aggressive behaviour becomes more likely when people are under the influence of alcohol. Alcohol exerts a disinhibiting effect by undermining people's awareness of the anti-normative character of aggression that would prevent them from lashing out if they were sober. In addition, alcohol reduces individuals' capacity for information processing, making them more responsive to salient situational cues, such as provocations, without engaging in a careful analysis of the other person's motives or intentions. Although alcohol is not necessarily a cause of intimate partner violence, it is likely to lower the threshold for aggressive behaviour in conflict situations with a partner.

Foran and O'Leary (2008) conducted a meta-analysis of 50 studies linking alcohol use and intimate partner violence. For men's violence towards a female partner, they found a significant effect size of $r = 0.23$. For women's violence towards a male partner, the effect size was also significant, but smaller with $r = 0.14$. In combination, these findings show a small to moderate association between drinking and perpetration of intimate partner violence for both men and women. Parallel findings for a range of drugs other than alcohol were obtained in the meta-analysis by Moore et al. (2008), who found that the association with intimate partner violence was strongest for cocaine.

Further evidence suggests that physical violence when the perpetrator, the victim, or both are drunk tends to be more severe and more likely to lead to serious harm. In a study by Graham, Bernards, Wilsnack, and Gmel (2011), in which data were collected from 13 countries around the world, participants were asked to think about the most severe incident of violence from a partner (if any) that they had experienced in the last 2 years. They were then asked to indicate the severity of the incident and to report whether they, the aggressor, or both had been drinking when the incident occurred. As predicted, incidents in which one or both partners had been drinking were rated as more severe by both men and women across all participating countries.

Finally, there are specific *relationship variables* that have been found to affect the likelihood of physical aggression between partners. Low levels of marital satisfaction were identified as a risk factor for physical partner violence in both men and women in the meta-analysis by Stith et al. (2004). Furthermore, abuse is more likely to occur in relationships based on patriarchal attitudes and role divisions in which the man dominates the relationship and has power over his female partner physically, materially, and in terms of decision making. This is particularly true for cultures that link male dominance to the concept of honour, in which a man's social status and reputation are defined by the extent to which he has control over his female partner (Vandello & Cohen, 2003).

There is also evidence that the legal status of the relationship is linked to rates of intimate partner violence. Survey data have revealed higher prevalence rates of partner abuse in couples who are cohabiting than in legally married couples, although this difference has been shown to decline in recent years as cohabitation has become more common (Brownridge, 2008).

Consequences of physical partner violence

Intimate partner violence is costly for societies as a whole. A report by the World Health Organization describes the economic burden of different forms of partner abuse (Waters et al., 2004). For example, Miller, Cohen, and Rossman (1993) estimated the costs of rape in the USA in terms of medical treatment as well as impairment of mental health, productivity, and quality of life to be 47000 US$ per case. In a survey of over 3000 women in the USA, Rivara et al. (2007) found that annual healthcare costs were 19% higher among victims of intimate partner violence than among non-victimised women. Based on a victimisation rate of 44% in their sample, they estimated that for every 100000 women in the healthcare system, excess healthcare costs of 19.3 million US$ are incurred each year as a result of intimate partner violence.

This section focuses on the psychological impact of partner abuse on the victim's mental health and well-being at the individual level. Intimate partner violence leads to a variety of physical consequences, including serious injuries, a higher incidence of stress-related physical illnesses, and economic effects, such as poverty resulting from leaving an abusive relationship or due to employment instability (Coker, Williams, Follingstad, & Jordan, 2011). Many victims of physical partner violence are traumatised by the experience, especially as severe forms of partner abuse tend to persist over time. A meta-analysis by Golding (1999) revealed that the mean rate of PTSD among female victims of physical partner abuse was 63%, the mean rate of depression was 47%, and the mean rate of suicidality was 17%. These figures were substantially higher than the prevalence rates for the respective symptomatologies in comparison samples from the general population of women.

Evidence on male victims of intimate partner violence is more limited and less clear. The review by Randle and Graham (2011) identified several studies that showed higher rates of PTSD in victimised compared with non-victimised men, but a longitudinal study by Ehrensaft, Moffitt, and Caspi (2006) failed to corroborate this conclusion. For depression and suicidal ideation the evidence was more conclusive, showing higher rates among victimised compared with non-victimised men, paralleling the findings for female victims. Even fewer data are currently available on the effects of intimate partner abuse in same-sex relationships, but what little evidence there is suggests similar effects to those in heterosexual couples (Randle & Graham, 2011).

Overall, there is overwhelming evidence that partner abuse may lead to long-term psychological distress and impairment. To ameliorate these adverse effects, a critical first step is to stop the continuation of abuse. Becoming trapped in abusive relationships because of psychological mechanisms such as denial, self-blame, and adaptation to violence is a common fate of victims of partner abuse. Of those who make an attempt to break away and seek refuge in shelters for battered women, about a third eventually return to their abusive partners, and some studies suggest even higher figures (Barnett et al., 2011). Thus, empowering women to gain independence from abusive partners, both psychologically and in terms of managing their everyday lives, must be a key objective of intervention work with victims of partner abuse. Interventions to reduce violent behaviour towards partners will be discussed in Chapter 11.

Elder abuse

When people think or hear about family violence, images of abused children or battered partners come to mind as prototypical examples of this type of aggression. Another form of family violence is less prominent in public awareness as well as in research: the abuse of elderly people. As the average life expectancy continues to rise throughout the western world, a growing number of people are becoming dependent on the care of younger relatives, most commonly their children, or of professional caregivers. Looking after dependent elders can be a highly demanding and strenuous task, sometimes leading to abusive behaviour of the caregivers towards the elderly person in their care. In this section we shall summarise some of the evidence on elder abuse in the family that has accumulated since the problem first attracted research attention about 20 years ago.

Forms and prevalence of elder abuse

In order to study elder abuse, the two terms involved need to be properly defined. This obvious requirement turns out to be problematic with respect to the term "elder." Unlike children, partners, or siblings, who can be identified with relative ease, there is no clear-cut criterion as to when a person becomes an elder. As recent summaries have revealed, studies vary widely with regard to the age of entry into the category of elders (e.g., De Donder et al., 2011), ranging from 55 years or older to 75 years or older across different European studies. It is obvious that variations in defining the age range for elder abuse make it more difficult to establish prevalence rates and to compare them across different studies. As far as the second term, "abuse," is concerned, definitions are more consistent. In general, five main forms of elder abuse are distinguished in the literature (e.g., Krug et al., 2002).

(1) *Physical abuse* involves behaviour carried out with the intention of causing physical pain or injury to an elderly person, such as battering, restraining, or bruising.
(2) *Sexual abuse* denotes non-consensual sexual contact and sexual attention of any kind, from unwanted sexual touching to sexual intercourse.
(3) *Psychological* or *emotional abuse* is defined as inflicting mental pain, anguish, or distress through verbal and non-verbal behaviour, such as name calling, verbal threats, or infantilising (e.g., by using baby talk).
(4) *Financial abuse* involves the illegal and improper exploitation of the elderly person's property or assets. Since many elderly people are unable to handle their own financial affairs for physical or mental reasons, they have to trust their caregivers to do this for them.
(5) *Neglect* refers to the withholding of adequate care to meet a dependent elder's physical, medical, and psychological needs. Whereas the previous forms of elder abuse referred to acts of *commission*, neglect represents a form of elder abuse through *omission*. Refusal or failure to meet the elderly person's physical needs (e.g., regular provision of food, personal hygiene), their need for respect, or their need for financial support are forms of abuse that can be just as damaging to the victim as the active commission of abusive acts.

Prevalence rates are even more difficult to establish for elder abuse than for the other forms of family violence considered so far. One reason is that victims are usually confined to the domestic setting, and have limited contact with people in the outside world who might be alerted to their situation. In addition, the very fact that they are dependent on the care provided by the abuser often makes victims reluctant to disclose the abuse to a third party. Furthermore, elders abused by their children may be embarrassed or even feel guilty about having brought up children who turn against their parents in this way. Therefore elder abuse is regarded as a "hidden" form of family violence, and established prevalence rates reflect the lower limits rather than the full scale of the problem.

Recent figures for the USA are available from the National Elder Mistreatment Study, conducted in 2008, which included almost 6000 participants aged 60 or over (Acierno et al., 2010). In this sample, 11.4% of the participants reported at least one form of abuse in the past year, with 4.6% reporting emotional abuse, 1.6% reporting physical abuse, 0.6% reporting sexual abuse, and 5.1% reporting neglect. Although the figures do not refer specifically to family members as perpetrators, additional data asking for the perpetrator of the most recent incident revealed that the majority of abusive acts were committed by a family member. For physical abuse, for example, 57% of the most recent incidents were committed by the partner or spouse, and a further 19% by children or other relatives (Arcierno, Hernandez-Tejada, Muzzy, & Steve, 2009, p. 45).

Data from ten European countries compiled by De Donder et al. (2011) revealed overall incidence rates for the last 12 months in the range 5.6–29.3%. For physical abuse, incidence rates were in the range of 0.1–6.2%. Again, these figures do not differentiate between perpetrators within and outside the family, and the studies vary not only by country but also in terms of the age range included. A summary of 49 studies by Cooper, Selwood, and Livingston (2008) found an overall incidence rate for physical elder abuse of 5.9% in the last 12 months.

Risk factors for elder abuse

As with other forms of family violence, a central task for researchers has been to establish vulnerability factors that increase the risk of elder abuse victimisation, and to identify characteristics associated with an increased likelihood of becoming a perpetrator of elder abuse. In terms of vulnerability factors for victimisation, the review by Amstadter, Cisler, McCauley, Hernandez, Muzzy, and Acierno (2011) concluded that victims of elder abuse are more likely to be female, to be in poor health, and to be divorced or separated rather than married or widowed. On the perpetrator side, a number of risk factors were found to increase the likelihood of abusing a dependent elder, as described below.

Gender

Men were found to be over-represented among abusers, especially in relation to the perpetration of physical abuse. This finding is due at least in part to the fact that men who abuse their elderly spouses account for a relatively large proportion of elder abuse cases (Biggs, Manthorpe, Tinker, Doyle, & Erens, 2009).

Psychopathology

Abusers were found to be more likely to have a history of mental illness and psychiatric hospitalisation (Pillemer & Suitor, 1988).

Substance abuse

Anetzberger, Korbin, and Austin (1994), for example, found that compared with a non-abusive comparison group, individuals who physically abused elderly parents in their care reported higher alcohol consumption and were more likely to have a drinking problem.

Dependency of the abuser on the victim

Abusers may need the support of their victims both financially and emotionally (Pillemer & Suitor, 1988). It has been suggested that abuse may take place in response to the sense of powerlessness experienced by grown-up children who are dependent on their parents (Gelles, 1997).

Transgenerational transmission of violent behaviour

The victim-to-perpetrator cycle identified with regard to both child abuse and intimate partner violence has also been proposed as an explanation for elder abuse. Evidence, albeit limited, suggests that elder abuse is more frequently committed by individuals who were themselves victims of family violence (e.g., Steinmetz, 1978).

External stress

Life stress that originates outside the family context has been linked to elder abuse. Unemployment and financial difficulties were identified as more prevalent external stressors in abusive than non-abusive carers (e.g., Bendik, 1992).

However, it is important to bear in mind that these individual risk factors may be present in many caregiving relationships, only a small number of which will become abusive. How different risk factors add up or interact to produce abusive behaviour, and whether there are protective factors which buffer the negative impact of risk factors has yet to be investigated.

The consequences of elder abuse

The adverse effects of abuse on elderly victims refer to different aspects of physical, psychological, and social functioning. Compared with non-abused older persons, victims of abuse have been found to have higher levels of depression, to show symptoms of learned helplessness, and to experience feelings of shame and guilt about the behaviour of their children or partner (Amstadter et al., 2011). These feelings are closely related to denial, which is a way for victims to cope with the trauma of abuse. A review of the literature on the effects of elder abuse on victims by Anetzberger (1997) identified a large number of physical, psychological, behavioural, and social effects of elder abuse. Her summary is presented in Table 7.7.

Although the list is not exhaustive, it demonstrates that victims of elder abuse experience serious impairments of their physical and mental health and their social functioning. In addition, Table 7.7 shows that the consequences of elder abuse are very similar to the negative effects of other forms of family violence. Similar parallels can be observed with respect to the precipitating factors for abuse. Therefore many of the causes and mechanisms proposed to explain one form of family violence can also be applied to other

Table 7.7 Consequences of elder abuse (Adapted from Anetzberger, 1997, p. 505. Copyright Sage Publications).

Psychological effects	*Behavioural effects*
• Denial	• Mental confusion
• Resignation	• Expression of anger
• Fear, anxiety	• Suicidal actions
• Hopelessness, depression	• Helplessness
• Embarrassment, self-blame	• Impaired coping
• Phobias	
• Dissociation	
Physical effects	*Social effects*
• Sleep disturbances	• Fewer contacts
• Eating problems	• Violent actions
• Headaches	• Dependence
	• Withdrawal

manifestations, and several overarching explanatory concepts have been discussed in the literature. In the next section we shall discuss the main explanations for family violence in its various facets.

Explaining aggression in the family

As noted at the beginning of this chapter, the different forms of family violence share a number of common characteristics (see Table 7.1). These include:

(1) an imbalance of power between perpetrator and victim, supported by economic factors, which enables the dominant person to enforce his or her needs through the use of aggression and get away with this
(2) childhood experiences of family violence by the abuser, promoting the use of violence as a strategy for conflict resolution that leads to the transmission of aggressive behaviour from one generation to the next
(3) both short-term and enduring behaviour patterns of the victim, such as difficult behaviour of the child or dependent elder.

Accordingly, a common core of risk factors for the different forms of family violence has emerged (Tolan, Gorman-Smith, & Henry, 2006). In this section we shall review the explanations for family violence that may help us to understand how these factors operate and interact in leading to aggression in the family. Explanations of family violence can be assigned to one of four levels: (a) the macro-level of the society, or social group, in which family violence occurs, (b) the level of family functioning, (c) the interpersonal level of interaction patterns between family members, and (d) the individual level of the perpetrator. A summary of variables that affect the risk of family violence at each level is presented in

Table 7.8 A multilevel approach to understanding domestic violence (Based on Barnett et al., 2011; Gelles, 2007; Wolfe, 2011)

Level of operation	Core assumption: domestic violence arising out of . . .	Explanatory constructs
Macro level	. . . cultural norms, values, and practices in a society	• Patriarchal gender relationships, with men dominating women • Cultural acceptance of physical punishment
Family level	. . . specific constellations and living conditions in a family	• Economic stress • Crowded housing • Lack of communication skills • Transgenerational transmission
Interpersonal level	. . . relationships and behavioural patterns between individual family members	• Low level of relationship satisfaction • Difficult behaviour by victim (e.g., child, elder) • Unfavourable cost–benefit analysis • Insecure attachment style
Individual level	. . . personality, biographical experience, learning history of perpetrators . . . vulnerability factors of victims	• History of victimisation • Abuser psychopathology • Insecure attachment style • Social learning processes reinforcing aggressive behaviour • Misperceptions and deficits in information processing

Table 7.8.

Macro-level explanations

Theories in this group look for the causes of family violence in the social structure and value systems of a society or a particular social group. The extent to which violence is culturally accepted in a society is thought to affect the prevalence of violence against family members. For example, if there is a general consensus that spanking is an accepted and effective way of disciplining children, the use of corporal punishment is seen as a legitimate child-rearing practice. Another social norm that lowers the threshold for family violence is the view that how parents treat their children, or husbands treat their wives, is nothing but their own business and that it is inappropriate for outside observers to intervene in family conflicts. In addition, the patriarchal structure of societies has been identified as promoting family violence, not least in feminist accounts of men's violence against female partners (Marin & Russo, 1999).

Patriarchal societies are characterised by a clear-cut power differential between men and women, with men dominating women in most areas of public and private life. Male dominance is linked to a positive evaluation of male assertiveness and aggressiveness. In these societies, social institutions are dominated by men, making it hard for women to be acknowledged as victims of male violence, to secure help, and to enforce the legal prosecution of perpetrators. Although linking violence in the family to power differentials in society would seem plausible, there is limited empirical evidence from psychology to support this notion (Eckhardt, 2011). An exception is the work by Vandello and Cohen (2008), who examined differences in the acceptability of physical partner abuse in cultures that differ in their endorsement of a "culture of honour" (see also Chapter 4). In honour cultures, it is important for men to uphold an image of toughness, which includes their ability to make sure that their female partner behaves in a socially accepted way based on prevailing standards of female decency. If women are seen as violating the honour code by undermining men's authority or reputation, men's use of physical violence can serve to restore their threatened manhood. In addition, indirect support for the idea of patriarchal power structures as a structural variable that promotes family violence comes from research linking masculinity to family violence at the individual level (Moore & Stuart, 2005). Theories focusing on male dominance over women are limited in that they cannot explain aggressive behaviour by women in the context of family relationships, nor can they explain violence in same-sex relationships.

Macro-level explanations postulate that there are certain societal conditions under which domestic violence can emerge and develop. They do not address the issue of why domestic violence occurs in some families but not others, and is performed by some individuals and not others.

Family-level explanations

At this level, explanations look at the family as the unit of analysis and try to identify structural features of family functioning that increase the likelihood of domestic aggression in addition to the characteristics of the individuals involved. Intra-familial stress, resulting from limited economic resources and environmental stressors, such as crowded housing conditions and poor access to childcare or other social services, was proposed as a risk factor for family violence. Moreover, it was argued that members of a family may learn aggressive behaviour patterns through mutual reinforcement and imitation. If abusers learn that their violent actions lead to the intended consequences and victims learn that the violence can be stopped by complying with the perpetrator's demands, interaction routines develop that reinforce aggressive behaviour. In abusive families, children learn that aggressive behaviour is rewarded in that the abusers usually achieve their objectives, and they may incorporate aggression into their own patterns of behaviour (Gelles, 2007). Aggression replaces more constructive forms of conflict resolution through negotiation, and precludes the development of appropriate communication skills.

These processes of learning through observation and reinforcement can explain the transgenerational transmission of violence documented in the literature (Cui, Durtschi, Donnellan, Lorenz, & Conger, 2010). Children who experience or witness violence at home are at greater risk of showing aggressive behaviour themselves in subsequent relationships with partners and children, because they adhere to their acquired patterns of conflict resolution by means of aggressive behaviour.

Interpersonal-level explanations

Explanations at this level consider the nature of the interactions between individual family members as precipitators of family violence. Interpersonal stress resulting from relationship dissatisfaction, and reciprocal provocation (e.g. between a difficult child and a punitive parent) has been proposed as a risk factor for domestic violence. From the point of view of *social exchange theory*, satisfaction with interpersonal relationships within the family is based on a cost-benefit analysis in which family members weigh their investments in the relationship (e.g., emotional commitment, time, money) against the perceived benefits (e.g., emotional rewards, material goods, social status) (Gelles, 2007). If the investments are perceived as outweighing the benefits (e.g., when expectations about the partner are not fulfilled or when children place high demands on their parents' attention and care), the theory predicts that dissatisfaction will be experienced and alternative relationships will be explored. Given that marital relationships are not easily terminated and parent-child relationships are even harder if not impossible to dissolve, aggression has been explained as a response to the dissatisfaction that results from relationships in which the costs are seen as exceeding the benefits.

Individual-level explanations

Finally, research has explored the causes of family violence at the level of the individual perpetrator. One line of explanation has focused on psychopathology to explain abusive behaviour. From this perspective, individuals who suffer from personality disorders or mental illness have a higher risk of abusing family members, particularly because they have problems controlling hostile feelings and aggressive impulses (Eckhardt, 2011). In a similar vein, personality characteristics such as low self-esteem, insecurity, and feelings of vulnerability have been proposed to explain why individuals behave aggressively towards family members, who are typically less powerful than themselves (for a discussion of the link between self-esteem and aggression, see Chapter 4). Finally, socio-cognitive explanations have stressed the importance of cognitions in understanding domestic violence. In particular, misperceptions and misguided expectations have been shown to play a role in both child abuse and partner abuse. For example, misinformed expectations about children's age-normative behaviour and abilities at different ages can lead parents to perceive their child's behaviour as unreasonable and inadequate, resulting in excessive discipline. In child sexual abuse, the abuser may misperceive the child's lack of resistance as an indication of consent. Misperceptions have also been shown to play a role in intimate partner violence. For example, Neighbors et al. (2010) found that physically abusive men significantly overestimated the rate of physical partner abuse in the population at large relative to the rates obtained in representative surveys. The General Aggression Model (GAM) introduced in Chapter 2 has recently been applied to individual-level processes that give rise to family violence. The GAM conceptualises person variables, such as attitudes condoning violence, and situational influences, such alcohol and drug use, as input variables. They elicit cognitive processes, such as hostile attributions, affective processes, such as anger, and arousal, undermining self-control, that pave the way for aggressive behaviour towards a partner or family member (DeWall et al., 2011).

The explanations discussed in this section have addressed different variables associated with an increased likelihood of family violence. None of them can aspire nor indeed claims to predict precisely who will show abusive behaviour and who will not, and what social and situational conditions precipitate family violence. Not every man who grows up in a patriarchal society turns into an abuser, nor does everyone who is exposed to external stress or aggressive role models within the family. Macro-level factors, such as cultural norms, are relatively stable and permanent. They provide the background against which aggressive behaviour is carried out. Family-level, interpersonal, and individual factors, such as distressed family relationships, external stress, and also victim-produced stress, have a more immediate impact on the unfolding of aggressive interactions. For example, children who are going through the temper-tantrum stage or elders who are losing control over their vital faculties and need full-time care may create tensions within the family and frustration in the individual carer, both increasing the likelihood of aggressive behaviour. It is the combination and interaction of these different risk factors that eventually precipitates aggressive behaviour against family members.

Summary

- This chapter has reviewed the evidence on the prevalence, risk factors, and consequences of major forms of family violence: child abuse in the form of physical, sexual, and emotional maltreatment and witnessing family violence, violence towards intimate partners, and abuse of elders in the family.
- Because domestic violence is shielded from outside detection and there is a general reluctance to intervene in family affairs, under-reporting is a particular problem when trying to establish the scale of violence in the family. Nonetheless, the available sources (official reports, survey data, and clinical studies) have presented substantial prevalence rates for each form of domestic violence.
- A controversial issue refers to gender differences in family violence perpetration, particularly with regard to intimate partner violence. Whereas surveys and crime statistics suggest that men are more likely to show physical aggression against a female partner, data based on the Conflict Tactics Scales indicate that women are just as involved as perpetrators of intimate partner violence, if not more so. However, there is consistent evidence of a greater risk of injury to female victims. The distinction between different types of intimate partner violence, in the form of situational couple violence, controlling coercive violence, and violent resistance, may help to create a more differentiated picture of the perpetration of intimate partner violence by men and women.

- Explanations of family violence discuss causes located at the societal level (e.g., acceptance of corporal punishment), at the level of the family system (e.g., economic stress), at the interpersonal level between family members (e.g., poor communication skills of family members, unrealistic expectations of parents about their children's behaviour), and at the level of the individual perpetrator (e.g., psychopathology, childhood experience of family violence).
- The effects of family violence on the victims are similar across different types of abuse. Post-traumatic stress disorder, depressive symptoms, and impairment of physical health are commonly identified in child and adult victims of family violence. In addition, there is consistent evidence that early exposure to violence in the family makes individuals more vulnerable to victimisation in later life, and also puts them at greater risk of perpetrating domestic violence in their own family.

Tasks to do

(1) Look up the legal definition of child sexual abuse and the age of consent in your country, and find out what the latest figures are for physical and sexual abuse of children in your national crime statistics.

(2) Ask ten male and ten female students from your year to complete (anonymously) the items of the CTS2 shown in Box 7.1. Do not ask for any additional information except respondent gender. Then collect the responses in a sealed envelope and calculate the mean score on each item for the male and female participants, using the scores from 1 to 6. Important: Do not reveal the classification of the items as representing minor and severe physical assault to your participants. Can you replicate the finding that (a) women score higher on the physical assault scale of the CTS2 and (b) men score higher on the injury scale?

(3) Find out what resources are available in your community for victims of intimate partner violence.

Suggested reading

Archer, J. (2000). Sex differences in aggression between heterosexual partners: A meta-analytic review. *Psychological Bulletin, 126*, 651–680.

Barnett, O. W., Miller-Perrin, C. L., & Perrin, R. D. (2011). *Family violence across the lifespan* (3rd edn). Thousand Oaks, CA: Sage.

White, J. W., Koss, M. P., & Kazdin, A. E. (Eds) (2011). *Violence against women and children. Volume 1. Mapping the terrain.* Washington, DC : American Psychological Association.

8   Sexual aggression

Beyond the sexual abuse of children, discussed in the previous chapter, a large and interdisciplinary body of research has been devoted to the problem of sexual aggression in adolescence and adulthood. The majority of this work addressed sexual aggression by male perpetrators against female victims, but there is growing recognition that sexual aggression is also committed by women towards men, as well as in same-sex relationships. In this chapter we shall look at the scale of sexual aggression in different victim-perpetrator constellations, present current explanations of the causes of sexual aggression, ask what factors may increase a person's vulnerability to sexual victimisation, and review evidence on the effects of sexual aggression on victims' mental and physical health. The focus will be on sexual aggression in face-to-face interactions, but it should be noted that recent research has also investigated sexual harassment over the Internet as a new form of sexual aggression (Mitchell, Wolak, & Finkelhor, 2007).

Definitions and scale of sexual aggression

As a summary term, "sexual aggression" refers to a range of sexual activities, such as sexual intercourse, oral sex, kissing, and sexual touching imposed on another person against her or his will. It involves a range of coercive strategies, such as threat or use of physical force, exploitation of the victim's inability to resist, or verbal pressure. Sexual aggression also includes unwanted sexual attention in the form of sexual harassment, stalking, and obscene phone calls (Post, Biroscak, & Barboza, 2011; for a discussion of sexual harassment in the context of workplace bullying, see Chapter 6). A comprehensive definition of sexual violence is given in the "World Report on Violence and Health" commissioned by the World Health Organization, which states:

> Sexual violence is defined as: any sexual act, attempt to obtain a sexual act, unwanted sexual comments or advances, or acts to traffic, or otherwise directed, against a person's sexuality using coercion, by any person regardless of their relationship to the victim, in any setting, including but not limited to home and work. Coercion can cover a whole spectrum of degrees of force. Apart from physical force, it may involve psychological

intimidation, blackmail or other threats – for instance, the threat of physical harm, of being dismissed from a job or of not obtaining a job that is sought. It may also occur when the person aggressed is unable to give consent – for instance, while drunk, drugged, asleep or mentally incapable of understanding the situation.

(Krug et al., 2002, p. 149)

Beyond this broad definition, specifying exactly what behaviours qualify as sexual aggression and how to distinguish between different forms of sexual aggression is not a straightforward task, and there are at least three frameworks in which definitions of sexual aggression can be located. The first is the *legal framework* that distinguishes between different forms of sexual violence in accordance with legal provisions. For example, rape is defined in many jurisdictions in terms of obtaining sexual acts involving the penetration of the body through the threat or use of physical force, whereas sexual acts that do not involve penetration of the body qualify as sexual assault or coercion. The second framework is provided by *research definitions* that guide conceptual and empirical work on the extent of and risk factors for sexual aggression. Research definitions often include forms of sexual aggression that are not considered to be criminal offences, such as verbal pressure and psychological manipulation. The third framework is the socially shared, *common-sense definition* of sexual aggression that is informed by stereotypical notions of "real rape" and plays a role in social responses to victims of sexual assault.

In contrast to intimate partner violence (see Chapter 7), it is undisputed that sexual violence is gender-asymmetrical, with men featuring primarily as perpetrators and women as victims of sexual aggression. As will be shown, this gender imbalance is reflected both in rapes recorded by the police and in large-scale victimisation surveys. Nonetheless, the problem of women's sexual aggression against male victims, although it is far less common, entails similarly adverse consequences for the victims. We shall review the evidence on women's sexual aggression against men in a separate section later in this chapter.

Legal definitions of rape and crime statistics

Legal definitions vary with regard to the type of sexual acts and coercive strategies that constitute rape, and in distinguishing between other forms of sexual aggression that are considered to be criminal offences. In this section, exemplary evidence will be provided for the USA, England and Wales, and Germany to show how rape is defined as a criminal offence and represented in annual crime statistics recorded by the police. Crime statistics yield incidence rates of the number of cases reported annually to the law enforcement agencies.

For the purposes of nationwide statistics on recorded crime, the Federal Bureau of Investigation (FBI) in the USA defines rape as "the carnal knowledge of a female forcibly and against her will. Attempts or assaults to commit rape by force or threat of force are also included; however, statutory rape (without force) and other sex offenses are excluded" (Federal Bureau of Investigation, 2011a). In 2009, 88 097 cases of rape according to this definition were recorded in the database, amounting to a rate of 56.6 per 100 000 female inhabitants. It is noteworthy that the FBI definition excludes male rape. Most states in the USA have adopted legislation in which rape is defined more broadly in terms of oral, anal, or vaginal penetration through threat, force, or intentional incapacitation, and that allows for both women and men to be victims (and perpetrators) of sexual violence (Koss & Cook, 1998). The restriction of legal definitions to extramarital acts of sexual aggression was removed in all US states in 1993, thereby instituting "marital rape" as a criminal offence (Bergen, 1996).

In England and Wales, rape is legally defined in the Sexual Offences Act of 2003 as intentional vaginal, anal, or oral penetration with the penis when the other person does not consent to the penetration and the actor does not reasonably believe that the other person consents. This definition of rape covers both marital rape and rape of male victims, but is limited to male perpetrators. Official crime statistics showed that in the year from April 2010 to March 2011, a total of 14 624 cases of rape of a female were recorded by the police in England and Wales. In the same period, 1310 cases of rape of a male were recorded (Chaplin et al., 2011).

In Germany, rape was legally defined until 1997 as the use or threat of violence against a woman to force her into extramarital sexual intercourse. In a revision that came into effect in 1997, a broader definition was adopted that removed the restriction to female victims and non-marital intercourse. The current legal definition in Article 177 of the Criminal Code includes the use or threat of violence or the exploitation of the victim's helpless state to force another *person* into sexual activities. Forced sexual activities qualify as rape if the act involves penetration of the victim's body, which is no longer restricted to vaginal intercourse. Figures for 2009 show that 7314 cases of rape were reported to the police, representing a rate of 9 per 100 000 inhabitants. Of the victims, 96.1% were female and 3.9% were male, of the perpetrators, 99% were male (Bundeskriminalamt, 2010).

Comparing annual incidence rates across countries is difficult because of variations in the legal definitions of rape and other sexual offences. This variability is reflected, for example, in the recent fourth edition of the *European Sourcebook of Crime and Criminal Justice Statistics*, which includes data from 37 countries. Whereas 19 countries had converging definitions of rape, the definitions in the remaining countries differed in various respects. Annual incidence rates of police-recorded rapes ranged from less than 1 in 100 000 inhabitants in Armenia to 11 per 100 000 in France (Aebi et al., 2010, p. 72). Part of this variation is due to differences in the scope of legal definitions.

Research definitions and victimisation surveys

Definitions of rape and sexual assault used as a basis for large-scale victimisation surveys and research studies on sexual aggression also show considerable variability, which makes it difficult to compare findings across different studies. For example, Wiehe and Richards (1995, p. 5) defined rape as "any sexual activity that one experiences without giving consent." In contrast, Koss et al. (2007), in their revised version of the Sexual Experiences Survey

(SES), distinguished between completed and attempted rape, defined as penetrative sexual acts obtained through the use of threat of force or the deliberate incapacitation of the victim, and other forms of sexual aggression, such as sexual coercion, defined as sexual penetration through the use of verbal pressure or manipulation, and sexual contact (i.e., non-penetrative sexual acts) (see also Chapter 1, Table 1.4, for the items of the SES). As demonstrated by Spitzberg (1999), estimates of the scale of sexual aggression and victimisation are strongly influenced by differences in the breadth or narrowness of the definitions on which the questions are based.

It is generally agreed that crime statistics reflect only a small minority of cases of sexual aggression. To come closer to estimating the true scale, representative surveys have been conducted to elicit reports of sexual aggression from the perspective of victims and/or perpetrators irrespective of whether or not they were reported to the police (for a review of female victimisation studies, see Post et al., 2011; for a review of male victimisation studies, see Peterson, Voller, Polusny, & Murdoch, 2011). By comparing the rates of sexual aggression and victimisation detected in these studies with official crime statistics, it is possible to gauge the number of cases of rape and other forms of sexual aggression that go unreported.

Surveys of community samples

Regular crime victimisation surveys are conducted in the USA and the UK. These surveys question representative samples from the general population about experiences of criminal victimisation, including rape and sexual assault, in the last 12 months. In the USA, the National Crime Victimization Survey (NCVS) provides estimates of criminal victimisation in the general population from the age of 12, including both heterosexual and homosexual rape. For 2006, the survey yielded an estimate of 110 incidents of rape or sexual assault per 100 000 individuals, of which 41% had been reported to the police (Rand & Catalano, 2007). Another representative survey of 3000 women from the general public addressed the prevalence of forcible rape, incapacitated rape (sexual penetration when the victim had consumed drugs or alcohol), and drug- or alcohol-facilitated rape (involving the deliberate administration of alcohol or drugs to the victim) (Kilpatrick, Resnick, Ruggiero, Conoscenti, & McCauley, 2007). On the basis of national census data, lifetime and 1-year prevalence rates obtained in the study were extrapolated to the female population as a whole. The findings indicated that 18% of women in the USA would experience one or more forms of rape during their lifetime, of which no more than 16% would be reported to the police. More than one million women (0.9%) would have been raped in the 12 months prior to the survey. In the subgroup of female college students, the lifetime prevalence was lower, at 11.5%, as would be expected because of their younger age, but past-year prevalence rates of 5.1% were substantially higher than in the general population sample. The prevalence rates for the different types of rape in the general population and among college women are presented in Figure 8.1.

For incapacitated and drug-related rape, college women are at greater risk of victimisation than the general population of women, in terms of both lifetime and past-year prevalence.

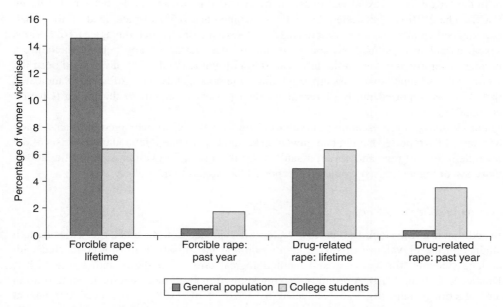

Figure 8.1 Estimated lifetime and past-year prevalence rates of rape in the general population of women and in female college students. Drug-related rape includes both incapacitated rape (in which the victim voluntarily consumed alcohol or drugs) and drug-facilitated rape (in which the perpetrator administered alcohol or drugs to the victim). (Adapted from Kilpatrick et al., 2007, p. 3).

The same is true for the past-year rate of forcible rape. For lifetime forcible rate, the figures are higher for the general population sample that included older women with a longer lifetime prevalence period and therefore a higher probability of victimisation. The fact that college women had lower lifetime rates of forcible rape but not drug-related rape may be explained at least partly by the more prominent role of alcohol and drug use as a lifestyle variable among college-age women (Abbey, Zawacki, Buck, Clinton, & McAuslan, 2004).

Including both genders, the National Intimate Partner and Sexual Violence Survey (NISVS), which surveyed 9086 women and 7421 men, revealed that 18.3% of women and 1.4% of men had been raped at some time in their life, in terms of experiencing completed forced penetration, attempted forced penetration, or alcohol- or drug-facilitated completed penetration (Black et al., 2011). More than 80% of the victims had been raped by someone they knew as an intimate partner or an acquaintance. More than 40% of the female victims experienced their first rape before the age of 18. It should be noted that the figures include a substantial proportion of rapes that occurred when the victims were below the age of consent (for example, 25% of male victims and 12% of female victims experienced their first rape before the age of 10), so these cases count as child sexual abuse.

In the UK, data on sexual victimisation are provided by the annual British Crime Survey (BCS). The 2010 BCS revealed that 5.1% of women and 0.5% of men aged 16 to 59 had experienced an attempted or completed serious sexual assault since the age of 16. Serious sexual assault was defined as rape or assault by penetration by any person, including a partner or family member. In the last year, 0.6% of women and 0.1% of men had been the victim of a serious sexual assault (including attempts). Only 11% of victims indicated that they had reported the most recent incident of sexual assault to the police (Chaplin et al., 2011).

For Germany, a representative survey of more than 10 000 women aged between 16 and 85 years, 13% reported having had unwanted sexual experiences, defined on the basis of the legal definition of rape and sexual assault, since the age of 16 (Müller & Schröttle, 2004). Only 8% of the victimised women had reported the assault to the police.

Surveys of college students

In addition to crime victimisation surveys, there is evidence from several large-scale research studies on the prevalence of sexual aggression and victimisation, mostly conducted with college students (for a review and methodological critique of these studies, see Fisher, Daigle, & Cullen, 2010). A ground-breaking study on sexual aggression and victimisation among college students was conducted by Koss et al. (1987), who used the Sexual Experiences Survey (SES) to elicit women's self-reports of sexual victimisation and men's self-reports of perpetration. They found that more than 50% of female students reported some form of sexual victimisation since the age of 14. More than 25% of the male students indicated that they had coerced a woman to engage in sexual acts at some point after the age of 14. The distribution of prevalence rates for different forms of sexual victimisation and aggression obtained by Koss et al. (1987) is shown in Table 8.1.

It is important to note that although multiple responses were possible in the survey, the figures in Table 8.1 are based on each respondent's most serious form of sexual victimisation or aggression, as defined by the authors, regardless of whether they reported less severe forms as well. Thus they present a conservative picture of the scale of sexual aggression. Koss et al. also asked women about sexual victimisation and men about perpetration in the 6 months prior to the survey, and found a rate of 83 per 1000 women for rape victimisation and a rate of 34 per 1000 men for the perpetration of rape.

In a later study by Fisher, Cullen, and Turner (2000), 4446 female students were surveyed about their experience of rape, defined as penetration of the body by force or threat of harm, since the beginning of the academic year (covering an average incidence period of 7 months). In total, 1.7 % of the respondents reported experiences amounting to completed rape, and a further 1.1% reported attempted rape. These figures are equivalent to a victimisation rate of 27.7 rapes or attempted rapes per 1000 female students. Fewer than 5% of the completed rapes were reported to the police. In addition, 24.1 per 100 000 college women reported completed sexual coercion, defined as unwanted sexual intercourse or sexual contact through the use of verbal pressure or threats of non-physical punishment. In another study obtaining

Table 8.1 Percentage prevalence rates of sexual aggression against women: victim and perpetrator reports. (Adapted from Koss, Gidycz, & Wisniewski, 1987, Table 4, p. 168. Copyright American Psychological Association).

	Women's victimisation reports (n = 3187)	*Men's perpetration reports* (n = 2972)
No victimisation/aggression	46.3	74.8
Sexual contact	11.4	10.2
Sexual coercion	11.9	7.2
Attempted rape	12.1	3.3
Rape	15.4	4.4

Note: Based on participants' most serious form of reported aggression/victimisation. Unweighted rates are reported.

Sexual contact: sexual behaviour other than penetrative sex against the woman's will through the use of verbal pressure, physical force (or threat thereof), or misuse of authority.
Sexual coercion: sexual intercourse against the woman's will through menacing verbal pressure or misuse of authority.
Attempted rape and rape: penetrative sexual acts through the use or threat of force or the deliberate incapacitation of the victim (e.g., through alcohol or other drugs).

prevalence data from almost 24 000 female undergraduates, almost 1 in 20 women (4.7%) were found to have been raped through the use or threat of force or by exploiting the fact that they were too intoxicated to consent (Mohler-Kuo, Dowdall, Koss, & Wechsler, 2004).

Including both female and male college students in a multinational study across 38 sites, Hines (2007) established that 2.3% of women had experienced forced sex and 24.5% had experienced verbal coercion by an intimate partner in the previous year. There was considerable variation between sites, with victimisation rates for forced sex ranging from 0% to 13%. The corresponding rates for men were 2.8% and 22%, respectively, with a range for forced sex of 0–12%.

Surveys of high-school students

It is becoming increasingly clear from large surveys of adolescents that sexual aggression and victimisation start well before college age. In a sample of over 1000 middle-school and high-school students, Young, Grey, and Boyd (2009) found that 37% of middle-school girls and 28% of middle-school boys had experienced unwanted sexual touch by a peer. In the high-school sample, the rates were 50% for girls and 26% for boys. In this older sample, 12% of girls and 3% of boys reported experiences classified as rape. Representative data for students in grades 9 to 12 are available from the Youth Risk Behavior Surveillance System (YRBSS). In the 2009 survey, 10.5% of girls and 4.5% of boys reported having been made to engage in sexual intercourse against their will through the use of force (Eaton et al., 2010).

Using a broader question, 2,800 adolescents in a representative sample of 14- to 17-year olds in Germany, 22% of sexually active German girls and 30% of sexually active girls from ethnic minorities reported that a boy or man had tried to make them engage in sexual acts or sexual touch by putting pressure on them (Bundeszentrale für gesundheitliche Aufklärung, 2010).

Sexual aggression in same-sex relationships

Compared with male-on-female sexual aggression, far less evidence is available from surveys and research studies on sexual aggression in same-sex relationships among men, and even less so among women. A review by Rothman, Exner, and Baughman (2011) of prevalence studies on sexual assault against gays, lesbians, and bisexuals found rates of adult sexual assault among gay and bisexual men ranging between 10% and 17% and rates among lesbian and bisexual women ranging between 11% and 53%. Analysing data from the National Violence Against Women Survey (NVAWS), which also included victimisation reports from male participants, Messinger (2011) found that the rate of sexual victimisation by an intimate partner in same-sex relationships was significantly higher than in heterosexual relationships for men (3.1% vs. 0.2%), and slightly lower for women (3.5% vs. 4.5%). However, homosexual men were no more likely to be victimised than homosexual women, which suggests that perpetrator gender alone cannot explain the higher victimisation rates of homosexual compared with heterosexual men. Data from the Youth Risk Behavior Surveillance System found that, between 2001 and 2009, the percentage of young people who reported that they had been physically forced into sexual intercourse when they did not want to was 23% for gay or lesbian participants and 22% for bisexual participants, compared with 7.2% for heterosexual participants (Kann et al., 2011). Lower victimisation rates for heterosexual than for homosexual men and women were also found by Balsam, Rothblum, and Beauchaine (2005). Victimisation rates for bisexual participants were substantially higher than those for homosexual participants in their sample.

A German study with a young adult sample of homosexual men used an adapted version of the Sexual Experiences Survey to obtain prevalence rates for sexual aggression and victimisation (Krahé, Schütze, Fritsche, & Waizenhöfer, 2000). The victimisation rates for different forms of sexual acts revealed that 16.1% of the respondents reported oral and anal sex involving the use or threat of force or the exploitation of their incapacitated state following the consumption of alcohol or drugs. The overall prevalence rate for any sexual victimisation, including non-penetrative sexual acts as well as coercion through verbal pressure, was 44.5% (Krahé, Scheinberger-Olwig, & Schütze, 2001). Parallel to victimisation rates, participants were also asked about the perpetration of sexually aggressive acts against another man (Krahé, Schütze, Fritsche, & Waizenhöfer, 2000). Prevalence rates were lower than the corresponding victimisation figures, but more than 5% of the respondents indicated that they had used, or threatened to use, physical force to make an unwilling man comply with their sexual demands, over 16% reported exploiting another man's inability to resist their advances, and over 6% admitted that they had used verbal coercion.

In a Canadian study on the perpetration of sexual coercion, 41% of homosexual men reported at least one incident in which they had used physical coercion, and 34% reported at least one incident in which they had used non-physical coercion (VanderLaan & Vasey, 2009). These figures were lower than the corresponding rates for heterosexual men (55% for physical coercion and 48% for non-physical coercion). This finding is at odds with the figures for the sexual victimisation of an intimate partner reported by Messinger (2011), which showed higher rates of sexual victimisation by an intimate partner for homosexual than for heterosexual men. VanderLaan and Vasey (2009) compared perpetration rates for heterosexual and homosexual women and did find that homosexual women were somewhat more likely to engage in physical and non-physical sexual coercion compared with heterosexual women, matching the victimisation data reported by Messinger (2011). Overall, though, the data base for sexual aggression in men's and women's same-sex relationships is limited, and further studies are needed to establish the similarities and differences in sexual aggression and victimisation in same-sex and heterosexual victim-perpetrator constellations.

Everyday discourse and the "real rape" stereotype

In addition to legal definitions of sexual aggression and definitions for the purposes of surveys and research studies, there is a third context in which the meaning of sexual aggression is defined. This is the context of everyday discourse, reflecting people's intuitive understanding of sexual aggression, most notably rape. Definitions in everyday discourse lead to classifications and interpretations that are at odds with legal and research definitions. This is illustrated, for example, by findings from the Fisher et al. (2000) survey of female college students mentioned earlier. The authors identified 86 women in their database who had reported experiences of forced sexual intercourse meeting the legal definition of rape. When they asked these women whether or not they considered their experience as rape, more than half of them said no.

Compared with legal and research definitions, everyday discourse is less concerned with the nature of the sexual acts or the coercive strategies employed to force a non-consenting person into sexual contacts. Instead, greater importance is attached to the circumstances and the relationship between aggressor and victim when deciding whether an incident qualifies as a "real rape." In everyday understanding, a "real rape" is seen as an attack in the dark by a stranger on an unsuspecting victim who puts up physical resistance against her attacker (Rozee, 1999). The more an incident differs from this prototypical representation, the less prepared people are to see it as rape (Krahé, 1991).

Findings from large-scale surveys in different countries consistently disconfirm the "real rape" stereotype by showing that the majority of sexual assaults take place between individuals who already knew each other. For example, the study by Kilpatrick et al. (2007) found that only 11% of cases of forcible rape and 18% of cases of incapacitated or drug- or alcohol-facilitated rape reported by women were committed by strangers. In the German study by Müller and Schröttle (2004), only 14.5% of victimised women had been assaulted by a stranger, and current or former partners accounted for almost 50% of all perpetrators. The British Crime Survey confirmed this finding by showing that, for female victims of serious sexual assault, the perpetrator had been a current or former partner in 54%

of the cases (Smith, Coleman, Eder, & Hall, 2011). In fact, Martin, Taft, and Resick (2007) concluded from their review of the evidence that marital rape is the most common form of rape.

As a result of excluding non-stranger rape from the everyday definition of a "real rape," prevalence estimates for this type of sexual assault are particularly affected by the problem of under-reporting. One reason is that individuals who were sexually assaulted by assailants whom they knew are less likely to identify themselves as victims, especially if they subscribe to the "real rape" stereotype (Peterson & Muehlenhard, 2004). Another reason is that victims of acquaintance or partner rape do not expect that others will accept their experience as rape, and are even less likely to report the assault to the police than are victims of stranger rape (Chen & Ullman, 2010). The "real-rape" stereotype also contributes to negative social reactions towards victims of rape, particularly in terms of holding women responsible for rape or accusing them of making false complaints. These social reactions are often experienced as a "second assault" by victims of rape (Temkin & Krahé, 2008; Ullman, 2010).

Taken together, the data presented in this section make it abundantly clear that sexual aggression is a reality in the lives of many women and also – although much less researched – in the lives of men. Of particular concern is the consistent finding that the majority of sexual assaults take place between people who are known to each other – as casual acquaintances, dates, or intimate partners. This brings home the threat of rape to the private sphere, making it far more pervasive than is implied by the "real rape" stereotype of the stranger attack in the dark alleyway. Trying to understand why men commit acts of sexual aggression has been a prime objective of psychological research. This is true not least because a better understanding of the causes that lead to sexual aggression may provide directions for the development of prevention strategies, which will be discussed in Chapter 11.

Explaining sexual aggression

To understand sexual aggression as a social problem, an explanatory framework is required that considers risk factors at different levels, ranging from the societal level to the individual perpetrator. An overview of variables that affect the likelihood of sexual aggression is presented in Table 8.2, based on a comprehensive review of the literature compiled in the "World Report on Violence and Health" (Krug et al., 2002).

Societal factors, such as policies related to gender equality or criminal justice responses to sexual assault, and community factors that lower the threshold for sexual violence need to be considered as background factors to understand patterns of interpersonal relationships and individual characteristics conducive to sexual aggression. Therefore a multi-level perspective considering these different factors is required to provide an explanation for sexual aggression. Rather than discussing all of the aspects listed in Table 8.2, this section provides a summary of the current state of knowledge about the major factors associated with an increased likelihood of sexual aggression. For the purposes of this review, explanations of sexual

Table 8.2 Risk factors for male sexual aggression (Based on the WHO *World Report on Violence and Health*, Krug et al., 2002, p. 159)

Societal factors	Community factors	Relationship factors	Individual factors
• Social norms condoning sexual violence • Social norms supportive of male superiority and sexual entitlement • Weak laws and policies against sexual violence • Weak laws and policies related to gender equality • High levels of violent crime	• Poverty mediated through crisis of male identity • Lack of employment opportunities • Lack of institutional support from police and justice system • Tolerance of sexual violence in the community • Weak community sanctions against perpetrators of sexual violence	• Association with sexually aggressive peers • Violent family environment • Patriarchal family structures • Emotionally unsupportive family environment • Strong emphasis on family honour	• Alcohol and drug use • Coercive sexual fantasies • Rape-supportive attitudes and beliefs • Impulsive and antisocial tendencies • Preference for impersonal sex • Hostility towards women • History of child sexual abuse • Witnessing family violence

aggression will be divided into two groups. The first group will be called "macro-level" explanations, because they locate the causes of sexual aggression in general aspects of societal functioning or in evolutionary development. The second group will be called "micro-level" explanations, because they focus on the individual perpetrator's interpersonal relationships, biographical experiences, and cognitive as well as affective processes as risk factors for sexually aggressive behaviour.

Macro-level explanations

In this section, two models of sexual aggression will be discussed which propose very different processes leading to sexual aggression: the *sociocultural approach* and the *evolutionary approach*. The sociocultural approach highlights societal features as creating the breeding ground for sexual aggression and allowing it to persist. By contrast, the evolutionary approach suggests a biological explanation of sexual aggression by placing modern-day sexual aggression within the developmental history of the human species. What the two approaches have in common is their emphasis on general mechanisms of societal functioning that promote sexual aggression.

The sociocultural approach

According to this approach, the roots of sexual aggression are to be found in the fabric of a society, most notably in the way in which gender relationships are defined (White &

Kowalski, 1998). This perspective has been advanced in particular by feminist authors, who have argued that the built-in power differential between men and women in many societies fosters the emergence of sexual aggression. By virtue of their greater social power, men claim the right to seek sexual satisfaction regardless of the woman's wishes. Moreover, sexual aggression is instrumental in perpetuating male dominance by instilling a sense of fear and vulnerability in women.

Support for the proposition that sexual aggression is the product of socio-structural characteristics that may vary between societies comes from cross-cultural research comparing western societies with societies in which sexual aggression is far less frequent or even non-existent. For example, Sanday (1981) conducted an ethnographic study of 95 tribal societies, about half of which (47%) she identified as "rape free" (i.e., showing no or only a minimal prevalence of sexual aggression). In contrast, 18% of societies were classified as "rape prone," with a high prevalence of sexual aggression. In the remaining societies, there were reports of rape, but no frequency information was available. In the rape-prone societies, sexual aggression served a ceremonial function (e.g., as a rite of passage for adolescent males) and/or functioned as a means of domination and punishment of women. Rape-free societies were found to have low levels of aggression overall and to place a high value on the contribution of women to the reproduction and continuity of the society.

Studies linking variations in rape rates within the USA to women's social status, defined in terms of economic, educational, employment, and occupational indicators, yielded inconsistent findings (for a review, see Martin, Vieraitis, & Britto, 2006). Whereas some studies found higher rape rates the lower the status of women compared to men, others found higher rates when women had a higher status, and yet others found no link at all. In their own analysis, which included 238 cities in the USA, Martin et al. (2006) found that the rates of police-recorded rapes were lower the higher the status of women.

A multinational study by Hines (2007) including 19 countries examined the prediction that the lower the status of women in the respective countries, the higher the rates of sexual aggression against women would be. Conversely, victimisation of men was expected to be higher in countries where women's status was high. An index of women's status in society was computed based on national-level data on women's participation in education, in the workforce, and in government. This index was related to men's and women's reports of sexual victimisation. As predicted, women's victimisation rates decreased, and men's victimisation rates increased, the higher the country-level status of women, lending support to the sociocultural model. In addition, Hines (2007) developed a country-level measure of adversarial sexual beliefs – that is, the tendency to view the relationship between men and women as hostile and manipulative and to see members of the opposite sex as adversaries. The average level of endorsement of adversarial sexual beliefs within a country was significantly correlated with sexual victimisation rates. The greater women's hostility towards men, the higher male victimisation rates, and the higher men's hostility towards women, the higher female victimisation rates.

Cross-cultural analyses suggest that sexual aggression must be seen in the context of general patterns of gender relations and sexual interactions within a society. With regard to sexual behaviour, cultural norms are reflected in "sexual scripts" that provide socially shared representations of sexual encounters (Krahé, 2000b). Some authors have seen rape as a variant of sexual behaviour accommodated within the normal sexual script based on the notions of male initiative and female receptivity. This view is expressed by Jackson (1978, p. 37), for example, who stated: "Sexual relationships are built around sexual inequalities, are scripted for actors whose roles have been predefined as subordinate and superordinate, and hence involve the exercise of power which may be manifested in the sexual act itself. . . . Rape, then, is simply an extreme manifestation of our culturally accepted patterns of male-female relationships."

Differences in the criminal prosecution of rape can also be seen as a socio-cultural variable related to the perpetration of sexual aggression. For example, the use of force to coerce a married partner into sexual intercourse used to be excluded from the legal definition of rape in many countries, and the abolition of the marital rape exemption is a fairly recent achievement in the western world. Similarly, there is considerable variation between countries in the percentage of rape cases reported to the police that are dropped at various stages of the criminal justice process, with as few as 5% of reported cases ending in a conviction in some countries, such as England and Wales (Lovett & Kelly, 2009; Temkin & Krahé, 2008).

The sociocultural view outlines conditions that impinge on the members of a particular society and create a platform for the development of rape-supportive attitudes and sexual scripts. It seeks to explain how socially shared conceptions, such as rape myths and gender stereotypes of male dominance and female subordination, are fed into the socialisation experiences of individual members of the society. Clearly, only a small number of men exposed to these sociocultural influences turn into sexual aggressors. The question of why some men seem to be more strongly affected by these influences than others is addressed by individual difference approaches which will be considered later in this section.

The evolutionary approach

At the core of the evolutionary approach, also known as the sociobiological approach, is the assumption that rape is a product of differences in men's and women's evolved sexuality. The general rationale of the evolutionary explanation of human aggression was outlined in Chapter 2. It refers to the *function* that a particular behaviour has for the survival of members of a species and/or for the species as a whole. With regard to sexual aggression, the argument is that for some men, and under certain circumstances, rape may be an adaptive strategy that enhances the genetic "fitness" of the aggressor by increasing his chances of passing on his genes to future generations. A less prominent variant of the evolutionary approach is the idea that sexual aggression has evolved as a by-product of a strong male sex drive, rather than being an adaptive mechanism in its own right for enhancing reproductive fitness (for a discussion of this issue, see Travis, 2003b).

The mainstream evolutionary argument holds that rape is a facultative mating strategy that is part of the behaviour potential of any man (McKibbin, Shakelford, Goetz, & Starratt, 2008). According to this view, rape is an option in the reproductive behaviour of all men.

However, it represents a high-cost mating strategy because most societies impose sanctions on rape, such as prison sentences and social stigma, which ultimately restrict a man's reproductive opportunities even further. Moreover, the chances of conception from a single sexual act are lower than from repeated sexual contacts with a consenting partner. Therefore sexual aggression will be used only if less risky options are not available. In line with this reasoning, evidence is quoted that rape is more prevalent among men who are at a reproductive disadvantage due to low status, lack of financial resources, or lack of physical attractiveness, which make them undesirable mating partners (Thornhill & Palmer, 2000).

To support the evolutionary model of rape, two main data sources are used: (a) findings from animal studies providing observational data on forced copulation in various species (e.g., orang-utans), as reviewed by McKibbin et al. (2008), and (b) statistical reports on the prevalence of rape in different demographic groups. For example, the over-representation of women of reproductive age among victims and of low-status men among perpetrators is quoted in support of the evolutionary model (Shields & Shields, 1983).

However, limitations have been noted for both data sources in terms of explaining human sexual aggression. As noted by Harding (1985), the operational definition of what constitutes rape in animal behaviour is inconsistent across studies. In addition, the very use of the term rape, which implies constructs such as "without consent" or "against the female's will," to describe animal behaviour is problematic. With regard to rape in humans, relying on statistical information about rape prevalence is problematic because these sources represent a distorted picture of the true prevalence of sexual aggression. For example, the fact that low-status and ethnic-minority men feature more prominently in official statistics on sexual violence than high-status or majority-group members of society may reflect the operation of social class stereotyping and ethnic bias (for detailed critiques of the evolutionary approach, see Lenington, 1985; Sunday & Tobach, 1985; and Travis, 2003a). Moreover, the evolutionary explanation is confined to explaining sexual violence against women of reproductive age, and therefore cannot easily account for several manifestations of sexual aggression: sexual assault on children, on post-menopausal women, on men, and on individuals who are genetically related to the assailant. None of these forms of sexual aggression are functional in enhancing the reproductive fitness of the aggressor, and therefore they fall outside the scope of the evolutionary explanation of rape.

A major source of disagreement between proponents of the evolutionary and feminist views on rape has been that, from the evolutionary perspective, rape is seen primarily as a result of male sexual reproduction strategies, whereas the feminist view sees rape primarily as a result of male power and dominance over women. However, as Vandermassen (2011) has argued in a recent paper, sexual and power motives for rape are not incompatible and may both be accommodated within an evolutionary framework that focuses on men's control over women. From that point of view, rape may be seen as a strategy serving men's reproductive interests under certain circumstances, a strategy that is related to a more general capacity of men to dominate others in a hierarchy of power (Buss, 1996). Other authors have argued for an integration of evolutionary thinking and psychological analyses of the individual-level risk factors for sexual aggression. A prominent example is Malamuth's (1998) "confluence model" of sexual aggression which will be discussed later.

Individual-level explanations

Sociocultural and evolutionary explanations focus on general mechanisms, rooted in social traditions and biological processes, which facilitate sexual aggression. In order to understand why only a few members of the species or a minority of people living under certain societal conditions engage in sexual aggression, individual-level explanations are required that identify risk factors for sexual aggression in the perpetrator. Studies addressing individual-level variables have been directed primarily at identifying differences between male aggressors and non-aggressors in terms of biographical experiences, sexual behaviour patterns, as well as affective and cognitive variables, as presented in Table 8.2.

Hall and Hirschman (1991) proposed that sexually aggressive men a differ from non-aggressive men with regard to four central aspects:

(1) the extent to which they are physiologically aroused by sexual stimuli
(2) the way they perceive and process stimuli pertinent to sexual behaviour in general and sexual aggression in particular
(3) their ability to control their affective responses
(4) their socialisation experiences and personality characteristics.

These aspects may be used as a framework for summarising the available evidence on individual-level risk factors for sexual aggression.

Sexual arousal

Several studies have looked for differences between known sexual aggressors and non-aggressive comparison groups in terms of sexual arousal following exposure to sexually explicit stimuli (Barbaree & Marshall, 1991). Sexual arousal is assessed by phallometry, which measures blood flow to the penis following exposure to sexual stimuli. Two processes have been examined: *stimulus control* (i.e., whether different types of sexual stimuli – consensual vs. coercive – elicit different patterns of physiological arousal) and *response control* (i.e., whether sexual arousal can be suppressed in response to sexually aggressive stimuli). With regard to stimulus control, a meta-analysis by Hall, Shondrick, and Hirschman (1993) confirmed that sexually aggressive men respond with a higher level of sexual arousal to depictions of coercive as compared with consensual sexual contacts. When sexual stimuli are combined with aggressive cues (e.g., by exposing respondents to violent pornography), non-aggressive men show a *decrease* in sexual arousal compared to depictions of consensual sex, which does not occur in sexually aggressive men. In terms of response control, sexually aggressive men were less able to deliberately suppress sexual arousal. Moreover, the incompatibility of sexual arousal and aggressive arousal, which is characteristic of non-aggressive men, was not found in sexual aggressors. Thus there are indications that sexual aggressors exhibit distinctive patterns of sexual arousal, most notably in response to sexually aggressive stimuli.

Lack of impulse control

Sexually aggressive men frequently display strong feelings of hostility and anger towards women (Lisak & Roth, 1990). The stronger these negative feelings, the greater the likelihood that they will override inhibitory factors against sexual aggression, such as moral standards or fear of sanctions. According to Kanin (1985), sexual frustration resulting from exaggerated, "hypersexual" needs is a primary cause of date rape. Lack of impulse control leads to spontaneous and particularly violent sexual assaults, and it is also seen as playing a role in sexual transgressions against children (Browne, 1994).

Cognitive processes

Cognitive processes also play an important role in differentiating between sexually aggressive and non-aggressive men (for a review, see Drieschner & Lange, 1999). Sexually aggressive men were found to have greater problems than non-aggressive men in shifting attention away from sexual stimuli, as reflected in longer response latencies when they were instructed to switch to an unrelated cognitive task (Yoon & Knight, 2011). The findings of a study by Bargh, Raymond, Pryor, and Strack (1995) suggest that sexual aggressors develop a cognitive association between sex and power that is not apparent in non-aggressors. Bargh et al. conducted two reaction-time experiments in which men who scored high or low on rape proclivity (i.e., the self-reported likelihood of raping a woman if certain not to be caught and punished; Malamuth, 1981) were exposed to subliminal word primes that referred to power or sex or were neutral with regard to the two domains. Participants then had to pronounce a target word that was also sex related, power related, or neutral. Shorter reaction times for pronouncing a sex-related word following the presentation of a power-related prime (compared with reaction times for pronouncing neutral words following a power-related prime, or sex-related words following a neutral prime) were taken as an indication of an automatic cognitive association of power and sex. As predicted, such shorter reaction times for the power-prime/sex-target combination were found only for respondents who scored high on rape proclivity. Moreover, sexually aggressive men are more likely to misperceive women's friendly behaviour as sexually suggestive (Farris, Treat, Viken, & McFall, 2008).

Attitudes

Sexually aggressive men were found to differ from non-aggressive men on a range of attitudes related to sexual violence, acceptance of aggression in general, and gender relations. A meta-analysis by Murnen, Wright, and Kaluzny (2002) that included 38 studies found significant correlations in the range of r = 0.20–0.30 between 11 different facets of a masculine gender role ideology and men's self-reported sexual aggression and likelihood to rape. The role of attitudinal variables in predicting sexual aggression was corroborated in longitudinal studies. Loh, Gidycz, Lobo, and Luthra (2005) found that the more men endorsed the belief that the relationship between men and women is adversarial in nature, the more likely they were to engage in sexual aggression in the next 7 months. Another longitudinal study which followed male students over a period of 12 months found that hostile gender-role beliefs and normative acceptance of verbal pressure to obtain sex were significantly higher among sexually assaultive than among non-assaultive men (Abbey & McAuslan, 2004). Rape-supportive attitudes, such as agreeing with the statement "When women talk and act sexy, they are inviting rape," were significantly linked to men's sexual aggression measured 8 months later (Thompson, Koss, Kingree, Goree, & Rice, 2011). Although all of these studies measured beliefs in male patriarchy at the individual level, the findings are in line with the sociocultural model of sexual aggression that stresses the role of male dominance in society as a risk factor for sexual aggression.

Biographical experiences and personality traits

In the search for variables that predict sexual aggression, particular attention has been paid to childhood experiences of abuse (see also Chapter 7 for a discussion of the effects of sexual abuse on later sexual aggression). Several longitudinal studies have demonstrated that male victims of childhood sexual abuse have a higher risk of engaging in sexual aggression as adults (for a review, see Thomas & Fremouw, 2009). In a large sample of men from a nationally representative survey followed over a period of 6 years, significant pathways were found from childhood experiences of sexual abuse, measured retrospectively at the first data wave, to sexually aggressive behaviour measured 6 years later (Casey, Beadnell, & Lindhorst, 2009). In addition to a direct path from sexual abuse to later sexual aggression, an indirect pathway was found via age at first sexual intercourse. Victims of childhood sexual abuse had their first sexual intercourse at a younger age, and early onset of sexual activity increased the risk of sexual aggression. Physical abuse in childhood was also linked to later sexual aggression in an indirect way through a higher tendency to engage in delinquent behaviour. The multinational study by Hines (2007) established sexual abuse as a predictor of sexual aggression among both men and women. In addition, the meta-analysis by Seto and Lalumière (2010) found elevated rates of childhood sexual abuse among adolescent sex offenders in 29 out of 31 studies.

In terms of personality variables, the concept of psychopathy has been introduced to distinguish sexual aggressors from non-aggressors. Psychopathy is defined as a "constellation of personality traits and socially deviant behaviors, including a narcissistic, grandiose sense of self; lack of empathy, remorse or concern for others; poor impulse control; manipulative approach to interpersonal relationships; and antisocial behavior" (Abbey, Jacques-Tiura, & LeBreton, 2011, p. 451). Supporting earlier research (for a review, see Lalumière, Harris, Quinsey, & Rice, 2005), Abbey et al. found significant links between personality traits related to psychopathy and men's sexual aggression via two pathways: hostile masculinity and impersonal sex, (i.e., a dissociation of sex from emotional bonds).

Alcohol and drinking habits

In addition to the stable individual differences between aggressors and non-aggressors, situational factors operate as another type of micro-level influence affecting sexual aggression. A powerful situational precipitator of sexual aggression is alcohol consumption. We saw in Chapter 4 that alcohol is generally associated with a greater likelihood of aggression, and sexual aggression is part of this general pattern. It is estimated that about half of all sexual assaults are committed by men who are under the influence of alcohol, and half of all victims of sexual aggression had been drinking at the time of the assault (Abbey et al., 2004). Both situational drinking and general habits of heavy drinking have been identified as a risk factor for sexual aggression in several longitudinal studies (e.g., Abbey & McAuslan, 2004; Swartout & White, 2010). As noted in Chapter 4, one of the pathways through which alcohol increases the odds of aggression is by reducing the person's information-processing capacities, creating a state of "alcohol myopia." This makes men's perceptions of women's cues less accurate, and increases their likelihood of misperceiving women's friendly behaviour as signalling sexual interest (Farris et al., 2008).

The "confluence model" of sexual aggression

A theoretical framework that integrates different risk factors for sexual aggression is the confluence model of sexual aggression by Malamuth (1998; Malamuth, Linz, Heavey, Barnes, & Acker, 1995). This model seeks to reconcile the evolutionary explanation of sexual aggression with the sociocultural approach, and accommodates several of the risk factors discussed in this section. The component of the model that is taken from evolutionary theory highlights *sexual promiscuity* as an antecedent of sexual aggression. Seeking sexual intercourse with a large number of women is seen as an adaptive strategy for maximising reproductive success, and the willingness to engage in sexual contact without closeness or commitment is seen as lowering the threshold for sexual coercion. The component that reflects the feminist account of sociocultural norms of male dominance is *hostile masculinity*, seeing sexual aggression as the result of an insecure male gender role and a desire to hurt and humiliate women. The confluence model is presented in Figure 8.2.

Different antecedents are specified for the two paths in the model. Sexual promiscuity is seen as deriving from a general tendency towards delinquent behaviour, which is in turn promoted by childhood experiences of harsh parental punishment and abuse. Hostile masculinity is influenced by attitudes that support the use of violence, including rape myth acceptance. Either path may lead to sexual aggression independently, but the model assumes that the probability of sexual aggression is higher in men who are both promiscuous and hostile towards women. In a large-scale study involving 3000 men, the two paths differentiated well between aggressive and non-aggressive men, explaining 78% of the variance in coerciveness against women (Malamuth, Sockloskie, Koss, & Tanaka, 1991). In terms of discriminant validity, men who were sexually aggressive towards women showed elevated levels of both sexual promiscuity and hostile masculinity, whereas men who showed physical

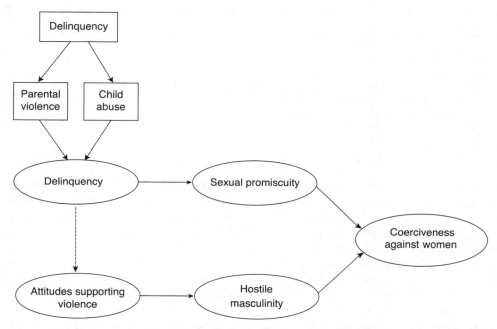

Figure 8.2 The "confluence model" of sexual aggression. (Adapted from Malamuth, 1998, p. 535. Copyright Academic Press).

aggression towards women scored higher on hostile masculinity but not on sexual promiscuity.

   In an experimental study, men who scored high on hostile masculinity delivered more aversive noise blasts as a measure of non-sexual aggression towards women, but not to men, corroborating the role of hostile masculinity as a specific predictor of aggression towards women (Anderson & Anderson, 2008). Several authors have proposed extensions of the confluence model. Knight and Sims-Knight (2004) introduced a third pathway, behavioural impulsivity, that included the use of alcohol (see also Abbey et al., 2011). Anderson and Anderson (2008) illustrated how the confluence model as a domain-specific explanation for sexual aggression can be accommodated in the General Aggression Model by treating sexual promiscuity and hostile masculinity as person variables that combine with situational variables to elicit aggressive behaviour (see Chapter 2, Figure 2.6).

Vulnerability factors for sexual victimisation

A number of studies have examined factors associated with an increased vulnerability to sexual victimisation, with most of the research concerned with female victims (for a review,

Table 8.3 Factors that increase women's vulnerability to sexual victimisation (Based on the WHO *World Report on Violence and Health*, Krug et al., 2002, p. 157)

- Being married or cohabiting with a partner
- Being young
- Being poor
- Becoming more educated and economically empowered, at least where sexual violence perpetrated by an intimate partner is concerned
- Having previously been raped or sexually abused
- Having many sexual partners
- Consuming alcohol or drugs
- Being involved in sex work

see Ullman & Najdowski, 2011a). It is important to clarify that this line of research is directed at understanding why the probability of experiencing sexual aggression is higher under some conditions and for some individuals, without thereby suggesting in any way that victims might be to blame. Accumulating evidence on risk factors for victimisation may help women, as well as men, to develop a realistic perception of potentially dangerous situations and behaviours and to protect themselves against sexual victimisation. Table 8.3 presents variables associated with an increased vulnerability of women to sexual assault based on the international literature analysed for the "World Report on Violence and Health" (Krug et al., 2002).

We shall look more closely at vulnerability factors for sexual victimisation from two broad categories: behavioural patterns and biographical experiences. For both sets of variables, remarkably consistent findings have emerged across a range of studies. Among the behavioural variables, alcohol consumption in the context of sexual encounters, the ambiguous communication of sexual intentions, and level of sexual activity (defined by age of onset of sexual activity and number of sexual partners) were identified as risk factors for sexual victimisation. Among the biographical variables, the most widely studied variable increasing vulnerability to sexual victimisation is a history of sexual abuse in childhood.

Across a large number of studies, alcohol consumption emerged as a consistent risk factor for sexual victimisation (Testa & Livingston, 2009). As noted earlier, it is estimated that about half of all victims of sexual assault had been drinking at the time of the assault (Abbey et al., 2004). Prospective studies that used measures of general drinking habits to predict subsequent victimisation rates found that regular drinking was linked to an increased risk of sexual victimisation (e.g., Combs-Lane & Smith, 2002; Messman-Moore, Coates, Gaffey, & Johnson, 2008). One explanation for this link is that alcohol impairs women's ability to process danger cues and assess risks (Gidycz, McNamara, & Edwards, 2006). In addition to actual drinking behaviour, alcohol-related expectancies were found to play a role in increasing the risk of victimisation. Alcohol-related expectancies refer to the belief that alcohol will have positive effects in sexual encounters, such as relaxation, reduction of inhibitions ("liquid courage"), and the enhancement of sexual pleasure. The more women expect alcohol to have positive effects in a sexual encounter, the higher their risk of sexual victimisation (Messman-Moore et al., 2008; Palmer, McMahon, Rounsaville, & Ball, 2010).

Palmer et al. (2010) found that positive alcohol expectancies went hand in hand with lower use of protective strategies, suggesting that positive alcohol expectancies may prevent women from perceiving themselves as at risk and taking precautions to mitigate the effects of intoxication. In addition, a woman's consumption of alcohol may indirectly increase the risk of victimisation by contributing to men's misperception of sexual intent. A woman's friendliness is more likely to be interpreted as sexual intent when she is drinking alcohol (Abbey, 2002).

The ambiguous communication of sexual intentions is another factor increasing the vulnerability to sexual victimisation. In particular, this is true for "token resistance" ("saying 'no', when you mean 'yes'"), which refers to the apparent rejection of sexual advances despite being willing to engage in sexual contacts. Muehlenhard and Hollabaugh (1988) argued that token resistance is likely to have negative consequences: it discourages honest communication, makes women appear manipulative, and encourages men to ignore women's refusals. Several studies have shown that token resistance is widely used by women and men in sexual encounters (e.g., Loh et al., 2005). It has also been established that women who use token resistance are more likely to experience sexual victimisation (Krahé, 1998; Krahé, Scheinberger-Olwig & Kolpin, 2000; Shotland & Hunter, 1995).

Certain sexual lifestyle variables were consistently found to increase women's risk of sexual victimisation. Women who start becoming sexually active at a younger age, have more sexual partners and engage in casual sex with men were found to have a higher risk of experiencing unwanted sexual contacts in a number of prospective studies. In these studies, a high level of sexual activity measured at the beginning of the study was significantly associated with a higher rate of unwanted sexual experiences at a later point (e.g., Combs-Lane & Smith, 2002; Gidycz, Hanson, & Layman, 1995; Messman-Moore et al., 2008). High levels of sexual activity put women at risk because they increase the likelihood of encountering sexually aggressive men.

Among the biographical experiences linked to sexual victimisation, sexual abuse in childhood stands out as a major risk factor for subsequent revictimisation (Krahé, 2000a; for reviews, see Classen, Palesh, & Aggarwal, 2005; Messman-Moore & Long; 2003). Support for the revictimisation hypothesis from the literature on childhood sexual abuse was reviewed in some detail in Chapter 7. This evidence is corroborated by studies of adolescent and adult sexual victimisation that looked at childhood abuse as an antecedent risk factor (e.g., Barnes, Noll, Putnam, & Trickett, 2009). Although the majority of studies addressed the risk of revictimisation in female victims of child sexual abuse, there is limited evidence that male victims of sexual abuse also have a higher risk of sexual victimisation as adolescents and adults (Aosved et al., 2011; Krahé, Scheinberger-Olwig, & Schütze, 2001).

Research addressing the underlying mechanisms of the pathway from childhood or adolescent sexual victimisation to later revictimisation has emphasised the role of alcohol and high levels of sexual activity, described earlier in this chapter as risk factors for sexual victimisation. Perhaps counterintuitively, victims of childhood sexual abuse and adolescent sexual victimisation have been shown to be more sexually active in terms of earlier onset of sexual activity and greater number of sexual partners across a wide range of studies (for a

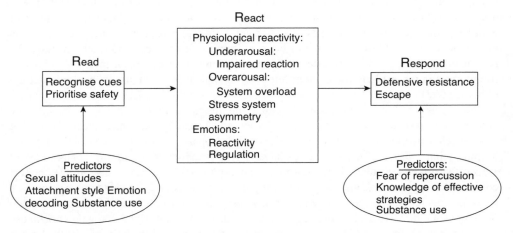

Figure 8.3 The Read–React–Respond Model of sexual revictimisation. (Reprinted from Noll & Grych, 2011, p. 208. Copyright American Psychological Association).

review, see Senn et al., 2008). Given the link between high levels of sexual activity and sexual victimisation described earlier, abuse victims' higher levels of sexual activity functions as a mediator of the link between childhood abuse and later revictimisation. Similarly, heavy drinking was identified as a mediating variable in a longitudinal study by Testa et al. (2010). An integrative framework for understanding sexual revictimisation has been offered by Noll and Grych (2011). In their Read-React-Respond model, presented in Figure 8.3, they proposed that victims of sexual aggression are vulnerable to revictimisation because of impairments in three essential areas of functioning.

The first problem for victims of child sexual abuse is a failure to properly "Read" the situation in which an assault may occur. This mis-reading of the situation is due to a greater propensity to engage in risky sexual behaviour, a higher likelihood of alcohol or drug use, an insecure attachment style, and problems in decoding the emotional signals of others. The second phase of problematic functioning is the "React" stage, which refers to physiological and affective reactions in the face of imminent harm. Victims of sexual abuse were found to show physiological underarousal in response to threat, which is dysfunctional in terms of undermining effective resistance behaviour. Finally, in the "Respond" stage, which requires a behavioural reaction to the threat of sexual assault, a history of prior victimisation may impede effective forms of resistance or escape. Evidence from past research supports each of the three stages, but the full model has yet to be tested within a single design.

With regard to the prevention of sexual victimisation, two important messages emerge from the findings discussed in this section. First, evidence that behaviours such as high levels of sexual activity, alcohol consumption, and ambiguous communication strategies are associated with an increased vulnerability to victimisation can be incorporated into rape awareness programmes to enable women to make informed behavioural choices. As Testa and Livingston (2009, p. 1349) have argued, "prevention programs targeting drinking may prove more efficacious than programs targeting sexual vulnerability." Secondly, the evidence on revictimisation identifies victims of childhood abuse as a risk group for subsequent victimisation that should be specifically targeted by rape prevention programmes. Unfortunately, programmes that were successful for non-victimised women had little or no effect on women with a history of childhood sexual abuse or adolescent victimisation (e.g., Hanson & Gidycz, 1993). The potential and limitations of rape prevention programmes will be discussed in more detail in Chapter 11.

Consequences of sexual victimisation

Many immediate and long-term adverse effects of sexual victimisation have been identified in the research literature, including the economic costs for healthcare provision and lost productivity at the societal level (for a review, see Martin, Macy, & Young, 2011). In the weeks and months following the assault, many victims develop the symptomatology of post-traumatic stress disorder (PTSD) (for the definition of PTSD, see Chapter 7). Sexual assault has been identified as one of the strongest risk factors for PTSD in women (Klump, 2008). In fact the finding that women in the general population show higher rates of PTSD than men has been attributed to the higher prevalence of sexual violence in this gender group (Tolin & Foa, 2006). Women who have experienced sexual assault also have a higher risk of suicidal behaviour, according to a review by Ullman (2004). Women who have experienced revictimisation had higher rates of PTSD than first-time victims (Najdowski & Ullman, 2011).

The evidence is limited for male victims of sexual assault, but the findings are largely in line with research on female victims. In a sample of both heterosexual and gay victims of male sexual assault, more than 90% of respondents reported feelings of depression, anxiety, and loss of self-respect in the weeks and months following the assault (Walker, Archer, & Davies, 2005). A cross-sectional study with gay and bisexual men found an increased risk of alcohol abuse, suicidal ideation, and depression among victims of adult sexual assault compared with non-victimised men (Ratner et al., 2003). The meta-analysis of gender differences in PTSD by Tolin and Foa (2006) found no difference in the rates of PTSD between female and male survivors of adult sexual assault.

Several factors moderate the adverse consequences of sexual aggression on victims' psychological health. The closer the relationship between victim and perpetrator, the more adversely victims are affected, as reflected in PTSD symptoms (Culbertson & Dehle, 2001). Unacknowledged rape victims (i.e., those who reported they had been forced by a man to have sexual intercourse but answered 'no' to the question of whether they had ever been raped) reported more severe psychological symptoms, such as anxiety, than women who identified their experience as rape (Clements & Ogle, 2009). Another factor associated with coping problems is the tendency for victims to see the assault as their own fault, blaming it on their behaviour or on characterological faults (Janoff-Bulman, 1979). Rape victims' tendency to blame themselves for the assault has been linked to lower feelings of self-worth, greater distress, and dysfunctional coping patterns in terms of denial and avoidance (Arata & Burkhart, 1998; Frazier, 2003; Littleton, Horsley, John, & Nelson, 2007).

Attributions of self-blame may be reinforced by negative social reactions that hold victims responsible for precipitating the sexual assault. The tendency to blame the victim of sexual aggression has been documented in a large body of evidence, amounting to a "secondary victimisation" (for a review, see Temkin & Krahé, 2008). A longitudinal study assessed victims at two points in time separated by a 1-year interval (Ullman & Najdowski, 2011b). Negative social reactions measured at Time 1 predicted victims' characterological self-blame 1 year later. At the same time, victims who blamed their own character for being assaulted at Time 1 reported fewer positive social reactions from others 1 year later. These findings suggest a downward spiral in which negative social responses reinforce self-blame, and self-blame reduces the likelihood of receiving positive responses from others. As shown by Campbell, Sefl, Barnes, Ahrens, Wasco, & Zaragoza-Diesfold (1999), victims of non-stranger rape, whose experience fell outside the "real-rape" stereotype described earlier, were particularly likely to encounter victim-blaming responses from legal or medical professionals, and had significantly higher levels of PTSD.

Women as perpetrators of sexual aggression against men

Although sexual aggression is predominantly committed by men against women, women also engage in sexual aggression against men. Reversing the traditional gender roles of aggressive men and victimised women, several authors have explored the prevalence, antecedents, and consequences of women's sexual aggression against men (Anderson & Struckman-Johnson, 1998). Whether or not women's sexual aggression needs to and should be investigated, given the predominance of male perpetration, has been a controversial issue. A balanced assessment has been provided by Muehlenhard (1998), who sees the study of women's sexual aggression as important for three main reasons: to avoid research bias, to challenge gender stereotypes, and to acknowledge the reality of men's victimisation experiences. At the same time, she warns about taking a gender-neutral approach as victim and perpetrator roles are not evenly distributed between men and women.

Several studies obtained prevalence rates for women's sexual aggression, but many of these failed to specify the gender of the target person (for a review of earlier studies, see Anderson & Savage, 2005). For example, Schatzel-Murphy, Harris, Knight, and Milburn (2009) found that 30% of women compared with 40% of men in their college sample reported having made an unwilling person engage in sexual acts by exploiting the other person's intoxicated state. For the use of force, the rate was 5.4% for women compared with 4.3% for men. Lower rates were found in another study with college students by Palmer et al. (2010), where the self-reported perpetration rate across different coercive strategies was 6% among women compared with 13% among men. None of the women in their sample reported having used force to engage another person in sexual activity, compared with 2% of the men. As neither of these studies specified the gender of the target person, they cannot distinguish between heterosexual and same-sex victim-perpetrator constellations.

Comparing women's sexual aggression towards men with male-on-female sexual aggression, Struckman-Johnson, Struckman-Johnson, and Anderson (2003) found that more men (13%) than women (5%) reported having engaged in sexual contact with an unwilling partner by exploiting her/his intoxicated state. Although men were also more likely than women to use emotional manipulation and lies to coerce an unwilling partner (32% vs. 15%), these tactics were used by a substantial minority of women. Krahé, Waizenhöfer, and Möller (2003) found in a German sample that 10% of women reported having made, or having attempted to make, a man engage in sexual acts against his will. These figures include verbal pressure, exploiting the man's intoxicated state, and using or threatening force. For the same strategies, the corresponding perpetration rate for men was almost 50% (Krahé, Scheinberger-Olwig, & Kolpin, 2000).

A Canadian study by VanderLaan and Vasey (2009) found substantially higher rates of sexual assault perpetration in their heterosexual samples, with 55% of men and 33% of women reporting at least one incident of using physical coercion in a heterosexual encounter. However, their measure of physical coercion was defined more broadly, and included "making constant physical attempts to have sexual activity with another person." Taken together, studies comparing perpetration rates for sexual aggression against a person of the opposite sex showed that although men consistently scored higher than women, women do employ various coercive strategies to make men engage in sexual contacts against their will.

Similarly, studies comparing men's and women's sexual victimisation often fail to specify the gender of the perpetrator, and therefore do not conclusively address the issue of men's sexual victimisation by women. Surveying a sample of over 3000 Los Angeles residents, Sorenson, Stein, Siegel, Golding, and Burnam (1987) found prevalence rates of adult sexual victimisation of 9.4% for men and 16.7% for women. A greater proportion of assaulted men had been victimised by friends, compared with women, who were more likely to have experienced assault by a stranger. In the study by Poppen and Segal (1988), 44% of men reported victimisation, compared with 74% of women. Struckman-Johnson (1988) found that 16% of men and 22% of women reported sexual victimisation by a dating partner. Finally, Larimer, Lydum, Anderson, and Turner (1999) found that 20% of men, compared with 27% of women, reported experiences of unwanted sexual contact during the year prior to the survey. However, the figures in all of these studies combined both male and female perpetrators.

In a study by Struckman-Johnson and Struckman-Johnson (1994) focusing on sexual victimisation by women, 10.2% of men reported at least one incident of being coerced into unwanted sexual touch or sexual intercourse by a woman since the age of 16, in 90% of cases committed by an acquaintance or girlfriend. Much higher rates were found in a study by Turchik (2012), where 48% of college men reported at least one experience of sexual victimisation by a woman since the age of 16. Looking specifically at forcible rape, Tjaden and Thoennes (2000) found that 0.2% of men had been victimised by a female partner. In two samples of heterosexual men in Germany, Krahé, Scheinberger-Olwig, and Bieneck (2003) studied the prevalence of unwanted sexual contact with women since the age of 14 through the use of verbal pressure, threat or use of physical force, or exploitation of their incapacitated state. In the younger sample (mean age 18 years) the prevalence rate was 25%, in the older sample (mean age 22 years) the prevalence rate was 30%. For completed sexual intercourse through the threat or use of force, the rates were 2.8% and 4.6%, respectively.

The literature reveals substantial variation in the rates of female sexual aggression towards men as well as male sexual victimisation by women across different studies, which is due in large part to differences in methodology and in the operational definition of sexual aggression. Nevertheless, the findings show that women's sexual aggression occurs on a scale that warrants closer research attention. The findings also disconfirm the commonly held belief that male rape is a "gay problem" (for a discussion of the discourse on male rape, see Graham, 2006).

Few studies have examined risk factors for female sexual aggression, but the available evidence found parallels to the risk factors identified for male perpetration. Childhood sexual abuse was linked to women's use of force as well as verbal coercion in the multinational study by Hines (2007). The same link was found in a German study that also established high levels of sexual activity and the ambiguous communication of sexual intentions as predictors of women's sexual aggression towards men (Krahé, Waizenhöfer, & Möller, 2003). A high level of sexual activity was also identified as a predictor of women's use of force (Anderson, Kontos, Tanigoshi, & Struckman-Johnson, 2005). For male victimisation by women, the evidence parallels the findings for female victimisation by men. For example, alcohol consumption was identified as a risk factor for male sexual victimisation in the same way as it was shown to increase the risk of sexual victimisation for women (Larimer et al., 1999),

Regarding the consequences of male sexual victimisation by women, there is some evidence that men may be less adversely affected than women. In the sample studied by Struckman-Johnson (1988), 27% of the male victims said that they had felt "bad" or "very bad" about the experience, while the corresponding figure for female victims was 88%. Further studies confirmed the finding that men do not report strong negative reactions following sexual coercion by a woman (Struckman-Johnson & Struckman-Johnson, 1994; Krahé, Scheinberger-Olwig, & Bieneck, 2003). Other studies found that male victims of sexual aggression scored higher on a range of health risk behaviours, such as alcohol or drug use, and on a measure of sexual dysfunction, compared with non-victims (Turchik, 2012). It would be premature to conclude that male victims are unaffected by sexual assault by women. Qualitative interviews have shown that many men are left severely traumatised by the experience of sexual victimisation (e.g., Sarrel & Masters, 1982). Measures used in quantitative studies may not be sufficiently sensitive to detect the psychological impact of men's unwanted sexual contact with women. Moreover, the possibility must be considered that men may be reluctant to acknowledge a negative impact of being sexually assaulted by a woman, which would be tantamount to acknowledging their vulnerability. Sarrel and Masters (1982, p. 121) quote one of their male victims who was terrified that if his friends found out about his "disgrace," they would think him "less than a man" because he had been "raped by a woman." Parallel tendencies to deny the trauma of sexual assault in male victims have been found in research with sexually abused boys (e.g., Friedrich, Berliner, Urquiza, & Beilke, 1988). Current evidence on the adverse effects of sexual victimisation on men rests entirely on self-reports of the extent to which they experienced the incident as distressing. In order to clarify whether these responses reflect a genuine lack of impact or a reluctance to acknowledge distress, self-reports must be complemented by other indicators, such as a clinical assessment of physical and psychological symptoms.

Summary

- Legal definitions of sexual assault specify those forms of sexual aggression that constitute criminal offences (such as rape, attempted rape, and sexual coercion). Research definitions cover a wider range of coercive strategies and sexual acts, including non-criminal forms of sexual aggression (such as verbal pressure). In everyday discourse, sexual assault is defined primarily in terms of the "real rape" stereotype, characterising rape as an attack by a stranger who uses physical violence to force the victim to engage in sexual acts.
- Prevalence studies demonstrate the widespread occurrence of sexual assault. Crime statistics, reflecting only reported cases, seriously under-represent the true scale of women's sexual victimisation, as evidenced by the much higher prevalence rates obtained in surveys of victims and perpetrators. The majority of sexual assaults are committed by perpetrators known to the victims, such as acquaintances, dates, or intimate partners, contradicting the "real rape" stereotype that designates stranger rape as the prototypical form of sexual assault.
- One group of explanations of sexual aggression refers to macro-level processes, such as sociocultural patterns of male-female power relationships or the evolution of sexual aggression as a strategy for enhancing male reproductive fitness. A second group concentrates on micro-level risk factors, most notably in the individual perpetrator. Sexual aggressors have been found to differ from non-aggressors in terms of sexual arousal patterns, rape-supportive attitudes, childhood experience of violence, and risky patterns of sexual as well as drinking behaviour.
- Without disputing that the responsibility for sexual aggression lies with the aggressor, research has identified factors associated with an increased vulnerability to sexual victimisation. High levels of sexual activity, alcohol consumption in the context of sexual encounters, and the ambiguous communication of sexual intentions have been shown to be behavioural risk factors for sexual victimisation. In addition, there is consistent evidence that childhood experiences of sexual abuse are linked to an increased risk of subsequent revictimisation.
- Sexual victimisation has a profound negative impact on victims' psychological well-being and mental health. The rate of post-traumatic stress disorder (PTSD) is high in victims of sexual assault. Victims who blame themselves for being assaulted have greater problems in coping with the assault. Moreover, responses by others to the disclosure of the assault often reflect the attribution of blame to the victim, and derogatory attitudes towards victims of rape held by laypersons, police, and legal professionals.

- Women also commit sexually aggressive behaviour towards men, albeit with lower prevalence rates. Even though the evidence shows that men rate their victimisation experiences as less distressing than do women, this does not necessarily mean they are less affected. For a man to accept that he has been sexually victimised by a woman is a threat to his self-esteem, undermining his sense of masculinity.

Tasks to do

(1) Look up the legal definition of rape in your country and find out how it differs from other forms of sexual aggression.
(2) Find recent figures from official crime statistics in your country about the number of rapes and other forms of sexual assault reported each year, and compare the numbers of male and female victims.
(3) Find out what agencies there are in your area to support victims of sexual aggression, and what types of services they offer.

Suggested reading

Fisher, B. S., Daigle, L. E., & Cullen, F. T. (2010). *Unsafe in the ivory tower: The sexual victimization of college women.* Thousand Oaks, CA: Sage.

Horvath, M., & Brown, J. (Eds) (2009). *Rape: Challenging contemporary thinking.* Cullompton, UK: Willan Publishing.

Temkin, J., & Krahé, B. (2008). *Sexual assault and the justice gap: A question of attitude.* Oxford: Hart Publications.

Ullman, S. E. (Ed.) (2010). *Talking about sexual assault. Society's response to survivors.* Washington, DC: American Psychological Association.

9 Aggression between social groups

The forms of aggression discussed in the previous chapters were manifestations of *interpersonal* aggression involving confrontations between individuals. In the present chapter, we turn to *intergroup* aggression originating in the context of encounters between social groups (Goldstein, 2002). Groups may become involved in violent conflict because they compete for resources, such as power or material profit, that only one party can obtain. However, even in the absence of such conflicts of interest, the mere categorisation of people into groups may produce feelings of intergroup hostility resulting from the desire to promote a positive view of their own group. Intergroup aggression can be both hostile (e.g., letting off steam after the defeat of one's favoured sports team) and instrumental (e.g., attacks by political activists to achieve a particular objective).

Collective violence is another term used to denote aggression in and between social groups. In the "World Report on Violence and Health" compiled by the World Health Organization (WHO), the term "collective violence" is used to refer to "the instrumental use of violence by people who identify themselves as members of a group . . . against another group or set of individuals, in order to achieve political, economic, or social objectives" (Krug et al., 2002, p. 215). Collective violence comprises (a) political conflicts within and between states (e.g. war, terrorism), (b) state-perpetrated violence (e.g., genocide, torture), and (c) organised violent crime (e.g., banditry, gang warfare). The WHO report identifies a range of conditions at the societal and political levels that make collective violence more likely. The main factors are summarised in Table 9.1.

At the political level, a lack of democratic participation and unequal access to power by different groups within a society increase the risk of collective violence. Inequality is also a risk factor at the societal and community level, through creating competition for material goods and status. Availability of weapons and population density are contextual variables that lower the threshold for violence (for a discussion of weapons as aggressive cues and the role of social density as a risk factor for aggression, see Chapter 4). Although these risk factors may not be sufficient individually to explain collective violence, in combination they create conditions that may precipitate aggressive confrontations between groups. Collective violence has dramatic consequences for people directly or indirectly involved in the conflict, in terms of their physical and mental health as well as their socio-economic welfare.

Table 9.1 Risk factors for collective violence (Based on the WHO *World Report on Violence and Health*, Krug et al., 2002, Chapter 8)

Political factors	• Lack of democratic processes
	• Unequal access to political power and to natural resources of different regions, social classes, religions, or ethnic groups
Societal and	• Inequality between groups in the allocation of goods and services
community factors	• Fuelling of group fanaticism along ethnic, national, or religious lines
	• Ready availability of weapons
Demographic factors	• Rapid demographic change, particularly increases in population density and in the proportion of young people

Whereas the risk factors shown in Table 9.1 operate at the level of society and political systems, from a social psychological perspective it is important to understand what happens to individuals to make them more prone to act aggressively as members of a group. We shall start by looking at theories that seek to explain the psychological processes involved in aggressive encounters between groups. Then we shall move on to the situational effects of group membership on individuals' readiness to engage in aggressive behaviour when they act as part of a crowd (e.g., in rallies or riots). In the second half of the chapter we will turn to more enduring processes of identification and affiliation with social groups, such as juvenile gangs, that lead to aggressive conflict with out-groups.

Theories of intergroup conflict and aggression

The social psychology of intergroup relations can offer two prominent theories for understanding the roots of aggression and violence between social groups: Sherif's (1958) *theory of realistic group conflict* and Tajfel's (1981) *social identity theory*. These theories address fundamental psychological processes underlying confrontations between groups, and provide general explanations of intergroup aggression that apply to a wide variety of groups.

Theory of realistic group conflict

An obvious answer to the question of why groups get into conflict is because they often compete for goals that only one party can achieve. Aggressive clashes between rivalling sports teams from different local schools are as much a case in point as are wars between countries fought over political influence and territorial claims. Although aggression in conflicts of this kind clearly serves an instrumental function, it is typically accompanied by hostile feelings towards the opposing group. In his *theory of realistic group conflict*, Sherif (1958, 1966) explained how intergroup hostility arises from competition over scarce resources. A basic assumption of his theory is that attitudes and behaviour towards an out-group depend on the functional relationships between the groups involved. If the relationships are cooperative, positive attitudes and behaviours are developed towards the out-group, but if the relationships are competitive, negative attitudes and discriminating behaviour develop. These negative evaluations then become ingrained in the collective beliefs of the group and are passed on to new members, who will come to share the prejudicial attitudes and discriminating behaviour even though they may not have had any direct negative experience with the out-group.

In a series of field experiments, Sherif and his colleagues examined these propositions under natural conditions (Sherif, Harvey, White, Hood, & Sherif, 1961). In the famous "Robbers Cave" experiment, named after the park in Oklahoma where it took place (www. stateparks.com/robbers_cave.html), they studied the behaviour of 11- to 12-year-old psychologically healthy boys who participated in a summer camp set up by the researchers for the purposes of their studies. In the first phase of the experiment, which lasted for about a week, groups were formed consisting of previously unacquainted boys. These groups engaged in coordinated activities and quickly developed a sense of in-group identity, calling themselves the "Rattlers" and the "Eagles." In the second phase, which lasted another week, the researchers deliberated created friction between the two groups. This was achieved by introducing a series of competitive events in which attractive prizes could be won by the victorious group, and by creating frustrations for each group that appeared to have been caused by the other group. During this phase, the Rattlers and the Eagles developed increasingly negative and hostile attitudes towards each other, up to the point where one group burnt the other's flag (see Figure 9.1). At the same time, in-group solidarity became stronger, widening the gap between the in-group and the out-group. The third stage was designed to reduce intergroup conflict by changing the functional relationships between the groups from competition to cooperation. This was achieved by introducing a series of

Figure 9.1 Banner from the original Robbers Cave experiment. (Copyright Archives of the History of American Psychology, The Center for the History of Psychology, University of Akron. Reprinted with permission).

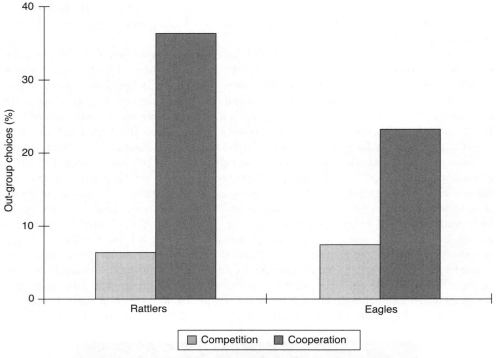

Figure 9.2 Percentage of friends chosen from the out-group following competition and cooperation. (Based on Sherif et al., 1961, Chapter 6, Table 1, and Chapter 7, Table 2).

"superordinate goals" that could only be reached through the joint efforts of both groups. For example, the researchers made the truck bringing the provisions for a picnic break down so that the joint efforts of both groups were required to pull it up the hill and get it moving again. Cooperating with the out-group on these superordinate goals reduced intergroup hostility and promoted positive attitudes and behaviour between the Rattlers and the Eagles. Beyond observational data showing the changes in intergroup attitudes, friendship choices were obtained from the boys at the end of the second and third stages. The percentage of friends chosen from the out-group at both points in time is shown in Figure 9.2.

In both groups, hardly anyone chose an out-group member as a friend when there was competition between the groups, but out-group friendship choices increased significantly following cooperation. This finding supports the assumption that realistic conflicts between groups produce hostile attitudes towards out-group members, and also points to the role of common goals in promoting positive attitudes between groups.

However, an important qualification needs to be made regarding the effectiveness of introducing superordinate goals as a way of defusing intergroup conflict. Working together towards a common goal does little per se to relieve tensions between hostile groups. Its positive effects depend on the *success* of the joint efforts. If the groups fail to reach their superordinate goal, relationships may deteriorate even further because each group is likely to blame the other for the failure. In Sherif's controlled experiments, the successful realisation of the superordinate goal in the third stage was under the control of the researchers, so there was no risk of a boomerang effect. By contrast, in many real-life contexts, success in reaching a superordinate goal is not guaranteed, and the risks of exacerbating the conflict in the event of failure need to be carefully considered.

Striving towards superordinate goals and doing so in a cooperative way are part of the optimal conditions specified by Allport (1954) for reducing intergroup prejudice. In addition, he proposed that contact is most likely to reduce out-group prejudice if the groups have equal status, and if intergroup contact is embedded in a supportive institutional framework. Pettigrew and Tropp (2006) conducted a meta-analysis of 515 studies and found that studies investigating intergroup contact that took place under these optimal conditions showed greater effects of contact on prejudice reduction than studies of contact that did not meet these conditions.

As conflicts of interest are omnipresent in intergroup relations, Sherif's theorising applies to a wide range of intergroup constellations. By studying groups that were formed for his experiment and had no prior history, he was able to demonstrate the causal role of introducing conflicts of interest between groups in eliciting hostility and aggression in a naturalistic context. Furthermore, he showed that intergroup attitudes improved as a result of reaching superordinate goals, pointing to a potential strategy for reducing aggression between groups.

Social identity theory

Sherif (1958, p. 351) already pointed out that individuals are inclined to assign positive attributes to their in-group, which "tend to be praiseworthy, self-justifying, and even self-glorifying." The idea that a positive evaluation of one's in-group may be linked to the individual members' feelings of self-worth features prominently in Tajfel's (1981) "social identity theory" (SIT), which is the second influential explanation for intergroup conflict. Tajfel started from the proposition that a conflict of interest is a sufficient but by no means necessary condition for eliciting intergroup hostility and aggression. He argued that discrimination and hostility between groups arise even in the absence of tangible conflicts of interest, merely as a result of social categorisation into in-groups and out-groups.

From the perspective of social identity theory (Tajfel, 1981), intergroup aggression is placed in the context of the psychological need to establish and maintain a positive identity. In addition to a positive sense of personal identity based on their individual qualities, people seek to establish a sense of self-worth through the social groups to which they belong. For example, being a member of a national group is a source of personal pride for many people, and they are keen to stress the positive qualities of their in-group. At the same time, they seek to minimise the positive qualities and emphasise the shortcomings of other groups, thereby achieving positive distinctiveness for their own group (Brown, 2010). Feeling close to in-group members and distancing oneself from out-groups gives rise to *in-group favouritism*, which is defined as preferential treatment and evaluation of in-group members solely on the basis of their shared group membership.

The desire to achieve a positive social identity through seeing one's social group in a positive light is so strong that it even works in so-called "minimal groups." These are groups with no common history or face-to-face contact, to which research participants are randomly assigned. Group members have only the most superficial attribute in common, such as sharing the same group name. In a classic study, Billig and Tajfel (1973) told participants they would be assigned to either Group X or Group W based on the toss of a coin. They were then given the task of allocating money to members of Group X and Group W (without any personal gains for themselves), whereby they could allocate equal sums to members of both groups, or give members of one group more than members of the other group. The results showed a significant shift away from a fair, equal treatment of both groups towards an unfair favouring of members of their own group with whom they had nothing in common but the letter designating their group. This finding showed that social categorisation based on minimal criteria was sufficient to elicit preferential treatment of the in-group, as suggested by social identity theory.

If group membership determined by chance is capable of eliciting in-group favouritism (and, by implication, out-group discrimination), the impact should be far greater in groups that share a common history and fate. The conflict between Protestants and Catholics in Northern Ireland is a case in point. As shown by Cairns, Kenworthy, Campbell, and Hewstone (2006), members of each religious group had more positive feelings for their own community than for the other community, and this pattern was particularly evident for those who identified strongly with their religious community.

Devaluing the out-group is a stronger form of intergroup bias than merely favouring the in-group. Out-group derogation promotes feelings of hostility that may lower the threshold for aggressive behaviour towards out-group members, even when there is no material conflict of interest between the groups. The minimal group experiments have shown that mere social categorisation can produce in-group favouritism in the form of a moderate preference for members of one's own group. Hostility towards an out-group is a much stronger feeling, and, as Brown (1986, Chapter 15) has argued, it is unlikely to be produced by minimal group distinctions alone. For hostility towards an out-group to develop, a further condition is important, namely a sense of unfair distribution of resources that discriminates against the in-group. This sense of unfairness is likely to arise from a combination of two psychological processes: social comparison with similar rather than dissimilar groups, and the formation of a positive social identity through stressing the positive distinctiveness of the in-group compared with the out-group. As Lickel, Miller, Stenstrom, Denson, and Schmader (2006) have shown, there is even a tendency for in-group members to engage in "vicarious retribution" against out-groups (i.e., to show an aggressive response to an out-group member after a member of their own group has been the target of aggression from another person in that out-group). For example, if a German boy sees a member of his national group being verbally abused by a Turkish classmate, he may retaliate by yelling abuse next time he meets another Turkish boy, even though neither he nor the other boy were involved in the initial confrontation.

The link between social identity and aggression towards out-groups has been further supported by the findings of a study by Fischer, Haslam, and Smith (2010) in the UK. In their all-female sample, they either made participants' *national* identity salient (by asking them to list three things they had in common with other British people) or they made their *gender* identity salient (by asking them to list three things they had in common with other women). Half of the participants were subsequently given a text and photos about the terrorist attacks in London on 7 July 2005, representing a threat to national identity, while the other half received a text and photos referring to the oppression of women by the Taliban, posing a threat to gender identity. In response to the terrorist scenario, participants perceived a greater threat from terrorists and were more in favour of retaliatory action when their national identity was salient than when their gender identity was salient. Conversely, women whose gender identity was salient perceived a greater threat from the Taliban and greater readiness for aggression than those whose national identity had been made salient. These findings suggest that a threat to social identity is more likely to elicit aggression in contexts in which the particular identity is salient. For example, meeting a student from a university that has a rival sports team should be more likely to trigger hostility in the context of a sports event, when fan identity is salient, than in a neutral context not associated with sports rivalry between the two universities.

Social identity theory offers a broad theoretical approach for understanding hostility and aggression between groups. Seeing the in-group in a positive light and attributing negative qualities to the out-group creates positive distinctiveness of the in-group that is a source of self-esteem for its members. The desire for a positive social identity is apparently so strong that even minimal criteria for defining group membership are sufficient to elicit in-group favouritism and out-group discrimination.

Although the theoretical approaches by Sherif and Tajfel focus on different underlying processes, it is clear that realistic conflicts of interest and social identity concerns often go hand in hand in intergroup conflicts. As we shall see in the following sections, this is true for intergroup relations that are relatively stable over time as well as for transient social groups that involve short-term changes in identity and social interests. As examples of intergroup violence between groups that are relatively stable over time, we shall examine evidence on gang violence and on hate crimes against members of minority groups, before looking at research on crowd behaviour as an example of more transient intergroup encounters.

Gang violence

As noted by Decker (2007, p. 388), "gangs and violence have become interchangeable terms in the last decade." A gang has been defined as "an age-graded peer group that exhibits some permanence, engages in criminal activity, and has some symbolic representation of membership" (Decker & van Winkle, 1996, p. 31). Gangs often adopt particular visible features, such as dress, hair style, or insignia, which serve to reinforce cohesion within the gang, present a unified group image to others, and help to achieve visible distinctiveness from other gangs. Although gang violence is by no means confined to adolescence, research has focused primarily on juvenile gangs, not least because membership of a juvenile gang may well be the pathway into an adult criminal career. Gangs operate primarily in the neighbourhood of the gang members, including their schools, and hostility and violence between local gangs are a key element of gang activities.

A picture of the scale of gang-related violence in the USA and its changes over time can be gleaned from the annual National Youth Gang Survey of 2500 US law enforcement agencies that has been conducted since 1996. The most recent available data estimate that approximately 774 000 gang members and 27 900 gangs were active in the USA in 2008. In the period from 2002 to 2008, the number of gangs increased by 28%, and the number of gang members increased by 6% (Egley, Howell, & Moore, 2010). In a nationwide survey of students aged between 12 and 18 conducted in 2007, 23% of respondents reported that gangs were active at their school, a rate that has remained stable since 2001 (Dinkes, Kemp, & Baum, 2009, pp. 32–33).

A report by the Metropolitan Police in London in 2006 identified 169 youth gangs, of which about 25% had been involved in murders, and which were responsible for more than 20% of all youth crime in the UK capital that year (http://news.bbc.co.uk/2/hi/uk_news/england/london/6383933.stm). In addition to accounting for a large number of violent crimes, gang violence shows a distinctive pattern with regard to individual and situational characteristics. For example, Decker (2007) concluded that compared with other homicides, homicides committed by gangs are far more likely to involve male perpetrators, members of racial or ethnic minorities, and the use of guns, and to occur outside and with multiple participants.

According to a review by Goldstein (1994a), males outnumber females by a ratio of 20:1 as members of violent gangs. Moreover, Chesney-Lind (1997) has shown that when girls are organised in gangs, they do not display violence at the same rate as do male gangs. Rather than forming gangs of their own, girls are more commonly involved in auxiliary roles in boys' gangs, as girlfriends, "little sisters," and helpers in the fight against other gangs. Furthermore, there is evidence that female gang members are exposed to physical and sexual violence by male members of their gang (Molidor, 1996).

According to several authors, the average age of gang members has gone up over the years, not least because drug-trafficking has been playing an increasing role in juvenile gangs (Cairns, Cadwallader, Estell, & Neckerman, 1997). In a sample of 101 gang members interviewed by Decker and van Winkle (1996), making money and selling drugs were cited as the most common reasons for staying in the gang.

Theories seeking to explain gang violence either focus on social-structural variables in a community that facilitate the formation and activity of gangs, or they look at psychological processes underlying intergroup encounters (for a comprehensive review, see Wood & Alleyne, 2010). In terms of structural conditions, poor socio-economic background, which prevents legitimate forms of access to material resources and status symbols, is an important factor explaining why young people are attracted to gangs. This may also account for the high proportion of juvenile gang members from ethnic minorities, who are affected by both adverse socio-economic conditions and lack of acceptance by the dominant social group. Several studies conducted across the USA, summarised by Decker (2007), have found a concentration of gang homicides in areas characterised by poverty and social disorganisation. The term "postcode gangs" refers to the fact that gangs sometimes name themselves after the postcode of their area as a marker of territorial claims, which underlines the intergroup nature of gang violence (e.g., http://news.bbc.co.uk/2/hi/uk_news/7232344.stm).

In terms of the social psychological processes involved, conditions of disorganisation and marginalisation facilitate the emergence of social norms that make violence and criminal behaviour acceptable or even imperative. These norms are passed on to new members through observational learning and peer pressure. In addition, gang members were found to have shown more deviant behaviour (e.g., starting a fight, damaging property) than non-members even before joining a gang, leading to an accumulation of individuals who mutually reinforce pro-deviance norms (Eitle, Gunkel, & Van Gundy, 2004). At the same time, however, there is evidence that gangs may also acknowledge conventional social norms, for example, by providing assistance to weaker members of the community or ensuring security during neighbourhood events (Wood & Alleyne, 2010).

Decker and van Winkle (1996) have offered an explanation of gang violence based on the construct of *threat*. According to their view, gangs often originate in response to perceived or genuine threats from individuals or other groups in a particular neighbourhood. This process is promoted by the failure of legal and community institutions to offer effective protection in crime-prone neighbourhoods. Threats may be, or are perceived to be, directed at gang members' physical safety, their territorial claims, and/or their psychological identity. To the extent that rival gangs adopt similar perceptions of threat and try to pre-empt their opponents' attacks, gang violence has a strong potential for escalation. Furthermore, the gang's violent actions alienate its members from legitimate social institutions. This marginalisation gives rise to feelings of vulnerability, which are likely to enhance the psychological significance of gang membership for the individual and strengthen affiliation with the gang. Decker and van Winkle's (1996) model of the role of threat in gang violence is depicted in Figure 9.3.

By virtue of their ability to threaten potential opponents, neighbourhood gangs can present themselves as attractive social groups. Group membership offers both instrumental benefits (e.g., protection, or the opportunity for material profit through illegal gang actions) and symbolic benefits (e.g., sharing in the power and prestige attributed to the gang). The presence of rival gangs constitutes an additional element of threat that increases the commitment of the members to their group and sharpens intergroup boundaries. These dynamics of gang behaviour in response to external threat are reflected in the observation that the arrest and incarceration of gang members reinforces gang cohesiveness.

The analysis offered by Decker and van Winkle (1996) ties in with both the theory of realistic group conflict and social identity theory described earlier in this chapter. Rival gangs compete for material gains, such as profits from drug sales, and for symbolic status, such as dominance in their neighbourhood, and the threat of defeat inherent in the competitive

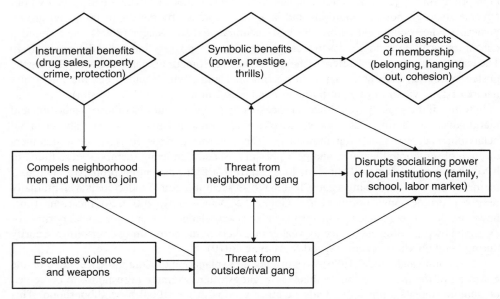

Figure 9.3 The role of threat in gang violence. (Reprinted with permission from Decker & van Winkle, 1996, p. 25. Copyright Cambridge University Press.)

nature of intergroup interactions can account for violent confrontations between them. At the same time, gangs can be seen as a means of defining a positive social identity for the individual both through identification with the in-group, reflected in catchy group names and distinctive regalia, and through the derogation of out-groups.

The important role of in-group identification in explaining gang violence has been further highlighted by Vasquez, Lickel, and Hennigan (2010), who examined gang members' readiness to engage in displaced aggression. Displaced aggression, similar to vicarious retribution discussed earlier, denotes retaliatory aggression towards an out-group member who was not involved in the initial confrontation or who is treated with a level of violence that is disproportionate to the initial provocation (for a discussion of displaced aggression, see Chapter 2). These researchers identified group-based retribution as a source of escalation in gang-related violence, suggesting that when a gang sees itself as the target of violent actions from another gang, a strong motivation is elicited to retaliate against members of the other gang (who may not have been involved in the original incident), even in those members of the target group who were not directly affected by the initial act of violence. Vasquez et al. (2010) have identified a sequence of cognitive and affective processes that underlie displaced aggression in confrontations between gangs.

(1) First, it is important that the initial provocation is perceived by the target group as an instance of intergroup aggression by virtue of the opponents' group membership, rather than an instance of interpersonal aggression between two individuals. Given that gangs typically have a history of rivalry, it is likely that any provocation between individual members will be construed as an act of intergroup aggression.

(2) Once the event is construed as an intergroup confrontation, the likelihood of engaging in aggressive action depends on group members' motivation to retaliate, which is strongly related to their identification with the in-group. The more individuals use group membership to define a positive social identity for themselves, the more empathy they will feel for group members who become victims of an attack by the out-group, and the greater their anger will be towards the out-group in general, not just towards those out-group members who were responsible for the initial attack. Identification with the in-group can also explain why gang members feel that their need for retribution has been satisfied even if they have not personally participated in the retaliatory action. In addition, in-group identification entails the acceptance of in-group norms and a readiness to respond to pressure to engage in direct or displaced aggression on behalf of the gang.

(3) Finally, one or more targets need to be chosen against whom to direct retaliative aggression. Although direct retaliation against the provocateur appears to be the most obvious choice, it may be precluded for various reasons. For example, the provocateur may be unavailable or too strong. In this case, the need for retribution can be satisfied by displacing aggression on to other out-group targets. Vasquez et al. (2010) argued that displaced aggression is more likely the more the out-group is seen as a cohesive entity in which members form a tightly knit community and are therefore blamed collectively for violent actions carried out by parts of their group.

Based on this conceptual analysis, Vasquez et al. (2010) suggested that a potential strategy for reducing gang violence is to weaken social identification with the gang. One possibility would be to strengthen a *positive personal identity* so as to override the social identity as a gang member. This could be achieved, for example, through job programmes that enable gang members to boost their self-esteem based on personal achievements rather than affiliation with a deviant group. In support of this idea, there is some indication that dropping out of gangs is facilitated by life events associated with social participation in the mainstream of society, such as forming a stable relationship with a partner outside the gang or becoming a parent, but it only works if these changes come with the possibility of supporting a family with legal income (Moloney, MacKenzie, Hunt, & Joe-Laidler, 2009).

Taken together, the research reviewed in this section shows that gangs have a high potential for violent action, much of which happens in an intergroup context as a result of rivalry with other gangs. Although structural conditions, such as poverty and social disorganisation, play an important role in explaining attraction to gangs, an analysis of the social psychological processes that operate within and between groups further adds to the understanding of gang violence. Gangs offer a means of defining a positive social identity, particularly for those who find it difficult to develop a positive personal identity based on participation in legitimate social institutions. Group identity is consolidated within the gang by shared norms and is communicated among gang members as well as to the outside world through symbolic means, such as names or dress codes. Categorical divisions between "them" and "us" promote out-group derogation as well as the perception of the out-group as a homogeneous entity, which facilitates displaced aggression.

Hate crimes

In this section we shall examine instances of violence in which the group membership of the *target person* motivates or triggers aggressive acts. Violence against members of particular social groups defined, for instance, by ethnicity, religion, sexual orientation, or disability, is happening on a large scale across the world and is summarised under the label of "hate crimes." Hate crimes can be distinguished from other forms of aggression and violence by a number of characteristics. Craig (2002) has identified a set of defining features of hate crimes that are presented in Table 9.2.

Compared with crimes that are unrelated to the group membership of the victims, hate crimes have a symbolic function in terms of publicly identifying the target group as the object of hate. They have an instrumental function in terms of reducing the targets' social participation by making them avoid certain places and events. They are typically perpetrated by groups of attackers, and they undermine social relationships in the community by spreading suspicion and fear, and, it might be added, by reinforcing in-group-out-group boundaries. Craig further suggested that hate crimes are associated with greater distress for the victims, as indicated in a study by Herek, Gillis, and Cogan (1999), but the empirical basis for this claim is as yet limited.

To establish the prevalence of hate crimes in the USA, hate crime statistics are reported annually by the Federal Bureau of Investigation (FBI), which include "incidents, offenses, victims, and offenders in reported crimes that were motivated in whole or in part by a bias against the victim's perceived race, religion, ethnicity, sexual orientation, or disability"

Table 9.2 Characteristics that distinguish hate crimes from other forms of aggression (Based on Craig, 2002)

Targets	• Hate crimes are directed specifically at members of negatively stereotyped social groups
Symbolic function	• A message of hate is communicated to the community
Instrumental function	• Behaviour of the disliked target groups is controlled and restricted (e.g., by keeping them away from certain locations)
Presence of multiple perpetrators	• Hate crimes are typically committed as group actions
Increased distress	• Hate crime victims may be more traumatised than victims who are not targeted for their group membership
Deteriorating social relations	• Hate crimes spread a climate of suspicion and fear in communities

(Federal Bureau of Investigation, 2011b). For 2009, the FBI recorded 6604 hate crime incidents, of which 48.5% were motivated by racial bias, 19.7% resulted from religious bias, 18.5% were linked to sexual-orientation bias, 11.8% stemmed from ethnicity/national origin bias, and 1.5% involved disability bias. A much higher figure was reported for England, Wales, and Northern Ireland. In 2009, a total of 52 028 crimes were recorded in which the offence was motivated by prejudice (Home Office, 2011). Of these, the vast majority of victims (83%) were targeted because of their race, 9.3% because of their sexual orientation, 4% because of their religion, and 2.7% because of a disability. To explain this staggering difference in the number of hate crimes recorded, it is important to take a close look at how hate crimes are defined in the two databases. In the UK data, incidents are recorded "that were perceived as hate crimes by the victim or any other person" (Home Office, 2011). By contrast, a much more stringent definition is used for the FBI statistics: "Only when law enforcement investigation reveals sufficient evidence to lead a reasonable and prudent person to conclude that the offender's *actions* were motivated, in whole or in part, by his or her bias, should an incident be reported as a hate crime" (Federal Bureau of Investigation, 2011b). Once again, this example highlights the importance of paying close attention to the methodologies on which data on aggression are based. Jurisdictions in other countries, such as Germany, do not recognise "hate crime" as a separate criminal offence, but deal with violent actions based on targets' group membership under a range of different offence categories, making it even more difficult to assess the scale of the problem.

For the purpose of our discussion, establishing the prevalence of hate crimes is less important than looking at the psychological processes that lead to acts of aggression against people on the basis of their group membership. Societal and individual factors must be considered jointly to understand hate crimes. For example, the 9/11 terrorist attacks created a general social climate of hostility against Muslims that translated into an increase in anti-Muslim attitudes at the individual level, and was accompanied by an increase in hate crimes against members of this group (Christie, 2006; see also Chapter 10). Similarly, a societal ideology of heterosexism may provide the basis for the stigmatisation of alternative sexual orientations and justify the expression of anger and hostility towards sexual minorities (Alden & Parker, 2005; Parrott & Peterson, 2008).

At the individual level, the extent to which these socially shared ideologies are internalised defines a person's racial, religious, or sexual prejudice. Prejudice is generally conceptualised in social psychology as a negative evaluation of others by virtue of their membership of a certain social group, and it is linked to discrimination at the behavioural level (Brown, 2010). Both Sherif's theory of realistic group conflict and Tajfel's social identity theory discussed at the beginning of this chapter are relevant to understanding the roots of prejudice. The former suggests that negative attitudes towards out-groups arise from conflicts of interest between competing groups, and it would explain hate crimes against members of ethnic or racial out-groups as a result of competition for material resources and social status. The latter emphasises the role of in-group favouritism and out-group discrimination in individuals' search for a positive social identity – for example, heterosexual men's attribution of positive characteristics to their in-group and their derogation of the out-group of gay men. Along these lines, Herek (2000) proposed that developing hostile attitudes towards members of sexual minorities is a way of coping with the threat posed by these groups to traditional gender roles and to the masculine self-concept of heterosexual men.

Prejudicial attitudes against members of out-groups defined by race, ethnicity, or sexual orientation have been linked to discrimination against members of those groups (for a meta-analytic review, see Six & Schütz, 1996). In a longitudinal analysis of survey data in Germany, Wagner, Christ, and Pettigrew (2008) found that ethnic prejudice predicted negative out-group behaviour over time. Several studies have demonstrated significant associations between sexual prejudice and aggression towards sexual minorities (for a review, see Parrott & Peterson, 2008). However, as Baron and Richardson (1994) have pointed out, there is no straightforward relationship between prejudice and aggression. Whether or not prejudiced people will respond more aggressively towards members of the rejected groups depends on the influence of mediating factors, such as fear of retaliation and anonymity. When white Americans who held strong prejudicial attitudes towards African Americans had to perform aggressive behaviour in public, they showed "reverse discrimination" (i.e., acted less aggressively towards a black than towards a white target person). However, if their behaviour was recorded anonymously they showed more aggression towards the black person (e.g., Donnerstein & Donnerstein, 1978).

Drawing on the General Aggression Model proposed by Anderson and colleagues (DeWall & Anderson, 2011) that identifies aggressive affect (anger) as a driving mechanism of aggression (see Chapter 2), Parrott and Peterson (2008) examined the role of anti-gay anger in the link between sexual prejudice and aggression. In their all-male sample, the higher the participants' level of sexual prejudice, the greater was their anger about gay men and the more anti-gay aggression they reported to have shown in the past (e.g., "I have spread negative talk about someone because I suspected that he or she was gay" or "I have gotten into a physical fight with a gay person because I thought he or she had been making moves on me"). Moreover, the link between sexual prejudice and anti-gay aggression was no longer significant when anti-gay anger was included in the analysis, supporting the claim that men holding anti-gay prejudice tend to behave more aggressively towards this group because they are angrier with them.

It has been demonstrated that rather than behaving aggressively towards members of a particular out-group, prejudiced people show a higher tendency to engage in aggressive behaviour in general – that is, against targets from all kinds of social out-groups. According to Bar-Tal (1990), *delegitimisation* is an important process mediating between the devaluation of out-groups and the performance of harmful action against out-group members. Delegitimisation refers to the "categorization of a group or groups into extremely negative social categories that are excluded from the realm of acceptable norms and/or values" (Bar-Tal, 1990, p. 65). If the perception of an out-group as different and inferior is accompanied by feelings of fear, then delegitimisation is likely to occur. Its function is (a) to maximise the difference between one's own in-group and the out-group, and (b) to provide a justification for the exploitation or other ill treatment of the out-group. The treatment of Jews in Nazi

Germany or of black citizens under the South African apartheid regime provide extreme examples of how delegitimisation creates a basis for justifying the oppression, persecution, and killing of out-group members (see also Bar-Tal, 1997).

Delegitimisation strategies are also reflected in the tendency to shift responsibility for aggressive behaviour from the actor on to the target persons who are said to elicit, or at least deserve, the negative actions directed at them. Using a jury simulation paradigm, Plumm, Terrance, Henderson, and Ellingson (2010) showed that participants who held negative views about gay people assigned greater blame to the victim of an alleged anti-gay hate crime than participants who held more positive views, confirming an earlier finding by Lyons (2006). Comparing the role of prejudice in attributions of victim blame in hate crimes and non-hate crimes, Rayburn, Mendoza, and Davison (2003) found that members of the white majority group assigned more blame to the victims of a racial, anti-Semitic, or anti-gay hate crime scenario than to victims of a crime unrelated to a particular out-group membership of the victim.

The research on hate crimes reviewed in this section underlines the psychological role of in-group identification and out-group derogation in securing a positive social identity. Out-groups become the collective targets of hostility and anger because they have characteristics, such as religious beliefs or sexual orientation, that are perceived as threatening the identity of the in-group. The fact that many of the target groups of hate crimes represent numerical minorities with limited social power and yet attract such intense feelings of hostility, further attests to the impact of psychological variables related to identity construction on this form of aggression.

Crowd behaviour

In contrast to groups that exist permanently, such as ethnic or religious groups, or over pro-longed periods of time, such as gangs, crowds are transient collectives that are formed on specific occasions. It has long been recognised that people's behaviour changes as they become members of larger groups, and our everyday experience confirms this observation. For example, everyone will have witnessed members of a large party in a restaurant who talked so loudly that they entertained the entire room without being aware of the noise level they created, or people who walk through the streets in groups, stepping into the road completely oblivious of traffic. In a tragic example, 12 young people were killed in Spain in 2010 when they crossed a live railway track and were hit by a passing train. Eyewitnesses said the teenagers had crossed the line "in a wave" (http://en.wikipedia.org/wiki/Castelldefels_train_accident).

There is plenty of anecdotal evidence that people lose their inhibitions when they are in a group, and engage in aggressive and antisocial behaviours, such as setting cars on fire or throwing stones, that they would never have shown on their own. In this section we shall look at research on aggressive behaviour by crowds of people, asking what can explain the change in behaviour when people move from being on their own to becoming a member of a crowd.

Building on the work of LeBon (1896), a French sociologist seen as the founder of "mass psychology," Zimbardo (1969) proposed three conditions that give rise to aggression in crowds: (a) anonymity, (b) diffusion of responsibility, and (c) large group size. Under these conditions, people are thought to engage in actions characterised by impulsiveness, irrationality, and regression to primitive forms of behaviour. To explain why ordinary people engage in behaviours that are totally out of character for them as individuals, Zimbardo (1969) introduced the concept of "de-individuation." His *de-individuation theory* claims that individuals acting in a large group lose their sense of personal identity and responsibility and may show aggressive behaviour that would normally be inhibited by their internal standards. He investigated this phenomenon with dramatic results in his famous "Stanford Prison Experiment" in 1971. In this experiment he recruited a group of mentally healthy young men, randomly assigned them to the roles of prisoners or prison guards, and asked them to enact their respective roles in a mock prison established in his laboratory at Stanford University. The experiment that had been planned to last for 2 weeks had to be aborted after 6 days because the guards engaged in increasingly cruel treatment of their prisoners, and the prisoners developed symptoms of severe trauma. The study was re-created in the UK in a BBC programme under the supervision of social psychologists Steve Reicher and Alex Haslam in 2001, albeit with much less dramatic results (Reicher & Haslam, 2006). In their study, the guards failed to identify with their roles and the guard-prisoner hierarchy eventually collapsed. However, Zimbardo (2006) pointed out that the BBC version differed from the original Stanford prison experiment in a number of ways, not least in the degree to which the experimental setting mirrored the constraints associated with the roles of guards and prisoners in a real prison situation. For example, in the BBC study, prisoners could be promoted to guards on the basis of good behaviour, something that is not normally possible in real prisons.

In an analysis of 500 violent assaults that occurred in Northern Ireland, Silke (2003) compared incidents in which attackers were disguised (wearing masks, hoods, or other clothing to cover their face) with those in which the attackers' faces could be identified. He established that significantly more serious injuries were inflicted, more acts of vandalism were committed, and more people were assaulted in the incidents involving attackers who were disguised.

A change in attentional focus has been proposed as a key mechanism for explaining aggression by members of a crowd (Diener, 1980; Mullen, 1983). When people are on their own, their attention is typically focused on the self, and they monitor their own behaviour against the standard of their personal norms and values. By contrast, being part of a larger group shifts attention away from the self on to the situation, reducing people's ability to regulate their behaviour in accordance with their personal norms. Instead, they pay more attention to the situational cues, particularly the aggressive behaviour of other group members. On the basis of his self-attention perspective, Mullen (1983) argued that the larger the crowd, the more difficult it would be for members to retain the self-focused attention that is important for inhibiting violent behaviour. His analysis of newspaper reports of 60 lynchings in the USA between 1899 and 1946 confirmed this line of reasoning. Mullen

(1986) demonstrated that lynch mobs were more savage in their atrocities as the size of the mob became larger relative to the number of victims. A later study used photographic records of 22 lynching events between 1890 and 1935. The number of mob members and the number of victims in each photograph were counted, and ratings were made of the level of atrocity of the victims' injuries (Leader, Mullen, & Abrams, 2007; Study 2). The results confirmed the earlier finding that the atrocities by lynch mobs became more savage as the size of the mob relative to the number of victims increased.

Explaining violent crowd behaviour as resulting from a breakdown of individual inhibitions implies a view of crowd behaviour as essentially unregulated by norms that might modulate aggressive behaviour. This view of crowd behaviour as characterised by the absence of social norms has been challenged by an alternative account arguing in favour of a *shift* rather than a *loss* of normative control. *Emergent norm theory* (Turner & Killian, 1972) proposed that crowd members base their behaviour on what they perceive to be the specific norms shared among the group. This means that behaviour may become either more or less aggressive depending on the normative stance towards aggression that is associated with the group. If being in a large group involves a shift from individual norms to perceived group norms, it follows that group behaviour should only be more violent than individual behaviour if the group norms are seen as promoting or at least condoning aggression. This is exactly what the study by Johnson and Downing (1979) showed. They de-individuated their participants either by dressing them in the uniform of the Ku Klux Klan, a group that is strongly associated with aggressive norms, or by dressing them in the uniform of nurses, a group closely associated with prosocial values. In two further individuated conditions, participants also wore the uniforms, but with large name tags attached to make them personally identifiable ("individuated"). The intensity of shocks delivered to an alleged co-participant in a teacher-learner task was the dependent variable in the experiment (see Chapter 1). Participants were told that a shock level for each error made by the learner would be set by default and that they could decide to increase or decrease that level. Selection of shock levels lower than the default setting therefore represented instances of prosocial behaviour, whereas shock levels above the default setting represented instances of aggressive behaviour. Participants in the individuated conditions believed that other group members would be able to identify the intensity of the shocks they delivered, whereas those in the de-individuated conditions believed that their shock settings would not be disclosed. Figure 9.4 presents the findings.

Participants in the Ku Klux Klan uniforms showed more aggression than those in the nurses' uniforms under both individuated and de-individuated conditions. However, as expected, the difference was greater under de-individuation, as indicated by a significant interaction between de-individuation and type of uniform. Thus, under conditions of de-individuation, participants' behaviour was affected to a greater extent by the antisocial and prosocial cues associated with the groups of Ku Klux Klan and nurses, respectively. These findings contradict the notion that de-individuation leads to a general breakdown of normative inhibitions against aggression, and support the view that it creates greater responsiveness to situational norms.

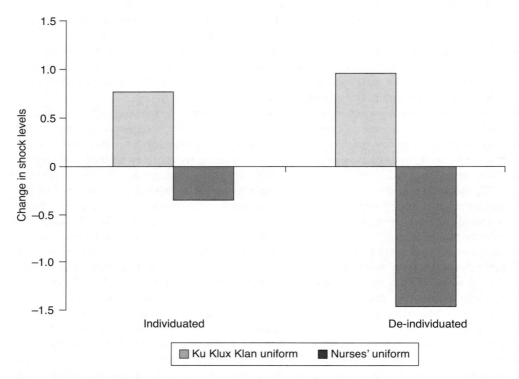

Figure 9.4 Effects of de-individuation and prosocial vs. aggressive situational norms on prosocial or aggressive choices of shock intensity. Possible range of scores was from –3 (maximal reduction of shock level) to +3 (maximal increase in shock level). (Adapted from Johnson & Downing, 1979, Table 1. Copyright American Psychological Association).

Sensitivity to group norms is also central to the explanation of crowd aggression based on social identity theory. The *social identity model of de-individuation effects (SIDE)* proposed by Reicher and colleagues stipulates that immersion in a group elicits a shift from personal identity to social identity that increases the salience of group norms (Reicher, Spears, & Postmes, 1995). Postmes and Spears (1998) conducted a meta-analysis of 60 de-individuation studies to contrast the prediction of de-individuation theory that aggressive crowd behaviour is a function of anonymity, reducing adherence to social norms, with the prediction that aggressive behaviour is related to situational norms in favour of, or against, aggression. They found little evidence that de-individuation promoted aggressive behaviour. However, they confirmed that under de-individuation, individuals' behaviour was more affected by situational norms, resulting in more aggression in the presence of pro-aggression norms and less aggression when the perceived situational norms inhibited aggression.

Beyond laboratory settings, historical analyses of riots also disconfirm the view that crowd action is uncontrolled, disorganised, and irrational, and support the importance of shared group norms. Rioting can be defined as a form of collective violence that involves "hostile collective action by a group of about 50 or more people who physically assault persons or property or coerce someone to perform an action" (Bohstedt, 1994, p. 259). For example, Bohstedt pointed out that in early modern Europe, food riots were common in times of food shortages, such as when harvests were poor and crops destroyed by bad weather conditions. These riots were restrained and organised, based on the idea of a "moral economy," and they were usually successful in bringing down food prices.

In a detailed case study of a riot in the St Paul's area of the city of Bristol in the UK in 1980, Reicher (1984) showed that the riot was confined to specific targets within a circumscribed geographical area, and that the rioters had developed a sense of shared identity vis-à-vis their common enemy (i.e., the police). In his sociological analysis of 341 urban riots in the USA during the 1960s, McPhail (1994) rejected the view that rioting is the result of structural strains particularly affecting young black males living in socially deprived ghettos. Instead he proposed a model of rioting as a behavioural response adopted by a person to achieve a particular aim (e.g., pursuing a political goal, acting out aggressive feelings against another group). In summarising his "purposive action model," McPhail concluded that "violent actors are neither the hapless victims of structural strain nor of psychological de-individuation. Purposive actors adjust their behaviours to make their perceptions match their objectives. They bear responsibility for those violent objectives and for the violent actions in which they engage" (McPhail, 1994, p. 25).

Summary

- Intergroup aggression and collective violence refer to a range of different forms of aggressive behaviour carried out by groups of individuals whose behaviour is shaped by the fact that they are acting as part of a group.
- Intergroup conflict arises out of competition when groups have incompatible goals, and it can be reduced by making groups engage in superordinate goals that require cooperation. This was argued in Sherif's theory of realistic group conflict and demonstrated in his famous Robbers Cave experiment. However, as argued by Tajfel in his social identity theory, intergroup aggression arises even in the absence of realistic conflicts as a result of social categorisations into in-group and out-group that enable individuals to establish a positive social identity through seeing their in-group as more positive than the out-group.
- Gang violence often involves extreme forms of intergroup violence, and represents a significant social problem. In addition to structural conditions, such as poverty, concerns for social identity also play a role in explaining why people become involved with violent gangs. Much of the violent behaviour shown by gangs is directed against rival gangs and therefore qualifies as intergroup aggression. Favouring the in-group and derogating the out-group in the service of achieving a positive social identity from gang

membership are potent psychological processes that fuel violent confrontations between gangs.

- Hate crimes are a form of intergroup aggression in which victims are targeted because of their ethnic, racial, or religious group membership, or their sexual orientation. They are driven by societal ideologies that marginalise or derogate the out-groups, which in turn gives rise to prejudicial attitudes against these groups at the individual level. By devaluing out-groups and questioning their legitimate rights of social participation, the basis is formed for justifying aggressive treatment of minority groups.

- Crowd violence and rioting are forms of collective violence that occur in specific contexts in transient social groups. Whereas earlier research on de-individuation explained aggressive crowd behaviour as the result of a breakdown of self-regulation and normative control, subsequent explanations stressed a shift from individual norms to group norms. According to this view, crowd behaviour is more aggressive than individual behaviour to the extent that the crowd endorses norms that disinhibit aggressive behaviour. Case studies of riots suggest that these forms of collective violence only superficially appear unregulated and anarchic. In fact they are often based on a normative structure evolved within the group, such as limiting aggression to specific target groups or locations.

Tasks to do

(1) Look at the detailed description of the Robbers Cave experiment by Sherif et al., including original photos, on http://psychclassics.yorku.ca/Sherif/index.htm.
(2) Visit the websites of the National Gang Center (www.nationalgangcenter.gov) and the Eurogang Project (www.umsl.edu/~ccj/eurogang/euroganghome.htm) for more information about the problem of gang violence and attempts to curb it.
(3) Watch the original video footage from Zimbardo's Stanford Prison Experiment on the official website (www.prisonexp.org). Also visit the website of the BBC Prison Study (www.bbcprisonstudy.org) and look out for differences between the two studies.

Suggested reading

Billig, M., & Tajfel, H. (1973). Social categorization and similarity in intergroup behaviour. *European Journal of Social Psychology, 3*, 27–52.

Reicher, S. D. (1984). The St. Paul's riot: An explanation of the limits of crowd action in terms of a social identity model. *European Journal of Social Psychology, 14*, 1–21

Sherif, M. (1958). Superordinate goals in the reduction of intergroup conflict. *American Journal of Sociology, 63*, 349–356.

Vasquez, E., Lickel, B., & Hennigan, K. (2010). Gangs, displaced, and group-based aggression. *Aggression and Violent Behavior, 15*, 130–140.

10 Terrorism

Terrorism is a special form of group-based aggression that poses a threat to the sense of safety and well-being of people around the globe. Despite the worldwide notoriety achieved by individual terrorists, such as Osama bin Laden, terrorism is for the most part an intergroup phenomenon (McCauley & Segal, 2009). Terrorism refers to violence that arises out of conflict between social groups that differ in ethnicity, religion, national or cultural identity, or political aims. It is intended to spread fear in communities (ranging from local to worldwide) in order to influence the decisions or behaviour of political agents. This chapter summarises a prolific research literature that has addressed the causes, manifestations, and consequences of terrorist violence as reflected, for example, in a recent collection of scholarly articles by Victoroff and Kruglanski (2009). In trying to understand the phenomenon of terrorist violence, the following discussion is divided into five sections.

First, a working definition of terrorism will be provided to identify the characteristic features of this form of aggression and to see its overlap with, and differences from, other types of group-based violence.

Secondly, although social, political, and historical background conditions provide a basis on which terrorism develops and may be sustained, only a minority of people living under these conditions engage in terrorism. Therefore explanations will be presented seeking to understand what turns individuals into terrorists and what the psychological processes are that lead them to be drawn to terrorist groups and to commit atrocious acts of violence against innocent targets.

Thirdly, we shall consider why it is that people accept and endorse terrorist violence, creating both the moral and practical support that is needed by terrorist groups to operate effectively.

Fourthly, a growing body of evidence will be reviewed that has examined the impact of terrorist violence on the attitudes, behaviour, and mental health of people who experience and witness terrorist attacks, both in the countries or regions immediately affected and in the population worldwide.

Finally, we shall ask how terrorism may be overcome and what strategies hold potential for reducing this form of intergroup aggression.

It is clearly the case that terrorist movements differ from one another in many respects, from the historical, political, and societal context in which they operate to the specific tactics they employ. Bearing this diversity in mind, the following discussion seeks to shed light on some common features from a social psychological point of view, trying to understand the individual and intergroup factors involved in terrorist violence.

Defining terrorism

In attempting to define terrorism, it is more useful to consider acts than to consider persons. Labelling a group of people as terrorists is ambiguous, because it is heavily dependent on the perspective and affiliation of those who make the categorisation, as reflected in the well-known saying that "one person's terrorist is another person's freedom fighter" (Friedland, 1988). By contrast, defining terrorism in behavioural terms is easier, because it narrows down the broad issue of what causes terrorism to the more tractable question of what makes individuals engage in terrorist acts. Although there is no consensus in the literature on how exactly to define terrorist acts (Strom & Irvin, 2007), two main features have been suggested as characteristic of these behaviours. First, terrorist acts are acts of violence that are used not only as direct means to achieve political aims, but also as instruments to achieve publicity and spread fear and intimidation. Secondly, they are directed at harming targets other than the direct opponents in the underlying political conflict, most notably targets in the civilian population.

Both criteria highlight that it is not the direct physical harm which is the primary objective of terrorist acts, but the psychological effects in terms of attracting public attention and undermining the authority of the state in ensuring the safety of its citizens. A succinct definition reflecting these criteria characterises terrorism as "politically motivated violence, perpetrated by individuals, groups, or state-sponsored agents, intended to instill feelings of terror and helplessness in a population in order to influence decision making and to change behavior" (Moghaddam, 2005, p. 161).

In addition to describing what defines terrorist violence, it is necessary to distinguish it from other forms of violent behaviour. Strom and Irvin (2007) have identified several ways in which terrorist violence differs from other forms of criminal violence.

(1) *Motivation*. Unlike the typical criminal offender whose acts of violence are motivated by personal gain, terrorist violence is motivated primarily by political or moralistic goals.

(2) *Publicity*. Whereas criminal offenders typically attempt to hide their violent acts from others, terrorists seek media attention to alert the world to their cause.

(3) *Organised structure*. Terrorist organisations typically operate in social networks united by a common political goal and a common enemy. Although this is also true for certain forms of organised crime, such as gang violence, Strom and Irvin (2007) have pointed out that terrorist groups are much more dependent for their cohesion on the presence of a defined leader, and are more likely to break down than criminal organisations when their leader is captured or killed (see also Post, 2005).

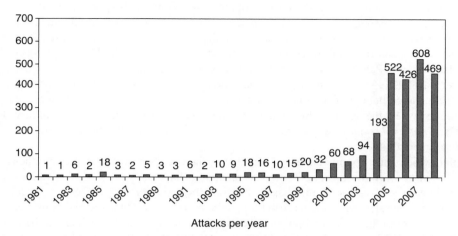

Figure 10.1 Incidence of suicide attacks around the world from 1981 to 2007. The figures were derived from a database covering suicide attacks around the world which is maintained by the first author of the study. Only attacks where the suicide bomber actually tried to kill him- or herself were counted. In almost all cases (98.7%) the suicide bomber died in the attack. (Reprinted with permission from Merari et al., 2010, p. 88. Copyright Taylor & Francis.)

(4) *Symbolic meaning.* Finally, as noted above, terrorist acts are intended to send out a message to a wider audience well beyond the immediate incidents and targets, something that does not typically apply to criminal violence.

A further feature that distinguishes terrorist acts from criminal violence is that they are often carried out by individuals who are willing, or even desire, to sacrifice their own life. These so-called *suicide attacks* are defined as assaults "intended to achieve a political objective, performed outside the context of a conventional war, in which the assailant intentionally kills himself for the purpose of killing others" (Merari, Diamant, Bibi, Broshi, & Zakin, 2010, p. 89). As shown in Figure 10.1, the incidence of suicide attacks has increased dramatically in the last 10 years, which can be attributed in large part to the numerous incidents in Iraq and Afghanistan.

Suicide attacks differ from non-suicidal terrorist violence in that they are embedded in a culture of martyrdom that promises special rewards to those who are willing to sacrifice their life in the service of the "good cause."

Psychological processes underlying terrorist violence

Our discussion will focus on the *psychological* aspects of terrorist violence that may help to explain what attracts people to terrorism, up to the point of sacrificing their own life, and what makes them willing to commit violent acts against innocent civilians. However, it is clear that the historical and material dimensions of intergroup conflict also play a critical role in providing the breeding ground for terrorist action (Hinde, 1997). This is highlighted, for example, in analyses of the genocide in Ruanda (Smith, 1998), as well as the long-standing conflicts between Catholics and Protestants in Northern Ireland (Cairns & Darby, 1998) or between Israelis and Palestinians in the Middle East (Fields, Elbedour, & Hein, 2002; Rouhana & Bar-Tal, 1998). As Singer (1989) has noted, *systemic conditions* (e.g., material resources, allegiance bonds) at the multi-national level, *dyadic conditions* in the bilateral relationship between the groups involved (e.g., trade relationship, balance of military strength), and *national conditions* within a country (e.g., economic instability) all interact to bring about terrorist violence.

To explain when and why movements directed at social change resort to violence rather than non-violent forms of political activism, several authors have transferred the frustration-aggression hypothesis, discussed in Chapter 2, from the individual to the group level. According to this view, terrorist violence can be explained as the result of perceived injustice, combined with a sense of social and political deprivation. In some cases, such as the Irish Republican Army (IRA) or the Palestine Liberation Organization (PLO), the frustrations leading to the emergence of terrorist movements are immediately traceable to a history of oppression. The actions of other terrorist groups, such as the Red Army Faction in Germany in the 1970s and 1980s, are more difficult to attribute to the blocking of specific goals. As noted by several scholars, the evidence linking terrorist violence to frustration and deprivation has been far from conclusive, not least because individuals from better educated and more privileged social classes are over-represented among the members of many terrorist groups (Kruglanski & Fishman, 2009; Victoroff, 2009).

To understand why individuals associate with terrorist groups and engage in acts of violence, especially suicide attacks, an obvious hypothesis to consider is that they are mentally disturbed and suffer from some form of psychopathology. However, evidence to support this view is sparse and has largely failed to yield consistent results, leading some authors to conclude that "terrorist psychopathology is a dead issue" (Silke, 2009, p. 96). Studies attempting to find evidence of psychopathology in the special group of suicide bombers are complicated by the fact that they have to rely mostly on second-hand evidence, such as interviews with relatives after the attacks were carried out.

In a rare exception, Merari et al. (2010) studied 15 survivors whose suicide attacks had been foiled and compared them with a group of 14 organisers of suicide attacks and a control sample of 12 men who had been convicted of violent acts in the context of political protests. On the basis of extensive clinical assessments, Merari et al. established that 40% of the participants in the suicide group displayed suicidal tendencies, whereas none of the organisers or the control participants did so. Depressive tendencies were also found more often in the suicide group (53%) than in the organiser group (21.4%) and the control group (8.3%). At the same time, the suicide group showed significantly less ego strength (defined as the ability to cope with stress and regulate affective states) than the organisers and the control group, and were more likely to display a tense and anxiety-ridden personality style.

As Lankford (2010) has pointed out, the personality characteristics and symptoms identified in suicide bombers show some overlap with the correlates of suicidality identified in the clinical literature outside the context of terrorism. However, Merari et al. (2010) did not find evidence of a history of mental illness in their sample of suicide attackers, which would be expected as a common precursor of suicide. They concluded: "Hence, although suicidality is perhaps a contributing factor in a significant minority of the terrorist martyrs, suicide bombers' motivating and background factors are different from those of ordinary people who commit suicide" (p. 100). Beyond the search for psychopathological characteristics, attempts to establish a profile of the prototypical terrorist have been equally unsuccessful. Neither demographic factors, such as level of education or economic status, nor personality traits have been found to reliably distinguish terrorists from individuals not involved in this form of violence (Kruglanski & Fishman, 2009).

However, failure to establish a psychological profile of the typical terrorist is not to say that psychological processes are irrelevant to the understanding of terrorism. Rather than focusing on stable personality traits or demographic characteristics, it would seem more promising to explore the processes by which individuals become attracted to terrorist groups. In this context, it is useful to distinguish between *attitudes* related to terrorism and manifest *behaviour* in terms of planning or carrying out acts of terrorist violence. Although, in general, the association between attitudes and behaviour is far from perfect, it is reasonable to propose that developing a positive attitude towards violence and a normative belief that acts of violence are acceptable and appropriate is a precursor to, or prerequisite for, engaging in terrorist behaviour. A process of radicalisation takes place to the extent that individuals (or groups) move from initially non-violent forms of protest or pursuance of political goals to the use of violence towards civilian targets, and this process involves a shift in attitudes and normative beliefs condoning violent action. It is also likely to involve an increase in anger as an emotional underpinning of terrorist behaviour, generated at least in part by frustration over the apparent failure of non-violent forms of action.

In his analysis of the developmental processes that may drive a person towards terrorist violence, Huesmann (2010b, p. 3) began by stating that people who commit acts of violence are not "just like you and me", and that their behaviour is not normal in the human adult. The challenge therefore is to understand how individuals grow up to be attracted to, and willing to engage in, terrorist violence, while recognising that no single influence is likely to be able to explain these extreme forms of behaviour. Huesmann applied his social-cognitive model of aggression, presented in Chapter 2, to the explanation of terrorist violence, stressing the convergence of individual predispositions and precipitating situational conditions. According to the social-cognitive model, aggressive behaviour is guided by aggressive scripts acquired through observational learning in the process of socialisation. The more prominent aggression and violence are in the social environment of a child and the more acceptable they appear to be, the more firmly they become ingrained in his or her cognitive script for dealing with conflict situations, and the more they promote a hostile world schema (i.e., the belief that the world is a violent and hostile place) (for a discussion of the hostile attribution bias, see Chapter 3). Aggressive scripts include normative beliefs about the appropriateness and legitimacy of aggression and about the situational cues that prompt an aggressive response. Emotions, such as anger or fear, play a critical role in the activation, evaluation, and enactment of aggressive scripts. Not only do people select scripts that are congruent with their current emotional state, but they also base the decision as to which script to follow in a given situation on their emotional responses. For example, an aggressive script is more likely to be activated when the person is angry, and it is more likely to be chosen as a course of action when the person feels good about it.

The script model can explain how being exposed to violence in the course of socialisation may precipitate violent behaviour through the promotion of aggressive scripts and hostile world schemata. However, additional personal dispositions need to be considered to explain why only a small number of individuals holding aggressive scripts turn to terrorist violence. Huesmann (2010b) identified three predisposing personal characteristics associated with an increased susceptibility to terrorist violence. The first characteristic is *narcissism*, defined as a grandiose view of the self and a sense of entitlement that leads to aggression when challenged by others (see Chapter 3). As Baumeister, Smart, and Boden (1996) have noted, terrorists often cultivate an attitude of moral superiority over their victims, from which they derive justification for their violent actions. Moreover, engagement in terrorism, especially suicide attacks, holds the promise of recognition by their in-group as martyrs or heroes, which has particular appeal for narcissistic individuals. The second personal characteristic is *proneness to negative emotional states*, as captured in constructs such as irritability and trait anger (see Chapter 3), which lowers the threshold for the activation of aggressive scripts. The third characteristic is *low arousal* in response to depictions of violence, which enables the person to engage in violent behaviour without remorse and concern for the victims. As noted in Chapter 2, under-reactivity, indicated by low levels of resting cortisol, has been identified as a precursor to aggressive behaviour. In addition, being exposed to violence in the process of socialisation may lead to reduced reactivity to violence through a process of desensitisation. If these individual predisposing factors meet with a social context in which violence is common and even encouraged – for example, by a charismatic leader – violent behaviour becomes more likely. Although this conceptual framework has not yet been applied systematically to the study of terrorist violence, there is support from studies on exposure to high levels of violence in the community (e.g., Guerra, Huesmann, & Spindler, 2003) and from a longitudinal study in Northern Ireland showing that exposure to terrorism in childhood was a predictor of terrorist activities in adulthood (Fields, 1979). In addition, a study with relatives of suicide bombers in Indonesia found normative support for their violent actions from the immediate family members, especially among those who had strong anti-western sentiments (King, Noor, & Taylor, 2011).

Beyond the acquisition of aggressive scripts and normative beliefs condoning the killing of civilian targets, the question arises of the motivations that drive people to perform terrorist acts. Researchers have identified a diversity of motives underlying terrorists' activities, which can be broadly subsumed under three different headings: (a) *ideological reasons* (e.g., the aim of promoting particular religious and political beliefs), (b) *personal causes* (e.g. a desire for revenge), and (c) a sense of *social duty* (e.g. protecting one's country against enemies) (for a summary, see Kruglanski, Chen, Dechesne, Fishman, & Orehek, 2009).

In an attempt to integrate these different motives, Kruglanski et al. (2009) proposed an overarching motivation, namely the *search for significance*, as the driving force behind terrorists' activities. Focusing on suicide bombers, they argued that sacrificing one's life in the service of a common cause provides a means of achieving personal significance beyond death by becoming a martyr and living on in the collective memory of one's group. According to an influential social psychological model termed *terror management theory (TMT)*, the terror invoked by the knowledge of mortality induces people to identify more strongly with their cultural norms and world views as a way of becoming part of a lasting collective identity that transcends their own physical existence (Pyszczynski, Solomon, & Greenberg, 2003). Being reminded of their mortality induces individuals to respond favourably to people who share their world view, and to react with hostility towards those who threaten it (see Burke, Martens, & Faucher, 2010, for a meta-analysis of mortality salience effects). Alerting people to their mortality is a strong cue to insignificance, and the prospect of achieving immortality through an act of martyrdom, coupled with the promise of paradise in some religious ideologies, decreases death anxiety by reducing the threat of insignificance. Furthermore, the quest for significance can explain why feelings of relative deprivation, the sense of being denied their fair share of resources such as wealth or status, may lead people to engage in terrorist activities. Being deprived of what one is entitled to is a clear indication of personal insignificance, eliciting the need to restore significance by other, potentially violent means. Finally, experiences of frustration and loss can also be seen as creating a threat of insignificance, with self-sacrificing behaviours being a way of re-establishing personal importance. If the individual quest for significance meets with an ideology that presents violence against out-groups as a way of gaining significance, terrorism becomes a salient option.

Finally, the fact that terrorist violence is to a large extent an intergroup phenomenon points to social identity theory (SIT) as a framework for understanding engagement in terrorist violence (Schwartz, Dunkel, & Waterman, 2009). This theory, described in detail in Chapter 9, proposes that individuals seek to achieve a positive social identity through assigning positive qualities to the groups to which they belong and through the derogation of out-groups. Although SIT argues that even categorisation based on minimally important criteria is enough to elicit in-group favouritism and out-group derogation, hostility against out-groups is stronger the more they are seen as a threat, for example, to territorial claims or cultural values. Under conditions of intergroup conflict, differences between in-group and out-groups are highlighted, presenting the in-group as superior and leading to categorical distinctions between "them" and "us." The fact that single incidents highlighting intergroup boundaries can have dramatic effects on people's willingness to join terrorist groups underlines this point. For example, when the British Army killed 26 unarmed civil rights protesters in Northern Ireland in 1972 in what came to be known as "Bloody Sunday", the number of new recruits into the IRA showed a sharp increase.

Defining out-groups as "inferior", "evil", or even as less human serves an important function in disabling inhibitions against violence directed towards out-group targets, such as innocent civilians. Willingness to die for one's group in a suicide attack may be seen as the ultimate expression of loyalty to the in-group, but as noted by Schwartz et al. (2009), it requires a particular constellation of cultural conditions: a strong commitment to collectivist values that put the needs of the group above those of the individual, the promise of rewards, and a high value placed on martyrdom for the sake of the group cause.

Pathways into terrorism: the "staircase model"

Societal-level variables cannot explain why out of all the people living under the same adverse conditions, only very few end up becoming terrorists. Similarly, individual-level variables cannot explain why out of all the people to whom particular individual characteristics apply, only very few turn to terrorism. Given the widespread nature of social and political injustice that affects large numbers of people without turning them into terrorists, individual and intergroup characteristics must be considered in conjunction to explain how these conditions at the macro level of society are channelled into terrorist activities. Friedland (1988, p. 111) has presented an interactionist model, arguing that terrorism is a joint function of both situational and individual factors. The origin, in most instances, is a widespread social protest movement. Confrontations, often violent, with authorities and failure to elicit an acceptable response lead to disillusion and deterioration of the movement. Remnants of the movement form small, clandestine groups that maintain little external contact and a fierce in-group loyalty and cohesion. These circumstances enhance the status of violent individuals within the groups, elevate them to leadership positions, and allow them to establish terrorism as the groups' preferred mode of operation.

More recently, Moghaddam (2005) used the metaphor of a staircase to conceptualise the interplay of societal, intergroup, and individual variables, and to describe the stages through which people are drawn into terrorism. The staircase becomes narrower at each floor, and only a very few people eventually climb to the top. Moghaddam's *staircase model* is depicted in Figure 10.2.

The *ground floor* is occupied by all members of society who evaluate their living conditions in terms of fairness and justice. Those who perceive their conditions to be fair and just remain on the ground floor, while those who see them as unjust move on to the first floor. On the *first floor* they evaluate the options for improving their conditions. Those who conclude that there are options for them as individuals to improve their position and influence decision makers through non-violent participation leave the staircase to terrorism at this level and pursue alternative paths. Those who are dissatisfied with the available options for redressing injustices move on to the second floor.

On the *second floor*, feelings of anger and frustration about not being able to improve their situation predominate, activating the search for a target – an "enemy" – to blame for their misfortune. This enemy can be either a direct opponent, such as a central government denying autonomy to an ethnic group or region, or a third party towards whom aggression is shifted, such as reflected in the widespread anti-Americanism in the Middle East. People on this level, who believe that there is an enemy towards whom they can direct their aggressive tendencies, will then climb up to the next floor.

By the time they arrive on the *third floor*, individuals have developed a certain readiness towards violence that can now be exploited by terrorist organisations through offering a

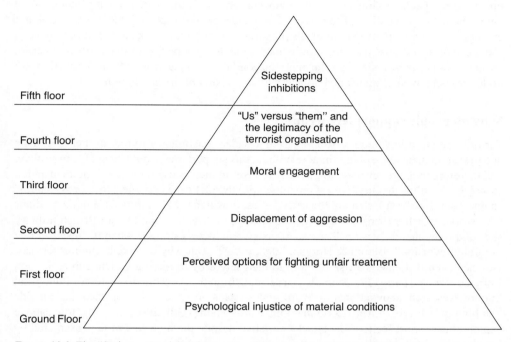

Figure 10.2 The "Staircase Model" of terrorism. (Based on Moghaddam, 2005).

sense of "moral engagement" to their potential new recruits. Violent actions against the alleged enemy are presented as morally acceptable or even imperative, and recruits are offered a new and appealing social identity as members of a highly selective in-group of fighters for freedom and justice. Those for whom this offer is attractive climb up to the next floor.

On the *fourth floor*, categorical thinking in terms of "us" and "them" is promoted by isolating new recruits from their families and friends, imposing strict secrecy, and emphasising the legitimacy of the terrorist organisation. There is virtually no chance for people who have climbed up to this floor to withdraw and exit alive. Therefore they have no choice but to move up to the *fifth floor*, which involves carrying out the terrorist act. In order to operate effectively on this floor, inhibitions against killing innocent people must be overcome, and this is achieved by two well-established psychological mechanisms: *categorisation*, stressing the differentiation between in-group and out-group, and *distancing*, which exaggerates the differences between the in-group and the targets that are seen as the enemy.

The staircase metaphor is useful for conceptualising the process by which a small number of individuals from large groups of disaffected people living under adverse conditions end up committing acts of violence against innocent targets. At the same time, it provides some clues about the prevention of terrorism. Moghaddam (2005) has pointed out that it is not enough to try to identify the individuals prepared to carry out terrorist acts before they get a chance to do so, because that would only make room for new people to step forward. Instead, terrorism can only be ended by reforming the conditions on the ground floor so that they are no longer perceived as unjust and hopeless by large parts of the population.

Why do people support terrorism?

Terrorist organisations require support from a wider constituency to recruit their members and to sustain their sense of legitimacy. Without this support they would be unable to survive, and therefore they are sensitive to public responses to their activities and willing to abandon strategies that alienate those who sympathise with them. A case in point is the "proxy bomb" campaign in Northern Ireland in the early 1990s, in which the IRA forced Catholic civilians who worked for the British army (i.e., the enemy) to drive car bombs into British military sites and blow themselves up. The use of proxy bombs was stopped when it caused "a tide of public revulsion" (Bloom & Horgan, 2008, p. 599). But why do people support terrorist violence even if it entails a risk of harm to themselves by triggering violence in retaliation from the attacked party? For example, survey data from the Palestinian Center for Policy and Survey Research showed that 69% of Palestinians interviewed supported the suicide bombing in Tel Aviv in April 2006 that killed 11 civilians (Gill, 2007, p. 150). How can we explain this support for terrorist attacks on Israel despite the high risk of being targeted by Israeli retaliation?

Several social psychological theories may prove useful for understanding public support for terrorist violence. Social identity theory, beyond helping to explain why people are prepared to engage in terrorist violence against an out-group, also offers an explanation of why people support terrorism. According to this theory, a positive evaluation of terrorist acts committed by members of the in-group towards targets of a disliked out-group helps members of that in-group to achieve a positive identity. In line with this reasoning, Levin, Henry, Pratto, and Sidanius (2009) showed, in a study with Lebanese students at the American University of Beirut, that the stronger the participants' Arab identification, the more they supported the 9/11 attack on the World Trade Center.

A strong in-group identification also affects attributions of the causes of behaviour shown by members of the in-group versus the out-group. Negative behaviour by in-group members is likely to be attributed to external or uncontrollable factors, whereas negative behaviour by out-group members is attributed to internal factors. Moreover, negative behaviour by a member of the in-group is seen as atypical of the group as a whole (the so-called "black sheep" effect), whereas negative behaviour by an out-group member is generalised to the group as a whole. This "intergroup attribution bias" (Hewstone, 1990) may explain why people make external attributions for terrorist acts by in-group members with whom they share religious, political, or ethnic affiliations. They see terrorist violence by in-group members as caused by external forces, such as wrongdoing by the out-group, and also as uncharacteristic of the in-group as a whole, whereas they attribute behaviour by members of the out-group to negative qualities that are typical of the out-group in general. A series of studies by Doosje, Zebel, Scheermeijer, and Mathyi (2007) conducted in the Netherlands found support for the intergroup attribution bias in explaining terrorist violence. They compared Islamic and non-Islamic participants' attributions for the murder of the Dutch film-maker Theo van Gogh by an Islamic terrorist in 2004. Non-Islamic participants attributed more responsibility to the assailant and also to the Islamic world in general than did Islamic participants. Non-Islamic participants also perceived the assailant as a more typical member of the Islamic world than did Islamic participants, and this tendency was stronger the more they identified with being Dutch (i.e., their own national in-group).

Research by Tarrant, Branscombe, Warner, and Weston (2012) has shown that people are more accepting of violence when it is perpetrated by an in-group rather than an out-group member. Participants in two studies conducted with British and American students received an alleged newspaper report on a suspected terrorist who had been tortured by a member of the security force. They were asked to rate how morally justified the torture was and how much empathy they felt for the target. When the torturer was presented as belonging to the in-group (a member of the British security services for British participants and a member of the US security services for American participants), they found torturing the suspect more morally justified and reported less empathy for the target than if the torturer was presented as belonging to the respective out-group.

Terror management theory (TMT), introduced earlier as an explanation for suicide bombers' willingness to give up their lives, is another useful approach for explaining public support for terrorist violence. Briefly, the theory stipulates that the existential terror associated with the knowledge of one's mortality activates the desire to achieve a symbolic sense of immortality through the endorsement of consensually shared cultural values. Seeing oneself as part of a system of values that is passed on through the generations can provide an anxiety-buffering function, counteracting the fear of death (Pyszczynski, Abdollahi, Solomon, Greenberg, Cohen, & Wiese, 2009). Two implications follow from this line of reasoning. First, the higher the level of awareness of one's mortality (e.g., because of attacks by a political enemy), the greater the need for affiliation with the predominant value system. Secondly, the more that value system is questioned and threatened by outside forces, the greater the willingness to defend it. In combination, these two mechanisms would suggest that the more terrorist violence is framed as a way of defending the cultural values of the in-group against an enemy, the more support it should attract from the terrorists' community. Research by Pyszczynski et al. (2009) with Islamic students in Iran confirmed this prediction. In the first study, participants were asked to evaluate a fellow student who allegedly either supported martyrdom attacks against the USA or opposed such attacks, and to indicate their willingness to consider joining the martyrdom cause. Before reading about the fellow student's attitudes, those in the mortality salience condition were asked "to describe the emotions that the thought of your own death arouses in you" and to "jot down, as specifically as you can, what will happen to you as you physically die" (Pyszczynski et al., 2009, p. 285). A control condition was included in which participants were given the same instructions with regard to dental pain rather than their own death. The findings are presented in Figure 10.3.

As expected, support for terrorist violence, indicated by a positive evaluation of the person holding pro-martyrdom views and by their own willingness to consider joining the martyrdom cause, was significantly higher when participants had thought about their own death (the mortality salient condition) than in the control condition. Mortality salience did not significantly affect the evaluation of the person holding an anti-martyrdom attitude or their own willingness to consider joining the anti-martyrdom cause. These findings are in line with the proposition that reminders of death make people more susceptible to threats to their world view and more willing to support actions designed to defend it. This tendency is reinforced by a rhetoric, adopted by many terrorist movements, which designates the groups that are seen as the source of the threat as evil, and the fight against them as a holy cause.

Effects of terrorism on attitudes, behaviour, and mental health

Terrorist violence is designed to spread fear and intimidation among civilian populations, and there is no doubt that it is successful in achieving this goal. In this section we shall look at the effects of terrorist violence on three areas of psychological functioning and well-being. First, we shall examine the effects of terrorist violence on attitudes towards the ethnic, religious, or political groups to which terrorists belong, and towards threats to the social order more generally. Secondly, we shall ask what kind of behavioural responses people adopt to adjust to the terrorist threat. Finally, we shall look at the impact of terrorist violence on mental health, particularly in terms of the development of post-traumatic stress disorder.

Changes in attitude

Several studies have shown that terrorist attacks lead to a deterioration in attitudes towards the group to which the terrorists belong and, in addition, to a general increase in prejudicial attitudes towards out-groups. A quasi-experimental study conducted in Spain demonstrated that attitudes towards Arabs became more negative after the Islamic terrorist attack in Madrid in 2004. In addition, there was a rise in anti-Semitism as well as in authoritarianism, and endorsement of conservative values and a decrease in support for liberal values (Echebarria-Echabe & Fernández-Guede, 2006). American research by Carnagey and Anderson (2007) demonstrated that attitudes towards war became more positive immediately after the attacks of 9/11, and remained elevated a year later. An experimental study conducted in the Netherlands confirmed that exposure to news about terrorist attacks carried out by Muslims increased anti-Muslim prejudice among non-Muslims, just as exposure to news about terrorism by non-Muslims increased prejudicial attitudes against them among Muslims (Das, Bushman, Bezemer, Kerkhof, & Vermeulen, 2009). The effect was mediated by an increase in death-related thoughts after reading the news items, lending support to the prediction of terror management theory that awareness of one's mortality increases in-group affiliation. Not only does mortality salience increase support for terrorist violence, as shown

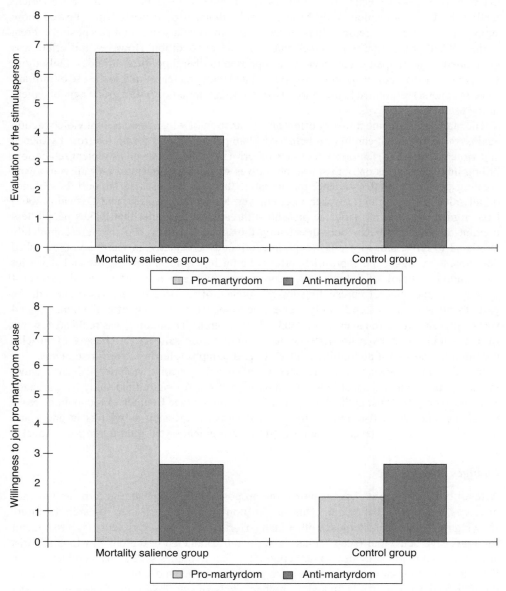

Figure 10.3 Iranian students' support for martyrdom attacks on the USA. Higher values indicate a more positive evaluation of the stimulus person and/or a greater willingness to consider joining the pro-martyrdom cause. (Reprinted with permission from Pyszczynski et al., 2009, p. 287. Copyright Psychology Press.)

in the study by Pyszczynski et al. (2009) described above, it also increases support for violent retaliation. In a companion study by the same authors, American students showed more support for the use of extreme military force against individuals and countries posing a threat to the USA after a mortality reminder than in a control condition. However, this effect was moderated by participants' conservative as opposed to liberal political attitudes. Only those with a conservative political orientation (associated with greater affinity to the use of military force in general) responded to the mortality salience manipulation with a greater endorsement of the use of violence.

Thus terror management theory offers an explanation of why people accept violent action against out-groups that can in turn help to explain public support for both terrorist violence and violent retaliation. Unfortunately, acts of terrorist violence as well as violent retaliation, killing innocent targets on both sides, themselves work as reminders of mortality, in a way creating a natural mortality salience manipulation that serves to escalate support for violence on all sides of the conflict. Fischer, Greitemeyer, Kastenmüller, Frey, and Osswald (2007) have argued that terrorist violence presents a threat to social order that makes people less tolerant towards any behaviours threatening the social order, even if they are completely unrelated to terrorism. In a quasi-experimental study conducted in Germany, they asked participants to suggest an appropriate criminal punishment for a car thief either 1 day after the London bombing of 7 July 2005 (representing high salience of terrorist threat), or 4 weeks after the attack (representing lower salience of terrorist threat). As predicted, the participants assigned a significantly higher fine to the car thief 1 day after the attack than 4 weeks after the attack (an average of 8503 vs. 5996 euros). The finding was replicated in two further studies that experimentally induced high terror salience by means of articles highlighting the risk of an imminent attack or photographs referring to terrorist attacks.

In addition to changes in attitude, there is evidence that terrorist violence also has a wider impact on personality dispositions related to aggression. A longitudinal study by Carnagey and Anderson (2007) using the Aggression Questionnaire (see Chapter 1) found an increase in college students' self-reported physical and verbal aggression as well as in anger and hostility from pre-9/11 levels to the post-9/11 measurement a year after the terrorist attacks.

Changes in behaviour

A small body of research has examined the proposition that exposure to terrorist violence increases aggressive behaviour. This proposition draws on a wider research literature showing that exposure to violence other than terrorism (e.g., family violence) is a risk factor for aggressive behaviour (see Chapter 7). Research conducted in regions in which terrorist attacks are common provides some support for this hypothesis. A study conducted with Palestinian youths showed that exposure to political conflict and violence, either directly or through media reports, was linked to higher levels of aggression, as measured by peer nominations, over and above the influence of exposure to violence in the community (Dubow et al., 2010). Even-Chen and Itzhaky (2007) compared adolescents from parts of Israel with high vs. low levels of exposure to terrorism, and obtained self-reports of their sense of personal danger as well as changes in their behaviour following terrorist attacks. They found that exposure to terrorism predicted higher levels of interpersonal aggression, even when controlling for exposure to violence in the family and in the community. However, an interesting finding emerged when hope about the future was considered as an additional variable. Only in the group who scored low on hope for the future was a sense of danger related to higher levels of violence, whereas for those who scored high on hope for the future the correlation was non-significant.

In addition to studies looking at responses among groups directly exposed to terrorist violence, other research has examined changes in behaviour among populations that witnessed terrorist violence through the media without being directly affected. The largest research literature is available on responses by citizens in the USA following the attacks of 9/11. For example, in a survey by Torabi and Seo (2004), 29.2% of participants reported that their behaviour "had changed as a result of 9/11." The different areas in which behavioural changes were reported are depicted in Figure 10.4.

As shown in Figure 10.4, changes in mode of transportation were among the most frequently reported behavioural adaptations following 9/11 in the Torabi and Seo (2004)

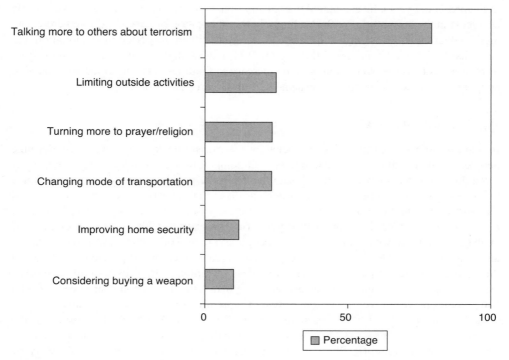

Figure 10.4 Changes in behaviour as a result of 9/11. (Based on Torabi & Seo, 2004).

survey. Similarly, in a survey of Londoners in the wake of the bombings of 7 July 2005, 32.5% of respondents indicated that they intended to travel less on underground transport, trains, and buses in or into central London (Rubin, Brewin, Greenberg, Simpson, & Wessely, 2005). When the same participants were interviewed again 7 months later, 19% of them still said that they intended to use public transport less than before the attacks (Rubin, Brewin, Greenberg, Hughes, Simpson, & Wessely, 2005).

Two studies by Gigerenzer (2004, 2006) examined the consequences of behavioural adaptations to the threat of terrorism based on an analysis of terrorism as a "dread risk" – that is, an event that has a low probability of occurring but a high risk of harm. Gigerenzer pointed out that terrorist violence not only causes direct effects, most notably injuries and loss of life, but also has indirect effects, such as job losses in the tourism industry, which are not under the immediate control of the terrorist agents. Examining a particular type of indirect effect resulting from the 9/11 terrorist attacks, namely people's fear of flying and avoidance of plane journeys, Gigerenzer investigated whether the shift from air travel to car journeys would be reflected in the rate of fatal road traffic accidents. Calculating the mean number of fatal road traffic accidents in the USA between 1996 and 2000 and comparing them with the figures for 2001, he found significantly higher rates for the months in the wake of 9/11 (i.e., October to December 2001). Extrapolating from the figures for the same period in the preceding years, he calculated that an additional 353 people were killed in road traffic accidents in the 3 months after 9/11, outnumbering the toll of 246 passengers and crew who died on board the planes crashed by the 9/11 terrorists. When the period of examination was extended to the full 12 months following the 9/11 attacks, and data on the average number of road miles travelled were included, the increase in fatalities was confirmed and linked to an increase in road traffic during the same period (Gigerenzer, 2006).

Effects on mental health

In addition to affecting attitudes and behaviour, terrorist attacks may severely undermine people's mental health and psychological well-being. One way of addressing this issue is through large-scale surveys in which samples from the general population are questioned about psychological symptoms, such as depression and anxiety, typically based on standard diagnostic criteria, such as the *Diagnostic and Statistical Manual of Mental Disorders, Fourth Edition (DSM-IV)* (American Psychiatric Association, 1994). For example, DeLisi et al. (2003) interviewed a sample of 1009 people living or working in New York between 3 and 6 months after the 9/11 attack. They used a validated measure of psychological trauma that addressed the frequency and severity of 17 symptoms, such as painful memories, avoidance of feelings, and sleep problems. More than half of the people surveyed (56.3%) had at least one very severe symptom or two or more mild or moderate symptoms.

A substantial body of literature, reviewed by Fischer and Ai (2008), has examined the traumatic effects of terrorist violence as conceptualised in the symptomatology of post-traumatic stress disorder (PTSD). As noted in Chapter 7, PTSD is defined in the DSM-IV by three main criteria, all of which must persist for more than 1 month: (a) re-experiencing of the traumatic event, (b) avoidance of stimuli associated with the trauma and numbing of general responsiveness, and (c) symptoms of increased arousal. Several studies conducted in the first few months after the 9/11 attacks found elevated rates of PTSD in general population samples. In the study by Schlenger et al. (2002), which included more than 2000 adults in New York and Washington, DC, the prevalence rate of PTSD was 11.2%, a figure that was higher than the national average of 4.2%. However, findings with regard to the persistence of symptoms beyond the first few weeks after the attack are inconclusive. Several studies suggest that the elevated rates of PTSD in general population samples returned to baseline levels within a few months after the attacks (e.g., Galea et al., 2003; Silver, Holman, McIntosh, Poulin, & Gil-Rivas, 2002). On the other hand, a longitudinal study found that the level of stress and the number of PTSD symptoms remained elevated for up to 1 year, relative to pre-9/11 levels (Silver, Poulin, Holman, McIntosh, Gil-Rivas, & Pizarro, 2005). Studies with people immediately involved at the scene of the attacks, such as firemen and rescue workers, showed that the PTSD rates in these groups even increased over time (e.g., Brackbill et al., 2009).

Research conducted in parts of the world where terrorist violence is a constant threat, such as the Middle East, has also shown increased levels of PTSD. A study by Besser, Neria, and Haynes (2009) conducted in Israel compared a group who had been exposed to ongoing terrorist violence with a group who had not been exposed to terrorist threat. They found significantly higher levels of perceived stress and a significantly higher association between perceived stress and PTSD in the former sample. The problem with much of this research literature is that it is unclear whether the experience of terrorism is *causally* related to PTSD, because the data were collected after the event. In one of the few studies that were able to relate symptoms to measures obtained prior to a terrorist attack, Rosen, Tiet, Cavella, Finney, and Lee (2005) found that patients diagnosed with PTSD before 9/11 did not show a deterioration of their symptoms when studied again post 9/11. However, this finding does not address the question of whether the rate of PTSD increased in populations that did not show signs of the disorder prior to 9/11.

In addition to the obvious negative effects of terrorist violence on mental health and well-being, the experience of collective trauma may also entail positive aspects, as captured in the construct of "post-traumatic growth. Post-traumatic growth refers to the experience of positive change that occurs as a result of the struggle with highly challenging life crises (Tedeschi & Calhoun, 2004). It is intuitively plausible that post-traumatic growth could be a protective factor against developing PTSD, so that the more people saw the trauma as allowing personal growth, the better they would cope, reflected in lower susceptibility to PTSD. However, the evidence on this issue is not clear, as many studies have found positive correlations between post-traumatic growth and PTSD (for a review, see Pat-Horenczyk & Brom, 2007). For example, Hobfoll et al. (2008) found in a sample of Israeli Jews directly exposed to terrorist violence that those who reported a high level of post-traumatic growth, defined in terms of an increase in social resources, were at greater risk of developing PTSD symptoms. However, no such link was found for Israeli Arabs directly exposed to violence. Again, cross-sectional studies such as this one are unable to address the possibility that people who are more adversely affected by exposure to terrorism are more motivated to seek post-traumatic growth, rather than post-traumatic growth being maladaptive in the sense of increasing the risk of PTSD. A longitudinal analysis, again conducted in Israel, found no significant pathway over time from post-traumatic growth to PTSD symptoms (Johnson et al., 2009). However, more longitudinal research is needed to examine the relationship between post-traumatic growth and PTSD as a process of coming to terms with the experience of terrorist violence. The findings of a longitudinal study by Updegraff, Silver, and Holman (2008) showed that *searching* for meaning shortly after the 9/11 attacks was linked to higher levels of PTSD a year later, whereas a sense of *finding* meaning was linked to a reduction in symptoms. It may well be that people's beliefs about personal growth as a result of exposure to trauma change in the course of the coping process. Perhaps they move from "wishful thinking," as a way of seeking comfort in the initial stages when post-traumatic stress levels are high, to a more constructive re-examination of core beliefs and values that may attenuate the negative impact of the trauma (Tedeschi, Calhoun, & Cann, 2007).

Psychological strategies for preventing terrorist violence

Finding effective ways of responding to terrorist violence is a global challenge, and as reflected in reports of new acts of terrorism coming in almost daily, it has so far had limited success. In this section no attempt will be made to discuss the strategies adopted at the political and military level – for example, by engaging in violent retaliation as a means of deterrence, or by reducing opportunities for attacks by reinforcing air travel security (see, for example, Victoroff & Kruglanski, 2009, Section VIII). Instead we shall briefly examine two approaches at the individual and intergroup levels that exemplify a social psychological perspective on preventing terrorist violence.

Many of the processes that explain an increased readiness for aggression can also be applied to the aim of reducing support for, and commitment of, terrorist violence. Terror management theory is a case in point. As discussed earlier, this theory proposes that terrorist threat functions as a reminder of mortality that increases commitment to prevailing cultural value systems and world views in an attempt to cope with the existential fear of death. This reasoning suggests that if the prevailing world view proclaims values which promote peace and compassion, mortality salience should decrease support for terrorist violence. A study by Rothschild, Abdollahi, and Pyszczynski (2009) has provided support for this prediction. It was found that reading a passage from the Koran which emphasises compassion reduced the endorsement of aggressive attitudes against the West in a sample of Shiite Muslims.

Another approach that is relevant to the prevention of terrorism is provided by social identity theory. As noted above, engaging in violence to express feelings of hatred towards out-groups and to protect the in-group against material or symbolic harm is a way of maintaining a positive social identity. Experiencing violent retaliation from the target group serves to strengthen in-group solidarity, and increases the willingness to commit further attacks. From this perspective, trying to undermine the identity construction that gives rise to terrorism may be a way forward. According to Schwartz et al. (2009), this challenge can be broken down into more specific tasks. The first task is to address the grievances that motivate out-group hostility through political changes. For example, Moghaddam (2006) has outlined ways of establishing a "contextualised democracy" that builds upon existing cultural traditions. The second task is the weakening of the intergroup boundaries that separate "them" and "us" by promoting cooperative contact between the conflicting groups (Cohen & Insko, 2008; see also Chapter 9). Finally, it is important to offer more attractive social identities than that of being a terrorist by providing mainstream forms of social participation that make individuals less susceptible to terrorist ideologies. None of these tasks will be easy or sufficient in themselves to prevent terrorist violence. However, they may help to shape an agenda for reducing the global threat of terrorism in the long term, and stop potential terrorists on their way up the staircase that leads to extreme forms of violence.

Summary

- Terrorism is defined as politically motivated violence, perpetrated by individuals, groups, or state-sponsored agents, that is intended to instil feelings of terror and helplessness in a population in order to influence decision making and change behaviour.
- There is little evidence to support the view that terrorists suffer from psychopathological disorders. Instead, psychological analyses have proposed that the learning of aggressive scripts through exposure to violence, the search for significance as a motivational basis, and the striving for a positive social identity are critical psychological processes that draw individuals towards terrorist groups. The "staircase model" was developed to explain why out of the large number of people who are disenchanted with their personal or social circumstances, only a small minority eventually engage in terrorist violence.
- *Social identity theory*, stressing the influence of in-group solidarity and out-group derogation, and *terror management theory*, focusing on the impact of terrorist violence as a mortality salience cue that instigates the need to affirm one's cultural values, offer explanations of why people support terrorist violence.
- Terrorist attacks elicit changes in attitudes, behaviour, and mental health both in the targeted communities and beyond. Attitudes towards the ethnic, religious, or political groups to which terrorists belong become more negative, and support for war and military action increases. At the behavioural level, exposure to terrorist violence has been linked to increased aggression as well as to changes in behaviour that may lead to alternative risks, such as changes in transportation behaviour associated with increases in road traffic fatalities. In terms of the effects on mental health, there is evidence of post-traumatic stress responses even in people not directly exposed to terrorist violence, although it is not clear how persistent the effects are. Research on post-traumatic growth points to a potentially constructive way of coping with terrorist violence, but the links between post-traumatic growth and post-traumatic stress responses are not yet clear.
- Social psychological theories of intergroup behaviour suggest strategies for reducing the likelihood of terrorist violence by capitalising on the activation of non-violent world

views to reduce support for terrorism under conditions of mortality salience, and by weakening intergroup boundaries as well as offering alternative, non-violent social identities to people who might otherwise be attracted to terrorist groups.

Tasks to do

(1) Visit the website of START, the National Consortium for the Study of Terrorism and Responses to Terrorism, to find out more about their work (www.start.umd.edu/start/research/investigators/investigator.asp?id=24).

(2) On the START website, look at the Global Terrorism Database, which contains a systematic collection of more than 87 000 incidents of terrorism (www.start.umd.edu/gtd).

(3) Visit the websites of two leading journals that specialise in the subject of terrorism to see the range of research topics addressed in this field: *Studies in Conflict and Terrorism*, started in 1977 (www.informaworld.com/smpp/title~content=t713742821) and *Terrorism and Political Violence*, started in 1989 (www.informaworld.com/smpp/title~content=t713636843).

Suggested reading

Huesmann, L. R. (2010). How to grow a terrorist without really trying: The psychological development of terrorism from childhood to adulthood. In D. Antonius, A. D. Brown, T. K. Walters, J. M. Ramirez, & S. J. Sinclair (Eds), *Interdisciplinary analyses of terrorism and political aggression* (pp. 1–21). Newcastle upon Tyne: Cambridge Scholars Publishing.

Moghaddam, F. (2006). *From the terrorists' point of view*. New York: Praeger.

Victoroff, J., & Kruglanski, A. W. (Eds) (2009). *Psychology of terrorism*. New York: Psychology Press.

Scholarly Content on the Impact of 9/11: a website containing free journal articles and book chapters (http://eu.wiley.com/WileyCDA/Section/id-611707.html).

11 Preventing and reducing aggressive behaviour

In the course of the last chapters, is has become abundantly clear that aggressive behaviour is rife in many areas of social life and brings misery and long-term suffering to large numbers of people. In addition, the economic costs of aggression and violence for health services, the labour market, and the criminal justice system are immense. Therefore, exploring effective ways to prevent and reduce aggressive behaviour is a pressing task. Even though the causes of aggressive behaviour are still not fully understood, the research brought together in this volume has accumulated a large body of knowledge that can be used to design strategies for prevention that are grounded in theory and based on empirical evidence.

This chapter offers a selective overview of approaches designed to tackle the problem of reducing aggression and violence. To systematise the large literature on the prevention of aggression, a distinction is made between general approaches and specific approaches. *General approaches* are designed to influence processes involved in many different forms of aggressive behaviour, such as affective and cognitive antecedents of aggression. *Specific approaches* are custom-tailored to address particular forms of aggressive behaviour, such as sexual abuse of children or bullying in the workplace. Within each of the two categories, a further distinction can be made between measures that target the *individual* person and measures that are implemented at the *societal* level. Table 11.1 illustrates these distinctions.

In the first part of this chapter we shall examine general strategies for reducing aggression that are directed at the individual person or implemented at the societal level. In addition to strategies that have been shown to be successful in reducing aggression, we shall also take a critical look at approaches that, despite their common-sense appeal and popularity in everyday discourse, have been demonstrated to be ineffective or even counterproductive. In the second part of the chapter, examples of prevention and intervention efforts to tackle specific forms of aggression, such as gang violence, domestic violence, and sexual aggression, will be discussed.

General strategies for preventing and reducing aggression

Theories of aggression specify the mechanisms by which aggressive behaviour is elicited and maintained, both in the course of individual development and in the immediate situation (see

Table 11.1 Approaches to prevention: illustrative examples

	Level of implementation	
Scope	*Individual*	*Society/community*
General	• Anger management • Eliciting incompatible responses • Modelling and reinforcement	• Capital punishment • Gun control • Alcohol restrictions

Domain-specific
   Gang violence
   Child abuse
   Sexual violence
	
	• Training of effective refusal skills
	• Promoting parenting skills
	• Rape prevention classes
		
		• Imposing curfews
		• Mandatory reporting
		• Restricting opportunities

Chapter 2). By implication, these theories can also be used as a basis for the development of strategies for preventing and modifying aggressive behaviour. For example, the view that aggression is the result of anger arousal points to the potential effectiveness of programmes designed to promote anger control. Explaining aggression as a response to aggressive situational cues suggests that limiting the influence of such cues (e.g., by keeping children and adolescents away from violent media contents) may be effective in reducing aggression. In the present section, general prevention strategies such as these are discussed that are applicable to many manifestations of aggressive behaviours. We shall begin by looking at strategies implemented at the societal level, and then move on to measures targeting the individual.

Societal-level approaches

Every society is under an obligation to offer its members the best possible protection against aggression and violence. Despite the fact that aggressive behaviour must ultimately be changed at the level of the individual aggressor, societal norms and practices can have a profound effect on the scale of aggression displayed by its individual members. Two studies of the link between alcohol use and aggression (see also Chapter 4) illustrate this point. The first study, conducted in Australia, found a positive association between the number of outlets selling alcohol and the rate of domestic violence in the neighbourhood (Livingston, 2011). The second study, conducted in Canada, showed that an intervention named "Safer Bars" implemented at the level of bars in Toronto was successful in reducing the level of physical aggression in bars (Graham et al., 2004). The intervention was designed to improve staff members' risk assessment skills and to train them to de-escalate and pre-empt violent incidents.

A general approach towards prevention at the societal level is to reduce opportunities for carrying out aggressive behaviours through influencing the social and physical environment (Goldstein, 1994b). Examples of measures implemented at the societal or community level to reduce opportunities for aggression are presented in Table 11.2.

For example, tightening security controls at airports worldwide was introduced in the wake of the 9/11 attacks to stop terrorists from carrying weapons and explosives on board

Table 11.2 Examples of societal measures for reducing opportunities for aggressive behaviour

- Airport security controls
- Alcohol bans in public
- Designated women's spaces in public car parks
- Dispersal zones for curbing antisocial behaviour
- Gun-control measures
- Neighbourhood watch schemes
- Restraining orders for stalkers or violent partners
- Strategic seating areas that separate fan groups at sports events
- Surveillance cameras in public places

planes. In the UK, measures designed to reduce aggressive and antisocial behaviour at the community level include neighbourhood watch schemes, in which residents cooperate to reduce violent and criminal behaviour in their local area, and the designation of "dispersal zones," which give police special powers to tell people in groups to disperse in certain designated areas for specified periods of time.[1] Apart from the difficulty of establishing the effectiveness of these measures, few of them have been subjected to systematic evaluations. A crucial question in evaluating their effectiveness is whether these strategies actually reduce the overall level of aggressive behaviour or simply shift it to less well-protected targets or areas. Fritsch, Caeti, and Taylor (1999) evaluated the effects of policing measures designed to reduce gang violence. They found that imposing a curfew and truancy enforcement significantly reduced gang violence, whereas merely increasing the presence of police patrols had no effect. A more effective way of preventing aggression may be to remove stressors known to enhance aggressive tendencies via the elicitation of negative affect, such as high temperature, noise, and crowded living conditions (see Chapter 4). This could be achieved, for example, by installing air conditioning systems in schools or by reducing spatial density in prisons (Anderson et al., 2000).

A central way in which societies seek to prevent and control aggressive behaviour is by means of legal regulations. The law is used to enforce adherence to social norms, not only by punishing individual lawbreakers but also by deterring future perpetrators from committing acts of aggression. In addition, as illustrated by some of the examples in Table 11.2, legal regulations are used to reduce the opportunities for aggressive behaviour (e.g., by prohibiting public drinking, or by banning abusive partners from approaching their victims).

Capital punishment

Whether or not legal sanctions have a deterrent effect on violence can be assessed with respect to the effectiveness of capital punishment. Deterrence theory assumes that "preventing

---

1 See: http://www.camden.gov.uk/ccm/content/press/2009/february/new-dispersal-zone-introduced-to-reduce-antisocial-behaviour–.en;jsessionid=587D3BDAAA60C6027C8A481BDBACC13E

crime requires the development of a system of punishment that will teach the lesson that 'crime does not pay'" (Bailey & Peterson, 1999, p. 258). Furthermore, it proposes that criminal acts are preceded by a rational decision-making process in which the potential offender weighs the presumed benefits of the criminal act against the cost of punishment. With few exceptions, studies that have examined the deterrent effect of capital punishment on homicides are limited to the USA as the only western nation still carrying out the death penalty in 34 states (www.deathpenaltyinfo.org).

Two main strategies have been employed to assess the deterrence potential of capital punishment: comparing homicide rates between US states with and without capital punishment, and comparing homicide rates before and after the abolition of capital punishment within a state (for reviews, see Bailey & Peterson, 1999; Land, Teske, & Zheng, 2009). Findings from both paradigms have disconfirmed the deterrence hypothesis by failing to provide evidence of lower homicide rates in states with capital punishment and increases in states that abolished capital punishment. However, as noted by Land et al. (2009), any inferences are fragile, given the small number of executions in many of the jurisdictions. Focusing on Texas as a state with a comparatively high execution rate, these authors found a small short-term dip in the number of homicides following executions, but this was followed by an increase in the subsequent months.

Further disconfirmation of the deterrence hypothesis comes from findings which show that neither the certainty nor the speed with which the death penalty was imposed was related to homicide rates (Wright, 2010). Even when enforced swiftly and with high certainty, capital punishment failed to act as a deterrent against future crimes. This was true for different types of murder, including police killings and homicides committed by female perpetrators. Critics have also proposed that rather than acting as a deterrent to homicide, the death penalty may have a brutalising effect, increasing homicide rates, by suggesting that it is appropriate to kill others against whom one has a grievance. There is some support for the brutalisation hypothesis in the evidence reviewed by Land et al. (2009).

Bailey and Peterson (1999, p. 274) concluded "that policy makers would do well to consider means *other* than capital punishment to significantly reduce the rate of homicide in the United States." More recent evidence reviewed above has confirmed this conclusion. The findings also send a clear message to those countries that have abolished capital punishment but in which public opinion regularly calls for its re-introduction following high-profile murder cases.

Gun-control legislation

Another example of how legal regulations are used to curtail the level of violence in a community is provided by gun-control legislation. Two out of three victims of homicide are killed with firearms (Miller, Hemenway, & Azrael, 2007), but whether reducing access to firearms would also bring down homicide rates has been a controversial issue, as illustrated, for example, by Michael Moore's well-known film *Bowling for Columbine* (2002). It has been argued that restricting access to firearms might not only be ineffective, but could in fact increase violence by limiting citizens' right and ability to defend themselves. Isolating the effects of gun-control legislation from the complex network of variables associated with the role of firearms, particularly in American society, is a difficult task. Nonetheless, there is consistent evidence of a positive link between gun prevalence and homicide rates both from the USA and from other parts of the world. For example, a study that included 26 high-income countries yielded a substantial correlation in the region of $r = 0.70$ between rates of gun ownership and rates of homicide, indicating that about 50% of the variance in homicide rates can be attributed to variations in the prevalence of firearms (Hemenway & Miller, 2000; for a review, see Hemenway & Hepburn, 2004).

However, such comparisons suffer from the problem that both firearm prevalence and homicide could be driven by other variables, such as cultural norms about violence, so that they do not necessarily suggest that reducing the availability of firearms would bring down homicide rates. Vigdor and Mercy (2006) examined changes in intimate partner homicide in different US states contingent upon the introduction of legal regulations restricting violent partners' access to firearms. They found that intimate partner homicides, especially those with female victims, decreased after states had passed such laws. Another study found that intimate partner homicide rates were 50% lower in states that require a waiting period of up to a week before a firearm is issued, which may allow the aggressors to "cool off" in the interim (Roberts, 2009).

Thus there is some evidence to suggest that making it harder for people to get hold of firearms reduces the risk of fatal violence. Even if gun-control legislation does not bring down violence rates, as some authors have claimed (e.g., Kleck & Hogan, 1999), it seems to have a positive effect on reducing fatality rates. However, it is clear that in order to have long-term effects, gun-control measures must be complemented by efforts to change public attitudes towards firearms, and to enhance citizens' sense of personal security in their communities so that guns are no longer seen as vital means of self-protection.

Measures directed at the individual

Ultimately, aggressive behaviour is performed by individual actors. Therefore a central objective is to influence the individual person so as to reduce the likelihood that he or she will show aggressive behaviour, both as a habitual pattern of behaviour over time and in a specific situation. As discussed in Chapter 2, psychological theories conceptualise aggressive behaviour as the result of an individual's learning history in the course of socialisation and the interplay of affective, physiological, and cognitive processes in a specific situation. Thus, influencing these processes would seem like a promising approach for reducing the likelihood of aggressive behaviour.

Unlearning aggression

There is ample evidence that aggression is a form of learned behaviour shaped by direct reinforcement and observational learning (see Chapter 2). Therefore, it follows that aggression can also potentially be reduced using the same mechanisms. The principle of reinforcement suggests that aggression should decrease and eventually be extinguished if it is followed by negative consequences, such as punishment. Indeed punishment is widely used to deter people from engaging in aggressive behaviour, both at the individual and the societal level. However, learning theory tells us that the effectiveness of punishment in stopping people from acting aggressively is dependent on several critical preconditions (Berkowitz, 1993).

(1) The anticipated punishment must be seen as adverse, so that the desire to avoid it is sufficiently strong.
(2) It must have a high probability of being imposed, which implies that the odds of being detected must be high.
(3) It must be imposed swiftly after the aggressive behaviour for the connection to be made between the offending behaviour and the negative consequence.
(4) The person's level of affective arousal must not be so high that it prevents him or her from engaging in a rational calculation of the costs of an aggressive behaviour in terms of the likely punishment.
(5) The person has to see alternative behavioural options in the given context.

If these conditions are met, punishment may be an effective strategy for stopping people from behaving aggressively on future occasions. However, the probability that these necessary conditions will co-occur in a given situation is relatively low, which limits the scope of punishment as a strategy for controlling aggression at the individual level. In addition to this practical limitation, a more fundamental criticism of punishment must be raised. Punitive responses, particularly in the form of verbal and corporal punishment, may in themselves instigate aggression by functioning as aggressive cues. They may reinforce aggressive scripts by presenting aggressive behaviour as an acceptable way of regulating interpersonal and intergroup conflict. This has been shown by a large number of studies which have demonstrated that harsh parental discipline is associated with higher levels of aggressive behaviour in children (e.g., Gershoff et al., 2010; see also Chapters 3 and 7). To make punishment a viable strategy for reducing aggression, imposing negative consequences to reduce aggression needs to be embedded within a more general approach towards social-emotional learning in which the primary aim is to reward desirable rather than to penalise undesirable behaviour (Jones, Brown, & Aber, 2011).

Observational learning

An alternative approach based on learning theory for preventing and reducing aggressive behaviour is observational learning. Exposure to non-violent role models is directed at the acquisition of new behavioural repertoires by which aggressive response patterns can be replaced in a more lasting way. Seeing people behaving in a non-aggressive fashion has been found to decrease the performance of aggressive acts by the observers

(Baron & Richardson, 1994). However, as Eron (1986) pointed out with regard to role models on the TV screen, the mere observation of non-aggressive models is less effective in changing aggressive response patterns than an integrated approach in which observation is combined with strategies for implementing the observed behaviour, such as role playing and performance feedback.

Both reinforcement and observational learning theories suggest that promoting the use of non-aggressive discipline strategies by parents should be a viable strategy for reducing children's aggressive behaviour. This objective is an integral part of *parent management trainings* designed to teach parents to interact with their children in a way that reinforces positive social behaviour (Eckenrode, 2011; Kazdin, 2005). Parent management trainings were shown in a wide range of studies to be successful in terms of changing children's antisocial behaviour patterns (e.g., Pearl, 2009).

Anger control

At the level of affective processes, anger has been identified as a critical antecedent of aggressive behaviour, which suggests that promoting people's ability to control their anger (e.g., in response to a provocation) should reduce their readiness to show an aggressive response. Anger management training aims to achieve just that. It is primarily directed at individuals with a history of poor anger control, but may also be used in the general population to promote anger regulation skills. The focus of anger management approaches is on conveying to the aggressive individual "an understandable model of anger and its relationship to triggering events, thoughts, and violent behaviour itself" (Howells, 1989, p. 166). Anger management approaches draw heavily on the principles of cognitive-behavioural therapy, in particular Meichenbaum's (1975) "*stress inoculation training*" (*SIT*), which was adapted to anger management by Novaco (1975). The central features of the anger-related SIT, as summarised by Beck and Fernandez (1998), are presented in Table 11.3.

In the course of the training, participants first learn to identify the cues that arouse their anger and to reduce their angry affect by interpreting the situation in a de-escalating way. Next, they are trained to use relaxation techniques to calm themselves, which are then

Table 11.3 The "stress inoculation training" approach to anger management (Based on Beck & Fernandez, 1998, p. 64)

Phase 1	• Identification of situational triggers which precipitate the onset of the anger response
	• Rehearsal of self-statements intended to reframe the situation and facilitate healthy responses (e.g., "I can handle this. It isn't important enough to blow up over this")
Phase 2	• Acquisition of relaxation skills
	• Coupling cognitive self-statements with relaxation after exposure to anger triggers, with clients attempting to mentally and physically soothe themselves
Phase 3	• Exposure to trigger utilising imagery or role play
	• Practising cognitive and relaxation techniques until the mental and physical responses can be achieved automatically and on cue

combined with the cognitive strategies for self-appeasement. The two strategies are rehearsed through role playing and practised repeatedly so that they can be activated on cue in anger-eliciting situations.

A meta-analysis of anger management studies based on the stress inoculation approach was conducted by Beck and Fernandez (1998). Their analysis included a total of 50 studies, the majority of which used self-reported anger as the dependent variable. The remaining studies used behavioural observation of aggression as the criterion. In total, 40 studies compared differences in anger or aggressive behaviour between an anger management group and a control group, and 10 studies explored intra-individual changes in the critical variable (anger or aggression) from a pre-test to a post-test subsequent to the anger management training. The meta-analysis yielded a large effect size across the set of studies (average weighted $d = 0.70$), suggesting that anger management is an effective strategy for reducing anger-based aggression. Other meta-analyses of school-based interventions (Robinson, Smith, Miller & Brownell, 1999) and studies of adults with clinical levels of anger (Del Vecchio & O'Leary, 2004) found effect sizes of a similar magnitude, also demonstrating the effectiveness of anger management interventions.

However, a less optimistic appraisal of the anger management approach comes from studies evaluating anger management trainings for violent offenders (Watt & Howells, 1999), juvenile male offenders (St. Lawrence, Crosby, Belcher, Yazdani, & Brasfield, 1999), and adolescents at high risk of aggression (McWhirter & Page, 1999), which largely failed to support the effectiveness of these interventions. These studies highlight a critical limitation of anger management interventions: they can only work with individuals who are aware of the fact that their aggressive behaviour results from a failure to control their aggressive impulses, and who are motivated to change their inadequate handling of these impulses (Howells & Day, 2003). Unfortunately, these requirements are rarely met in those high-risk groups who experience the greatest problems with anger control.

Whereas anger management interventions are specifically designed to enable individuals to control their angry affect, a more general approach is to promote individuals' self-control beyond anger management. In a study by Denson, Capper, Oaten, Friese, and Schofield (2011), participants in the intervention condition underwent 2 weeks of self-control training that involved a physical regulation task when engaging in everyday activities (e.g. when brushing their teeth or carrying items). In a subsequent experimental session, those in the training condition were less likely to respond aggressively to a provocation and reported less anger towards the provocateur than untrained participants in the control condition.

Eliciting incompatible responses

Whereas anger management interventions are designed to promote a person's ability to control anger in the longer term, evidence suggests that it is also possible to counteract anger-based aggressive behaviour situationally. This is done by eliciting affective states and cognitions that are incompatible with anger, and thereby buffer the effects of aggression-eliciting stimuli on angry affect and anger-related cognitions (Tyson, 1998). For example,

Krahé and Bieneck (2012, Study 1) showed that participants who listened to music rated as pleasant in a pilot study (e.g. Grieg's *Peer Gynt Suite*) while receiving a provocation subsequently reported less anger than did participants who listened to music rated as aversive (a mix of Hardcore and Techno) or those in a no-music control condition. Addressing the buffering role of music in a real-life context, Wiesenthal et al. (2000) assigned a sample of commuters to either a group that listened to self-selected music while driving to work, or to a no-music group. Depending on the level of traffic congestion on the route to work, participants were classified as experiencing low vs. high traffic congestion, representing different stress levels. Self-reported driver stress was the dependent variable. Under low traffic congestion conditions, listening to music made no difference, but under high congestion conditions, participants in the music group reported significantly lower levels of stress than those in the no-music condition (for a discussion of research on the link between driver stress and aggressive driving, see Chapter 6). Overall, this research suggests that eliciting positive affect may be an effective strategy for buffering the effects of frustration and provocation in triggering aggressive responses.

Eliciting incompatible responses to suppress aggression can also work via the cognitive route. In another study by Krahé and Bieneck (2012, Study 2), participants who were listening to pleasant music while receiving a provocation took significantly longer to recognise aggressive words in a lexical decision task than did provoked participants who were listening to aversive music or no music at all. A study by Bremner, Koole, and Bushman (2011) showed that priming religious thoughts decreased anger following a provocation. After receiving a provocation in the form of a negative essay evaluation (for the essay evaluation paradigm, see Chapter 1), their participants were either asked to pray for a sick fellow student or just to think about her. Those who had engaged in praying subsequently reported less anger than those who had merely thought about the sick student. A second study found a buffering effect of praying on aggressive behaviour measured by the noise blast paradigm.

Greitemeyer and Osswald (2009, Study 2) asked participants to play either a prosocial video game (*Lemmings*) or a neutral game (*Tetris*) before administering a word completion task as a measure of aggressive cognitions. Participants who had played the prosocial game produced significantly fewer aggressive word completions than those who had played the neutral game. In a subsequent set of studies, Greitemeyer (2011) showed a parallel effect for music with prosocial as opposed to neutral lyrics. Furthermore, participants reported lower state hostility and showed less relational and physical aggression after listening to music with prosocial as compared with neutral lyrics.

Research into the concept of disgust provides further support for the buffering effect of emotions that are incompatible with aggression. Pond, DeWall, Lambert, Deckman, Bonser, and Fincham (2012) argued that whereas anger and aggression are approach oriented, disgust is avoidance oriented, eliciting withdrawal behaviour. Therefore the urge to withdraw should interfere with aggression that requires approach, so that people who are sensitive to the experience of disgust should be less inclined to show aggressive behaviour. Supporting this line of reasoning, a series of studies showed that high disgust sensitivity was linked to less aggressive behaviour across different measures of aggression.

Catharsis

According to a widely accepted notion, bottling up one's angry feelings carries the risk of uncontrolled outbursts of aggression. Therefore many people believe that releasing aggressive tension through physical activity in sport or in symbolic ways, such as through sarcastic humour or acting aggressively in the virtual reality of a video game, is a successful strategy for "letting off steam" and reducing aggression (Bushman & Whitacker, 2010). As we saw in Chapter 2, Freud (1920) used the concept of catharsis to argue that the venting of hostile feelings can lead to a discharge of aggressive impulses that reduces the likelihood of aggressive behaviour. Similarly, the idea that aggressive urges can be channelled into harmless forms of expression is part of Lorenz's (1966) steam boiler model of aggression, also described in Chapter 2.

The term "catharsis" refers to the idea in Greek tragedy that watching the unfolding and resolution of tragic conflict on stage leads to a purification or "cleansing" of the emotions (pity and fear) in the audience, and brings about spiritual renewal or release from tension. However, empirical evidence shows that symbolic engagement in aggressive thoughts or actions is not only ineffective but even counterproductive for reducing aggression (Schaefer & Mattei, 2005). There is plenty of evidence that the imaginary performance of aggressive behaviour (e.g., in pretend play or when watching media violence) is more likely to promote aggression than to reduce it (e.g., Bushman, 2002). Several theoretical explanations can account for this finding (see Chapter 2). Social learning theory would hold that thinking about the positive effects of aggression has a reinforcing quality, and script theory would argue that engaging in mental simulations of aggressive behaviour rehearses aggressive scripts. Furthermore, symbolic acts of aggression can be regarded as aggressive cues that prime hostile thoughts and feelings, and thereby pave the way for aggressive behaviour. It is clear from a number of studies that aggressive fantasising is positively linked to aggressive behaviour (e.g., Guerra et al., 2003).

Focusing on the arousal component of catharsis, Verona and Sullivan (2008) conducted a study in which they made participants engage in aggressive behaviour by delivering unpleasant air blasts to a confederate, and recorded the participants' heart rate before and after they showed the aggressive behaviour. They found that those participants who showed the greatest reduction in heart rate after performing the aggressive behaviour – that is those who could be said to have experienced most catharsis – were most aggressive in the next phase of the experiment. This finding indicates that the reduction in arousal experienced after an aggressive act makes people more rather than less aggressive in a subsequent situation.

The evidence discussed so far suggests that the idea of catharsis is a popular myth for which there is little empirical evidence. However, there are some recent findings that point to a more complex role for engaging in aggressive thoughts or symbolic action in reducing aggression. Studies by Denzler, Förster, and Liberman (2009) showed that imagining aggressive responses or performing symbolic aggressive behaviour reduced the accessibility of aggressive thoughts, in line with the catharsis hypothesis, but only when the imagined aggression was successful in achieving the actor's goal. They asked their participants to imagine a scenario in which they found their romantic partner in bed with their best friend. One group was asked to imagine that they managed to take revenge on the friend (goal fulfilment), whereas the other group was told that their attempt at taking revenge was thwarted (no goal fulfilment). Those who had imagined that they would successfully take revenge had longer reaction times for recognising aggressive words in a lexical decision task, indicating a reduced accessibility of aggressive cognitions, compared with those who had imagined that their attempts at revenge would be thwarted. Among participants in the successful goal condition, those who stabbed a voodoo doll, (i.e. engaged in symbolic aggression) showed longer response times in the lexical decision task than those who had merely looked at the voodoo doll. These results suggest that, under certain conditions, the imaginary or symbolic enactment of aggression may lead to a short-term reduction in the accessibility of aggressive thoughts. Whether this strategy is effective in the long term is a different matter. From the perspective of social learning and script theory, it would appear unlikely that habitually responding to provocation by imagining successful acts of revenge would be effective in reducing aggressive behaviour, as it involves the rehearsal and reinforcement of aggressive thoughts.

Several approaches for preventing aggression by targeting the individual have been discussed in this section. Support was shown for changing aggressive behaviour through observational learning, improving anger control, and eliciting responses that are incompatible with aggression in reducing aggressive behaviour. The evidence suggests a more critical view of punishment, because it only works under certain conditions and it sends out the message that coercion is an acceptable strategy. Finally, the idea that the imaginary or symbolic expression of aggression can serve to inhibit aggression has largely been refuted.

Approaches directed at specific forms of aggression and violence

In addition to strategies designed to reduce aggression and violence in a wide range of domains, custom-tailored approaches have been developed to address specific forms of aggression. To illustrate this approach, the present section will offer a brief review of strategies directed at three types of aggression: gang violence, domestic violence, and sexual aggression.

Tackling gang violence

As noted in Chapter 9, many acts of gang violence take place in and around school settings where children and adolescents spend a large proportion of their time and conduct many of their social relationships. Therefore schools are "aggression hot spots", and at the same time would seem to lend themselves as settings for the implementation of intervention programmes.

An example of a school-based approach for the prevention of gang membership and delinquency is the Gang Resistance Education and Training (G.R.E.A.T.) programme (Esbensen et al., 2011). It was chosen as an example from a wide range of gang violence prevention programmes because it is rooted in psychological theories of gang-related aggression and was subjected to two rounds of evaluations using state-of-the-art methods. G.R.E.A.T. is a school-based intervention delivered by law enforcement personnel that consists of a curriculum of 13 lessons, presented in Table 11.4.

It is clear from the modules listed in Table 11.4 that G.R.E.A.T. is a programme targeting the individual. In addition to providing background information about the problem of gang-related violence, the programme aims to promote social skills that enable adolescents to resist peer pressure to join gangs, and to find non-aggressive ways of dealing with interpersonal conflict. Two large-scale evaluations were conducted to assess the effectiveness of the programme. The first round of evaluation of the initial curriculum included longitudinal comparisons of programme groups and control groups over a 4-year period. It yielded some intended effects, such as more negative views about gangs, but failed to demonstrate lower levels of violence, delinquency, or gang membership (Esbensen, Osgood, Taylor, Peterson, & Freng (2001). The curriculum presented in Table 11.4 is the result of a thorough revision of the programme based on the evaluation results. In addition to improving the contents and teaching methods of the school-based intervention, the main change was to incorporate it in a wider approach that includes a summer programme and a family-based training component. An evaluation of the revised programme using a randomised controlled trial yielded more

Table 11.4 Curriculum of the G.R.E.A.T. Programme for preventing gang membership.(Reprinted with permission from Esbensen et al., 2011, p. 70. Copyright Sage Publications)

1. *Welcome to G.R.E.A.T.*: An introductory lesson designed to provide students with basic knowledge about the connection between gangs, violence, drug abuse, and crime.
2. *What's the Real Deal?*: Designed to help students learn ways to analyze information sources and develop realistic beliefs about gangs and violence.
3. *It's About Us*: A lesson to help students learn about their communities (e.g., family, school, residential area) and their responsibilities.
4. *Where Do We Go From Here?*: Designed to help students learn ways of developing realistic and achievable goals.
5. *Decisions, Decisions, Decisions*: A lesson to help students develop decision-making skills.
6. *Do You Hear What I Am Saying?*: Designed to help students develop effective verbal and nonverbal communication skills.
7. *Walk in Someone Else's Shoes*: A lesson to help students develop active listening and empathy skills, with a particular emphasis on understanding victims of crime and violence.
8. *Say It Like You Mean It*: Designed to help students develop effective refusal skills.
9. *Getting Along Without Going Along*: A lesson to reinforce and practice the refusal skills learned in Lesson 8.
10. *Keeping Your Cool*: A lesson to help students understand signs of anger and ways to manage the emotion.
11. *Keeping It Together*: Designed to help students use the anger management skills learned in Lesson 10 and apply them to interpersonal situations where conflicts and violence are possible.
12. *Working It Out*: A lesson to help students develop effective conflict-resolution techniques.
13. *Looking Back*: Designed to conclude the G.R.E.A.T. program with an emphasis on the importance of conflict resolution skills as a way to avoid gangs and violence; students also present their projects aimed at improving their schools.

positive findings, as reported by Esbensen et al. (2011). Compared with the non-intervention control group, participants in the programme group showed less positive attitudes about gangs, more frequent use of refusal skills, greater resistance to peer pressure, and lower rates of gang membership at the follow-up assessment 1 year after the intervention. In fact, participants in the intervention group were less than half as likely to identify themselves as members of a gang as those in the control group. Whether the positive effects of the intervention are sustainable over longer periods will be established in the course of the evaluation that is still ongoing.

The complexity of designing and evaluating school-based interventions is further illustrated by another project, incidentally also called GREAT (for "Guiding Responsibility and Expectations in Adolescents Today and Tomorrow"), that included the risk of violence perpetration and the risk of violent victimisation as target variables (Simon et al., 2009). An evaluation was conducted that addressed these target variables in schools where the programme was implemented for unselected groups of students (the "universal" condition), in schools where it was implemented as a family-based intervention for students with an increased risk of aggression (the "selected" condition), or in schools that used a combination of both approaches. The three groups were compared with a no-intervention control group. Over a 2-year period, no positive programme effects on aggression were found in the intervention groups. In fact the decrease in aggression that occurred in the control group over time was not seen in either the universal or the selected intervention groups. There was little evidence of a decrease in victimisation in the intervention groups compared with the control group, and the combined intervention was no more effective than the universal and selected conditions on their own.

Taken together, the two studies reported here illustrate that changing aggressive behaviour by means of theory-based interventions is a difficult task that may even carry the risk of counterproductive outcomes, such as apparently interfering with the decline in aggression shown by the no-intervention group. At the same time, the two examples lend themselves as prototypical designs for the implementation of theory-based interventions using state-of-the art methods of programme development and evaluation.

Preventing family violence

The experience of family violence may lead to a wide range of negative consequences that affect the victim's future development in many ways (see Chapter 7). Therefore finding effective ways of preventing aggression against children, partners, and elders is a primary concern of practitioners and policy makers, and researchers can help them to achieve this goal. Just as theories of domestic violence were classified as pertaining to the macro level, the micro level, or the individual level in Chapter 7, strategies designed to prevent domestic violence can be located at these levels. As different forms of domestic violence are often related and can be traced back to a common set of underlying causes and facilitating conditions, measures suggested for tackling domestic violence show a high degree of similarity across different types of abuse. Therefore the approaches presented in this section were selected because of their relevance to the prevention of different forms of domestic violence, rather than being specific to just one particular manifestation.

Societal-level interventions

Changing the societal conditions that allow domestic violence to occur requires, first and foremost, establishing a consensus that violence is unacceptable. Gelles (1997, p. 166) noted that "we need to cancel the hitting license in society," and Schwartz and DeKeseredy (2008) stressed the widespread peer support for violence as a major factor in explaining violence against women. Challenging the societal acceptance of aggression involves measures directly related to domestic violence, such as creating an awareness that corporal punishment is not an adequate child-rearing technique. It also includes wider issues, such as restricting the availability of firearms and challenging media presentations of violence as masculine, entertaining, and ultimately rewarding (see Chapter 5). It further involves the removal of the traditional gender gap in the distribution of power, both within relationships and in society at large. To the extent that social structures become more egalitarian (e.g., by providing equal pay and job opportunities), women will gain a stronger position in society, and patriarchal attitudes will become less influential.

One more specific way in which domestic violence can be tackled at the societal level is by means of the legal system. Legal regulations have been introduced to enhance the protection of victims and improve the detection of domestic violence. For example, many countries now have the instrument of imposing *restraining orders* on individuals who have used or threatened to use violence against an intimate partner. This instrument prohibits abusers from getting close to the persons they threaten to attack, and enforces legal sanctions in the event that the order is violated. Other legal regulations are designed to increase the likelihood of criminal prosecution of domestic violence offenders in the form of *warrantless arrests* or *mandatory arrest* policies in cases of domestic violence. In their review of criminal justice responses to violence, Goodman and Epstein (2011) describe these efforts as highly successful. Evaluations of success are mostly based on official records, indicating increases in the number of arrests and criminal prosecutions in domestic violence incidents. At the same time, there have also been critical voices. For example, critics have argued that restraining orders may serve to escalate rather than de-escalate domestic conflicts because they create frustration, and that mandatory arrest policies have increased the number of victims arrested alongside the aggressor (e.g., Hovmand, Ford, Flom, & Kyriakakis, 2009). The file analysis by Muller, Desmarais, and Hamel (2009) showed that temporary restraining orders in cases of low-level intimate partner aggression were more likely to be granted to female than to male applicants, leading those authors to ask whether men are discriminated against as targets of aggression by female partners. However, this imbalance may also reflect the fact that men's aggression towards intimate partners is more likely to lead to injuries than is women's aggression, as discussed in Chapter 7.

Another legal tool for addressing domestic violence is the *mandatory reporting* of suspected cases of abuse (Matthews & Kenny, 2008). Mandatory reporting laws put professionals, such as social workers, medical staff, and mental health professionals, under a legal obligation to report suspected cases of abuse. The introduction of mandatory reporting of childhood abuse as well as elder abuse has led to a substantial increase in the number of recorded cases of alleged abuse (Leveque, 2011). However, a large proportion of cases are later dropped as unsubstantiated, raising the question of unintended side effects associated with this measure (e.g., Morton & Oravecz, 2009). If mandatory reporting is to expose cases of abuse that would otherwise have gone unrecognised while at the same time keeping the number of false alarms low, it is essential that the professionals mandated to report abuse are sufficiently well educated about the different forms of abuse to read the warning signs, and to avoid raising false alarms.

The third approach for dealing with domestic violence as a society consists of improving *protective services* that offer support to the victims. Measures include the provision of sheltered accommodation for women and children who have suffered domestic violence, regular visits by social workers to families identified as "at risk" to pre-empt the development of abusive situations, provisions for placing abused children and elders in high-quality care, and providing treatment programmes for the perpetrators of abuse (Barnett et al., 2011).

Evaluating the effectiveness of such macro-level responses to domestic violence is not easy, not least because the criteria for success are hard to define. For example, it is almost impossible to establish whether the introduction of restraining orders causes rates of intimate partner homicide to decline, given the many factors that affect the incidence of such assaults. Similarly, it is hard to decide whether mandatory reporting leads to an increased rate of detection of genuine child abuse cases that outweighs the increase in the number of false alarms. In the case of intimate partner violence, it has been argued that mandatory reporting laws undermine the autonomy of victims and put them at risk of further violence from the abusive partner (for a balanced discussion, see Bledsoe, Yankeelov, Barbee, & Antle, 2004,).

Family-level measures

Measures directed at preventing abuse or ameliorating its consequences by influencing the micro system of the family focus on changing dysfunctional interaction patterns (Staggs & Schewe, 2011). One aspect of this work is the development of instruments for identifying families at risk for child abuse. One such measure is the Parenting Stress Index (PSI) (Abidin, 1995). The short form of the PSI consists of two subscales: "personal distress", captured by items such as "I feel trapped in parenting responsibilities", and "childrearing stress", including items such as "My child does not like me or want to be close" (Haskett, Ahern, Ward, & Allaire, 2006). The higher parents scored on these scales, the less sensitivity to their children's needs they displayed as observed in standardised parent-child interactions. Another widely used measure is the Child Abuse Potential Inventory (CAPI) (Milner & Wimberly, 1980), which measures three parental risk factors for child abuse: rigidity, unhappiness, and problems with child and self. Milner and Wimberley (1980) showed that scores on the CAPI were able to discriminate between abusive and non-abusive parents.

Once families have been identified as at risk for abuse, *behavioural family interventions* can set in as a micro-level strategy for stopping or preventing the abuse (Turner & Sanders, 2006). Thomas and Zimmer-Gembeck (2011) evaluated a parent-child interaction training in families with a history of child maltreatment. Recognising the dynamic interaction of parent and child behaviour, the training was aimed at both parents (promoting self-confidence in their parenting skills and changing attributions about their child's problem behaviour) and children (reducing their externalising behaviour). Critical variables of parent and child behaviour were measured before the start of the intervention and 12 weeks after the end of the intervention. Parents in the intervention group were observed to show an increase in positive behaviours towards their children, and reported a significant decrease in their child's externalising behaviour from pre-test to post-intervention, whereas no change was observed in the waiting-list control group. A meta-analysis of 24 intervention studies that used the parent-child interaction training or the Triple P Positive Parenting Programme (Sanders, Cann, & Markie-Dadds, 2003) found both approaches to be effective in reducing parenting stress and children's externalising behaviour (Thomas & Zimmer-Gembeck, 2007).

Individual-level interventions

At this level, the focus of interventions is on the individual person who commits aggressive acts towards a family member. Several approaches have been developed and evaluated in the literature (Babcock, Green, & Robie, 2004). The first is the psycho-educational approach designed to increase men's understanding of the detrimental effects of violence and to challenge role perceptions of male dominance. The second approach draws on cognitive-behavioural therapy to help abusers to "unlearn" violent behaviour through improving their communication skills and anger management. Two meta-analyses have investigated the effectiveness of interventions, mainly based on these two approaches, targeting male perpetrators of intimate partner violence. Babcock et al. (2004) included 44 effect sizes from 22 treatment studies that compared treated abusers either with a non-treatment control group or with dropouts who failed to complete the intervention. Treatment efficacy was measured by the rate of recidivism in terms of the proportion of participants who committed further acts of physical violence during the post-treatment period, as indicated by police records and partner reports. For both sources the average effect size was $d = 0.18$.

The second meta-analysis, by Feder and Wilson (2005), considered 10 rigorously conducted studies in which participants had been mandated by a court to take part. Whether or not abusers engaged in further intimate partner violence, established through official records or through victim reports, was the outcome variable. For recidivism rates as established by official records, a significant effect size of $d = 0.26$ was found in the experimental studies between treatment and control groups, indicating that participants in the treatment groups had a lower rate of continuing violence. The effect size was considerably higher for the comparison between participants in the treatment groups who completed the intervention and those who dropped out ($d = 0.97$). However, no effects of the treatment were found in official records for the non-experimental studies. Studies using victim reports as a source of information on recidivism failed to show a significant treatment effect, regardless of study design. Assuming that victim reports provide a more accurate reflection of repeat abuse, as only a small proportion of abusive incidents are reported to official agencies, it appears that these programmes were largely ineffective.

In addition to treating offenders, interventions can be directed at potential victims of domestic violence to enable them to better protect themselves from the risk of aggression. This approach is exemplified by programmes directed at the prevention of childhood sexual abuse. Educational programmes have been designed to empower children to resist sexual exploitation (e.g., by teaching them to enforce their right to privacy, to be assertive in rejecting unwanted touch, and to seek support from other adults) (Krahé & Knappert, 2009). The outcome measures in most of the evaluation studies are changes at the level of social skills and cognitive variables, such as knowledge about sexual abuse, perception of risk, self-protection, and willingness to disclose abuse experiences. There is virtually no evidence addressing programme efficacy in reducing the number of children who become victims of sexual abuse. Although they found substantial variation in programme success in their review of 22 studies evaluating school-based interventions, Topping and Barron (2009) concluded that participation in sexual abuse prevention programmes leads to moderate increases in targeted knowledge and skills variables, at least immediately after the intervention. A study by Krahé and Knappert (2009) that evaluated a theatre play for elementary-school children found positive intervention effects that were sustained over a period of 30 weeks. Systematic reviews have found little evidence that the programmes have detrimental side-effects, such as frightening or upsetting children (Finkelhor & Dziuba-Leatherman, 1995; Topping & Barron, 2009).

Preventing sexual aggression

Given the widespread occurrence of sexual aggression and the lasting negative effects it has on the victims (see Chapter 8), it is clear that the development of measures for preventing sexual aggression is a key challenge for researchers and policy makers alike. Approaches aimed at reducing the risk of sexual aggression can be broadly located at the societal and the individual level. This section will discuss some illustrative examples from both categories.

Societal measures designed to reduce sexual aggression

Measures in this category seek to influence established risk factors by changing the social context that allows sexual violence to occur (for a discussion of society-level risk factors, see Chapter 8). Drawing on research on the links between alcohol use and sexual aggression, for example, enforcing stricter observation of age limits on the sale of alcohol could be a possible measure for reducing the likelihood of sexual aggression. Similarly, as we saw in Chapter 5, there is considerable evidence that exposure to violent pornography is linked to a higher risk of engaging in sexually aggressive behaviour. This suggests that restricting access to violent pornography, especially for an underage audience, could contribute to the prevention of sexual aggression. Although such measures have been adopted as part of youth protection legislation and policies (e.g., Hingson, 2010), there is a shortage of rigorous evaluations of their effectiveness in reducing the rate of sexual aggression.

A widely used societal-level approach draws on mass media campaigns to raise awareness of the problem of sexual violence and to dispel common misconceptions about sexual aggression (for a review, see Lonsway et al., 2009). In the USA, for example, the National Online Resource Center on Violence against Women provides a range of online learning tools on violence against women (www.vawnet.org/special-collections/OnlineLearning. php). Public service announcements in the form of posters, postcards, and websites have also been widely used to remind men of the unacceptability and legal consequences of rape, and to alert women to the risk of sexual assault associated with drinking and other risky behaviours (for an example, see www.thisisnotaninvitationtorapeme.co.uk). Although such campaigns may intuitively seem valuable, there have been few rigorous examinations of their effects. In addition to establishing that people take notice of the campaigns and their messages, it is critical to establish whether they serve the purpose of changing attitudes and behaviours related to sexual aggression. An experimental evaluation of two posters used in a campaign by the British Home Office to raise awareness of the need to obtain consent before sex showed that the posters failed to increase the understanding that non-consensual sex qualifies as a crime (Temkin & Krahé, 2008, Study 3). The two posters are shown in Figure 11.1.

Participants who saw the posters while reading a rape scenario that contained a clear statement of the woman's non-consent were no more inclined to hold the perpetrator responsible than participants in a control condition who did not see the posters. In fact, ratings of the man's criminal liability were significantly reduced in the condition that showed the prison poster compared with the control group. This finding shows that public messages designed to change attitudes must be carefully assessed in terms of their effectiveness, including the possibility of producing counterproductive effects.

A further societal response to the problem of rape is to address the low conviction rates in the criminal prosecution of rape by implementing changes in the treatment of rape victims by the police and the medical system (see also Chapter 8). Although these measures are directed in the first instance at survivors of sexual assault, they are also intended to have a wider effect on increasing reporting rates by removing the expectation of secondary victimisation by police and medical staff as a barrier to reporting. In the UK, specialised Sexual Assault Referral Centres (SARCs) were introduced to better meet the needs of victims and improve the chances of criminal prosecution, and further recommendations for change were made in an independent report to the government (Stern, 2010). In the USA, initiatives have been developed to ensure that sexual assault victims are examined by specialised teams, such as sexual assault nurse examiners (the SANE programme) (Campbell & Patterson, 2011; Campbell, Patterson, & Lichty, 2005).

Finally, the notoriously low conviction rates in sexual assault cases in the adversarial criminal justice system have led to a search for alternative models for responding to sexual assault based on the idea of restorative justice. For example, the RESTORE programme pioneered by Koss (Koss, 2010; Koss, Bachar, Hopkins, & Carlson, 2004) brings together

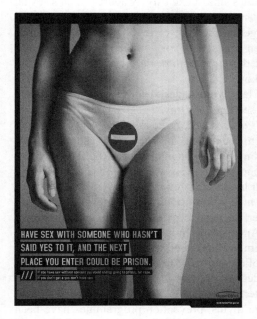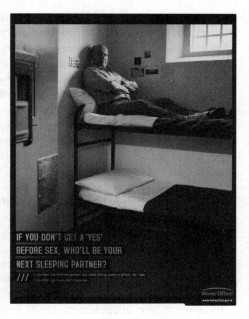

Figure 11.1 Posters used in the evaluation of a rape awareness campaign (Temkin & Krahé, 2008; http://www.homeoffice.gov.uk/documents/consent-campaign/).

victims, offenders, and their communities of care in face-to-face conferencing to work out ways of achieving material and personal reparation. In its mission statement, the aim of RESTORE is described as facilitating "a victim-centered, community-driven resolution of selected individual sex crimes that creates and carries out a plan for accountability, healing, and public safety" (Koss et al., 2004, p. 1448). The victim's satisfaction with the extent of her or his involvement, the degree of reparation, and the fairness of the outcome is the main criterion of success. The restorative justice approach requires a fundamental change of thinking compared to established criminal justice responses to sexual assault. Although first evaluations indicate that restorative justice procedures may be a viable option for certain forms of sexual assault, and that the majority of victims are satisfied with the outcome, wider implementation and evaluation is required to appraise the potential and limitations of this approach.

Individual-level approaches to the prevention of sexual aggression

Targeting the individual, rape prevention programmes implemented in schools and universities are designed to educate men and women about sexual assault by challenging rape-supportive attitudes and increasing awareness of the risk factors for sexual assault (Gidycz,

Orchowski, & Edwards, 2011). These programmes almost exclusively address men's sexual aggression towards women, with the aim of "enlightening men and empowering women" (Rozee, 2011). Accordingly, interventions targeting men are called "rape prevention programmes" and interventions targeting women are called "risk reduction programmes." Findings from evaluation studies suggest that these programmes are best implemented in single-sex groups (Gidycz, Orchowski, & Berkowitz, 2011).

Many studies have been conducted over the last two decades to address the effectiveness of rape prevention programmes (for reviews, see Paul & Gray, 2011; Vladutiu, Martin, & Macy, 2011). In terms of *reducing rape myth acceptance*, a meta-analysis by Flores and Hartlaub (1998) found evidence for short-term reductions in rape myth acceptance, and more recent studies have confirmed this finding (e.g., Langhinrichsen-Rohling, Foubert, Brasfield, Hill, & Shelley-Tremblay, 2011). Some studies have shown that the effects of the programmes are stronger for participants with high initial levels of rape myth acceptance (Pacifici, Stoolmiller, & Nelson, 2001) and for men with a prior history of sexual aggression (O'Donohue, Yeater, & Fanetti, 2003). However, the results are less encouraging with regard to the sustainability of intervention effects (Anderson & Whiston, 2005; Schewe, 2002). Rape myth acceptance is typically measured immediately before and after participation in the intervention, with some studies including follow-ups of up to 2 months post-intervention. The reviews concluded that the effects tended to disappear within a few weeks post-intervention, with attitudes returning to pre-intervention levels.

In addition to challenging the belief in rape myths, prevention programmes have been directed at *changing social norms about sexual violence*. Based on evidence that men tend to overestimate the extent to which their peers accept and use sexual aggression, the "social norms approach" considers a correction of these misperceptions as a central element of rape prevention (Fabiano, Perkins, Berkowitz, Linkenbach, & Stark, 2003). The aim of this approach is to counter the rape-supportive normative environment by engaging men as social justice allies, both in terms of challenging misperceptions and in promoting active intervention to stop other men from engaging in sexual aggression. An evaluation of a theory-based rape prevention programme that included a social norms component and sought to increase men's willingness to intervene as bystanders on behalf of sexual assault victims was conducted by Gidycz et al. (2011). The specific aims of the programme are shown in Table 11.5.

The authors conducted an evaluation with over 600 first-year college men in which they compared changes on the critical outcome variables from baseline at 4 and 7 months after the end of the intervention between an intervention group and a control group. The results, also presented in Table 11.5, yielded a mixed picture. Although the programme was clearly successful in changing the perception of sexual aggression as normative and in decreasing the rate of sexual aggression, little effect was found for rape myth acceptance and the promotion of bystander intervention. Other programmes have reported more success in increasing men's readiness to intervene as bystanders (e.g., Langhinrichsen-Rohling et al., 2011), but the outcome variable typically measured in this research is self-reported confidence and willingness to intervene, not actual behaviour. The extent to which participants translate

Table 11.5 Aims and success of a theory-based rape prevention programme directed at men (Based on Gidycz, Orchowski, & Berkowitz, 2011)

Intervention aims		Treatment success*	
		4-month follow-up	7-month follow-up
Aim 1	Decrease rape myth acceptance and negative attitudes towards women by challenging rape myths and stereotypical gender roles	No	No
Aim 2	Increase the accuracy of men's perceptions of other men's attitudes and behaviors through		
	• changing perceptions of peer disapproval of sexual violence	No	No
	• perceived peer engagement in bystander intervention	Yes	Yes
Aim 3	Create more appropriate norms regarding sexually aggressive behavior through:		
	• changing the perception that their friends would engage in sexual aggression,	Yes	Yes
	• reducing exposure to sexually aggressive role models, e.g., in the media, and	Yes	Yes
	• reducing the perceived reinforcement value of engaging in sexual aggression	Yes	Yes
Aim 4	Increase prosocial bystander behaviour and support for victims by	No	No
	• promoting personal engagement in bystander intervention	No	No
	• providing support for rape prevention efforts		
Aim 5	Increase the understanding of consent through accurate identification in rape scenarios	No	Yes
Aim 6	Reduce the perpetration of sexual aggression	Yes	No

* Significant interaction between time (pre- and post-test) and condition (intervention vs. control group).

their intentions into behaviour and a decrease in sexual violence rates can be found following bystander interventions has yet to be established by further research. Evidence from research on prosocial behaviour has identified processes that inhibit bystander intervention, such as diffusion of responsibility, evaluation apprehension, and pluralistic ignorance (i.e., the shared misinterpretation of the situation). This research can be used to design evidence-based interventions that maximise the chance of increasing actual bystander intervention (Banyard, Plante, & Moynihan, 2004).

Another line of intervention research has examined the effectiveness of *risk reduction programmes* directed at women (Fisher, Daigle, & Cullen, 2008). These programmes address two main aspects: (a) increasing women's awareness and understanding of the risk factors that lead to sexual aggression, and (b) enabling them to engage in more effective resistance when faced with a situation in which a sexual assault may be imminent. For example, understanding that most sexual assaults are committed by someone known to the victim may increase women's sensitivity to warning signs in interactions with dates, acquaintances, and partners. In addition, promoting bystander intervention has also been explored as an effective way of pre-empting sexual aggression in programmes targeting women (Foubert, Langhinrichsen-Rohling, Brasfield, & Hill, 2010; Moynihan, Banyard, Arnold, Eckstein, & Stapleton, 2011).

As we saw in Chapter 8, several behavioural variables, such as high levels of sexual activity, alcohol consumption in the context of sexual encounters, and the ambiguous communication of sexual intentions are linked to an increased risk of sexual victimisation. At the same time, women who engage in high-risk behaviours often fail to realise their vulnerability. For example, women with a habit of binge-drinking estimated their efficacy in avoiding a sexual assault in a situation where they had been drinking to be higher than women without a habit of binge-drinking. Conversely, they estimated their ability to resist a sexual assault in a situation in which they had not been drinking to be lower (McCauley & Calhoun, 2008). Given the well-established finding that alcohol increases the risk of sexual assault, it seems that women who are prone to binge-drinking underestimate the risk of sexual assault when under the influence of alcohol, and there is a need to correct this false estimation through risk awareness measures.

Earlier evaluations of risk reduction programmes for women revealed that their success was limited. For example, Hanson and Gidycz (1993) found that their rape prevention programme reduced the incidence of first-time assaults on women, but was ineffective in reducing the risk of revictimisation in women who had experienced a prior sexual assault. Gidycz et al. (2001) found no difference between participants in their intervention group and those in a control group on any of the outcome measures at a follow-up 2 months later, although they did find a reduced revictimisation rate between the follow-up and a later assessment in the intervention group. However, more recent studies that tested revised programmes with a focus on promoting self-protective behaviour and overcoming barriers to resistance yielded a more positive picture (Ullman, 2007). For example, Gidycz, Orchowski, Probst, Edwards, Murphy, and Tansill (2012) evaluated a risk reduction intervention directed at women that was implemented concurrently with the programme for men described in Table 11.5. The specific goals of this programme are listed in Table 11.6.

Significant increases in self-protective dating behaviours, more assertive communication in sexual interactions, greater self-efficacy in rejecting unwanted sexual advances, and greater use of resistance tactics were found in programme participants from pre-test to the 4- and 7-month follow-ups compared with a control group. Victimisation rates did not differ between the intervention group and the control group, but victimised women in the intervention group were less likely to engage in self-blame and more likely to blame the perpetrator. Another study found that participation in a risk reduction programme buffered the psychological distress experienced after a subsequent sexual victimisation (Mouilso, Calhoun, & Gidycz, 2011).

Many rape risk reduction programmes for women seek to strengthen women's sense of self-efficacy in resisting a sexual assault. In addition, they address barriers to active resistance rooted in traditional female gender roles, such as the fear of negative evaluation by

Table 11.6 Aims and success of a theory-based risk reduction programme directed at women (Based on Gidycz et al., 2012)

Intervention aims		Treatment success*	
		4-month follow-up	7-month follow-up
Aim 1	Increase women's assertiveness in sexual situations	Yes	Yes
Aim 2	Promote women's confidence in responding to potential attackers	Yes	Yes
Aim 3	Increase women's use of self-protective strategies through		
	• self-protective dating behaviour	Yes	Yes
	• self-defence tactics	Yes	Yes
Aim 4	Reduce the incidence of sexual assault among programme participants	No	No
Aim 5	Reduce the frequency of assault among participants who were victimised	No	Yes
Aim 6	Increase victims' use of resistance tactics during an assault	Yes	Yes
Aim 7	Decrease self-blame among women who experience sexual victimisation	No	Yes

* Significant interaction between time (pre- and post-test) and condition (intervention vs. control group).

others or the tendency to blame themselves for having been sexually assaulted. Evidence suggests that responding to a sexual attack with verbal and physical resistance is an effective strategy without increasing the risk of serious injury (Fisher et al., 2008; Ullman, 2007). However, it is important to bear in mind that the positive evaluation of active resistance is based on probability estimates for *samples* of assault victims, and does not guarantee that resistance is the best strategy in any single case. Therefore, when recommending active resistance, it needs to be stressed that the decision for or against fighting back in an assault situation must be based, in the final instance, on an assessment of the particular circumstances of the attack. For example, actively resisting an assailant who is far stronger than the victim or in a remote place where it is unlikely that others will come to the victim's aid, may well be counterproductive. Recommendations on how to respond to a sexual attack can therefore only serve as guidelines that enable women to think about adequate responses to an attack in advance, rather than being faced with the need to make instantaneous decisions under the extreme stress of an assault situation (Fischhoff, 1992).

A research matrix for the prevention of aggression and violence

The research reviewed in this chapter has illustrated the challenges of finding effective ways to reduce the pervasiveness of aggression in many domains of life. Some firmly entrenched beliefs about effective control mechanisms, such as the role of cathartic release of aggressive

Table 11.7 Characteristics of aggression and violence as "wicked problems" (Based on Kazdin, 2011)

- Multiple stakeholders have divergent views about what the problem "really" is.
- Aggression and violence do not result from any single cause but from a set of interrelated causes that influence each other.
- Aggression and violence are not isolated problems but are embedded in other critical social issues.
- There is no single solution that will eliminate the problem.
- Action needs to be taken on the basis of insufficient evidence.
- The problem is unlikely ever to be completely resolved.

---

feelings or the deterrent function of punishment, need to be revised on the basis of this research. New courses of action have been developed that address aggressive behaviour at the societal, interpersonal, and individual levels, but these are still awaiting more extensive evaluations. In the words of Kazdin (2011), aggression and violence can be seen as "wicked problems" that are characterised by a number of problematic features, listed in Table 11.7.

Taken together, the features listed in Table 11.7 illustrate why it is so difficult to find successful ways of reducing aggression. They also point to a tension between seeking broad solutions that pertain to many forms of aggression, and specialised responses that are geared towards more narrowly defined forms of aggression. Specialisation runs the risk of producing fragmented lines of research that fail to acknowledge the common roots and consequences of different forms of aggression, whereas broader approaches may lose sight of the unique causes and outcomes of particular forms of aggression. Therefore general strategies for intervention need to be combined with domain-specific approaches for preventing particular forms of aggression.

Mercy and Hammond (1999) have presented an organising framework for homicide prevention that can also serve as a more general agenda for the prevention of aggression and violence. It illustrates how different subsystems interact in the emergence of aggression, and how effective prevention measures need to target each of these subsystems. Their model is presented in Table 11.8.

The model acknowledges that the causes of aggression and violence lie at different levels from the individual person to the interpersonal encounter of two or more individuals and from the micro-system of social groups to the macro-level of society. It also reflects the recognition that measures need to be tailored to the needs of different target groups. First, it is critical to reduce the odds of aggression and violence universally (i.e., in societies as a whole) by promoting individual development and well-being, strengthening interpersonal skills for non-violent conflict resolution, and creating a social consensus that aggression and violence are unacceptable. However, it is equally important to develop selective measures that are specifically directed at persons and situations with an increased risk for aggression and violence. Finally, measures are required for reducing the risk of further aggression and violence among groups with a history of aggression and violence, which have a special

Table 11.8 An integrative matrix for violence prevention (Reprinted with permission from Mercy & Hammond, 1999, p. 306. Copyright Sage Publications)

System influencing violence	Type of preventive measure		
	Universal	Selective	Indicated
Individual factors	• Provide violent risk education for all students • Teach children to recognize and report sexual abuse • Provide enriched preschool education for all children	• Provide therapy for children who witness violence • Teach convenience store clerks techniques to avoid injury during robberies	• Treat sex offenders • Provide psychotherapy for violent offenders • Use former perpetrators to influence nonconforming peers through social marketing programs
Close interpersonal Relationships	• Provide parenting education for all new parents • Teach adolescents how to form healthy relationships with the opposite sex	• Use peer mediation to resolve disputes in schools • Increase adult mentoring of high-risk youth • Visit families at high risk of child abuse	• Improve parent-management strategies and parent–child bonding in the families of violent children
Proximal social contexts	• Use metal detectors to keep weapons out of schools • Initiate after-school programs to extend adult supervision of youths	• Create safe havens for children in homes and businesses on high-risk routes to and from school • Establish violence prevention coalitions in high-risk neighborhoods	• Provide adequate shelter space for battered women • Disrupt illegal gun markets in communities • Train health care professionals in identification and referral of family violence victims
Social macrosystems	• Reduce violence in the media • Reduce income inequality	• Deconcentrate lower-income housing • Establish meaningful job creation programs for inner-city youths	• Increase severity of penalties for violent crimes • Reduce illegal interstate transfer of firearms by limiting purchases to one gun a month

indication for interventions. These measures also need to include the protection of victims from further experiences of aggression.

Many of the strategies discussed in the course of this chapter can be placed within this matrix and become part of a broader prevention framework. In that sense, the matrix provides a format for integrating research from individual studies and lines of research into the emerging knowledge base of effective prevention efforts at multiple levels. At the same time, it can be seen as mapping out an agenda for future research on the prevention of aggression.

Concluding comment

The present volume has focused on the contribution of social psychological research to understanding the causes and consequences of aggression between individuals and groups. This focus does not in any way imply that the aggression-related problems of today's world can be comprehensively addressed and fully explained from the perspective of a single psychological discipline or, for that matter, by psychology as a whole. Aggression and violence are the products not only of cognitions, emotions, and actions of individual persons, acting alone or in groups, but also of historical developments (as in the case of conflicts between nations and ethnic groups), predominant value systems (as in pitting the role of civil liberties against gun control and media restrictions), and cultural traditions (as in the much-quoted "Southern culture of honour"). Approaches from a variety of disciplines need to be brought together to a greater extent than they are at present to arrive at a comprehensive analysis of aggression, including the historical and cultural roots of this antisocial behaviour.

Not all the findings and conclusions generated by the research presented in this volume will be gladly accepted outside the academic debate. This is true, for example, for evidence linking media violence to aggression, and for evidence on the effects of tightening gun-control legislation on reducing violent crime, neither of which has been, or will be, translated into policy responses without strong opposition from the respective interest groups. In addition to accumulating knowledge about the scale, causes, and consequences of aggression, psychological aggression research is therefore faced with the challenge of spreading this knowledge beyond the scientific community to inform both policy makers and public opinion.

In terms of its standing within psychology, the large number of recent studies reviewed in this volume indicates that aggression research is alive and well. This conclusion, which would be seen as an unreservedly positive development in most other fields of research, has a sad side to it in the case of aggression. It highlights the pressing need to find answers to the questions of causation and prevention of aggression and violence, which bring immeasurable suffering to victims and their families. Therefore gaining a better understanding of the processes that lead individuals and groups to engage in aggressive, often lethal actions against each other, and then using this understanding to develop strategies for their prevention and control, remains one of the greatest challenges for both basic and applied research in psychology.

Summary

- Compared with the wealth of research into the causes of and precipitating factors for aggressive behaviour, evidence on how to prevent and reduce it is more limited. Measures designed to reduce the scale of aggression and violence may be classified into two groups: general strategies for preventing aggression in its variety of manifestations, and specific strategies custom-tailored to reduce particular forms of aggression. Within each of the two approaches, measures can be implemented either at the level of society or at the level of individuals and their immediate social environment.
- At the societal level, reducing the opportunity for crime (e.g., by restricting access to firearms) and using capital punishment to deter violent offenders were discussed as general measures that were found to have limited success. Evidence on the effects of capital punishment on homicide rates provides little support for the deterrence hypothesis. In contrast, limiting the availability and use of firearms has been shown to reduce the fatal effects of violent attacks.
- Approaches directed at changing the general propensity towards aggressive behaviour in the individual can build on the principles of reinforcement and observational learning. Trying to reduce aggressive behaviour through punishment is of limited value because it requires several preconditions that rarely co-occur in a given context. Instead, reinforcing positive social behaviour and providing non-aggressive behavioural models are more promising avenues for prevention. These aspects are captured in parent management trainings designed to teach parents constructive forms of discipline and conflict resolution.
- Eliciting responses that are incompatible with angry arousal and aggressive cognitions (e.g., through prosocial behaviour or using pleasant music to buffer stress and anger) is a way of reducing aggression by influencing affective and cognitive antecedents of aggressive behaviour. Anger management and observational learning can also be used to modify aggressive behaviour. Rather than suppressing aggression, they replace aggressive responses with more adequate ways of dealing with frustration and provocation.
- Contrary to popular wisdom, catharsis (i.e., acting out aggressive impulses in a symbolic or innocuous way) is largely counterproductive in reducing aggression. It generally leads to an increase rather than a decrease in aggressive responses.
- As an example of tailored interventions directed at specific forms of aggression, school-based programmes have been developed for tackling gang violence. Over a 1-year period they were found to be successful in reducing attraction to violent gangs.
- Strategies for the prevention of domestic violence are located at three levels. At the societal level, legal instruments can be used for protecting potential victims and for improving the detection of abuse. At the family level, interventions for improving communication skills among family members are promising measures for breaking up inadequate patterns of conflict resolution. Finally, at the individual level, programmes directed at abusive partners with the aim of teaching them anger management skills and

alternative strategies for resolving conflicts with children and partners had some success. In addition, preventive measures directed at the potential victims of domestic violence seek to empower them to successfully defend their physical, sexual, and emotional integrity.

• Strategies for preventing sexual assault at the societal level, such as improving the treatment of rape victims by the police and the medical system, and increasing reporting rates, are designed to create a social climate in which the seriousness of sexual assault is recognised and victims are treated with sympathy and respect. Individual-level measures are directed at changing men's rape-supportive attitudes and challenging misconceptions about the acceptability of sexual aggression. Risk reduction interventions that target women seek to raise their awareness about risky behaviours and situations and to promote effective rape-resistance strategies.

Tasks to do

(1) Find out what the policy is in your country, state, or city about carrying and drinking alcohol in public.

(2) Visit the website of neighbourhoodwatch.net (www.neighbourhoodwatch.net/index.php ?StoryId=8&Type=Resource&func=PageResourceStory) and find out whether similar schemes exist in your community.

(3) Conduct an Internet search using the key words "rape awareness websites" to find out about rape awareness initiatives around the world.

Suggested reading

Esbensen, F. A., Peterson, D., Taylor, T. J., Freng, A., Osgood, D. W., Carson, D., & Matsuda, K. N. (2011). Evaluation and evolution of the Gang Resistance Education and Training (G.R.E.A.T.) program. *Journal of School Violence, 10*, 53–70.

Hemenway, D., & Hepburn, L. M. (2004). Firearm availability and homicide: A review of the literature. *Aggression and Violent Behavior, 9*, 417–440.

Koss, M. P., White, J. W., & Kazdin, A. E. (Eds) (2011). *Violence against women and children. Volume 2. Navigating solutions*. Washington, DC: American Psychological Association.

References

Abbey, A. (2002). Alcohol-related sexual assault: A common problem among college students. *Journal of Studies on Alcohol, Suppl. 14*, 118–128.

Abbey, A., Jacques-Tiura, A. J., & LeBreton, J. M. (2011). Risk factors for sexual aggression in young men: An expansion of the confluence model. *Aggressive Behavior, 37*, 450–464.

Abbey, A., & McAuslan, P. (2004). A longitudinal examination of male college students' perpetration of sexual assault. *Journal of Consulting and Clinical Psychology, 72*, 747–756.

Abbey, A., Zawacki, T., Buck, P. O., Clinton, A. M., & McAuslan, P. (2004). Sexual assault and alcohol consumption: What do we know about their relationship and what types of research are still needed? *Aggression and Violent Behavior, 9*, 271–303.

Åberg, L., & Rimmö, P.-A. (1998). Dimensions of aberrant driver behaviour. *Ergonomics, 41*, 39–56.

Abidin, R. R. (1995). *Parenting Stress Index (PSI) manual* (3rd edn). Charlottesville, VA: Pediatric Psychology Press.

Acierno, R., Hernandez, M. A., Amstadter, A. B., Resnick, H. S., Steve, K., Muzzy, W. et al. (2010). Prevalence and correlates of emotional, physical, sexual, and financial abuse and potential neglect in the United States: The National Elder Mistreatment Study. *American Journal of Public Health, 100*, 292–297.

Acierno, R., Hernandez-Tejada, M., Muzzy, W., & Steve, K. (2009). *Final report: The National Elder Mistreatment Study*. Washington, DC: U.S. Department of Justice. Available online: www.ncjrs.gov/pdffiles1/nij/grants/226456.pdf

Adams, T. M., & Fuller, D. B. (2006). The words have changed but the ideology remains the same: Misogynistic lyrics in rap music. *Journal of Black Studies, 36*, 938–957.

Aebi, M. F. et al. (2010). *European Sourcebook of Crime and Criminal Justice Statistics* – 4th ed. Available online: http://europeansourcebook.org/ob285_full.pdf

Aldarondo, E., & Castro-Fernandez, M. (2011). Risk and protective factors for domestic violence perpetration. In J. W. White, M. P. Koss, & A. E. Kazdin (Eds), *Violence against women and children. Volume 1. Mapping the terrain* (pp. 221–242). Washington, DC: American Psychological Association.

Alden, H. L., & Parker, K. F. (2005). Gender role ideology, homophobia and hate crime: Linking attitudes to macro-level anti-gay and lesbian hate crimes. *Deviant Behavior, 26*, 321–343.

Alexy, E. M., Burgess, A. W., & Prentky, R. A. (2009). Pornography use as a risk marker for an aggressive pattern of behavior among sexually reactive children and adolescents. *Journal of the American Psychiatric Nursing Association, 14*, 442–453.

Alink, L. P., Mesman, J., van Zeijl, J., Stolk, M. N., Juffer, F., Koot, H. M. et al. (2006). The early childhood aggression curve: Development of physical aggression in 10- to 50-month-old children. *Child Development, 77*, 954–966.

Allen, M., D'Alessio, D., & Brezgel, K. (1995). A meta-analysis summarizing the effects of pornography. II. Aggression after exposure. *Human Communication Research, 22*, 258–283.

Allen, M., Emmers, T., Gebhardt, L., & Giery, M. A. (1995). Exposure to pornography and acceptance of rape myths. *Journal of Communication, 45*, 5–26.

Allport, G. H. (1954). *The nature of prejudice*. Reading, MA: Addison-Wesley.

American Psychiatric Association (1994) *Diagnostic and statistical manual of mental disorders* (4th edn). Washington, DC. Available online: www.psychnet-uk.com/dsm_iv/posttraumatic_stress_disorder.htm

Amstadter, A. B., Cisler, J. M., McCauley, J. L., Hernandez, M. A., Muzzy, W., & Acierno, R. (2011). Do incident and perpetrator characteristics of elder mistreatment differ by gender of the victim? Results from the National Elder Mistreatment Study. *Journal of Elder Abuse & Neglect, 23*, 43–57.

Anderson, C. A. (1989). Temperature and aggression: Ubiquitous effects of heat on occurrence of human violence. *Psychological Bulletin, 106*, 74–96.

Anderson, C. A. (1997). Effects of violent movies and trait hostility on hostile feelings and aggressive thoughts. *Aggressive Behavior, 23*, 161–178.

Anderson, C. A. (2001). Heat and violence. *Current Directions in Psychological Science, 10*, 33–38.

Anderson, C. A. (2004). An update on the effects of playing violent video games. *Journal of Adolescence, 27*, 113–122.

Anderson, C. A., & Anderson, K. B. (1998). Temperature and aggression: Paradox, controversy, and a (fairly) clear picture. In R. G. Geen, & E. Donnerstein (Eds), *Human aggression: Theories, research and implications for social policy* (pp. 247–298). San Diego, CA: Academic Press.

Anderson, C. A., & Anderson, K. B. (2008). Men who target women: Specificity of target, generality of aggressive behavior. *Aggressive Behavior, 34*, 605–622.

Anderson, C. A., Anderson, K. B., Dorr, N., DeNeve, K. M., & Flanagan, M. (2000). Temperature and aggression. *Advances in Experimental Social Psychology. 32*, 63–133.

Anderson, C. A., Benjamin, A. L., & Bartholow, B. D. (1998). Does the gun pull the trigger? Automatic priming effects of weapon pictures and weapon names. *Psychological Science, 9*, 308–314.

Anderson, C. A., Berkowitz, L., Donnerstein, E., Huesmann, L. R., Johnson, J. D., Linz, D., Malamuth, N. M., & Wartella, E. (2003). The influence of media violence on youth. *Psychological Science in the Public Interest, 4*, 81–110.

Anderson, C. A., & Bushman, B. J. (1997). External validity of "trivial" experiments: The case of laboratory aggression. *Review of General Psychology, 1*, 19–41.

Anderson, C. A., & Bushman, B. J. (2001). Effects of violent video games on aggressive behavior, aggressive cognition, aggressive affect, physiological arousal, and prosocial behavior: A meta-analytic review of the scientific literature. *Psychological Science, 12*, 353–359.

Anderson, C. A., & Bushman, B. J. (2002a). Human aggression. *Annual Review of Psychology, 53*, 27–51.

Anderson, C. A., & Bushman, B. J. (2002b). Media violence and the American public revisited. *American Psychologist, 57*, 448–450.

Anderson, C. A., Bushman, B. J., & Groom, R. W. (1997). Hot years and serious and deadly assaults: Empirical tests of the heat hypothesis. *Journal of Personality and Social Psychology, 73*, 1213–1223.

Anderson, C. A., & Carnagey, N. L. (2004). Violent evil and the general aggression model. In A. Miller (Ed.), *The social psychology of good and evil* (pp. 168–192). New York: Guilford Press.

Anderson, C. A., & Carnagey, N. L., (2009). Causal effects of violent sports video games on aggression: Is it competitiveness or violent content? *Journal of Experimental Social Psychology, 45*, 731–739.

Anderson, C. A., & DeLisi, M. (2011). Implications of global climate change for violence in developed and developing countries. In J. P. Forgas, A. W. Kruglanski, & K. D. Williams (Eds), *The psychology of social conflict and aggression* (pp. 249–265). New York: Psychology Press.

Anderson, C. A., & Dill, K. E. (2000). Video games and aggressive thoughts, feelings, and behavior in the laboratory and in life. *Journal of Personality and Social Psychology, 78*, 772–790.

Anderson, C. A., Gentile, D. A., & Buckley, K. E. (2007). *Violent video game effects on children and adolescents*. New York: Oxford University Press.

Anderson, C. A., Ihori, N., Bushman, B. J., Rothstein, H. R., Shibuya, A., Swing, E. L., Sakamoto, A., & Saleem, M. (2010). Violent video game effects on aggression, empathy, and prosocial behavior in Eastern and Western countries: A meta-analytic review. *Psychological Bulletin, 136*, 151–173.

Anderson, C. A., & Murphy, C. R. (2003). Violent video games and aggressive behavior in young women. *Aggressive Behavior, 29*, 423–429.

Anderson, L.A., & Whiston, S. C. (2005). Sexual assault education programs: A meta-analytic examination of their effectiveness. *Psychology of Women Quarterly, 29*, 374–388.

Anderson, P. B., Kontos, A. P., Tanigoshi, H., & Struckman-Johnson, C. (2005). An examination of sexual strategies used by urban Southern and rural Midwestern university women. *Journal of Sex Research, 42*, 335–341.

Anderson, P. B., & Savage, J. (2005). Social, legal, and institutional context of heterosexual aggression by college women. *Trauma, Violence, & Abuse, 6*, 130–140.

Anderson, P. B., & Struckman-Johnson, C. (Eds) (1998). *Sexually aggressive women*. New York: The Guilford Press.

Anetzberger, G. L. (1997). Elderly adult survivors of family violence. *Violence Against Women, 3*, 499–514.

Anetzbeger, G. L., Korbin, J. E., & Austin, C. (1994). Alcoholism and elder abuse. *Journal of Interpersonal Violence, 9*, 184–193.

Annerbäck, E. M., Wingren, G., Svedin, C. G., & Gustafsson, P. A. (2010). Prevalence and characteristics of child physical abuse in Sweden: Findings from a population-based youth survey. *Acta Paediatrica, 99*, 1229–1236.

Aosved, A. C., Long, P. J., & Voller, E. K. (2011). Sexual revictimization and adjustment in college men. *Psychology of Men & Masculinity, 12*, 285–296.

Aquino, K., & Thau, S. (2009). Workplace victimization: Aggression from the target's perspective. *Annual Review of Psychology, 60*, 717–741.

Arata, C. M., & Burkhart, B. M. (1998). Coping appraisals and adjustment to nonstranger sexual assault. *Violence Against Women, 4*, 224–239.

Archer, J. (1988). *The behavioural biology of aggression*. Cambridge: Cambridge University Press.

Archer, J. (1991). The influence of testosterone on human aggression. *British Journal of Psychology, 8*, 1–28.

Archer, J. (1995). What can ethology offer the psychological study of human aggression? *Aggressive Behavior, 21*, 243–255.

Archer, J. (2000). Sex differences in aggression between heterosexual partners: A meta-analytic review. *Psychological Bulletin, 126*, 651–680.

Archer, J. (2002). Sex differences in physically aggressive acts between heterosexual partners: A meta-analytic review. *Aggression and Violent Behavior, 7*, 313–351.

Archer, J. (2004). Sex differences in aggression in real-world settings: A meta-analytic review. *Review of General Psychology, 8*, 291–322.

Archer, J. (2006). Cross-cultural differences in physical aggression between partners: A social-role analysis. *Personality and Social Psychology Review, 10*, 133–153.

Archer, J. (2009). The nature of human aggression. *International Journal of Law and Psychiatry, 32*, 202–208.

Archer, J., Birring, S. S., & Wu, F. C. W. (1998). The association between testosterone and aggression among young men: Empirical findings and a meta-analysis. *Aggressive Behavior, 24*, 411–420.

Archer, J., & Browne, K. (1989). Concepts and approaches to the study of aggression. In J. Archer & K. Browne (Eds), *Human aggression: Naturalistic approaches* (pp. 3–24). London: Routledge.

Archer, J., & Coté, S. (2005). Sex differences in aggressive behavior. In R. E. Tremblay, W. W. Hartup, & J. Archer (Eds), *Developmental origins of aggression* (pp. 425–443). New York: Guilford Press.

Archer, J., & Coyne, S. M. (2005). An integrated review of indirect, relational, and social aggression. *Personality and Social Psychology Review, 9*, 212–230.

Archer, J., Fernández-Fuertes, A., & Thanzami, V. L. (2010). Does cost-benefit analysis or self-control predict involvement in two forms of aggression? *Aggressive Behavior, 36*, 292–304.

Archer, J., Holloway, R., & McLoughlin, K. (1995). Self-reported physical aggression among young men. *Aggressive Behavior, 21*, 325–342.

Archer, D., & McDaniel, P. (1995). Violence and gender: Differences and similarities across societies. In B. R. Ruback, & N. A. Weiner (Eds), *Interpersonal violent behaviors* (pp. 63–87). New York: Springer.

Archer, J., & Thanzami, V. (2007). The relation between physical aggression, size and strength, among a sample of young Indian men. *Personality and Individual Differences, 43*, 627–633.

Arms, R. L., Russell, G. W., & Sandilands, M. L. (1979). Effects on the hostility of spectators of viewing aggressive sports. *Social Psychology Quarterly, 42*, 275–279.

Arriola, K. J., Louden, T., Doldren, M., & Fortenberry, R. M. (2005). A meta-analysis of the relationship of child sexual abuse to HIV risk behavior among women. *Child Abuse & Neglect, 29*, 725–746.

Asbridge, M., Smart, R. G., & Mann, R. E. (2006). Can we predict road rage? *Trauma, Violence, & Abuse, 7*, 109–121.

Averill, J. R., Malstrom, E. J., Koriat, A., & Lazarus, R. S. (1972). Habituation to complex emotional stimuli. *Journal of Abnormal Psychology, 80*, 20–28.

Ayar, A. (2006). Road rage: A psychological disorder. *Journal of Psychiatry and the Law, 34*, 123–150.

Ayduk, Ö., Gyurak, A., & Luerssen, A. (2008). Individual differences in the rejection-aggression link in the hot sauce paradigm. *Journal of Experimental Social Psychology, 44*, 775–782.

Babcock, J. C., Green, C.E., & Robie, C. (2004). Does batterers' treatment work? A meta-analytic review of domestic violence treatment. *Clinical Psychology Review, 23*, 1023–1053.

Bailey, W. C., & Peterson, R. D. (1999). Capital punishment, homicide, and deterrence. In M. D. Smith & M. A. Zahn (Eds), *Homicide. A sourcebook of social research* (pp. 257–276). Thousand Oaks, CA: Sage.

Balsam, K. F., Rothblum, E. D., & Beauchaine, T. P. (2005). Victimization over the life span: A comparison of lesbian, gay, bisexual, and heterosexual siblings. *Journal of Consulting and Clinical Psychology, 73*, 477–487.

Bandura, A. (1983). Psychological mechanisms of aggression. In R. G. Geen, & E. I. Donnerstein (Eds), *Aggression: Theoretical and empirical reviews. Volume 1* (pp. 1–40). New York: Academic Press.

Bandura, A., Ross, D., & Ross, S. A. (1961). Transmission of aggression through imitation of aggressive models. *Journal of Abnormal and Social Psychology, 63*, 575–582.

Bandura, A., Ross, D., & Ross, S. A. (1963). Vicarious reinforcement and imitative learning. *Journal of Abnormal and Social Psychology, 67*, 601–607.

Banyard, V. L., Plante, E. G., & Moynihan, M. M. (2004). Bystander education: Bringing a broader community perspective to sexual violence prevention. *Journal of Community Psychology, 32*, 61–79.

Barbaree, H. E., & Marshall, W. L. (1991). The role of male sexual arousal in rape: Six models. *Journal of Consulting and Clinical Psychology, 59*, 621–630.

Bargh, J. A., & Pietromonaco, P. (1982). Automatic information processing and social perception: The influence of trait information presented outside of conscious awareness on impression formation. *Journal of Personality and Social Psychology, 43*, 437–449.

Bargh, J. A., Raymond, P., Pryor, J. B., & Strack, F. (1995). Attractiveness of the underling: An automatic power → sex association and its consequences for sexual harassment and aggression. *Journal of Personality and Social Psychology, 68*, 768–781.

Barker, E. D., Seguin, J. R., White, H. R., Bates, M., Lacourse, E., Carbonneau, R. et al. (2007). Developmental trajectories of male physical violence and theft. *Archives of General Psychiatry, 64*, 592–599.

Barlett, C. P., Anderson, C. A., & Swing, E. L. (2009). Video game effects – confirmed, suspected, and speculative. *Simulation & Gaming, 40*, 377–403.

Barlett, C. P., Branch, O., Rodeheffer, C., & Harris, R. (2009). How long do the short-term violent video game effects last? *Aggressive Behavior, 35*, 225–236.

Barlett, C. P., Harris, R. J., & Baldassaro, R. (2007). Longer you play, the more hostile you feel: Examination of first person shooter video games and aggression during video game play. *Aggressive Behavior, 33*, 486–497.

Barlett, C. P., Harris, R. J., & Bruey, C. (2008). The effect of the amount of blood in a violent video game on aggression, hostility, and arousal. *Journal of Experimental Social Psychology, 44*, 539–546.

Barnes, J. E., Noll, J. G., Putnam, F. W., & Trickett, P. K. (2009). Sexual and physical revictimization among victims of severe childhood sexual abuse. *Child Abuse & Neglect, 33*, 412–420.

Barnett, O. W., Miller-Perrin, C. L., & Perrin, R. D. (2011). *Family violence across the lifespan* (3rd edn). Thousand Oaks, CA: Sage.

Barnwell, S. S., Borders, A., & Earleywine, M. (2006). Alcohol-aggression expectancies and dispositional aggression moderate the relationship between alcohol consumption and alcohol-related violence. *Aggressive Behavior, 32*, 517–527.

Baron, R. A. (1976). The reduction of human aggression. A field study of the influence of incompatible reactions. *Journal of Applied Social Psychology, 6*, 260–274.

Baron, R. A., & Bell, P. A. (1976). Aggression and heat: The influence of ambient temperature, negative affect, and a cooling drink. *Journal of Personality and Social Psychology, 33*, 245–255.

Baron, R. A., & Richardson, D. R. (1994). *Human aggression* (2nd edn). New York: Plenum Press.

Bar-Tal, D. (1990). Causes and consequences of delegitimization: Models of conflict and ethnocentrism. *Journal of Social Issues, 46*, 65–81.

Bar-Tal, D. (1997). The monopolization of patriotism. In D. Bar-Tal, & E. Staub (Eds), *Patriotism in the lives of individuals and nations* (pp. 246–270). Chicago: Nelson-Hall.

Bartholomew, K., Regan, K. V., White, M. A., & Oram, D. (2008). Patterns of abuse in male same-sex relationships. *Violence and Victims, 23*, 617–636.

Bartholow, B. D., & Anderson, C. A. (2002). Effects of violent video games on aggressive behavior: Potential sex differences. *Journal of Experimental Social Psychology, 38*, 283–290.

Bartholow, B. D., Anderson, C. A., Carnagey, N. L., & Benjamin, A. J. (2005). Interactive effects of life experience and situational cues on aggression: The weapons priming effect in hunters and nonhunters. *Journal of Experimental Social Psychology, 41*, 489–60.

Bartholow, B. D., Bushman, B. J., & Sestir, M. R. (2006). Chronic violent video game exposure and desensitization to violence: Behavioral and event-related brain potential data. *Journal of Experimental Social Psychology, 42*, 532–539.

Bartholow, B. D., Sestir, M. A., & Davis, E. B. (2005). Correlates and consequences of exposure to video game violence: Hostile personality, empathy, and aggressive behavior. *Personality and Social Psychology Bulletin, 31*, 1573–1586.

Basile, K. C., Espelage, D. L., Rivers, I., McMahon, P. M., & Simon, T. R. (2009). The theoretical and empirical links between bullying behavior and male sexual violence perpetration. *Aggression and Violent Behavior, 14*, 336–347.

Baumeister, R. F., & Boden, J. M. (1998). Aggression and the self: High self-esteem, low self-control, and ego-threat. In R. G. Geen, & E. Donnerstein (Eds), *Human aggression: Theories, research and implications for social policy* (pp. 111–137). San Diego, CA: Academic Press.

Baumeister, R. F., Bushman, B. J., & Campbell, W. K. (2000). Self-esteem, narcissism, and aggression: Does violence result from low self-esteem or from threatened egotism? *Current Directions in Psychological Science, 9*, 26–29.

Baumeister, R. F., Smart, L., & Boden, J. M. (1996). Relation of threatened egotism to violence and aggression: The dark side of high self-esteem. *Psychological Review, 103*, 5–33.

Bauserman, R. (1996). Sexual aggression and pornography: A review of correlational research. *Basic and Applied Social Psychology, 18*, 405–427.

Beck, R., & Fernandez, E. (1998). Cognitive-behavioral therapy in the treatment of anger: A meta-analysis. *Cognitive Therapy and Research, 22*, 63–74.

Becker, G. (2007). The Buss-Perry Aggression Questionnaire: Some unfinished business. *Journal of Research in Personality, 41*, 434–452.

Bégue, L., & Subra, B. (2008). Alcohol and aggression: Perspectives on controlled and uncontrolled social information processing. *Social and Personality Psychology Compass, 2*, 511–538.

Beitchman, J. H., Zucker, K. J., Hood, J. E., daCosta, G. A., & Akman, D. (1991). A review of the short-term effects of childhood sexual abuse. *Child Abuse and Neglect, 15*, 537–556.

Bem, S. L. (1981). Gender schema theory: A cognitive account of sex typing. *Psychological Review, 88*, 354–364.

Bendik, M. F. (1992). Reaching the breaking point: Dangers of mistreatment in elder caregiving situations. *Journal of Elder Abuse and Neglect, 4*, 39–59.

Bensley, L., & Van Eenwyk, J. (2001). Video games and real-life aggression: A review of the literature. *Journal of Adolescent Health, 29*, 244–257.

Benton, D. (1992). Hormones and human aggression. In K. Bjorkqvist & P. Niemelä (Eds), *Of mice and women: Aspects of female aggression* (pp. 37–48). San Diego, CA: Academic Press.

Berdahl, J. L. (2007). Harassment based on sex: Protecting social status in the context of gender hierarchy. *Academy of Management Review, 32*, 641–658.

Bergen, R. K. (1996). *Wife rape: Understanding the responses of survivors and service providers.* Thousand Oaks, CA: Sage.

Berkowitz, L. (1962). *Aggression. A social psychological analysis.* New York: McGraw-Hill.

Berkowitz, L. (1989). Frustration-aggression hypothesis: Examination and reformulation. *Psychological Bulletin, 106,* 59–73.

Berkowitz, L. (1993). *Aggression: Its causes, consequences, and control.* Philadelphia, PA: Temple University Press.

Berkowitz, L. (1997). On the determinants and regulation of impulsive aggression. In S. Feshbach & J. Zagrodzka (Eds), *Aggression: Biological, developmental, and social perspectives* (pp. 187–211). New York: Plenum Press.

Berkowitz, L. (1998). Affective aggression: The role of stress, pain, and negative affect. In R. G. Geen & E. Donnerstein (Eds), *Human aggression: Theories, research and implications for social policy* (pp. 49–72). San Diego, CA: Academic Press.

Berkowitz, L. (2008). On the consideration of automatic as well as controlled psychological processes in aggression. *Aggressive Behavior, 34,* 117–129.

Berkowitz, L., & Harmon-Jones, E. (2004). Toward an understanding of the determinants of anger. *Emotion, 4,* 107–130.

Berkowitz, L., & LePage, A. (1967). Weapons as aggression-eliciting stimuli. *Journal of Personality and Social Psychology, 7,* 202–207.

Berlin, L. J., Appleyard, K., & Dodge, K. A. (2011). Intergenerational continuity in child maltreatment: Mediating mechanisms and implications for prevention. *Child Development, 82,* 162–176.

Bernhardt, P. C., Dabbs, J. M., Fielden, J. A., & Lutter, C. D. (1998). Testosterone changes during vicarious experiences of winning and losing among fans at sporting events. *Physiology & Behavior, 65,* 59–62.

Besser, A., Neria, Y., & Haynes, M. (2009). Adult attachment, perceived stress, and PTSD among civilians exposed to ongoing terrorist attacks in Southern Israel. *Personality and Individual Differences, 47,* 851–857.

Bettencourt, B. A., & Kernahan, C. (1997). A meta-analysis of aggression in the presence of violent cues: Effects of gender differences and aversive provocation. *Aggressive Behavior, 23,* 447–456.

Bettencourt, B. A., & Miller, N. (1996). Gender differences in aggression as a function of provocation: A meta-analysis. *Psychological Bulletin, 119,* 422–447.

Bettencourt, B. A., Talley, B. A. J., & Valentine, J. (2006). Personality and aggressive behavior under provoking and neutral conditions: A meta-analytic review. *Psychological Bulletin, 132,* 751–777.

Biggs, S., Manthorpe, J., Tinker, A., Doyle, N., & Erens, B. (2009). Mistreatment of older people in the United Kingdom: Findings from the First National Prevalence Study. *Journal of Elder Abuse & Neglect, 21,* 1–14.

Bijvank, M. N., Konijn, E. A., Bushman, B. J., & Roelofsma, P. H. M. P. (2009). Age and violent-content labels make video games forbidden fruits for youth. *Pediatrics, 123,* 870–876.

Billig, M., & Tajfel, H. (1973). Social categorization and similarity in intergroup behaviour. *European Journal of Social Psychology, 3,* 27–52.

Björkqvist, K., Lagerspetz, K., & Österman, K. (1992). *The direct and indirect aggression scales.* Vasa, Finland: Abo Akademi University, Department of Social Sciences.

Black, M. C., Basile, K. C., Breiding, M. J., Smith, S. G., Walters, M. L., Merrick, M. T. et al. (2011). *The National Intimate Partner and Sexual Violence Survey (NISVS): 2010 Summary Report.* Atlanta, GA: National Center for Injury Prevention and Control, Centers for Disease Control and Prevention. Available online: www.cdc.gov/ViolencePrevention/pdf/NISVS_Report2010-a.pdf

Blackhart, G. C., Nelson, B. C., Knowles, M. L., & Baumeister, R. F. (2009). Rejection elicits emotional reactions but neither causes immediate distress nor lowers self-esteem: A meta-analytic review of 192 studies on social exclusion. *Personality and Social Psychology Bulletin, 13,* 269–309.

Blackwell, L. M., Lynn, S. J., Vanderhoff, H., & Gidycz, C. (2004). Sexual assault revictimization: Toward effective risk-reduction programs. In L. J. Koenog, L.S. Doll, A. O'Leary, & W. Pequegnat (Eds), *From child sexual abuse to adult sexual risk: Trauma, revictimization, and intervention* (pp. 269–295). Washington, DC: American Psychological Association.

Bledsoe, L. K., Yankeelov, P. A., Barbee, A. P., & Antle, B. F. (2004). Understanding the impact of intimate partner violence mandatory reporting law. *Violence Against Women, 10,* 534–560.

Blockley, P. N., & Hartley, L. R. (1995). Aberrant driving behaviour: Errors and violations. *Ergonomics, 38,* 1759–1771.

Bloom, M., & Horgan, J. (2008). Missing their mark: The IRA's proxy bomb campaign. *Social Research, 75,* 579–614.

Blosnich, J. R., & Bossarte, R. M. (2009). Comparisons of intimate partner violence among partners in same-sex and opposite-sex relationships in the United States. *American Journal of Public Health, 99,* 2182–2184.

Bluemke, M., Friedrich, G., & Zumbach, J. (2010). The influence of violent and nonviolent computer games on implicit measures of aggressiveness. *Aggressive Behavior, 36,* 1–13.Bösche, W. (2010). Violent content enhances video game performance. *Journal of Media Psychology, 21,* 145–150.

Bohstedt, J. (1994). The dynamics of riots: Escalation and diffusion/contagion. In M. Potegal & J. F. Knutson (Eds), *The dynamics of aggression* (pp. 257–306). Hillsdale, NJ: L. Erlbaum.

Bonino, S., Ciairano, S., Rabaglietti, E., & Cattelino, E. (2006). Use of pornography and self-reported engagement in sexual violence among adolescents. *European Journal of Developmental Psychology, 3,* 265–288.

Borders, A. Barnwell, S. S., & Earleywine, M. (2007). Alcohol-aggression expectancies and dispositional rumination moderate the effect of alcohol consumption on alcohol-related aggression and hostility. *Aggressive Behavior, 33,* 327–338.

Bowling, N. A., & Beehr, T. A. (2006). Workplace harassment from the victim's perspective: A theoretical model and meta-analysis. *Journal of Applied Psychology, 91,* 998–1012.

Brackbill, R. M., Hadler, J. L., DiGrande, L., Ekenga, C. C., Farfel, M. R., Friedman, S., et al. (2009). Asthma and posttraumatic stress symptoms 5 to 6 years following exposure to the World Trade Center terrorist attack. *Journal of the American Medical Association, 302,* 502–516.

Brathwaite, B. (2007). *Sex in video games*. Boston, MA: Charles River Media.

Braun, C. M., & Giroux, J. (1989). Arcade video games: Proxemic, cognitive and content analyses. *Journal of Leisure Research, 21,* 92–105.

BRAVO (2009). *Dr. Sommer Studie 2009: Liebe! Körper! Sexualität!* München: Bauer Media Group.

Brehm, J. (1966). *A theory of psychological reactance*. Oxford: Academic Press.

Bremner, R. H., Koole, S. L., & Bushman, B. J. (2011). "Pray for those who mistreat you": Effects of prayer on anger and aggression. *Personality and Social Psychology Bulletin, 37,* 830–837.

Bridges, A. J., Wosnitzer, R., Scharrer, E., Sun, C., & Liberman, R. (2010). Aggression and sexual behavior in best-selling pornography videos: A content analysis update. *Violence Against Women, 16,* 1065–1085.

Broidy, L. M., Nagin, D. S., Tremblay, R. E., Bates, J. E., Brame, B., Dodge, K. A., et al. (2003). Developmental trajectories of childhood disruptive behaviors and adolescent delinquency: A six-site, cross-national study. *Developmental Psychology, 39,* 222–245.

Brown, G. R. (2000). Can studying non-human primates inform us about human rape? A zoologist's perspective. *Psychology, Evolution & Gender, 2*, 321–324.

Brown, J., Cohen, P., Johnson, J. G., & Salzinger, S. (1998). A longitudinal analysis of risk factors for child maltreatment: Findings of a 17-year prospective study of officially recorded and self-reported child abuse and neglect. *Child Abuse and Neglect, 22*, 1065–1078.

Brown, J. D., & L'Engle, K. L. (2009). X-rated. Sexual attitudes and behaviors associated with U.S. early adolescents' exposure to sexually explicit media. *Communication Research, 36*, 129–151.

Brown, R. (1986). *Social psychology* (2nd edn). New York: The Free Press.

Brown, R. (2010). *Prejudice: Its social psychology* (2nd edn). Chichester: Wiley-Blackwell.

Browne, A., & Finkelhor, D. (1986). Impact of child sexual abuse: A review of the research. *Psychological Bulletin, 99*, 66–77.

Browne, K. D. (1994). Child sexual abuse. In J. Archer (Ed.), *Male violence* (pp. 210–230). London: Routledge.

Browne, K. D., & Hamilton-Giachritsis, C. (2005).The influence of violent media on children and adolescents: A public health approach. *The Lancet, 365*, 702–710.

Brownridge, D. A. (2008). The elevated risk for violence against cohabitating women. *Violence Against Women, 14*, 809–832

Bryant, F. B., & Smith, B. D. (2001). Refining the architecture of aggression: A measurement model for the Buss-Perry Aggression Questionnaire. *Journal of Research in Personality, 35*, 138–167.

Bundeskriminalamt (Ed.) (2010). *Polizeiliche Kriminalstatistik 2009*. Bundesrepublik Deutschland. Available online: www.bka.de/nn_193232/DE/Publikationen/PolizeilicheKriminalstatistik/ PksJahrbuecher/pksJahrbuecher__node.html?__nnn=true

Bundeszentrale für gesundheitliche Aufklärung (2010). *Jugendsexualität 2010. Reprä sentative Wiederholungsbefragung von 14- bis 17-Jährigen und ihren Eltern – Aktueller Schwerpunkt Migration*. Köln: BZgA. Available online: www.bzga.de/infomaterialien/studien/ jugendsexualitaet-2010/

Burke, B. L., Martens, A., & Faucher, E. H. (2010). Two decades of terror management theory: A meta-analysis of mortality salience effects. *Personality and Social Psychology Review, 14*, 155–195.

Burks, V. S., Laird, R. D., Dodge, A., Pettit, G. S., & Bates, J. E. (1999). Knowledge structures, social information processing, and children's aggressive behavior. *Social Development, 8*, 220–236.

Burt, S. A. (2009). Are there meaningful etiological differences within antisocial behavior? Results of a meta-analysis. *Clinical Psychology Review, 29*, 163–178.

Bushman, B. J. (1993). Human aggression while under the influence of alcohol and other drugs: An integrative research review. *Current Directions in Psychological Science, 2*, 148–152.

Bushman, B. J. (1995). Moderating role of trait aggressiveness in the effects of violent media on aggression. *Journal of Personality and Social Psychology, 69*, 950–960.

Bushman, B. J. (1997). Effects of alcohol on human aggression. Validity of proposed explanations. *Recent Developments in Alcoholism, 13*, 227–243.

Bushman, B. J. (1998). Priming effects of media violence on the accessibility of aggressive constructs in memory. *Personality and Social Psychology Bulletin, 24*, 537–545.

Bushman, B. (2002). Does venting anger feed or extinguish the flame? Catharsis, rumination, distraction, anger, and aggressive responding. *Personality and Social Psychology Bulletin, 28*, 724–731.

Bushman, B. J., & Anderson, C. A. (1998). Methodology in the study of aggression: Integrating experimental and nonexperimental findings. In R. G. Geen, & E. Donnerstein (Eds), *Human aggression: Theories, research and implications for social policy* (pp. 24–48). San Diego, CA: Academic Press.

Bushman, B. J., & Anderson, C. A. (2001). Is it time to pull the plug on the hostile versus instrumental aggression dichotomy? *Psychological Review, 108*, 273–279.

Bushman, B. J., & Anderson, C. A. (2002). Violent video games and hostile expectations: A test of the General Aggression Model. *Personality and Social Psychology Bulletin, 28*, 1679–1686.

Bushman, B. J., Baumeister, R. F., Thomaes, S., Ryu, E., Begeer, S., & West, S. G. (2009). Looking again, and harder, for a link between low self-esteem and aggression. *Journal of Personality, 77*, 427–446.

Bushman, B. J., Bonacci, A. M., Pedersen, W. C., Vasquez, E. A., & Miller, N. (2005). Chewing on it can chew you up: Effects of rumination on triggered displaced aggression. *Journal of Personality and Social Psychology, 88*, 969–983.

Bushman, B. J., & Cantor, J. (2003). Media ratings for violence and sex. *American Psychologist, 58*, 130–141.

Bushman, B. J., & Cooper, H. M. (1990). Effects of alcohol on human aggression: An integrative research review. *Psychological Bulletin, 107*, 341–354.

Bushman, B. J., & Huesmann, L. R. (2006). Short-term and long-term effects of violent media on aggression in children and adults. *Archives of Pediatrics and Adolescent Medicine, 160*, 348–352.

Bushman, B. J., Ridge, R. D., Das, E., Key, C. W., & Busath, G. L. (2007). When God sanctions killing: Effects of scriptural violence on aggression. *Psychological Science, 18*, 204–207.

Bushman, B. J., & Wells, G. L. (1998). Trait aggressiveness and hockey penalties: Predicting hot tempers on the ice. *Journal of Applied Psychology, 83*, 969–974.

Bushman, B. J., & Whitacker, J. L. (2010). Like a magnet: Catharsis beliefs attract angry people to violent video games. *Psychological Science, 21*, 790–792.

Buss, A. H. (1961). *The psychology of aggression.* New York: John Wiley.

Buss, A. H., & Durkee, A. (1957). An inventory assessing different kinds of hostility. *Journal of Consulting Psychology, 21*, 343–348.

Buss, A. H., & Perry, M. (1992). The aggression questionnaire. *Journal of Personality and Social Psychology, 63*, 452–459.

Buss, A. H., & Warren, W. L. (2000). *The aggression questionnaire manual.* Los Angeles, CA: Western Psychological Services.

Buss, D. M. (1996). Sexual conflict: Evolutionary insights into feminism and the "battle of the sexes". In D. M. Buss, & N. Malamuth (Eds), *Sex, power, conflict: Evolutionary and feminist perspectives* (pp. 296–328). New York: Oxford University Press.

Buss, D. M., & Shakelford, T. K. (1997). Human aggression in evolutionary psychological perspective. *Clinical Psychology Review, 17*, 605–619.

Byrne, S. (2009). Media literacy interventions: What makes them boom or boomerang? *Communication Education, 58*, 1–14.

Cahill, C., Llewelyn, S. P., & Pearson, C. (1991). Long-term effects of sexual abuse which occurred in childhood: A review. *British Journal of Clinical Psychology, 30*, 117–130.

Cairns, E., & Darby, J. (1998). The conflict in Northern Ireland. *American Psychologist, 53*, 754–760.

Cairns, R. B., Cadwallader, T. W., Estell, D., & Neckerman, H. J. (1997). Groups to gangs: Developmental and criminological perspectives and relevance for prevention. In D. M. Stoff, J. Breiling, & J. D. Maser (Eds), *Handbook of antisocial behavior* (pp. 194–204). New York: John Wiley & Sons, Inc.

Cairns, R. B., & Cairns, B. D. (1994). *Lifelines and risks. Pathways of youths in our time*. Cambridge: Cambridge University Press.

Cairns, E., Kenworthy, J., Campbell, A., & Hewstone, M. (2006). The role of in-group identification, religious group membership and intergroup conflict in moderating in-group and out-group affect. *British Journal of Social Psychology, 45*, 701–716.

Campbell, A. (2006). Sex differences in direct aggression: What are the psychological mediators? *Aggression and Violent Behavior, 11*, 237–264.

Campbell, R., & Patterson, D. (2011). Services for victims of sexual violence. In M. P. Koss, J. W. White, & A. E. Kazdin (Eds), *Violence against women and children. Volume 2. Navigating solutions* (pp. 95–114). Washington, DC: American Psychological Association.

Campell, R., Patterson, D., & Lichty, L. F. (2005). The effectiveness of sexual assault nurse examiner (SANE) programs: A review of psychological, medical, legal, and community outcomes. *Trauma, Violence, & Abuse, 6*, 313–329.

Campbell, R., Sefl, T., Barnes, H. E., Ahrens, C. E., Wasco, S. M. & Zaragoza-Diesfeld, Y. (1999). Community services for rape survivors: Enhancing psychological well-being or increasing trauma? *Journal of Consulting and Clinical Psychology, 67*, 847–858.

Cantor, J., & Wilson, B. J. (2003). Media and violence: Intervention strategies for reducing aggression. *Media Psychology, 5*, 363–403.

Caprara, G. V., Cinnani, V., D'Imperio, G., Passerini, S., Renzi, P., & Travaglia, G. (1985). Indicators of impulsive aggression: Present status of research on irritability and emotional susceptibility scales. *Personality and Individual Differences, 6*, 665–674.

Caprara, G. V., Perugini, M., & Barbaranelli, C. (1994). Studies of individual differences in aggression. In M. Potegal, & J. F. Knutson (Eds), *The dynamics of aggression* (pp. 123–153). Hillsdale, NJ: Lawrence Erlbaum.

Card, N. A., & Little, T. D. (2006), Proactive and reactive aggression in childhood and adolescence: A meta-analysis of differential relations with psychosocial adjustment. *International Journal of Behavioral Development, 30*, 466–480.

Card, N. A., Stucky, B. D., Sawalani, G. M., & Little, T. D. (2008). Direct and indirect aggression during childhood and adolescence: A meta-analytic review of gender differences, intercorrelations, and relations to maladjustment. *Child Development, 79*, 1185–1229.

Carlson, M., Marcus-Newhall, A., & Miller, N. (1989). Evidence for a general construct of aggression. *Personality and Social Psychology Bulletin, 15*, 377–389.

Carlson, M., Marcus-Newhall, A., & Miller, N. (1990). Effects of situational aggression cues: A quantitative review. *Journal of Personality and Social Psychology, 58*, 622–633.

Carnagey, N. L., & Anderson, C. A. (2005). The effects of reward and punishment in violent video games on aggressive affect, cognition, and behavior. *Psychological Science, 16*, 882–889.

Carnagey, N. L., & Anderson, C. A. (2007). Changes in attitudes towards war and violence after September 11, 2001. *Aggressive Behavior, 33*, 118–129.

Carnagey, N. L., Anderson, C. A., & Bushman, B. J. (2007). The effect of video game violence on physiological desensitization to real-life violence. *Journal of Experimental Social Psychology, 43*, 489–496.

Carney, A. G., & Merrell, K. W. (2001). Bullying in schools: Perspectives on understanding and preventing an international problem. *School Psychology International, 22*, 364–382.

Carrasco, M. A., Holgado, F. P., Rodriguez, M. A., & del Barrio, M. V. (2009). Concurrent and across-time relations between mother/father hostility and children's aggression: A longitudinal study. *Journal of Family Violence, 24*, 213–220.

Casey, E. A., Beadnell, B., & Lindhorst, T. P. (2009). Predictors of sexually coercive behavior in a nationally representative sample of adolescent males. *Journal of Interpersonal Violence, 24*, 1129–1147.

Caspi, A., Elder, G. H., & Bem, D. J. (1987). Moving against the world: Life-course patterns of explosive children. *Developmental Psychology, 23*, 308–313.

Centers for Disease Control and Prevention (2010). *Web-based Injury Statistics Query and Reporting System (WISQARS)*. Atlanta, GA: National Center for Injury Prevention and Control. Available online: www.cdc.gov/injury/wisqars/index.html

Chan, D. K. S., Lam, C. B., Chow, S. Y., & Cheung, S. F. (2008). Examining the job-related, psychological, and physical outcomes of workplace sexual harassment: A meta-analytic review. *Psychology of Women Quarterly, 32*, 362–376.

Chan, Y.-C., & Yeung, J. W. (2009). Children living with violence within the family and its sequel: A meta-analysis from 1995 to 2006. *Aggression and Violent Behavior, 14*, 313–322.

Chandy, J. M., Blum, R. W., & Resnick, M. D. (1996). Female adolescents with a history of sexual abuse. *Journal of Interpersonal Violence, 11,* 503–518.

Chaplin, R., Flatley, J., & Smith, K. (2011). *Crime in England and Wales 2010/11. Findings from the British Crime Survey and police recorded crime*. London: Home Office Statistical Bulletin HOSB1011. Available online: www.homeoffice.gov.uk/publications/science-research-statistics/research-statistics/crime-research/hosb1011/hosb1011?view=Binary

Chen, Y., & Ullman, S. E. (2010). Women's reporting of sexual and physical assaults to police in the National Violence Against Women Survey. *Violence Against Women, 16*, 262–279.

Chermack, S. T., & Giancola, P. R. (1997). The relation between alcohol and aggression: An integrated biopsychosocial conceptualization. *Clinical Psychology Review, 17*, 621–649.

Chesney-Lind, M. (1997). *The female offender. Girls, women, and crime*. Thousand Oaks, CA: Sage.

Christensen, E. (1999). The prevalence and nature of abuse and neglect in children under four: A national survey. *Child Abuse Review, 8*, 109–119.

Christensen, P. N., & Wood, W. (2007). Effects of media violence on viewers' aggression in unconstrained social interaction. In R. W. Preiss, B. M. Gayle, N. Burrell, M. Allen, & J. Bryant (Eds), *Mass media effects research: Advances through meta-analysis* (pp. 145–168). New York: Lawrence Erlbaum Associates.

Christie, D. J. (2006). 9/11 Aftershocks: An analysis of conditions ripe for hate crimes. In P. R. Kimmel, & C. E. Stout (Eds), *Collateral damage: The psychological consequences of America's war on terrorism* (pp. 19–44). Westport, CT: Praeger.

Chu, A. T., Pineda, A. S., DePrince, A. P., & Freyd, J. J. (2011). Vulnerability and protective factors for child abuse and maltreatment. In J. W. White, M. P. Koss, & A. E. Kazdin (Eds), *Violence against women and children. Volume 1. Mapping the terrain* (pp. 55–75). Washington, DC: American Psychological Association.

Classen, C. C., Palesh, O. G., & Aggarwal, R. (2005). Sexual revictimization: A review of the literature. *Trauma, Violence, and Abuse, 6*, 103–129.

Clements, C. E., & Ogle, R. L. (2009). Does acknowledgement as an assault victim impact post-assault psychological symptoms and coping? *Journal of Interpersonal Violence, 24*, 1595–1614.

Cohen, D., Nisbett, R. E., Bowdle, B. F., & Schwarz, N. (1996). Insult, aggression, and the southern culture of honor: An "experimental ethnography". *Journal of Personality and Social Psychology, 70*, 945–960.

Cohen, J. (1988). *Statistical power analysis for the behavioral sciences* (2nd edn). New York: Academic Press.

Cohen, L. E., & Felson, M. (1979). Social change and crime rate trends: A routine activity approach. *American Sociological Review, 44*, 588–608.

Cohen, T. R., & Insko, C. A. (2008). War and peace. Possible approaches to reducing intergroup conflict. *Perspectives on Psychological Science, 3*, 87–93.

Coker, A. L., Williams, C. M., Follingstad, D. R., & Jordan, C. E. (2011). Psychological, reproductive and maternal health, behavioral, and economic impact of intimate partner violence. In J. W. White, M. P. Koss, & A. E. Kazdin (Eds), *Violence against women and children. Volume 1. Mapping the terrain* (pp. 265–284). Washington, DC: American Psychological Association.

Collins, R. (2008). *Violence. A micro-sociological theory*. Princeton, NJ: Princeton University Press.

Collinshaw, S., Pickles, A., Messer, J., Rutter, M., Shearer, C., & Maughan, B. (2007). Resilience to adult psychopathology following childhood maltreatment: Evidence from a community sample. *Child Abuse & Neglect, 31*, 211–229.

Combs-Lane, A. M., & Smith, D. W. (2002). Risk of sexual victimization in college women: The role of behavioral intentions and risk-taking behaviors. *Journal of Interpersonal Violence, 17*, 165–183.

Conroy, D. E., Silva, J. M., Newcomer, R., Walker, B. W., & Johnson, M. S. (2001). Personal and participatory socializers of the perceived legitimacy of aggressive behavior in sport. *Aggressive Behavior, 27*, 405–418.

Cook, C. R., Williams, K. R., Guerra, N., Kim, T. E., & Sadek, S. (2010). Predictors of bullying and victimization in childhood and adolescence: A meta-analytic investigation. *School Psychology Quarterly, 25*, 65–83.

Coons, C. J. (1995). College sports and fan aggression: Implications for residence hall discipline. *Journal of College Student Development, 36*, 587–593.

Cooper, C., Selwood, A., & Livingston, G. (2008). The prevalence of elder abuse and neglect: A systematic review. *Age and Ageing, 37*, 151–160.

Corvo, K., & deLara, E. (2010). Towards an integrated theory of relational violence: Is bullying a risk factor for domestic violence? *Aggression and Violent Behavior, 15*, 181–190.

Coulomb-Cabagno, G., & Rascle, O. (2006). Team sports players' observed aggression as a function of gender, competitive level, and sport type. *Journal of Applied Social Psychology, 36*, 1980–2000.

Coyne, S. M. , Robinson, S.L., & Nelson, D. A. (2010). Does reality backbite? Physical, verbal, and relational aggression in reality television programs. *Journal of Broadcasting & Electronic Media, 54*, 282–294.

Coyne, S. M., & Whitehead, E. (2008). Indirect aggression in animated Disney films. *Journal of Communication, 58*, 382–395.

Craig, K. M. (2002). Examining hate-motivated aggression: A review of the social psychological literature on hate crimes as a distinct form of aggression. *Aggression and Violent Behavior, 7*, 85–101.

Craig, W., Harel-Fisch, Y., Fogel-Grinvald, H., Dostaler, S., Hetland, J., Simons-Morton, B. et al. (2009). A cross-national profile of bullying and victimization among adolescents in 40 countries. *International Journal of Public Health, 54, Supplement 2*, 216–224.

Crick, N. R., Casas, J. F., & Mosher, M. (1997). Relational and overt aggression in preschool. *Developmental Psychology, 33*, 579–588.

Crick, N. R., & Grotpeter, J. K. (1995). Relational aggression, gender, and social-psychological adjustment. *Child Development, 66*, 710–722.

Crick, N. R., Ostrov, J. M., & Kawabata, Y. (2007). Relational aggression and gender: An overview. In D. J. Flannery, A. T. Vazsonyi, & I. D. Waldman (Eds), *The Cambridge handbook of violent behavior and aggression* (pp. 245–259). New York: Cambridge University Press.

Cross, C. P., & Campbell, A. (2011). Women's aggression. *Aggression and Violent Behavior, 16,* 390–398.

Cross, C. P., Copping, L. T., & Campbell, A. (2011). Sex differences in impulsivity: A meta-analysis. *Psychological Bulletin, 137,* 97–130.

Crown · Prosecution Service (2010). *Violence against Women crime report 2009–2010.* Available online: www.cps.gov.uk/publications/docs/CPS_VAW_report_2010.pdf

Cui, M., Durtschi, J. A., Donnellan, M. B., Lorenz, F. O., & Conger, R. D. (2010). Intergenerational transmission of relationship aggression: A prospective longitudinal study. *Journal of Family Psychology, 24,* 688–697.

Culbertson, K. A., & Dehle, C. (2001). Impact of sexual assault as a function of perpetrator type. *Journal of Interpersonal Violence, 16,* 992–1007.

Currie, C., Gabhaim, S. N., Godeau, E., Roberts, C., Currie, D., Picket, W. et al. (2008). *Inequalities in young people's health. HBSC International report from the 2005/2006 survey.* Available online: www.euro.who.int/__data/assets/pdf_file/0005/53852/E91416.pdf

Cutajar, M., Mullen, P. E., Ogloff, J. P., Thomas, S. D., Wells, D. L., & Spataro, J. (2010). Psychopathology in a large cohort of sexually abused children followed up to 43 years. *Child Abuse & Neglect, 34,* 813–822.

Daly, M., & Wilson, M. (1994). Evolutionary psychology of male violence. In J. Archer (Ed.), *Male violence* (pp. 253–288). London: Routledge.

Darwin, C. (1859). *On the origin of species.* London: Murray.

Das, E., Bushman, B. J., Bezemer, M. D., Kerkhof, P., & Vermeulen, I. E. (2009). How terrorism news reports increase prejudice against outgroups: A terror management account. *Journal of Experimental Social Psychology, 45,* 453–459.

Davis, K. C. (2010). The influence of alcohol expectancies and intoxication on men's aggressive unprotected sexual intentions. *Experimental and Clinical Psychopharmacology, 18,* 418–428.

Decker, S. H. (2007). Youth gangs and violent behavior. In D. J. Flannery, A. T. Vazsonyi, & I. D. Waldman (Eds), *The Cambridge handbook of violent behavior and aggression* (pp. 388–401). New York: Cambridge University Press.

Decker, S. H., & van Winkle, B. (1996). *Life in the gang.* New York: Cambridge University Press.

De Donder, L., Luoma, M.-L., Penhale, B., Lang, G., Santos, A, J., Tamutiene, I. et al. (2011). European map of prevalence rates of elder abuse and its impact for future research. *European Journal of Ageing, 8,* 129–143.

Deffenbacher, J. L., Deffenbacher, D. M., Lynch, R. S., & Richards, T. L. (2003). Anger, aggression and risky behavior: A comparison of high and low anger drivers. *Behaviour Research and Therapy, 41,* 701–718.

Deffenbacher, J. L., Filetti, L. B., Lynch, R. S., Dahlen, E. R., & Oetting, E. R. (2002). Cognitive-behavioral treatment of high anger drivers. *Behaviour Research and Therapy, 40,* 895–910.

Deffenbacher, J. L., Lynch, R. S., Oetting, E. R., & Swaim, R. C. (2002). The Driving Anger Expression Inventory: A measure of how people express their anger on the road. *Behaviour Research and Therapy, 40,* 717–737.

Deffenbacher, J. L., Lynch, R. S., Oetting, E. R., & Yingling, D. A. (2001). Driving anger: Correlates and a test of state-trait theory. *Personality and Individual Differences, 31,* 1321–1331.

DeLisi, L. E., Maurizio, A., Yost, M., Papparozzi, C. F., Fulchino, C., Katz, C. L. et al. (2003). A survey of New Yorkers after the Sept. 11, 2001, terrorist attacks. *American Journal of Psychiatry, 160,* 780–783.

Del Vecchio, T., & O'Leary, K. D. (2004). Effectiveness of anger treatments for specific anger problems: A meta-analytic review. *Clinical Psychology Review, 24,* 15–34.

Denson, T. F., Capper, M. M., Oaten, M., Friese, M., & Schofield, T. P. (2011). Self-control training decreases aggression in response to provocation in aggressive individuals. *Journal of Research in Personality, 45,* 252–256.

Denson, T. F., Pedersen, W. C., Friese, M., Hahm, A., & Roberts, L. (2011). Understanding impulsive aggression: Angry rumination and reduced self-control capacity are mechanisms underlying the provocation-aggression relationship. *Personality and Social Psychology Bulletin, 37,* 850–862.

Denson, T. F., Pedersen, W. C., & Miller, N. (2006). The Displaced Aggression Questionnaire. *Journal of Personality and Social Psychology, 90,* 1032–1051.

Denzler, M., Förster, J., & Liberman, N. (2009). How goal-fulfilment decreases aggression. *Journal of Experimental Psychology, 45,* 90–100.

Department for Children, Schools, and Families (2007). *A study into the views of parents on the physical punishment of children.* Available online: www.education.gov.uk/publications// eOrderingDownload/Section58-Parental-Survey.pdf

Department for Education (2010). *Children in need in England, including their characteristics and further information on children who were the subject of a child protection plan.* Statistical Release ORS28/2010. Available online: www.education.gov.uk/rsgateway/DB/STR/d000970/osr28-2010. pdf

DePaul, J., & Domenech, L. (2000). Childhood history of abuse and child abuse potential in adolescent mothers: A longitudinal study. *Child Abuse & Neglect, 24,* 701–713.

Deselms, J. L., & Altman, J. D. (2003). Immediate and prolonged effects of videogame violence. *Journal of Applied Social Psychology, 33,* 1553–1563.

DeWall, C. N., & Anderson, C. A. (2011). The General Aggression Model. In P. Shaver, & M. Mikulincer (Eds), *Human aggression and violence: Causes, manifestations, and consequences* (pp. 15–33). Washington, DC: American Psychological Association.

DeWall, C. N., Anderson, C. A., & Bushman, B. J. (2011). The General Aggression Model: Theoretical extensions to violence. *Psychology of Violence, 1,* 245–258.

DeWall, C. N., Baumeister, R. F., Stillman, T. F., & Gailliot, M. T. (2007). Violence restrained: Effects of self-regulation and its depletion on aggression. *Journal of Experimental Social Psychology, 43,* 62–76.

DeWall, C. N., Bushman, B. J. Giancola, P. R., & Webster, G. D. (2010). The big, the bad and the boozed-up: Weight moderates the effect of alcohol on aggression. *Journal of Experimental Social Psychology, 46,* 619–623.

DeWall, C. N., Twenge, J. M., Gitter, S. A., & Baumeister, R. F. (2009). It's the thought that counts: The role of hostile cognition in shaping aggressive responses to social exclusion. *Journal of Personality and Social Psychology, 96,* 45–59.

Diener, E. (1980). Deindividuation: The absence of self-awareness and self-regulation in group members. In P. B. Paulus (Ed.), *Psychology of group influence* (pp. 209–242). Hillsdale, NJ: Lawrence Erlbaum.

Dietz, T. L. (1998). An examination of violence and gender role portrayals in video games: Implications for gender socialization and aggressive behavior. *Sex Roles, 38,* 425–442.

DiLalla, L. F., & Gottesman, I. I. (1991). Biological and genetic contributions to violence – Widom's untold tale. *Psychological Bulletin, 109*, 125–129.

Dill, K. E., Anderson, C. A., Anderson, K. B., & Deuser, W. E. (1997). Effects of aggressive personality on social expectations and social perceptions. *Journal of Research in Personality, 31*, 272–292.

Dinkes, R., Kemp, J., & Baum, K. (2009). *Indicators of school crime and safety: 2009*. National Center for Education Statistics, Institute of Education Sciences, U.S. Department of Education, and Bureau of Justice Statistics, Office of Justice Programs, U.S. Department of Justice. Washington, DC. Available online: http://nces.ed.gov/pubs2010/2010012.pdf

Dodge, K. A. (2006). Translational science in action: Hostile attributional style and the development of aggressive behavior problems. *Development and Psychopathology, 18*, 791–814.

Dollard, J., Doob, L. W., Miller, N. E., Mowrer, O. H., & Sears, R. R. (1939). *Frustration and aggression*. New Haven, CT: Yale University Press.

Donnerstein, E. (1984). Pornography: Its effect on violence against women. In N. M. Malamuth & E. Donnerstein (Eds), *Pornography and sexual aggression* (pp. 53–81). Orlando, FL: Academic Press.

Donnerstein, E., & Wilson, D. W. (1976). The effects of noise and perceived control on ongoing and subsequent aggressive behaviour. *Journal of Personality and Social Psychology, 34*, 774–781.

Donnerstein, M., & Donnerstein, E. (1978). Direct and vicarious censure in the control of interracial aggression. *Journal of Personality, 46*, 162–175.

Dooley, J. J., Pyzalski, J., & Cross, D. (2009). Cyberbullying versus face-to-face bullying: A theoretical and conceptual review. *Zeitschrift für Psychologie/Journal of Psychology, 21*, 182–188.

Doosje, B., Zebel, S., Scheermeijer, M., & Mathyi, P. (2007). Attributions of responsibility for terrorist attacks: The role of group membership and identification. *International Journal of Conflict and Violence, 1*, 127–141.

Drieschner, K., & Lange, A. (1999). A review of cognitive factors in the etiology of rape. *Clinical Psychology Review, 19*, 57–77.

Dubow, E., Boxer, P., Huesmann, L. R., Shikaki, K., Landau, S., Gvirsman, S. D. et al. (2010). Exposure to conflict and violence across contexts: Relations to adjustment among Palestinian children. *Journal of Clinical Child and Adolescent Psychology, 39*, 103–116.

Duda, J. L., Olson, L. K., & Templin, T. J. (1991). The relationship of task and ego orientation to sportsmanship attitudes and the perceived legitimacy of injurious acts. *Research Quarterly for Exercise and Sport, 62*, 79–87.

Duffy, M. (2009). Preventing workplace mobbing and bullying with effective organizational consultation, policies, and legislation. *Consulting Psychology Journal: Practice and Research, 61*, 242–262.

Dunning, E., Murphy, P. & Williams, J. (1986). Spectator violence at football matches: Towards a sociological explanation. *British Journal of Sociology, 37*, 221–244.

Eagly, A. H. (1987). *Sex differences in social behavior: A social role interpretation*. Hillsdale, NJ: Lawrence Erlbaum.

Eagly, A. H., & Steffen, F. J. (1986): Gender and aggressive behavior: A meta-analytic review of the social psychological literature. *Psychological Bulletin, 100*, 309–330.

Eagly, A. H., & Wood, W. (1999). The origins of sex differences in human behaviour. Evolved dispositions versus social roles. *American Psychologist, 54*, 408–423.

Eastin, M. R. (2006). Video game violence and the female game player: Self- and opponent gender effects on presence and aggressive thoughts. *Human Communication Research, 32*, 351–372.

Eaton, D. K. et al. (2010). *Youth Risk Behavior Surveillance – United States, 2009*. Atlanta, GA: Centers for Disease Control and Prevention. Available online: www.cdc.gov/mmwr/pdf/ss/ss5905.pdf

Echebarria-Echabe, A., & Fernández-Guede, E. (2006). Effects of terrorism on attitudes and ideological orientation. *European Journal of Social Psychology, 36*, 259–265.

Eckenrode, J. (2011). Primary prevention of child abuse and maltreatment. In M. P. Koss, J. W. White, & A. E. Kazdin (Eds), *Violence against women and children. Volume 2. Navigating solutions* (pp. 71–91). Washington, DC: American Psychological Association.

Eckhardt, C. (2011). Intimate partner violence: Cognitive, affective, and relational factors. In J. P. Forgas, A. W. Kruglanski, & K. D. Williams (Eds), *The psychology of social conflict and aggression* (pp. 167–184). New York: Psychology Press.

Eckhardt, C., Norlander, B., & Deffenbacher, J. (2002). The assessment of anger and hostility: A critical review. *Aggression and Violent Behavior, 7*, 1–27.

Edguer, N., & Janisse, M. P. (1994). Type A behavior and aggression: Provocation and cardiovascular responsivity in the Buss teacher-learner paradigm. *Personality and Individual Differences, 17*, 377–393.

Edwards, K. M., Desai, A. D., Gidycz, C. A., & VanWynsberghe, A. (2009). College women's aggression in dating relationships: The role of childhood and adolescent victimization. *Psychology of Women Quarterly, 33*, 255–265.

Egley, A., Howell, J. C., & Moore, J. P. (2010). *Highlights of the 2008 National Youth Gang Survey.* Washington, DC: U.S. Department of Justice. Available online: www.ncjrs.gov/pdffiles1/ojjdp/229249.pdf

Ehrensaft, M. K., Moffitt, T. E., & Caspi, A. (2006). Is domestic violence followed by an increased risk of psychiatric disorders among women but not among men? A longitudinal cohort study. *American Journal of Psychiatry, 163*, 885–892.

Einarsen, S., Hoel, H., & Notelaers, G. (2009). Measuring exposure to bullying and harassment at work: Validity, factor structure and psychometric properties of the Negative Acts Questionnaire-Revised. *Work & Stress, 23*, 24–44.

Eisenberger, N. I., Lieberman, M. D., & Williams, K. D. (2003). Does rejection hurt? An fMRI study of social exclusion. *Science, 302*, 290–292.

Eitle, D., Gunkel, S., & Van Gundy, K. (2004). Cumulative exposure to stressful life events and male gang membership. *Journal of Criminal Justice, 32*, 95–111.

Ekstein, R. (1949). A biographical comment on Freud's dual instinct theory. *American Imago, 6*, 211–216.

Ellison-Potter, P. A., Bell, P. A., & Deffenbacher, J. L. (2001). The effects of trait driving anger, anonymity, and aggressive stimuli on aggressive driving behaviour. *Journal of Applied Social Psychology, 31*, 431–443.

Erdley, C. A., & Asher, S. R. (1998). Linkages between children's beliefs about the legitimacy of aggression and their behavior. *Social Development, 7*, 321–339.

Eron, L. D. (1986). Interventions to mitigate the psychological effects of media violence on aggressive behavior. *Journal of Social Issues, 42*, 155–169.

Eron, L.D. (1987). The development of aggressive behavior from the perspective of a developing behaviorism. *American Psychologist, 42*, 435–442.

Eron, L. D. (1994). Theories of aggression: From drives to cognitions. In L. R. Huesmann, (Ed.), *Aggressive behavior: Current perspectives* (pp. 3–11). New York: Plenum Press.

Esbensen, F. A., Osgood, D. W., Taylor, T. J., Peterson, D., & Freng, A. (2001). How great is G.R.E.A.T.? Results from a longitudinal quasi-experimental design. *Criminology & Public Policy, 1*, 87–118.

Esbensen, F. A., Peterson, D., Taylor, T. J., Freng, A., Osgood, D. W., Carson, D. et al. (2011). Evaluation and evolution of the Gang Resistance Education and Training (G.R.E.A.T.) program. *Journal of School Violence, 10*, 53–70.

Evans, S. E., Davies, C., & DiLillo, D. (2008). Exposure to domestic violence: A meta-analysis of child and adolescent outcomes. *Aggression and Violent Behavior, 13*, 131–140.

Even-Chen, M., & Itzhaky, H. (2007). Exposure to terrorism and violent behavior among adolescents in Israel. *Journal of Community Psychology, 35*, 43–55.

Fabiano, P. M., Perkins, H. W., Berkowitz, A., Linkenbach, J., & Stark, C.(2003). Engaging men as social justice allies in ending violence against women: Evidence for a social norms approach. *Journal of American College Health, 52*, 105–112.

Fagan, A. A. (2005). The relationship between adolescent physical abuse and criminal offending: Support for an enduring and generalized cycle of violence. *Journal of Family Violence, 20*, 279–290.

Fargo, J. D. (2009). Pathways to adult sexual revictimization: Direct and indirect behavioral risk factors across the lifespan. *Journal of Interpersonal Violence, 24*, 1771–1791.

Farrington, D. P. (2007). Origins of violent behavior over the life span. In D. J. Flannery, A. T. Vazsonyi, & I. D. Waldman (Eds), *The Cambridge handbook of violent behavior and aggression* (pp. 19–48). New York: Cambridge University Press.

Farrington, D. P., Ttofi, M. M., & Coid, J. W. (2009). Development of adolescence-limited, late-onset, and persistent offenders from age 8 to age 48. *Aggressive Behavior, 35*, 150–163.

Farris, C., Treat, T. A., Viken, R. J., & McFall, R. M. (2008). Sexual coercion and the misperception of sexual intent. *Clinical Psychology Review, 28*, 48–66.

Featherstone, B. (1996). Victims or villains? Women who physically abuse their children. In B. Fawcett, B. Featherstone, J. Hearn, & C. Toft, (Eds), *Violence and gender relations* (pp. 178–189). London: Sage.

Feder, L., & Wilson, D. B. (2005). A meta-analytic review of court-mandated batterer intervention programs: Can courts affect abusers' behavior? *Journal of Experimental Criminology, 1*, 239–262.

Federal Bureau of Investigation (2009). *Crime in the United States. Expanded homicide data*. Available online: www2.fbi.gov/ucr/cius2009/offenses/expanded_information/data/shrtable_10.html

Federal Bureau of Investigation (2011a). *Forcible rape 2009*. Available online: www2.fbi.gov/ucr/cius2009/offenses/violent_crime/forcible_rape.html

Federal Bureau of Investigation (2011b). *Hate crime statistics 2009*. Available online: www2.fbi.gov/ucr/hc2009/index.html

Feiring, C., Simon, V. A., & Cleland, C. M. (2009). Childhood sexual abuse, stigmatization, internalizing symptoms, and the development of sexual difficulties and dating aggression. *Journal of Consulting and Clinical Psychology, 77*, 127–137.

Ferguson, C. J. (2007a). Evidence for publication bias in video game violence effects literature: A meta-analytic review. *Aggression and Violent Behavior, 12*, 470–482.

Ferguson, C. J. (2007b) The good, the bad and the ugly: A meta-analytic review of positive and negative effects of violent video games. *Psychiatric Quarterly, 78*, 309–316.

Ferguson, C. J. (2010). Blazing angels or resident evil? Can violent video games be a force for good? *Review of General Psychology, 14*, 68–81.

Ferguson, C. J., & Beaver, K. M. (2009). Natural born killers: The genetic origins of extreme violence. *Aggression and Violent Behavior, 14*, 286–294.

Ferguson, C. J., & Hartley, R. D. (2009). The pleasure is momentary . . . the expense damnable? The influence of pornography on rape and sexual assault. *Aggression and Violent Behavior, 14*, 323–329.

Ferguson, C. J., & J. Kilburn. (2009). The public health risks of media violence: A meta-analytic review. *Journal of Pediatrics, 154*, 759–763.

Ferguson, C. J., & Ruda, S. M. (2009). Examining the validity of the modified Taylor competitive reaction time test of aggression. *Journal of Experimental Criminology, 5*, 121–137.

Ferguson, C. J., San Miguel, C., Kilburn, J. C., & Sanchez. P. (2007). The effectiveness of school-based anti-bullying programs: A meta-analytic review. *Criminal Justice Review, 32*, 401–414.

Ferriday, C., Vartanian, O., & Mandel, D. R. (2011). Public but not private ego threat triggers aggression in narcissists. *European Journal of Social Psychology, 41*, 564–568.

Fields, R. M. (1979). Child terror victims and adult terrorists. *Journal of Psychohistory, 7*, 71–75.

Fields, R. M., Elbedour, S., & Hein, F. A. (2002). The Palestinian suicide bomber. In C. E. Stout (Ed.), *The psychology of terrorism* (pp. 193–223). Westport, CT: Praeger.

Finkelhor, D. (1986). *A sourcebook on child sexual abuse*. Beverly Hills, CA: Sage.

Finkelhor, D. (1987). The trauma of child sexual abuse: Two models. *Journal of Interpersonal Violence, 2*, 348–366.

Finkelhor, D. (1994). The international epidemiology of child sexual abuse. *Child Abuse and Neglect, 18*, 409–417.

Finkelhor, D. (2011). Prevalence of child victimization, abuse, crime, and violence exposure. In J. W. White, M. P. Koss, & A. E. Kazdin (Eds), *Violence against women and children. Volume 1. Mapping the terrain* (pp. 9–29). Washington, DC: American Psychological Association.

Finkelhor, D., & Dziuba-Leatherman, J. (1995). Victimization prevention programs: A national survey of children's exposure and reactions. *Child Abuse and Neglect, 19*, 19–28.

Finkelhor, D., Turner, H., Ormrod, R., & Hamby, S. (2009). Violence, abuse, and crime exposure in a national sample of children and youth. *Pediatrics, 124*, 1411–1423.

Finkelhor, D., Turner, H., Ormrod, R., Hamby, S., & Kracke, K. (2009). *Children's exposure to violence: A comprehensive national survey*. Washington, DC: U.S. Department of Justice. Available online: www.ncjrs.gov/pdffiles1/ojjdp/227744.pdf

Finzi-Dottan, R., & Karu, T. (2006). From emotional abuse in childhood to psychopathology in adulthood: A path mediated by immature defense mechanisms and self-esteem. *Journal of Nervous and Mental Disease, 194*, 616–621.

Fischer, P., & Ai, A. L. (2008). International terrorism and mental health. *Journal of Interpersonal Violence, 23*, 339–361.

Fischer, P., & Greitemeyer, T. (2006). Music and aggression: The impact of sexual-aggressive song lyrics on aggression-related thoughts, emotions, and behavior towards the same and the opposite sex. *Personality and Social Psychology Bulletin, 32*, 1165–1176.

Fischer, P., Greitemeyer, T., Kastenmüller, A., Frey, D., & Osswald, S. (2007). Terror salience and punishment: Does terror salience induce threat to social order? *Journal of Experimental Social Psychology, 43*, 964–971.

Fischer, P., Greitemeyer, T., Kastenmüller, A., Vogrincic, C., & Sauer, A. (2011). The effects of risk-glorifying media exposure on risk-positive cognitions, emotions, and behaviors: A meta-analytic review. *Psychological Bulletin, 137*, 367–390 .

Fischer, P., Greitemeyer, T., Morton, T., Kastenmüller, A., Postmes, T., Frey, D., et al. (2009). The racing-game-effect: Why do video racing games increase risk-taking inclinations? *Personality and Social Psychology Bulletin, 35*, 1395–1409.

Fischer, P., Haslam, S. A., & Smith, L. (2010). "If you wrong us, shall we not revenge?" Social identity salience moderates support for retaliation in response to collective threat. *Group Dynamics: Theory, Research, and Practice, 14*, 143–150.

Fischer, P., Kastenmüller, A., & Greitemeyer, T. (2010). Media violence and the self: The impact of personalized gaming characters in aggressive video games on aggressive behavior. *Journal of Experimental Social Psychology, 46*, 192–195.

Fischer, P., Kubitzki, J., Guter, S., & Frey, D. (2007). Virtual driving and risk taking: Do racing games increase risk-taking cognitions, affect, and behaviors? *Journal of Experimental Psychology: Applied, 13*, 22–31.

Fischhoff, B. (1992). Giving advice: Decision theory perspectives on sexual assault. *American Psychologist, 47*, 577–588.

Fisher, B. S., Cullen, F. T. & Turner, M. G. (2000). *The sexual victimization of college women.* Research Report NJC 182369, U.S. Department of Justice. Available online: www.ncjrs.gov/pdffiles1/nij/182369.pdf

Fisher, B. S., Daigle, L. E., & Cullen, F. T. (2008). Rape against women: What can research offer to guide the development of prevention programs and risk reduction interventions? *Journal of Contemporary Criminal Justice, 24*, 163–177.

Fisher, B. S., Daigle, L. E., & Cullen, F. T. (2010). *Unsafe in the ivory tower: The sexual victimization of college women.* Los Angeles, CA: Sage.

Fite, P. J., Raine, A., Stouthamer-Loeber, M., Loeber, R., & Pardini, D. A. (2010). Reactive and proactive aggression in adolescent males: Examining differential outcomes 10 years later in early adulthood. *Criminal Justice and Behavior, 37*, 141–157.

Fitzgerald, L. F. (1993). Sexual harassment: Violence against women in the workplace. *American Psychologist, 48*, 1070–1076.

Fitzgerald, L. F., Magley, V. J., Drasgow, F., & Waldo, C. R. (1999). Measuring sexual harassment in the military: The SEQ-DOD. *Military Psychology, 11*, 243–263.

Fitzgerald, L. F., & Ormerod, A. J. (1993). Breaking the silence: The sexual harassment of women in academia and the workplace. In F. Denmark & M. Paludi (Eds), *Psychology of women: A handbook of issues and theories* (pp. 553–581). Westport, CT: Greenwood Press.

Flannery, D. J. Vazsonyi, A. T., & Waldman, I. D. (Eds) (2007). *The Cambridge handbook of violent behavior and aggression.* New York: Cambridge University Press.

Flatley, J., Kershaw, C., Smith, K., Chaplin, R., & Moon, D. (Eds) (2010). *Crime in England and Wales 2009/10.* Home Office Statistical Bulletin 1210. Available online: http://rds.homeoffice.gov.uk/rds/pdfs10/hosb1210.pdf

Flores, S. A., & Hartlaub, M. G. (1998). Reducing rape-myth acceptance in male college students: A meta-analysis of intervention studies. *Journal of College Student Development, 39*, 438–448.

Fontaine, N., Carbonneau, R., Barker, E. D., Vitaro, F., Hébert, M., Coté, S. et al. (2008). Girls' hyperactivity and physical aggression during childhood and adjustment problems in adulthood. *Archives of General Psychiatry, 65*, 320–328.

Fontaine, R. G., & Dodge, K. A. (2009). Social information processing and aggressive behavior: A transactional perspective. In A. Sameroff (Ed.), *The transactional model of development: How children and contexts shape each other* (pp. 117–135). Washington, DC: American Psychological Association.

Foran, H., & O'Leary, K. D. (2008). Alcohol and intimate partner violence: A meta-analytic review. *Clinical Psychology Review, 28*, 1222–1234.

Forgas, J. P., Kruglanski, A. W., & Williams, K. D. (Eds) (2011). *The psychology of social conflict and aggression.* New York: Psychology Press.

Forgyas, D. G., Forgyas, D. K., & Spielberger, C. D. (1997). Factor structure of the State–Trait Anger Expression Inventory. *Journal of Personality Assessment, 69*, 497–507.

Fortin, A., & Chamberland, C. (1995). Preventing the psychological maltreatment of children. *Journal of Interpersonal Violence, 10,* 275–295.

Forrest, S., Eatough, V., & Shevlin, M. (2005). Measuring adult indirect aggression: The development and psychometric properties of the Indirect Aggression Scales. *Aggressive Behavior, 31,* 84–97.

Foubert, J. D., Langhinrichsen-Rohling, J., Brasfield, H., & Hill, B. (2010). Effects of a rape awareness program on college women: Increasing bystander efficacy and willingness to intervene. *Journal of Community Psychology, 38,* 813–827.

Frank, M. G., & Gilovich, T. (1988). The dark side of self- and social perception: Black uniforms and aggression in professional sports. *Journal of Personality and Social Psychology, 54,* 74–85.

Frazier, P. A. (2003). Perceived control and distress following sexual assault: A longitudinal test of a new model. *Journal of Personality and Social Psychology, 84,* 1257–1269.

Freud, S. (1920). *Beyond the pleasure principle.* New York: Bantam Books.

Friedland, N. (1988). Political terrorism: A social psychological perspective. In W. Stroebe et al. (Eds), *The social psychology of intergroup conflict* (pp. 103–114). New York: Springer.

Friedrich, W. N., Berliner, L., Urquiza, A. J., & Beilke, R. L. (1988). Brief diagnostic group treatment of sexually abused boys. *Journal of Interpersonal Violence, 3,* 331–343.

Frieze, I. H. (2000). Violence in close relationships – development of a research area: Comment on Archer (2000). *Psychological Bulletin, 126,* 681–684.

Fritsch, E. J., Caeti, T. J., & Taylor, R. W. (1999). Gang suppression through saturation patrol, aggressive curfew and truancy enforcement: A quasi-experimental test of the Dallas anti-gang initiative. *Crime and Delinquency, 45,* 122–139.

Funk, J. B., Baldacci, H. B., Pasold, T., & Baumgardner, J. (2004). Violence exposure in real-life, video games, television, movies, and the internet: Is there desensitization? *Journal of Adolescence, 27,* 23–39.

Funk, J. B., Buchman, D. D., Jenks, J., & Bechtoldt, H. (2003). Playing violent video games, desensitization, and moral evaluation in children. *Applied Developmental Psychology, 24,* 413–436.

Funk, J. B., Flores, G., Buchman, D. D., & Germann, J. N. (1999). Rating electronic games. Violence is in the eye of the beholder. *Youth & Society, 30,* 283–312.

Galea, S., Vlahov, D., Resnick, H., Ahern, J., Susser, E., Gold, J., et al. (2003). Trends of probable post-traumatic stress disorder in New York City after the September 11 terrorist attacks. *American Journal of Epidemiology, 158,* 514–524.

Galovski, T. E., Malta, L. S., & Blanchard, E. B. (2006). *Road rage: Assessment and treatment of the angry, aggressive driver.* Washington, DC: American Psychological Association.

Geen, R. G. (1995). Violence. In A. S. R. Manstead & M. Hewstone (Eds), *Blackwell dictionary of social psychology* (p. 669). Oxford: Blackwell.

Geen, R. G. (1998). Aggression and antisocial behavior. In D. T. Gilbert, S. T. Fiske & G. Lindzey (Eds), *The Handbook of Social Psychology. Volume II* (4th edn) (pp. 317–356). Boston, MA: McGraw-Hill.

Geen, R. G., & McCown, E. J. (1984). Effects of noise and attack on aggression and physiological arousal. *Motivation and Emotion, 8,* 231–241.

Geen, R. G., & O'Neal, E. C. (1969). Activation of cue-elicited aggression by general arousal. *Journal of Personality and Social Psychology, 11,* 289–292.

Gelles, R. J. (1997). *Intimate violence in families* (3rd edn). Thousand Oaks, CA: Sage.

Gelles, R. J. (2007). Family violence. In D. J. Flannery, A. T. Vazsonyi, & I. D. Waldman (Eds), *The Cambridge handbook of violent behavior and aggression* (pp. 403–417). New York: Cambridge University Press.

Geneva Declaration on Armed Violence and Development (Ed.) (2011). *Global Burden of Armed Violence 2011*. Available online: www.genevadeclaration.org/measurability/global-burden-of-armed-violence/global-burden-of-armed-violence-2011.html

Gentile, D. A. (2010). Are motion picture ratings reliable and valid? *Journal of Adolescent Health, 47*, 423–424.

Gentile, D. A., & Anderson, C. A. (2006). Violent video games: The effects on youth, and public policy implications. In N. Dowd & D. G. Singer (Eds), *Handbook of children, culture and violence* (pp. 225–246). Thousand Oaks, CA: Sage.

Gentile, D. A., & Gentile, J. R. (2008). Violent video games as exemplary teachers: A conceptual analysis. *Journal of Youth and Adolescence, 37*, 127–141.

Gentile, D. A., Lynch, P. J., Linder, J. L., & Walsh, D. A. (2004). The effects of violent video game habits on adolescent hostility, aggressive behaviors, and school performance. *Journal of Adolescence, 27*, 5–22.

Georgiou, S. N., & Stavrimides, P. (2008). Bullies, victims and bully-victims: Psychosocial profiles and attribution styles. *School Psychology International, 29*, 574–589.

Gershoff, E. T. (2002). Corporal punishment by parents and associated child behaviors and experiences: A meta-analytic and theoretical review. *Psychological Bulletin, 128*, 539–579.

Gershoff, E. T., Grogan.Kaylor, A., Lansford, J. E., Chang, L., Zelli, A., Deater-Deckard, K. et al. (2010). Parent discipline practices in an international sample: Associations with child behaviors and moderation by perceived normativeness. *Child Development, 81*, 487–502.

Giancola, P. R. (2002a). Irritability, acute alcohol consumption and aggressive behavior in men and women. *Drug and Alcohol Dependence, 68*, 263–274.

Giancola, P. R. (2002b). The influence of trait anger on the alcohol-aggression relation in men and women. *Alcoholism: Clinical and Experimental Research, 26*, 1350–1358.

Giancola, P. R., & Corman, M. D. (2007). Alcohol and aggression: A test of the attention-allocation model. *Psychological Science, 18*, 649–655.

Giancola, P. R., Josephs, R. A., Parrott, D. J., & Duke, A. A. (2010). Alcohol myopia revisited: Clarifying aggression and other acts of disinhibition through a distorted lens. *Perspectives on Psychological Science, 5*, 265–278.

Giancola, P. R., Levinson, C. A., Corman, M. D., Godlaski, A. J., Morris, D. H., Philipps, J. P. et al. (2009). Men and women, alcohol and aggression. *Experimental and Clinical Psychopharmacology, 17*, 154–164.

Giancola, P. R., & Parrott, D. J. (2008). Further evidence for the validity of the Taylor aggression paradigm. *Aggressive Behavior, 34*, 214–229.

Giancola, P. R., & Zeichner, A. (1995). An investigation of gender differences in alcohol-related aggression. *Journal of Studies on Alcohol, 56*, 573–579.

Gidycz, C. A., Hanson, K., & Layman, M. J. (1995). A prospective analysis of the relationships among sexual assault experiences. *Psychology of Women Quarterly, 19*, 5–29.

Gidycz, C. A., Layman, M. J., Rich, C. L., Crothers, M., Gylys, J., Matorin, A. et al. (2001). An evaluation of an acquaintance rape prevention program. *Journal of Interpersonal Violence, 16*, 1120–1138.

Gidycz, C. A., McNamara, J. R., & Edwards, K. M. (2006). Women's risk perception and sexual victimization: A review of the literature. *Aggression and Violent Behavior, 11*, 441–456.

Gidycz, C. A., Orchowski, L. M., & Berkowitz, A. D. (2011). Preventing sexual aggression among college men: An evaluation of a social norms and bystander intervention program. *Violence against Women, 17*, 720–742.

Gidycz, C. A,, Orchowski, L. M., & Edwards, K. M. (2011). Primary prevention of sexual violence. In M. P. Koss, J. W. White, & A. E. Kazdin (Eds), *Violence against women and children. Volume 2. Navigating solutions* (pp. 159–179). Washington, DC: American Psychological Association.

Gidycz, C. A., Orchowski, L. M., Probst, D., Edwards, K., Murphy, M., & Tansill, E. (2012). Concurrent administration of sexual assault prevention and risk reduction programming: Outcomes for women. *Journal of Interpersonal Violence, 27*, in press.

Gigerenzer, G. (2004). Dread risk, September 11, and fatal traffic accidents. *Psychological Science, 15*, 286–287.

Gigerenzer, G. (2006). Out of the frying pan into the fire: Behavioral reactions to terrorist attacks. *Risk Analysis, 26*, 347–351.

Gilbert, R., Widom, K. S., Browne, K., Fergusson, D., Webb, E., & Janson, S. (2009). Burden and consequences of child maltreatment in high-income countries. *The Lancet, 373*, 68–81.

Gill, P. (2007). A multi-dimensional approach to suicide bombing. *International Journal of Conflict and Violence, 1*, 142–159.

Gini, G., & Pozzoli, T. (2009). Association between bullying and psychosomatic problems: A meta-analysis. *Pediatrics, 123*, 1059–1065.

Giumetti, G. W., & Markey, P. M. (2007). Violent video games and anger as predictors of aggression. *Journal of Research in Personality, 41*, 1234–1243.

Glass, G. V., McGaw, B., & Smith, M. L. (1981). *Meta-analysis in social research*. Beverly Hills, CA: Sage.

Golding, J. M. (1999). Intimate partner violence as a risk factor for mental disorders: A meta-analysis. *Journal of Family Violence, 14*, 99–132.

Goldstein, A. P. (1994a). Delinquent gangs. In L. R. Huesmann (Ed.), *Aggressive behavior: Current perspectives* (pp. 255–273). New York: Plenum Press.

Goldstein, A. P. (1994b). *The ecology of aggression*. New York: Plenum Press.

Goldstein, A. P. (2002). *The psychology of group aggression*. Chichester: John Wiley & Sons Ltd.

Gollwitzer, M., Banse, R., Eisenbach, K., & Naumann, A. (2007). Effectiveness of the Vienna social competence training on explicit and implicit aggression: Evidence from an aggressiveness-IAT. *European Journal of Psychological Assessment, 23*, 150–156.

Goodman, L. A., & Epstein, D. (2011). The justice system response to domestic violence. In M. P. Koss, J. W. White, & A. E. Kazdin (Eds), *Violence against women and children. Volume 2. Navigating solutions* (pp. 215–235). Washington, DC: American Psychological Association.

Gottfredson, M. R. (2007). Self-control theory and criminal violence. In D. J. Flannery, A. T. Vazsonyi, & I. D. Waldman (Eds), *The Cambridge handbook of violent behavior and aggression* (pp. 533–544). New York: Cambridge University Press.

Graham, K., Bernards, S., Wilsnack, S. C., & Gmel, G. (2011). Alcohol may not cause partner violence but it seems to make it worse: A cross-national comparison of the relationship between alcohol and the severity of partner violence. *Journal of Interpersonal Violence, 26*, 1503–1523.

Graham, K., Osgood, D. W., Zibrowski, E., Purcell, J., Gliksman, L., Leonard, K. et al. (2004). The effect of the Safer Bars programme on physical aggression in bars: Results of a randomized controlled trial. *Drug and Alcohol Review, 23*, 31–41.

Graham, K., & Wells, S. (2001). Aggression among young adults in the social context of the bar. *Addiction Research & Theory, 9*, 193–219.

Graham, R. (2006). Male rape and the careful construction of the male victim. *Social & Legal Studies, 15*, 187–208.

Green, J., & Plant, M. A. (2007). Bad bars: A review of risk factors. *Journal of Substance Use, 12,* 157–189.

Greenwald, A. G., McGhee, D. E., & Schwartz, J. K. L. (1998). Measuring individual differences in implicit cognition: The Implicit Association Test. *Journal of Personality and Social Psychology, 74,* 1464–1480.

Greitemeyer, T. (2011). Exposure to music with prosocial lyrics reduces aggression: First evidence and test of the underlying mechanisms. *Journal of Experimental Social Psychology, 47,* 28–36.

Greitemeyer, T., & Osswald, S. (2009). Prosocial video games reduce aggressive cognitions. *Journal of Experimental Social Psychology, 45,* 896–900.

Griffin, R. S., & Gross, A. M. (2004). Childhood bullying: Current empirical findings and future directions for research. *Aggression and Violent Behavior, 9,* 379–400.

Grimm, P., Kirste, K., & Weiβ, J. (2005). *Gewalt zwischen Fakten und Fiktionen. Eine Untersuchung von Gewaltdarstellungen im Fernsehen unter besonderer Berücksichtigung ihres Realitäts- bzw. Fiktionalitätsgrades.* Berlin: Vistas.

Gross, A. B., & Keller, H. R. (1992). Long-term consequences of childhood physical and psychological maltreatment. *Aggressive Behavior, 18,* 171–185.

Guerra, N. G., Huesmann, L. R., & Spindler, A. (2003). Community violence exposure, social cognition, and aggression among urban elementary school children. *Child Development, 74,* 1507–1522.

Gunter, B. (2008). Media violence: Is there a case for causality? *American Behavioral Scientist, 51,* 1061–1122.

Gustafson, R. (1994). Alcohol and aggression. *Journal of Offender Rehabilitation, 21,* 41–80.

Hald, G. M., Malamuth, N. M., & Yuen, C. (2010). Pornography and attitudes supporting violence against women: Revisiting the relationship in nonexperimental studies. *Aggressive Behavior, 36,* 14–20.

Hale, W. W., VanderValk, I., Akse, J., & Meeus, W. (2008). The interplay of early adolescents' depressive symptoms, aggression and perceived parental rejection: A four-year community study. *Journal of Youth and Adolescence, 37,* 928–940.

Hall, G. C. N., & Hirschman, R. (1991). Toward a theory of sexual aggression: A quadripartite model. *Journal of Consulting and Clinical Psychology, 59,* 662–669.

Hall, G. C. N., Shondrick, D. D., & Hirschman, R. (1993). The role of sexual arousal in sexually aggressive behavior: A meta-analysis. *Journal of Consulting and Clinical Psychology, 61,* 1091–1095.

Halligan, S. L., & Philips, K. J. (2010). Are you thinking what I'm thinking? Peer group similarities in adolescent hostile attribution tendencies. *Developmental Psychology, 46,* 1385–1388.

Halpern, C. T., Udry, R. J., Campbell, B., & Suchindran, C. (1993). Relationships between aggression and pubertal increases in testosterone: A panel analysis of adolescent males. *Social Biology, 40,* 8–24.

Hamberger, L. K., & Holtzworth-Munroe, A. (2009). Psychopathological correlates of male aggression. In K. D. O'Leary & E. M. Woodin (Eds), *Psychological and physical aggression in couples: Causes and interventions* (pp. 79–98). Washington, DC: American Psychological Association.

Haninger, K., & Thompson, K. M. (2004), Content and ratings of teen-rated video games. *Journal of the American Medical Association, 291,* 856–865.

Hanson, K. A., & Gidycz, C. A. (1993). Evaluation of a sexual assault prevention program. *Journal of Consulting and Clinical Psychology, 61,* 1046–1052.

Harding, C. F. (1985). Sociobiological hypotheses about rape: A critical look at the data behind the hypotheses. In S. R. Sunday & E. Tobach (Eds), *Violence against women: A critique of the sociobiology of rape* (pp. 23–85). New York: Gordian Press.

Harris, M. B. (1974). Mediators between frustration and aggression in a field experiment. *Journal of Experimental Social Psychology, 10,* 561–571.

Harris, P. B., & Houston, J. M. (2010). Recklessness in context: Individual and situational correlates of aggressive driving. *Environment and Behavior, 42,* 44–60.

Haskett, M. E., Ahern, L. S., Ward, C. S., & Allaire, J. C. (2006). Factor structure and validity of the Parenting Stress Index-Short Form. *Journal of Clinical Child and Adolescent Psychology, 35,* 302–312.

Hawker, D. S., & Boulton, M. J. (2000). Twenty years' research on peer victimization and psychosocial maladjustment: A meta-analytic review of cross-sectional studies. *Journal of Child Psychology and Psychiatry, 41,* 441–455.

Hay, D. F. (2007). The gradual emergence of sex differences in aggression: Alternative hypotheses. *Psychological Medicine, 37,* 1527–1537.

Hay, D. F., Perra, O., Hudson, K., Waters, C. S., Mundy, L., Philipps, R. et al. (2010). Identifying early signs of aggression: Psychometric properties of the Cardiff Infant Contentiousness Scale. *Aggressive Behavior, 36,* 351–357.

Heilbron, N., & Prinstein, M. J. (2010). Adolescent peer victimization, peer status, suicidal ideation, and nonsuicidal self-injury: Examining concurrent and longitudinal associations. *Merrill Palmer Quarterly, 56,* 388–419.

Hemenway, D., & Hepburn, L. M. (2004). Firearm availability and homicide: A review of the literature. *Aggression and Violent Behavior, 9,* 417–440.

Hemenway, D., & Miller, M. (2000). Firearm availability and homicide rates across 26 high-income countries. *Journal of Trauma, Injury, Infection, and Critical Care, 49,* 985–988.

Hennessy, D. A., & Wiesenthal, D. L. (1999). Traffic congestion, driver stress, and driver aggression. *Aggressive Behavior, 25,* 409–423.

Hennessy, D. A., & Wiesenthal, D. L. (2001). Gender, driver aggression, and driver violence: An applied evaluation. *Sex Roles, 44,* 661–676.

Hennessy, D. A., & Wiesenthal, D. L. (2002). Aggression, violence, and vengeance among male and female drivers. *Transportation Quarterly, 56,* 65–75.

Hennessy, D. A., Wiesenthal, D. L., & Kohn, P. M. (2000). The influence of traffic congestion, daily hassles, and trait stress susceptibility on state driver stress: An interactive perspective. *Journal of Applied Biobehavioral Research, 5,* 162–179.

Herek, G. M. (2000). The psychology of sexual prejudice. *Current Directions in Psychological Science, 9,* 19–22.

Herek, G. M., Gillis, J. R., & Cogan, J. C. (1999). Psychological sequelae of hate-crime victimization among lesbian, gay, and bisexual adults. *Journal of Consulting and Clinical Psychology, 67,* 945–951.

Hershcovis, S. M., & Barling, J. (2010). Towards a multi-foci approach to workplace aggression: A meta-analytic review of outcomes from different perpetrators. *Journal of Organizational Behavior, 31,* 24–44.

Herzberg, P. Y. (2003). Faktorstruktur, Gütekriterien und Konstruktvalidität der deutschen Übersetzung des Aggressionsfragebogens von Buss und Perry. *Zeitschrift für Differentielle und Diagnostische Psychologie, 24,* 311–323.

Hewstone, M. (1990). The "ultimate attribution error"? A review of the literature on intergroup causal attribution. *European Journal of Social Psychology, 20,* 311–336.

Hillberg, T., Hamilton-Giachritsis, C., & Dixon, L. (2011). Review of meta-analyses on the association between child sexual abuse and adult mental health difficulties: A systematic approach. *Trauma, Violence, & Abuse, 12*, 38–49.

Hill, C., & Silva, E. (2005). *Drawing the line: Sexual harassment on campus.* Washington, DC: American Association of University Women. Available online: www.aauw.org/learn/research/upload/DTLFinal.pdf

Hinde, R. (1997). Is war a consequence of human aggression? In S. Feshbach & J. Zagrodzka (Eds), *Aggression: Biological, developmental, and social perspectives* (pp. 177–183). New York: Plenum Press.

Hinduja, S., & Patchin, J. W. (2010). Bullying, cyberbullying and suicide. *Archives of Suicide Research, 14*, 206–221.

Hines, D. A. (2007). Predictors of sexual coercion against women and men: A multilevel, multinational study of university students. *Archives of Sexual Behavior, 36*, 403–422.

Hingson, R. W. (2010). Magnitude and prevention of college drinking and related problems. *Alcohol Research & Health, 33*, 45–54.

Hittner, J. B. (2005). How robust is the Werther effect? A re-examination of the suggestion-imitation model of suicide. *Mortality, 10*, 193–200.

Hobfoll, S. E., Canetti-Nisim, D., Johnson, R. J., Palmieri, P. A., Varley, J. D., & Galea, S. (2008). The association of exposure, risk, and resiliency factors with PTSD among Jews and Arabs exposed to repeated acts of terrorism in Israel. *Journal of Traumatic Stress, 21*, 9–21.

Hoel, H., Rayner, C., & Cooper, C. L. (1999). Workplace bullying. *International Review of Industrial and Organizational Psychology, 14*, 195–230.

Höynck, T., Mößle, T., Kleimann, M., Pfeiffer, C., & Rehbein, F. (2007). *Jugendmedienschutz bei gewalthaltigen Computerspielen.* Forschungsbericht Nr. 101. Hannover: Kriminologisches Forschungsinstitut Niedersachsen (http://www.kfn.de/Publikationen/KFN-Forschungsberichte.htm).

Hogben, M. (1998). Factors moderating the effect of televised aggression on viewer behavior. *Communication Research, 25*, 220–247.

Holtzworth-Munroe, A., Meehan, J. C., Herron, K., Rehman, U., & Stuart, G. L. (2000). Testing the Holtzworth-Munroe and Stuart (1994) batterer typology. *Journal of Consulting and Clinical Psychology, 68*, 1000–1019.

Holtzworth-Munroe, A., Meehan, J. C, Herron, K., Rehman, U., & Stuart, G. L.(2003). Do subtypes of maritally violent men continue to differ over time? *Journal of Consulting and Clinical Psychology, 71*, 728–740.

Holtzworth-Munroe, A., & Stuart, G. L. (1994). Typologies of male batterers: Three subtypes and the differences among them. *Psychological Bulletin, 116*, 476–497.

Home Office (2011). *Total of recorded hate crime from regional forces in England, Wales and Northern Ireland during the calendar year 2009.* Available online: www.report-it.org.uk/files/e_crime_from_regional_forces_in_england_wales_and_northern_ireland_during_the_calendar_year_2009.pdf

Houston, J. M., Harris, P. B., & Norman, M. (2003). The Aggressive Driving Behavior Scale: Developing a self-report measure of unsafe driving practices. *North American Journal of Psychology, 5*, 269–278.

Hovmand, P. S., Ford, D. N., Flom, I., & Kyriakakis, S. (2009). Victims arrested for domestic violence: Unintended consequences of arrest policies. *System Dynamics Review, 25*, 161–181.

Howells, K. (1989). Anger management methods in relation to the prevention of violent behaviour. In J. Archer & K. Browne (Eds), *Human aggression: Naturalistic approaches* (pp. 153–181). London: Routledge.

Howells, K., & Day, A. (2003). Readiness for anger management: Clinical and theoretical issues. *Clinical Psychology Review, 23*, 319–337.

Hsiang, S. M., Meng, K. C., & Cane, M. A. (2011). Civil conflicts are associated with the global climate. *Nature, 476*, 438–441.

Huang, S., Trapido, E., Fleming, L., Arheart, K., Crandall, L., French, M. et al. (2011). The long-term effects of childhood maltreatment experiences on subsequent illicit drug use and drug-related problems in young adulthood. *Addictive Behaviors, 36*, 95–102.

Hubbard, J. A., McAuliffe, M. D., Morrow, M. T., & Romano, L. J. (2010). Reactive and proactive aggression in childhood and adolescence: Precursors, outcomes, processes, experiences, and measurement. *Journal of Personality, 78*, 95–118.

Hubbard, J. A., Smithmyer, C. M., Ramsden, S. R., Parker, E. H., Flanagan, K., Dearing, K. F. et al. (2002). Observational, physiological, and self-report measures of children's anger: Relations to reactive versus proactive aggression. *Child Development, 73*, 1101–1118.

Huesmann, L. R. (1988). An information processing model for the development of aggression. *Aggressive Behavior, 11*, 13–24.

Huesmann, L. R. (1998). The role of social information processing and cognitive schema in the acquisition and maintenance of habitual aggressive behavior. In R. G. Geen, & E. Donnerstein (Eds), *Human aggression: Theories, research and implications for social policy* (pp. 73–109). San Diego, CA: Academic Press.

Huesmann, L. R. (2010a). Nailing the coffin shut on doubts that violent video games stimulate aggression: Comment on Anderson et al. (2010). *Psychological Bulletin, 136*, 179–181.

Huesmann, L. R. (2010b). How to grow a terrorist without really trying: The psychological development of terrorism from childhood to adulthood. In D. Antonius, A. D. Brown, T. K. Walters, J. M. Ramirez & S. J. Sinclair (Eds), *Interdisciplinary analyses of terrorism and political aggression* (pp. 1–21). Newcastle upon Tyne: Cambridge Scholars Publishing.

Huesmann, L. R., Dubow, E. F., & Boxer, P. (2009). Continuity of aggression from childhood to early adulthood as a predictor of life outcomes: Implications for the adolescent-limited and life-course-persistent models. *Aggressive Behavior, 35*, 136–149.

Huesmann, L. R., Dubow, E. F., & Boxer, P. (2011). The transmission of aggressiveness across generations: Biological, contextual, and social learning processes. In P. R. Shaver & M. Mikulincer (Eds), *Human aggression and violence: Causes, manifestations, and consequences* (pp. 123–142). Washington, DC: American Psychological Association.

Huesmann, L. R., & Eron, L. D. (Eds) (1986). *Television and the aggressive child: A cross-national comparison*. Hillsdale, NJ: Lawrence Erlbaum.

Huesmann, L. R. & Guerra, N. G. (1997). Children's normative beliefs about aggression and aggressive behavior. *Journal of Personality and Social Psychology, 72*, 408–419.

Huesmann, R. L., & Kirwil, L. (2007). Why observing violence increases the risk of violent behavior by the observer. In D. J. Flannery, A. T. Vazsonyi, & I. D. Waldman (Eds), *The Cambridge handbook of violent behavior and aggression* (pp. 545–570). New York: Cambridge University Press.

Huesmann, L. R., & Miller, L. S. (1994). Long-term effects of the repeated exposure to media violence in childhood. In L. R. Huesmann (Ed.), *Aggressive behavior: Current perspectives* (pp. 153–186). New York: Plenum Press.

Huesmann, L. R., Moise-Titus, J., Podolski, C. L., & Eron, L. (2003). Longitudinal relations between children's exposure to TV violence and their aggressive and violent behavior in young adulthood. *Developmental Psychology, 39*, 201–229.

Hull, J. G., Levenson, R. W., Young, R. D., & Sher, K. J. (1983). Self-awareness-reducing effects of alcohol consumption. *Journal of Personality and Social Psychology, 44*, 461–473.

Hunter, C., & McClelland, K. (1991). Honoring accounts for sexual harassment: A factorial survey analysis. *Sex Roles, 24*, 725–751.

Hyde, J. S. (1984). How large are gender differences in aggression? A developmental meta-analysis. *Developmental Psychology, 20*, 722–736.

Ito, T. A., Miller, N., & Pollock, V. E. (1996). Alcohol and aggression: A meta-analysis of the moderating effects of inhibitory cues, triggering cues, and self-focused attention. *Psychological Bulletin, 120*, 60–82.

Jackson, S. (1978). The social context of rape: Sexual scripts and motivation. *Women's Studies International Quarterly, 1*, 27–38.

Jaffe, D. S. (1982). Aggression: Instinct, drive, behavior. *Psychoanalytic Inquiry, 2*, 77–94.

Jaffee, D., & Straus, M.A. (1987). Sexual climate and reported rape: A state-level analysis. *Archives of Sexual Behavior, 16*, 107–123.

Janoff-Bulman, R. (1979). Characterological versus behavioral self-blame: Inquiries into depression and rape. *Journal of Personality and Social Psychology, 37*, 1798–1809.

Johnson, R. D., & Downing, L. L. (1979). Deindividuation and valence of cues: Effects on prosocial and antisocial behavior. *Journal of Personality and Social Psychology, 37*, 1532–1538.

Johnson, R. J., Canetti, D., Palmieri, P. A., Galea, S., Varley, J., & Hobfoll, S. E. (2009). A prospective study of risk and resilience factors associated with posttraumatic stress symptoms and depression symptoms among Jews and Arabs exposed to repeated acts of terrorism in Israel. *Psychological Trauma: Theory, Research, Practice, and Policy, 1*, 291–311.

Jones, J. W. (1978). Adverse emotional reactions of nonsmokers to secondary cigarette smoke. *Environmental Psychology and Nonverbal Behavior, 3*, 125–127.

Jones, S. M., Brown, J. L., & Aber, J. L. (2011). Two-year impacts of a universal school-based social-emotional and literacy intervention: An experiment in translational developmental research. *Child Development, 82*, 533–554.

Jones, T. S., & Remland, M. S. (1992). Sources of variability in perceptions of and responses to sexual harassment. *Sex Roles, 27*, 358–383.

Kanin, E. J. (1985). Date rapists: Sexual socialization and relative deprivation. *Archives of Sexual Behaviour, 14*, 219–231.

Kann, L., Olsen, E. O., McManus, T., Kinchen, S., Chyen, D., Harris, W. A. et al. (2011). *Sexual identity, sex of sexual contacts, and health-risk behaviors among students in grades 9–12 – Youth Risk Behavior Surveillance, Selected Sites, United States, 2001–2009*. Atlanta, GA: Center for Disease Control. Available online: www.cdc.gov/mmwr/pdf/ss/ss60e0606.pdf

Kazdin, A. E. (2005). *Parent management training: Treatment for oppositional, aggressive, and antisocial behavior in children and adolescents*. New York: Oxford University Press.

Kazdin, A. E. (2011). Conceptualizing the challenge of reducing interpersonal violence. *Psychology of Violence, 1*, 166–187.

Keenan, K., Wroblewski, K., Hipwell, A., Loeber, R., & Stouthamer-Loeber, M. (2010). Age of onset, symptom threshold, and expansion of the nosology of conduct disorder for girls. *Journal of Abnormal Psychology, 119*, 689–698.

Kelly, J. B., & Johnson, M. P. (2008). Differentiation among types of intimate partner violence: Research update and implications for interventions. *Family Court Review, 46*, 476–499.

Kendall-Tackett, K., & Marshall, R. (1998). Sexual victimization of children. In R. K. Bergen (Ed.), *Issues in intimate violence* (pp. 47–63). Thousand Oaks, CA: Sage.

Kendall-Tackett, K. A., Williams, L. M., & Finkelhor, D. (1993). Impact of sexual abuse of children: A review and synthesis of recent empirical studies. *Psychological Bulletin, 113*, 164–180.

Kilpatrick, D. G., Resnick, H. S.,, Ruggiero, K. J., Conoscenti, L. M, & McCauley, J. (2007). *Drug-facilitated, incapacitated, and forcible rape: A national study*. Washington. DC: U.S. Department of Justice. Available online: www.ncjrs.gov/pdffiles1/nij/grants/219181.pdf

Kimble, N. B., Russo, S. A., Bergman, B. G., & Galindo, V. H. (2010). Revealing an empirical understanding of aggression and violent behavior in athletics. *Annual Review of Psychology, 15*, 446–462.

King, M., Noor, H., & Taylor, D. M. (2011). Normative support for terrorism: The attitudes and beliefs of immediate relatives of Jema'ah Islamiyah members. *Studies in Conflict and Terrorism, 34*, 402–417.

Kingston, D. A., Fedoroff, P., Firestone, P., Curry, S., & Bradford, J. M. (2008). Pornography use and sexual aggression: The impact of frequency and type of pornography use on recidivism among sexual offenders. *Aggressive Behavior, 34*, 341–351.

Kingston, D. A., Malamuth, N. M., Fedoroff, P., & Marshall, W. L. (2009). The importance of individual differences in pornography use: Theoretical perspectives and implications for treating sexual offenders. *Journal of Sex Research, 46*, 216–232.

Kingston, L., & Prior, M. (1995). The development of patterns of stable, transient, and school-age onset aggressive behavior in young children. *Journal of the American Academy of Child and Adolescent Psychiatry, 34*, 348–358.

Kirsh, S. J. (2010). *Media and youth: A developmental perspective*. Oxford: John Wiley & Sons Ltd.

Kirsh, S. J. (2012). *Children, adolescents, and media violence* (2nd edn). Thousand Oaks, CA: Sage.

Kitzmann, K. M., Gaylord, N. K., Holt, A. R., & Kenny, E. D. (2003). Child witnesses to domestic violence: A meta-analytic review. *Journal of Consulting and Clinical Psychology, 71*, 339–352.

Kleck, G., & Hogan, M. (1999). National case–control study of homicide offending and gun ownership. *Social Problems, 46*, 275–293.

Klinesmith, J., Kasser, T., & McAndrew, F. T. (2006). Guns, testosterone, and aggression. *Psychological Science, 17*, 568–571.

Klomek, A. B., Sourander, A., Niemelä, S., Kumpulainen, K., Piha, J., Tamminen, T. et al. (2009). Childhood bullying behaviors as a risk for suicide attempts and completed suicides: A population-based birth cohort study. *Journal of the American Academy of Child and Adolescent Psychiatry, 48*, 254–261.

Klump, M. S. (2008). Posttraumatic stress disorder and sexual assault in women. *Journal of College Student Psychotherapy, 21*, 67–83.

Knight, G. P., Fabes, R. A., & Higgins, D. A. (1996). Concerns about drawing causal inferences from meta-analyses: An example in the study of gender differences in aggression. *Psychological Bulletin, 119*, 410–421.

Knight, R. A., & Sims-Knight, J. E. (2004). Testing an etiological model for male juvenile sexual offending against females. *Journal of Child Sexual Abuse, 13*, 33–55.

Knutson, J. F., Lawrence, E., Taber, S. M., Bank, L., & DeGamo, D. S. (2009). Assessing children's exposure to intimate partner violence. *Clinical Child and Family Psychology Review, 12*, 157–173.

Kokko, K., Pulkkinen, L., Huesmann, L. R., Dubow, Eric F., & Boxer, P. (2009). Intensity of aggression in childhood as a predictor of different forms of adult aggression: A two-country (Finland and the United States) analysis. *Journal of Research on Adolescence, 19*, 9–34.

Koss, M. P. (2010). Restorative justice for acquaintance rape and misdemeanor sex crimes. In J. Ptacek (Ed.), *Restorative justice and violence against women* (pp. 218–238). New York: Oxford University Press.

Koss, M. P., Abbey, A., Campbell, R., Cook, S., Norris, J., Testa, M. et al. (2007). Revising the SES: A collaborative process to improve assessment of sexual aggression and victimization. *Psychology of Women Quarterly, 31*, 357–370.

Koss, M. P., Bachar, K. J., Hopkins, C. Q., & Carlson, C. (2004). Expanding a community's justice response to sex crimes through advocacy, prosecutorial, and public health collaboration: Introducing the RESTORE program. *Journal of Interpersonal Violence, 19*, 1435–1463.

Koss, M. P., & Cook, S. L. (1998). Facing the facts. Date and acquaintance rape are significant problems for women. In R. K. Bergen (Ed.), *Issues in intimate violence* (pp. 147–156). Thousand Oaks, CA: Sage.

Koss, M. P., Gidycz, C. A., & Wisniewski, N. (1987). The scope of rape: Incidence and prevalence of sexual aggression and victimization in a national sample of higher education students. *Journal of Consulting and Clinical Psychology, 55*, 162–170.

Koss, M. P., & Oros, C. J. (1982). Sexual Experiences Survey: A research instrument investigating sexual aggression and victimization. *Journal of Consulting and Clinical Psychology, 50*, 455–457.

Krafka, C., Linz, D., Donnerstein, E., & Penrod, S. (1997). Women's reactions to sexually aggressive mass media depictions. *Violence Against Women, 3*, 149–181.

Krahé, B. (1991). Social psychological issues in the study of rape. *European Review of Social Psychology, 2*, 279–309.

Krahé, B. (1998). Sexual aggression among adolescents: Prevalence and predictors in a German sample. *Psychology of Women Quarterly, 22*, 537–554.

Krahé, B. (2000a). Childhood sexual abuse and revictimization in adolescence and adulthood. *Journal of Personal and Interpersonal Loss, 5*, 149–165.

Krahé, B. (2000b). Sexual scripts and heterosexual aggression. In T. Eckes & H. M. Trautner (Eds), *The developmental social psychology of gender* (pp. 273–292). Mahwah, NJ: Lawrence Erlbaum Associates, Inc.

Krahé, B. (2005). Predictors of women's aggressive driving behavior. *Aggressive Behavior, 31*, 537–546.

Krahé, B. (2011). Pornografiekonsum, sexuelle Skripts und sexuelle Aggression im Jugendalter. *Zeitschrift für Entwicklungspsychologie und Pädagogische Psychologie, 43*, 133–141.

Krahé, B., & Berger, A. (2005). Sex differences in relationship aggression among young adults in Germany. *Sex Roles, 52*, 829–839.

Krahé, B., & Bieneck, S. (2012). The de-escalating effect of music on aggressive affect, cognition, and behavior. *Journal of Applied Social Psychology, 42*, 271–290.

Krahé, B., Bieneck, S., & Möller, I. (2005). Understanding gender and intimate partner violence from an international perspective. *Sex Roles, 52*, 807–827.

Krahé, B., Bieneck, S., & Scheinberger-Olwig, R. (2007). The role of sexual scripts in sexual aggression and victimization. *Archives of Sexual Behavior, 36*, 687–701.

Krahé, B., & Fenske, I. (2002). Predicting aggressive driving behaviour. The role of macho personality, age and power of car. *Aggressive Behavior, 28*, 21–29.

Krahé, B., & Knappert, L. (2009). A group-randomized evaluation of a theatre-based sexual abuse prevention programme for primary school children in Germany. *Journal of Community and Applied Social Psychology, 19*, 321–329.

Krahé, B., & Möller, I. (2011). Links between self-reported media violence exposure and teacher ratings of aggression and prosocial behavior among German adolescents. *Journal of Adolescence, 34*, 279–287.

Krahé, B., Möller, I., Huesmann, L. R., Kirwil, L., Felber, J., & Berger, A. (2011). Desensitization to media violence: Links with habitual media violence exposure, aggressive cognitions and aggressive behavior. *Journal of Personality and Social Psychology, 100*, 630–646.

Krahé, B., Scheinberger-Olwig, R., & Bieneck, S. (2003). Men's reports of nonconsensual sexual interactions with women: Prevalence and impact. *Archives of Sexual Behavior, 32*, 165–175.

Krahé, B., Scheinberger-Olwig, R., & Kolpin, S. (2000). Ambiguous communication of sexual intentions as a risk marker of sexual aggression. *Sex Roles, 42*, 313–337.

Krahé, B., Scheinberger-Olwig, R., & Schütze, S. (2001). Risk factors of sexual aggression and victimization among homosexual men. *Journal of Applied Social Psychology, 31*, 1385–1408.

Krahé, B., Scheinberger-Olwig, R., Waizenhöfer, E. & Kolpin, S. (1999). Childhood sexual abuse and revictimization in adolescence. *Child Abuse and Neglect, 23*, 383–394.

Krahé, B., Schütze, S., Fritsche, I., & Waizenhöfer, E. (2000). The prevalence of sexual aggression and victimization among homosexual men. *Journal of Sex Research, 37*, 142–150.

Krahé, B., Waizenhöfer, E., & Möller, I. (2003). Women's sexual aggression against men: Prevalence and predictors. *Sex Roles, 49*, 219–232.

Kraus, S. W., & Russell, B. (2008). Early sexual experiences: The role of Internet access and sexually explicit material. *Cyberpsychology & Behavior, 11*, 162–168.

Kretschmar, J. M., & Flannery, D. J. (2007). Substance use and violent behavior. In D. J. Flannery, A. T. Vazsonyi, & I. D. Waldman (Eds), *The Cambridge handbook of violent behavior and aggression* (pp. 647–663). New York: Cambridge University Press.

Krug, E. G., Dahlberg, L. L., Mercy, J. A., Zwi, A. B., & Lozano, R. (2002). *World report on violence and health*. Geneva: World Health Organization. Available online: http://whqlibdoc.who.int/hq/2002/9241545615.pdf

Kruglanski, A. W., Chen, X., Dechesne, M., Fishman, S., & Orehek, E. (2009). Fully committed: Suicide bombers' motivation and the quest for personal significance. *Political Psychology, 30*, 331–357.

Kruglanski, A. W., & Fishman, S. (2009). The psychology of terrorism: "syndrome" versus "tool" perspectives. In J. Victoroff & A. W. Kruglanski (Eds), *Psychology of terrorism* (pp. 35–53). New York: Psychology Press.

Lahm, K. F. (2008). Inmate-on-inmate assault: A multilevel examination of prison violence. *Criminal Justice and Behavior, 35*, 120–137.

Lajunen, T., & Parker, D. (2001). Are aggressive people aggressive drivers? A study of the relationship between self-reported general aggressiveness, driver anger and aggressive driving. *Accident Analysis and Prevention, 33*, 243–255.

Lalumière, M. L., Harris, G. T., Quinsey, V. L., & Rice, M. E. (2005). Antisociality and mating effort. In M. L. Lalumière, G. T. Harris, V. L. Quinsey & M. E. Rice (Eds), *The causes of rape: Understanding individual differences in male propensity for sexual aggression* (pp. 61–103). Washington, DC: American Psychological Association.

Land, K. C., Teske, R. H., & Zheng, H. (2009). The short-term effects of executions on homicides: Deterrence, displacement, or both. *Criminology: An Interdisciplinary Journal, 47*, 1009–1043.

Langhinrichsen-Rohling, J., Foubert, J. D., Brasfield, H. M., Hill, B., & Shelley-Tremblay, S. (2011). The Men's Program: Does it impact college men's self-reported bystander efficacy and willingness to intervene? *Violence Against Women, 17*, 743–759.

Langley, T., O'Neal, E. C., Craig, K. M., & Yost, E. A. (1992). Aggression-consistent, -inconsistent, and -irrelevant priming effects on selective exposure to media violence. *Aggressive Behavior, 18,* 349–356.

Lanier, C. A. (2001). Rape-accepting attitudes: Precursors to or consequences of forced sex. *Violence Against Women, 7,* 876–885.

Lankford, A. (2010). Do suicide terrorists exhibit clinically suicidal risk factors? A review of initial evidence and call for future research. *Aggression and Violent Behavior, 15,* 334–340.

Lansford, J. E., Malone, P. S., Dodge, K. A., Pettit, G. S., & Bates, J. E. (2010). Developmental cascades of peer rejection, social information processing biases, and aggression during middle childhood. *Development and Psychopathology, 22,* 593–602.

Lansford, J. E., Miller-Johnson, S., Berlin, L. J., Dodge, K. A., Bates, J. E., & Pettit, G. S. (2007). Early physical abuse and later violent delinquency: A prospective longitudinal study. *Child Maltreatment, 12,* 233–245.

Laplace, A., Chermack, S. T., & Taylor, S. P. (1994). Effects of alcohol and drinking experience on human physical aggression. *Personality and Social Psychology Bulletin, 20,* 439–444.

Larimer, M. E., Lydum, A. R., Anderson, B. K., & Turner, A. P. (1999). Male and female recipients of unwanted sexual contact in a college student sample: Prevalence rates, alcohol use, and depression symptoms. *Sex Roles, 40,* 295–308.

Larrick, R. P., Timmerman, T. A., Carton, A. M., & Abrevaya, J. (2011). Temper, temperature, and temptation: Heat-related retaliation in baseball. *Psychological Science, 22,* 423–428.

Lawrence, C., & Andrews, K. (2004). The influence of perceived prison crowding on male inmates' perception of aggressive events. *Aggressive Behavior, 30,* 273–283.

Lawton, R., Parker, D., Manstead, A. S. R., & Stradling, S. G. (1997). The role of affect in predicting social behaviors: The case of road traffic violations. *Journal of Applied Social Psychology, 27,* 1258–1276.

Leader, T., Mullen, B., & Abrams, D. (2007). Without mercy: The immediate impact of group size on lynch mob atrocity. *Personality and Social Psychology Bulletin, 33,* 1340–1352.

Leary, M., R., Kowalski, R. M., Smith. L., & Philipps, S. (2003). Teasing, rejection, and violence: Case studies of the school shootings. *Aggressive Behavior, 29,* 202–214.

Leary, M. R., Tambor, E. S., Terdal, S. K., & Downs, D. L. (1995). Self-esteem as an interpersonal monitor: The sociometer hypothesis. *Journal of Personality and Social Psychology, 68,* 518–530.

Leary, M., R., Twenge, J. M., & Quinlivan, E. (2006). Interpersonal rejection as a determinant of anger and aggression. *Personality and Social Psychology Review, 10,* 111–132.

LeBon, G. (1896). *The crowd: A study of the popular mind.* London: T. Fisher Unwin.

Leibman, M. (1970). The effects of race and sex norms on personal space. *Environment and Behavior, 2,* 208–246.

Lenhart, A., Kahne, J., Middaugh, E., Macgill, A. R., Evans, C., & Vitak, J. (2008). *Teens, video games, and civics.* Pew Internet and American Life Project. Available online: http://pewinternet.org/~/media//Files/Reports/2008/PIP_Teens_Games_and_Civics_Report_FINAL.pdf.pdf

Lenhart, A., & Macgill, A. R. (2008). *Over half of American adults play video games, and four out of five young adults play.* Pew Internet and American Life Project. Available online: www.pewinternet.org/~/media//Files/Reports/2008/PIP_Adult_gaming_memo.pdf.pdf

Lenington, S. (1985). Sociobiological theory and the violent abuse of women. In S. R. Sunday & E. Tobach (Eds), *Violence against women: A critique of the sociobiology of rape* (pp. 13–22). New York: Gordian Press.

Lennings, H. B., & Warburton, W. A. (2011). The effect of auditory versus visual violent media exposure on aggressive behaviour: The role of song lyrics, video clips, and musical tone. *Journal of Experimental Social Psychology, 47*, 794–799.

Leonard, K. E. (1989). The impact of explicit aggressive and implicit nonaggressive cues on aggression on intoxicated and sober males. *Personality and Social Psychology Bulletin, 15*, 390–400.

Leonard, K. E., Collins, R. L., & Quigley, B. M. (2003). Alcohol consumption and the occurrence and severity of aggression: An event-based analysis of male-to-male barroom violence. *Aggressive Behavior, 29*, 346–365.

Leonard, K. E., & Roberts, L. J. (1998). The effects of alcohol on the marital interactions of aggressive and nonaggressive husbands and their wives. *Journal of Abnormal Psychology, 107*, 602–615.

Leveque, R. (2011). Justice responses to child abuse and maltreatment. In M. P. Koss, J. W. White & A. E. Kazdin (Eds), *Violence against women and children. Volume 2. Navigating solutions* (pp. 47–69). Washington, DC: American Psychological Association.

Levin, S., Henry, P. J., Pratto, F., & Sidanius, J. (2009). Social dominance and social identity in Lebanon: Implications for support of violence against the West. In J. Victoroff, & A. W. Kruglanski (Eds), *Psychology of terrorism* (pp. 253–267). New York: Psychology Press.

Lewis-O'Connor, A., Sharps, P. W., Humphreys, J., Gary, F. A., & Campbell, J. (2006). Children exposed to intimate partner violence. In M. M. Feerick & G. B. Silverman (Eds), *Children exposed to violence* (pp. 3–28). Baltimore, MD: Paul H. Brookes.

Leymann, H. (1993). *Mobbing: Psychoterror am Arbeitsplatz und wie man sich dagegen wehren kann.* Reinbek: Rowohlt.

Lickel, B., Miller, N., Stenstrom, D. M., Denson, T. F., & Schmader, R. (2006). Vicarious retribution: The role of collective blame in intergroup aggression. *Personality and Social Psychology Review, 10*, 372–390.

Lieberman, J. D., Solomon, S., Greenberg, J., & McGregor, H. A. (1999). A hot new way to measure aggression: Hot sauce allocation. *Aggressive Behavior, 25*, 331–348.

Lightdale, J. R., & Prentice, D. A. (1994). Rethinking sex differences in aggression: Aggressive behavior in the absence of social roles. *Personality and Social Psychology Bulletin, 20*, 34–44.

Lim, S., & Cortina, L. M. (2005). Interpersonal mistreatment in the workplace: The interface and impact of general incivility and sexual harassment. *Journal of Applied Psychology, 90*, 483–496.

Lindsay, J. J., & Anderson, C. A. (2000). From antecedent conditions to violent actions: A general affective aggression model. *Personality and Social Psychology Bulletin, 26*, 533–547.

Linz, D. (1989). Exposure to sexually explicit materials and attitudes toward rape: A comparison of study results. *Journal of Sex Research, 26*, 50–84.

Linz, D., Donnerstein, E., & Adams, S. (1989). Physiological desensitization and judgments about female victims of violence. *Human Communication Research, 15*, 509–522.

Linz, D., & Malamuth, N. M. (1993). *Pornography.* Newbury Park, CA: Sage.

Lisak, D., Roth, S, (1990). Motives and psychodynamics of self-reported, unincarcerated rapists. *American Journal of Orthopsychiatry, 60*, 268–280.

Litrownik, A. J., Newton, R., Hunter, W. M., English, D., & Everson, M. D. (2003). Exposure to family violence in young at-risk children: A longitudinal look at the effects of victimization and witnessed physical and psychological aggression. *Journal of Family Violence, 18*, 59–73.

Littleton, H., Horsley, S., John, S., & Nelson, D. V. (2007). Trauma coping strategies and psychological distress: A meta-analysis. *Journal of Traumatic Stress, 20*, 977–988.

Livingston, M. (2011), A longitudinal analysis of alcohol outlet density and domestic violence. *Addition, 106*, 919–925.

Lochman, J. E., & Dodge, K. A. (1994). Social-cognitive processes of severely violent, moderately aggressive, and nonaggressive boys. *Journal of Consulting and Clinical Psychology, 62*, 366–374.

Loeber, R., & Hay, D. (1997). Key issues in the development of aggression from childhood to early adulthood. *Annual Review of Psychology, 48*, 371–410.

Loeber, R., & Stouthamer-Loeber, M. (1998). Development of juvenile aggression and violence. Some common misconceptions and controversies. *American Psychologist, 53*, 242–259.

Loh, C., Gidycz, C. A., Lobo, T. R., & Luthra, R. (2005). A prospective analysis of sexual assault perpetration. *Journal of Interpersonal Violence, 20*, 1325–1348.

Lonsway, K., Banyard, V., Berkowitz, A. D., Gidycz, C. A., Jackson, K., Koss, M. P. et al. (2009). *Rape prevention and risk reduction: Review of the research literature for practitioners*. Available online: www.vawnet.org/Assoc_Files_VAWnet/AR_RapePrevention.pdf

Lore, R. K. & Schultz, L. A. (1993). Control of human aggression. A comparative perspective. *American Psychologist, 48*, 16–25.

Lorenz, K. (1966). *On aggression*. London: Routledge.

Lovett, B. J., & Sheffield, R. A. (2007). Affective empathy deficits in aggressive children and adolescents: A critical review. *Clinical Psychology Review, 27*, 1–13.

Lovett, J., & Kelly, L. (2009). *Different systems, similar outcomes? Tracking attrition in reported rape cases across Europe*. London: Child and Woman Abuse Studies Unit. Available online: www.cwasu.org/publication_display.asp?pageid=PAPERS&type=1&pagekey=44&year=2009

Lubek, I. (1995). Aggression research. *Theory and Psychology, 5*, 99–129.

Lustman, M., Wiesenthal, D. L., & Flett, G. L. (2010). Narcissism and aggressive driving: Is an inflated view of the self a road hazard? *Journal of Applied Social Psychology, 40*, 1423–1449.

Lyons, C. J. (2006). Stigma or sympathy? Attributions of fault to hate crime victims and offenders. *Social Psychology Quarterly, 69*, 39–59.

McBurnett, K., Lahey, B. B., Rathouz, P. J., & Loeber, R. (2000). Low salivary cortisol and persistent aggression in boys referred for disruptive behavior. *Archives of General Psychiatry, 57*, 38–43.

McCauley, C. R., & Segal, M. E. (2009). Social psychology of terrorist groups. In J. Victoroff & A. W. Kruglanski (Eds), *Psychology of terrorism* (pp. 331–346). New York: Psychology Press.

McCauley, J. L., & Calhoun, K. S. (2008). Faulty perceptions? The impact of binge drinking history on college women's perceived rape resistance efficacy. *Addictive Behaviors, 33*, 1540–1545.

McDonald, P. (2012). Workplace sexual harassment 30 years on: A review of the literature. *International Journal of Management Reviews, 14*, 1–17.

McGregor, H. A., Lieberman, J. D., Greenberg, J., Solomon, S., Arndt, J., Simon, L. et al. (1998). Terror management and aggression: Evidence that mortality salience motivates aggression against worldview-threatening others. *Journal of Personality and Social Psychology, 74*, 590–605.

McKibbin, W. F., Shakelford, T. K., Goetz, A. T., & Starratt, V. G. (2008). Why do men rape? An evolutionary psychology perspective. *Review of General Psychology, 12*, 86–97.

McPhail, C. (1994). The dark side of purpose: Individual and collective violence in riots. *The Sociological Quarterly, 35*, 1–32.

McWhirter, B. T., & Page, G. L. (1999). Effects of anger management and goal setting group interventions on state-trait anger and self-efficacy beliefs among high risk adolescents. *Current Psychology, 18*, 223–237.

Maas, C., Herrenkohl, T. I., & Sousa, C. (2008). Review of research on child maltreatment and violence in youth. *Trauma, Violence, & Abuse, 9*, 56–67.

Malamuth, N. M. (1981). Rape proclivity among males. *Journal of Social Issues, 37,* 138–157.

Malamuth, N. M. (1998). The confluence model as an organizing framework for research on sexually aggressive men: Risk moderators, imagined aggression, and pornography consumption. In R. G. Geen & E. Donnerstein (Eds), *Human aggression: Theories, research and implications for social policy* (pp. 229–245). San Diego, CA: Academic Press.

Malamuth, N. M., Addison, T., & Koss, M. P. (2000). Pornography and sexual aggression: Are there reliable effects and can we understand them? *Annual Review of Sex Research, 11,* 26–91.

Malamuth, N. M., & Heilmann, M. F. (1998). Evolutionary psychology and sexual aggression. In C. H. Crawford & D. L. Krebs (Eds), *Handbook of evolutionary psychology* (pp. 515–542). Mahwah, NJ: Lawrence Erlbaum.

Malamuth, N. M., Linz, D., Heavey, C. L., Barnes, G., & Acker, M. (1995). Using the confluence model of sexual aggression to predict men's conflict with women: A 10-year follow-up study. *Journal of Personality and Social Psychology, 69,* 353–369.

Malamuth, N. M., Sockloskie, R. J., Koss, M. P., & Tanaka, J. S. (1991). Characteristics of aggressors against women: Testing a model using a national sample of college students. *Journal of Consulting and Clinical Psychology, 59,* 670–681.

Mann, R. E., Zhao, J., Stoduto, G., Adlaf, E. M., Smart, R. G., & Donovan, J. (2007). Road rage and collision involvement. *American Journal of Health Behavior, 31,* 384–391.

Marcus-Newhall, A., Pedersen, W. C., Carlson, M., & Miller, N. (2000). Displaced aggression is alive and well: A meta-analytic review. *Journal of Personality and Social Psychology, 78,* 670–689.

Marin, A. J., & Russo, N. F. (1999). Feminist perspectives of male violence against women: Critiquing O'Neil and Harway's model. In M. Harway & J. M. O'Neil (Eds), *What causes men's violence against women?* (pp. 18–35). Thousand Oaks, CA: Sage.

Martin, E. K., Taft, C. T., & Resick, P. A. (2007). A review of marital rape. *Aggression and Violent Behavior, 12,* 329–347.

Martin, K., Vieraitis, L. M., & Britto, S. (2006). Gender equality and women's absolute status: A test of the feminist models of rape. *Violence Against Women, 12,* 321–339.

Martin, S. L., Macy, R. J., & Young, S. K. (2011). Health and economic consequences of sexual violence. In J. W. White, M. P. Koss & A. E. Kazdin (Eds), *Violence against women and children. Volume 1. Mapping the terrain* (pp. 173–195). Washington, DC: American Psychological Association.

Martino, S. C., Ellickson, P. L., Klein, D. J., McCaffrey, D., & Edelen, M. O. (2008). Multiple trajectories of physical aggression among adolescent boys and girls. *Aggressive Behavior, 34,* 61–75.

Mattaini, M. A., McGowan, B. G., & Williams, G. (1996). Child maltreatment. In M. A. Mattaini & B. A. Thyer (Eds), *Finding solutions to social problems* (pp. 223–266). Washington, DC: American Psychlogical Association.

Mattaini, M.A., Twyman, J.S., Chin, W., & Lee, K.N. (1996). Youth violence. In M.A. Mattaini & B. A. Thyer (Eds), *Finding solutions to social problems* (pp. 75–111). Washington, DC: American Psychological Association.

Matthews, B., & Kenny, M. C. (2008). Mandatory reporting legislation in the United States, Canada, and Australia: A cross-jurisdictional review of key features, differences, and issues. *Child Maltreatment, 13,* 50–63.

Maxwell, J. P. (2004). Anger rumination: An antecedent of athlete aggression? *Psychology of Sport and Exercise, 5,* 279–289.

Medienpädagogischer Forschungsverbund Südwest (2010). *JIM 2010. Jugend, Information, (Multi-) Media.* Stuttgart: MPFS. Available online: www.mpfs.de/fileadmin/JIM-pdf10/JIM2010.pdf

Meichenbaum, D. H. (1975). *Stress inoculation training.* New York: Pergamon Press.

Meier, B. P., & Hinsz, V, B. (2004). A comparison of human aggression committed by groups and individuals: An interindividual-intergroup discontinuity. *Journal of Experimental Social Psychology, 40*, 551–559.

Merari, A., Diamant, I., Bibi, A., Broshi, Y., & Zakin, G. (2010). Personality characteristics of "self martyrs"/"suicide bombers" and organizers of suicide attacks. *Terrorism and Political Violence, 22*, 87–101.

Mercy, J. A., & Hammond, W. R. (1999). Combining action and analysis to prevent homicide: A public health perspective. In M. D. Smith & M. A. Zahn (Eds), *Homicide. A sourcebook of social research* (pp. 297–310). Thousand Oaks, CA: Sage.

Merrell, K. W., Gueldner, B. A., Ross, S. W., & Isava, D. M. (2008). How effective are school bullying intervention programs? A meta-analysis of intervention research. *School Psychology Quarterly, 23*, 26–42.

Merrill, L. L., Thomsen, C. J., Crouch, J. L., May, P., Gold, S. R., & Milner, J. S. (2005). Predicting adult risk of child physical abuse from childhood exposure to violence: Can interpersonal schemata explain the association? *Journal of Social and Clinical Psychology, 24*, 981–1002.

Messinger, A. M. (2011). Invisible victims: Same-sex IPV in the National Violence Against Women Survey. *Journal of Interpersonal Violence, 26*, 2228–2243.

Messman-Moore, T. L., Coates, A. A., Gaffey, K. J., & Johnson, C. F. (2008). Sexuality, substance use, and susceptibility to victimization. *Journal of Interpersonal Violence, 23*, 1730–1746.

Messman-Moore, T. L., & Long, P. J. (2003). The role of childhood sexual abuse sequelae in the sexual revictimization of women: An empirical review and theoretical reformulation. *Clinical Psychology Review, 23*, 537–571.

Messman-Moore, T. L., Walsh, K. L., & DiLillo, D. (2010). Emotion dysregulation and risky sexual behavior in revictimization. *Child Abuse & Neglect, 34*, 967–976.

Miles, D. R., & Carey, G. (1997). Genetic and environmental architecture of aggression. *Journal of Personality and Social Psychology, 72*, 207–217.

Milgram, S. (1974). *Obedience to authority*. New York: Harper & Row.

Miller, B. C., Monson, B. H., & Norton, M. C. (1995). The effects of forced sexual intercourse on white female adolescents. *Child Abuse and Neglect, 19*, 1289–1301.

Miller, M., Hemenway, D., & Azrael, D. (2007). State-level homicide victimization rates in the US in relation to survey measures of household firearm ownership, 2001–2003. *Social Science and Medicine, 64*, 656–664.

Miller, N., Pedersen, W. C., Earleywine, M., & Pollock, V. E. (2003). A theoretical model of triggered displaced aggression. *Personality and Social Psychology Review, 7*, 75–97.

Miller, N. E. (1941). The frustration-aggression hypothesis. *Psychological Review, 48*, 337–342.

Miller, P., & Eisenberg, N. (1988). The relation of empathy to aggressive and externalizing/antisocial behavior. *Psychological Bulletin, 103*, 324–344.

Miller, T. R., Cohen, M. A., & Rossman, S. B. (1993). Victim costs of violent crime and resulting injuries. *Health Affairs, 12*, 186–197.

Miller-Perrin, C. L., & Perrin, R. D. (2007). *Child maltreatment*. Thousand Oaks, CA: Sage.

Milletich, R. J., Kelley, M. L., Doane, A. N., & Pearson, M. R. (2010). Exposure to interparental violence and childhood physical and emotional abuse as related to physical aggression in undergraduate dating relationships. *Journal of Family Violence, 25*, 627–637.

Milner, J. S., & Crouch, J. L. (1999). Child physical abuse: Theory and research. In R. L. Hampton (Ed.), *Family violence: Prevention and treatment* (2nd edn) (pp. 33–65). Thousand Oaks, CA: Sage.

Milner, J. S., & Wimberly, R. C. (1980). Prediction and explanation of child abuse. *Journal of Clinical Psychology, 36,* 875–884.

Mitchell, K. J., Wolak, J., & Finkelhor, D. (2007). Trends in youth reports of sexual solicitations, harassment and unwanted exposure to pornography on the Internet. *Journal of Adolescent Health, 40,* 116–126.

Möller, I., & Krahé, B. (2009). Exposure to violent video games and aggression in German adolescents. *Aggressive Behavior, 35,* 75–89.

Möller, I., Krahé, B., Busching, R., & Krause, C. (2011). Efficacy of an intervention to reduce the use of media violence and aggression: An experimental evaluation with adolescents in Germany. *Journal of Youth and Adolescence, 41.*

Moffitt, T. E. (1993). Adolescent-limited and life-course persistent antisocial behavior: A developmental taxonomy. *Psychological Review, 100,* 674–701.

Moffitt, T. E. (2007). A review of research on the taxonomy of life-course persistent versus adolescence-limited antisocial behavior. In D. J. Flannery, A. T. Vazsonyi & I. D. Waldman (Eds), *The Cambridge handbook of violent behavior and aggression* (pp. 49–74). New York: Cambridge University Press.

Moffitt, T. E., Caspi, A., Harrington, H., & Milne, B. J. (2002). Males on the life-course-persistent and adolescence-limited antisocial pathways: Follow-up at age 26 years. *Development and Psychopathology, 14,* 179–207.

Moghaddam, F. M. (2005). The staircase to terrorism: A psychological exploration. *American Psychologist, 60,* 161–169.

Moghaddam, F. (2006). *From the terrorists' point of view.* New York: Praeger.

Mohler-Kuo, M., Dowdall, G. W., Koss, M. P., & Wechsler, H. (2004). Correlates of rape while intoxicated in a national sample of college women. *Journal of Studies on Alcohol, 65,* 37–45.

Moloney, M., MacKenzie, K., Hunt, G., & Joe-Laidler, K. (2009). The path and promise of fatherhood for gang members. *British Journal of Criminology, 49,* 305–325.

Molidor, C. E. (1996). Female gang members: A profile of aggression and victimization. *Social Work, 41,* 251–257.

Moore, S. C., Shepherd, J. P., Eden, S., & Sivarajasingam, V. (2007). The effect of rugby match outcome on spectator aggression and intention to drink alcohol. *Criminal Behaviour and Mental Health, 17,* 118–127.

Moore, T. M., & Stuart, G. L. (2005). A review of the literature on masculinity and partner violence. *Psychology of Men and Masculinity, 6,* 46–61.

Moore, T. M., Stuart, G. L., Meehan, J. C., Rhatigan, D., Hellmuth, J. C., & Keen, S. M. (2008). Drug abuse and aggression between intimate partners: A meta-analytic review. *Clinical Psychology Review, 28,* 247–274.

Morton, G. M., & Oravecz, L. M. (2009). The mandatory reporting of abuse: Problem creation through problem solution? *Journal of Feminist Family Therapy, 21,* 177–197.

Mosher, D. L., & Sirkin, M. (1984). Measuring a macho personality constellation. *Journal of Research in Personality, 18,* 150–163.

Mouilso, E., Calhoun, K. S., & Gidycz, C. A. (2011). Effects of participation in a sexual assault risk reduction program on psychological distress following revictimization. *Journal of Interpersonal Violence, 26,* 769–788.

Moynihan, M. M., Banyard, V. L., Arnold, J. S., Eckstein, R. P., & Stapleton, J. G. (2011). Sisterhood may be powerful for reducing sexual and intimate partner violence: An evaluation of the Bringing in the Bystander in-person program with sorority members. *Violence Against Women, 17,* 703–719.

Muehlenhard, C. L. (1998). The importance and danger of studying sexually aggressive women. In P. B. Anderson & C. Struckman-Johnson (Eds), *Sexually aggressive women* (pp. 19–48). New York: The Guilford Press.

Muehlenhard, C. L., & Hollabaugh, L. C. (1988). Do women sometimes say no when they mean yes? The prevalence and correlates of women's token resistance to sex. *Journal of Personality and Social Psychology, 54*, 872–879.

Müller, U., & Schröttle, M. (2004). *Health, well-being and personal safety of women in Germany. A representative study of violence against women in Germany*. Available online: http://webapps01. un.org/vawdatabase/uploads/Germany%20-%20A%20representative%20study%20on%20 violence%20against%20women.pdf.

Mullen, B. (1983). Operationalizing the effect of the group on the individual: A self-attention perspective. *Journal of Experimental Social Psychology, 19*, 295–322.

Mullen, B. (1986). Atrocity as a function of lynch mob composition: A self-attention perspective. *Personality and Social Psychology Bulletin, 12*, 187–197.

Muller, H. J., Desmarais, S. L., & Hamel, J. M. (2009). Do judicial responses to restraining order requests discriminate against male victims of domestic violence? *Journal of Family Violence, 24*, 625–637.

Mullin, C. R., & Linz, D. (1995). Desensitization and resensitization to violence against women: Effects of exposure to sexually violent films on judgments of domestic violence victims. *Journal of Personality and Social Psychology, 69*, 449–459.

Murnen, S. K., Wright, C., & Kaluzny, G. (2002). If "boys will be boys", then girls will be victims? A meta-analytic review of the research that relates masculine ideology to sexual aggression. *Sex Roles, 46*, 359–375.

Murphy, P., Williams, J., & Dunning, E. (1990). *Football on trial: Spectator violence and development in the football world*. London: Routledge.

Murray, J. P. (2008). Media violence: The effects are both real and strong. *American Behavioral Scientist, 51*, 1212–1230.

Najdowski, C. J., & Ullman, S. E. (2011). The effects of revictimization on coping and depression in female sexual assault victims. *Journal of Traumatic Stress, 24*, 218–221.

Nalkur, P. G., Jamieson, P. E., & Romer, D. (2010). The effectiveness of the Motion Picture Association of America's rating system in screening explicit violence and sex in top-ranked movies from 1950 to 2006. *Journal of Adolescent Health, 47*, 440–447.

National Television Violence Study (1997). Vol. 1. Thousand Oaks, CA: Sage.

National Society for the Prevention of Cruelty to Children (2011). *Child cruelty in the UK 2011*. Available online: www.coe.int/t/dg3/children/news/nspcc/NSPCC_summary_14Feb.pdf

Neighbors, C., Walker, D. D., Mbilinyi, L. F., O'Rourke, A., Edleson, J. L., Zegree, J. et al. (2010). Normative misperceptions of abuse among perpetrators of intimate partner violence. *Violence Against Women, 16*, 370–386.

Nesbit, S. M., Conger, J. C., & Conger, A. J. (2007). A quantitative review of the relationship between anger and aggressive driving. *Aggression and Violent Behavior, 12*, 156–176.

Niederkrotenthaler, T., Till, B., Kapusta, N. D., Voracek, M., Dervic, K., & Sonneck, G. (2009). Copycat effects after media reports on suicide: A population-based ecologic study. *Social Science and Medicine, 69*, 1085–1090.

Niedhammer, I., David, S., Degioanni, S., Drummond, A., Philip, P., Acquarone, D. et al. (2009). Workplace bullying and sleep disturbances: Findings from a large-scale cross-sectional survey in the French working population. *Sleep, 32*, 1211–1219.

Nisbett, R. E. (1993). Violence and U.S. regional culture. *American Psychologist, 48*, 441–449.

Noll, J. G., & Grych, J. H.(2011). Read–React–Respond: An integrative model for understanding sexual revictimization. *Psychology of Violence, 1*, 200–215.

Noll, J. G., Shenk, C. E., & Putnam, K. T. (2009). Childhood sexual abuse and adolescent pregnancy: A meta-analytic update. *Journal of Pediatric Psychology, 34*, 366–378.

Notelaers, G., De Witte, H., & Einarsen, S. (2010). A job characteristics approach to explain workplace bullying. *European Journal of Work and Organizational Psychology, 1*, 487–504.

Novaco, R. W. (1975). *Anger control. The development and evaluation of an experimental treatment.* Lexington, MA: D. C. Heath.

O'Brennan, L. M., Bradshaw, C. P., & Sawyer, A. L. (2009). Examining development differences in the social-emotional problems among frequent bullies, victims, and bully/victims. *Psychology in the Schools, 46*, 100–115.

O'Donohue, W., Downs, K., & Yeater, E. A. (1998). Sexual harassment: A review of the literature. *Aggression and Violent Behavior, 3*, 111–128.

O'Donohue, W., Yeater, E. A., & Fanetti, M.. (2003). Rape prevention with college males. *Journal of Interpersonal Violence, 18*, 513–531.

O'Hagan, K.P. (1995). Emotional and psychological abuse: Problems of definition. *Child Abuse and Neglect, 19*, 449–461.

O'Hare, E. O., & O'Donohue, W. (1998). Risk factors relating to sexual harassment: An examination of four models. *Archives of Sexual Behavior, 27*, 561–580.

O'Keefe, M. (1995). Predictors of child abuse in maritally violent families. *Journal of Interpersonal Violence, 10*, 3–25.

O'Leary-Kelly, A. M., Bowes-Sperry, L., Bates, C. A., & Lean, E. R. (2009). Sexual harassment at work: A decade (plus) of progress. *Journal of Management, 35*, 503–536.

Ohbuchi, K., Ikeda, T., & Takeuchi, G. (1994). Effects of violent pornography upon viewers' rape myth beliefs: A study of Japanese males. *Psychology, Crime and Law, 1*, 71–81.

Olweus, D. (1978). *Aggression in the schools. Bullies and whipping boys.* Washington, DC: Hemisphere Press.

Olweus, D. (1979). Stability of aggressive reaction patterns in males. A review. *Psychological Bulletin, 86*, 852–875.

Olweus, D. (1994). Bullying at school. Long-term outcomes for the victims and an effective school-based intervention program. In L. R. Huesmann (Ed.), *Aggressive behavior: Current perspectives* (pp 97–130). New York: Plenum Press.

Orobio de Castro, B. , Veerman, J. W., Koops, W., Bosch, J. D., & Monshouwer, H. J. (2002). Hostile attribution of intent and aggressive behaviour: A meta-analysis. *Child Development, 73*, 916–934.

Ostrov, J. M., & Godleski, S. A. (2009). Impulsivity–hyperactivity and subtypes of aggression in early childhood: An observational and short-term longitudinal study. *European Child and Adolescent Psychiatry, 18*, 477–483.

Ostrov, J. M., & Keating, C. F. (2004). Gender differences in preschool aggression during free play and structured interactions: An observational study. *Social Development, 13*, 255–277.

Ostrowsky, M. K. (2010). Are violent people more likely to have low self-esteem or high self-esteem? *Aggression and Violent Behavior, 15*, 69–75.

Özkan, T., & Lajunen, T. (2005). Why are there sex differences in risky driving? The relationship between sex and gender-role on aggressive driving, traffic offences, and accident involvement among young Turkish drivers. *Aggressive Behavior, 31*, 547–558.

Pacifici, C., Stoolmiller, M., & Nelson, C. (2001). Evaluating a prevention program for teenagers on sexual coercion: A differential effectiveness approach. *Journal of Consulting and Clinical Psychology, 69*, 552–559.

Paik, H., & Comstock, G. (1994). The effects of television violence on antisocial behavior: A meta-analysis. *Communication Research, 21*, 516–546.

Palmer, R. S., McMahon, T. J., Rounsaville, B. J., & Ball, S. A. (2010). Coercive sexual experiences, protective behavioral strategies, alcohol expectancies and consumption among male and female college students. *Journal of Interpersonal Violence, 25*, 1563–1578.

Paludi, M. A. (Ed.), (1990). *Ivory power: Sexual harassment on campus*. Albany, NY: SUNY Press.

Parker, D., Lajunen, T., & Summala, H. (2002). Anger and aggression among drivers in three European countries. *Accident Analysis and Prevention, 34*, 229–235.

Parker, R. N., & Auerhahn, K. (1999). Drugs, alcohol, and homicide. In M. D. Smith & M. A. Zahn (Eds), *Homicide. A sourcebook of social research* (pp. 176–191). Thousand Oaks, CA: Sage.

Parrott, D. J., & Giancola, P. R. (2004). A further examination of the relation between trait anger and alcohol-related aggression: The role of anger control. *Alcoholism: Clinical and Experimental Research, 28*, 855–864.

Parrott, D. J., & Giancola, P. R. (2007). Addressing "the criterion problem" in the assessment of aggressive behavior: Development of a new taxonomic system. *Aggression and Violent Behavior, 12*, 280–299.

Parrott, D. J., & Peterson, J. L. (2008). What motivates hate crimes based on sexual orientation? Mediating effects of anger on antigay aggression. *Aggressive Behavior, 34*, 306–318.

Patchin, J. W., & Hinduja, S. (2006). Bullies move beyond the schoolyard: A preliminary look at cyberbullying. *Youth Violence and Juvenile Justice, 4*, 148–169.

Pat-Horenczyk, R., & Brom, D. (2007). The multiple faces of post-traumatic growth. *Applied Psychology, 56*, 379–385.

Patterson, G. R., DeBaryshe, B. D., & Ramsey, E. (1989). A developmental perspective on antisocial behavior. *American Psychologist, 44*, 329–335.

Patterson, M. L., Mullens, S., & Romano, J. (1971). Compensatory reactions to spatial intrusion. *Sociometry, 34*, 114–121.

Paul, L. A., & Gray, M. J. (2011). Sexual assault programming on college campuses: Using social psychological belief and behavior change principles to improve outcomes. *Trauma, Violence, and Abuse, 12*, 99–109.

Pearl, E. S. (2009). Parent management training for reducing oppositional and aggressive behavior in preschoolers. *Aggression and Violent Behavior, 14*, 295–305.

Pedersen, W. C., Aviles, F. E., Ito, T. A., Miller, N., & Pollock, V. E. (2002). Psychological experimentation on alcohol-induced human aggression. *Aggression and Violent Behavior, 7*, 293–312.

Pedersen, W. C., Gonzales, C., & Miller, N. (2000). The moderating effect of trivial triggering provocation on displaced aggression. *Journal of Personality and Social Psychology, 78*, 913–927.

Peled, M., & Moretti, M. (2010). Ruminating on rumination: Are rumination on anger and sadness differentially related to aggression and depressed mood? *Journal of Psychopathology and Behavioral Assessment, 32*, 108–117.

Pellegrini, A. D., & Long, J. D. (2003). A sexual selection theory longitudinal analysis of sexual segregation and integration in early adolescence. *Journal of Experimental Child Psychology, 85*, 257–278.

Pereda, N., Guilera, G., Forns, M., & Gómez-Benito, J. (2009a). The prevalence of child sexual abuse in community and student samples: A meta-analysis. *Clinical Psychology Review, 29,* 328–338.

Pereda, N., Guilera, G., Forns, M., & Gómez-Benito, J. (2009b). The international epidemiology of child sexual abuse: A continuation of Finkelhor (1994). *Child Abuse & Neglect, 33,* 331–342.

Perilla, J. L., Lippy, C., Rosales, A., & Serrata, J. V. (2011). Prevalence of domestic violence. In J. W. White, M. P. Koss & A. E. Kazdin (Eds), *Violence against women and children. Volume 1. Mapping the terrain* (pp. 199–220). Washington, DC: American Psychological Association.

Perry, E. L., Schmidtke, J. M., & Kulik, C. T. (1998). Propensity to sexually harass: An exploration of gender differences. *Sex Roles, 38,* 443–460.

Peter, J., & Valkenburg, P. M. (2007). Adolescents' exposure to a sexualized media environment and their notions of women as sex objects. *Sex Roles, 56,* 381–395.

Peter, J., & Valkenburg, P. M. (2008). Adolescents' exposure to sexually explicit internet material, sexual uncertainty, and attitudes toward uncommitted sexual exploration. Is there a link? *Communication Research, 35,* 579–601.

Peterson, Z. D., & Muehlenhard, C. L. (2004). Was it rape? The function of women's rape myth acceptance and definitions of sex in labeling their own experiences. *Sex Roles, 51,* 129–144.

Peterson, Z. D., Voller, E. K., Polusny, M. A., & Murdoch, M. (2011). Prevalence and consequences of adult sexual assault of men: Review of empirical findings and state of the literature. *Clinical Psychology Review, 31,* 1–24.

Pettigrew, T. F., & Tropp, L. R. (2006). A meta-analytic test of intergroup contact theory. *Journal of Personality and Social Psychology, 90,* 751–783.

Phil, R. O., & Sutton, R. (2009). Drugs and aggression readily mix; so what now? *Substance Use and Misuse, 44,* 1188–1203.

Philippe, F. L., Vallerard, R. J., Richer, I., Vallières, E., & Bergeron, J. (2009). Passion for driving and aggressive driving behavior: A look at their relationship. *Journal of Applied Social Psychology, 29,* 3020–3043.

Pillemer, K., & Suitor, J. J. (1988). Elder abuse. In V. B. van Hasselt, R. L. Morrison, A. S. Bellack & M. Hersen (Eds), *Handbook of family violence* (pp. 247–270). New York: Plenum Press.

Pinker, S. (2011). *The better angels of our nature: The decline of violence in history and its causes.* London: Allen Lane.

Plumm, K. M., Terrance, C. A., Henderson, V. R., & Ellingson, H. (2010). Victim blame in a hate crime motivated by sexual orientation. *Journal of Homosexuality, 57,* 267–286.

Polman, H., Orobio de Castro, B., & van Aken, M. (2008). Experimental study of the differential effects of playing versus watching violent video games on children's aggressive behavior. *Aggressive Behavior, 34,* 256–264.

Pond, R. S., DeWall, C. N., Lambert, N. M., Deckman, T., Bonser, I. M., & Fincham, F. D. (2012). Repulsed by violence: Disgust sensitivity buffers trait, behavioral, and daily aggression. *Journal of Personality and Social Psychology, 102,* 175–188.

Poppen, P. J., & Segal, N. J. (1988). The influence of sex and sex role orientation on sexual coercion. *Sex Roles, 19,* 689–701.

Post, J. M. (2005). When hatred is bred in the bone: Psycho-cultural foundations of contemporary terrorism. *Political Psychology, 26,* 615–636.

Post, L. A., Biroscak, B. J., & Barboza, G. (2011). Prevalence of sexual violence. In J. W. White, M. P. Koss & A. E. Kazdin (Eds), *Violence Against Women and Children. Volume 1. Mapping the terrain* (pp. 101–123). Washington, DC: American Psychological Association.

Postmes, T., & Spears, R. (1998). Deindividuation and antinormative behavior: A meta-analysis. *Psychological Bulletin, 123,* 238–259.

Potter, W. J., & Byrne, S. (2007). What are media literacy effects? In S. R. Mazzarella (Ed.), *20 questions about youth and the media* (pp. 197–208). New York: Peter Lang.

Prino, C. T., & Peyrot, M. (1994). The effect of child physical abuse and neglect on aggressive, withdrawn, and prosocial behavior. *Child Abuse and Neglect, 18,* 871–884.

Privitera, C., & Campbell, A. (2009). Cyberbullying: The new face of workplace bullying? *Cyberpsychology & Behavior, 12,* 395–400.

Pyszczynski, T., Abdollahi, A., Solomon, S., Greenberg, J., Cohen, F., & Wiese, D. (2009). Mortality salience, martyrdom, and military might: The Great Satan versus the Axis of Evil. In J. Victoroff & A. W. Kruglanski (Eds), *Psychology of terrorism* (pp. 281–297). New York: Psychology Press.

Pyszczynski, T., Solomon, S., & Greenberg, J. (2003).Terror management theory: An evolutionary existential account of human behavior. In T. Pyszczynski, S. Solomon & J. Greenberg (Eds), *In the wake of 9/11: The psychology of terror* (pp. 11–35). Washington, DC: American Psychological Association.

Quigley, B. M., & Leonard, K. E. (2006). Alcohol expectancies and intoxicated aggression. *Aggression and Violent Behavior, 11,* 484–496.

Raine, A. (1996). Autonomic nervous system activity and violence. In D. M. Stoff & R. B. Cairns (Eds), *Aggression and violence* (pp. 145–168). Mahwah, NJ: Lawrence Erlbaum.

Rand, M., & Catalano, S. (2007). *Criminal victimization, 2006.* Washington, DC: U.S. Department of Justice, Available online: www.rainn.org/pdf-files-and-other-documents/News-Room/press-releases/2006-ncvs-results/NCVS%202006–1.pdf

Randall, P. (1997). *Adult bullying.* London: Routledge.

Randle, A. A., & Graham, C. A. (2011). A review of the evidence on the effects of intimate partner violence on men. *Psychology of Men and Masculinity, 12,* 97–111.

Raskauskas, J., & Stoltz, A. D. (2007). Involvement in traditional and electronic bullying among adolescents. *Developmental Psychology, 43,* 564–575.

Raskin, R., & Terry, H. (1988). A principal-components analysis of the Narcissistic Personality Inventory and further evidence of its construct validity. *Journal of Personality and Social Psychology, 54,* 890–902.

Ratner, P. A., Johnson, J. L., Shoveller, J. A., Chan, K., Marindale, S. L., Schilder, A. J. et al. (2003). Non-consensual sex experienced by men who have sex with men: Prevalence and association with mental health. *Patient Education and Counseling, 49,* 67–74.

Rayburn, N. R., Mendoza, M., & Davison, G. C. (2003). Bystanders' perceptions of perpetrators and victims of hate crime: An investigation using the person perception paradigm. *Journal of Interpersonal Violence, 18,* 1055–1074.

Rayner, C. (1997). The incidence of workplace bullying. *Journal of Applied and Community Psychology, 7,* 199–208.

Regoeczi, W. C. (2008). Crowding in context: An examination of the differential responses of men and women to high-density living environments. *Journal of Health and Social Behavior, 49,* 254–268.

Rehbein, F., Kleimann, M., & Mößle, T. (2009). *Computerspielabhängigkeit im Kindes- und Jugendalter.* KFN-Forschungsbericht No. 108. Hannover: Kriminologisches Forschungsinstitut Niedersachsen e.V. Available online: www.kfn.de/versions/kfn/assets/fb108.pdf.

Rehm, J., Steinleitner, M., & Lilli, W. (1987). Wearing uniforms and aggression: A field experiment. *European Journal of Social Psychology, 17,* 357–360.

Reicher, S. D. (1984). The St. Paul's riot: An explanation of the limits of crowd action in terms of a social identity model. *European Journal of Social Psychology, 14*, 1–21.

Reicher, S., & Haslam, S. A. (2006). Rethinking the psychology of tyranny: The BBC Prison Study. *British Journal of Social Psychology, 45*, 1–40.

Reicher, S., Spears, R., & Postmes, T. (1995). A social identity model of deindividuation phenomena. *European Review of Social Psychology, 6*, 161–198.

Reidy, D. E., Foster, J. D., & Zeichner, A. (2010). Narcissism and unprovoked aggression. *Aggressive Behavior, 36*, 414–422.

Reidy, D. E., Shirk, S. D., Sloan, C. A., & Zeichner, A. (2009). Men who aggress against women: Effects of feminine gender role violation on physical aggression in hypermasculine men. *Psychology of Men and Masculinity, 10*, 1–12.

Reidy, D. E., Zeichner, A., Foster, J. D., & Martinez, M. (2008). Effects of narcissistic entitlement and exploitativeness on human physical aggression. *Personality and Individual Differences, 44*, 865–875.

Reifman, A. S., Larrick, R. P., & Fein, S. (1991). Temper and temperature on the diamond: The heat–aggression relationship in major league baseball. *Personality and Social Psychology Bulletin, 17*, 580–585.

Rennison, C. M., & Welchans, S. (2000). *Intimate partner violence.* Bureau of Justice Statistics Special Report, May 2000. Available online: http://bjs.ojp.usdoj.gov/content/pub/pdf/ipv.pdf

Rhee, S. H., & Waldman, I. D. (2002). Genetic and environmental influences on antisocial behavior: A meta-analysis of twin and adoption studies. *Psychological Bulletin, 128*, 490–529.

Rhodes, S. D., McCoy, T. P., Wilkin, A. M., & Wolfson, M. (2009). Behavioral risk disparities in a random sample of self-identifying gay and non-gay male university students. *Journal of Homosexuality, 56*, 1083–1100.

Richardson, D. S., & Green, L. R. (2003). Defining direct and indirect aggression. The Richardson Conflict Response Questionnaire. *International Review of Social Psychology, 16*, 11–23.

Richardson, D. S., Green, L. R., & Lago, T. (1998). The relationship between perspective-taking and nonaggressive responding in the face of an attack. *Journal of Personality, 66*, 235–256.

Richardson, D. S., & Hammock, G. S. (2007). Social context of human aggression: Are we paying too much attention to gender? *Aggression and Violent Behavior, 12*, 417–426.

Richardson, D. R., Hammock, G. S., Smith, S., Gardner, W. L., & Signo, M. (1994). Empathy as a cognitive inhibitor of interpersonal aggression. *Aggressive Behavior, 20*, 275–289.

Richetin, J., & Richardson, D. S. (2008). Automatic processes and individual differences in aggressive behavior. *Aggression and Violent Behavior, 13*, 423–430.

Richetin, J., Richardson, D., & Mason, G. D. (2010). Predictive validity of IAT aggressiveness in the context of provocation. *Social Psychology, 41*, 27–34.

Riddle, K., Potter, J. W., Metzger, M. J., Nabi, R. L., & Linz, D. G. (2011). Beyond cultivation: Exploring the effects of frequency, recency, and vividness of autobiographical memories for violent media. *Media Psychology, 14*, 168–191.

Rideout, V. J., Foehr, U. G., & Roberts, D. F. (2010). *GENERATION M²: Media in the lives of 8- to 18-year-olds.* Menlo Park, CA: Henry J. Kaiser Family Foundation. Available online: www.kff.org/entmedia/upload/8010.pdf

Rigby, K., & Johnson, B. (2006). Expressed readiness of Australian schoolchildren to act as bystanders in support of children who are being bullied. *Educational Psychology, 26*, 425–440.

Ritter, D., & Eslea, M. (2005). Hot sauce, toy guns, and graffiti: A critical account of current laboratory aggression paradigms. *Aggressive Behavior, 31*, 407–419.

Rivara, F. P., Anderson, M. L., Fishman, P., Bonomi, A. E., Reid, R. J., Carrell, D. et al. (2007). Healthcare utilization and costs for women with a history of intimate partner violence. *American Journal of Preventive Medicine, 32*, 89–96.

Roberts, D. W. (2009). Intimate partner homicide: Relationships to alcohol and firearms. *Journal of Contemporary Criminal Justice, 25*, 67–88.

Robinson, T. N., Wilde, M. L., Navracruz, L. C., Haydel, K. F., & Varady, A. (2001). Effects of reducing children's television and video game use on aggressive behavior. *Archives of Pediatrics and Adolescent Medicine, 155*, 17–23.

Robinson, T. W., Smith, S. W., Miller, M. D., & Brownell, M. T. (1999). Cognitive behavior modification of hyperactivity–impulsivity and aggression: A meta-analysis of school-based studies. *Journal of Educational Psychology, 91*, 195–203.

Roisman, G. I., Monahan, K. C., Campbell, S. B., Steinberg, L., Cauffman, E. & the National Institute of Child Health and Human Development Early Child Care Research Network (2010). Is adolescence-onset antisocial behavior developmentally normative? *Development and Psychopathology, 22*, 295–311.

Romano, E., & De Luca, R. (2001). Male sexual abuse: A review of effects, abuse characteristics, and links with later psychological functioning. *Aggression and Violent Behavior, 6*, 55–78.

Rosen, C., Tiet, C., Cavella, S., Finney, J., & Lee, T. (2005). Chronic PTSD patients' functioning before and after the September 11 attacks. *Journal of Traumatic Stress, 18*, 781–784.

Rosenkoetter, L. I., Rosenkoetter, S. E., & Acock, A. C. (2009). Television violence: An intervention to reduce its impact on children. *Applied Developmental Psychology, 30*, 381–397.

Rosenkoetter, L. I., Rosenkoetter, S. E., Ozretich, R. A., & Acock, A. C. (2004). Mitigating the harmful effects of violent television. *Journal of Applied Developmental Psychology, 25*, 25–47.

Rosenthal, R. R. (1990). Media violence, antisocial behavior, and the social consequences of small effects. In R. Surette (Ed.), *The media and criminal justice policy: Recent research and social effects* (pp. 53–61). Springfield, IL: C. C. Thomas.

Rosenzweig, P. (1945). The picture-association method and its application in a study of reactions to frustration. *Journal of Personality, 14*, 3–23.

Rosenzweig, P. (1976). Aggressive behavior and the Rosenzweig Picture-Frustration (P-F) Study. *Journal of Clinical Psychology, 32*, 885–891.

Rosenzweig, S., Fleming, E. E., & Rosenzweig, L. (1948). The children's form of the Rosenzweig Picture-Frustration Study. *Journal of Psychology: Interdisciplinary and Applied, 26*, 141–191.

Rosenzweig, S., Ludwig, D. J., & Adelman, S. (1975). Retest reliability of the Rosenzweig Picture-Frustration Study and similar semiprojective techniques. *Journal of Personality Assessment, 39*, 3–12.

Rothman, E. F., Exner, D., & Baughman, A. L. (2011). The prevalence of sexual assault against people who identify as gay, lesbian, or bisexual in the United States: A systematic review. *Trauma, Violence, & Abuse, 12*, 55–66.

Rothschild, Z. K., Abdollahi, A., & Pyszczynski, T. (2009). Does peace have a prayer? The effect of mortality salience, compassionate values, and religious fundamentalism on hostility toward out-groups. *Journal of Experimental Social Psychology, 45*, 816–827.

Rotten, J., Frey, J., Barry, T., Milligan, M., & Fitzpatrick, M. (1979). The air pollution experience and physical aggression. *Journal of Applied Social Psychology, 9*, 397–412.

Rouhana, N. N., & Bar-Tal, D. (1998). Psychological dynamics of intractable ethnonational conflicts: The Israeli-Palestinian case. *American Psychologist, 53*, 761–770.

Rozee, P. (1999). Stranger rape. In M. A. Paludi (Ed.), *Sexual victimization* (pp. 97–115). Westport, CT: Greenwood Press.

Rozee, P. (2011). I. New views of rape prevention and resistance: Enlightening men, empowering women. *Feminism & Psychology, 21*, 257–261.

Rubin, G. J., Brewin, C. R., Greenberg, N., Hughes, J. H., Simpson, J., & Wessely, S. (2005). Enduring consequences of terrorism: 7-month follow-up survey of reactions to the bombings in London on 7 July 2005. *British Journal of Psychiatry, 190*, 350–356.

Rubin, G. J., Brewin, C. R., Greenberg, N., Simpson, J., & Wessely, S. (2005). Psychological and behavioural reactions to the bombings in London on 7 July 2005: Cross-sectional survey of a representative sample of Londoners. *British Medical Journal, 331 (7517)*, 606.

Rudman, L. A., & Glick, P. (2008). *The social psychology of gender*. New York: Guilford Press.

Russell, G. W. (1993). *The social psychology of sport*. New York: Springer.

Russell, G. W. (2004). Sport riots: A social-psychological review. *Aggression and Violent Behavior, 9*, 353–378.

Russell, G. W. (2008). *Aggression in the sports world*. New York: Oxford University Press.

Saam, N. (2010). Interventions in workplace bullying: A multilevel approach. *European Journal of Work and Organizational Psychology, 19*, 51–75.

Sabina, C., Wolak, J., & Finkelhor, D. (2008). The nature and dynamics of Internet pornography exposure for youth. *Cyberpsychology & Behavior, 11*, 691–693.

Sachs, C. J., & Chu, L. D. (2000). The association between violent football games and domestic violence in Los Angeles County. *Journal of Interpersonal Violence, 15*, 1192–1201.

Salmivalli, C. (2010). Bullying and the peer group: A review. *Aggression and Violent Behavior, 15*, 112–120.

Salmivalli, C., Lagerspetz, K., Björkqvist, K., Österman, K., & Kaukiainen, A. (1996). Bullying as a group process: Participant roles and their relations to social status within the group. *Aggressive Behavior, 22*, 1–15.

Salzinger, S., Rosario, M., Feldman, R. S., & Ng-Mak, D. S. (2007). Adolescent suicidal behavior: Associations with preadolescent physical abuse and selected risk and protective factors. *Journal of the American Academy of Child and Adolescent Psychiatry, 46*, 859–866.

Samara, M., & Smith, P. K. (2008). How schools tackle bullying, and the use of whole school policies: Changes over the last decade. *Educational Psychology, 28*, 663–676.

Sanday, P. R. (1981). The social cultural context of rape. *Journal of Social Issues, 37*, 5–27.

Sanders, M. R., Cann, W., & Markie-Dadds, C. (2003). The Triple P Positive Parenting Programme: A universal population-level approach to the prevention of child abuse. *Child Abuse Review, 12*, 155–171.

Santisteban, C., Alvarado, J. M., & Recio, P. (2007). Evaluation of a Spanish version of the Buss and Perry aggression questionnaire: Some personal and situational factors related to the aggression scores of young subjects. *Personality and Individual Differences, 42*, 1453–1465.

Sarrel, P. M., & Masters, W. H. (1982). Sexual molestation of men by women. *Archives of Sexual Behavior, 11*, 117–131.

Savage, J. (2008). The role of exposure to media violence in the etiology of violent behavior. *American Behavioral Scientist, 51*, 1123–1136.

Savage, J., & Yancey, C. (2008). The effects of media violence exposure on criminal aggression: A meta-analysis. *Criminal Justice and Behavior, 35*, 772–791.

Schachter, S. (1964). The interaction of cognitive and physiological determinants of emotional state. In L. Berkowitz (Ed.), *Advances in experimental social psychology. Volume 1* (pp. 49–80). New York: Academic Press.

Schaefer, C. E., & Mattei, D. (2005). Catharsis: Effectiveness in children's aggression. *International Journal of Play Therapy, 14*, 103–109.

Schank, R., & Abelson, R. (1977). *Scripts, plans, goals, and understanding: An inquiry into human knowledge structures*. Hillsdale, NJ: Lawrence Erlbaum.

Schat, A. C. H., & Kelloway, E. K. (2005). Workplace violence. In J. Barling, E. K. Kelloway & M. Frone (Eds), *Handbook of work stress* (pp. 189–215). Thousand Oaks, CA: Sage.

Schatzel-Murphy, E. A., Harris, D. A., Knight, R. A., & Milburn, M. A. (2009). Sexual coercion in men and women: Similar behaviors, different predictors. *Archives of Sexual Behavior, 38*, 974–986.

Scheithauer, H., Haag, N., Mahlke, J., & Ittel, A. (2008). Gender and age differences in the development of relational/indirect aggression: First results of a meta-analysis. *International Journal of Developmental Science, 2*, 176–189.

Schewe, P. A. (2002). Guidelines for developing rape prevention and risk reduction interventions. In P. A. Schewe (Ed.), *Preventing violence in relationships* (pp. 107–136). Washington, DC: American Psychological Association.

Schlenger, W. E., Caddell, J. M., Ebert, M., Jordan, B. K., Rourke, K. M., Wilson, D. et al. (2002). Psychological reactions to terrorist attacks: Findings from the national study of Americans' reactions to September 11. *Journal of the American Medical Association, 228*, 581–588.

Schneider, K. T., Swan, S., & Fitzgerald, L. F. (1997). Job-related and psychological effects of sexual harassment in the workplace: Empirical evidence from two organizations. *Journal of Applied Psychology, 82*, 401–415.

Schuster, B. (1996). Rejection, exclusion, and harassment at work and in schools. *European Psychologist, 1*, 293–317.

Schwartz, M., & DeKeseredy, W. S. (2008). Interpersonal violence against women: The role of men. *Journal of Contemporary Criminal Justice , 24*, 178–185.

Schwartz, S., Dunkel, C. S., & Waterman, A. S. (2009). Terrorism: An identity theory perspective. *Studies in Conflict & Terrorism, 32*, 537–559.

Scott, J. E., & Schwalm, L. (1988). Rape rates and the circulation rates of adult magazines. *Journal of Sex Research, 24*, 241–250.

Sedlak, A. J. Mettenburg, J., Basena, M., Petta, I., McPherson, K., Greene, A. et al. (2010). *The Fourth National Incidence Study of Child Abuse and Neglect*. Washington, DC: US Department of Health and Human Services. Available online: www.acf.hhs.gov/programs/opre/abuse_neglect/natl_incid/ nis4_report_congress_full_pdf_jan2010.pdf

Senn, T. E., Carey, M. P., & Vanable, P. A. (2008). Childhood and adolescent sexual abuse and subsequent sexual risk behavior: Evidence from controlled studies, methodological critique, and suggestions for research. *Clinical Psychology Review, 28*, 711–735.

Seto, M. C., & Lalumière, M. L. (2010). What is so special about male adolescent sexual offending? A review and test of explanations through meta-analysis. *Psychological Bulletin, 136*, 526–575.

Seto, M. C., Maric, A., & Barbaree, H. E. (2001). The role of pornography in the etiology of sexual aggression. *Aggression and Violent Behavior, 6*, 35–53.

Shaver, P. R., & Mikulincer, M. (Eds) (2011). *Human aggression and violence: Causes, manifestations, and consequences*. Washington, DC: American Psychological Association.

Sherer, Y. C., & Nicholson, A. B. (2010). Anti-bullying practices in American schools: Perspectives of school psychologists. *Psychology in the Schools, 47*, 217–229.

Sherif, M. (1958). Superordinate goals in the reduction of intergroup conflict. *American Journal of Sociology, 63*, 349–356.

Sherif, M. (1966). *In common predicament: Social psychology in intergroup conflict and cooperation.* Boston, MA: Houghton Mifflin.

Sherif, M., Harvey, O. J., White, B. J., Hood, W. R., & Sherif, C. W. (1961). *Intergroup conflict and cooperation: The Robbers Cave experiment.* Norman, OK: University of Oklahoma Book Exchange. Available online: http://psychclassics.yorku.ca/Sherif/

Sherry, J. L. (2001). The effects of violent games on aggression: A meta-analysis. *Human Communication Research, 27*, 309–331.

Shibuya, A., Sakamoto, A., Ihori, N., & Yukawa, S. (2008). The effects of the presence and contexts of video game violence on children: A longitudinal study in Japan. *Simulation & Gaming, 39*, 528–539.

Shields, W. M., & Shields, L. M. (1983). Forcible rape: An evolutionary perspective. *Ethology and Sociobiology, 4*, 115–136.

Shoal, G. D., Giancola, P. R., & Kirillova, G. P. (2005). Salivary cortisol, personality, and aggressive behavior in adolescent boys: A five-year longitudinal study. *Journal of the American Academy of Child and Adolescent Psychiatry, 42*, 1101–1107.

Shotland, R. L., & Hunter, B. A. (1995). Women's "token resistant" and compliant sexual behaviors are related to uncertain sexual intentions and rape. *Personality and Social Psychology Bulletin, 21*, 226–236.

Shrum, L. J. (1996). Psychological processes underlying cultivation effects: Further tests of construct accessibility. *Human Communication Research, 22*, 482–509.

Sidebotham, P., Bailey, S., Belderson, P., & Brandon, M. (2011). Fatal child maltreatment in England, 2005–2009. *Child Abuse & Neglect, 35*, 299–306.

Silke, A. (2003). Deindividuation, anonymity, and violence: Findings from Northern Ireland. *Journal of Social Psychology, 143*, 493–499.

Silke, A. (2009). Cheshire-cat logic: The recurring theme of terrorist abnormality in psychological research. In J. Victoroff & A. W. Kruglanski (Eds), *Psychology of terrorism* (pp. 95–107). New York: Psychology Press.

Silver, R. C., Holman, E. A., McIntosh, D. N., Poulin, M., & Gil-Rivas, V. (2002). Nationwide longitudinal study of psychological responses to September 11. *Journal of the American Medical Association, 288*, 1235–1244.

Silver, R., Poulin, M., Holman, E. A., McIntosh, D. N., Gil-Rivas, V., & Pizarro, J. (2005). Exploring the myths of coping with a national trauma: A longitudinal study of responses to the September 11th terrorist attacks. *Journal of Aggression, Maltreatment and Trauma, 9*, 129–141.

Simon, T. R., Ikeda, R. M., Smith, E. P., Reese, L. E., Rabiner, D. L., Miller, S. et al. (2009). The ecological effects of universal and selective violence prevention programs for middle school students: A randomized trial. *Journal of Consulting and Clinical Psychology, 77*, 526–542.

Simons, Y., & Taylor, J. (1992). A psychosocial model of fan violence in sport. *International Journal of Sports Psychology, 23*, 207–226.

Sims, C. S., Drasgow, F., & Fitzgerald, L. F. (2005). The effects of sexual harassment on turnover in the military: Time-dependent modeling. *Journal of Applied Psychology, 90*, 1141–1152.

Singer, J. D. (1989). The political origins of international war: A multifactorial review. In J. Groebel & R. A. Hinde (Eds), *Aggression and war: Their biological and social bases* (pp. 202–220). Cambridge: Cambridge University Press.

Six, B., & Schütz, H. (1996). How strong is the relationship between prejudice and discrimination? A meta-analytic answer. *International Journal of Intercultural Relations, 20*, 441–462.

Slater, M. D., Henry, K. L., Swaim, R. C. & Anderson, L. L. (2003). Violent media content and aggressiveness in adolescents: A downward spiral model. *Communication Research, 30*, 713–736.

Smith, C. A., Ireland, T. O., Park, A., Elwyn, L., & Thornberry, T. P. (2011). Intergenerational continuities and discontinuities in intimate partner violence: A two-generational prospective study. *Journal of Interpersonal Violence, 26*, 3720–3752.

Smith, D. M. (1998). The psychocultural roots of genocide. Legitimacy and crisis in Ruanda. *American Psychologist, 53*, 743–753.

Smith, K., Coleman, K., Eder, S., & Hall, P. (Eds) (2011). *Homicides, firearm offences and intimate violence 2009/10. Supplementary Volume 2 to Crime in England and Wales 2009/10.* London: Home Office Statistical Bulletin HOS 01/11. Available online: www.homeoffice.gov.uk/publications/science-research-statistics/research-statistics/crime-research/hosb0111/hosb0111?view=Binary

Smith, P. K., Cowie, H., Olafsson, R. F., & Liefooghe, A. P. D. (2002). Definitions of bullying: A comparison of terms used, and age and gender differences, in a fourteen-country international comparison. *Child Development, 73*, 1119–1133.

Smith, P. K., Singer, M., Hoel, H., & Cooper, C. L. (2003). Victimization in the school and the workplace: Are there any links? *British Journal of Psychology, 94*, 175–188.

Smith, S. L., & Boyson, A. R. (2002). Violence in music videos: Examining the prevalence and context of physical aggression. *Journal of Communication, 52*, 61–83.

Smith, S. L., & Donnerstein, E. (1998). Harmful effects of exposure to media violence: Learning of aggression, emotional desensitization, and fear. In R. G. Geen & E. Donnerstein (Eds), *Human aggression: Theories, research and implications for social policy* (pp. 168–202). San Diego, CA: Academic Press.

Smith, S. L., Lachlan, K., Pieper, K. M., Boyson, A. R., Wilson, B. J., Tamborini, R. et al. (2004). Brandishing guns in American media: Two studies examining how often and in what context firearms appear on television and in popular video games. *Journal of Broadcasting & Electronic Media, 48*, 584–606.

Smith, S. L., Lachlan, K., & Tamborini, R. (2003). Popular video games: Quantifying the presentation of violence and its context. *Journal of Broadcasting & Electronic Media, 47*, 58–76.

Sorenson, S. B., Stein, J. A., Siegel, J. M., Golding, J. M., & Burnam, M. A. (1987). The prevalence of adult sexual assault. *American Journal of Epidemiology, 126*, 1154–1164.

Sousa, C., Herrenkohl, T. I., Moylan, C. A., Tajima, E. A., Klika, J. B., Herrenkohl, R. C. et al. (2011). Longitudinal study on the effects of child abuse and children's exposure to domestic violence, parent–child attachments, and antisocial behavior in adolescence. *Journal of Interpersonal Violence, 26*, 111–136.

Soyer, R. B., Rovenpor, J. L., Kopelman, R. E., Mullins, L. S., & Watson, P. J. (2001). Further assessment of the construct validity of four measures of narcissism: Replication and extension. *Journal of Psychology, 135*, 245–258.

Sparks, G. G., & Sparks, C. W. (2002). Effects of media violence. In J. Bryant & D. Zillmann (Eds), *Media effects: Advances in theory and research* (2nd edn) (pp. 269–285). Mahwah, NJ: Lawrence Erlbaum.

Spertus, I. L., Yehuda, R., Wong, C. M., Halligan, S., & Seremetis, S. V. (2003). Childhood emotional abuse and neglect as predictors of psychological and physical symptoms in women presenting to a primary care practice. *Child Abuse & Neglect, 27*, 1247–1258.

Spielberger, C. D. (1996). *Manual for the State–Trait Anger Expression Inventory (STAXI)*. Odessa, FL: Psychological Assessment Resources.

Spitzberg, B. H. (1999). An analysis of empirical estimates of sexual aggression victimization and perpetration. *Violence and Victims, 14*, 241–260.

St Lawrence, J. S., Crosby, R. A., Belcher, L., Yazdani, N., & Brasfield, T. L. (1999). Sexual risk reduction and anger management interventions for incarcerated male adolescents: A randomized controlled trial of two interventions. *Journal of Sex Education and Therapy, 24*, 9–17.

Stadler, C., Rohrmann, S., Steuber, S., & Poustka, F. (2006). Effects of provocation on emotions and aggression: An experimental study with aggressive children. *Swiss Journal of Psychology, 65*, 117–124.

Staggs, S. L., & Schewe, P. A. (2011). Primary prevention of domestic violence. In M. P. Koss, J. W. White & A. E. Kazdin (Eds), *Violence against women and children. Volume 2. Navigating solutions* (pp. 237–257). Washington, DC: American Psychological Association.

Steele, C., & Josephs, R. (1990). Alcohol myopia: Its prized and dangerous effects. *American Psychologist, 45*, 921–933.

Steinmetz, S. K. (1978). Battered parents. *Society, 15*, 54–55.

Stern, V. (2010). *A report by Baroness Vivien Stern CBE of an independent review into how rape complaints are handled by public authorities in England and Wales.* Available online: www.policesupers.com/uploads/news/100315%20Stern_Review_of_Rape_Reporting_1FINAL.pdf

Stith, S. M., Liu, T., Davies, L. C., Boykin, E. L., Alder, M. C., Harris, J. M. et al. (2009). Risk factors in child maltreatment: A meta-analytic review of the literature. *Aggression and Violent Behavior, 14*, 13–29.

Stith, S. M., Smith, D. B., Penn, C. E., Ward, D. B., & Tritt, D. (2004). Intimate partner abuse perpetration and victimization risk factors: A meta-analytic review. *Aggression and Violent Behavior, 10*, 65–98.

Stott, C., Hutchison, P., & Drury, J. (2001). 'Hooligans' abroad? Inter-group dynamics, social identity and participation in collective 'disorder' at the 1998 World Cup Finals. *British Journal of Social Psychology, 40*, 359–384.

Straus, M. A. (1979). Measuring intrafamily conflict and violence: The Conflict Tactics Scales. *Journal of Marriage and the Family, 41*, 75–88.

Straus, M. A., Hamby, S. L. Boney-McCoy, S., & Sugarman, D. B. (1996). The revised Conflict Tactics Scales (CTS2). *Journal of Family Issues, 17*, 283–316.

Straus, M. A., Hamby, S. L., Finkelhor, D., Moore, D. W., & Runyan, D. (1998). Identification of child maltreatment with the Parent-Child Conflict Tactics Scales: Development and psychometric data for a national sample of American parents. *Child Abuse and Neglect, 22*, 249–270.

Straus, M. A., & Paschall, M. J. (2009). Corporal punishment by mothers and development of children's cognitive ability: A longitudinal study of two nationally representative age cohorts. *Journal of Aggression, Maltreatment & Trauma, 18*, 459–483.

Strom, K. J., & Irvin, C. (2007). Terrorism as a form of violence. In D. J. Flannery, A. T. Vazsonyi, & I. D. Waldman (Eds), *The Cambridge handbook of violent behavior and aggression* (pp. 583–601). New York: Cambridge University Press.

Struckman-Johnson, C. (1988). Forced sex on dates: It happens to men, too. *Journal of Sex Research, 24*, 234–241.

Struckman-Johnson, C., & Struckman-Johnson, D. (1994). Men pressured and forced into sexual experience. *Archives of Sexual Behavior, 23*, 93–114.

Struckman-Johnson, C., Struckman-Johnson, D., & Anderson, P. B. (2003). Tactics of sexual coercion: When men and women won't take no for an answer. *Journal of Sex Research, 40*, 76–86.

Stucke, T., & Baumeister, R. F. (2006). Ego depletion and aggressive behavior: Is the inhibition of aggression a limited resource? *European Journal of Social Psychology, 36*, 1–13.

Subra, B., Muller, D., Bègue, L., Bushman, B. J., & Delmas, F. (2010). Automatic effects of alcohol and aggressive cues on aggressive thoughts and behaviors. *Personality and Social Psychology Bulletin, 36*, 1052–1057.

Sunday, S. R., & Tobach, E. (Eds) (1985). *Violence against women: A critique of the sociobiology of rape*. New York: Gordian Press.

Swartout, K. M., & White, J. W. (2010). The relationship between drug use and sexual aggression in men across time. *Journal of Interpersonal Violence, 25*, 1716–1735.

Tafrate, R. C., Kassinove, H., & Dundin, L. (2002). Anger episodes in high- and low-trait-anger community adults. *Journal of Clinical Psychology, 58*, 1573–1590.

Taft, C. T., Schumm, J. A., Marshall, A. D., Panuzio, J., & Holtzworth-Munroe, A. (2008). Family-of-origin maltreatment, posttraumatic stress disorder symptoms, social information processing deficits, and relationship abuse perpetration. *Journal of Abnormal Psychology, 117*, 637–646.

Tajfel, H. (1981). *Human groups and social categories: Studies in social psychology*. Cambridge: Cambridge University Press.

Takarangi, M. K. T., Polaschek, D. L. L., Hignett, A., & Garry, M. (2008). Chronic and temporary aggression causes hostile false memories for ambiguous information. *Applied Cognitive Psychology, 22*, 39–49.

Tarrant, M., Branscombe, N. R., Warner, R. H., & Weston, D. (2012). Social identity and perceptions of torture: It's moral when we do it. *Journal of Experimental Social Psychology, 48*, 513–518.

Taylor, L. D., Davis-Kean, P., & Malanchuk, O. (2007). Self-esteem, academic self-concept, and aggression at school. *Aggressive Behavior, 33*, 130–136.

Taylor, S. P. (1967). Aggressive behavior and physiological arousal as a function of provocation and the tendency to inhibit aggression. *Journal of Personality and Social Psychology, 35*, 297–310.

Taylor, S. P., Gammon, C. B., & Capasso, D. R. (1976). Aggression as a function of the interaction of alcohol and threat. *Journal of Personality and Social Psychology, 34*, 938–941.

Tedeschi, R. G. & Calhoun, L. G., (2004). Posttraumatic growth: Conceptual foundations and empirical evidence. *Psychological Inquiry, 15*, 1–18.

Tedeschi, J., Calhoun, L. G., & Cann, A. (2007). Evaluating resource gain: Understanding and misunderstanding posttraumatic growth. *Applied Psychology, 56*, 396–406.

Tedeschi, J. T., & Felson, R. B. (1994). *Violence, aggression, and coercive actions*. Washington, DC: American Psychological Association.

Temcheff, C. E., Serbin, L. A., Martin-Storey, A., Stack, D. M., Hodgins, S., Ledingham, J. et al. (2008). Continuity and pathways from aggression in childhood to family violence in adulthood: A 30-year longitudinal study. *Journal of Family Violence, 23*, 231–242.

Temkin, J., & Krahé, B. (2008). *Sexual assault and the justice gap: A question of attitude*. Oxford: Hart Publishing.

Terburg, D., Morgan, B., & van Honk, J. (2009). The testosterone-cortisol ratio: A hormonal marker for proneness to social aggression. *International Journal of Law and Psychiatry, 32*, 216–223.

Testa, M., Hoffman, J. H., & Livingston, J. A. (2010). Alcohol and sexual risk behaviors as mediators of the sexual victimization-revictimization relationship. *Journal of Consulting and Clinical Psychology, 78*, 249–259.

Testa, M., & Livingston, J. A. (2009). Alcohol consumption and women's vulnerability to sexual victimization: Can reducing women's drinking prevent rape? *Substance Use and Misuse, 44*, 1349–1376.

Thomaes, S., Bushman, B. J., Orobio de Castro, B., Cohen, G. L., & Denissen, J. A. (2009). Reducing narcissistic aggression by buttressing self-esteem. *Psychological Science, 20*, 1536–1542.

Thomas, R., & Zimmer-Gembeck, M. J. (2007). Behavioral outcomes of Parent-Child Interaction Therapy and Triple P-Positive Parenting Program: A review and meta-analysis. *Journal of Abnormal Child Psychology, 35*, 475–495.

Thomas, R., & Zimmer-Gembeck, M. J. (2011). Accumulating evidence for parent–child interaction therapy in the prevention of child maltreatment. *Child Development, 82*, 177–192.

Thomas, T. A., & Fremouw, W. (2009). Moderating factors of the sexual "victim to offender cycle" in males. *Aggression and Violent Behavior, 14*, 382–387.

Thompson, M. P., Koss, M. P., Kingree, J. B., Goree, J., & Rice, J. (2011). A prospective mediational model of sexual aggression among college men. *Journal of Interpersonal Violence, 26*, 2716–2734.

Thornhill, R., & Palmer, C. T. (2000). *A natural history of rape: Biological bases of sexual coercion*. Cambridge, MA: MIT Press.

Thornhill, R., & Thornhill, N. W. (1991). Coercive sexuality of men: Is there psychological adaptation to rape? In E. Grauerholz & M. A. Koralewski (Eds), *Sexual coercion* (pp. 91–107). Lexington MA: Lexington Books.

Tjaden, P., & Thoennes, N. (2000). Prevalence and consequences of male-to-female and female-to-male intimate partner violence as measured by the National Violence Against Women Survey. *Violence Against Women, 6*, 140–159.

Todorov, A., & Bargh, J. A. (2002). Automatic sources of aggression. *Aggression and Violent Behavior, 7*, 53–68.

Tolan, P., Gorman-Smith, D., & Henry, D. (2006). Family violence. *Annual Review of Psychology, 57*, 557–583.

Tolin, D. F., & Foa, E. B. (2006). Sex differences in trauma and posttraumatic stress disorder: A quantitative review of 25 years of research. *Psychological Bulletin, 132*, 959–962.

Topping, K. J., & Barron, I. G. (2009). School-based child sexual abuse prevention programs: A review of effectiveness. *Review of Educational Research, 79*, 431–463.

Torabi, M. R., & Seo, D. C. (2004). National study of behavioral and life changes since September 11. *Health Education & Behavior, 31*, 179–192.

Travis, C. B. (Ed.) (2003a). *Evolution, gender, and rape*. Cambridge, MA: MIT Press.

Travis, C. B. (2003b). Theory and data on rape and evolution. In C. B. Travis (Ed.), *Evolution, gender, and rape* (pp. 207–220). Cambridge, MA: MIT Press.

Tremblay, R. E., Japel, C., Péruss, D., McDuff, P., Boivin, M., Zoccolillo, M. et al. (1999). The search for the age of 'onset' of physical aggression: Rousseau and Bandura revisited. *Criminal Behaviour and Mental Health, 9*, 8–23.

Trickett, P. K., Noll, J. G., & Putnam, F. W. (2011). The impact of sexual abuse on female development: Lessons from a multigenerational, longitudinal research study. *Development and Psychopathology, 23*, 453–476.

Turchik, J. A. (2012). Sexual victimization among male college students: Assault severity, sexual functioning, and health risk behaviors. *Psychology of Men and Masculinity, 13*, 243–255.

Turcotte-Seabury, C. A. (2010). Anger management and the process mediating the link between witnessing violence between parents and partner violence. *Violence and Victims, 25*, 306–318.

Turner, K. M., Sanders, M. R. (2006). Dissemination of evidence-based parenting and family support strategies: Learning from the Triple P-Positive Parenting Program system approach. *Aggression and Violent Behavior, 11*, 176–193.

Turner, R. H., & Killian, L. M. (1972). *Collective behavior* (2nd edn). Englewood Cliffs, NJ: Prentice Hall.

Twenge, J. M,, Baumeister, R. F., Tice, D. M., & Stucke, T. S. (2001). If you can't join them, beat them: Effects of social exclusion on aggressive behavior. *Journal of Personality and Social Psychology, 81*, 1058–1069.

Twenge, J. M., & Campbell, W. K. (2003). 'Isn't it fun to get the respect that we're going to deserve?' Narcissism, social rejection, and aggression. *Personality and Social Psychology Bulletin, 29*, 261–272.

Twenge, J. M., Konrath, S., Foster, J. D., Campbell, W. K., & Bushman, B. J. (2008). Egos inflating over time: A cross-temporal meta-analysis of the Narcissistic Personality Inventory. *Journal of Personality, 76*, 875–902.

Tyson, P. D. (1998). Physiological arousal, reactive aggression, and the induction of an incompatible relaxation response. *Aggression and Violent Behavior, 3*, 143–158.

Uhlmann, E., & Swanson, J. (2004). Exposure to violent video games increases automatic aggressiveness. *Journal of Adolescence, 27*, 41–52.

Ullman, S. E. (2004). Sexual assault victimization and suicidal behavior in women: A review of the literature. *Aggression and Violent Behavior, 9*, 331–351.

Ullman, S. E. (2007). A 10-year update of 'review and critique of empirical studies of rape avoidance.' *Criminal Justice and Behavior, 34*, 411–429.

Ullman, S. E. (2010). *Talking about sexual assault: Society's response to survivors*. Washington, DC: American Psychological Association.

Ullman, S. E., & Najdowski, C. J. (2011a). Vulnerability and protective factors for sexual assault. In J. W. White, M. P. Koss & A. E. Kazdin (Eds), *Violence against women and children. Volume 1. Mapping the terrain* (pp. 151–172). Washington, DC: American Psychological Association.

Ullman, S. E., & Najdowski, C. J. (2011b). Prospective changes in attributions of self-blame and social reactions to women's disclosure of adult sexual assault. *Journal of Interpersonal Violence, 26*, 1934–1962.

Uniform Crime Reports (2009). *Crime in the United States*. Washington, DC: U.S. Department of Justice. Available online: www2.fbi.gov/ucr/cius2009/index.html

Updegraff, J. A., Silver, R. C., & Holman, E. A. (2008). Searching for and finding meaning in collective trauma: Results from a national longitudinal study of the 9/11 terrorist attacks. *Journal of Personality and Social Psychology, 95*, 709–722.

U.S. Department of Health and Human Services (2009). *Child maltreatment 2009*. Available online: www.acf.hhs.gov/programs/cb/pubs/cm09/cm09.pdf#page=109

U.S. Department of Justice (Ed.) (2010). *Crime in the United States*. Available online: www2.fbi.gov/ucr/cius2009/arrests/index.html.

Vaillancourt, T. (2005). Indirect aggression among humans. In R. E. Tremblay, W. W. Hartup & J. Archer (Eds), *Developmental origins of aggression* (pp. 158–177). New York: Guilford Press.

Vandello, J. A., & Cohen, D. (2003). Male honor and female fidelity: Implicit cultural scripts that perpetuate domestic violence. *Journal of Personality and Social Psychology, 84*, 997–1010.

Vandello, J. A., & Cohen, D. (2008). Culture, gender, and men's intimate partner violence. *Social and Personality Psychology Compass, 2*, 652–667.

Van Goozen, S. H. M. (2005). Hormones and the developmental origins of aggression. In R. E. Tremblay, W. W. Hartup & J. Archer (Eds), *Developmental origins of aggression* (pp. 281–306). New York: Guilford Press.

Van Goozen, S., Fairchild, G., Snoek, H., & Harold, G. T. (2007). The evidence for a neurobiological model of childhood antisocial behavior. *Psychological Bulletin, 133*, 149–182.

Van Hiel, A., Hautman, L., Cornelis, I., & De Clercq, B. (2007). Football hooliganism: Comparing self-awareness and social identity theory explanations. *Journal of Community and Applied Social Psychology, 17*, 169–186.

VanderLaan, D. P., & Vasey, P. L. (2009). Patterns of sexual coercion in heterosexual and homosexual men and women. *Achives of Sexual Behavior, 38*, 987–999.

Vanlaar, W., Simpson, H., Mayhew, D., & Robertson, R. (2008). Aggressive driving: A survey of attitudes, opinions, and behaviors. *Journal of Safety Research, 39*, 375–381.

Vandermassen, G. (2011). Evolution and rape: A feminist Darwinian perspective. *Sex Roles, 64*, 732–747.

Van Rooy, D. L., Rotton, J., & Burns, T. M. (2006). Convergent, discriminant, and predictive validity of aggressive driving inventories: They drive as they live. *Aggressive Behavior, 32*, 89–98.

Van Vugt, M. (2011). The male warrior hypothesis. In J. P. Forgas, A. W. Kruglanski & K. D. Williams (Eds), *The psychology of social conflict and aggression* (pp. 233–248). New York: Psychology Press.

Vasquez, E., Denson, T. F., Pedersen, W., Stenstrom, D. M., & Miller, N. (2005). The moderating effect of trigger intensity on triggered displaced aggression. *Journal of Experimental Social Psychology, 41*, 61–67.

Vasquez, E., Lickel, B., & Hennigan, K. (2010). Gangs, displaced, and group-based aggression. *Aggression and Violent Behavior, 15*, 130–140.

Vega,V., & Malamuth, N. M. (2009). Predicting sexual aggression: The role of pornography in the context of general and specific risk factors. *Aggressive Behavior, 33*, 104–117.

Verlinden, S., Hersen, M., & Thomas, J. (2000). Risk factors in school shootings. *Clinical Psychology Review, 20*, 3–56.

Verona, E., & Sullivan, E. A. (2008). Emotional catharsis and aggression revisited: Heart rate reduction following aggressive responding. *Emotion, 8*, 331–340.

Victoroff, J. (2009). The mind of the terrorist: A review and critique of psychological approaches. In J. Victoroff & A. W. Kruglanski (Eds), *Psychology of terrorism* (pp. 55–86). New York: Psychology Press.

Victoroff, J., & Kruglanski, A. W. (Eds) (2009). *Psychology of terrorism*. New York: Psychology Press.

Vigdor, E. R., & Mercy, J. A. (2006). Do laws restricting access to firearms by domestic violence offenders prevent intimate partner homicide? *Evaluation Review, 30*, 313–346.

Vissing, Y. M., Straus, M. A., Gelles, R. J., & Harrop, J. W. (1991). Verbal aggression by parents and psychosocial problems of children. *Child Abuse and Neglect, 15*, 223–238.

Vladutiu, C. J., Martin, S. L., & Macy, R. (2011). College- or university-based sexual assault prevention programs: A review of program outcomes, characteristics, and recommendations. *Trauma, Violence, & Abuse, 12*, 67–86.

Vrij, A., van der Steen, J., & Koppelaar, L. (1994). Aggression of police officers as a function of temperature: An experiment with the fire arms training system. *Journal of Community and Applied Social Psychology, 4*, 365–370.

Wagner, U., Christ, O., & Pettigrew, T. F. (2008). Prejudice and group-related behavior in Germany. *Journal of Social Issues, 64*, 403–416.

Walker, S., Archer, J., & Davies, M. (2005). Effects of rape on men: A descriptive analysis. *Archives of Sexual Behavior, 34*, 69–80.

Walker, J. S., & Bright, J. A. (2009). False inflated self-esteem and violence: A systematic review and cognitive model. *Journal of Forensic Psychiatry and Psychology, 20*, 1–32.

Walsh, D. A., & Gentile, D. A. (2001). A validity test of movie, television, and video game ratings. *Pediatrics, 107*, 1302–1308.

Wann, D. L., Carlson, J. D., Holland, L. C., Jacob, B. E., Owens, D. A., & Wells, D. D. (1999). Beliefs in symbolic catharsis: The importance of involvement with aggressive sports. *Social Behavior and Personality, 27*, 155–164.

Wann, D. L., Carlson, J. D., & Schrader, M. P. (1999). The impact of team identification on the hostile and instrumental verbal aggression of sport spectators. *Journal of Social Behavior and Personality, 14*, 279–286.

Wann, D. L., Culver, Z., Akanda, R., Daglar, M., De Divitiis, C., & Smith, A. (2005). The effects of team identification and game outcome on willingness to consider anonymous acts of hostile aggression. *Journal of Sport Behavior, 28*, 282–294.

Wann, D. L., Haynes, G., McLean, B., & Pullen, P. (2003). Sport team identification and willingness to consider anonymous acts of hostile aggression. *Aggressive Behavior, 29*, 406–413.

Warburton, W. A., Williams, K. D., & Cairns, D. R. (2006). When ostracism leads to aggression: The moderating effects of control deprivation. *Journal of Experimental Social Psychology, 42*, 213–220.

Waters, H., Hyder, A., Rajkotia, Y., Basu, S., Rehwinkel, J. A., & Butchart, A. (2004). *The economic dimensions of interpersonal violence*. Geneva: World Health Organization. Available online: http://whqlibdoc.who.int/publications/2004/9241591609.pdf

Watt, B. D., & Howells, K. (1999). Skills training for aggression control: Evaluation of an anger management programme for violent offenders. *Legal and Criminological Psychology, 4*, 285–300.

Wehby, J. H., & Symons, F. J. (1996). Revisiting conceptual issues in the measurement of aggressive behavior. *Behavioral Disorders, 22*, 29–35.

Weinstein, M. D., Smith, M. D., & Wiesenthal, D. L. (1995). Masculinity and hockey violence. *Sex Roles, 33*, 831–847.

Wells, S., Mihic, L., Tremblay, P. F., Graham, K., & Demers, A. (2008). Where, with whom, and how much alcohol is consumed on drinking events involving aggression? Event-level associations in a Canadian national survey of university students. *Alcoholism: Clinical and Experimental Research, 32*, 522–533.

Welsh, S. (2000). The multidimensional nature of sexual harassment. *Violence Against Women, 6*, 118–141.

Werner, N. E., Bumpus, M. F., & Rock, D. (2010). Involvement in internet aggression during early adolescence. *Journal of Youth and Adolescence, 39*, 607–619.

Wesselmann, E. D., Butler, F. A., Williams, K. D., & Pickett, C. L. (2010). Adding injury to insult: Unexpected rejection leads to more aggressive responses. *Aggressive Behavior, 36*, 232–237.

West, C. M. (2002). Lesbian intimate partner violence: Prevalence and dynamics. *Journal of Lesbian Studies, 6*, 121–127.

White, G. F., Katz, J., & Scarborough, K. E. (1992). The impact of professional football games upon violent assaults on women. *Violence and Victims, 7*, 157–181.

White, J. W., Koss, M. P., & Kazdin, A. E. (Eds) (2011). *Violence against women and children. Volume 1. Mapping the terrain*. Washington, DC: American Psychological Association.

White, J. W., & Kowalski, R. M. (1998). Male violence toward women: An integrated perspective. In R. G. Geen & E. Donnerstein (Eds), *Human aggression: Theories, research and implications for social policy* (pp. 203–228). San Diego, CA: Academic Press.

Widman, L., & McNulty, J. K. (2010). Sexual narcissism and the perpetration of sexual aggression. *Archives of Sexual Behavior, 39*, 926–939.

Widom, C. S. (1989). Does violence beget violence? A critical examination of the literature. *Psychological Bulletin, 106*, 3–28.

Wiehe, V. R., & Richards, A. L. (1995). *Intimate betrayal.* Thousand Oaks, CA: Sage.

Wiesenthal, D. L., Hennessy, D. A., & Totten, B. (2000). The influence of music on driver stress. *Journal of Applied Social Psychology, 30*, 1709–1719.

Wiesenthal, D. L., & Janovjak, D. P. (1992). *Deindividuation and automobile driving.* LaMarsh Research Programme Report Series, No. 46. Toronto, Canada: York University.

Wilkowski, B. M., & Robinson, M. D. (2008). The cognitive basis of trait anger and reactive aggression: An integrative analysis. *Personality and Social Psychology Review, 12*, 3–21.

Williams, J. R., Ghandour, R. M., & Kub, J. E. (2008). Female perpetration of violence in heterosexual intimate relationships. *Trauma, Violence, & Abuse, 9*, 227–249.

Williams K. D. (1997). Social ostracism. In R. M. Kowalski (Ed.), *Aversive interpersonal behaviors* (pp. 133–170). New York: Plenum Press.

Williams, K. D. (2007a). Ostracism. *Annual Review of Psychology, 58*, 425–452.

Williams, K. D. (2007b). Ostracism: The kiss of social death. *Social and Personality Psychology Compass, 1*, 236–247.

Williams, K. D. (2011). The effects of homophily, identification, and violent video games on players. *Mass Communication and Society, 14*, 3–24.

Williams, K. D., Cheung, C. K. T., & Choi, W. (2000). Cyberostracism: Effects of being ignored over the Internet. *Journal of Personality and Social Psychology, 79*, 748–762.

Williams, K. D., & Warburton, W. A. (2003). Ostracism: A form of indirect aggression that can result in aggression. *Revue Internationale de Psychologie Sociale, 16*, 101–124.

Williams, K. D., & Wesselmann, E. D. (2011). The link between ostracism and aggression. In J. P. Forgas, A. W. Kruglanski & K. D. Williams (Eds), *The psychology of social conflict and aggression* (pp. 37–51). New York: Psychology Press.

Williams, S. T., Conger, K. J., & Blozis, S. A. (2007). The development of interpersonal aggression during adolescence: The importance of parents, siblings, and family economics. *Child Development, 78*, 1526–1542.

Willness, C. R., Steel, P., & Lee, K. (2007). A meta-analysis of the antecedents and consequences of workplace sexual harassment. *Personnel Psychology, 60*, 127–162.

Wilson, B. J., Smith, S. L., Potter, W. J., Kunkel, D., Linz, D., Colvin, M. et al. (2002). Violence in children's television programming: Assessing the risks. *Journal of Communication, 52*, 5–35.

Wolfe, D. A. (2011). Risk factors for child abuse perpetration. In J. W. White, M. P. Koss & A. E. Kazdin (Eds), *Violence against women and children. Volume 1. Mapping the terrain* (pp. 31–53). Washington, DC: American Psychological Association.

Wolfe, D. A., Crooks, C. V., Lee, V., McIntyre-Smith, A., & Jaffe, P. (2003). The effects of children's exposure to domestic violence: A meta-analysis and critique. *Clinical Child and Family Psychology Review, 6*, 171–187.

Wong, W., Wong, F. Y., & Chachere, J. G. (1991). Effects of media violence on viewers' aggression in unconstrained social interaction. *Psychological Bulletin, 10*, 371–383.

Wood, J., & Alleyne, E. (2010). Street gang theory and research: Where are we now and where do we go from here? *Aggression and Violent Behavior, 15*, 100–111.

World Health Organization (2004). *Young people's health in context.* Available online: www.euro.who.int/__data/assets/pdf_file/0008/110231/e82923.pdf

World Health Organization (2006). *Preventing child maltreatment.* Available online: http://whqlibdoc. who.int/publications/2006/9241594365_eng.pdf

Worth, K. A., Chambers, J. G., Nassau, D. H., Rakhra, B. K., & Sargent, J. D. (2008). Exposure of US adolescents to extremely violent movies. *Pediatrics, 122,* 306–312.

Wright, V. A. (2010). *Celerity, capital punishment, and murder: Do quicker executions deter criminal homicides?* Dissertation Abstracts International Section A: Humanities and Social Sciences, Vol. 70 (11-A), 2010. pp. 4464. Graduate School, Ohio State University.

Yao, M. Z., Mahood, C., & Linz, D. (2010). Sexual priming, gender stereotyping, and likelihood to sexually harass: Examining the cognitive effects of playing a sexually explicit video game. *Sex Roles, 62,* 77–88.

Ybarra, M., Mitchell, K., Hamburger, M., Diener-West, M., & Leaf, P. (2011). X-rated material and the perpetration of sexually aggressive behavior among children and adolescents: Is there a link? *Aggressive Behavior, 37,* 1–18.

Yokota, F., & Thompson, K. M. (2000). Violence in G-rated films. *Journal of the American Medical Association, 283,* 2716–2720.

Yoon, J., & Knight, R. A. (2011). Sexual material perception in sexually coercive men: Disattending deficit and its covariates. *Sexual Abuse, 23,* 275–291.

Young, A. M., Grey, M., & Boyd, C. J. (2009). Adolescents' experiences of sexual assault by peers: Prevalence and nature of victimization occurring within and outside of school. *Journal of Youth and Adolescence, 38,* 1072–1083.

Young, K. (2012). *Sport, violence and society.* London: Routledge.

Younger, J. C., & Doob, A. N. (1978). Attribution and aggression: The misattribution of anger. *Journal of Research in Personality, 12,* 164–171.

Zadro, L. (2011). Silent rage: When being ostracized leads to aggression. In J. P. Forgas, A. W. Kruglanski & K. D. Williams (Eds), *The psychology of social conflict and aggression* (pp. 201–216). New York: Psychology Press.

Zadro, L., Williams, K. D., & Richardson, R. (2004). How low can you go? Ostracism by a computer is sufficient to lower self-reported levels of belonging, control, self-esteem, and meaningful existence. *Journal of Experimental Social Psychology, 40,* 560–567.

Zani, B., & Kirchler, E. (1991). When violence overshadows the spirit of sporting competition: Italian football fans and their clubs. *Journal of Community and Applied Social Psychology, 1,* 5–21.

Zillmann, D. (1979). *Hostility and aggression.* Hillsdale, NJ: Lawrence Erlbaum.

Zillmann, D. (1998). *Connections between sexuality and aggression* (2nd edn). Mahwah, NJ: Lawrence Erlbaum Associates.

Zillmann, D., Baron, R., & Tamborini, R. (1981). Social costs of smoking: Effects of tobacco smoke on hostile behavior. *Journal of Applied Social Psychology, 11,* 548–561.

Zillmann, D., & Bryant, J. (1974). Effect of residual excitation on the emotional response to provocation and delayed aggressive behavior. *Journal of Personality and Social Psychology, 30,* 782–791.

Zimbardo, P. G. (1969). The human choice: Individuation, reason, and order versus deindividuation, impulse, and chaos. In W. J. Arnold & D. Levine (Eds), *Nebraska Symposium on Motivation. Volume 17* (pp. 273–307). Lincoln, NB: University of Nebraska Press.

Zimbardo, P. G. (2006). On rethinking the psychology of tyranny: The BBC Prison Study. *British Journal of Social Psychology, 45,* 47–53.

Zolotor, A. J., & Puzia, M. E. (2010). Bans against corporal punishment: A systematic review of the laws, changes in attitudes and behaviours. *Child Abuse Review, 19,* 229–247.

Zuckerman, M. (2007). *Sensation seeking and risky behavior.* Washington, DC: American Psychological Association.

Zuravin, S., McMillen, C., DePanfilis, D., & Risley-Curtiss, C. (1996). The intergenerational cycle of child maltreatment: Continuity versus discontinuity. *Journal of Interpersonal Violence, 11,* 315–334.

Zurbriggen, E. L., Gobin, R. L., & Freyd, J. J. (2010). Childhood emotional abuse predicts late adolescent sexual aggression perpetration and victimization. *Journal of Aggression, Maltreatment & Trauma, 19,* 204–223.

Author Index

Subject Index